NANZAN GUIDE TO JAPANESE RELIGIONS

NANZAN GUIDE TO JAPANESE RELIGIONS

EDITED BY

PAUL L. SWANSON
AND CLARK CHILSON

UNIVERSITY OF HAWAI'I PRESS
HONOLULU

11 10 09 08 07 06   6 5 4 3 2

Library of Congress Cataloging-in-Publication Data

Nanzan guide to Japanese religions / edited by Paul L. Swanson and Clark Chilson.
     p. cm. — (Nanzan library of Asian religion and culture)

    Includes bibliographical references and index.
    ISBN 13 : 978-0-8248-3002-1 (cloth : alk. paper)
    ISBN 10 : 0-8248-3002-4 (cloth : alk. paper)
    1. Japan—Religion—Study and teaching. 2. Japan—Religion—Sources. 3. Japan—
    Religion—Research. I. Title. II. Series.
BL2210.5 .N36 2006
200'.952 22—dc22

                                 2005050169

The typesetting for this book was done by the Nanzan Institute for Religion and Culture.

Printed by IBT Global

Contents

Editors' Introduction

To paraphrase J. R. R. Tolkien's comment with regard to his monumental *The Lord of the Rings*, this book grew in the making. The project germinated as an ambitious suggestion many years ago (in the mid-1990s) by Okuyama Michiaki to produce a multivolume English-language history of Japanese religions, including a practical "handbook" of advice on resources, sources of funding, bibliographies, and so forth. Since such a multi-volume project was too grand and unwieldy, the goal was limited to the more modest and practical plan of first producing a single-volume handbook. This handbook then grew to become the wide-ranging introduction and critical analysis of the field of Japanese religions that you now hold in your hands as the *Nanzan Guide to Japanese Religions*. A brief outline of this process will illustrate some of the issues we struggled with, and which reflect ongoing concerns and issues in the field of Japanese religions.

The preliminary rationale for this project was stated in an internal Nanzan Institute memo as follows:

> There has not been a scholarly overview of religion in Japanese history in English for over thirty years, since J. Kitagawa's book *Religion in Japanese History* (1966). The books in English that give overviews on Japanese Buddhism and Shinto are based largely on the scholarship of the 1960s and 1970s. Consequently, many of the ideas contained within them are no longer accepted, and many of the issues they concentrate on are no longer the most important issues in the field.

Originally named the "History of Japanese Religions Guidebook Project," the goals were further defined in a meeting of Clark Chilson, Robert Kisala, and Okuyama Michiaki in October 1998, at which it was decided to "put together a research guidebook for the study of religion in Japanese history from ancient times to 1945." The original concept was that

> the book should contain an introduction, review articles, appendices, and bibliographies. The introduction will delineate the major trends and debates in the field, and point out the main areas and problems that need to be researched in the future. The review articles will give an overview of the work done in a particular subfield of the history of Japanese religions (e.g., Tokugawa Buddhism, Shinto in medieval times) by pointing out the key problems and sources. The review articles should also give suggestions for further research. The number and content of the appendices has yet to be decided. OM suggested an annotated list of journals. CC suggested an appendix on how to access sources, particularly primary sources [and so forth]....

Paul Swanson, who was on sabbatical at Indiana University at the time, was contacted, and he agreed to participate in the project, eventually taking on a leading role as organizer and editor. As various ideas were tried out (translating review articles from the Japanese, adapting material from the *Japanese Journal of Religious Studies*, producing bibliographical lists, etc.) through the summer and autumn of 1999, Clark Chilson agreed to write a formal book proposal, and Okuyama Michiaki took responsibility for preparing an application for a three-year grant from the Japanese Monbukagakushō. Chilson's proposal became the working model for the project:

> The book is intended to help students and scholars find what they need to do research on the history of Japanese religions. It will be the first research guide in any language to allow a researcher to navigate the whole field of the history of Japanese religions. Because no book maps out the entire field, most researchers become familiar with a particular area of the field in rather unsystematic ways, and are often only vaguely aware of what exists in the rest of the field. Over a period of time of working on specific academic problems, a researcher learns what resources are available in an area by being pointed in profitable directions by senior colleagues or by serendipitously finding sources in the research process. This rather inefficient method pinions researchers, especially less experienced ones, and circumscribes their lines of inquiry. By providing a reference for finding resources in the field, from manuals to money, we can provide beginners and specialists with a reference that will allow them to research more efficiently and in greater depth.

Our proposal for a research grant was approved in the spring of 2000, allowing us to provide minimum payment to authors of essays, and giving us access to funds for travel, equipment, and books to support the project.

Lengthy discussions were held through the summer and fall of 2000 on the evolving contents of the book. One of the issues debated was whether or not to use the traditional categories of "Shinto," "Buddhism," and so forth. Some of the problems associated with these traditional categories are discussed in the essays (see, e.g., Havens on "Shinto"), but it was decided that, if only for the sake of convenience, we would use the categories to provide familiar handles on the field, and authors were solicited to contribute essays on the six "traditions" of our section one. The letters requesting a contribution included the following description:

> Our intent with these essays is to provide an overview of key issues and important topics of research with regard to Japanese religions. The essay should be an overview of the subject, with attention given to issues in that area that have received special attention or have been controversial or the subject of debate in recent years. The essay should be structured along the following lines:
>
>   1. Definition of key terms.
>   2. Overview of the field and the main areas of interest.
>   3. Recent publications, and a general outline of the state of research, in this area.
>   4. Important topics and controversial issues in the area, and points that need further research in the future.
>
> In addition to your cited references, we would also like to have the author provide a select bibliography of primary sources in the area that have been translated into Western languages. Limited space means that the essays must be short and to the point. Please bear in mind that the intent is to help the student or scholar gain a wide yet incisive perspective on this topic. The essay should contain many "pointers" that would lead the reader to think "This is an important issue, this is an area that needs more work, this is an interesting point to follow up on, this is an important publication in this area," and so forth.

A key event in the evolution of the project was a "working session" conducted at the annual conference of the American Academy of Religion at Nashville on 20 November 2000. Armed with our list of six essays on the "traditions" and a tentative list of twelve possible thematic essays (e.g., mythology, archaeology and material culture, syncretism, historiography, ritual and *matsuri*, etc.), we presented our ideas to an eager audience and solicited their advice. A lively discussion ensued over the contents and purpose of the book, with numerous suggestions for additional themes. Duncan Williams suggested having three sections—on traditions, history, and themes—each with six interrelated essays, and this eventually became the basic framework of the book.

After the AAR consultation, the structure of the book finally approached its final form. The remaining issues were to decide on the periodization for the historical essays in section two, and to select the representative themes for section three. A seminar was held in January 2001 to discuss the issue of historical periodization, and Yoshida Kazuhiko and Hayashi Makoto were invited to outline the issues and provide advice. A decision was made to avoid the usual "era" divisions (Nara, Heian, Kamakura, etc.) and instead aim for discussion of general, overlapping swaths of history. Thus, the essay on "ancient" Japan includes comments on events in the Nara period, "classical" covers from Asuka-Nara and into early Kamakura, "medieval" from late Heian to early Tokugawa, "early modern" from Tokugawa to Meiji, "modern" from the Bakumatsu (late Tokugawa) through Shōwa, and "contemporary" from post-wwii to the present. This approach, we felt, minimized arbitrary breaks in long-term trends that overlapped conventional historical eras, and allowed for a more sweeping analysis of religion throughout Japanese history.

The choice of themes was refined from a list of "Religion and the Arts," "…Literature," "…Gender," "…Philosophy," "…Politics," and "…Economics," to the six themes now in section three. This is not meant to be a comprehensive list of "themes in Japanese religions," and surely everyone will be able to come up with some topic that "should" have been included ("why not an essay on *matsuri*," or "what happened to institutional history," we can hear ringing in our ears…). Our aim was to cover as much ground as possible while still addressing specific issues. Admittedly, at times the theme (and the resulting contents of the essay) was much influenced by the individual author.

Posting the essays on the Nanzan homepage (as they were submitted and with a preliminary edit) allowed authors to consult and compare what others had done, and over time to revise their essays accordingly. As a result, though the essays retain their individual flavors, there is a great deal of natural cross-referencing, and, we believe, an unexpectedly high level of cohesiveness. The authors were given relatively free rein (with only the rather ambiguous "guidelines" quoted above), and we were very gratified when they went beyond our expectations to provide instructive, provocative, and insightful treatments of their subject, sometimes quite different from the content we envisioned when we first solicited the essays. Thus there is quite a variety in style, from the literary flavor (and annotated bibliography) of Morrell, the revisioning analyses of Havens and Yoshida, the sweeping overviews of Reader and Bodiford, the new perspectives and insights of Payne and Kasulis, the personal experiential touch of Schnell, and so forth. Again, our original intent was to compile a single comprehensive bibliography to which all the essays would refer, but the differences in style and content convinced us to leave each essay with its own list of sources. This resulted in some repetition, but the appearance of the same reference in more than one essay serves to underscore the importance of that work, and also the continuity between essays.

As time went on it became clear that many of the objectives of our original plan—specialized bibliographies, information on sources of funding for research, lists of academic societies and universities in Japan involved in religious studies, and so forth—could now be better undertaken on the internet rather than in a printed format, since the information is being constantly updated and revised. (Believe it or not, "Google" was as yet unknown when this book project began, and searches on the internet were still crude and unreliable.) Some of the materials compiled over the years are already outdated and replaced by better resources on the internet (e.g., a list of research sources on Buddhism compiled by Swanson) and will be laid to rest. The following collections of information that were compiled for the

Guide and are still useful, but were left out of the final printing, will be provided on the Nanzan Institute homepage (www.nanzan-u.ac.jp/SHUBUNKEN/publications/).

1. List of educational institutions in Japan involved in the study of Japanese religions (Okuyama and Terao)
2. List of academic societies in Japan for the study of Japanese religion (Okuyama and Terao)
3. List of major sources of funding for research on Japanese religions (Okuyama)
4. Bibliography of Japanese-language works on Christianity in Japan (Terao)
5. List of primary sources in Western languages (Okuyama and Swanson)

On the other hand, an essay on fieldwork was added late in the process to supplement the essays on libraries and archives in section four, and William Bodiford volunteered to provide his valuable "Chronology of Religion in Japan."

As a result, we now have a book that is neither a comprehensive introduction to Japanese religions, nor just a collection of research resources. Instead, we have a *Guide* that we think can serve as an overview of Japanese religions and help both beginning students and seasoned researchers navigate the field by providing overviews of scholarship in different subfields, different time periods, and on select themes, and by offering practical techniques for accessing relevant information. We hope the book will be useful as a supplementary textbook for undergraduates taking courses on Japanese religions and as a reference for graduate students that will help them carry out their research projects more efficiently. For specialists of Japanese religions, the book can serve as an inventory of the field, showing how the field has developed and its current state. We believe that historians and social scientists of Japan who do not specialize in religion, but whose research relates to it, will also find beneficial material in the book.

ACKNOWLEDGMENTS

First, we would like to thank our contributors for their extraordinary essays, especially those who submitted their essays on schedule and then waited patiently while the book evolved and underwent a long period of revision, updating, and final editing. We would also like to acknowledge the Japan Society for the Promotion of Science (JSPS, Nihon Gakujutsu Shinkōkai 日本学術振興会) for its generous three-year research grant (April 2000–March 2003; 文部科学省科学研究費補助金, on the theme "Promoting the Internationalization of Research through the Editing and Publication of Basic Research Materials concerning the History of Japanese Religions" 日本宗教史に関する基礎的な研究資料の編集刊行による研究の国際化の推進) that allowed us to pay authors a minimum remuneration for their essays, buy computer equipment and software, purchase books, and travel to international conferences. Thomas Kasulis provided the photos that appear on the divider pages. We would like to express a special thanks to Kawahashi Seishu, head priest of Reiganji (in Toyota) and photographer extraordinaire (see www.msk-gallery.com), who made a special effort to produce the cover photo of Daruma dolls.

The editors (who get to have their names on the cover of this *Guide*) would like to express their appreciation to the "project team" that, especially in the early stages, worked hard on various aspects of the project (many of whose results, for one reason or another, do not appear on the surface), and without which the *Guide* would never have coalesced:

Trevor Astley	Robert Kisala	Horo Atsuhiko
Okuyama Michiaki	Terao Kazuyoshi	

The following essays were submitted in Japanese and translated into English: "Ancient Japan and Religion" by Matsumura Kazuo, translated by Benjamin Dorman; "Religion in the Classical Period" by Yoshida Kazuhiko, translated by Paul L. Swanson; "Religion in the Modern Period" by Hayashi Makoto, translated by Clark Chilson; and "Contemporary Japanese Religions" by Shimazono Susumu, translated by Robert Kisala.

We also appreciate the advice and encouragement we received on numerous occasions from Yoshida Kazuhiko and Hayashi Makoto. Finally, James Heisig provided his usual invaluable services in designing the layout of the book, assisting with the layout, and offering crucial advice at various stages of the editorial process.

April 2005

Paul L. Swanson
Nagoya, Japan

Clark Chilson
Ithaca, New York

PHOTO CREDITS

Cover photo by Kawahashi Seishu

Photos on divider pages by Thomas Kasulis:

  p. 1, "sunrise at wedded rocks near Ise"
  p. 129, "pilgrims at Tōdaiji in Nara"
  p. 233, "lion mask ritual costume"
  p. 337, "Fudō-myōō temple lanterns"
  p. 393, "statue of Zenkōji founder carrying Buddha image"

Traditions

Robert KISALA

Japanese Religions

In contrast to the situation in many of the European countries and some other areas of the West, where we see relatively high levels of at least nominal religious affiliation and low levels of participation in religious rites, religion in Japan is marked by almost universal participation in certain rites and customs but low levels of self-acknowledged affiliation to a religious group. It has become commonplace to say that Japanese are born Shinto, marry as Christians, and die Buddhists, a phrase that indicates both the high level of participation in religious rites of passage as well as the eclectic nature of Japanese religiosity. Note is also often made of the fact that nearly ninety percent of the Japanese observe the custom of annual visits to ancestral graves, and seventy-five percent have either a Buddhist or Shinto altar in their home. However, surveys consistently show that only thirty percent of the population identify themselves as belonging to one of the religions active in Japan—this despite the fact that the religions themselves claim an overall total membership that approaches twice the actual population of 126 million. This is mainly due to the fact that much of the population is automatically counted as parishioners of both the local Shinto shrine and the ancestral Buddhist temple.

Although identified today as the major religious traditions of Japan, Buddhism and Shinto have been so closely intertwined throughout much of Japanese history that the forced separation of the two at the beginning of the modern period in the mid-nineteenth century resulted in a great upheaval in Japanese religious practice, and continues to have repercussions today. In addition, these religious traditions have been combined with elements of Taoism and Confucianism from China, issuing in a kind of common or popular religiosity that is not easily contained in any one religious tradition. Christianity, introduced to Japan in the fifteenth century by the Catholic missionaries who accompanied the Spanish and Portuguese explorers, was actively persecuted throughout the early modern period (seventeenth century to mid-nineteenth century), and small groups of "hidden Christians" continue to preserve a secret faith tradition that they trace back to the time of persecution. Reintroduced in the modern period, Christianity has had little success in attracting members in Japan, with less than one percent of the population belonging to one of the Christian churches. Christian influence is generally acknowledged as greater than those membership numbers would indicate, however, especially in the fields of education and social welfare.

The modern period has seen the proliferation of new religious movements in Japan, leading at times to widely exaggerated estimates of their number and strength. To varying degrees these groups often incorporate folk religious practices, Buddhist doctrinal elements, and, more recently, ideas and practices from a wide range of religions and independent spiritualist practices. Given this religious ferment, it is hard to describe Japan as a secular society. However, many Japanese would prefer to see themselves as secular or unconcerned with religion. In a recent survey, for example, only twenty-six percent of the respondents in Japan described themselves as religious. In part this is due to the controversy surrounding some religious groups, particularly the new religions that have become so prominent in the modern period. The already poor image of these groups was further damaged by the terrorist activities of Aum Shinrikyō in the mid-1990s, contributing to the rise of an anticult movement in Japan. However, the attitude towards religion in Japan is also influenced by differences in the understanding of "religion" as compared to the West, differences that arise from the history of the use of the term *shūkyō* 宗教, or religion, in that country.

Modernity, as it is understood in Japan, is closely associated with the country's contact with the West. What is commonly referred to as the early modern period followed the arrival of Portuguese and Spanish explorers in the sixteenth century, and was marked by the attempt to limit contact with the West during the two-and-a-half-century Tokugawa Shogunate (1603–1867). The modern period was ushered in by the collapse of that regime in the face of the forced opening of the country by American and other Western powers, leading to a mad rush to catch up with the West economically, technologically, and militarily. The desire to build a nation strong enough to avoid Western colonization contributed greatly to emergence of Japanese nationalism and Japanese colonialism, and

TRADITIONS

impacted on religious developments during this period. Government attempts to separate Buddhism from Shinto and establish Shinto as the moral and spiritual basis for Japanese nationalism provided the background against which religion as a concept was debated and understood.

In considering what "religion" means in Japan, we will first take a look at popular images of religion as reflected in recent surveys on the subject. From there we will turn to the history of the concept in Japan, and consider how that continues to influence popular and public discourse on the subject. In the wake of the Aum Affair, religion and its future have once again become a popular topic of debate by scholars and media commentators. We will take a look at two influential arguments, before returning to survey results to draw some of our own conclusions on the state of religion in Japan.

POPULAR IMAGE OF RELIGION

Since 1995, the Religious Awareness Project of the Japanese Association for the Study of Religion and Society has conducted an annual survey of university students' attitudes towards religion.[1] The results of this survey bring into stark relief the image-problem that religion suffers under in Japan. The number of respondents who profess belief in any particular religion hovers around seven percent, much lower than the thirty percent that most national surveys in Japan yield. Around sixty percent say that they have little or no interest in religion, but only three percent of these respondents attribute their negative feelings toward religion to a personal experience. The vast majority, usually around seventy percent, say they just don't see any need for religion.

These numbers indicate that very few university students have had a personal experience of "religion," with only seven percent saying they believe in a religion and three percent claiming to have had a negative experience of religion. The low degree of interest in religion would seem to be a result then of shared popular images. Another survey, conducted in the wake of the Aum Affair in 1995 by the *Yomiuri Shinbun*, a national newspaper, indicates what some of these images might be.[2] Offered the opportunity to make multiple choices regarding their opinion on religious groups, forty percent of the respondents said that religious groups "are just out to make money," and thirty-seven percent said that they "prey on people's fears" to encourage them to join the group. Other complaints were that religion was "only for show" (18%) or that religious groups are "too involved in politics" (20%).

A broader survey[3] on contemporary values conducted by the Nanzan Institute for

---

1. *Shūkyō to shakai gakkai shūkyō ishiki chōsa purojekuto* 「宗教と社会」学会・宗教意識調査プロジェクト, 1995–2000. While the survey does not use a random sample, the number of respondents range between four and eleven thousand, which should yield reliable results. The annual reports on the survey results are available from the author.

2. The results of this survey can be found in Ishii 1997, p. 180.

3. The survey was conducted in 1998 using a random sample of three hundred from the Tokyo and Osaka metropolitan areas, weighted for sex and age. Preliminary reports on the results of the survey can be found in Kisala 1999a and 1999b.

Religion and Culture also yielded interesting results regarding the meanings assigned to religion in Japan. Twenty-nine percent of the respondents to this survey acknowledged that they belong to some religious group, consistent with the results of surveys conducted throughout much of the postwar period. Despite this rather low level of religious affiliation, however, one-half the respondents said that they believe in the existence of gods or buddhas, and nearly two-thirds professed that they believe in an "unseen higher power." Perhaps the most startling result was that one-quarter of those who described themselves as atheists (*mushinronsha* 無神論者, 19% of the total respondents) also professed some belief in God. It would appear that "atheist" has different connotations in Japan, identified more with a rejection of "religion" than a lack of belief in the divine.

The Nanzan study also confirmed the low popular image of religion in Japan, in a most definitive manner. A question was included in the survey regarding the level of trust afforded certain social institutions. While respondents gave high marks to the police (69%), the legal system (63%), and the military (52%), religion came in dead last, with only thirteen percent finding it trustworthy, considerably lower than the twenty-percent level given to politicians in the national parliament.

What these survey results clearly indicate is that "religion" is associated with religious institutions in Japan today, and the vast majority of people have a very low opinion of these institutions. What might normally be conceived as religious beliefs, practices, and feelings have been divorced from the concept of religion in Japan, as illustrated by the case of professed atheists acknowledging a belief in God. Although the surveys we have looked at here were conducted in the years following the Aum Affair, which led to a further erosion of religion's place in Japanese society, the meanings assigned to religion in Japan have a longer history, going back at least to the final determination of a translation for the term in the 1870s. We turn to these historical issues next.

THE CONCEPT OF "RELIGION" IN MODERN JAPAN

As Shimazono Susumu points out, it was around 1873 that the Japanese word *shūkyō* was fixed as the translation for "religion" (SHIMAZONO 1998). The meanings attached to the term religion and its Japanese counterpart were profoundly influenced by debates in the emerging Science of Religion in the West, as well as the particular institutional and political situation in Japan.

Under the influence of the evolutionary paradigm, many of the early theorists of the modern study of religion in the West worked under the assumption that there was one "elementary" form of religion, and all past and present religious expressions could be placed on a spectrum from least developed to most advanced as that elementary form evolved throughout human history. Occasionally this advanced form of religion was identified with morality or ethics, cleansed of magical, superstitious, or irrational elements found in lower religious forms. Often contained in this evolutionary view of religious forms was the assumption, either explicit or implicit, that religion itself would ultimately give way to the rational, scientific methods that these researchers themselves employed. Under the influence of romanticism, however, the situation was further complicated by the desire to reappraise the value of the irrational, frequently identified with folk or popular religious forms. Finally, the question of the definition of religion itself was a perennial problem for religious researchers, with differing views regarding the importance of beliefs in God or the presence of organizational structures as necessary elements of that definition.

Modern religious studies in Japan emerged at the end of the nineteenth century, as one result of the interest in the Parliament of Religions held in Chicago in 1893. A Comparative Religions Society was founded in 1896, and a course in Religious Studies was begun at Tokyo Imperial University in 1898, with a chair in Religious Studies established at the same university in 1905. Public and intellectual discourse on religion, however, preceded the founding of the academic discipline, since it was seen as crucial to the establishment of a modern state after the collapse of the Tokugawa political system.

From early in the nineteenth century the presence of foreign ships off the coast of Japan was seen as a threat to the enforced isolation of the country imposed at the beginning the Tokugawa period. Aizawa Seishisai, a retainer of the Mito domain, composed in 1825 the *Shinron* 新論, or *New Theses*, as a kind of manifesto calling on the regime to defend the nation from this threat.[4] Aizawa proposed that in addition to a military defense the times called for a spiritual defense as well, and, indeed, the latter would ultimately be more important. Drawing heavily on the arguments of the Kokugaku movement, he called for the propagation of beliefs based on Japanese mythology, centered on the emperor, in order to unite the nation against its enemies. These beliefs were to be combined with national rites to constitute a national religion that would play a role in society comparable to that of Christianity in the West.

Aizawa's proposals were adopted by the Meiji reformers, and from the earliest days of the modern period *saisei itchi* 祭政一致, or the unification of rites and government, was promoted as official government policy. While the implementation of this policy took various forms as the government adapted to the changing situation and engaged in a kind of trial-and-error strategy, its unifying purpose was the promotion of Shinto, both *jinja shintō* 神社神道, or Shrine Shinto, and what later came to be called *kokka shintō* 国家神道, or State Shinto.[5]

In the early Meiji period, the prohibition against Christianity, instituted prior to the establishment of the Tokugawa regime and enforced vigorously throughout the early modern period, remained in force. This became a problem, however, as the government tried to renegotiate the treaties forced on Japan by the Western powers in the final years of the Tokugawa government. These powers demanded that the prohibition be lifted under the principle of religious freedom, a principle that was eventually enshrined in the Imperial Constitution promulgated in 1889. To preserve Shinto's favored position under

4. On Aizawa and the *Shinron* see WAKABAYASHI 1986.
5. Shimazono Susumu has pointed out that the term *kokka shintō* appears in the records of parliamentary debates in 1908, and that the English translation State Shinto was used by the religious scholar Katō Genchi in his *A Study of Shinto*, published in 1926. This information is taken from a presentation by Shimazono at the 59th Annual Conference of the Japanese Association for Religious Studies held in September 2000.

these circumstances, there was a movement toward the redefinition of Shinto as a non-religious set of native beliefs and customs, a distinction that was reflected institutionally in the reorganization of the religious affairs office of the Interior Ministry into the Agency for Shrine Affairs (Jinjakyoku 神社局) and the Agency for Religious Affairs (Shūkyōkyoku 宗教局) in 1900.

Public and scholarly discourse on the non-religious nature of Shinto reached a climax of sorts in the aftermath of the promulgation of the Imperial Rescript on Education in 1890 and the controversy surrounding the refusal of Uchimura Kanzō and other Christians to reverence the Rescript. In focusing on one of the Shinto proponents in this debate, Inoue Tetsujirō, Shimazono points out that although the Rescript takes on the character of a "sacred text" in Inoue's attacks on Christianity, the terms of debate for Inoue are always the opposition of religion (Christianity) to education, morality, the state, or the "teaching of the East" (SHIMAZONO 1998). In Inoue's argument all of these are equated with Shinto.

As State Shinto and Shrine Shinto thus became identified with national morality, customs, and patriotic duties, religion was characterized by the presence of an individual founder and denominational organization. In addition to Christianity and the Buddhist sects, so-called Sect Shinto, the new religious movements that were able to gain government recognition by incorporating officially sanctioned beliefs, were included in the latter category. As Isomae Jun'ichi points out, this was a convenient way to both account for the "religious" elements of Shinto, as well as to at least implicitly denigrate these elements as magical or superstitious beliefs inferior to the national morality promoted by the government.[6]

While some of the leading scholars of Religious Studies in Japan argued for the religious nature of Shinto, Shinto Studies emerged as an independent discipline early in the twentieth century, and argued forcefully for the government's position. The profound impact that non-religious theories of Shinto have had on modern Japanese society is reflected in the fact that they have been recognized by the courts in the postwar period as justification for the use of Shinto rites in groundbreaking ceremonies for government buildings and visits by government officials to Shinto shrines.

TWO RECENT VIEWS OF "RELIGION" IN JAPANESE SOCIETY

Ama Toshimaro is a lecturer in Japanese intellectual history, particularly respected for his views on the development of the idea of religion in Japan. In a popular book published in 1996, *Nihonjin wa naze mushūkyō na no ka* [Why are the Japanese "non-religious"?], he argues that the self-conception of the Japanese as non-religious has its roots in a distinction between "founded religions" (*sōshō shūkyō* 創唱宗教) and "folk (natural) religions" (*shizen shūkyō* 自然宗教).[7] Largely under the influence of the historical

---

6. From a presentation at the Annual Meeting of the Association for Asian Studies, held in Washington D.C., March 1998.

7. *Shizen* would normally be translated as "nature," but AMA himself points out that he is not referring to the worship of nature, but rather religions that emerge "naturally," without any distinguishable founder (1996, p. 11). Folk religion seems to be a better conveyor of this meaning.

developments outlined above, "religion" in Japan has come to mean the founded religions of Christianity, Buddhism, Islam, and the New Religions, while the practices of folk religion that the vast majority of the population engage in—New Year's visits to shrines and temples, funeral rites, visits to ancestral graves—are viewed as social customs, devoid of "religious" meaning. For this reason, seventy percent of the population considers itself non-religious, because they don't belong to one of the founded religions, while seventy-five percent of these "non-religious" Japanese say that being "religious" is important (*shūkyōshin wa taisetsu*) (AMA 1996, p. 8).

Expanding the argument beyond the question of the definition of religion in the modern period, Ama finds the roots of Japanese non-religiosity in several trends evident in the early modern period. He claims that the spread of Confucian ideas, with its emphasis on the cultivation of morals, led to an emphasis on life in this world and a consequent decrease in concern in the Buddhist concept of the afterlife. This trend was further aided by the establishment of "funeral Buddhism" (*sōshiki Bukkyō* 葬式仏教), the parochial system eventually enforced by the Tokugawa government that mandated registration with a Buddhist temple to perform the funeral and later veneration rites. Ama argues that the reassurance of prayers after death, guaranteeing the achievement of Buddhahood—as seen in the spread of the practice of calling all the dead *hotoke*, or Buddha—also served to alleviate concern with the afterlife. This lack of concern in the afterlife is illustrated by the spread of the concept of *ukiyo,* or the transitory nature of life, and especially its accompanying interest in the pleasures of life, as seen in the life of Ihara Saikaku, a poet and popular fiction writer of the late seventeenth century. Here Ama makes mention of *Kōshoku ichidai otoko* [Life of an Amorous Man], a popular novel written by Saikaku in 1682 that details, in its first chapter, the sexual conquests of the hero Yonosuke, amounting to 3,724 women and 725 boys. Ama concludes that "funeral Buddhism is Japanese folk religion in Buddhist clothing" (AMA 1996, p. 66) and its development in the early modern period is yet another reason why contemporary Japanese have little interest in founded religion, and identify themselves as non-religious.

Yamaori Tetsuo, a scholar specializing in the history of religion, argues that two events in 1995 will lead to the death of religion in Japan, or, more accurately, that they have revealed that religion in Japan is already dead. These events were the Kobe Earthquake in January of that year, and, of course, the release of poison gas on the Tokyo subways by members of Aum Shinrikyō in March. Yamaori says that in the first incident religious believers showed the bankruptcy of their own faith by failing to offer a specifically religious response to the catastrophe, content to provide the same aid as non-religious volunteers and counselors. And the Aum case only served to confirm popular suspicion of religion in general, leading to calls to restrict the activities of religious groups and reform the law governing officially registered religious corporations.

Yamaori identifies three factors that have contributed to the perilous position of religion in Japanese society: the hollowing out of Buddhism, the "dereligionization" of Shinto, and widespread disdain for religion among the intelligentsia and media. Buddhism has been hollowed out by the development of "funeral" Buddhism, and Shinto dereligionized in an attempt to preserve its privileged place in the modern state, both processes discussed above. Intellectual and media contempt for religion is traced to Western rationalism, and a knee-jerk reaction on the part of Japanese elites to conform to Western trends.

These three trends have been exacerbated by two modern "separation policies": the separation of Shinto and Buddhism at the beginning of the modern period, and the separation of religion and state in the postwar period. Yamaori argues that the coexistence of the kami and buddhas throughout Japanese history led to a popular religiosity based on both Shinto and Buddhism, and the forced question of either-or, based on an exclusivity found in the Christian concept of religion foreign to the Japanese, leaves many wondering how they should respond. The Japanese have been forced to "examine their own psyches through Christian eyes... they have observed the innermost Japanese soul through the lens of a foreign concept of religion,"[8] and so they respond that they have no belief corresponding to that image of religion. The second separation, that of religion and state in the postwar period, likewise forced Western distinctions of private (religious belief) and public (government), sacred and secular—distinctions that are themselves rarely rigorously enforced in the West, where the British monarch is officially titled the Defender of the Faith, Western European countries provide financial support to churches, and the U. S. president takes his oath of office on a Bible—on a culture that is not used to making these distinctions, and thus has enforced them to a ridiculous, or perhaps dangerous, degree. Yamaori cites the case of Doi Takako, the former head of Japan's Socialist Party, whose Christian belief was concealed by the media and by Doi herself, presumably in the interest of preserving this separation, and observes that it illustrates a "strange mélange of unconscious contempt of religion and credulous susceptibility to the ambience of Western civilization" (YAMAORI 2000, p. 236).

One gets the feeling that Yamaori is swept up in his own arguments, dramatically proclaiming the death of religion in Japan and placing the blame on an ill-fitting Western concept of what the term means. Recent studies on the history of religious conflict in Japan temper the supposed religious plurality that premises his arguments, and court cases in Japan and the United States indicate that the separation of religion and state is a developing concept, in both the East and the West. His arguments are provocative, however, in pointing out, once again, the poor image of religion in Japan, and how this image even affects the activities of religious groups and believers themselves. While the roots of this problem seem to lie in the cultural clash in the concept of religion, as Yamaori maintains, Ama's more nuanced argument, focusing on the difference between "founded" religion and folk religion seems closer to the point, while raising questions of its own regarding the characteristics that make folk religion "religious" and its future in a modern society (see also Ian Reader's essay in this *Guide*). Ama's *shizen shūkyō* does not remain on the level of amorphous religious sentiments, but is expressed in concrete actions: shrine visits, weddings and funerals, veneration of the ancestors at the household altar, participation in local festivals. All of these acts involve some degree of participation in religious institutions,

8. YAMAORI, 2000, p. 231. The article was first published in Japanese (*Oumu jiken to Nihon no shūkyō no shūen*) in *Shokun*, June 1995. An English translation was published by Japan Echo the same year and is reprinted in the volume cited here.

and without these institutions Ama's folk religion would be an empty concept. We turn, finally, to a consideration of the state of institutional religion in Japan.

THE STATE OF RELIGIOUS INSTITUTIONS IN JAPAN

The Agency for Cultural Affairs of the Ministry of Education and Science publishes annual statistics on the number of officially registered religious groups and the number of believers claimed by these groups. The numbers, especially those regarding membership, can be misleading, since there are no uniform criteria for membership and it is assumed that at least some groups will inflate their numbers to give added weight to their importance. On the other hand, the numbers can be taken as revealing the differing meanings assigned to religion that we have been discussing here, and in that sense they need to be considered alongside the survey data introduced at the beginning of this article. At the very least they indicate the relative strength of the various religious groups active in Japan.

At the end of 1998 there were more than 183,000 officially registered religious corporations in Japan. However, the vast majority of these are individual Shinto shrines (86,000) or Buddhist temples (78,000). In addition there were four thousand Christian corporations, including individual dioceses and Catholic religious orders, and sixteen thousand corporations were classified as "other." In addition to the statistics on registered corporations, the agency gives numbers of individual groups; in some instances the corporation will represent a number of groups. Among the Buddhist groups, the largest representation is found in the Pure Land sects (30,000), followed by the Zen sects (21,000), Shingon (15,000), Nichiren sects (12,000), Tendai (5,000), and Nara Buddhism (500), giving some indication of the relative number of temples affiliated with various schools of Buddhism in Japan.

In terms of membership, the Shinto shrines claim a following of over 106,000,000, and the Buddhist temples over 96,000,000. The Shinto membership reflects the number of those considered *ujiko* 氏子, or parishioners, by the shrines, usually including all the residents in the area of the shrine. The Buddhist membership is based on the number of *danka* 檀家, or families registered with the individual temples, usually for funeral and memorial rites. Clearly most of the population is considered as belonging to both of these categories. Christian groups, based on their own definition of membership through individual choice, report a total of almost 1.8 million believers, and the groups classified as "other" claim over eleven million adherents.

The above statistics are inclusive of all religious corporations registered either with the Minister for Education and Science or with the local prefecture office. Under a revision of the Religious Corporations Law following the Aum Affair, all groups active in more than one prefecture must register with the central government, while local groups have the option of registering either with the prefecture or the central government. In a separate set of numbers reflecting the membership of only those groups registered with the central government, a breakdown given by sect is a further indication of the relative strength of these groups. Here, out of a total Buddhist membership of almost 58,000,000, the largest group is once again the Pure Land sects (19,000,000), followed closely by the Nichiren sects (18,000,000),[9] Shingon (13,000,000), and Zen and Tendai with over 3,000,000 apiece.

In a sense it can be said that these numbers, yielding a total religious membership of almost twice the population of Japan, reflect the differing meaning of religion in the country that Ama and Yamaori have pointed out; shrines and temples claim the same people as members, in accordance with Ama's idea of folk religion and Yamaori's claims for religious pluralism. Neither group seems wanting for participants in its religious functions, with the shrines bustling during the New Year holiday, in mid-November for traditional blessings of young children, and a steady stream of young couples coming for marriage ceremonies or to mark the birth of children, and the Buddhist clergy particularly busy at the spring and fall equinoxes and at the end of the year with memorial rites. Neither group, moreover, seems to lack for financial support, an observation that can be extended to new religious groups and Christian churches as well. On these terms, institutional religion seems to be at least holding its own, if not, indeed, prospering, despite the professed lack of interest in "religion" by a large majority of Japanese.

The problem of the image of these religious institutions, however, continues to have a profound effect on how "religion" is perceived in Japan today. Religious institutions have made some attempts to address the issue, or at least have given indications that they are aware of the presence of a problem. Perhaps the best example of this is the discussions in some Buddhist groups on how to reform the practice of *kaimyō* 戒名, or the charging of substantial amounts of money for the granting of a posthumous Buddhist name. In general, however, religious groups have shied away from the problem, choosing to remain anonymous in their activities, as Yamaori points out in the case of the Kobe Earthquake, refraining from engaging in public discourse on current problems, even the problem of religion itself, as in the case of Aum Shinrikyō.[10] There are indications that the public expects religious institutions to play a more active role in such discourse, and that the image of religion would improve if it were seen as more engaged (see KISALA 1999c, pp. 184–86). Despite the ambiguities reflected in survey data on religion, it would appear that reports on its death are still premature.

BIBLIOGRAPHY

AMA Toshimaro 阿満利麿, 1996. *Nihonjin wa naze mushūkyō na no ka* 日本人はなぜ無宗教なのか. Tokyo: Chikuma Shobō.

AGENCY FOR CULTURAL AFFAIRS, 2000. *Shūkyō nenkan* 宗教年鑑. Tokyo: Gyōsei.

ISHII Kenji 石井研士, 1997. *Dētabukku gendai Nihonjin no shūkyō: Sengo gojūnen no shūkyō ishiki to shūkyōkōdō* データブック現代日本人の宗教——戦後五〇年の宗教意識と宗教行動. Tokyo: Shinyōsha.

9. Some of the large new religious groups, such as Risshō Kōseikai, are included in this number.

10. On the general lack of religious responses to the Aum Affair, see KISALA 2001.

KISALA, Robert, 1999a. Asian Values Study. *Bulletin of the Nanzan Institute for Religion and Culture* 23: 59–73.

_____, 1999b. Japanese Religiosity and Morals. In *Religion in Secularizing Society: The Europeans' Religion at the End of the 20th Century,* ed. Loek Halman and Ole Riis, pp. 173–88. Tilburg: Tilburg University Press.

_____, 1999c. *Prophets of Peace: Pacifism and Cultural Identity in Japan's New Religions.* Honolulu: University of Hawai'i Press.

_____, 2001. Religious Responses to the "Aum Affair." In *Religion and Social Crisis in Japan: Understanding Japanese Society through the Aum Affair,* ed. Robert J. Kisala and Mark R. Mullins, pp. 107–32. Houndmills, UK: Palgrave.

SHIMAZONO Susumu 島薗 進, 1998. *Nihon ni okeru "shūkyō" gainen no keisei: Inoue Tetsujirō no Kirisutokyō hihan o megutte* 日本における「宗教」概念の形成——井上哲次郎のキリスト教批判をめぐって. In *Nihonji wa Kirisutokyō o dono yō ni juyō shita ka* 日本人はキリスト教をどのように受容したか, ed. Yamaori Tetsuo 山折哲雄 and Osada Toshiki 長田俊樹, pp. 61–75. Kyoto: Kokusai Nihon Bunka Kenkyū Sentā.

WAKABAYASHI, Bob Tadashi, 1986. *Anti-Foreignism and Western Learning in Early-Modern Japan: The New Theses of 1825.* Cambridge: Harvard University Press.

YAMAORI Tetsuo, 2000. Aum Shinrikyō Sounds the Death Knell of Japanese Religion. In *Years of Trial: Japan in the 1990s,* ed. Masuzoe Yōichi. Tokyo: Japan Echo. Originally published 1995 in *Japan Echo* 22/3: 48–53.

Norman HAVENS

Shinto

By one account, the field of Shinto studies has changed little since 1988 when Joseph M. KITAGAWA (1988, p. 227) introduced a special issue of *History of Religions* dedicated to Shinto with the warning that the subject presents "some very difficult and disconcerting questions" for the historian of religions. The trouble starts with our first attempts at defining an object of study. As recently described by INOUE Nobutaka (1988, pp. 245), "Shinto is ordinarily understood as Japan's traditional religion, or indigenous form of religion, but there exists no firm agreement as to what should be included within the rubric of Shinto." He then states that definitions of Shinto run the gamut from those that include "the entirety of the Japanese people's way of life," to others claiming that "Japanese religious behavior (*shinkō* 信仰) is virtually all a collection or adaptation of elements taken from foreign religions, making it impossible to extract any coherent unity deserving the name 'Shinto.'" Most researchers, Inoue

14

states, lie between these two extremes, feeling that "it is possible to distinguish a form of religion called Shinto possessing a certain degree of particularity (*koyūsei* 固有性)."

The three approaches suggested by Inoue might be called the "air," "onion," and "pearl" strategies of definition, reflecting the views that Shinto is variously the "air we breathe," an onion that, once peeled, leaves nothing behind, or, is rather like a pearl—lots of accretions around a small but distinct core. Even this tripartite categorization, however, remains too simplistic, since elements of the definitions are not always mutually exclusive. At any rate, the paradox in approaching this subject is that, in the context of the other essays in this *Guide*, and depending on one's perspective, Shinto might easily be taken as the sum total of all the other essays here, or, perhaps, no more than part of the chapter on Buddhism.

WHAT IS SHINTO?

Traditional *emic* descriptions of Shinto are those given by modern Shintoists themselves, and by extension, Western observers who rely on predominantly Shintoist sources. They frequently start with a variation on "*Shinto is the indigenous religion of Japan.*" One recent introductory work in English thus states that Shinto is one of "two major faiths" espoused in Japan (the other being Buddhism): "Shinto is indigenous to Japan, and…the religion still permeates almost every aspect of Japanese life" (LITTLETON 2002, p. 6). The traditional accounts frequently go on to describe Shinto as a natural polytheism that evolved within the specific ecology and communal lifestyle common to the Japanese islands (SONODA 2000). Rather than individual belief, religious life is focused on seasonal festivals or *matsuri* involving ageless agricultural rites dedicated to tutelary deities (kami) enshrined in *jinja* of each locality. Parishioners and other worshipers visit the shrines at times of major festivals, during initiatory and life-crisis rites, and at other times of extraordinary need. Other conventional details might include the fact that while Shinto was subordinate to Buddhism through most of its history and underwent syncretism with Buddhism from the late ancient period on, it developed an increasing sense of self-identity and awareness from the medieval period, culminating in the early modern nativist program of Motoori Norinaga and Hirata Atsutane, both of whom attempted to purify kami ritual of all specious (primarily Confucian) and vulgarly religious (primarily Buddhist) taint. By throwing off such accretions, the architects of the Meiji Restoration succeeded in restoring Shinto to its "pure" form—yet without the religious content that ironically had made the earlier cult popular (GRAPARD 1984). Following the Restoration (1868), brief attempts were made to raise Shinto to the equivalent of a national church, but it was then divorced once again from "religion" and defined as a system of patriotic national ethics and civic morality, a non-religious vehicle for the mystical national polity called *kokutai* 国体.

Other features may be enumerated, but *doctrine* is rarely addressed. In fact, Shinto is known for its doctrinal latitude and the minimal level of creedal demands placed on its adherents. These last characteristics are in fact some of what makes Shinto so difficult to grasp as a *religion*. Ueda Kenji, for example, notes that "as a national religion or 'natural religion,' Shinto originally had no need for establishing doctrines," yet that very characteristic has meant, contrarily, that "the development of scholastic theology within Shinto has always been in response to stimulation from outside" (UEDA 1987). Perhaps even more important, the post-Meiji promulgation of Restoration Shinto as a non-religious system of national rite and vehicle for Japan's *kokutai* led to strict prohibitions on the production of speculative teachings. Following World War II, when Shrine Shinto was disestablished and forced into the status of an independent religion on the same footing with other religions, suggestions were made toward the end of establishing a uniform body of Shinto doctrine, yet with disappointing results. The conclusion of the 1947 document, "Principles for the Treatment of Doctrinal Inquiry," was to recommend that "no specific doctrinal stance be established," and as late as 1965, a survey of "some three-hundred selected priests, scholars and laypersons" could not even provide a basis for deciding whether Shinto was polytheistic or monotheistic (UEDA 1987, pp. 77–81; see also UEDA 1991, pp. 16ff).

Descriptions of this type can be said to use elements of both the "pearl" and "air" strategies. Namely, they claim that Shinto has existed throughout Japanese history, though over time it has become overlain with accretions from other religions and philosophies. The work of the restorationists was to dig down through, and peel off, the accretions in order to reveal the pure essence underneath.

Unfortunately, in the process, the core thus revealed frequently appears so bereft of *substantiality* that it can barely support the weight of a discrete institutional identity, and tends to be defined instead as the mystical spiritual foundation of all Japanese culture, the "national essence" or *kokutai*. For example, while Ueda states that "it is difficult to capture Shinto in a definition…" he then continues by suggesting that Shinto, "in the most comprehensive sense of the term, represents the value orientation of the Japanese people in the various forms it has taken and the developments it has undergone throughout Japanese history—including contacts with foreign cultures." When Ueda says "in the various forms it has taken and the developments it has undergone," he leaves little out, thus implying that whatever is Japanese, is Shinto. Similarly, ASOYA Masahiko (1999, p. 55) states, "It is very difficult" to define Shinto, since it is equivalent to the "Japanese way of living" and thus for the Japanese traditionally "needs no explanation in words." Here again, Shinto, once distilled of accretions, is seen through "meta-religious" lenses as the wordless "air we breathe," and thus in one sense, beyond critique. As a result, although recent scholars in the West may assume that the notion of Shinto as an identifiable, perduring institution of indigenous Japanese culture has been thoroughly discredited, the belief continues to strongly color the work of many scholars working *within* the tradition.

Finally, one aspect of the emic account not always emphasized in Western treatments of Shinto as a religion, yet deeply rooted in the status of modern Shinto as a non-religious system of civic ritual is the role of the modern emperor (BREEN and TEEUWEN 2000, p. 2). The emperor's place within Shinto, and more broadly the role of Shinto in legitimating a particularistic socio-political system of authority, has been a constant issue for modern Shinto theorists. While outlining historical views of the definition of Shinto, Asoya Masahiko first quotes Kōno Seizō as an examplar of prewar "Kokutai Shinto":

> Shinto is the "Way of the Kami." The Way of the Kami is the basic principle of life since the times of the ancestors of the Japanese race. The Japanese race considered the act of

glorifying, enhancing, and worshipping the heavenly virtues of Amaterasu Okami the principle of life, and the principle of the Japanese nation. (ASOYA 1999, p. 59)

ASOYA then continues, "In other words, Shinto is the principle of life for the Japanese people. Put in more concrete terms, it is for the subject to serve the emperor, who is the descendant of the heavenly *kami*" (1999, p. 59). While Asoya brackets these comments in the context of historical (prewar) definitions of Shinto, there is little doubt that many proponents of Shrine Shinto today would agree with their sentiment. The Association of Shinto Shrines (Jinja Honchō), umbrella organization for the 80,000 shrines throughout Japan, has set forth a minimal creed in the form of Principles of a Life of Reverence for the Kami (*Keishin seikatsu no kōryō* 敬神生活の綱領); the third of these states, "Gratefully *accepting the emperor's mind and will*, I shall live in amity and goodwill with my fellows, praying for the prosperity of the nation and the mutual coexistence and welfare of the entire world." When Anzu Motohiko claims that "the Japanese who … take a rather serious view of this life know *through experience* [and] *through historical fact* … the existence of the Emperor as the absolute condition of the life of the Japanese race," it seems only natural to respond with Kitagawa that "neither Anzu nor anyone else has the right to superimpose his Shintō belief on non-Shintō Japanese…" (KITAGAWA 1988, p. 230). But given the breadth of the definitions involved, can there be such a thing as a "non-Shintō Japanese"? If Shinto is indeed equivalent to the "Japanese way of living" ("the air we breathe"), then by extension all true Japanese are bound to submit to the emperor's will.

In sum, the debate over common claims that Shinto is Japan's "indigenous religion" is not primarily a matter of academic quibbles about the correct parsing of the words *indigenous* or *religion*, what part of Shinto is truly home grown and what part imported, or whether Shinto is *a religion* in the sense of the Buddhism with which it is usually contrasted. These are all legitimate and relevant concerns, but they are secondary to the issue of the political use which such claims serve, specifically as a legitimation of demands for subservience on the part of *all* Japanese to established institutions of authority. Claims for Shinto's ahistorical meta-religious inclusivity thus have implications that may go beyond those of ordinary religions toward fellow members of a religious communion; claiming that "the entire Japanese way of life is Shinto" can be called "conversion by definition," something that sits uneasily with non-Shintoist scholars, and that has made them in turn extremely critical toward issues of bias in the area of historical claims. After noting the early modern nativist origins of restoration Shinto and its offspring, Shrine Shinto, Wilhelmus Creemers stated in 1968 that "in view of the bias underlying many such interpretations and treatises, it is very difficult to decide whether or not they can be accepted as reliable sources of information." He concluded that "to find out what Shinto is, therefore, it seems wise to disregard the writings of most prewar and many postwar Shinto theorists" (CREEMERS 1968, p. xvi).

A harsh judgment, but one that helps explain why much writing has been directed either toward "softening" (universalizing) Shinto through the use of motifs akin to "perennial philosophy" or Bergsonian theories of subconscious creativity (MASON 1935, PICKEN 1980, YAMAMOTO 1987), or subjecting Shinto's claims for indigeneity, inclusivity, and historical continuity to rigorous skepticism (KURODA 1975, 1981).

"HISTORY BEGINS AT KURODA"

It is here that the "onion" strategy comes in. This definitional approach claims that once relieved of its historical "accretions," little remains of an immutable entity worthy of the name "Shinto," at least not until the creation of Shrine Shinto in the modern period. Needless to say, the person most closely associated with this kind of description is Kuroda Toshio. If Samuel Noah Kramer's cliché is true that "history begins at Sumer," it might be equally said that, particularly for those in the West, "the history of modern Shinto studies begins at Kuroda," a reflection of the immense impact his work has had on the field. With regard to Shinto, Kuroda and his interpreters have argued that the term "Shinto" 神道 (or *jindō* as it was likely pronounced until the medieval period; see TEEUWEN 2002) was not used in ancient times to describe an independent "religion," but primarily the "way (or condition) of being a kami," and its historical usage consistently takes for granted the Buddhist conceptual vocabulary then current (KURODA 1981, TEEUWEN 2002). While we assume that prehistoric rituals were oriented toward non-everyday potencies, their first historical organization as *jingi saishi* 神祇祭祀 took place under the influence of Chinese models and Buddhist theory and practice. In the words of TEEUWEN and SCHEID (2002, p. 205), the *jingi* system was not "Shinto," but rather "the canvas onto which Shinto was to be drawn" centuries later. As a result, the history of Japanese religion should not be considered the story of the relationship between "two major faiths," but rather a tableau, or an ever-shifting kaleidoscopic pattern of forces, constantly within the conceptual limits of the comprehensive theoretical discourse and practical institutional structure that Kuroda called variously *kenmitsu shisō* 顕密思想 ("exo-esoteric discourse"), and *kenmitsu taisei* 顕密体制 ("exo-esoteric regime"). The term *kenmitsu* here refers to the combination of exoteric and esoteric Buddhist thought and practice as it developed within the Tendai and Shingon schools from around the mid-Heian period on, and which formed the basic condition of knowledge throughout Japan's history up to at least the late medieval to early modern periods, until Shrine Shinto was reinvented as a modern national religion in the late nineteenth century. One result of Kuroda's theory is that it has freed scholars from the need to wrestle with the ambiguous nature of essentialist definitions of the Shinto "tradition," viewing it instead through most of Japanese history as "rituals directed toward kami," namely, one vector within a phenomenal "field" ruled by the *kenmitsu* discourse, similar to the way in which anthropologists such as Victor Turner and Stanley Tambiah have utilized the "field" concept in their studies of religion (TURNER 1974; TAMBIAH 1970; see also TEEUWEN and RAMBELLI 2003, p. 2).

Since this new understanding flies in the face of received wisdom regarding Shinto's independence and existence as an independent tradition, it remains controversial—particularly within the Shinto religious establishment itself—but is gaining acceptance among the younger generation of scholars. For example, in a recent work by Itō Satoshi, Endō Jun, and Mori Mizue, the authors state that "we do not think of 'Shinto' as an independent religious tradition. On the contrary, we believe that kami worship was established within a 'field' (*ba* 場) representing the seamless integration of a variety of cults and discourses which today are viewed as discrete traditions, including Buddhism, Confucianism, Taoism, and the way of Yin-Yang" (ITŌ et al. 2002, p. 2).

As a result, most Western research on Shinto in recent years has at minimum displayed an awareness of the Kuroda thesis, and increasingly concentrated research has been directed toward the thesis itself (TEEUWEN and RAMBELLI 2003; also the special issues of *Japanese Journal of Religious Studies* 23/3–4 in 1996 and 29/3–4 in 2002). In sum, this—the "onion" definition of Shinto—tends to be the ruling definitional paradigm in use today.

THE HISTORICAL TRAJECTORY OF SHINTO

Based on recent trends in research and the study of religion, how can we "reenvision" the history of "Shinto"?

Religion in Japan's prehistoric epoch was, based on archaeological evidence, probably not dissimilar from that found in hunter-gatherer cultures elsewhere in eastern Asia, namely, the observance of ritualized behavior to placate a variety of natural powers, in Japan called variously *kami*, *mono*, *chi*, *mi*, and *tama* (ITŌ 1998, YOSHIDA 2003). Taken alone, the word kami is not believed to have been used to refer to anthropomorphic beings until the production of a discourse of ritual-political power that began in the late seventh century. Kami attributed with the kind of human personality found in the eighth-century *Kojiki* 古事記 and *Nihon shoki* 日本書紀 were the products of relatively late, sophisticated speculation, and on the whole not characteristic of the earliest usage (HAVENS 1998, pp. 236–7). Kami were believed to "inhabit" specific, particular phenomena of nature—including trees, mountains, and rivers—and this belief in the sacrality of concrete natural phenomena is one of the keys to understanding the way in which Japanese space was later sacralized within Buddhist discourse. At the same time, while associated with such natural phenomena, kami made their appearance only erratically, or in response to specific acts of worship, and were not enshrined in permanent man-made structures until after the coming of Buddhism (MATSUMAE 1993). Traditional interpretations of ancient Japan tend to portray kami in almost exclusively pacific and beneficent terms (REISCHAUER 1980); more recent research, however, has thrown doubts on that sanguine portrayal, and suggest a darker apprehension of kami in the pre-historic and ancient periods. Rather than munificent bestowers of the blessings of nature, the most striking aspect of ancient kami was, in SATŌ Hiroo's words, their "unpredictable nature" (2000, p. 20). Other scholars are even more emphatic. Itō Satoshi states that the ancient association of kami activity with epidemic disease, floods, and drought was so close as to conclude that "the activity of performing worship to kami was for no other reason than placating the kami's ire; it is not excessive to say the essence of kami worship (*jingi saishi*) in Japan can be sought in the avoidance of the kami's violent apparitions (*tatari*). It was only later that kami came to be viewed as beings that had compassion on humans—a concept unknown to those of the ancient period" (ITŌ et al. 2002, p.4; see also NAKAMURA 1994, p. 109). This characteristic is important since it helps in understanding the interpretation of the place of kami within subsequent Buddhist discourse.

The patterns of ritual conduct oriented toward such non-everyday powers no doubt became more systematized in the first centuries of the common era, together with the advent of widespread hydraulic rice agriculture and the gradual merger of tribes into a confederation centering on the Yamato clan and its "great kings" (*daiō* 大王 or *ōkimi* 大君). Debate remains regarding the nature and incidence of so-called "dual-gender pair" rule (sometimes called the *himehiko* 姫彦 system), wherein a woman and man ruled together with joint control over the sacred (non-everyday) and secular (everyday) realms, although the evidence suggests that women were frequently viewed as being particularly susceptible to sacred induction (PIGGOTT 1997).

As with other preliterate peoples, no conception was made of a "religious" realm strictly divorced from the "secular" or political. Referring to the ritual practices of that period as a "religion" is meaningful only in the same sense that one speaks of "Nuer religion" or "the religion of the Maoris," which is to say that to the degree that government dealt with the control over and wielding of *power,* it inevitably involved "religion." In reflection of this holistic worldview, an early term for government, *matsurigoto* 政 meant literally the "business of ritual worship." In the words of Allan GRAPARD, "ritual was the locus of a discourse of power through which legitimacy was enforced and communicated" (1988, p. 256; see also *idem* 1999, p. 521). Observance of ceremonial worship by the *ōkimi* was, in short, a crucial act legitimizing his status as great king. The ritual practices involved were developed locally as well as imported from China in the form of Taoist and Yin-Yang cults, and later Buddhism (BARRETT 2000; see also TEEUWEN 2002).

As a natural corollary of this holistic worldview, the introduction of Buddhism in the sixth century should not be thought of as representing a clash of *religions* (TAMURA 2000, p. 26), but rather a conflict over which ritual objects and techniques were the more powerful, and thus more efficacious. Attempts to understand the newly arriving buddhas within the local idiom as "visiting kami" or "foreign kami"—and thus not essentially different in nature from the non-everyday powers found locally—were quickly overwhelmed, however, as the Japanese were confronted with the sophisticated cosmology associated with Buddhism's advanced thought. Buddhism brought with it an immense and developed soteriological and philosophical literature, and even to the uneducated eye, it added distinct human personality to its concept of supranormal power in the concrete shape of anthropomorphic sculpture and other arts. Permanent architectural structures (*tera* 寺, *jiin* 寺院) housed these images, hinting that Buddhist powers were accessible to entreaty at all times, and such structures formed the model for the subsequent construction of permanent "shrines" (*jinja* 神社) to house local kami. But as noted above, Buddhism was viewed initially within the same construct of concepts that had governed pre-Buddhist Japan, so while its introduction signaled the replacement, for example, of burial tumuli by Buddhist architecture, the new structures were initially treated as serving a purpose similar to the previous burial mounds, namely, memorials to the powerful dead. Beneath the pagoda of one of the earliest temples, Asukadera, for example, have been found interred not only Buddhist relics, but mirrors, swords, and other articles normally interred with a deceased ruler (BROWN 1993, p. 511).

Politically, the introduction of Buddhism provoked internecine conflict between those clans desiring closer ties to the cosmopolitan culture of the continent and those wishing to

TRADITIONS

preserve local traditions and estates of power. With the ascendancy of the group favoring the liturgical system of Buddhist objects of worship, the government began systematizing bureaucratic and ritual practice along Chinese and Buddhist lines, leading to the ritual and legal institutions known as the *ritsuryō*, enacted from the late seventh century onward (PIGGOTT 1997, p. 208ff). Within that system, the Jingikan or Department of Kami, while holding a position nominally superior to the Department of State, did not represent an indigenous "religion," but an application of the Chinese model of the "Ministry of Rites" and T'ang ritual protocols that implemented styles for the worship of powers considered crucial to the imperial Yamato clan and its various confederated kinship groups (NAUMANN 2000; GRAPARD 1988, 1999, 2000, 2002; YOSHIDA 2003). The newly named *tennō*, or "heavenly sovereign" of the post–seventh-century period acted, in Joan Piggott's words, as a "ritual coordinator" responsible for fine-tuning the requirements of the two ritual systems, namely, the kami shrines and Buddhist temples (PIGGOTT 1997, p. 208). The establishment of the Grand Shrines of Ise and adoption of a Sun Deity as an imperial ancestral kami are believed to have occurred roughly in this same period, between the late fifth and seventh centuries, although much of the history of the shrines' establishment and the purpose of their location in Ise remain controversial (see TAMURA 1996; OKADA 1985).

In short, the official introduction of Buddhism in the mid-sixth century corresponds to the period in which the Yamato "great king" (*ōkimi*) adopted the new, possibly Taoist, title of Tennō 天皇 (see BARRETT 2000), permanent shrine structures began to appear modeled after Buddhist counterparts, and a systematic body of kami ritual came to be established after Chinese and Buddhist models. Within this fluctuating intellectual and institutional crucible, the very concepts of "kami" and "buddha" were fluid and, contrary to conventional assumptions, not necessarily discriminated in the way we think of today.

As pointed out by SATŌ Hiroo (2000), although the content of concepts like kami and buddha have undergone immense changes through the years, traditional research has basically ignored those changes and continued to assume that a simple dichotomy can continue to be made between the two. This situation is reflected in the expression used to refer to the process, *shinbutsu shūgō* 神仏習合, since it proposes the distinction between two simple entities, *shin* 神 (kami) and *butsu* 仏 (buddhas), which are then "syncretized," thus already assuming part of what the research might want to prove. As a result, Satō states that researchers have "merely attempted to measure the *degree* of amalgamation (*shūgō* 習合) or estrangement between kami and buddhas," rather than questioning the validity of the basic dichotomy itself. Fundamentally, the early Japanese were reacting to, and attempting to make sense of, a wide variety of powers perceived within a holistic world. The conceptual vocabulary they used in that attempt was provided by Chinese thought and Buddhism. As a result, the attempt to understand the relationship between the various kinds of powers, and the "truths" they represented, occupied the Japanese mind and served as a seminal theme through succeeding centuries.

Early hints of the attempt to comprehend the relationship between naturalistic local kami and the potencies introduced by Buddhism are expressed in Japan's early myths and legendary tales. In the mythology of the *Nihongi*, for example, a camphor-wood boat is the vehicle used when an early creative failure, the kami Hiruko no mikoto, is cast away in the sea. The motif of the camphor-wood "boat" returns later in the account of the transmission of Buddhism as recorded in both *Nihongi* and *Nihon ryōiki* 日本霊異記 (ca. early 9th c.); here, a miraculously glowing camphor log is found arriving on the sea and is subsequently used for carving into Buddhist images (ASTON 1972, p. 268; KANDA 1985, p. 10; NAKAMURA 1973, pp. 111–12; also GRAPARD 1992b, 151–54). The *Ryōiki* likewise records the story of a tree felled for use in making Buddhist images, and which reveals a sign of supranormal sentience (NAKAMURA 1973, p. 196). Other records relate the power of Buddhism in pacifying the wrath of kami when shrine trees were exploited for Buddhist purposes. In all these stories, one can sense the attempt to relate trees, a prototypical vehicle or hierophany of local kami, to the new personalized powers of Buddhism (see TEEUWEN and RAMBELLI 2003, pp. 7–12).

Throughout the *Ryōiki*'s tales are revealed the diverse ways in which Japanese of the early centuries of Buddhist contact attempted to formulate a paradigm that could account for the variety of supranormal powers and forces that filled their world, whether kami, Buddhist, Taoist, or other. While nominally a "Buddhist" work, the *Ryōiki* wove its stories from numerous religious traditions in the attempt to understand in a comprehensive way the supranormal. For example, Nakamura Kyōko suggests that the *Ryōiki*'s author Kyōkai understood Buddhist truth or Dharma through the Chinese concept of an ultimate principle or *tao* 道, one that incorporated not only Buddhism but the other "ways" of Yin-Yang and local kami as well (NAKAMURA 1973, p. 49).

The concept of a universal *tao* points to a feature of Buddhism and Taoism that was likely new to Japan, namely, a clear sense of what might be called a "gnostic" view of two realities or "two truths," what NAKAMURA Ikuo (1994, p. 102) calls the "Buddhist paradigm of the provisional (*gon* 権) and the real (*jitsu* 実)" (see also MATSUNAGA 1969, pp. 116ff). That the Japanese were intrigued with the concept, basically that "what you see may not be real," and that a deeper layer of ultimate truth lies behind the apparent surface, is found in many of the *Ryōiki*'s tales. The karmic transformations encountered in the work thus involve kami, human beings, natural objects, Buddho-Taoist sages, and bodhisattvas: what appears to be a natural log turns out to be a sentient buddha image in disguise. An apparent beggar might in fact be a noble or sage. A supranormal human child is revealed to be a reborn thunder-kami, and later goes on to become a Buddhist Dharma master (LIN 2003). While some aspects of the concept of two realities may not be entirely absent in any "animism" (the idea that some kind of invisible life force exists within or behind all phenomena), it is certain that early Japan was influenced by specifically Taoist-related teachings regarding immortals and "wizards" (*shinsen* 神仙), while the *Lotus Sūtra*, in particular, introduced the concept of provisional versus absolute truth. And only those who had developed suprahuman abilities could easily discern the difference:

> We learn that a sage recognizes a sage, whereas an ordinary man cannot recognize a sage. The ordinary man sees nothing but the outer form of a beggar, while the sage has a penetrating eye able to recognize the hidden essence. (NAKAMURA 1973, p. 110; see also KURODA 1996a, p. 245).

As suggested above, the overall process whereby the Japanese attempted to construct a comprehensive understanding of the variety of phenomenal powers around them has traditionally been referred to as the evolution of *shinbutsu shūgō*, or the "amalgamation (or syncretism) of kami and buddhas." Based on the pioneering work of Tsuji Zennosuke 辻善之助, modern *shinbutsu shūgō* theory has been conceptualized as a process passing through several "stages," although recent research emphasizes that the process was not a unilinear progress, but more akin to the activity of bricolage, in which ad hoc theories were assembled from teachings at hand, with the result that succeeding "stages" did not necessarily displace previous theories, and phenomena characteristic of earlier periods continued to coexist in the relationship between kami and buddhas of later times. The number of "steps" proposed in the evolution varies depending on the scholar, but is usually three or four (the best recent treatment of this topic is TEEUWEN and RAMBELLI 2003; see also TEEUWEN 2000, p. 95; NAKAMURA 1994, p. 97ff; MURAYAMA 1974).

In the earliest period of contact, Buddhist powers were assumed to be fundamentally of the same nature as local kami, powerful but unpredictable beings who would produce *tatari* or violent apparitions (plague and disasters) if not placated with worship (NAKAMURA 1994, p. 110). The conceptual fluidity within which kami and buddha were grasped seems evident, for example, in the aforementioned tales of kami trees being appropriated for the purpose of making Buddhist images or structures. At times, this contact provoked violent apparitions from the kami as Buddhism spread, and its powers encroached upon the existing prerogatives or lands of the local potencies (TEEUWEN and RAMBELLI 2003, p. 8). But while the traditional kami ritualists appear to have possessed little more than a theology of territoriality, Buddhism furnished a new cosmology, ontology, and theoretical rationale that opened new vistas for understanding the relationship. By the eighth century, the Buddhist doctrine of karma was already being used to explain the status of local kami. According to the new view, kami were *sentient beings in need of salvation.* In response, Buddhist temples, called *jingūji* 神宮寺 or "shrine-temples," began to be built on or near the grounds of kami shrines, for the purpose of worshiping the kami according to Buddhist liturgical style, thus "aiding" the kami toward achievement of salvation. The famous Tado shrine oracle of 763 thus related that the kami wished to "shed the *kami*-body, and cling to the Three Treasures [Buddhism]" (MURAYAMA 1974, p. 37). Such early shrine-temples were forerunners of what have been termed the religious "multiplexes" that characterized Japanese religion through the succeeding centuries. In this process, it is important to remember that the conceptual rapproachment was occasioned by access to a Buddhist theory that explained the origin and nature of these powers. The old motif whereby a kami indicated its will through the medium of a violent apparition (*tatari*) was now reinterpreted by Buddhism as an indication of the kami's pain, and its desire for release from its suffering status (ITŌ et al. 2002, p. 51).

At virtually the same time, a second style of rapprochement appeared, according to which kami were interpreted as being divine tutelaries of Buddhism. Based on its historical origins in India, Buddhism had adopted numerous deva from Hinduism as protectors of the Dharma, and this practice was continued and expanded upon as the religion passed through China and entered Japan (MATSUNAGA 1969). The most famous early case is undoubtedly that of the Usa Hachiman, which issued an oracle in honor of the completion of the Great Buddha of Nara's Tōdaiji in 749, relating that it wished to "pay homage to the Great Buddha" (SONODA 1993, p. 412). The case of Hachiman is additionally striking for the fact that it is believed to be one of the first cases in which a kami was depicted in sculpture (*shinzō* 神像), specifically, in the fashion of a Buddhist monk. TEEUWEN and RAMBELLI note that this practice was "inspired directly by the statues of Buddhist divinities worshiped at temples" (2003, p.14); but the specific mode of the depiction was also likely influenced by the concept of miraculous transformations noted earlier, namely, that a kami could make its appearance in the guise of a Buddhist thaumaturge or other figure.

According to the traditional account, the final way in which local kami and Buddhist figures were accommodated appeared within the development of the doctrine generally known as *honji suijaku* 本地垂迹 ("original ground and manifest traces"). This doctrine proposed the appearance of various phenomenal beings as *avatars*, incarnations or embodiments of the immaterial noumenon or Buddhist truth. In what might be compared to a limited application of Platonic emanationist theories, *honji suijaku* appeared in Japan from the Heian period within the Tendai and Shingon schools of Buddhism as part of the mystical apprehension of the Buddhist theory of "two truths." Central to this discourse was the *Lotus Sūtra*, which had been interpreted in Chinese T'ien-t'ai 天台 as divided into two halves, appropriately called "ground" and "trace" (MATSUNAGA 1969; STONE 1999). The "ground" represented the Buddha in its immaterial form of ultimate truth, while the "trace" aspect was represented by the ways in which ultimate truth made its phenomenal appearance, the Buddha's "means" (Skt. *upāya*, Jpn. *hōben* 方便) meant to lead suffering sentient beings to ultimate salvation. As this doctrine developed in the late Heian period, it became the *leit motif* of what Kuroda calls the *kenmitsu* discourse.

Throughout this development, it is important to recall that while the specifics of the *honji suijaku* doctrine were apprehended as new, the development itself was part of the same ongoing process that had, from the days of earliest contact, worked to analyze and accommodate conflicting sources of power and experiences of reality. Once again, the conceptual tools for the analysis are provided almost entirely by Buddhism. Further, the impact of this combinatory kind of thought is evident in the fact that it was eventually extended from religious potencies in the narrow sense (kami and buddhas) to other areas of experience, including geography, society, and nature. As a result, not only were local deities given new stature and identity as avatars of buddhas and bodhisattvas, but mountains and other traditional Japanese ritual sites were valorized as physical equivalents of immaterial geographies (pure lands), a process that has been called the "mandalization" of space in Japan (GRAPARD 1982; RAMBELLI 1996, p. 395). And while the connection with *honji suijaku* may be less clear, the relationship between secular law (*ōbō* 王法) and Buddhist truth (*buppō* 仏法) was likewise expressed as "heart and mind," or mutually supporting halves of a single whole, another way in which Buddhist cosmology fit into the overall discourse on power (KURODA 1996b). Eventually the very geography of "Japan" came to be viewed as the locus for a discourse on the notion of *shinkoku* 神国 or "the land of kami," one which coincided with the development of independent Shinto schools and nativist thought (KURODA 1996b, 1996c; RAMBELLI 1996). But like the "reverse *honji suijaku*" theory promoted at the Outer Shrine of Ise (see below), the medieval *shinkoku* discourse did not indicate nascent consciousness of a metahistorical Japanese "nation" or "Shinto" as an indigenous tradition. Rather, it was largely the product of the internecine wars of early medieval Buddhism, used as a tool by the older sects to criticize the new *nenbutsu* and other "single-practice" sects' refusal to show devotion to native kami as Buddhist avatars (KURODA 1996c; NAKAMURA 1994).

The identification of the phenomenal entities with their immaterial ground in *honji sui-jaku* reached its peak with the appearance and spread of Tendai "original enlightenment" (*hongaku* 本覚) thought in the Kamakura period. Based on the key Mayayana doctrine of *śūnyatā* (emptiness of all dharmas, the lack of ultimate self-nature in all phenomena), original enlightenment thought is usually described as the expression of a non-dualistic understanding that identifies the phenomenal world, *as it is*, with the state of ultimate enlightenment (STONE 1999). As Robert MORRELL describes the medieval monk Mujū Ichien, the conviction lying behind this kind of syncretistic view was that "truth not only can, but must, assume a variety of forms" (1985, p. 59). Usually considered to imply a thoroughgoing valorization of the physical world, this doctrine furnished a new twist to the use of *honji suijaku* in identifying local Japanese kami with their ultimate Buddhist counterparts. As noted earlier, according to original *honji suijaku* doctrine, Japanese kami were interpreted as the "provisional" (*gon*) revelations of immaterial or "real" (*jitsu*) Buddhist truth. With the flowering of original enlightenment thought, however, it became possible to view the provisional manifestations (*suijaku*) not only as identical in nature to their grounds (*honji*), but even superior to them, due to their greater accessibility and compassion for humans expressed in the act of "dimming their light and mingling with the dust" (*wakō dōjin* 和光同塵). This was expressed as what is conventionally called the "reverse *honji suijaku*" doctrine, which influenced the appearance of both Watarai Shinto, which developed from the thirteenth century among the priests of the Outer Shrine (Gekū) at Ise, and Yoshida Shinto in later centuries.

Another influence on the Watarai School was Ryōbu (dual) Shinto, a current of kami cult promoted by the Shingon and esoteric Tendai schools and applied specifically to the Grand Shrines of Ise (Inner Shrine) in order to rationalize or counteract the traditional taboo of Buddhism at the shrine, and thus allow for pilgrimage by Buddhist clergy. According to this doctrine, the deity of Ise, Amaterasu, was in fact the "spirit" of Mahāvairocana Buddha (TEEUWEN and VEERE 1998), and thus not opposed to Buddhism. Like *shinkoku* thought, "reverse *honji suijaku*" doctrine in general, and Watarai Shinto in particular, have frequently been interpreted as representing an embryonic "Shinto" revolution against Buddhism, due to the way in which kami were raised to a status superior to the buddhas. In his exhaustive study of this school, however, Mark TEEUWEN argues that Watarai Shinto in fact represented one particular shrine cult still operating within the broader conceptual vocabulary and limits of the *kenmitsu* discourse, with the result that the Ise argument that Buddhism was unnecessary at Ise was not intended to "establish the primacy of Shintō over Buddhism, but rather to construe an exclusive link between the Ise shrines and esoteric teaching as the highest form of Buddhism, and thus to further enhance the sanctity of the shrines" (1996, p. 128). These new schools of combinatory kami cult arose against the background of declining economic conditions stemming from the disintegration of the state-supported religious system of the *ritsuryō*. The process continued into the later medieval period as not only Ise, but most other religious institutions as well were forced to widen their catchments so as to cater to warriors and other commoners.

Much more remains to be understood about the specific ways in which the combinatory religion of this period was understood, however, not only at Ise, where the controversial rationale behind Buddhist taboo words remains unclear, but also more generally to the development within kami cults of concepts like "honesty" (*shōjiki* 正直), "sincerity" (*makoto* 誠, *magokoro* 真心) and "purity" (*shōjō* 清浄).

In any event, Teeuwen's work on Ise, together with that of Fabio Rambelli and Allan Grapard on other aspects of medieval Shinto, has been instrumental in revising our knowledge of Japanese combinatory religion of the period, shaking Western Shinto studies out of the complacent assumption regarding Shinto and Buddhist identities that has plagued so much writing for the past century. Grapard's studies have placed new focus on the close relationship of cult organization to geography, and the way identities of physical and ideal locales acted in a mutually reinforcing way with religious and mundane systems of authority. His institutional study of the Kasuga "multiplex" (1992c) thus serves as a counterpart to Royall Tylers's study of the *Kasuga gongen genki* 春日権現験記 (1990), one of the texts of that combinatory cult that also places heavy emphasis on geographic specificity. Rambelli (2002), in turn, has made striking observations regarding a variety of buddho-kami "initiatiatory rituals" (*kanjō* 灌頂), showing how they served as part of the "cultural hegemony" of the *kenmitsu* regime that coopted potential rivals, each new text or cultural artifact being understood "as a potential esoteric symbol endowed with several levels of secret meanings," thus drawing and preserving all possible knowledge within the limits of the exo-esoteric discourse.

Our knowledge of late medieval developments in combinatory religion through Western sources is not well understood, and few specific studies have been directed to the kami religion of the period, with work on Yoshida Shinto by Grapard (1992a, 1992b) and Scheid (2000), and Morrell on the *Shasekishū* (1985) being important exceptions.

Known best merely as Yoshida Shinto, the "Unique and Singular Shinto" founded by Yoshida Kanetomo (1435–1511) is usually thought to represent a turning point in the development of Shinto "self-awareness." Kanetomo founded his Shinto upon a notion introduced from Sung China, namely that of "the unity of the three lands," according to which (in the Japanese version), the kami cult of Japan was the "root," Confucianism was the branch, and Buddhism was the "flower." The fact that Buddhism was so widely spread in Japan, he said, was because all things "return" to their root (Itō et al. 2002, p. 212ff). Based on that notion, he proclaimed a version of "Shinto" that he insisted existed prior to and was superior to Buddhism. Bernhard Scheid's study of Kanetomo's chief work, *Myōbō yōshū* 名法要集, however, makes it abundantly clear that while Kanetomo's use of the term "Shinto" at times appeared to refer to a "teaching," more often than not it referred instead to "the deeds or activities of the kami" (200, p. 119) in the same way as earlier usages, and Kanetomo's denial of Buddhist influence is belied by, among other things, the thoroughgoing exo-esoteric paradigm running through the work. Kanetomo's success at gaining intimate influence in the court, however, was crucial to the success of Yoshida

Shinto at gaining near-monopolistic privileges to license shrines and priests under the subsequent period of the Tokugawa (Edo), and the school had a strong impact on later Shinto movements and popular religion. Kanetomo's insistence that the kami of Ise had "flown" to his center at Mt. Yoshida in Kyoto, for example, was a model for later *tobi shinmei* 飛び神明 ("flying deities") that formed an important motif of popular religion in the Edo period. Yoshida doctrines were also a primary source for the so-called "Japanese Analects" (*Warongo*), and the school was responsible for the broad popularization of the "Oracles of the Three Shrines" (*Sanja takusen* 三社託宣), both elements of kami-centered popular religion that placed new emphasis on moral virtues (OOMS 1985, p. 96ff; BOCKING 2000, 2001).

The Edo period revealed two particularly noteworthy trends in regard to Shinto. First is the continuing spread of knowledge and practice of shrine and kami cults through the populace and the growth of popular movements and groups based on them. The other was the growing rejection of the earlier Buddhist discourse in favor of academic studies of the kami traditions by scholars unaffiliated with specific shrines and their cults, and who tended to draw their intellectual paradigms from various Confucian persuasions. These two trends culminated in the Nativist (Kokugaku) movement, which aimed at "purifying" Shinto (and its deities) of both the "vulgar" religious elements of Buddhist origin found in the popular cults, and simultaneously of the rationalist foreign elements represented by Confucianism.

Bernard Scheid claims that, already in the early part of the period, Yoshida Shinto had managed to establish a typology of Shinto that represented a third, independent, discourse alongside Buddhism and Confucianism, and that suggested a way out of the *kenmitsu* paradigm of *honji suijaku*. This independent, or "kami-only" Shinto implies, for SCHEID, that "Shinto had become conceivable as a religion of its own and as an alternative to Buddhism" (2003, p. 205). If so, then it represents an area that demands further close study as we attempt to unpack the various currents leading to the creation of modern "Shrine Shinto."

Overall, however, as the object of growing academic interest through the period, "Shinto" remains somewhat an enigma. On the one hand, due in part to its disassociation from active life at shrines, academic Shinto of the period is usually treated as a minor topic within more general studies of (mostly Confucian) intellectual history (see especially NOSCO 1984, 1990; OOMS 1985; DE BARY and BLOOM 1979; HAROOTUNIAN 1988; two recent major edited volumes on Shinto studies include no articles devoted to Confucian Shinto—see BREEN and TEEUWEN 2000, and TEEUWEN and SCHEID 2002). Needless to say, that fact is not unrelated to the historically tenuous or insecure status of "Shinto" as a tradition at that time. It was precisely in the Edo-period crucible of Confucian and Nativist studies that the contours of modern Shinto took their shape. While figures such as Hayashi Razan, Nakae Tōju, Kumazawa Banzan, and Yamaga Sokō all criticized Buddhism from the standpoint of the newly burgeoning field of Confucian studies, they, like many Buddhist predecessors, searched for a universal Way that would encompass and give prominence to the kami of Japan. Their visions of an orderly Way, however, eschewed otherworldly salvation for the goal of a "secular sagehood" that was firmly grounded in the order of everyday life (DE BARY 1979), and their inquiries thus tended to the nature of human ethics, and how to conform the reality of Japanese patterns of governing to Chinese principles of sagely rule (KITAGAWA 1987, p. 161).

Yamazaki Ansai (1618–1682), by contrast, while likewise a Confucianist originally without shrine affiliation, developed a school of Shinto that combined a strong ethico-political orientation with distinctly religious kami worship. His Suika Shintō, called by Herman Ooms "the most dynamic force in the world of Shinto theology until the second half of the eighteenth century," produced a highly systematized view of Shinto and emphasized the principle of submissive reverence for authority, thus producing an influence far beyond its nominal lifetime as it served as one of the engines behind modern ultranationalist ideology (1985, p. 195).

One of the important features of all intellectual currents in the Edo period was the steady move away from medieval forms of secret transmission within closed family traditions to more open access to and discussion of scholarly materials. As part of this liberalization, the development of large-volume woodblock publishing enterprises provided wider access to texts, making necessary new methodologies that would allow common grounds for communication and study across nominal lines of intellectual affiliation. One principle adopted was the method of text-critical analysis generally called *kōshōgaku* 考証学, or "evidential learning" (INOUE, ed., 1996, p. 185; MCNALLY 2002, p. 360). Proponents of this new form of study engaged in word-by-word analyses of their texts' meanings, eschewing the "forced analogies" they claimed characterized the earlier Buddhist tradition. While the method was adopted by both Confucian and Nativist (Kokugaku) scholars through the period, it became more associated with the latter, as they attempted to leap over one thousand years of history and reclaim the "original meanings" of ancient texts. As a result, scholars such as Kamo no Mabuchi and Motoori Norinaga condemned both Buddhists and Confucianists alike for adding artificed and rationalistic interpretations to the purity of ancient documents, claiming that the job of the Japanese scholar was to eliminate such foreign contrivances as he rendered a purified version of ancient Japanese spirituality, what Peter NOSCO calls the "élan vital with which the age was infused" (1990, p. 128). Motoori's crucial place in the subsequent "restoration" of Shinto is slowly becoming more accessible as the result of a number of translations of his shorter works, including *Uiyamabumi* うひ山ぶみ (NISHIMURA 1987), *Tamakushige* 玉くしげ(匣) (BROWNLEE 1988), and *Naobi no mitama* 直毘霊 (NISHIMURA 1991), as well as the first book of his monumental *Kojikiden* 古事記伝 (MOTOORI 1997), although relatively little of the work of other Nativists has been translated.

In addition to academic studies involving Shinto, the Edo period also saw a continuously growing body of popular religious faith centered on the earlier Buddho-Shinto religious multiplexes and shrines. The same economic incentives that had caused religious multiplexes to appeal to warrior and other non-noble families in the medieval period continued into the Edo, as shrines and temples developed networks and systems of nationwide pilgrimage confraternities (*kō* 講) based on representatives of individual households at the local level (SAKURAI 1962). As part of their work in visiting distant "client" communities and promoting their ties to the distant objects of worship, clerical and quasi-clerical representatives of the shrines distributed thaumaturgic amulets and emblems to confraternity members; even more emblems were brought back by pilgrims themselves, and together, this influx of powerful religious symbols helped stimulate the near-universal spread of household "Shinto" altars (*kamidana* 神棚), pointing to a new degree of individual control over symbols of religious power that likely helped influence the development of the prophetic religious discourse of the new religions. This potential is hinted at obliquely by the fact that such religious participation was the target of criticism by Confucian theoreticians such as Dazai Shundai, who claimed that popular, home-centered worship of the kami was both vulgar and blasphemous (TEEUWEN 1996, p. 337).

In this way, pilgrimage confraternities and the burgeoning culture of religious travel not only contributed to the spread of knowledge regarding major religious multiplexes and their mythologies, but also represented an important social base and model for new Shinto religious organizations such as Kurozumikyō and Tenrikyō that emerged so vigorously from the late Edo into the modern period (HARDACRE 1986). This side of early modern popular combinatory religion has been covered in Japan most energetically by folklorists such as MIYATA Noboru (1970, 1972) and NISHIGAKI Seiji (1973, 1992), while historians such as FUJITANI Toshio have interpreted spectacular movements like the mass pilgrimages to the Grand Shrines of Ise (*okagemairi*) as budding revolutionary movements (1968).

In the sense of broader analyses of overall religious trends, Helen HARDACRE's model study (2002) of local religion in the nineteenth century limits its focus to the religious activity observed within a circumscribed geographical *field* as revealed through local gazetteers, a strategy that allows Hardacre to uncover the broad scope and kaleidoscopic variety of combinatory popular religion through the period, without sacrificing the phenomena to strict labels such as "Shinto" and "Buddhist."

MODERN SHINTO

The architects of the Meiji Restoration were concerned not only with restoring the imperial institution in place of the feudal institutions represented by the Tokugawa *bakufu*. They were equally intent upon suppressing those features of premodern Japanese religiosity associated with Buddhism and considered "vulgar" or "superstitious," and also with establishing a national ideology that could compete on an equal footing with the known success of Christianity in the West. Adopting the "restoration Shinto" (*fukko Shintō* 復古神道) variety of Nativism espoused by Hirata Atsutane and his followers, the government launched a series of religious policies—frequently inconsistent and disjointed—as it lurched toward the establishment of a modern national consciousness. The place of Shinto in this overall process has been described by MURAKAMI Shigeyoshi (1970, 1980) and Helen HARDACRE (1988, 1989), while individual personalities contributing to the development have been the focus of studies by John BREEN (1996, 2000b), and ISOMAE Jun'ichi (1998, 2000b). Discussion of modern Shinto has naturally been dominated by debate over its status as a national religion ("State Shinto") and its role in fostering xenophobic ultra-nationalism. The hardline view is often associated with scholars like MURAKAMI (1970, 1980), who tended to view State Shinto as an imperial "theocracy" composed of Shrine Shinto, imperial rites, the 1889 Constitution, and the Imperial Rescript on Education, and whose ultimate trajectory was virtually inherent in its Meiji origins. This monolithic view has been challenged in recent years, particularly by scholars within the Shinto tradition such as SAKAMOTO Koremaru (1987, 1994, 2000, 2001), INOUE and SAKAMOTO (1987), and NITTA Hitoshi (2000, 2003). Sakamoto argues that the treatment of shrines by the modern government was haphazard and contradictory, and that the nationalistic Shinto of the late 1930s and 1940s should be viewed as an aberration not characterizing the significance of modern Shinto as a whole. Such studies have also been linked to attempts to hammer out a "new Japanese model of church-state relations" (INOUE and SAKAMOTO 1987; ABE 1989) that transcends the spectre of the postwar Shinto Directive which disestablished Shinto from all state support. In this connection, little research has been done on the political involvement of the Association of Shinto Shrines (Jinja Honchō) and lobbying groups such as the Shintō Seiji Renmei (Shinseiren: established in 1969, this group bears the official English title "Shinto Association of Spiritual Leadership" or SAS), which have attempted to influence religious policies and lawmaking within the Diet. Particularly important objectives for such groups are the issues of revision of the postwar "peace" Constitution, changing of the Fundamental Education Law toward "reforming" school textbooks (specifically, the removal of episodes from the World War II period considered "embarrassing" or inimical to the establishment of a proud Japanese citizenry), and changing of the government's official stance toward the imperial house and Yasukuni Shrine. In short, many within the modern Shinto establishment continue to view the role of Shinto through the same normative lenses of prewar Nativist thought and its determinate mission of national integration as described thirty years ago by CREEMERS (1968, xvi).

On the popular front, a number of recent studies have focused on the practice of Shinto and festival traditions within the local community, including analyses of specific shrines and their traditions by Michael ASHKENAZI (1993), John NELSON (1996, 2000), Karen SMYERS (1999), and Scott SCHNELL (1999). These studies frequently point out exactly what establishment Shinto fails to, namely, the highly variegated and non-harmonious side of communal Shinto observances, and their modern tendency to revert to premodern combinatory forms that make little sense within the context of "orthodox" Shrine Shinto.

Recent years have also seen a growing awareness among Shintoists of the need to make Shinto more visible in the area of social and ethical debate. One of Japan's two "Shinto-related" universities, Kōgakkan University in Ise established a Faculty of Social Welfare in 1998. Since then, it has begun exploring the potential for greater Shinto involvement in the kind of social work normally associated with more missionary religions like Christianity and Buddhism (ITAI 2001; KŌGAKKAN 2002; FUJIMOTO 2004; KAWANO 2003, 2004). Also a reflection of new social concern, Shintoists have become more active in discussing the issue of brain death and organ transplants (JINJA HONCHŌ 1991), while other attempts have been made by Shinto organizations to secure a place for Shinto in the debates over ecology and environmental preservation in Japan, including programs to promote the preservation of shrine groves for their environmental function within Japanese ecology (JINJA HONCHŌ 1983, 1985), and participation by representatives of the Association of Shinto Shrines in the 1997 Harvard-hosted conference on "Shinto and Ecology" (BERNARD, forthcoming). Overall, however, such efforts have tended to be derivative, and remain subordinated to

Shrine Shinto's continuing self-understanding as a religion of communal and national integration, with the result that they have not received the degree of attention and concern one might expect.

On the education front, Kokugakuin University in Tokyo introduced a new Faculty of Shinto Studies—the only such university faculty in Japan—in 2002, and the new faculty was instrumental in winning for Kokugakuin a "Center of Excellence" (COE) grant from the Ministry of Education, Culture, Sports, Science and Technology (MEXT) for the purpose of research on and dissemination of information about Shinto and Japanese Culture. As part of that program, the university is planning to soon complete its English translation of the *Shintō jiten* 神道事典 (KOKUGAKUIN 1994; partial English editions IJCC 2001, 2004) and make it available in electronic form.

Finally, a large amount of new research has been stimulated by the International Shinto Foundation through its endowment of a chair in Shinto Studies at the University of California–Santa Barbara, as well as its hosting of numerous conferences and publications; unfortunately, the foundation's work has not been without controversy (ANTONI 2001) due to continuing allegations of a lack of transparency in the relationship of the Foundation to the religious group Worldmate (*aka* Cosmomate).

BIBLIOGRAPHY

ABE Yoshiya 阿部美哉, 1989. *Seikyō bunri: Nihon to America ni miru shūkyō no seijisei* 政教分離——日本とアメリカにみる宗教の政治性. Tokyo: The Simul Press. (English title in original: *State and Religion: A Religious Dimension of Politics in Japan and America*)

ANTONI, Klaus, 2001. Review of BREEN and TEEUWEN 2000, *Journal of Japanese Studies* 27: 405–9.

ANZU Motohiko 安津素彦, 1986. *Shintō to Nihonjin* 神道と日本人. Jinja Shinpō Bukkusu 1. Tokyo: Jinja Shinpōsha.

AOKI, Michiko Yamaguchi, 1971. *Izumo fudoki.* Monumenta Nipponica Monograph. Tokyo: Sophia University.

_____, 1997. *Records of Wind and Earth: A Translation of Fudoki, with Introduction and Commentaries.* Ann Arbor: Association of Asian Studies Monograph Series.

ASHKENAZI, Michael, 1993. *Matsuri: Festivals of a Japanese Town.* Honolulu: University of Hawai'i Press.

ASOYA Masahiko, 1999. What Is Shinto? In *The Religious Heritage of Japan,* ed. John Ross Carter, pp. 55–63. Portland: Book East.

ASTON, W. G., 1921. *Shinto: The Ancient Religion of Japan.* London: Constable & Company.

_____, 1972 (1924). *Nihongi.* Tokyo: Charles E. Tuttle.

BARRETT, Tim, 2000. Shinto and Taoism in Early Japan. In BREEN and TEEUWEN 2000, pp. 13–31.

BERNARD, Rosemarie, ed., forthcoming. *Shinto and Ecology.* World Religions and Ecology Series, ed. Mary Evelyn Tucker and John Grim. Harvard University Press.

BOCKING, Brian, 2000. Changing Images of Shinto: *Sanja takusen* or the Three Oracles. In BREEN and TEEUWEN 2000, pp. 167–85.

_____, 2001. *The Oracle of the Three Shrines: Windows on Japanese Religion*. Richmond, UK: Curzon Press.

BREEN, John, 1996. Accommodating the Alien: Ōkuni Takamasa and the Religion of the Lord of Heaven. In *Religion in Japan: Arrows to Heaven and Earth*, ed. P. F. Kornicki and I. J. McMullen, pp. 179–97. Cambridge: Cambridge University Press.

_____, 2000a. Nativism Restored. *Monumenta Nipponica* 55: 429–38.

_____, 2000b. Ideologues, Bureaucrats and Priests: On "Shinto" and "Buddhism" in Early Meiji Japan. In BREEN and TEEUWEN 2000, pp. 230–51.

BREEN, John, and Mark TEEUWEN, eds., 2000. *Shinto in History: Ways of the Kami*. Richmond, UK: Curzon Press.

BROWN, Delmer M., 1993. The Early Evolution of Historical Consciousness. In *The Cambridge History of Japan*, vol. 1: *Ancient Japan*, ed. Delmer M. Brown, pp. 504–48. Cambridge: Cambridge University Press.

BROWNLEE, John S., 1988. The Jeweled Comb-Box: Motoori Norinaga's Tamakushige. *Monumenta Nipponica* 43: 35–61.

CREEMERS, Wilhelmus H. M., 1968. *Shrine Shinto after World War II*. Leiden: E. J. Brill.

DE BARY, Wm. Theodore, 1979. Sagehood as Secular and Spiritual Ideal. In DE BARY and BLOOM 1979, pp. 127–88.

DE BARY, Wm. Theodore, and Irene BLOOM, eds., 1979. *Principle and Practicality: Essays in Neo-Confucianism and Practical Learning*. New York: Columbia University Press.

FUJIMOTO Yorio 藤本頼生, 2004. Sengo no jinjakai ni okeru shakai hōshi katsudō: Hansen-byō shisetsu no jinja saikō o megutte 戦後の神社界における社会奉仕活動——ハンセン病施設の神社再興をめぐって. *Kōgakkan Daigaku Shintō Kenkyūsho kiyō* 20: 39–55.

FUJITANI Toshio 藤谷俊雄, 1968. *Okage mairi to ee ja nai ka*「おかげまいり」と「ええじゃないか」. Tokyo: Iwanami Shoten.

GRAPARD, Allan, 1982. Flying Mountains and Walkers of Emptiness: Toward a Definition of Sacred Space in Japanese Religions. *History of Religions* 21: 195–221.

_____, 1984. Japan's Ignored Cultural Revolution: The Separation of Shinto and Buddhist Divinities in Meiji (*shinbutsu bunri*) and a Case Study: Tōnomine. *History of Religions* 23: 240–65.

_____, 1987. Linguistic Cubism: A Singularity of Pluralism in the Sannō Cult. *Japanese Journal of Religious Studies* 14: 211–34.

_____, 1988. Institution, Ritual, and Ideology: The Twenty-Two Shrine-Temple Multiplexes of Heian Japan. *History of Religions* 27: 246–69.

_____, 1992a. The Shinto of Yoshida Kanetomo. *Monumenta Nipponica* 47: 27–58.

_____, 1992b, tr. *"Yuiitsu Shintō Myōbō Yōshū"* [by] Yoshida Kanetomo. *Monumenta Nipponica* 47: 137–61.

_____, 1992c. *The Protocol of the Gods: A Study of the Kasuga Cult in Japanese History*. Berkeley: University of California Press.

_____, 1999. Religious Practices. Chapter 8 of *The Cambridge History of Japan*, vol. 2: *Heian Japan*, ed. Donald H. Shively and William H. McCullough, pp. 517–75. Cambridge: Cambridge University Press.

_____, 2000. The Economics of Ritual Power. In BREEN and TEEUWEN 2000, pp. 68–94.

TRADITIONS

_____, 2002. Shrines Registered in Ancient Japanese Law: Shinto or Not? *Japanese Journal of Religious Studies* 29: 209–32.

HARDACRE, Helen, 1986a. *Kurozumikyō and the New Religions of Japan*. Princeton: Princeton University Press.

_____, 1986b. Creating State Shinto: The Great Promulgation Campaign and the New Religions. *Journal of Japanese Studies* 12: 29–63.

_____, 1988. The Shintō Priesthood in Early Meiji Japan: Preliminary Inquiries. *History of Religions* 27: 294–320.

_____, 1989. *Shintō and the State: 1868–1988*. Princeton: Princeton University Press.

_____, 2002. *Religion and Society in Nineteenth-Century Japan*. Ann Arbor: Center for Japanese Studies, University of Michigan.

HAROOTUNIAN, H. D., 1978. The Consciousness of Archaic Form in the New Realism of Kokugaku. In *Japanese Thought in the Tokugawa Period: Methods and Metaphors*, ed. Tetsuo Najita and Irwin Scheiner, pp. 63–104. Chicago: University of Chicago Press.

_____, 1988. *Things Seen and Unseen: Discourse and Ideology in Tokugawa Nativism*. Chicago: Chicago University Press.

HAVENS, Norman, 1998. Immanent Legitimation: Reflections on the Kami Concept. In *Kami*, ed. Inoue Nobutaka, Contemporary Papers on Japanese Religion 4, pp. 227–46. Tokyo: Institute for Japanese Culture and Classics, Kokugakuin University.

HIRAI Naofusa, 1969. Understanding Japan: Japanese Shinto. *Bulletin of the International Society for Educational Information* 18.

_____, 1999. An Introduction to Shinto. In *The Religious Heritage of Japan*, ed. John Ross Carter, pp. 45–54. Portland: Book East.

IJCC, 2001. *Encyclopedia of Shinto*, vol. 1: *Kami*. Tokyo: Institute for Japanese Culture and Classics, Kokugakuin University.

_____, 2004. *Encyclopedia of Shinto*, vol. 2: *Jinja*. Tokyo: Institute for Japanese Culture and Classics, Kokugakuin University.

INOUE Nobutaka 井上順孝, 1990. Globalization and Modern Japanese Religion within the Context of Sect Shintō's Policy Toward Christianity. In *Japanese Civilization in the Modern World: VI Religion*, pp. 21–35. Senri Ethnological Studies 29. Osaka: National Museum of Ethnology.

_____, ed., 1998. *Shintō: Nihon umare no shūkyō shisutemu* 神道──日本生まれの宗教システム Tokyo: Shin'yōsha.

INOUE Nobutaka and SAKAMOTO Koremaru 阪本是丸, eds., 1987. *Nihongata seikyō kankei no tanjō* 日本型政教関係の誕生. Tokyo: Daiichi Shobō.

ISOMAE Jun'ichi 磯前順一, 1998. The Establishment of Modern Shintology and the Role of Tanaka Yoshitō. *Acta Asiatica* 75: 73–91.

_____, 2000a. Reappropriating the Japanese Myths: Motoori Norinaga and the Creation Myths of the *Kojiki* and *Nihon shoki*. *Japanese Journal of Religious Studies* 27: 15–39.

_____, 2000b. Tanaka Yoshitō and the Beginnings of Shintōgaku. In BREEN and TEEUWEN 2000, pp. 318–39.

ITAI Masanori 板井正斉, 2001. Fukushi bunka to matsuri: Shintō fukushi kenkyū no kanōsei 福祉文化と祭り──神道福祉研究の可能性, *Kōgakkan Daigaku Shintō Kenkyūsho kiyō* 17: 155–76.

ITŌ Mikiharu, 1998. Evolution of the Concept of *Kami*. Tr. Norman Havens. In *Kami*, ed. Inoue Nobutaka, pp. 20–41. Contemporary Papers on Japanese Religion 4. Tokyo: Institute for Japanese Culture and Classics, Kokugakuin University.

ITŌ Satoshi 伊藤聡 et al., 2002. *Nihonshi shōhyakka: Shintō* 日本史小百科・神道. Tokyo: Tōkyōdō Shuppan.

JINJA HONCHŌ 神社本庁, ed., 1983. *Jinja to midori* 神社とみどり. Tokyo: Jinja Shinpōsha.

_____, 1985. *Mamore: Chinju no midori* 護れ——鎮守のみどり. Tokyo: Jinja Shinpōsha.

_____, 1991. Shintō no shiseikan: Nōshi mondai to shinsōsai 神道の死生観——脳死問題と神葬祭. Jinja Honchō Kyōgaku Kenkyūsho katsudō hōkoku.

KANDA, Christine Guth, 1985. *Shinzō: Hachiman Imagery and Its Development*. Harvard East Asian Monographs. Cambridge: Harvard University.

KAWANO Satoshi 河野訓, 2003, 2004. Shintō-kei kyōdan no shakai hōshi katsudō to sono rinen (1, 2) 神道系教団の社会奉仕活動とその理念(一、二). *Kōgakkan Daigaku Shintō Kenkyūsho kiyō* 19, 20.

KITAGAWA, Joseph M., 1987. *Understanding Japanese Religion*. Princeton: Princeton University Press.

_____, 1988. Some Remarks on Shintō. *History of Religions* 27: 227–45.

KŌGAKKAN DAIGAKU 皇學館大学, 2002. "Shūkyō, chiiki, fukushi" o kangaeru (Heisei jūni-nendo Kōgakkan Daigaku Shintō Kenkyūsho kōkai gakujutsu shinpojiumu) 「宗教・地域・福祉」を考える (平成十二年度皇學館大学神道研究所公開学術シンポジウム). In *Kōgakkan Daigaku Shintō Kenkyūsho kiyō* 18: 25–87.

KOKUGAKUIN DAIGAKU NIHON BUNKA KENKYŪJO 國學院大學日本文化研究所, ed., 1994. *Shintō jiten* 神道事典. Tokyo: Kōbundō. (expanded edition, 1999)

KURODA Toshio 黒田俊雄, 1959. Gukanshō and Jinnō Shōtōki: Observations on Medieval Historiography. In *New Light on Early and Medieval Japanese Historiography*, ed. John A. Harrison, pp. 19–41. Gainesville: University of Florida Press.

_____, 1964. Shintō-setsu no hattatsu 神道説の発達. In *Shūkyōshi* 宗教史, ed. Kawasaki Mochiyuki 川崎庸之 and Kasahara Kazuo 笠原一男, pp. 256–61. Taikei Nihonshi Sōsho 18. Tokyo: Yamakawa Shuppansha.

_____, 1975. *Nihon chūsei no kokka to shūkyō* 日本中世の国家と宗教. Tokyo: Iwanami Shoten.

_____, 1981. Shinto in the History of Japanese Religion. Tr. James C. Dobbins and Suzanne Gay. *Journal of Japanese Studies* 7: 1–21.

_____, 1989. Historical Consciousness and Hon-Jaku Philosophy in the Medieval Period on Mount Hiei. In *The Lotus Sutra in Japanese Culture*, ed. George J. Tanabe, Jr., and Willa Jane Tanabe, pp. 143–58. Honolulu: University of Hawai'i Press.

_____, 1996a. The Development of the *Kenmitsu* System as Japan's Medieval Orthodoxy. Tr. James Dobbins. *Japanese Journal of Religious Studies* 23: 233–69.

_____, 1996b. The Imperial Law and the Buddhist Law. Tr. Jacqueline I. Stone. *Japanese Journal of Religious Studies* 23: 271–85.

_____, 1996c. The Discourse on the "Land of the Kami" (*Shinkoku*) in Medieval Japan. Tr. Fabio Rambelli. *Japanese Journal of Religious Studies* 23: 353–85.

LIN, Irene H., 2003. From Thunder Child to Dharma-Protector: Dōjō hōshi and the Buddhist Appropriation of Japanese Local Deities. In TEEUWEN and RAMBELLI 2003, 54–76.

TRADITIONS

LITTLETON, C. Scott, 2002. *Shinto: Origins, Rituals, Festivals, Spirits, Sacred Places.* Oxford: Oxford University Press.

LOWELL, Percival, 1894. *Occult Japan: Shinto, Shamanism and the Way of the Gods.* Boston: Houghton-Mifflin.

MASON, Joseph Warren Teets, 1935. *The Meaning of Shinto: The Primaeval Foundation of Creative Spirit in Modern Japan.* Fort Washington, N.Y. (reprint 1967 Kennikat Press; 2002 Matsuri Foundation of Canada)

MATSUMAE Takeshi, 1993. Early Kami Worship. In *The Cambridge History of Japan*, vol. 1: *Ancient Japan*, ed. Delmer M. Brown, pp. 317–58. Cambridge: Cambridge University Press.

MATSUNAGA, Alicia, 1969. *The Buddhist Philosophy of Assimilation.* Monumenta Nipponica Monographs. Tokyo: Sophia University.

MCNALLY, Mark. 2002. The *Sandaikō* Debate: The Issue of Orthodoxy in Late Tokugawa Nativism. *Japanese Journal of Religious Studies* 29: 359–78.

MIYATA Noboru 宮田 登, 1970. *Ikigami shinkō* 生き神信仰. Tokyo: Hanawa Shobō.

_____, 1972. *Kinsei no hayarigami* 近世の流行神. Nihonjin no Kōdō to Shisō 17. Tokyo: Hyōronsha.

MORRELL, Robert E., 1985. *Sand and Pebbles (Shasekishū).* SUNY Series in Buddhist Studies. Albany: SUNY Press.

MOTOORI Norinaga 本居宣長, 1997. *Kojiki-den* 古事記伝 Book I. Tr. and annot. Ann Wehmeyer. Ithaca: Cornell East Asia Series.

MURAKAMI Shigeyoshi 村上重良, 1970. *Kokka Shintō* 国家神道. Tokyo: Iwanami Shoten.

_____, 1980. *Japanese Religion in the Modern Century.* Tr. H. Byron Earhart. Tokyo: University of Tokyo Press.

MURAYAMA Shūichi 村山修一, 1974. *Honji suijaku* 本地垂迹. Tokyo: Yoshikawa Kōbunkan.

NAKAMURA Ikuo 中村生雄, 1994. *Nihon no kami to ōken* 日本の神と王権. Tokyo: Hōzōkan.

NAKAMURA, Kyoko Motomochi, tr., 1973. *Miraculous Stories from the Japanese Buddhist Tradition: The Nihon ryōiki of the Monk Kyōkai.* Cambridge: Harvard University Press.

NAUMANN, Nelly, 2000. The State Cult of the Nara and Early Heian Periods. In BREEN and TEEUWEN 2000, pp. 47–67.

NELSON, John K., 1996. *A Year in the Life of a Shinto Shrine.* Seattle: University of Washington Press.

_____, 2000. *Enduring Identities: The Guise of Shinto in Contemporary Japan.* Honolulu: University of Hawai'i Press.

NISHIGAKI Seiji 西垣晴次, 1973. *Ee ja nai ka* ええじゃないか. Tokyo: Shinjinbutsu Ōraisha.

_____, 1992. *O-Ise mairi* お伊勢参り. Tokyo: Iwanami Shoten.

NISHIMURA, Sey, 1987. First Steps into the Mountains: Motoori Norinaga's *Uiyamabumi. Monumenta Nipponica* 42: 449–93.

_____, 1991. The Way of the Gods: Motoori Norinaga's *Naobi no Mitama. Monumenta Nipponica* 46: 21–41.

NITTA Hitoshi 新田 均, 2000. Shinto as a "Non-Religion": The Origins and Development of an Idea. In BREEN and TEEUWEN 2000, pp. 252–71.

_____, 2003. *Arahitogami: Kokka Shintō to iu gensō* 現人神──国家神道という幻想. Tokyo: PHP Kenkyūsho.

Nosco, Peter, 1984. Masuho Zankō (1655–1742): A Shinto Popularizer between Nativism and National Learning. In *Confucianism and Tokugawa Culture*, ed. Peter Nosco, pp. 166–87. Princeton: Princeton University Press.

———, 1990. *Remembering Paradise: Nativism and Nostaligia in Eighteenth-Century Japan*. Cambridge: Council on East Asian Studies, Harvard University.

Okada Seishi 岡田精司, 1985. Ise Jingū no seiritsu to kodai ōken 伊勢神宮の成立と古代王権. In *Ise shinkō: Kodai, chūsei* 伊勢信仰　古代・中世, ed. Hagiwara Tatsuo 萩原龍夫, pp. 15–57. Tokyo: Yūzankaku.

Ono Sokyo, 1960. *Shinto: The Kami Way*. Tokyo: Charles E. Tuttle.

Ooms, Herman, 1985. *Tokugawa Ideology: Early Constructs, 1570–1680*. Princeton: Princeton University Press.

———, 1986. "Primeval Chaos" and "Mental Void" in Early Tokugawa Ideology: Fujiwara Seika, Suzuki Shosan, and Yamazaki Ansai. *Japanese Journal of Religious Studies* 13: 245–60.

Picken, Stewart D. B., 1980. *Shinto: Japan's Spiritual Roots*. Tokyo: Kodansha International.

Piggott, Joan, 1989. Sacral Kingship and Confederacy in Early Izumo. *Monumenta Nipponica* 44: 45–74.

———, 1997. *The Emergence of Japanese Kingship*. Stanford: Stanford University Press.

Rambelli, Fabio, 1996. Religion, Ideology of Domination, and Nationalism: Kuroda Toshio on the Discourse of *Shinkoku*. *Japanese Journal of Religious Studies* 23: 387–426.

———, 2002. The Ritual World of Buddhist "Shinto." *Japanese Journal of Religious Studies* 29: 265–97.

Reischauer, Edwin O., 1980. Introduction to Picken 1980.

Sakamoto Koremaru 阪本是丸, 1987. Religion and State in the Early Meiji Period (1868–1912). *Acta Asiatica* 51: 42–61.

———, 1994. *Kokka Shintō keisei katei no kenkyū* 国家神道形成過程の研究. Tokyo: Iwanami Shoten.

———, 2000. The Structure of State Shinto: Its Creation, Development and Demise. In Breen and Teeuwen 2000, pp. 272–94.

———, 2001. Kokka Shintō no seiritsu to shūen 国家神道の成立と終焉. In *Nihon no shūkyō to seiji: Kin-gendai 130-nen no shiza kara* 日本の宗教と政治——近・現代130年の視座から, ed. Kokugakuin Daigaku Nihon Bunka Kenkyūsho, pp. 83–120. Tokyo: Seibundō.

Sakurai Tokutarō 桜井徳太郎, 1962. *Kō shūdan seiritsu katei no kenkyū* 講集団成立過程の研究. Tokyo: Yoshikawa Kōbunkan.

Satō Hiroo 佐藤弘夫, 2000. *Amaterasu no henbō* アマテラスの変貌. Tokyo: Hōzōkan.

Satow, Ernest, 1874 (revised 1882). The Revival of Pure Shiñ-tau. *The Transactions of the Asiatic Society of Japan*. (reprints, vol. II [December 1927], p. 165; original in *TASJ* First Series, vol. III)

Scheid, Bernhard, 2000. Reading the *Yuiitsu Shintō myōbō yōshū*: A Modern Exegesis of an Esoteric Shinto Text. In Breen and Teeuwen 2000, pp. 117–43.

———, 2003. "Both Parts" or "Only One"? Challenges to the *honji suijaku* Paradigm in the Edo Period. In Teeuwen and Rambelli 2003, pp. 204–21.

Schnell, Scott, 1999. *The Rousing Drum: Ritual Practice in a Japanese Community*. Honolulu: University of Hawai'i Press.

TRADITIONS

SMYERS, Karen A., 1999. *The Fox and the Jewel: Shared and Private Meanings in Contemporary Japanese Inari Worship*. Honolulu: University of Hawai'i Press.

SONODA Kōyō, 1993. Early Buddha Worship. In *The Cambridge History of Japan*, vol. 1: *Ancient Japan*, ed. Delmer M. Brown, pp. 359–414. Cambridge: Cambridge University Press.

SONODA Minoru, 2000. Shinto and the Natural Environment. In BREEN and TEEUWEN 2000, pp. 32–46.

STONE, Jacqueline, 1999. *Original Enlightenment and the Transformation of Medieval Japanese Buddhism*. Studies in East Asian Buddhism 12. Honolulu: The Kuroda Institute, University of Hawai'i Press.

SUEKI Fumihiko, 1996. A Reexamination of the *Kenmitsu Taisei* Theory. *Japanese Journal of Religious Studies* 23: 449–66.

TAIRA Masayuki, 1996. Kuroda Toshio and the *Kenmitsu Taisei* Theory. *Japanese Journal of Religious Studies* 23: 427–48.

TAMBIAH, Stanley, 1970. *Buddhism and the Spirit Cults in North-East Thailand*. Cambridge: Cambridge University Press.

TAMURA Enchō 田村圓澄, 1996. *Ise Jingū no seiritsu* 伊勢神宮の成立. Tokyo: Yoshikawa Kōbunkan.

TAMURA Yoshiro, 2000. *Japanese Buddhism: A Cultural History*. Tr., Jeffrey Hunter. Tokyo: Kosei Publishing.

TEEUWEN, Mark, 1996. *Watarai Shinto: An Intellectual History of the Outer Shrine in Ise*. Leiden: Research School CNWS.

———, 2000. The Kami in Esoteric Buddhist Thought and Practice. In BREEN and TEEUWEN 2000, pp. 95–116.

———, 2002. From *Jindō* to Shinto. *Japanese Journal of Religious Studies* 29: 233–63.

TEEUWEN, Mark, and Bernhard SCHEID. 2002. Tracing Shinto in the History of Kami Worship: Editors' Introduction. *Japanese Journal of Religious Studies* 29: 196–207.

TEEUWEN, Mark, and Fabio RAMBELLI, eds., 2003. *Buddhas and Kami in Japan: Honji suijaku as a Combinatory Paradigm*. London: RoutledgeCurzon.

TEEUWEN, Mark, and Hendrik van der VEERE, 1998. *Nakatomi Harae Kunge: Purification and Enlightenment in Late-Heian Japan*. Buddhist Studies 1. Munich: Iudicium Verlag.

TURNER, Victor, 1974. *Dramas, Fields, and Metaphors: Ritual Action in Human Society*. Symbol Myth and Ritual Series. Ithaca: Cornell University Press.

TYLER, Royall, 1990. *The Miracles of the Kasuga Deity*. New York: Columbia University Press.

UEDA Kenji 上田賢治, 1987. The Monotheistic Tendency in Shinto Faith. *Acta Asiatica* 51: 77–95.

———, 1991. *Shintō shingaku ronkō* 神道神学論考. Tokyo: Taimeidō.

———, 1996. Shinto. In *Religion in Japanese Culture: Where Living Traditions Meet a Changing World*, ed. Tamaru Noriyoshi and David Reid, pp. 27–42. Tokyo: Kodansha International.

YAMAMOTO Yukitaka, 1987. *Kami no Michi: The Way of the Kami*. Stockton, Cal.: Tsubaki America Publications.

YOSHIDA Kazuhiko, 2003. Revisioning Religion in Ancient Japan. *Japanese Journal of Religious Studies* 30: 1–26. (reprinted as Yoshida essay in this *Guide*)

Jacqueline I. STONE

Buddhism

The academic field of "Japanese Buddhism" emerged in Japan roughly a century ago, centering around the disciplines of doctrinal studies and history. These two approaches were represented, respectively, by such pioneers as SHIMAJI Daitō 島地大等 (1875–1927) and TSUJI Zennosuke 辻善之助 (1877–1955), scholars whose work, read critically, is still valuable today. The field has also developed within a dual venue: at Japanese national universities originally established on the Western model, and at private sectarian Buddhist universities, which originated in the seminaries (*danrin* 檀林) of the Edo period and, in addition to their more recently acquired role as liberal arts colleges, retain the function of training priests. It is due in no small measure to the influence of sectarian scholarship (*shūgaku* 宗学) that, even outside Japan, the study of Japanese Buddhism was for decades structured around the life and thought of sectarian founders and the traditions descending from them.

Since about the 1970s, however, there have been some dramatic changes. Increased scholarly exchange across disciplinary boundaries has brought the study of Japanese Buddhism into dialogue with social history, folklore studies, art history, archaeology, women's studies, literature, and other fields. A specific stimulus for some of these developments can be found in the work of the late medieval historian Kuroda Toshio (discussed below), who drew new attention to Buddhism's political, economic, and ideological dimensions. At the same time, these trends may be seen as part of a broader move on the part of scholars worldwide toward cross-disciplinary approaches in Buddhist studies and in the humanities more generally. In a shift away from earlier modes of Buddhist studies emphasizing philological, textual, and doctrinal studies, Japanese Buddhism has come to be seen as embodied in specific historical, social, and institutional contexts. An earlier focus on elites and cultural centers has expanded to include attention to Buddhism at the peripheries, in the provinces and rural areas, and also among marginal groups. Increasingly varied approaches to the study of Japanese Buddhism have encouraged, and been encouraged by, a remarkable expansion in the range of sources. In addition to canonical or classic doctrinal texts, scholars have begun to look to ritual handbooks, temple records, and other local historical material, as well as to the evidence of art history and archaeological findings, greatly multiplying the perspectives from which Buddhism can be studied. A prominent example can be seen in recent studies of the Sōtō sect, where painstaking editing of secret transmission texts (*kirikami* 切紙) by Ishikawa Rikizan 石川力山, along with the recent publication of other, previously untapped sources, has made possible a new kind of Sōtō Zen studies emphasizing not the philosophical teachings of the founder Dōgen, but the social history and ritual practice of Sōtō in rural communities.[1]

An exhaustive account of specific developments in the study of Japanese Buddhism would be impossible in a brief essay. Rather than attempting a comprehensive survey, the following discussion focuses on a few selected areas of both new research and ongoing scholarly concern. For further discussion of sources and methods and a more detailed overview, see NIHON BUKKYŌ KENKYŪKAI 1996 and 2000, whose members have helped pioneer the interdisciplinary study of Japanese Buddhism. An innovative introductory text on "thirty-four keys to Japanese Buddhism" (ŌKUBO 2003) also provides a brief overview of new directions in scholarship.

HEIAN BUDDHISM: CHALLENGING OLD MODELS

Recent research on Buddhism in Japan's Heian period (794–1185) offers several striking examples of how older scholarly models, dating to the postwar period or even earlier, are now being revised. The standard narrative of Heian Buddhism was in essence one of the new schools or movements emerging in reaction against, and eventually displacing, decadent older ones. It typically began with the founding of the Tendai and Shingon schools by Saichō 最澄 (766/767–822) and Kūkai 空海 (774–835) respectively, a development often

---

1. For new directions in the history of Sōtō or of Zen more generally, see HIROSE 1988; FAURE 1991, 1996; BODIFORD 1993; HARADA 1998; WILLIAMS 2005.

said to have originated in their dissatisfaction with empty formalism of the "six schools of Nara" (*nanto rokushū* 南都六宗), whose doctrines had long constituted orthodoxy. The mid-Heian period, according to this narrative, saw the proliferation of Tendai and Shingon esoteric rites, sponsored by noble families for "this-worldly" aims, while the latter Heian was marked by the spread of Pure Land beliefs, representing a new concern with individual salvation in the next life. Otherworldly Pure Land faith is said to have attracted disaffected members of middle and lower aristocracy unable to win honor and promotion commensurate with their abilities and was also spread by *hijiri* 聖, monks based primarily at small retreats (*bessho* 別所) apart from major temples, who rejected the worldliness of the Buddhist establishment and its noble patrons and paved the way for the independent "popular" Pure Land movements of Hōnen and Shinran in the Kamakura period. However, new methodological perspectives have called into question major components of this "textbook" model of Heian Buddhism. Attention to the interplay of doctrine and institutional history, for example, has suggested that the "six Nara schools" did not represent a long established orthodoxy that Saichō and Kūkai rejected. Rather, it was not until the early ninth century, roughly when Saichō and Kūkai were formulating their teachings, that the Nara schools began to standardize their own respective doctrines in connection with reorganization of the system of court-allotted yearly ordinands (*nenbundosha* 年分度者) along sectarian lines. In this sense, the "eight schools"—the Nara schools along with Tendai and Shingon—took shape together and collectively represented a "new Buddhism" of the early Heian (SONE 2003; see also 2000). Kūkai himself has been reevaluated, not primarily as the founder of a "Shingon school," but as the formulator of a new mode of esoteric Buddhist ritual language adopted across sectarian lines and carrying profound social, political, and cultural ramifications (ABÉ 1999).

Studies are beginning to appear of hitherto neglected figures, important in their own age, but who do not figure prominently in received sectarian narratives. These include Ryōgen 良源 (912–985), eighteenth *zasu* 座主 or head of the Tendai monastery on Mt. Hiei, who left few doctrinal teachings but made vital innovations in monastic education, debate, and ritual practice (GRONER 2002) and the scholar-monk Jichihan (a.k.a. Jitsuhan or Jippan 実範, d. 1144), versed in esoteric Buddhism, precepts, and Pure Land thought, who is mentioned only cursorily in Pure Land histories today but was celebrated by the great medieval scholar Gyōnen 凝然 (1240–1321) as one of six patriarchs of Japanese Pure Land Buddhism (BUNJISTERS 1999). In addition, studies drawing on sources other than doctrinal writings and temple documents are beginning to recover a picture of Heian Buddhism as "lived religion" that bears little relation to schools and founders. MITSUHASHI Tadashi (2000) has used court diaries (*nikki* 日記) to investigate the role of Heian nobles in shaping patterns of Japanese religious life by appropriating Buddhist observances, in conjunction with kami worship and yin-yang practices, and their influence as patrons on the development of Buddhist ritual. Brian RUPPERT's attention to esoteric ritual manuals and material culture has shed light on the roles of relic worship in constructing imperial authority and ensuring the prosperity of family lineages (2000).

Another aspect of the standard narrative now being challenged is its tendency to characterize specific historical moments as represented by a single form of Buddhism having a

single constituency and a unitary aim. According to the traditional account, to oversimpli-
fy a bit, early Heian Buddhism was "state Buddhism," officially sponsored and concerned
chiefly with thaumaturgical protection of the emperor and the realm (on problems with
the category of "state Buddhism," see Yoshida's essay in this *Guide*); then in the mid-Heian,
with the decline of the *ritsuryō* system, "state Buddhism" was displaced by an "aristocratic
Buddhism" centered on esoteric rites sponsored by noble families for this-worldly prosperity, while the later Heian saw the emergence, via the spread of Pure Land faith, of
"popular Buddhism." Historical research has been chipping away at this linear depiction
for some time now, noting, for example, that Pure Land practices spread, not in reaction
to the "this-worldly" orientation of esoteric rites, but within the same framework of reception: the chanted *nenbutsu* 念仏 was widely understood by both clerics and laity in the
same manner as the *kōmyō shingon* 光明真言 and other esoteric mantras and *dhāraṇī*, as
a powerful spell for pacifying the deceased and effecting their salvation (Hayami 1975).
And concern for personal salvation in the next life did not have to await the Pure Land
faith of late Heian *hijiri* or lower level aristocrats but is well attested in the writings of
high-ranking clerics and court nobles from the ninth century on (Taira 1992). The trajectory of the old narrative—from "state Buddhism" to "aristocratic Buddhism" to "popular
Buddhism"—was a teleological one, suggesting a gradual shift in Buddhist concerns, from
politics and this-worldly benefits to individual liberation, and culminating in the teachings of the "new Buddhism" of the Kamakura period. It is now being challenged by the
recognition that Buddhism at each juncture of the Heian period (or any period, for that
matter) encompassed a range of both social bases and soteriological aims.

(STILL) RE-VISIONING "KAMAKURA BUDDHISM"

No era in the history of Japanese Buddhism has drawn more scholarly attention than the Kamakura period (1185–1333). Until recently such research focused not on
Kamakura Buddhism broadly conceived, but on the teachings and activities of a few individuals revered as the founders of new sectarian movements, collectively termed "Kamakura
new Buddhism" (*Kamakura shin-Bukkyō* 鎌倉新仏教): Hōnen 法然 (1133–1212), who initiated
the Jōdoshū 浄土宗 or Pure Land sect; his disciple Shinran 親鸞 (1173–1262), honored as the
founder of Jōdo Shinshū 浄土真宗 or the True Pure Land sect; Dōgen 道元 (1200–1253),
the patriarch of Japanese Sōtō Zen 曹洞禅; and Nichiren 日蓮 (1222–1282), from whom
the Nichiren sects trace their lineages. (To a lesser extent, Eisai or Yōsai 栄西, 1141–1215,
revered as the patriarch of Rinzai Zen 臨済禅, and Ippen 一遍, 1239–1289, founder of the
Jishū 時宗, are also grouped among the seminal figures of "Kamakura new Buddhism.")
These figures have been typically associated with a rejection of the ritual complexity characterizing the older Buddhist establishment; notions of an "easy path" to enlightenment or
salvation; and emphasis on personal faith and a single, exclusive form of practice held to
be uniquely efficacious and suitable to persons of all capacities—whether it was chanting
the *nenbutsu* or the *daimoku* 題目 (title) of the *Lotus Sūtra* or sitting in meditation (*za-
zen* 坐禅). Jōdoshū, Jōdo Shinshū, Sōtō Zen, and Nichirenshū number among the largest
Buddhist institutions in contemporary Japan, and scholarly emphasis on Hōnen, Shinran,

Dōgen, and Nichiren owes less to the influence of these teachers in the Kamakura period than to their importance as the founders of schools that predominate today. These figures have long been considered exemplars of the entire Japanese Buddhist tradition, though the reasons for this valorization have shifted over time. During the Meiji period (1868–1912), a time of nation formation, they were often celebrated as cultural heroes, initiators of distinctively "Japanese" forms of Buddhism, or as leaders of a Japanese analogue to the Protestant Reformation. In the postwar era, they have more frequently been characterized as democratic reformers championing the religious needs of the common people (*minshū* 民衆) or even as quasi-Marxist figures resisting a hegemonic religio-political establishment.[2]

Already evident in prewar scholarship, the category of "Kamakura new Buddhism" became central to postwar studies of medieval Japanese Buddhism, notably in the work of IENAGA Saburō 家永三郎 and INOUE Mitsusada 井上光貞, who focused in particular on the new Pure Land movements of Hōnen and Shinran. These scholars took the "new Buddhism" to be representative of the Buddhism of the medieval period, arising against and displacing an elitist, formalistic, and outmoded "old Buddhism" (*kyū-Bukkyō* 旧仏教). The popularity of this model owed much to the revulsion of thoughtful intellectuals against institutional Buddhism's recent support for militant imperialism and to their desire for social reform. In the postwar milieu, the official temples of Kamakura "old Buddhism," associated with rites of nation protection, were easily characterized as "corrupt," and the new movements that broke away from them, as reformist and egalitarian. In light of historical research since the 1970s, it is now generally recognized that the movements of Hōnen, Shinran, and Nichiren remained marginal during the Kamakura period and did not gain institutional prominence until later medieval times; thus their followings cannot be said to have represented the mainstream of medieval Japanese Buddhism. Nor, we now know, were they by any means the first to spread Buddhism among the masses. Buddhism was embraced across social classes from early on, and Kuroda Toshio's successors in particular have shed light on the popular support base of the major temple-shrine complexes. Nonetheless, the importance of the new movements, in terms of both Buddhist thought and later institutional development, remains undeniable. How to rethink these new movements and their place in the larger Kamakara-period Buddhist world has provoked a great deal of scholarly discussion.

First, attempts have been made to complicate, refine, or transcend models emphasizing the opposition of "old" and "new" Buddhism. Among the first of such challenges was serious study of the existing Buddhist establishment in its own right, rather than as a foil against which to highlight the new movements. The landmark publication of *Kamakura kyū Bukkyō* 鎌倉旧仏教 (KAMATA and TANAKA 1971) was soon followed by studies of specific figures deemed representative of the "old Buddhist" establishment, such as Myōe 明恵 (1173–1232) (see MORRELL 1987; GIRARD 1990; TANABE 1992). Other scholars have offered re-readings of "new" Buddhist figures, such as Christoph KLEIN's assessment of Hōnen, not as a reformer or sectarian founder, but as a radically heterodox thinker (1996). Still others

---

2. On representations of the Kamakura-period sectarian founders, see DOBBINS 1998; and STONE 1999a, pp. 55–62.

have sought to identify new patterns in medieval Buddhism transcending institutional or sectarian lines between "old" and "new" (e.g., PAYNE 1998). Such studies have, for example, noted a common trend toward simplified practices, new forms of religious organization, and new proselytizing techniques (FOARD 1980); transsectarian concerns with the role of the kami, the image of the *tennō* or ruler, and the position of Japan as a marginal country in the last age (*masse hendo* 末世辺土; TAKAGI 1982); and new concepts of enlightenment or liberation as readily accessible in the act of practice or even through faith alone, ideas which emerged across the "new Buddhism"/"old Buddhism" divide and were particularly distinctive, not just of the "new Buddhism," but of the medieval period (STONE 1999a).

Another approach to reconceiving Kamakura Buddhism has been to redraw the "old"/"new" configuration. SASAKI Kaoru has posited a "trans-establishment Buddhism" (*chō-taisei Bukkyō* 超体制仏教), represented by such figures as Saigyō 西行, Chōgen 重源, or Ippen, as constituting a third element cutting across the opposition between the "establishment Buddhism" (*taisei Bukkyō* 体制仏教) supporting the court and *bakufu* and the "anti-establishment Buddhism" (*han-taisei Bukkyō* 反体制仏教) represented by the single-practice movements of Hōnen, Shinran, and Nichiren (1988). A more thorough redefinition of "Kamakura new Buddhism" is that of MATSUO Kenji (1988, 1997). Matsuo identifies the "old Buddhism" with "official monks" (*kansō* 官僧), who were ordained on state-sponsored ordination platforms; were responsible for conducting rites of nation protection; observed pollution taboos; and were primarily concerned with community religion. In contrast, he argues, the "new Buddhism" was associated with "reclusive monks" (*tonseisō* 遁世僧), who adopted new forms of ordination independent of the state-sponsored ordination system; worked for the salvation of lepers and other outcastes; ordained women; conducted funerals; engaged in fundraising; and were concerned primarily with individual religion. Matsuo's definition is innovative in that it groups figures such as Myōe and the precept revival movements of Eison 叡尊 (1201–1290) and Ninshō 忍性 (1217–1303), along with the exclusive Pure Land and Nichiren movements, as "new Buddhism" (1988). While his distinction between official monks and reclusive monks has been criticized as overdrawn, his work has shed significant light on hitherto neglected aspects of Kamakura Buddhism, in particular, the activities of the Shingon-Ritsu movement. Matsuo's model also informs a landmark study by MINOWA Kenryō (1999) of the precept revival efforts of the Nara schools in the early medieval period.

The work of Kuroda Toshio and others has done much to de-center the Kamakura period as the focus of academic Buddhist studies. Outside sectarian scholarly circles, the category of "Kamakura new Buddhism" no longer enjoys its former prominence, nor is it treated as frequently as before in teleological fashion as the definitive historical moment toward which earlier forms were evolving and against which later developments are judged. Nonetheless, images of the "new Buddhist" founders as reformers persist, and—although not necessarily couched in terms of "old" and "new"—binary models of medieval Buddhism emphasizing the tension between reformist new movements and an entrenched Buddhist establishment continue to inform scholarship, a point to which we shall return below. Moreover, even in the narrowest definition of "Kamakura Buddhism" as the life and teachings of the new Buddhist founders, research topics have by no means been exhausted.

We have yet to see in English, for example, a definitive book-length study of Hōnen and the early development of Jōdoshū lineages. At the same time, the Kamakura period saw a flourishing in lineage formation, ritual practices, textual production, and doctrinal innovation within the Tendai, Shingon, and Nara schools as well as the spread of popular practices across denominational lines—all topics that cry out for further study.

THE THEORY OF THE "EXOTERIC-ESOTERIC SYSTEM"

One of the greatest paradigm shifts ever to occur in Japanese Buddhist studies, or in medieval studies more generally, is represented by the work of the late historian KURODA Toshio 黒田俊雄 (1926–1993) and his theory of the *kenmitsu taisei* 顕密体制 or "exoteric-esoteric system" that characterized the dominant medieval Buddhist institutions—Tendai, Shingon, and the Nara schools.[3] This system consisted of a shared and loosely unifying basis in esoteric teachings and practice, especially *mikkyō* thaumaturgical rites, which all Buddhist schools had incorporated, joined to an emphasis by each school on its particular exoteric doctrine.

Kuroda's *kenmitsu* theory has made numerous contributions. First, as already noted, it has served as a major corrective to postwar "Kamakura new Buddhism" centered approaches. Kuroda persuasively demonstrated that the overwhelmingly dominant forms of medieval Japanese Buddhism were not the new movements of Hōnen, Shinran, etc., but the *kenmitsu* Buddhism of the major temple-shrine complexes (*jisha* 寺社), which represented religious orthodoxy (*seitō-ha* 正統派). The new movements did not displace the preexisting Buddhist establishment but existed coevally with it as marginal heterodoxies (*itan-ha* 異端派).

Second, *kenmitsu taisei* theory has done much to clarify the integral relationship of medieval religion, economics, political power, and land ownership. Kuroda demonstrated how leading temple-shrine complexes received donations of extensive private estates (*shōen* 荘園) in return for esoteric rites of protection performed for powerful patrons. By amassing large portfolios of landholdings, *jisha* emerged as powerful economic and political forces in their own right; along with the court and *bakufu*, they were integral to the medieval system of ruling elites (*kenmon taisei* 権門体制). At the same time, "*kenmitsu* ideology" (*kenmitsu-shugi* 顕密主義) was deployed to legitimize the hierarchy of rule, from the management of local *shōen* to an overarching rhetoric of the mutual dependence of Buddhist law and the ruler's law (*ōbō buppō sōi ron* 王法仏法相依論).[4]

Third, *kenmitsu taisei* theory has provided the basis for an integrated view of different strands of Japanese religion. The perceived magical powers of esoteric ritual to invite prosperity and ward off danger enabled the *kenmitsu* system to incorporate local thaumaturgical rites, including the pacification of vengeful spirits (*goryō* 御霊), yin-yang divination practices, and cults of the kami, subsuming them all within a framework of Mahāyāna universalism. From this perspective, both medieval Shinto lore and doctrine, as well as discourse about Japan as a "land of the kami" (*shinkoku* 神国) are redefined as expressions

---

3. For an introduction to Kuroda's scholarship, see DOBBINS 1996.
4. On the political influence of elite Buddhist temples, see ADOLPHSON 2000.

of *kenmitsu* Buddhism, challenging earlier notions of a medieval Shinto arising in opposition to Buddhism. While not everyone has accepted Kuroda's argument that the existence of an independent Shinto tradition continuous since premodern times is no more than "a ghost image produced by a word linking together unrelated phenomenon (*sic*)" (KURODA 1981), his work has promoted a healthy tendency to consider premodern Buddhism, not in isolation, but in terms of its interactions with kami ritual and other non-Buddhist traditions, overcoming reified divisions in the academic world between "Buddhism," "Shinto," etc. Even the principle of the unity of "original forms and their manifest traces" (*honji suijaku* 本地垂迹), by which kami were understood to be the local forms of universal buddhas and bodhisattvas, now appears to have been far more than a simple binary logic equating specific Buddhist deities with corresponding kami; rather, it served as a "combinative paradigm" whose specifics varied from one site, text, or ritual setting to another and involved complex webs of association linking not only Buddhist divinities and kami but including yin-yang, esoteric, and other continental deities, demons, spirits, and cultural heroes (TEEUWEN and RAMBELLI 2003). Nor, it seems, was the distinction between buddhas and kami necessarily always the chief division among divinities in the medieval world. SATŌ Hiroo, for example, has argued for a distinction between what he terms "saving deities" (*sukuu kami* 救う神), or the transcendent buddhas and bodhisattvas who extend their universal compassion to all beings, and "wrathful deities" (*ikaru kami* 怒る神), who reward and punish in this world. While buddhas and bodhisattvas in their original forms are "saving deities," once enshrined and rendered physically present as "manifest traces" at specific sites—such as the Great Buddha of Tōdaiji or the Ishiyama Kannon—they could also function in the same manner as kami, to mete out reward and punishment (SATŌ 1998, pp. 348–76; trans. in TEEUWEN and RAMBELLI 2003, pp. 95–144).

A fourth contribution, one owing to Kuroda's intellectual heirs, is the use of his *kenmitsu* concept to identify and illuminate a pervasive medieval episteme. In this episteme, "exoteric" doctrines such as one mind, emptiness, the threefold truth, or original enlightenment provided notions of a wholly integrated, interpenetrating cosmos, while "esoteric" teachings and practices introduced the possibility of ritual control and transformation of the world through the manipulation of symbols. Any sphere of phenomenal activity could be "mandalized" as a realm where the wisdom and compassion of buddhas and bodhisattvas were expressed. Thus temple and shrine precincts and landholdings could be defined as realms of the buddhas and kami, immune from government incursion, while the disciplines of specific arts, professions, and trades could be constructed as "ways" (*michi* 道) of religious cultivation. Symbols of the sacred realm of Buddhist reality were mapped onto specific features of the phenomenal world via complex sets of correspondences and resemblances, both formal and linguistic, equating, for example, the three pagoda precincts of Mt. Hiei with the threefold truth or the five viscera of the human body with the five wisdom buddhas. The decoding (actually, encoding) of these resemblances formed the substance of secret transmissions passed down in master-disciple (or father-son) lineages of religious and worldly knowledge, esoteric rites, court precedents, and the arts. These identifications of specific sets of phenomena or activities with Buddhist principles—a paradigm that may perhaps be considered the "unity of original forms and their manifest traces" (*honji suijaku*) in a broad sense—is proving to have been central to the cognitive, aesthetic, and ideological dimensions of much of medieval Japanese culture (GRAPARD 1987; RAMBELLI 2003).

Kenmitsu taisei theory has also drawn some criticism. Kuroda's subsuming of Shinto within a Buddhist framework has been criticized for overlooking the extent to which Buddhism in Japan was shaped by kami-related practices (BREEN and TEEUWEN 2000, pp. 5–8). Some scholars have questioned how well the category of *kenmitsu* describes the Buddhism of eastern Japan; SASAKI Kaoru, for example, has proposed as a counter-theory a "Zen-esoteric" ideology (*zenmitsu shugi* 禅密主義) that provided thaumaturgical support and religious legitimation for the Kamakura *bakufu* (1997). Another set of critiques revolves around Kuroda's reified and inadequate definition of *mikkyō* as the basis of the *kenmitsu* system (SUEKI 1998; ABÉ 1999, pp. 416–28). Kuroda saw medieval Tendai original enlightenment thought (*hongaku shisō* 本覚思想) as "archetypical" of *kenmitsu* ideology (a claim that has itself been questioned), but appears to have overlooked earlier theoretical integrations of esoteric and exoteric Buddhism within the Nara schools, following the systematizing of *mikkyō* by Kūkai. It is not clear, in fact, whether Kuroda located early Heian Buddhism, when *mikkyō* was first formally established, within the *kenmitsu* system or not. In addition, a range of explanations of the relationship between esoteric and exoteric Buddhism were put forth over the course of the medieval period, not all of which support Kuroda's argument that *mikkyō* was invariably deemed fundamental. His claim that the thaumaturgical elements of *kenmitsu* Buddhism were rejected by the heterodox movements has been controverted in the case of Nichiren (DOLCE 2002), raising questions about the nature of the "orthodox"/"heterodox" distinction. Another question concerns how far Heian-period Pure Land thought, such as Genshin's, or the activities of independent *hijiri* or holy men can be understood within an esoteric framework. A more precise understanding of "esoteric Buddhism" and a closer integration of the approaches of intellectual and institutional history are among the challenges confronting *kenmitsu taisei* theorists.

One further point of controversy involves the status of the new Kamakura Buddhism in post-Kuroda scholarship. Kuroda himself tended to reject notions of a rigid opposition between "old" and "new" forms of Buddhism, for example, by noting points of continuity between the marginal sectarian movements (*itan-ha*) of Hōnen, Shinran, etc., and reform movements (*kaikaku-ha* 改革派) within mainstream Buddhist institutions. Some of his successors, however, see a radical disjuncture between the new heterodox movements and the orthodox *kenmitsu* establishment in terms of their respective stances toward dominant structures of authority and power. Such scholars argue that the all-encompassing nature of *kenmitsu* Buddhism served as an ideology of social control. For example, because all buddhas, bodhisattvas, or kami were understood as embodiments of Buddhist truth, taxes or corvée labor provided for temple-administered *shōen* could be defined as offerings to the particular Buddhist deity enshrined as a temple's object of worship, and peasant recalcitrance in providing such services could be countered with the threat of divine punishment. From this perspective, the absolutizing of a single practice and rejection of all other forms seen in the teachings of Hōnen, Shinran, or Nichiren is understood as ideological resistance to the entire *kenmitsu* establishment and to the order of authority that it legitimated (e.g., Taira 1992, 1994; Satō 1998). In contrast, Sueki Fumihiko (1998) has argued that the founders of the new Buddhist movements, despite their soteriologically egalitarian views, were not primarily social reformers, and that to characterize them as unique critics of *kenmitsu* authority simply replicates in the language of *kenmitsu taisei* theory the "new Buddhism"-centered approaches of earlier scholarship.[5]

A NOTE ON BUDDHISM AND THE ARTS

The interrelated view of Buddhism and social practice suggested by *kenmitsu* theory highlights a need for deeper understanding of the relation between religion and the literary, visual, and performing arts, as the modern disciplinary separation between "art" and "religion" does not reflect medieval realities. While scholars have long traced Buddhist influences upon specific works of literature, "Buddhist literature" (*Bukkyō bungaku* 仏教文学) is itself now emerging as a recognized subfield within the study of Japanese Buddhism, as seen, for example, in the *Journal of Comparative Buddhist Literature* (*Komazawa Daigaku Bukkyō bungaku kenkyū* 駒澤大学仏教文学研究) inaugurated in 1998. Recent studies have suggested a more integrated approach, in which abstract Buddhist teachings were shaped and concretized by *setsuwa*, *imayō*, Noh drama, and popular forms of preaching such as *jikidan* 直談 (see, for example, Hirota 1987). Such approaches shed light on the process by which poetry and music, once shunned by clerics as worldly distractions, were appropriated as forms of Buddhist practice in their own right (LaFleur 1983, pp. 1–25, 80–106; Ogi 1998), and artistic expressions, like the concrete forms of esoteric ritual (*ji* 事), came to be seen as instantiating formless principles (*ri* 理); thus the arts, too, could be conceived of as the "traces" (*suijaku*) of Buddhist truth (Sanford, LaFleur, and Nagatomi 1992, pp. 3–7; Misaki 1999). This move is in turn related to practices of initiation and secret transmission in the arts paralleling the formation of Buddhist ritual and teaching lineages—a subject in need of further research.

Recent interdisciplinary approaches to the study of Japanese Buddhist art have shed light on such areas as the politics of art patronage and the appropriation of Buddhism in specific localities, such as Mimi Yiengpruksawan's work relating the structures and icons of the Chūsonji 中尊寺 in Hiraizumi to Ōshū Fujiwara polity (1998). Other studies have investigated the cultic and ritual dimensions of Buddhist icons (McCallum 1994; Sharf and Sharf 2001). Such work promises to help rectify a longstanding aniconic bias in Western Buddhist studies, for example, by showing that images were not seen as purely "symbolic" or as aids to meditation or devotion, but rather, as actually instantiating the powerful sacred presences they represented.

WOMEN, GENDER, AND THE FAMILY

Stimulated by developments in the study of social history and the emergence of women's studies as an academic field, research into the roles and position of women and

---

5. Compare, for example, the perspectives of Taira 1996 and Sueki 1996.

gender in Japanese Buddhism has progressed remarkably since the 1980s.[6] Early impetus was provided by the Research Group on Women and Buddhism in Japan (Kenkyūkai: Nihon no Josei to Bukkyō 研究会・日本の女性と仏教) formed in 1984 by Nishiguchi Junko and Ōsumi Kazuo and consisting primarily of younger scholars representing a range of disciplines.[7]

One major focus of scholarly attention in this area has been the history of nuns. As described in Yoshida Kazuhiko's essay in this *Guide*, nuns played a key role in the introduction of Buddhism to Japan in the sixth century; they were active in court-sponsored rites and also helped to promote Buddhism in the provinces. From the latter part of the eighth century, however, their status began to decline. Nuns gradually disappeared from official ceremonies; nunneries came under the management of monks, declined, or were converted to monasteries. By the ninth century, formal ordination for women appears to have lapsed altogether (USHIYAMA 1990; GRONER 2002, pp. 245–88). Despite loss of formal ordination, however, renunciate women by no means disappeared. Research since the 1980s has done much to illuminate the varied activities and modes of life of privately ordained or self-ordained "unofficial" nuns throughout the Heian period. Many such women took the tonsure only after raising children, often on the death of a husband. Depending upon the individual, her class, and her personal resources, some nuns established private retreats, became mendicants, or supported themselves by washing and sewing robes for monks; many, however, continued to live in their family households while devoting themselves to Buddhist practice (KATSUURA 1995 and 2000). Elite women, especially of the court, developed their own ordination traditions independent of the Vinaya and the state-sponsored ordination system (NISHIGUCHI 1992; MEEKS 2003, pp. 209–33).

The Kamakura period witnessed efforts to revive official nuns' ordination and monastic institutions for women. These have drawn scholarly attention, especially in connection with Eison's Shingon Ritsu 真言律 precept revival movement (HOSOKAWA 1987, 1989; MATSUO 1995, pp. 379–401; GRONER 2005).[8] While most research on nuns to date has focused on premodern times, surveys of the archives of major Kansai area nunneries, chiefly holding Edo-period documents, are now in progress. These "*amadera chōsa*" may eventually yield vital information about Buddhist nuns in early modern Japan. A few studies have begun to examine the cultural and political influence exerted during the early modern period by elite nuns of the imperial house and the shogunal household (WRIGHT 2002; COGAN 2004). Modern and contemporary nuns, however, represent an almost wholly neglected area.[9]

The intersection of Buddhism and the family in the medieval period represents another

6. For a brief history of this subfield, see YOSHIDA 1999, pp. 6–34.

7. For the group's initial achievements, see ŌSUMI and NISHIGUCHI 1989; some of these essays have been translated and published with contributions from European and North American scholars (see RUCH 2002).

8. See also MEEKS 2003, who argues that the Ritsu nuns of this period were in substantial ways independent of Eison's community.

9. For a study of contemporary nuns, see ARAI 1999.

new research area. Despite traditional rhetoric of "leaving the household," many clerics continued to occupy themselves with family concerns. Monks from aristocratic families often performed rites for the welfare and prosperity of family members, who in turn commended private estates (*shōen*) to their temples; these in turn would often be passed down to disciples of the same family, a process contributing to the "aristocraticization" of the upper echelons of the clergy. Lines between monastic renunciation and family life were blurred in other ways as well. While private or self-ordination as a "lay nun" was virtually the sole option for women, for men in the medieval period as well, the most widely adopted model of renunciate life was not that of the monk who enters a temple as a child and receives formal ordination according to the Vinaya, but that of the *nyūdō* 入道 or lay novice. Such individuals typically shaved their heads and took vows later in life, devoting themselves to Buddhist practices, while at the same time remaining in the household and continuing to look after family interests. Lay nuns in particular were often responsible for memorial rites for family members (NISHIGUCHI 1997). Of particular interest are "monastic families" (see NISHIGUCHI 1987, pp. 183–218). Throughout the medieval period, numerous monks maintained homes in *sato-bō* 里坊 or towns below the precincts of mountain temples, had wives and children, administered personal property, and transferred monastic office and temple wealth to their biological sons. While the extent of such practices remains to be fully clarified, such research calls into question the notion of fixed distinctions between monastics and laity, and demands a fundamental re-imagining of medieval monastic life.

Yet another related research area concerns the ideology of Buddhist attitudes about gender. One major accomplishment has been the overturning of earlier claims that, where the "old Buddhism" of the establishment excluded women as karmically limited and difficult to save, teachers of the "new Buddhism" such as Hōnen and Shinran compassionately extended salvation to women as well as men (e.g., KASAHARA 1975). In fact, teachings asserting the possibility of women's salvation (*nyonin ōjō* 女人往生, *nyonin jōbutsu* 女人成仏) were common in the dominant *kenmitsu* Buddhism of the Heian period. Far from promoting soteriological egalitarianism, however, such teachings represented the obverse face of discriminatory rhetoric about the special karmic obstructions of women, which had begun to appear around the late ninth century, and were often enlisted in support of claims for the efficacy of particular practices, such as the *nenbutsu* or *kōmyō shingon*, in encompassing women's salvation (TAIRA 1992, pp. 391–426). Claims that a particular practice saves "even women"—which assume female soteriological hindrances—can also be found in the teachings of the Kamakura new Buddhist movements.

Lack of a clear counter-discourse in premodern times has led some scholars to assume that women passively accepted and internalized rhetoric about female hindrances to salvation. Others question this assumption. James DOBBINS (2004, pp. 74–106), for example, in studying the letters of Shinran's wife, the nun Eshinni 恵信尼 (1182–1268?), suggests that doctrinal axioms about female obstructions to salvation were not necessarily operative for women at the level of practiced religion, while Lori MEEKS (2003) has shown how elite nuns of Hokkeji in the Kamakura period developed rhetorical strategies for "talking past" male monastic rhetoric about women's soteriological hindrances without directly engaging

it. There are severe limitations to our sources, and how premodern Japanese women themselves received teachings about the alleged karmic burden of female gender remains an
open question.

The emergence in early medieval times of Buddhist discourses about women's special
hindrances was also accompanied by the exclusion of women from the precincts of certain
Buddhist temples. Why these *nyonin kekkai* 女人結界 were established, and why women
were banned from some temples but not others, have been the subject of considerable
scholarly discussion. Suggestions about possible factors contributing to the exclusion of
women from temple precincts include concern for protecting monastic celibacy; the rise
of Confucian values and the emergence of a patriarchal family system; local traditions
associating mountain ascetic practice with ritual purity; and new concepts of pollution
(*kegare* 穢れ) associated with the breakdown of the *ritsuryō* system, the vulnerability of
the capital to crime and disease, and the accompanying perceived need to establish ritually pure zones (such as Mt. Hiei) for thaumaturgical protection of the ruler's law (*ōbō*).
As noted by Kawahashi Noriko in her essay in this *Guide*, with some variation, scholarly
consensus now holds that the *nyonin kekkai* originated in regulations enforcing the precepts by prohibiting the presence of women at monasteries and of men at nunneries. As
nunneries disappeared, only the ban excluding women from monasteries remained and
was later rationalized in terms of female pollution (USHIYAMA 1996; YOSHIDA 1999, pp.
27–31; GRONER 2002, pp. 262–65). Researchers have also highlighted early modern concerns about female pollution, as expressed in practices associated with the *Ketsubon-kyō*
血盆経 (Blood bowl sutra), a sutra said to save women from a Blood Pool Hell into which
they would otherwise fall for the sin of pollution caused by their blood of menstruation
and childbirth (GLASSMAN 2001; KŌDATE 2004; WILLIAMS 2005, pp. 50–58, 125–28). Practices such as the *nyonin kekkai* and *Ketsubon-kyō* rites point out the need for clearer understanding of premodern notions of pollution and their complex variations with respect
to status groups, gender, place, and variation over time.

While research on women and Buddhism in Japan has focused on ancient and medieval
times, the modern period also represents a rich, largely untapped field for such studies.
Promising areas for research include the ambiguous status of *jizoku* 寺族 or temple wives
(KAWAHASHI 1995); feminist critiques of Buddhism (ŌGOSHI, MINAMOTO, and YAMASHITA
1990; MINAMOTO 1996); and the networks of Buddhist women—nuns, priests' wives,
teachers, researchers, and lay believers—working for internal, egalitarian reform of Buddhist institutions (JOSEI TO BUKKYŌ TŌKAI-KANTŌ NETTOWĀKU 1999).

RECONSIDERING EARLY MODERN BUDDHISM

During the unification campaigns of Oda Nobunaga (1534–1582) and Toyotomi Hideyoshi (1536/1537–1598), Buddhist temples were gradually stripped of the political, military, and economic power they had enjoyed during the medieval period, and, in
the Edo or Tokugawa period (1603–1868), were subjected to varying degrees of state control. This marked a radical break with the "mutual dependence of the Buddhist law and the
ruler's law" that had underlain state polity for centuries (see FUJII 1975; McMULLIN 1984).

TRADITIONS

The *bakufu* sought to regulate Buddhist institutions by organizing the temples of each sect as branch temples under the oversight of a single head temple. At the same time, all families were required to affiliate with a local temple, which would issue certificates testifying that they were not Christians or members of other proscribed religious groups. As patron families (*danka* 檀家), they were obliged to support their *danka* temple and participate in its regularly scheduled rites; in particular, they were required to hold Buddhist funerals for all family members and make offerings to the temple for an extended sequence of memorial rites. Thus on one hand, during the Edo period, Buddhist temples were subsumed within the official administrative apparatus for population surveillance, while on the other hand, this was the era when—largely through the medium of the *danka* system and Buddhist funerals—Buddhism for the first time truly penetrated all levels of society.

Citing the use of Buddhist temples to monitor the population and the compulsory affiliation of the laity, the influential historian Tsuji Zennosuke characterized the Buddhism of this period as ossified and corrupt, thus discouraging serious study for some time. Since the founding of the academic journal *Kinsei Bukkyō* 近世仏教 (1960–1965; second series 1979–1987), scholars working in this area have been struggling against Tsuji's characterization to gain a more precise understanding of early modern Buddhism, both as the matrix of Buddhist institutions in contemporary Japan and as a worthy object of historical inquiry in its own right.[10] Attempts to gain a more detailed and accurate picture of Edo Buddhism have been aided by numerous regional history projects, including the cataloguing of temple, family, and local government archives, which began in the 1970s and are yielding a wealth of documentation. Broadly speaking, scholarship since Tsuji in a social historical mode has tended to concentrate either on the role of Buddhist institutions in the Tokugawa regime's attempts at social control or on the development of popular Buddhist practices. As Duncan Williams notes in his essay in this *Guide*, these two trends characterize the study of early modern Japanese religion more generally.

The first of these two lines of inquiry has examined Buddhist institutional structures, such as the temple certification (*terauke seido* 寺請制度), parishioner (*danka seido* 檀家制度), and head temple–branch temple (*honmatsu seido* 本末制度) systems and their linkages to *bakufu* and domainal authority. Such studies have often emphasized the connection between Buddhist funerals and memorial rites, both institutionally and ideologically, in the maintainance of social order. TAMAMURO Taijō, who coined the term "funerary Buddhism" (*sōshiki bukkyō* 葬式仏教) in his study of the same name (1977), was among the first to stress this aspect of early modern Buddhism. More exhaustive research in this vein has been done by TAMAMURO Fumio, who has shown how mandatory temple certification and the performance of Buddhist funerals were connected to government suppression of Christianity and functioned as an instrument for monitoring the populace (1999). Nam-lin HUR (forthcoming) has argued that the spread of Buddhist funerals and ancestor cults served to help construct and maintain Tokugawa social order. Studies in the second vein, while acknowledging government use of Buddhist temples for population surveillance,

10. For an overview of these efforts, see ŌKUWA 1991, pp. 259–80.

have instead focused on the popular Buddhist culture, exploring, for example, the inseparable connection between "prayer" and "play," or entertainment, that characterized the urban Buddhism of Edo (Hur 2000); lay confraternities (*kō* 講) and their support for *kaichō* 開帳 or temples' public exhibition of sacred treasures (Kitamura 1989); the role of village priests in mediating peasant disputes and interceding with local authorities on behalf of their parishioners (Vesey 2003); and the practices for worldly benefits and management of the dead by which Sōtō Zen vastly expanded its regional parishioner bases (Williams 2005). Buddhist pilgrimage and popular preaching have also drawn scholarly attention (see the essays by Barbara Ambros and Duncan Williams in this *Guide*).

Though not yet as well studied as temple institutions or popular Buddhist culture, the intellectual history of Edo Buddhism is also beginning to draw scholarly attention. One area of research concerns Buddhist contributions to early modern social and political ideology. For a long time, scholarly assumptions that neo-Confucianism represented the official discourse made it possible to overlook the ongoing intellectual vitality of early modern Buddhism. However, historians such as Herman Ooms (1985) and Ōkuwa Hitoshi (1991), focusing on the case of Suzuki Shōzan 鈴木正三, have noted how Buddhist figures—like neo-Confucians, Nativists, and others—seeking a place for themselves and their traditions in the new regime, actively contributed to the formation of Tokugawa ideology. Sonehara Satoshi (1996) has examined the role of the eminent Tendai Buddhist cleric Tenkai 天海 (1536–1643) in the legitimation of the Tokugawa regime and divinization of the first Tokugawa shōgun, Ieyasu.

Japanese sectarian scholarship has provided numerous studies of specific Buddhist schools during the early modern period (see the essay by Williams in this *Guide*). Outside Japan, Zen has been the tradition most widely studied. In addition to major studies of Sōtō and Rinzai figures, the less well-known Ōbaku tradition has drawn scholarly attention (Schwaller 1989, 1996; Baroni 2000). Janine Sawada has investigated the integration of Zen with Neo-Confucianism in local Shingaku 心学 circles (1993) and in popular discourses and practices of "self-cultivation" (2004). Sawada's work is especially valuable in showing that "Buddhism" was not a self-contained entity but participated in broader early modern conceptual trends that crossed religious traditions, such as the enormously influential ideology of self-cultivation as the key to both personal religious attainment and social prosperity, still prominent in the discourse and practice of Japanese religions today.

Trends in early modern Buddhism that emerged across sectarian lines call out for investigation. Movements to revive the precepts occurred in a number of schools and have not yet been studied in a comprehensive manner. Another crucial but understudied topic is the formalization and solidification of sectarian identity, a salient feature of early modern Buddhism. The "discovery" during this era of sectarian founders as sources of normative authority; the compiling, editing, and publishing of sectarian canons, aided by the emergence of a sophisticated print culture; and the codification of sectarian doctrine continue to shape Buddhist institutional self-definitions down to the present. These developments occurred within the context of Edo-period intellectual currents, crossing religious traditions, that emphasized the uncovering of normative origins and the identification, collation, and publication of authoritative texts, which in some quarters began to displace medieval traditions of secret transmission (*kuden* 口伝) as sources of legitimizing knowledge. The place of Buddhist sectarianism in this early modern epistemological shift remains to be investigated.

MODERN AND CONTEMPORARY BUDDHISM

With the fall of the Tokugawa *bakufu* in 1868 and the establishment of the Meiji regime, Buddhist institutions confronted a number of threats and challenges: the disestablishment of Buddhism and the abrogation of mandatory temple affiliation, seriously affecting temples' economic base; the promulgation of edicts mandating "separation of Shinto and Buddhism" (*shinbutsu bunri* 神仏分離); and the ensuing outbreaks of anti-Buddhist violence (*haibutsu kishaku* 廃仏毀釈) in which numerous temples were destroyed and monks and nuns forcibly laicized. Documents relating to the "separation of Shinto and Buddhism" were collected by historians early on (MURAKAMI, TSUJI, and WASHIO, 1926–1929; this collection, along with more recent advances in regional history, has enabled some detailed studies of the impact of the separation edicts and the *haibutsu kishaku* movement in specific localities, e.g., TAMAMURO 1977; YASUMARU 1979; COLLCUTT 1986; NAKURA 1988; GRAPARD 1984; MURATA 1999). However, as Hayashi Makoto notes in his essay in this *Guide*, the study of "modern Buddhism" is chiefly a postwar phenomenon, beginning only in the late 1950s with the groundbreaking social historical research of YOSHIDA Kyūichi (1992). Since then, this field has gained considerable momentum, especially since the founding in 1992 of the Society for the Study of Modern Japanese Buddhist History (Nihon Kindai Bukkyōshi Kenkyūkai 日本近代仏教史研究会) and the inauguration of its yearly journal, *Kindai Bukkyō* 近代仏教.

Since the formation and development of "modern Buddhism" as an academic field are detailed in Hayashi's essay in this *Guide*, a brief summary will suffice here. One prominent trend in scholarship on modern Buddhism has been to examine Buddhist institutional changes and internal self-redefinitions in response to the challenges of modernity, beginning with the seminal developments of the Meiji period (1868–1912). Examples focusing on institutional change include research on Buddhism's social roles (YOSHIDA 1991); the formation of ground-level Buddhist teaching assemblies (*kyōkai* 教会) and lay societies (*kessha* 結社) and their impact on the formation of modern sectarian organization (IKEDA 1994); and the debates, conflicts, and practical problems arising from the decriminalization of clerical marriage in 1872 (JAFFE 2001). Others have focused on how influential Buddhist leaders reconfigured their tradition as a unique spiritual resource for the projects of modernization and nation-building. An early example was Kathleen STAGG's study (1983) of Inoue Enryō 井上円了 (1858–1919) and his attempts to redefine Buddhism as consistent with Western philosophy, scientific, and superior to Christianity. Broader treatments include James KETELAAR's pioneering study (1990) of the "definitional strategies" by which Meiji Buddhists reformulated their tradition as "modern Buddhism," and the work of ŌTANI Eiichi (2001) on the emergence of lay Nichirenism (*Nichirenshugi* 日蓮主義) as a politically involved, highly nationalistic movement. A ground-breaking, two-volume study by SUEKI Fumihiko (2004), including analyses of eleven key figures, explores the contributions of modern Buddhists in shaping the discourses and issues that engaged Meiji-period intellectuals more broadly, especially the relation of society and the individual, and of religion and the state. Another, more recent trend has been to consider modern Japanese Buddhism in a broader Asian context, investigating, for example, the role of Buddhism in Japan's colonial ventures in China and Manchuria (KOJIMA and AKESHI 1992; SUEKI 2004, vol. 2) or the development of modern Buddhism from the comparative perspective of Japan and China (SUEKI 2004, vol. 2). Richard JAFFE (2004) has investigated how global travel by Japanese Buddhists and interactions with their counterparts in other Asian countries from the late nineteenth through mid-twentieth centuries contributed to the formation of a pan-Asian Buddhist identity. Japanese versions of Buddhist pan-Asianism were deployed against hegemonic Western notions of culture and civilization and often, though not exclusively, enlisted in the service of Japanese imperialistic agendas. Such studies illuminate the place of Japanese Buddhist thinkers and activists in the formation of Buddhist modernism as a global as well as national phenomenon and promise to bring the study of modern Japanese Buddhism into dialogue with research in other cultural contexts on trans-nationalism and the emergence of modern Asian identities.

The subject of Buddhist institutional and ideological support for modern nationalism leads inevitably to the issue of Buddhist involvement in Japan's ventures of militant imperialism. Along with broader studies of religion under imperialism (e.g., YOSHIDA 1970), several articles and a few booklength studies have appeared on Buddhism's wartime role (ICHIKAWA 1970; NAKANO 1977; VICTORIA 1997). Wartime sectarian doctrinal materials have also been compiled (SENJI KYŌGAKU KENKYŪKAI 1988–1995). This subject was for a long time deeply painful, even taboo, in some academic quarters, and has only just begun to be addressed directly. More extensive research will be of value in illuminating issues of religion and the state, religion and violence, and the complex processes by which religious teachings are revised, reappropriated, and invoked to legitimize national aims. In addition to "top down" methodological approaches, stressing the actions of institutions and influential figures, one hopes also for studies shedding light on what Buddhist involvement in modernization, nation-building, and war meant for ordinary clerics and lay Buddhists.

Despite a persistent rhetoric of Buddhist "decadence," as well as some very real present challenges, temples of the traditional Buddhist sects still collectively represent the largest religious institutional presence in Japan. Yet until the 1990s there was little academic research on contemporary Buddhism, almost as though Buddhism in the postwar period lay outside the legitimate purview of Buddhist studies. Some initial work was done by scholars also affiliated with Buddhist institutions on topics such as Buddhist social work (TAMIYA, HASEGAWA, and MIYAGI 1994) and Buddhist funerary and mortuary practices (ITŌ and FUJII 1997). These studies combine historical inquiry with concern for the future direction of traditional Buddhism. At issue are questions of how temples can effectively contribute to redressing social problems, such as the effects of an aging population, or cope with loss of traditional roles brought about, for example, by the growth of secular funeral companies (*sōgiya* 葬儀屋 or *sōgisha* 葬儀社) that have assumed many of the functions once performed by temples and priests. In contrast to frequently expressed internal critiques and anxieties about institutional Buddhism's diminishing social role, a few scholars have stressed temples' ingenuity in devising new ways to maintain contemporary relevance and garner economic support, for example, by promoting pilgrimage, festivals, worldly benefits, and the sale of amulets (READER and TANABE 1998) or by initiating voluntary burial societies and other alternatives to the family grave system (ROWE 2004). Since the beginning of the present century, some illuminating studies of contemporary Buddhist institutions—incorporating along with archival research the anthropological and sociological methods used in the study of new religions—have begun to appear. Most noteworthy are Stephen COVELL's study of contemporary Tendai temples (forthcoming) and a significant collection of essays on the status of traditional Buddhism in contemporary Japan (COVELL and ROWE 2004), addressing such topics as popular ethical teachings, priestly education, Buddhism in civil society, and Japanese Buddhist NGOs.

More work is also needed on Buddhist-based new religions. Very little academic research has been conducted, for example, on the lay Buddhist organizations Sōka Gakkai 創価学会 and Risshō Kōseikai 立正佼成会, the two largest "new religions" in Japan. Such research might fruitfully adopt Buddhist studies and historical approaches, for example, by inquiring into Buddhist new religions' appropriation of traditional Buddhist doctrines (e.g., HUBBARD 1998) or the continuities between these movements and earlier forms, such as the lay confraternities of the early modern period.

ISSUES IN BUDDHIST THOUGHT

Outside sectarian circles, in recent years, social history has to some extent displaced Buddhist thought as the mainstream of the academic study of Japanese Buddhism. However, important contributions continue to appear in this area. In the West, the teachings of Shinran and of Zen, Dōgen in particular, have drawn scholarly attention from the standpoints of both philosophy and intellectual history. Shinran has inspired comparison with Protestant theologians, while philosophically oriented Dōgen studies have focused on his teachings about the Buddha nature, impermanence, and "being-time"; he has also been the subject of comparative studies, notably with Heidegger. The philosophers of the Kyoto school—Nishida Kitarō 西田幾多郎, Tanabe Hajime 田辺 元, and Nishitani Keiji 西谷啓治—have also inspired numerous discussions and comparative studies. Kyoto-school related studies and translations for a readership outside Japan include the work of D. A. Dilworth, Kevin Doak, Andrew Feenberg, Gereon Kopf, James Heisig, Christopher Ives, Agustin Jacinto Zavala, Thomas Kasulis, Lin Chen-Kuo, John Maraldo, Steve Odin, Taitetsu Unno, Jan Van Bragt, Michiko Yusa, Hans Waldenfels, Dale Wright, and others.

One recent trend, both in Japan and elsewhere, has been analysis of modern ideological uses of Buddhist thought, especially by Zen and the Kyoto school, to shape discourses of reverse orientalism, Japanese nationalism, and miltarism (FAURE 1993, pp. 52–88; SHARF 1993; HEISIG and MARALDO 1995). In a more polemical vein, the intellectual movement known as "Critical Buddhism" (hihan Bukkyō 批判仏教) has argued that the influential doctrine of original enlightenment (hongaku 本覚; some prefer "original awakening"), celebrated by some scholars as the "climax" of Japanese Buddhism as philosophy, in fact constitutes an oppressive ideology whose claim that "all things are enlightened just as they are" has served to legitimate social inequality and even militant imperialism.[11]

Popular debates stimulated by Critical Buddhism have also been paralleled by new scholarly research on the *hongaku* doctrine in its medieval Tendai contexts, based on close textual and historical study. Following in the pioneering footsteps of Shimaji Daitō, Hazama Jikō 硲 慈弘, Ōkubo Ryōjun 大久保良順, and Tamura Yoshirō 田村芳朗, several booklength essay collections and monographs have recently appeared (ASAI 1991; HABITO 1996; ŌKUBO 1998; STONE 1999a), as well as significant essays by HANANO (e.g., 1979, 1992) and SUEKI Fumihiko (e.g., 1987 and 1993). Collectively, such research can be expected to yield a more detailed and accurate picture of the nature of this influential doctrine; its relationship to practice, ritual, and institutions; and its broader impact on medieval Japanese thought and culture.

Continuities and differences between original enlightenment doctrine and esoteric Buddhist teachings, especially those of Tendai esotericism or Taimitsu 台密, need to be further investigated. Particular attention should be paid to how *hongaku* ideas were understood in their medieval context. As William Bodiford notes in his essay in this *Guide*, "original enlightenment thought" is a modern interpretive rubric, one whose heuristic nature is often overlooked, and the term tends to be bandied about in an excessively broad and reified fashion. Medieval texts do not necessarily agree in their interpretations of *hongaku* ideas, which are sometimes hard to distinguish from esoteric Buddhist thought or even more general Mahāyāna concepts of nonduality. Nor is there a distinct bibliographic category that can be designated as *hongaku* writings. "Original enlightenment thought" is a useful category in studying specific intellectual developments within medieval Tendai, but its utility as a broader interpretive model remains to be assessed.

Increased attention to Heian Buddhist doctrinal developments should also be noted. New research has explored, for example, the Tendai system of religious examination and debate (GRONER 2002); *mikkyō*, especially Taimitsu, thought and practice (MISAKI 1988; ŌKUBO 2004); and the influence upon Tendai thinkers of the *Ta-sheng ch'i-hsin lun* 大乗起信論 (Awakening of Mahāyāna Faith; see TAKE 1988). Challenging longstanding opinion that the Kamakura period represents the formative moment in Japanese Buddhist history, SUEKI Fumihiko has argued that, from the standpoint of the history of thought (*shisōshi* 思想史), the major ideas distinctive of Japanese Buddhism emerged in the early Heian period. His own study (1995) of Annen 安然 (841–?) discusses the origin and development of key concepts such as the Buddhahood of grasses and trees (*sōmoku jōbutsu* 草木成仏) and the realization of Buddhahood in this very body (*sokushin jōbutsu* 即身成仏).

Despite the sustained attention devoted to the thought of a few sectarian founders, Zen teachers, and Buddhist philosophers, vast areas in Japanese Buddhist intellectual history remain to be explored. Texts of unknown, questionable, or spurious authorship, or of traditions without a strong contemporary presence, have attracted less attention than

11. For an introduction to Critical Buddhism, see HUBBARD and SWANSON 1997; see also STONE 1999b.

the works of famous figures associated with major schools and sects. Medieval debate literature and transmission records, for example, have barely begun to be tapped. Japanese Hossō or Yogācara thought is another vast area calling out for scholarly investigation.

SOME CONCERNS AND FUTURE DIRECTIONS

A great many topics and issues in the field of Japanese Buddhism remain to be investigated. Several specific areas in need of further research have been noted in passing in this and other related essays in this volume. Rather than attempting an exhaustive list, this concluding section will raise only a few broad issues of concern.

First, we lack reliable booklength overviews or introductory works on Japanese Buddhism in English, suited to the non-specialist reader, for college and university teaching. The standbys on which we have relied so long (e.g., MATSUNAGA 1974–1976), as well as more recently available translations (TAMURA 2001) rest on older scholarly models and must now be used with care. More excellent translations of primary texts are also needed. While neither textbook writing nor translation does much to further academic careers, both remain areas of urgent need.

Another concern has to do with tensions between the methods of social history and the history of thought. Half a century ago, Buddhist studies—including the study of Japanese Buddhism—centered on textual and doctrinal research. The pendulum has now swung, however, and scholarship is becoming more historically grounded. Buddhism is no longer seen chiefly as a matter of abstract "thought" or as a quest for transcendent enlightenment, but as inextricably embedded in the political, ideological, and cultural specifics of Japanese society.

On one hand, this move has been salutary, and one would like to see it developed still further; "on the ground" studies of what Buddhist institutions, ritual practices, and ideas meant in the lives of actual people, both monastics and laity, are in short supply for almost every historical period. On the other hand, the shift toward social history has involved costs as well as gains. Especially when coupled with the pressures of shortened graduate programs, it often means (at least in North America) that graduate students complete their Ph.D. without acquiring the broad familiarity with Buddhist texts and doctrine that the last generation of specialists deemed essential. Some worry that the study of Japanese Buddhist thought may be irretrievably losing ground. One hopes, not only for the survival and prosperity of Japanese Buddhist thought as an academic subfield, but for studies that will bridge the two approaches, shedding light on the interrelation of doctrine and social practice.

As the field develops, it will become increasingly important to recognize that we can no longer consider Japan in isolation. A third desideratum would be for more studies considering Japanese Buddhism within the larger context of East Asia or even Asia more generally, juxtaposing specific Japanese developments with comparable ones in China, Korea, and—especially in relation to esoteric Buddhism—Tibet.

BIBLIOGRAPHY

ABÉ, Ryūchi, 1999. *The Weaving of Mantra: Kūkai and the Construction of Esoteric Buddhist Discourse.* New York: Columbia University Press.

ADOLPHSON, Mikhael S., 2000. *The Gates of Power: Monks, Courtiers, and Warriors in Premodern Japan.* Honolulu: University of Hawai'i Press.

ARAI, Paula Kane Robinson, 1999. *Women Living Zen: Japanese Sōtō Buddhist Nuns.* Oxford: Oxford University Press.

ASAI Endo 浅井圓道, ed., 1991. *Hongaku shisō no genryū to tenkai* 本覚思想の源流と展開. Kyoto: Heirakuji Shoten.

BARONI, Helen J., 2000. *Ōbaku Zen: The Emergence of the Third Sect of Zen in Tokugawa Japan.* Honolulu: University of Hawai'i Press.

BODIFORD, William M., 1993. *Sōtō Zen in Medieval Japan.* Honolulu: University of Hawai'i Press.

BREEN, John, and Mark TEEUWEN, eds., 2000. *Shinto in History: Ways of the Kami.* Honolulu: University of Hawai'i Press.

BUNJISTERS, Marc, 1999. Jichihan and the Restoration and Innovation of Buddhist Practice. *Japanese Journal of Religious Studies* 26: 39–82.

COGAN, Gina, 2004. Precepts and Power: Enshōji, Buddhism and the State in Seventeenth-Century Japan. Ph.D. dissertation, Columbia University.

COLLCUTT, Martin, 1986. Buddhism: The Threat of Eradication. In *Japan in Transition: From Tokugawa to Meiji,* ed. Marius B. Jansen and Gilbert Rozman, pp. 143–67. Princeton: Princeton University Press.

COVELL, Stephen G., forthcoming. *Japanese Temple Buddhism.* Honolulu: University of Hawai'i Press.

COVELL, Stephen G., and Mark ROWE, eds., 2004. *Traditional Buddhism in Contemporary Japan.* Special issue, *Japanese Journal of Religious Studies* 31/2.

DOBBINS, James C., 1998. Envisioning Kamakura Buddhism. In *Re-Visioning "Kamakura" Buddhism,* ed. Richard K. Payne, pp. 24–42. Honolulu: University of Hawai'i Press.

_____, 2004. *Letters of the Nun Eshinni: Images of Pure Land Buddhism in Medieval Japan.* Honolulu: University of Hawai'i Press.

DOBBINS, James C., ed., 1996. *The Legacy of Kuroda Toshio.* Special issue, *Japanese Journal of Religious Studies* 23/3–4.

DOLCE, Lucia Dora, 2002. Esoteric Patterns in Nichiren's Interpretation of the Lotus Sutra. Ph.D. dissertation, University of Leiden.

FAURE, Bernard, 1991. *The Rhetoric of Immediacy: A Cultural Critique of Chan/Zen Buddhism.* Princeton: Princeton University Press.

_____, 1993. *Chan Insights and Oversights: An Epistemological Critique of the Chan Tradition.* Princeton: Princeton University Press.

_____, 1996. *Visions of Power: Imagining Medieval Japanese Buddhism.* Princeton: Princeton University Press.

FOARD, James H., 1980. In Search of a Lost Reformation: A Reconsideration of Kamakura Buddhism. *Japanese Journal of Religious Studies* 7: 261–91.

TRADITIONS

FUJII Manabu 藤井 学, 1975. Kinsei shoki no seiji shisō to kokka ishiki 近世初期の政治思想と 国家意識. In *Iwanami kōza Nihon rekishi* 岩波講座日本歴史 10: *Kinsei* 近世 2, pp. 135–72. Tokyo: Iwanami Shoten.

GIRARD, Frédéric, 1990. *Un moine de la secte Kegon à l'Époque de Kamakura: Myōe (1173–1232) et le "Journal de ses Rêves."* Paris: École Francaise d'Extrème-Orient.

GLASSMAN, Hank, 2001. The Religious Construction of Motherhood in Medieval Japan. Ph.D. dissertation, Stanford University.

GRAPARD, Allan G., 1984. Japan's Ignored Cultural Revolution: The Separation of Buddhist and Shinto Divinities (*shinbutsu bunri*) and a Case Study: Tōnomine. *History of Religions* 23: 240–65.

_____, 1987. Linguistic Cubism: A Singularity of Pluralism in the Sannō Cult. *Japanese Journal of Religious Studies* 14: 211–34.

GRONER, Paul, 2002. *Ryōgen and Mount Hiei: Japanese Tendai in the Tenth Century.* Honolulu: University of Hawai'i Press.

_____, 2005. Tradition and Innovation: Eison's Self-Ordination and the Establishment of New Orders of Buddhist Practitioners. In *Going Forth: Visions of Buddhist Vinaya*, ed. William M. Bodiford, pp. 210–35. Honolulu: University of Hawai'i Press.

HABITO, Ruben L. F., 1996. *Originary Enlightenment: Tendai Hongaku Doctrine and Japanese Buddhism.* Tokyo: International Institute for Buddhist Studies.

HANANO Jūdō 化野充道 (*aka* Hanano Michiaki 花野充昭), 1979. *Chūko Tendai bunken to nenbutsu shisō* 中古天台文献と念仏思想. In *Eizan Jōdokyō no kenkyū* 叡山浄土教の研 究, ed. Satō Tetsuei 佐藤哲英, pp. 318–46. Kyoto: Hyakkaen.

_____, 1992. Nichiren no shōdai shisō to Danna-ryū no kanjō genshi kuden 日蓮の唱題思想 と檀那流の灌頂玄旨口伝. In *Nihon, Chūgoku Bukkyō shisō to sono tenkai* 日本・中国仏 教思想とその展開, ed. Misaki Ryōshū 三崎良周, pp. 115–58. Tokyo: Sankibō Busshorin.

HARADA Masatoshi 原田正俊, 1998. *Nihon chūsei no Zenshū to shakai* 日本中世の禅宗と社会. Tokyo: Yoshikawa Kōbunkan.

HAYAMI Tasuku 速水 侑, 1975. *Heian kizoku shakai to Bukkyō* 平安貴族社会と仏教. Tokyo: Yo-shikawa Kōbunkan.

HEISIG, James W., and John C. MARALDO, 1995. *Rude Awakenings: Zen, the Kyoto School, and the Question of Nationalism.* Honolulu: University of Hawai'i Press.

HIROSE Ryōkō 広瀬良弘, 1988. *Zenshū chihō tenkaishi no kenkyū* 禅宗地方展開史の研究. Tokyo: Yoshikawa Kōbunkan.

HIROTA Tetsumichi 廣田哲通, 1987. *Chūsei Bukkyō setsuwa no kenkyū* 中世仏教説話の研究. Tokyo: Benseisha.

HOSOKAWA Ryōichi 細川涼一, 1987. *Chūsei no Risshū jiin to minshū* 中世の律宗寺院と民衆. Tokyo: Yoshikawa Kōbunkan.

_____, 1989. *Onna no chūsei: Ono no Komachi, Tomoe, sono ta* 女の中世——小野小町・巴・そ の他. Tokyo: Nihon Editā Sukūru Shuppanbu.

HUBBARD, Jamie, 1998. Embarrassing Superstition, Doctrine, and the Study of New Religious Movements. *Journal of the American Academy of Religion* 66: 59–92.

Hubbard, Jamie, and Paul L. Swanson, eds., 1997. *Pruning the Bodhi Tree: The Storm over Critical Buddhism*. Honolulu: University of Hawai'i Press.

Hur, Nam-lin, 2000. *Prayer and Play in Late Tokugawa Japan: Asakusa Sensōji and Edo Society*. Cambridge: Harvard University Asia Center.

———, forthcoming. *Death and Social Order in Tokugawa Japan: Buddhism, Anti-Christianity, and the Danka System*. Cambridge: Harvard University Asia Center.

Ichikawa Hakugen 市川白弦, 1970. *Bukkyō no sensō sekinin* 仏教の戦争責任. Reprinted in *Ichikawa Hakugen chosakushū* 市川白弦著作集 3, 1993. Kyoto: Hōzōkan.

Ikeda Eishun 池田英俊, 1994. *Meiji Bukkyō kyōkai/kessha-shi no kenkyū* 明治仏教教会・結社史の研究. Tokyo: Tōsui Shobō.

Itō Yuishin 伊藤唯真 and Fujii Masao 藤井正雄, eds., 1997. *Sōsai Bukkyō: Sono rekishi to gendai-teki kadai* 葬祭仏教──その歴史と現代的課題. Tokyo: Nonburu.

Jaffe, Richard, 2001. *Neither Monk nor Layman: Clerical Marriage in Modern Japanese Buddhism*. Princeton: Princeton University Press.

———, 2004. Seeing Śākyamuni: Travel and the Reconstruction of Japanese Buddhism. *Journal of Japanese Studies* 30: 65–96.

Josei to Bukkyō Tōkai-Kantō Nettowāku 女性と仏教 東海・関東ネットワーク, ed., 1999. *Bukkyō to jendā: Onna tachi no nyoze gamon* 仏教とジェンダー──女たちの如是我聞. Osaka: Shuju Shobō.

Kamata Shigeo 鎌田茂雄 and Tanaka Hisao 田中久夫, eds., 1971. *Kamakura kyū-Bukkyō* 鎌倉旧仏教. Nihon Shisō Taikei 日本思想体系 15. Tokyo: Iwanami Shoten.

Kasahara Kazuo 笠原一男, 1975. *Nyonin ōjō shisō no keifu* 女人往生思想の系譜. Tokyo: Yoshikawa Kōbunkan.

Katsuura Noriko 勝浦令子, 1995. *Onna no shinjin: Tsuma ga shukke shita jidai* 女の信心──妻が出家した時代. Tokyo: Heibonsha.

———, 2000. *Nihon kodai no sōni to shakai* 日本古代の僧尼と社会. Tokyo: Yoshikawa Kōbunkan.

Kawahashi Noriko, 1995. *Jizoku* (Priests' Wives) in Sōtō Zen Buddhism: An Ambiguous Category. *Japanese Journal of Religious Studies* 22: 161–83.

Ketelaar, James E., 1990. *Of Heretics and Martyrs in Meiji Japan: Buddhism and Its Persecution*. Princeton: Princeton University Press.

Kitamura Gyōon 北村行遠, 1989. *Kinsei kaichō no kenkyū* 近世開帳の研究. Tokyo: Meicho Shuppan.

Klein, Christoph, 1996. *Hōnens Buddhismus des Reinen Landes: Reform, Reformation oder Häresie?* Frankfurt: Peter Lang.

Kōdate, Naomi, 2004. Aspects of *Ketsubonkyō* Belief. In *Practicing the Afterlife: Perspectives from Japan*, ed. Susanne Formanek and William R. LaFleur, pp. 121–43. Vienna: Verlag der Österreichischen Akademie der Wissenschaften.

Kojima Masaru 小島 勝 and Kiba Akeshi 木場明志, eds., 1992. *Ajia no kaikyō to kyōiku* アジアの開教と教育. Kyoto: Hōzōkan.

Kuroda Toshio, 1981. Shinto in the History of Japanese Religion. Trans. James C. Dobbins and Suzanne Gay. *Journal of Japanese Studies* 7: 1–21.

LaFleur, William R., 1983. *The Karma of Words: Buddhism and the Literary Arts in Medieval Japan*. Berkeley and Los Angeles: University of California Press.

Matsunaga, Daigan, and Alicia Matsunaga, 1974–1976. *Foundation of Japanese Buddhism*. 2 vols. Los Angeles: Buddhist Books International.

Matsuo Kenji 松尾剛次, 1988. *Kamakura shin-Bukkyō no seiritsu: Nyūmon girei to soshi shinwa* 鎌倉新仏教の成立——入門儀礼と祖師神話. Tokyo: Yoshikawa Kōbunkan.

———, 1995. *Kanjin to hakai no chūseishi: Chūsei Bukkyō no jissō* 勧進と破戒の中世史——中世仏教の実相. Tokyo: Yoshikawa Kōbunkan.

———, 1997. What is Kamakura New Buddhism? Official Monks and Reclusive Monks. *Japanese Journal of Religious Studies* 24: 179–89.

McCallum, Donald F., 1994. *Zenkōji and Its Icon: A Study in Medieval Japanese Religious Art*. Princeton: Princeton University Press.

McMullin, Neil, 1984. *Buddhism and the State in Sixteenth-Century Japan*. Princeton: Princeton University Press.

Meeks, Lori Rachelle, 2003. Nuns, Court Ladies, and Female Bodhisattvas: The Women of Japan's Medieval Ritsu-School Nuns' Revival Movement. Ph.D. dissertation, Princeton University.

Minamoto Junko 源淳子, 1996. *Feminizumu ga tou Bukkyō: Kyōken ni shūbaku sareta shizen to bosei* フェミニズムが問う仏教——教権に収縛された自然と母性. Tokyo: San'ichi Shobō.

Minowa Kenryō 蓑輪顕量, 1999. *Chūsei shoki Nanto kairitsu fukkō no kenkyū* 中世初期南都戒律復興の研究. Kyoto: Hōzōkan.

Misaki Gisen 三崎義泉, 1999. *Shikanteki bi-ishiki no tenkai: Chūsei geidō to hongaku shisō to no kanren* 止観的美意識の展開——中世芸道と本覚思想との関連. Tokyo: Perikansha.

Misaki Ryōshū 三崎良周, 1988. *Taimitsu no kenkyū* 台密の研究. Tokyo: Sōbunsha.

Mitsuhashi Tadashi 三橋正, 2000. *Heian jidai no shinkō to shūkyō girei* 平安時代の信仰と宗教儀礼. Tokyo: Zoku Gunsho Ruijū Kansei Kai.

Morrell, Robert E., 1987. *Early Kamakura Buddhism: A Minority Report*. Berkeley: Asian Humanities Press.

Murakami Senshō 村上専精, Tsuji Zennosuke 辻善之助, and Washio Junkyō 鷲尾順敬, eds., 1926–1929. *Meiji ishin, shinbutsu bunri shiryō* 明治維新・神仏分離史料. Tokyo: Tobō Shoin. (revised 1984 as *Shinpen Meiji ishin: Shinbutsu bunri shiryō* 新編明治維新——神仏分離史料. Tokyo: Meicho Shuppan)

Murata Yasuo 村田安穂, 1999. *Shinbutsu bunri no chihōteki tenkai* 神仏分離の地方的展開. Tokyo: Yoshikawa Kōbunkan.

Nakano Kyōtoku 中濃教篤, ed., 1977. *Senjika no Bukkyō* 戦時下の仏教. Tokyo: Kokusho Kankōkai.

Nakura Tetsuzō 名倉哲三, 1988. Haibutsu kishaku to minshū: Echigo Yahikosan Amida Nyoraizō shugo kōdō 廃仏毀釈と民衆——越後弥彦山阿弥陀如来像守護行動. In *Minshū to shakai: Henkaku no rinen to sezoku no rinri* 民衆と社会——変革の理念と世俗の倫理, ed. Murakami Shigeyoshi 村上重良, pp. 147–92. Tokyo: Shunjūsha.

Nihon Bukkyō Kenkyūkai 日本仏教研究会, ed., 1996. *Handobukku Nihon Bukkyō kenkyū* ハンドブック日本仏教研究. Nihon no Bukkyō 日本の仏教 5. Kyoto: Hōzōkan.

———, 2000. *Nihon Bukkyō no kenkyūhō: Rekishi to tenbō* 日本仏教の研究法——歴史と展望. Nihon no Bukkyō 日本の仏教 series 2, vol. 2. Kyoto: Hōzōkan.

Nishiguchi Junko 西口順子, 1987. *Onna no chikara: Kodai no josei to Bukkyō* 女の力——古代の女性と仏教. Tokyo: Heibonsha.

_____, 1992. Josei no shukke to jukai 女性の出家と受戒. *Kyōto Joshi Daigaku Shūkyō Bunka Kenkūjo kenkyū kiyō* 京都女子大学宗教文化研究所研究紀要 5: 79–103.

_____, 1997. Josei to mōja kinichi kuyō 女性と亡者忌日供養. In *Hotoke to onna* 仏と女, ed. Nishiguchi Junko, pp. 218–46. Tokyo: Yoshikawa Kōbunkan.

OGI Mitsuo 荻美津夫, 1998. Kodai ni okeru sōni to ongaku 古代における僧尼と音楽. In *Insei-ki no Bukkyō* 院政期の仏教, ed. Hayami Tasuku 速水 侑, pp. 192–222. Tokyo: Yoshikawa Kōbunkan.

ŌGOSHI Aiko 大越愛子, MINAMOTO Junko 源淳子, and YAMASHITA Akiko 山下明子, eds., 1990. *Sei sabetsu suru Bukkyō* 性差別する仏教. Kyoto: Hōzōkan.

ŌKUBO Ryōshun 大久保良峻, 1998. *Tendai kyōgaku to hongaku shisō* 天台教学と本覚思想. Kyoto: Hōzōkan.

_____, 2004. *Taimitsu kyōgaku no kenkyū* 台密教学の研究. Kyoto: Hōzōkan.

ŌKUBO Ryōshun et al., eds., 2003. *Nihon Bukkyō sanjū-yon no kagi* 日本仏教34の鍵. Tokyo: Shunjūsha.

ŌKUWA Hitoshi 大桑 斉, 1991. *Nihon kinsei no shisō to Bukkyō* 日本近世の思想と仏教. Kyoto: Hōzōkan.

OOMS, Herman, 1985. *Tokugawa Ideology: Early Constructs, 1570–1680*. Princeton: Princeton University Press.

ŌSUMI Kazuo 大隅和雄 and NISHIGUCHI Junko 西口順子, eds., 1989. *Shirīzu josei to Bukkyō* シリーズ女性と仏教. 4 vols. Tokyo: Heibonsha.

ŌTANI Eiichi 大谷栄一, 2001. *Kindai Nihon no Nichirenshugi undō* 近代日本の日蓮主義運動. Kyoto: Hōzōkan.

PAYNE, Richard K., ed., 1998. *Re-Visioning "Kamakura" Buddhism*. Honolulu: University of Hawai'i Press.

RAMBELLI, Fabio, 2003. *Honji suijaku* at Work: Religion, Economics, and Ideology in Pre-Modern Japan. In TEEUWEN and RAMBELLI 2003, pp. 255–86.

READER, Ian, and George J. TANABE, Jr., 1998. *Practically Religious: Worldly Benefits and the Common Religion of Japan*. Honolulu: University of Hawai'i Press.

ROWE, Mark, 2004. Where the Action Is: Sites of Contemporary Sōtō Buddhism. *Japanese Journal of Religious Studies* 31: 357–88.

RUCH, Barbara, ed., 2002. *Engendering Faith: Women and Buddhism in Premodern Japan*. Ann Arbor: Center for Japanese Studies, University of Michigan.

RUPPERT, Brian D., 2000. *Jewel in the Ashes: Buddha Relics and Power in Early Medieval Japan*. Cambridge: Harvard University Asia Center.

SANFORD, James H., William R. LAFLEUR, and Masatoshi NAGATOMI, eds., 1992. *Flowing Traces: Buddhism in the Literary and Visual Arts of Japan*. Princeton: Princeton University Press.

SASAKI Kaoru 佐々木馨, 1988. *Chūsei kokka no shūkyō kōzō* 中世国家の宗教構造. Tokyo: Yoshikawa Kōbunkan.

_____, 1997. *Chūsei Bukkyō to Kamakura bakufu* 中世仏教と鎌倉幕府. Tokyo: Yoshikawa Kōbunkan.

SATŌ Hiroo 佐藤弘夫, 1998. *Kami, hotoke, ōken no chūsei* 神・仏・王権の中世. Kyoto: Hōzōkan.

SAWADA, Janine, 1993. *Confucian Values and Popular Zen: Sekimon Shingaku in Eighteenth-Century Japan.* Honolulu: University of Hawai'i Press.

———, 2004. *Practical Pursuits: Religion, Politics, and Personal Cultivation in Nineteenth-Century Japan.* Honolulu: University of Hawai'i Press.

SCHWALLER, Dieter, 1989. *Der japanische Ōbaku-Mönch Tetsugen Dōkō: Leben, Denken, Schriften.* Bern: Peter Lang.

———, 1996. *Unreiner Zen? Zwei Texte des Ōbaku-Mönchs Chōon Dōkai (1628–1695).* Bern: Peter Lang.

SENJI KYŌGAKU KENKYŪKAI 戦時教学研究会, 1988–1995. *Senji kyōgaku to Shinshū* 戦時教学と真宗. 3 vols. Kyoto: Nagata Bunshōdō.

SHARF, Robert H., 1993. The Zen of Japanese Nationalism. *History of Religions* 33: 1–43.

SHARF, Robert H., and Elizabeth Horton SHARF, eds., 2001. *Living Images: Japanese Buddhist Icons in Context.* Stanford: Stanford University Press.

SONE Masato 曽根正人, 2000. *Kodai Bukkyōkai to ōchō shakai* 古代仏教界と王朝社会.Tokyo: Yoshikawa Kōbunkan.

———, 2003. Saichō, Kūkai to Nanto 最澄・空海と南都. In ŌKUBO 2003, pp. 32–39.

SONEHARA Satoshi 曽根原理, 1996. *Tokugawa Ieyasu shinkakuka e no michi* 徳川家康神格化への道. Tokyo: Yoshikawa Kōbunkan.

STAGGS, Kathleen M., 1983. "Defend the Nation and Love the Truth": Inoue Enryō and the Revival of Meiji Buddhism. *Monumenta Nipponica* 38: 251–81.

STONE, Jacqueline I., 1999a. *Original Enlightenment and the Transformation of Medieval Japanese Buddhism.* Honolulu: University of Hawai'i Press.

———, 1999b. Some Reflections on Critical Buddhism. *Japanese Journal of Religious Studies* 26: 159–88.

SUEKI Fumihiko 末木文美士, 1987. Tendai hongaku shisō kenkyū no shomondai 天台本覚思想研究の諸問題. In *Bukkyō kenkyū no shomondai* 仏教研究の諸問題, ed. Hirakawa Akira 平川 彰. Tokyo: Sankibō Busshorin.

———, 1993. Chūsei Tendai to hongaku shisō 中世天台と本覚思想. In *Nihon Bukkyō shisōshi ronkō* 日本仏教思想史論考, pp. 312–46. Tokyo: Daizō Shuppan.

———, 1995. *Heian shoki Bukkyō shisō no kenkyū: Annen no shisō keisei o chūshin toshite* 平安初期仏教思想の研究――安然の思想形成を中心として. Tokyo: Shunjūsha.

———, 1996. A Reexamination of the *Kenmitsu Taisei* Theory. *Japanese Journal of Religious Studies* 23: 449–66.

———, 1998. *Kamakura Bukkyō keisei ron: Shisōshi no tachiba kara* 鎌倉仏教形成論――思想史の立場から. Kyoto: Hōzōkan.

———, 2004. *Kindai Nihon no shisō, saikō* 近代日本の思想・再考. 2 vols. Tokyo: Transview.

TAIRA Masayuki 半 雅行, 1992. *Nihon chūsei no shakai to Bukkyō* 日本中世の社会と仏教. Tokyo: Hanawa Shobō.

———, 1994. Kamakura Bukkyō ron 鎌倉仏教論. In *Nihon tsūshi* 日本通史 8: *Chūsei* 中世 2, ed. Asao Naohiro 朝尾直弘 et al., pp. 255–301. Tokyo: Iwanami Shoten.

———, 1996. Kuroda Toshio and the *Kenmitsu Taisei* Theory. *Japanese Journal of Religious Studies* 23: 427–48.

Takagi Yutaka 高木 豊, 1982. *Kamakura Bukkyōshi kenkyū* 鎌倉仏教史研究. Tokyo: Iwanami Shoten.

Take Kakuchō 武 覚超, 1988. *Tendai kyōgaku no kenkyū* 天台教学の研究. Kyoto: Hōzōkan.

Tamamuro Fumio 圭室文雄, 1977. *Shinbutsu bunri* 神仏分離. Tokyo: Kyōikusha.

―――, 1999. *Sōshiki to danka* 葬式と檀家. Tokyo: Yoshikawa Kōbunkan.

Tamamuro Taijō 圭室諦成, 1977. *Sōshiki Bukkyō* 葬式仏教. Tokyo: Daihōrinkaku.

Tamiya Masashi 田宮 仁, Hasegawa Masatoshi 長谷川匡俊, and Miyagi Yōichirō 宮城洋一郎, eds., 1994. *Bukkyō to fukushi* 仏教と福祉. Tokyo: Keisuisha.

Tamura Yoshiro, 2001. *Japanese Buddhism: A Cultural History*. Tr. Jeffrey Hunter. Tokyo: Kōsei Publishing.

Tanabe, George J., Jr., 1992. *Myōe the Dreamkeeper: Fantasy and Knowledge in Early Kamakura Buddhism*. Cambridge: Council on East Asian Studies, Harvard University.

Teeuwen, Mark, and Fabio Rambelli, eds., 2003. *Buddhas and Kami in Japan: Honji suijaku as a Combinatory Paradigm*. London: RoutledgeCurzon.

Ushiyama Yoshiyuki 牛山佳幸, 1990. *Kodai chūsei jiin soshiki no kenkyū* 古代中世寺院組織の研究. Tokyo: Yoshikawa Kōbunkan.

―――, 1996. "Nyonin kinsei" sairon 『女人禁制』再論. *Sangaku shugen* 山岳修験 17: 1–11.

Vesey, Alexander Marshall, 2003. The Buddhist Clergy and Village Society in Early Modern Japan. Ph.D. dissertation, Princeton University.

Victoria, Brian (Daizen) A., 1997. *Zen at War*. New York: Weatherhill.

Williams, Duncan Ryūken, 2005. *The Other Side of Zen: A Social History of Sōtō Zen Buddhism in Tokugawa Japan*. Princeton: Princeton University Press.

Wright, Dianna, 2002. Mantokuji: More Than a "Divorce Temple." In Ruch 2002, pp. 247–76.

Yasumaru Yoshio 安丸良夫, 1979. *Kamigami no Meiji Ishin: Shinbutsu bunri to haibutsu kishaku* 神々の明治維新――神仏分離と廃仏毀釈. Tokyo: Iwanami Shoten.

Yiengpruksawan, Mimi Hall, 1998. *Hiraizumi: Buddhist Art and Politics in Twelfth-Century Japan*. Cambridge: Harvard University East Asia Center.

Yoshida Kazuhiko 吉田一彦, 1999. Josei to Bukkyō o meguru shomondai 女性と仏教をめぐる諸問題. In *Nihon no naka no josei to Bukkyō* 日本の中の女性と仏教, ed. Shinshū Bunka Kenkyūjo 真宗文化研究所, pp. 4–47. Kyoto: Hōzōkan.

Yoshida Kyūichi 吉田久一, 1970. *Nihon no kindai shakai to Bukkyō* 日本の近代社会と仏教. Nihonjin no Kōdō to Shisō 日本人の行動と思想 6. Tokyo: Hyōronsha.

―――, 1991. *Kaitei zōhoban Nihon kindai Bukkyō shakaishi kenkyū* 改訂増補版日本近代仏教社会史研究. *Yoshida Kyūichi chosakushū* 吉田久一著作集, vols. 5–6. Tokyo: Kawashima Shoten. (revision and expansion of 1964 edition from Yoshikawa Kōbunkan)

―――, 1992. *Nihon kindai Bukkyō kenkyū* 日本近代仏教研究. *Yoshida Kyūichi chosakushū*, vol. 4. Tokyo: Kawashima Shoten. (reprint of 1959 edition from Yoshikawa Kōbunkan)

TRADITIONS

Ian READER

Folk Religion

I t was once common in the academic study of Japanese religion to consider that "folk religion" (*minkan shinkō* 民間信仰 or *minzoku shūkyō* 民俗宗教, terms that contain significant differences of nuance to be discussed later) was somehow separate from other, formally established religious traditions such as Buddhism and Shinto. While they—and notably Buddhism—were discussed in terms of texts, doctrines, founders, and sectarian developments, folk religion was generally seen as something relating to an amorphous area of traditions, customs, practices, and superstitions that lacked doctrinal focus and that were largely the preserve of rural Japan.

Folk religion, as such, represented a survival of native customs and traditions that stood in contrast to the modernizing forces that were shaping Japan in the modern era. This perspective has influenced the development in Japan of the discipline of folk studies (*minzokugaku* 民俗学) which has had a higher profile as an academic discipline in Japan than in many other countries. At its core *minzokugaku,* as evidenced by the work of its Japanese founder-figure Yanagita Kunio, was concerned with *minkan shinkō,* a term normally translated as either folk or popular religion, but literally meaning the "faith of the (ordinary) people." Indeed, *minkan shinkō* has traditionally been the most comprehensively studied aspect of *minzokugaku* (Miyamoto 1978, p. 161). For Yanagita, such faith and folk customs indicated a "unique religiosity" (*koyū shinkō* 固有信仰) that marked the Japanese out from other peoples and that provided the bedrock of native Japanese culture and of the lives of its people (Sakurai 1978, p. 3, cited also in Shinno 1991a, p. 276, and in English translation in Shinno 1993, p. 193).[1] The main aim of the *minzokugaku* that Yanagita inspired was the collection and preservation of evidence relating to this unique "native culture" before it could be overwhelmed and destroyed by Western cultural influences and the processes of modernization. Its agenda was innately nationalist and was intent on emphasizing what Yanagita and his disciples saw as an indigenous native genius that was special to (and hence part of the emotional identity construction of) the Japanese people. On such levels, too, the early study of *minkan shinkō* had little time or need for comparative studies of folk religion, or for considering how Japanese folk religion might be compared to or fitted into any wider analytical framework: it was unique to Japan, while the concerns of those who studied it were wholly focused on the Japanese situation.

While such emphases remain an element in the agenda of Japanese folklore studies, the academic study of folk religion has moved beyond these early beginnings and, indeed, to develop critiques of early scholars such as Yanagita for their rather insular focus on Japan and their attempts to emphasize a "uniqueness" that cannot be sustained when Japanese phenomena are subjected to comparative analysis (see, e.g., Shinno 1991a, pp. 270–79). Folk religion is no longer seen solely as the preserve of folklorists intent primarily on collecting, classifying, preserving, and "discovering" the unique, but as a valid arena of study for scholars of religion and anthropologists intent on analyzing its interactions with established religious traditions and comparing and relating it to folk religious structures in broader contexts. The earlier separation of the folk from other traditions was based, ultimately, on concepts of high and low, or elite and popular, religion, and on the notion prevalent early in the development of religious studies and Buddhist studies that texts and doctrines constitute the core and essence of religions, and that the study of "primitive" phenomena such as religious practices and rituals were the field of folklorists and anthropologists rather than the scholar of religion. As the field of religious studies has developed, however, scholars have moved away from such narrow attitudes that made artificial distinctions between text and doctrine, on the one hand, and practice and custom on the other, and that used such artificial and judgemental concepts as "high" and "low" or "elite" and "popular" religion. In so doing, they have come to recognize that seemingly "folk" religious phenomena such as rituals, festivals, concepts relating to the spirits of the dead and to spirit possession, uses of talismans, amulets and divination practices, and beliefs in the wish-granting capacities of deities and the like, are central and critical elements

---

1. Shinno 1993 is a translation of the concluding chapter of Shinno 1991a.

within normative religious structures, of equal value and import as, for example, text and doctrine, and that they must, therefore, be studied and analyzed as such. Whether in the study of Buddhism (where beliefs and practices related to death and the ancestors are now widely acknowledged by scholars as being intrinsic parts of, rather than superstitious folk accretions to, or perversions of, Japanese Buddhism) or the study of new religions (whose debt, in terms of concepts of healing, spirit possession, and shamanism, to the folk religious world of Japan has received clear academic recognition), the folk religious tradition has widely come to be seen as the underlying basis of the entire religious structure of Japan (see, for example, MIYAKE 1974 and 1981).

In such ways the divisions that were formerly assumed to exist between different traditions have been reassessed. Equally, the study of folk religion has come to be seen as something that necessitates interdisciplinary perspectives (for example, combining historical and textual studies with anthropological approaches) so as to properly explore the workings of folk religion in the context of the traditions it has so heavily influenced.

As scholars have developed more textured and historically informed perspectives and analyses of folk religion in Japan, they have increasingly moved away from the static conceptualization implicit in the Yanagita model of an unchanging phenomenon associated with the past and with agrarian, pre-modern, and "traditional" Japan, and have come to recognize that it, like other religious traditions, has the capacity to change, adapt, and develop in line with changing situations and circumstances. Indeed, one of the themes consistently emphasized in more recent studies of folk religious phenomena focuses on the capacity of the folk tradition to change in accord with the times, and to reflect contemporary religious dynamics. Among the Japanese scholars who played important roles in thus opening out the field and taking it beyond its earlier narrow confines have been Gorai Shigeru, Miyata Noboru, Miyake Hitoshi, Sasaki Kōkan, Sakurai Tokutarō, and Shinno Toshikazu, all of whom, while having special interests in the study of folk religion, have grounded their research in such disciplines as anthropology and religious studies.

Equally, the focus on agrarian, rural areas that typified earlier studies of folk religion and folk lore, has changed as scholars have focused attention also upon manifestations of folk religion in modern urban contexts, thereby identifying the folk religious dynamic as an element in the religious structure of the modern, technologically oriented world of contemporary Japan as well as in its seemingly more "traditional" rural areas (e.g., SHŪKYŌ SHAKAIGAKU NO KAI 1985, 1987, 1999, 2002; see also DAVIS 1980 and READER 1991a).

As studies in the field of folk religion have thus advanced and taken on broader and more encompassing perspectives, the terminology initially used to describe "folk religion" (i.e., *minkan shinkō*) has been changed in order to bring the study of Japanese folk religion out of the restrictive arena implied by *minkan shinkō* and to allow it to be placed on a comparative basis with folk religious traditions elsewhere. The term that has become standard in the work of scholars such as Sakurai, Shinno, Miyake, and others, is *minzoku shūkyō*, a term which is also most readily translated in English as "folk religion," but which contains nuances of meaning in Japanese that differentiate it from *minkan shinkō* (see below) including the emphasis on "religion" (*shūkyō*) rather than "faith" (*shinkō*).

This terminological shift does not mean that discussions and debates about the terminology to use in the field have not continued to emerge. Recently, for example, questions have been asked in English language contexts as to whether the term "folk religion" itself is an appropriate term to use. Arguing that the English term (and by implication, the Japanese *minzoku shūkyō*) is too bound up with the problematic notions of high and low (or elite and popular) religion implicit within earlier religious studies, Ian READER and George TANABE, Jr. (1998) have argued that "common religion" (a term that they perceive as encompassing and incorporating text, liturgy, shared customs, beliefs, and practices) would be a more appropriate term for what they view as a shared stratum of religious notions and practices that permeate the Japanese religious world. This, too, has raised further debates, and led to further suggestions about, an appropriate terminology to describe what current scholars continue to regard as an intrinsic, central area of religious beliefs and practices that is integral to the study of the religious traditions extant in Japan.

EARLY STUDIES OF FOLK RELIGION:
TRADITION, SURVIVALS AND RESIDUAL CUSTOMS

As was noted above, early studies of folk religion in Japan centered on customs and local practices, especially in rural communities. They were especially concerned with capturing the essence and spirit of a Japan that they feared was rapidly disappearing in the face of modernization and cultural influences from the West, and in constructing a psychological portrait or profile of the Japanese through studies of (and compilations of the records of) its customs and traditions, thereby "preserving" the cultural ethos and spirit of traditional Japan and "saving" it from cultural erosion. Yanagita Kunio was central to this activity, and his foundational work in the field centered especially on oral traditions, such as folk tales (*mukashibanashi* 昔話) and legends (*densetsu* 伝説), which he and other folklorists collected in great quantities. Besides compiling, and thereby preserving, vast amounts of legends and stories in this way, Yanagita and his disciples sought also to identify what they saw as the essentially Japanese religious motifs articulated within such oral traditions and stories.[2] They also examined in detail a variety of beliefs, customs, and practices found throughout the Japanese archipelago (but primarily in rural areas), such as: those associated with life cycles, death and mortuary rituals, and the influences of the spirits of the dead; commemorative and celebratory events associated with the rhythms of life of communities, e.g., festivals (*matsuri* 祭り); the role and nature of various deities associated

2. See UENO 1978, esp. the chapter by Nomura (pp. 210–28) on the study of oral traditions in Japanese folk studies. Yanagita wrote extensively about oral traditions, and several volumes of his collected works (YANAGITA 1962–1963) pay particular attention to them, notably volume 4, which contains Yanagita's famous collection of tales from northern Japan, *Tōno monogatari*, and volumes 5 and 6, which focus on other folk tales that he collected. For a study of Yanagita's work and influences, see the series of essays in KOSHMANN, ŌIWA, and YAMASHITA 1985, which discuss Yanagita's work and influence at some length and focus particularly on his studies of folk tales, ancestors, and festivals. This volume also contains a translation of some of his work on festivals and is perhaps the most accessible overview and introduction to this important figure available in English.

with geographical features (e.g., *yama no kami* 山の神 and *ta no kami* 田の神—gods of the mountains and fields respectively); prohibitions and taboos; practices and beliefs relating to communications between this and other realms; and the roles of shamanic figures, diviners, and mediums.[3] Along with Yanagita, another seminal figure in the early foundations of Japanese folklore was Orikuchi Shinobu, whose main focus was to decipher and reconstruct what he viewed as the traditional culture of Japan based in its folk faith which was manifested in, and found through, studies of folk arts, practices, and religious beliefs (ORIKUCHI 1929–1930).

Such studies were carried out not only in academic institutes, but also by organizations such as the Japanese Folklore Society and by local and regional folklore societies and folklorists. These, too, have been active in the preservation and collection of materials and customs related to folk religious customs and, while not necessarily always "academic" in content, they have often provided important source materials for scholars in the field. In my research on the Shikoku pilgrimage, for example, I have found that local folklore studies can provide highly valuable information (e.g., the work by TAKEDA Akira 1972 and 1987) on folk tales and on death customs as they relate to pilgrimage in Shikoku, and the studies of TSURUMURA Shōichi (1978, 1979) on pilgrim activities and diaries (especially in earlier ages in Shikoku) has provided useful data for my studies. This indicates a critical matter for anyone intent on studying religious practices, customs, and beliefs in Japan: the need to delve deeply at local levels in the collection of information, for it is in such areas that one will often find some of the most valuable information and sources. Since local folklore societies and folklorists in Japan tend to publish locally (indeed, often through self-published works) one cannot rely on libraries, especially in larger cities, or on major bookshops, to acquire such materials. Much of the published material I have collected in my research has come from such sources, and has been picked up from stalls at popular shrines and temples, or at local shops on the streets leading up to them, or (especially in my pilgrimage work) from local folklore societies and individual folklorists in small towns and villages in Shikoku and elsewhere. The message is simple: collecting written sources is often done in the same places as those where one collects oral and anthropological evidence.

It was in the late 1930s that the first steps toward extended fieldwork on matters of folk religion in Japan were taken by Western scholars, with the study by John F. Embree of Suye Mura, a village in Kyushu. The first Western anthropologist to study Japanese village life, Embree's prime focus was on the social structure and dynamics of life in the village, and in his study he provided a detailed exposition of its religious life (EMBREE 1964 [1946], pp. 221–98). His account in essence emphasized the importance of a folk religious structure, in which he identified the key concerns as being not the formalized teachings of the established religious traditions, but practices and customs relating to the spirits of the dead, popular local deities, and cyclical rituals within the community. Indeed Embree intro-

3. There have been numerous volumes produced in Japanese assessing and surveying the field of folklore studies, along with many dictionaries focused on *minzokugaku*. Amongst the most useful are UENO 1978, FUKUDA and MIYATA 1983, and AKATA 1984, in the latter of which the chapter by MIYATA (pp. 113–34) is especially recommended.

duced his study of village religion through this observation, stating that the "only religious system … is the festival calendar" (p.221). Embree's interest in, and focus on, festivals and the festival calendar as a seminal element in religious and social life, reflected not just some of the prime concerns of Japanese folk studies at the time, but also a continuing area of interest for scholars in the field in the later eras, for whom calendrical cycles and rituals, as well as *matsuri* and their structures and social meanings, have remained a prime area of concern (see below).

OVERARCHING THEMATIC DEVELOPMENTS AND ACADEMIC PARADIGM SHIFTS: FROM *MINKAN SHINKŌ* TO *MINZOKU SHŪKYŌ*

The work done by Yanagita, his disciples, and others such as Orikuchi, was crucial in establishing the importance of "folk" practices, customs, and beliefs in the broader context of studies of Japanese religion and society. Their activities not only shaped the initial developments of Japanese folk studies but have had a lasting influence on its subsequent evolution, while also providing immense amounts of information and materials data that have been of use to subsequent scholars. Furthermore, the tradition they developed from the outset, based in extensive data gathering throughout the country, has continued to the present, and contemporary researchers continue to benefit from the enormous flow of materials and information that continues to be generated as a result. However, while later scholars have maintained the tradition of extensive data collection, they have also increasingly—especially from the late 1970s onwards—questioned whether the parameters that framed early Japanese folk studies and depictions of folk religion, which centered particularly on concepts of uniqueness, posed limitations for the subject. As a result there has been something of a paradigm shift in the field, accompanied by a significant change in terminology occasioned by the engagement of scholars other than those primarily identified as "folklorists" (a discipline that, in the ways it was established in Japan, had specifically Japanese orientations and concerns) in studying folk phenomena. Especially since the 1970s those who have engaged in the study of what were previously seen as folk phenomena, customs, and practices, have included scholars whose primary disciplinary focus has not been in folklore studies so much as anthropology, history, and religious studies. Such scholars have tended to relate their studies of folk religious phenomena in Japan to wider disciplinary issues in their fields, and in so doing, have moved away from the earlier focus on uniqueness, toward examinations of the relationship of folk practices to other religious traditions in Japan, and beyond that, to studies of folk religion in other parts of the world. Such studies took, as their basis, the view that folk religion and practices in Japan could be discussed in comparative contexts, and that a more comprehensive framework that recognized the potentially universal dimensions of folk religion, might be developed and applied to Japan.

This paradigm shift is symbolized by the replacement of the term *minkan shinkō* by that of *minzoku shūkyō*. While each of these terms may be (and, indeed, has commonly been) translated as "folk religion," the two contain important nuances of difference. The former indicates a folk religious world clearly parochial and localized in focus, related to customs and practices that were not systematically organized around doctrinal ideas, and that existed in contradistinction to organized and established religious traditions, which were presumed to be built and operate around doctrines, founders, and the like. These themes were emphasized by HORI Ichirō, whose postwar studies of folk religion in Japan built on Yanagita's work and sought to develop a systematic framework for *minkan shinkō*, folk religion, one which presented a clear and oppositional contrast between the folk and organized religious realms (HORI 1951, esp. pp. 8–10). Hori also argued that all religious tradition in Japan was based on an underlying folk religious stratum, while also seemingly reiterating the Yanagita legacy of the unique nature of Japanese folk religion by positing a unified and organic relationship between Japanese folk religion and social structure (e.g., HORI 1968).[4]

The latter term, with its use of *shūkyō* 宗教 ("religion"), indicates a potentially more coherent and cohesive structure, and locates folk religion within a universal frame of reference that relates not just to one specific culture (as was the case with *minkan shinkō*) but to the notion of a field of religious expression that may exist in *any* society and culture through the interaction of universalizing and local currents. It also recognizes the tensions that exist between doctrinally and textually constructed religious traditions with universalizing dimensions that are taught through the transmission of doctrines, texts, sermons, and the words of founders and teachers, and the shared, common customs, practices, and localized beliefs founded in specific cultural settings, that are imbibed through belonging to a specific cultural tradition, society, community, or locale. Indeed, it is in these areas of tension and intersection that, scholars in the field have argued, the creative dynamism of folk religion and its impact on established traditions may especially be found. Such arguments and perspectives can be found in the work of prominent Japanese scholars in the field, such as Sakurai, Miyake, Miyata, Gorai, and Shinno, who have already been mentioned as seminal figures in the development of *minzoku shūkyō* as a disciplinary category in Japan.[5]

The development of, and emphasis on, the notion of *minzoku shūkyō*, and the turn away from *minkan shinkō*, represented a gradual rather than a sudden change in perception over a number of years, during which time many in the field shifted their ground—a point illustrated by the fact that the anthropologist Sakurai Tokutarō (whose main research

---

4. Hori was Yanagita's son-in-law. This is an aspect of the study of Japanese folk religious studies that is of some interest, but that has as yet barely been discussed in academic studies: the ways in which studies in the field have also tended to produce family lineages in academic and intellectual terms. Two further scholars mentioned in this chapter as playing seminal roles in redefining the field and taking it beyond its early boundaries, namely Sakurai Tokutarō and Shinno Toshikazu, are also linked through marriage, with Shinno as Sakurai's son-in-law.

5. For a fuller exposition in English of the uses of the terms *minkan shinkō* and *minzoku shūkyō*, see HAYASHI and YOSHIHARA 1988, esp. pp. 90–92, and SHINNO 1993, esp. pp.188–89. See also the review of Shinno 1991a by READER (1991b). MIYAKE (1989, pp. 1–30, esp. 15–25, and 2002, pp. 2–23) provides valuable overviews of the field, its historical development, and its methodological orientations.

focus was on shamanism) used the term *minkan shinkō* in his writings from 1958 throughout the 1960s (e.g., SAKURAI 1958, 1966), and it is only near the end of his academic career
in the 1980s that he regularly used the term *minzoku shūkyō* (e.g., SAKURAI 1982). While
it is unclear exactly when this terminological and intellectual shift occurred, it is evident
that *minzoku shūkyō* really came into its own as an analytical term from the mid-1970s,
becoming fairly standard in the field by the early 1980s (see GORAI 1979).

This terminological and intellectual advance came about because Japanese scholars recognized that the realm of *minkan shinkō* was dated and limited to a disappearing world of
rural Japan, and that to study popular religious phenomena in a society that was changing rapidly necessitated new understandings and frameworks of analysis. Moreover, the
methods of study associated with *minkan shinkō* and, indeed, with Yanagita's folk studies
(largely based in collecting oral legends, customs, and accounts of popular practices) came
to be seen as less than academically rigorous and too heavily weighted in favor of placing
emphasis on uncorroborated oral testimonies from people in rural areas who were seen
as founts of disappearing knowledge. Those who sought a re-evaluation of the field in intellectual and terminological terms combined this with a recognition that more rigorous
disciplinary approaches, including the use of modern anthropological fieldwork methods
and historical research methodologies, necessitated the examination of textual materials,
archives, and historical texts and documents, which came to be seen as necessary for a comprehensive understanding of folk religion both in Japanese and comparative contexts.

FURTHER DEVELOPMENTS:
COMMON THREADS AND COLLAPSING BOUNDARIES

As Japanese scholarship moved from its former rather introverted absorption
with rural customs, it also began to influence Western scholarship in the field, while establishing the ground for both cooperative work between Japanese and Western scholars, and
for Western scholarship that has influenced the field in Japan. Two notable figures worthy
of mention here are H. Byron EARHART and Carmen BLACKER. Earhart has had a close academic association with Miyake Hitoshi, and while the latter's work has clearly influenced
Earhart, Earhart has done much to bring Miyake's scholarship to a Western audience (see
MIYAKE 2001, which is a collection of Miyake's essays, edited and with an Introduction
by Earhart). EARHART has also produced seminal studies of mountain religion (1970) in
which he identifies the importance of calendrical rituals within the religious traditions of
Japan, as well as writing a number of texts (EARHART 1974, 1982) that have provided the
basis for university courses on Japanese religion, and that draw attention to such unifying
themes in Japanese religious contexts as the folk tradition and the calendar of ritual events.
Carmen BLACKER, who worked closely with and was deeply influenced by the work of
such scholars as Gorai, Miyake, and Miyata, produced one of the most important studies of shamanism, asceticism, exorcism, and divination in Japan in her seminal study *The
Catalpa Bow* (1975, republished 1999). In this work Blacker shows how shamanic activities,
along with ascetic and exorcistic practices constitutes a vast and coherent arena of activity
in Japanese religious contexts, manifest in the new religions as well as at Buddhist temples

and Shinto shrines, as well as among practitioners specifically associated with none of these traditions. Despite the importance of shamanism and related phenomena, however, scant attention had been paid to it by Western scholars (who tended to follow the normative of earlier studies of religion by focusing on the established and identifiable traditions of Shinto and Buddhism and on doctrines and texts) prior to Blacker's study. The problems inherent in such approaches were evident to Blacker, however, in her comment that the subject of her study "makes nonsense of that conventional distinction hitherto observed by most Western writers on Japanese religion, the separation of Shinto from Buddhism" (1975, p. 33). She went on to note that there is in Japan a large area of religious practice that is common across the board, and which is shared by Shinto and Buddhism, to the extent that worshippers are rarely aware of whether a deity is Shinto or Buddhist. Blacker notes further that such issues were "either ignored or relegated to various snail patches with pejorative labels such as superstition, syncretism or magic" (1975, p. 33). What she is talking about, of course, is what has been discussed above as "folk religion," and the ways in which it intersected with (and thus cannot be ultimately differentiated from) the so-called established traditions. Blacker's study is important as the first in English to bring this point so clearly into the fore of studies of Japanese religion. Through it, shamanism and other aspects of folk religion could no longer be relegated to marginal "snail patches" but took their place in the center of the field of study.

INTERACTIONS AND INTERSTICES: FOLK RELIGION AND BUDDHISM

Such academic developments were also mirrored by developments in the study of established religions that facilitated increasing awareness of the extent to which such traditions have overlapped and been closely linked together. Of particular importance has been the understanding developed by Buddhist studies scholars in and beyond Japan that emphasizing or focusing only on textual, doctrinal, and sectarian traditions, restricted their understanding of Buddhism to what was, in effect, a highly selective aspect of that tradition (one dominated largely by a literate male monastic elite). As scholars of Buddhism have expanded their fields of interest to look at the interconnections between doctrine and practice, at the activities and practices carried out at Buddhist temples and by Buddhist ascetics, for example, they have come to recognize that many of these issues involve interactions between Buddhism and folk religion, and that many seemingly "folk" oriented beliefs, practices, and ritual processes (e.g., the rites relating to death and the spirits of the dead), are intrinsic elements in the structure of Japanese Buddhism, rather than as anomalous external accretions.[6] Thus, the expansion of the study of folk religion

6. This dynamic has come particularly from Western scholars both directly concerned with the study of East Asian Buddhism, and with scholars who specialize in the study of early Buddhism, and who have come to argue that earlier studies of Buddhism were based in Western preconceptions of, and attempts to construct, a Buddhism that would be palatable to particular Western interests. Gregory SCHOPEN was one of the earliest scholars to point to Buddhist origins far less associated with philosophy and doctrine than with cults of the dead

to include interactions with established traditions, has been paralleled by the expansion of the remit of Buddhist studies to take account of and analyze, within Buddhist contexts, folk religious practices. In such terms, one of the prime focuses of research across these fields in recent times has been the interrelationship between Buddhism and folk religion—an area which in many respects serves to demonstrate how problematic and, indeed, impractical it is to try to draw formal lines of differentiation between these two traditions that have overlapped and interpenetrated for many centuries. A sizeable general literature has developed in Japanese on such issues, represented by such extensive collected series as the ten-volume *Bukkyō Minzokugaku Taikei* 仏教民俗学大系 series published by Meicho Shuppan (1986–1993), which features volumes on topics such as the development of Buddhist folk studies (vol. 1), ancestor veneration and funerary rites (vol. 4), and Buddhist calendrical rituals (vol. 6) and whose contributors and editors include several scholars already mentioned such as Sakurai Tokutarō, Miyata Noboru, and Shinno Toshikazu.

THEMES OF STUDY: MOUNTAINS, ASCETICS, PILGRIMAGES, ANCESTORS, AND THE SPIRITS OF THE DEAD

Numerous themes and topics that sit, as it were, on the borders of organized, established religions and of folk religion (and, especially, in areas relating to the interface of Buddhism and folk religion) have been featured in studies of folk religion, and here it is only possible to mention a representative number of them. Here attention will be paid especially to mountain religion (generally regarded as an area in which Buddhist and folk themes are linked together), to individual practitioners and ascetic figures who might be termed "intermediary" religious practitioners who may be identified both with folk religion and with Buddhist institutions, to pilgrimages and pilgrimage customs, which offer extensive scope for folk religious practice yet are largely centered on Buddhist temples, and to an area central to Buddhist practice in Japan, but one with roots in folk beliefs and customs, namely funerary customs, ancestors, and the spirits of the dead.

The study of mountain religious customs and practices, and of the orders and practitioners associated with them, has been central to the work of some of the seminal scholastic figures already mentioned in this chapter, including Gorai, Miyata, Miyake, and Shinno. Their work recognizes how the mountain religious tradition, in the shape of Shugendō 修験道 and its practitioners, the *yamabushi* 山伏, operated in an area between the formalized religious structures of Buddhism and the world of folk religion, and how the tradition and its practitioners mediated between the worlds of the mountain and village, and, indeed, between formalized religious structures with their roots in Buddhism, and folk traditions centered on the roles assumed by the *yamabushi* at local and village levels, as diviners and healers. Studies of Shugendō and of *yamabushi* are central to much of MIYAKE Hitoshi's corpus of works, especially his comprehensive two volumes respectively on Shugendō rit-

and popular practices (see SCHOPEN 1997 for a collection of his papers on the issue), while the various contributors to LOPEZ 1995 have demonstrated how this construction of Buddhism came about.

uals and thought (1999a and 1999b). Perhaps the most notable and sizeable contribution in the context of mountain religion has been the 18-volume series *Sangaku Shūkyōshi Kenkyū sōsho* (1975–1989) published by Meicho Shuppan, in which individual volumes centered on aspects of Shugendō as well as on different Japanese mountains and the cults centered around them, including mountains regarded as *reizan* 霊山 (mountains that are considered to be the abodes of the spirits of the dead, and whose study also is related to other topics such as pilgrimage and issues relating to the spirits of the dead). Gorai Shigeru was a major contributor to this series, editing several of the volumes in it, but numerous other scholars previously mentioned, including Miyake Hitoshi, also made important contributions.

Other notable contributions to studies of mountains, mountain cults, and their relation to other areas of religious practice in Japan, include MIYATA Noboru's (1993) study of an often dichotomous relationship widely commented on in Japanese religious studies, that of the *yama* 山 and *sato* 里 (mountain and village), in which the former signifies the dangerous, wild, and uninhabited, and is the locus of ascetic practice, as well as being the realm of the spirits of the dead, and the latter represents the safe, inhabited world of ordinary society. Miyata's study of this relationship shows how the two are linked together, and he examines such topics as pilgrimages to mountainous regions and the role of local religious confraternities (*kō* 講) that are based in villages but conduct religious exercises and rituals in the mountains, and hence form a link between these two worlds. The significance of mountains as sacred locations—and the activities of confraternities that ascend and conduct religious exercises therein—is dealt with also by writers such as NISHIGAI Kenji (1984) who has studied religious cults and practices centered on Mt. Ishizuchi in Shikoku, and the relationships centered on it and linking it, via Ishizuchi religious confraternities and Shugendō groups, to local communities in northern Shikoku.

Western scholarship, too, has paid attention to Shugendō and mountain religion, both with Earhart's previously cited volume (1970) and, more recently, Irit AVERBUCH's (1995) study of *yamabushi* activities, that emphasizes another important area of study—that of the relationship between popular, folk religious practices, and artistic/cultural traditions. Averbuch examines how Shugendō ideas and practices are expressed through the performance of the ritual dance form *kagura*. In a similar vein, mention should also be made of the work of Jane Marie LAW (1997), who also examines artistic and cultural performances within the context of folk religion, in her study of the *bunraku* puppet theater of Awaji Island, with special reference to its religious dimensions and meanings.

A religious figure who has attracted a great deal of attention from Japanese scholars in the field has been the *hijiri* or wandering ascetic, whose role in spreading Buddhist practices and ideas through the Japanese populace and in the context of the encounter of Buddhism and folk religion has been discussed in Japanese by GORAI (1975, 1984) and SHINNO (1991a, 1991b, 1993). Shinno's studies of *hijiri* have especially focused on the legends relating to them, and their roles in spreading a popular Buddhist faith and in opening up pilgrimage routes. In discussing such issues he has put forward the argument that, since the *hijiri* were representatives of a universal religion (Buddhism) which they mediated and transmitted to local populaces, they could be seen as paradigmatic models of the process of interaction between overarching/universalizing and local traditions in general (SHINNO, 1993, p. 197).

Similar themes have been expressed in English on the topic of *hijiri* by Janet Goodwin (1994), who emphasizes the complementary roles of the *hijiri* in practical and spiritual terms, as proponents of both social welfare and salvation activities.

The *hijiri* cannot always be distinguished from the shamanic and ascetic figures discussed by Blacker and other scholars of shamanism in Japan, and Shinno not only reiterates such perspectives but also argues that elements of the *hijiri* figure (whose influence was especially notable in medieval times as Buddhist temples sought to spread their influence among the ordinary people) can also be found in the modern day activities of diviners and shamans in modern, urban settings. In this context, and in the course of his primarily pre-modern-based study of *hijiri*, Shinno draws attention to the work of the Osaka-based research group the Shūkyō Shakaigaku no Kai (whose studies of urban-based folk practices will be discussed later in this chapter), which has examined shaman-like figures and diviners in the Osaka region. Shinno sees such modern figures who, like pre-modern ascetics, perform austerities and also mediate religious messages to the populace, as "*hijiri*-like" figures and, hence, as modern continuations of a tradition that has been central to Japanese folk religion (1993, pp. 200–3).

By focusing attention on such shaman-like figures, Shinno implicitly reiterates and reaffirms the work carried out by scholars such as Sakurai Tokutarō, who discussed diviners and shamanic figures as mediators between this and other realms, and between established and folk traditions, and who examined the roles and activities of such figures as the *itako* or blind female diviners of northern Japan (Sakurai 1974, 1977). This focus on shamanic and ascetic figures—which reflects many of the themes in Blacker's work, mentioned earlier—and especially on female practitioners in northern Japan, who undergo austerities, and who claim the ability to divine the future and to communicate with the spirits of the dead, remains a prominent theme in Japanese studies of religion. Important works here include the studies by Kanda Yoriko (1992), who conducted detailed ethnographic studies of such figures in Iwate Prefecture, and Ikegami Yoshimasa (1999) who also examines figures such as the aforementioned *itako* and the divinatory roles they perform. In English, Ellen Schattschneider (2003) has also studied female practitioners in marginalized mountain locales in northern Japan, showing how mountains not only provide the setting for spiritual practice for such figures, but also serve as a meeting point between this and other worlds. It is in such marginalized contexts, and through austerities carried out in them, that such female figures can provide guidance for others, become spiritual authorities, and—at least in the context of the mountain—temporarily step outside the normative gender relations that privilege male over female and that normally govern their lives.

Related to this interest in individual religious figures such as *hijiri* and other such ascetic practitioners, has been a focus on the development and practice of pilgrimage in Japan, an area that has been widely regarded as a further example of the interaction between, and the common ground of, established traditions and the folk realm. Shinno (1991a, p. 91) , in discussing one of the most prominent pilgrimages in Japan, the Shikoku *henro* or 88-temple pilgrimage around the island of Shikoku, has commented that this has two faces, one related to established Shingon Buddhism (80 of the 88 pilgrimage temples are affiliated to the Shingon sect, Shingon images and notions permeate many areas of the pilgrimage, and Shingon authorities have made great attempts to portray it as a Shingon activity) and the other to folk religion, with pilgrims in general pursuing their own activities and manifesting folk religious beliefs and practices in the miracle working figure of Kōbō Daishi, who is at the heart of the pilgrimage. Although Kōbō Daishi is formally associated with the Shingon sect, in folkloric terms he is usually depicted and envisioned as a miraculous wanderer akin to the *hijiri,* and devotion to him is more commonly seen as being rooted in the folk tradition. KANEKO Satoru (1991) has made this point through his study of members of Jōdo Shin (True Pure Land) Buddhist temples who live in Shikoku, which indicates that a sizeable number of such people are (despite the tenets of their Buddhist sect, which theoretically prohibits devotion to other figures or practices other than those relating to faith in Amida) more likely than not to be devotees of Kōbō Daishi and to have either participated at some time or other in performing the Shikoku pilgrimage or in giving support and alms to other pilgrims. The pilgrimage and devotion to Kōbō Daishi are, in effect, elements in the folk religious structure of the island of Shikoku, and hence are likely to be adhered to by members of Buddhist organizations, even when official teachings appear to warn them against such practices.

Studies of pilgrimage in Japan have generally seen pilgrimage as a practice that is simultaneously associated with established traditions and yet is equally, and especially when viewed from the perspective of ordinary pilgrims, a manifestation of populist and folk traditions. Studies of mass pilgrimages to the shrines of Ise, for example, frequently reflect the extent to which these have been mass folk practices (NISHIGAKI 1983; DAVIS 1992, pp. 45–80). The work of HOSHINO Eiki has emphasized the dynamic nature of the folk religious tradition as a formative element in the Shikoku pilgrimage and pointed out the links between the formation of the Shikoku pilgrimage, and mountain ascetics (1979). More recently, HOSHINO (2001) has shown how pilgrims and religious authorities often have different perceptions of the pilgrimage and, while showing how Shikoku pilgrimage temple authorities have striven to emphasize the Shingon Buddhist elements of the pilgrimage, he emphasises the extent to which pilgrims in effect follow a folk interpretation of the pilgrimage by framing their journeys within populist beliefs and assumptions, including notions of salvation at death and the attainment of worldly benefits through pilgrimage, that are independent of the attempts made by religious authorities to control and organize the pilgrimage. Similar themes can be found in READER (2005), which examines the Shikoku pilgrimage in terms of how it has been "made" (i.e., constructed) through the engagement and activities of ordinary people over the centuries, and which shows how the two faces identified by Shinno, of folk faith and organized Buddhism, intersect and how the dynamism of the pilgrimage is in effect through such interactions.[7]

A further area that has traditionally been widely studied by Japanese scholars—and that relates very much to the intersection of Buddhism and folk practices and beliefs—has been that of practices relating to the dead, and especially to the role of ancestors (e.g.,

---

7. There is an extensive literature on pilgrimage in Japan, and much of it is discussed in the essay by Barbara Ambros in this *Guide.* For a general overview of the field, see also READER and SWANSON 1997 and the three-volume series edited by SHINNO (1996).

TAKEDA Chōshū 1971). SASAKI Kōkan, too, has written widely from anthropological perspectives about the relationship between Buddhism and the spirits of the dead (1991 and 1993). A notable Western contribution to this area has been Robert J. SMITH's (1974) study, which examined this issue both through historical and fieldwork research, and through an analysis of who was worshipped and memorialized as ancestors, through a study of the contents of family Buddhist altars in Tokyo. What Smith's study showed, amongst other things, was that not all who were so memorialized were family members and that the contents of urban Buddhist altars had a higher level of non-lineal memorial tablets in them than rural ones—data that led Smith to suggest that urbanization and changes in family structure were occasioning changes in ancestor worship, and that it was becoming a family rather than extended household centered practice (1974, pp. 152–86). His analysis, which has been highly influential in Japan, has been confirmed by scholars such as KŌMOTO Mistugu (1988, 2001) whose studies indicate a continuing process of extending the notion of who can be ancestors beyond traditional familial, and patrilineal, boundaries.

Among other areas that have especially concerned Japanese scholars is the study of festivals (*matsuri*), a major topic of interest for early folklorists that has continued to be important in the field of *minzoku shūkyō*. It has also become an area of interest for sociologists of religion, who saw in the structure of festivals symbolic articulations of important themes in the structure of modern Japanese (and comparative) religion. YANAGAWA Keiichi (1987), for example, sought to analyze, through his studies of *matsuri*, the symbolic interactions of concepts of sacred space and time, while questioning the extent to which what he saw as the "decline of traditional society" was impacting on religion in the modern age. Festivals have also attracted the attention of Western scholars, most notably in Scott SCHNELL's (1999) study of *matsuri* in Furukawa, which blends anthropological fieldwork with historical research to show how a ritual within the festival (often portrayed in tourist literature as an expression of enduring tradition) has developed in recent times as a result of social, economic, and political factors and changes within and around the Furukawa community. Schnell's work also challenges standard presentations of community festivals primarily as exhibitions of symbolic unity and harmony. While these elements do exist in the festival, Schnell shows that it also provides an important means through which people can challenge, temporarily, the hierarchic social order of the community, articulating their dissent and expressing grievances against and conflicts with others within the supposedly "harmonious" community.

Other topics central to early studies of folk religion that have been utilized by later scholars in more comparative and analytical interpretive frameworks include the subjects of purity and pollution. NAMIHARA Emiko (1984), for example, has analyzed folk religion as a unity, using a typological framework based on the perceptions of participants and centered in concepts of pollution (*kegare*) and its relationships with the concomitant ideas of *hare* (a term indicating the manifestation of sacred power and time) and *ke* (inherent life power).

FOLK RELIGION IN THE MODERN DAY:
URBAN SETTINGS AND NEW RELIGIONS

In the developing study of folk religion, one area that has come to the fore
in recent years has been the study of folk religious practices and beliefs in modern, urban
Japanese environments, along with considerations of their influence in the Japanese new,
and "new" new, religions. The development of research in such areas has moved the study
of folk religion beyond its earlier focus on the rural and has cast light on the ways in which
seemingly "folk" and traditional practices can not just survive but continue to display vitality in, and adapt to, modern times. One can perhaps draw parallels here with the patterns
of development of anthropology in general, which originated as a discipline focused on
the study of native, supposedly "primitive," subsistence/rural societies, and sought to
observe and discover the native, original, and primitive roots of human organization, but
which has in modern times also turned its attention to modern and urban societies and
communities.

In Japan, too, scholars have increasingly recognized that the urban environment offered
plentiful scope for the study of folk practices and beliefs. Attention has been drawn, for
example, to the prevalence of diviners and shamanic healers such as *ogamiyasan* who
operated and flourished either in or on the fringes of urban centers, with a clientele drawn
predominantly from the artisans, merchants, and workers of metropolises such as Tokyo
and Osaka. While, as has been discussed earlier, shamanic figures, diviners, and the like
have long been a focus of interest in studies of Japanese folk religion, this has normally
been done focused on figures in rural and marginal regions, for example, in northern
Japan, with such figures being seen somewhat as "survivals" of the past that are somehow
set apart from the modern world. Yet more recent studies have shown that such figures
remain very much part of the modern world, and present in and around major cities as
much as in more rural places. The interest shown in such figures has not been confined to
academia either, for the topic, and the continuing existence of a lively folk religious stratum in Japan, has become an item of interest and discussion among journalists in the mass
media from the 1970s onward.[8]

Academically, the study of folk religion in urban environs has been especially researched
in recent years by a network of scholars based in the Kansai region and working under the
group name Shūkyō Shakaigaku no Kai (Society for the Sociological Study of Religion).
This group has produced a series of studies of religious customs, practices, and networks
in the Kansai, centered on and around Osaka. Along with studies of shamans and healers, the Shūkyō Shakaigaku no Kai's work has focused on amulets, votive tablets, religious
practices among the *zainichi* (Koreans resident in Japan) community, and the dynamics
of small-scale religious centers based around charismatic faith-healing ascetics. These studies

8. See, e.g., MAINICHI SHINBUNSHA 1976–1977, which is a five-volume series investigating
religious issues in Japan in the 1970s, and which has several sections on shamanism, exorcism,
divination, and the like, and the various publications by members of the Asahi Shinbun's religious research center, such as ASAHI SHINBUN 1984, which focused on local deities and cults
of worship. See also ISHII Kenji's (1994) work on shrines in the urban Ginza area.

are based in intensive anthropological fieldwork and sociologically oriented statistical surveys and questionnaires, and they have gone a long way toward demolishing any notion that the "folk" tradition relates especially to the rural. Equally, the group's work illustrates clearly the vibrancy of folk religious practices in urban settings and thus demonstrates how such practices remain relevant to the changing patterns of modern life (SHŪKYŌ SHAKAIGAKU NO KAI 1985, 1987, 1999).

FOLK RELIGION AND THE NEW RELIGIONS OF JAPAN

The importance of folk practices and beliefs has also been emphasized in studies of the new religions. Here attention has been drawn to the ways in which the new religions have risen out of and drawn influences from, and have centered their teachings on practices and beliefs normally associated with, the folk religious stratum (e.g., issues of spirit possession, the role of the spirits of the dead, concepts of illness, healing, and psychic solutions to misfortune). While HORI Ichirō discussed the new religions in the context of survivals of earlier shamanic traditions (1968, pp. 217–51), later scholars such as NUMATA Kenya (1988) have shown that new religions can be viewed as modern, organized, and structured manifestations of folk religion articulated by charismatic leaders who are modern shamanic folk healers.

Similar themes appear in Western scholarship as well: in his study of Mahikari, Winston DAVIS draws attention to the importance of the folk tradition as a source for the new religions, and especially to the associations between Mahikari's exorcistic practices and the shamanic techniques found in Japanese folk religion (1980, pp. 84–88). Subsequent studies of the "new" new religions, which have often been characterized as being primarily focused on magic and mystery, have also indicated the debt these movements owe to folk religious cosmological views (e.g., READER 1991a, p. 208). Again, such studies effectively refute the notion that folk religion is an unchanging manifestation of the rural past and of "tradition." Rather, they indicate clearly its continuing relevance, its capacity to change and modify in accord with changing conditions, and its ability to influence and shape more formal and organized religious traditions in modern Japan.

WORKS IN OTHER LANGUAGES

While writings in Japanese and English may be the most numerous and widely read source of academic studies in the field, there are also extensive works in other languages such as French and German that require the attention of scholars in the field. Josef KYBURZ (1987), for example, has produced a detailed and comprehensive study of religion in a mountain region of central Japan, that is based on historical research and fieldwork research, and that provides an illuminating analysis of how local beliefs and practices have adapted and changed over the ages, especially in relation to changing economic priorities and patterns. Kyburz's work, which resembles Schnell's account, cited earlier, in its combination of anthropological insight with historical research, thus illustrates the importance of combining such disciplinary focuses together in order to fully perceive the workings of

TRADITIONS

folk traditions through time. His work is one example of the extensive tradition of French language studies of religion in Japan: others include a continuing interest in mountain religion illustrated by the work of Gaston RENONDEAU (1965) and Helmut ROTERMUND (1983), and François MACÉ's (1985) studies of death in early Japan. There is also a strong and continuing tradition in the study of folk religion in Germany, especially influenced by Nelly NAUMANN, who wrote extensively about Shinto and folk religion, in historical and folkloric contexts, as well as publishing some of her studies of folk tales and legends also in English.[9] Her tradition has been continued in Germany by scholars such as Klaus AN-TONI (1988), whose work includes studies of the significance of saké in religious and ritual contexts. An example of Antoni's work available in English is his examination of Yasukuni Shrine (1993), which shows how this shrine, in its emphasis on spirits of the dead, is located in the folk tradition and had antecedents predating the Meiji era.

Such examples of scholarship indicate that students of folk religion and other religious traditions in Japan should endeavor to move beyond the English-Japanese linguistic axis that seems to have become the norm nowadays, and, at the very least, to be aware that there are other languages (especially German and French) in which academic work is carried out. They certainly must not assume that, because no studies exist on a particular topic in English, no works have been published in that area in Western languages.

OTHER CHALLENGES AND NEW STUDIES

Through the work of Japanese scholars such as Miyake, Gorai, Sakurai, and others, along with contributions from a variety of Western scholars, the idea that the folk religious tradition is a common base for the Japanese religious world in general has become widely accepted in scholarship on Japanese religions in general (see READER 1991a, p. 23). As it has become more widely accepted as a mainstream area of study, further attempts to develop and provide broader theoretical frameworks and modes of analysis that move beyond the earlier shift from *minkan shinkō* to *minzoku shūkyō*, and that reflect the true potential of studies of folk religion in Japan to serve as an analytical framework for studies of religion in general, have been made. Perhaps the most comprehensive of these have been seen in the work of MIYAKE Hitoshi, both in earlier studies that, in discussing the structure of Japanese religion (e.g., 1974), paid special attention to folk practices and beliefs (spirit possession, worldly benefits, and local customs, and so forth), and in later publications that have aimed at developing a systematic theoretical overview of the topic in universal terms. In his book *Shūkyō minzokugaku* (1989), in particular, Miyake sought to discuss Japanese folk religion as a coherent entity that can be understood through an analytic framework that could equally be applied to any folk religious system. One should note also that here, in the title of his book, Miyake has moved on from the notion of *minzoku shūkyō*

---

9. Among Naumann's publications in German is her two-volume study of Shinto (which she terms "indigenous religion" (*einheimische Religion*) (1988, 1994). She has published numerous studies of folk tales in German, while examples in English can be found in *Asian Folklore Studies* (e.g., NAUMANN 1982).

("folk religion") as a field of study, toward developing the title of an academic field of studies, namely *shūkyō minzokugaku* 宗教民俗学 ("religious folk studies")—a nomenclature that has begun to be used widely and that seeks to impart a disciplinary framework on this field of study. In this work Miyake drew extensively on Western theoretical work, utilizing, for instance, Levi-Straussian concepts of the raw and cooked as means to discuss the relationships between the concepts of *hare, ke,* and *kegare* that have been widely used by Japanese scholars such as Namihira, and applying the semiotic studies of Sapir, Jacobsen, and others as a means of developing an extended linguistic/structuralist interpretation of the language and structure of rituals.[10]

Recently, too, challenges have been made regarding the terminology thus far widely used in the field, with questions being raised about the applicability and use of terms such as "folk religion" (and its occasional concomitant, "popular religion"). In their study of worldly benefits in Japan, for example, Ian READER and George TANABE (1998) consider the terms "folk" and "popular" religion are too based in divisive notions that presuppose an alternative (high/elite religion) to folk/popular religion. They, instead, seek to draw attention not to a base that underpins and provides the foundations for other religious traditions in Japan, but to what they see as a common core that is central to, and permeates, the entire Japanese religious structure. This they term "common religion," whose core, they argue, is founded in the beliefs and practices connected with the promise and pursuit of *genze riyaku* 現世利益 ("worldly benefits"), a topic that had, prior to their study, been marginalized in studies of Japanese religion and on which, prior to their book, no major or extended academic analysis had been developed. They examined *genze riyaku* through a combination of historical, textual, and anthropological research, to argue that it forms a "common religion" at the heart of the Japanese religious world, and one that transcends any notions of division implied in terms such as folk/popular/high/elite religion.

Thus far their analysis, and the need for a change in terminology, have not been challenged, although some commentators have wondered whether "common religion" is the most appropriate term to use. Terms suggested include "shared religion,"[11] while Bardwell SMITH, in commenting on Reader and Tanabe's work, wondered whether "collective religion," which he saw as "inclusive and embracing, without the unremarkable flavor of the term 'common religion," might not be a better term (2000, p. 456). More recently, IKEGAMI Yoshimasa (2004) has picked upon the concepts outlined by Reader and Tanabe relating to "common religion" and the notion of *genze riyaku* as a core analytical tool in the study of religion, and has sought to develop them in the broader context not just of Japanese religion but in the context of religions in general.

10. See READER 1990 for a review and outline of this book's contents, and MIYAKE 2002 for a more general and accessible overview of the subject written more with the general reader than the specialist in mind.

11. At a presentation of their arguments at the 1996 Association of Asian Studies conference in Honolulu, some in the audience made a case for "shared" rather than "common" religion, although READER and TANABE remained unconvinced, considering that "shared" involved a level of implied possession absent from "common" (1998, pp. 28–29).

FIELDS FOR FURTHER STUDY

The scope for research, and the potential fields of study in the context of folk religion in Japan, are, as the above account might suggest, vast. All the areas mentioned above, from the study of pilgrimage, to issues relating to the spirits of the dead, to the study of contemporary diviners, all offer immense scope for further research. I can only hint at a few that might be of interest for new research, and at the many areas that have already received attention but that continue to provide scope for further investigations. For example, the study of mortuary practices has always been highly favored in the study of folk religion, and it has recently seen a surge of new attention (see, e.g., KENNEY and GILDAY 2000). However there is still much scope for further investigations into how the dead are dealt with in the present day, in areas such as the development of new techniques for commemorating the dead (e.g., electronic altars); new modes for providing the dead with a repository or resting place (with the increasing unavailability of traditional graveyards and the development of new memorial halls); and the changing attitudes of new religions, which have in some cases begun to challenge the previous hegemonic role of Buddhism in dealing with the dead. In this area, too, it should be noted that Smith's seminal work on ancestor worship is over a quarter of a century old, and that it is perhaps a good time for new investigations into this topic, for example, on who is memorialized in family altars, how modern changes to family structures and lifestyles have affected this practice, and to what extent urban practices deviate from those in rural areas.

In Western languages, too, relatively little has been done on the cults of individual deities and figures of worship that, while enshrined in Shinto shrines or Buddhist temples, reach out to, or develop clienteles that are clearly associated with such deities on personal rather than through institutional channels. An important work in this context is Karen SMYERS's (1999) study of Inari, a deity venerated in Shinto and Buddhist contexts, but with clear folk dimension related, for instance, to spirit possession and healing. Through her study of Inari, Smyers shows how practitioners, while engaging in shared rituals relating to deities and figures of worship, develop highly individualized and personalized relationships with them. However, her book is a somewhat rare example of a Western language depth study of one deity or figure of worship, and there is much scope for further works in this area, to develop and/or challenge the analyses of Smyers with regard to popular figures of worship in Japan, based on her research into Inari.

Even in areas where much work has already been done, there is generally much uncharted ground to explore. A case in point is pilgrimage: while much research has been done on major pilgrimage routes, legends, and the like, comparatively little attention has been given to the widespread phenomenon in Japan of local and regional pilgrimages, especially those that replicate the patterns of major routes.[12] Areas such as those explored by the Shūkyō Shakaigaku no Kai (the roles of urban diviners, the religious ecology of regions

---

12. This is a topic in which I have had an interest for many years, yet I am unaware of any extended studies of this phenomenon except for a small number of articles I have written in English, and there are a number of articles in Japanese in SHINNO 1996, vol. 3. There is, as yet, no extended or sustained examination of this area.

surrounding cities) in their studies of the Osaka region have been less thoroughly investigated in relation to other conurbations—or, indeed, in smaller population centers. Here, too, there is much scope for fieldwork-based regional studies that could provide clearer pictures of the religious patterns of behavior within specific regions or population centers. One of the issues that concerned early folklore studies, was the variation in regional customs and practices—an issue that has been less overtly focused on in more recent times, but one that requires some thought. Scholars are aware that practices, beliefs, and customs are not necessarily uniform throughout Japan, yet relatively little analysis has occurred in more recent folk-based studies, to how and in what ways such variations occur, and how these might affect overarching analyses.

Given that the field of "folk studies" originated in investigations of rural Japan and was concerned with survivals and with trying to preserve dying traditions, and that subsequent scholarship has called attention to the inadequacies of its approaches, it is perhaps ironic to suggest that attention needs to be paid to the issues that underpinned the concerns of Yanagita and his contemporaries and that, in effect, stimulated them to engage in their data collecting in the hope of "saving" or preserving traditions from the threats of modernity. However, it is critical to consider the continuing impact of modernization and social change, and especially the processes of depopulation and the aging of rural areas, and to examine how these impact on local customs and beliefs. As studies of folk religion focus increasingly on its presence in the major areas of Japanese population (the urban areas), care must be taken not to neglect the increasingly depopulated rural areas of the country. Indeed, given the insights developed about the nature of folk religion over several decades of scholarship, and given the readiness of scholars now to analyze and observe the ways in which customs and traditions modify and develop over time and through circumstances, this would be an appropriate time to reconsider the dynamics of folk religion in villages and rural areas. Thus questions such as to what degree, for example, are population decline, the loss of young people, the closure of Buddhist temples and Shinto shrines, and so on—all phenomena widespread in parts of Japan—affecting the structure of religious beliefs and practices in rural and less highly developed areas of the country, are critical ones that need to be studied and addressed, and should be part of the academic agenda of scholars in the field in the coming years.

A further area as yet relatively little studied is the extent to which practices that we regard as "folk" have become the target of media attention, tourism, and consumption in the modern day. The festival at Osorezan in northern Japan, centered on the blind shamanesses (*itako*), is a good example of a "folk" event that has experienced massive interest and attention in recent times (see READER 1991a, p. 132; a recent visit by the author in 2003 indicated that business and commercial forces had advanced further in the development of the area around where the *itako* gather); the popularity of *matsuri* as a spectacle and as the focus of the tourist gaze is another. Schnell's study of the Furukawa festival, for example, indicates the ways in which the festival has been commodified for external consumption, and how this process is designed to increase tourism to Furukawa and hence provide the sort of local economic infrastructure necessary to stem the tide of depopulation. The irony, again, here is that many decades back Yanagita and his colleagues sought to "preserve" the customs and practices of rural Japan lest they be lost forever and in order to discover the essence of Japan in those very practices. In the modern day, the process of "preservation" is often conducted by tourist concerns, local authorities, and other commercial actors for commercial reasons. This has often been done against a rhetoric (articulated also by many popular writers on customs and traditions) that portrays such customs and practices (such as the colorful and tourist-friendly Furukawa festival) as illustrative of the essence of Japanese culture.[13] This process—of commodification and its impact on folk religious structures, beliefs, and practices—is thus another area that, in the context of the study of folk religion, is worthy of consideration and further research.

CONCLUDING COMMENTS

As this overview has indicated, the study of folk religion has moved on from its origins in folklore studies, with its emphasis on data collection and the preservation of a unique Japanese past, and has become an area of analytical concern for scholars of religion, historians, anthropologists, and sociologists alike. The growing recognition of the close integration of the different strands of religion in Japan has further necessitated a multidisciplinary approach to its study. Nowadays, as several of the leading works cited above indicate, scholars require the use of a variety of methodological tools and avenues of study if they are to properly study, for example, popular deities, festivals, and their development, the prevalence of practices related to worldly benefits and so on, all of which combine anthropological fieldwork with textual and historical research. Such developments, and particularly the paradigm shift from *minkan shinkō* to *minzoku shūkyō*—a shift in terminology that is far less easy to explicate in English translations of these terms than it is in Japanese—have opened up the way for greater comparative and cross-cultural studies that can place the study of Japanese religion in a more universal context.

While the study of *minkan shinkō* was initially useful in identifying many salient elements in Japanese folk religion, it was too theoretically limited, and too bound up with a particular ideological stance, to be of use in developing academic arguments beyond the narrow confines of Japan. The development of *minzoku shūkyō* (and subsequently the terminology used by Miyake, of *shūkyō minzokugaku* and its implications of an emergent disciplinary field) as the lens through which to study folk religion has, however, opened the field of study up greatly and enabled common ground to be established between Japanese folk religion and other folk religion(s), and helped to show the value of Japanese studies for the study of religion in general.

It is clear also from the above that there is widespread scholarly consensus about the centrality of folk religion within the Japanese religious world, about its role in shaping Japan's religious consciousness, and about its influences on organized religious traditions such as Buddhism and the new religions. Yet, as scholarly interest has focused on the inter-

---

13. See, for example, IVY 1995, ROBERTSON 1991, and READER 1987, for studies of how nostalgia and images of the "past" have been used in Japan to glamorize customs and portray them as manifestations of a pure and essential Japanese cultural heritage and tradition.

actions between religious currents in Japan, and on the shared and common elements in the Japanese religions, problems of definition have arisen, and some scholars have begun to question whether terms such as "folk religion" remain useful.

Equally, too, defining or identifying what constitutes the "folk" aspects of religion has become increasingly problematic. The question, for example, of whether venerating the ancestors is intrinsically a "folk" practice or one intrinsic to Buddhism (as evinced by Buddhism's involvement in services for the departed and mortuary rituals throughout Asia) is one of probably indeterminate resolution, as, indeed, is the question of whether studying *matsuri* means one is primarily studying folk religion or Shinto.[14] Few modern studies of religion in Japan have *not* centered particularly upon phenomena that might once have been regarded as marginal and the preserve of folklorists, but which have come to be regarded nowadays as normative elements in Japanese religious structure.

Moreover, while developments in the field have drawn attention to the continuing vibrancy of folk practices in modern Japan, they also have done much to collapse the categories around which the study of folk religion was founded. As the above comments about the interactions between various religious traditions, about the notions of common religion, and about the role of "folk religion" as a common denominator and bedrock in the Japanese religious world, indicate, it could easily be argued that there is, in reality, no such thing as "folk religion" at all in Japan. Rather, there is a common religious core of shared ideas, beliefs, practices, and assumptions that permeates in various degrees virtually every aspect and tradition in the spectrum. Folk religion, in such terms, is clearly a "common religion" that permeates all areas of Japanese religious life and consciousness and that is integral to, rather than separate from, the working of other influential religious traditions.

REFERENCES CITED IN THE TEXT

AKATA Mitsuo 赤田光男 et al., 1984. *Nihon minzokugaku* 日本民俗学. Tokyo: Kōbundō.

ANTONI, Klaus, 1988. *Miwa, der heilige Trank. Zur Geschichte und religiösen Bedeutung des alkoholischen Getränkes (Sake) in Japan.* Stuttgart: F. Steiner.

―――, 1993. Yasukuni-Jinja and Folk Religion. In *Religion and Society in Modern Japan*, ed. Mark Mullins, Shimazono Susumu, and Paul L. Swanson, pp. 121–32. Berkeley: Asian Humanities Press.

ASAHI SHINBUN, 1984. *Gendai no chiisana kamigami* 現代の小さな神々. Tokyo: Asahi Shinbunsha.

AVERBUCH, Irit, 1995. *The Gods Come Dancing: A Study of the Japanese Ritual Dance of Yamabushi Kagura.* Ithaca: Cornell East Asia Series.

BLACKER, Carmen, 1975. *The Catalpa Bow: A Study of Shamanistic Practices in Japan.* Richmond, UK: Curzon Press. (republished 1999)

TRADITIONS

14. Of course one could approach this topic from either angle: the respective studies of John K. NELSON (2000) and Scott SCHNELL (1999) are indicative here. Nelson is more concerned with "Shinto" and its relationship to issues of identity in his study of shrine practices, while Schnell, in his study of *matsuri*, is more focused on the "folk" tradition.

DAVIS, Winston B., 1980. *Dojo: Magic and Exorcism in Modern Japan*. Stanford: Stanford University Press.

_____, 1992. *Japanese Religion and Society: Paradigms of Structure and Change*. Albany: SUNY Press.

EARHART, H. Byron, 1970. *A Religious Study of the Mount Haguro Sect of Shugendo: An Example of Japanese Mountain Religion*. Tokyo: Sophia University.

_____, 1974. *Religion in the Japanese Experience*. Belmont, Cal.: Wadsworth.

_____, 1982. *Japanese Religion: Unity and Diversity*. Belmont, Cal.: Wadsworth.

EMBREE, John F., 1964. *Suye Mura: A Japanese Village*. Chicago: University of Chicago Press. (1st edition 1946)

FUKUDA Ajio 福田アジオ and MIYATA Noboru 宮田 登, eds., 1983. *Nihon minzokugaku gairon* 日本民俗学概論. Tokyo: Yoshikawa Kōbunkan.

GOODWIN, Janet R., 1994. *Alms and Vagabonds: Buddhist Temples and Popular Patronage in Medieval Japan*. Honolulu: University of Hawai'i Press.

GORAI Shigeru 五来 重, 1975. *Kōya hijiri* 高野聖. Tokyo: Kadokawa Sensho.

_____, 1984. *Bukkyō to minzoku* 仏教と民俗. Tokyo: Kadokawa Sensho.

_____, 1989 *Yugyō to junrei* 遊行と巡礼. Tokyo: Kadokawa Sensho.

GORAI Shigeru et al., eds., 1979. *Kōza Nihon no minzoku shūkyō* 講座日本の民俗宗教. Tokyo: Kōbundō.

_____, 1975–1989, *Sangaku shūkyōshi kenkyū sōsho* 山岳宗教史研究叢書. 13 vols. Tokyo: Meicho Shuppan.

HAYASHI Makoto and YOSHIHARA Kazuo, 1988. Editors' Introduction. Special issue on "Folk Religion and Religious Organizations in Asia," *Japanese Journal of Religious Studies* 15: 89–101.

HORI Ichirō 堀 一郎, 1951. *Minkan shinkō* 民間信仰. Iwanami Zensho 151. Tokyo: Iwanami Shoten.

_____, 1968. *Folk Religion in Japan: Continuity and Change*. Chicago: University of Chicago Press.

HOSHINO Eiki 星野英紀, 1979. Shikoku henro to sangakushinkō 四国遍路と山岳信仰. In *Daisen, Ishizuchi to Saigoku shugendō* 大山・石鎚と西国修験道, ed. Miyake Hitoshi 宮家 準, pp. 310–28. Sangaku Shūkyōshi Kenkyū 12. Tokyo: Meicho Shuppan.

_____, 2001. *Shikoku henro no shūkyōgakuteki kenkyū* 四国遍路の宗教学的研究. Kyoto: Hōzōkan.

IKEGAMI Yoshimasa 池上良正, 1999. *Minkan miko shinkō no kenkyū* 民間巫者信仰の研究. Tokyo: Miraisha.

_____, 2004. Genze riyaku to sekai shūkyō 現世利益と世界宗教. In *Shūkyō e no shiza* 宗教への視座, Iwanami Kōza: Shūkyō 2, ed. Ikegami Yoshimasa et al., pp. 167–92. Tokyo: Iwanami Shoten.

ISHII Kenji 石井研士, 1994. *Ginza no kamigami: Toshi ni tokekomu shūkyō* 銀座の神々――都市に溶け込む宗教. Tokyo: Shinyōsha.

IVY Marilyn, 1995. *Discourses of the Vanishing: Modernity, Phantasm, Japan*. Chicago: University of Chicago Press.

KANDA Yoriko 神田より子, 1992. *Miko no ie no onnatachi* 神子の家の女たち. Tokyo: Tōkyōdō Shuppan.

KANEKO Satoru 金児暁嗣, 1991. *Shinshū shinkō to minzoku shinkō* 真宗信仰と民俗信仰. Kyoto: Nagata Bunshōdō.

Kenney, Elizabeth, and Edmund T. Gilday, eds., 2000. Mortuary Rites in Japan. Special issue, *Japanese Journal of Religious Studies* 27/3–4.

Kōmoto Mitsugi 孝本 貢, 1988. Gendai toshi no minzoku shinkō: Kakyō saiken to chinkon 現代都市の民俗信仰——家郷再建と鎮魂. In *Gendaijin no shūkyō* 現代人の宗教, ed. Ōmura Eishō 大村英昭 and Nishiyama Shigeru 西山 茂. Tokyo: Yūhikaku.

_____, 2001. *Gendai nihon ni okeru senzo saishi* 現代日本における先祖祭祀. Tokyo: Ochano-mizu Shobō.

Koshmann, J. Victor, Ōiwa Keibō, and Yamashita Shinji, eds., 1985. *International Perspectives on Yanagita Kunio and Japanese Folklore Studies*. Cornell University East Asia Series 37. Ithaca: Cornell University.

Kyburz, Josef, 1987. *Cultes et croyances au Japon: Kaida, une commune dans les montagnes du Japon*. Paris: Maisonneuve & Larose.

Law, Jane Marie, 1997. *Puppets of Nostalgia: The Life, Death and Rebirth of the Awaji Ningyō*. Princeton: Princeton University Press.

Lopez, Donald S., ed., 1995. *Curators of the Buddha: The Study of Buddhism under Colonialism*. Chicago: University of Chicago Press.

Macé, François, 1985. *La mort et les funerailles dans le Japon Ancien*. Paris: Presses Orientalistes de France.

Mainichi Shinbunsha 毎日新聞社, ed., 1976–1977. *Shūkyō o gendai ni tou* 宗教を現代に問う. 5 vols. Tokyo: Mainichi Shinbunsha.

Miyake Hitoshi 宮家 準, 1974. *Nihon shūkyō no kōzō* 日本宗教の構造. Tokyo: Keiō Tsūshin.

_____, 1981. Folk Religion. In *Japanese Religion. A Survey by the Agency for Cultural Affairs*, ed. Hori Ichirō, pp. 121–43. Tokyo: Kodansha.

_____, 1989. *Shūkyō minzokugaku* 宗教民俗学. Tokyo: Tōkyō Daigaku Shuppan.

_____, 1999a. *Shugendō girei no kenkyū* 修験道儀礼の研究. Tokyo: Shunjūsha.

_____, 1999b. *Shugendō shisō no kenkyū* 修験道思想の研究. Tokyo: Shunjūsha.

_____, 2001. *Shugendō: Essays on the Structure of Japanese Folk Religion*. Edited with an Introduction by H. Byron Earhart. Ann Arbor: University of Michigan Press.

_____, 2002. *Shūkyō minzokugaku nyūmon* 宗教民俗学入門. Tokyo: Maruzen.

Miyamoto Kesao 宮本袈裟雄, 1978. Minkan shinkō 民間信仰. In *Minzoku kenkyū handobukku* 民俗研究ハンドブック, ed. Ueno Kazuo 上野和男 et al., pp. 161–84. Tokyo: Yoshikawa Kōbunkan.

Miyata Noboru 宮田 登, 1984. Shinkō denshō 信仰伝承. In Akata 1984, pp. 113–34.

_____, 1993. *Yama to sato no shinkōshi* 山と里の信仰史. Tokyo: Yoshikawa Kōbunkan.

Namihara Emiko 波平恵美子, 1984. *Kegare no kōzō* ケガレの構造. Tokyo: Seidosha.

Naumann, Nelly, 1982. Sakahagi: The "Reverse Flying" of the Heavenly Piebald Horse. *Asian Folklore Studies* 41: 7–38.

_____, 1988. *Die einheimische Religion Japans*, Teil 1. *Bis zum Ende der Heian-Zeit*. Leiden: Brill.

_____, 1994. *Die einheimische Religion Japans*, Teil 2. *Synkretistische Lehren und religiöse Entwicklungen von der Kamakura bis zum Beginn der Edo-Zeit*. Leiden: Brill.

Nelson, John K., 2000. *Enduring Identities: The Guise of Shinto in Contemporary Japan*. Honolulu: University of Hawai'i Press.

TRADITIONS

Nishigai Kenji 西海賢二, 1984. *Ishizuchisan to shugendō* 石鎚山と修験道. Tokyo: Meicho Shuppan.

Nishigaki Haruji 西垣晴次, 1983. *O-Ise mairi* お伊勢まいり. Tokyo: Iwanami Shoten.

Nomura Jun'ichi 野村純一, 1978. Kōshō bungei 口承文芸. In Ueno 1978, pp. 210–28.

Numata Kenya 沼田健哉, 1988. *Gendai Nihon no shinshūkyō* 現代日本の新宗教. Osaka: Sōgensha.

Orikuchi Shinobu 折口信夫, 1929–1930. *Kodai kenkyū* 古代研究 (vols. 1–3 of *Orikuchi Shinobu Zenshū*). Tokyo: Chūō Kōronsha.

Reader, Ian, 1987. Back to the Future: Images of Nostalgia and Renewal in a Japanese Religious Context. *Japanese Journal of Religious Studies* 14: 287–303.

_____, 1990. Review of Miyake Hitoshi, *Shūkyō minzokugaku*. *Japanese Journal of Religious Studies* 17: 433–38.

_____, 1991a. *Religion in Contemporary Japan*. London and Honolulu: Macmillan and University of Hawai'i Press.

_____, 1991b. Review of Shinno Toshikazu, *Nihon yugyō shūkyōron*. *Japanese Journal of Religious Studies* 19: 81–84.

_____, 2005. *Making Pilgrimages: Meaning and Practice in Shikoku*. Honolulu: University of Hawai'i Press.

Reader, Ian, and Paul L. Swanson, 1997. Editors' Introduction. Special issue on "Pilgrimage in Japan," *Japanese Journal of Religious Studies* 24: 225–70.

Reader, Ian, and George J. Tanabe, Jr., 1998. *Practically Religious: Worldly Benefits and the Common Religion of Japan*. Honolulu: University of Hawai'i Press.

Renondeau, G., 1965. *Le Shugendō: Histoire, Doctrine et Rites des Anachorètes dits Yamabushi*. Paris: Cahiers de la Société Asiatique.

Robertson, Jennifer, 1991. *Native and Newcomer: Making and Unmaking a Japanese City*. Berkeley: University of California Press.

Rotermund, Hartmut O., 1983. *Pèlerinage aux Neuf Sommets: Carnet de route d'un religieux itinérant dans le Japon du xixe siècle*. Paris: Centre National de la Recherche Scientifique.

Sakurai Tokutarō 桜井徳太郎, 1958. *Nihon minkan shinkōron* 日本民間信仰論. Tokyo: Yūzankaku.

_____, 1966. *Minkan shinkō* 民間信仰. Tokyo: Hanawa Shobō.

_____, 1974–1977. *Nihon no shāmanizumu* 日本のシャーマニズム. 2 vols. Yoshikawa Kōbunkan.

_____, 1978. Minkan shinkō no kinōteki kyōi: Sōshō shūkyō to koyū shinkō no setten 民間信仰の機能的境位――創唱宗教と固有信仰の接点. In *Nihon shūkyō no fukugōteki kōzō* 日本宗教の複合的構造, ed. Sakurai Tokutarō, pp. 3–22. Tokyo: Kōbundō.

_____, 1982. *Nihon minzoku shūkyōron* 日本民俗宗教論. Tokyo: Kōbundō.

Sasaki Kōkan 佐々木宏幹, 1991. Sōron: Hotoke to reikon no aida 総論――仏と霊魂のあいだ. In *Gendai to Bukkyō* 現代と仏教, ed. Sasaki Kōkan, pp. 3–63. Gendai Nihonjin no Seishin Kōzō to Bukkyō 現代日本人の精神構造と仏教 12. Tokyo: Shunjūsha. (reissued in 2000)

_____, 1993. *Hotoke to tama no jinruigaku: Bukkyō bunka no shinsō kōzō* 仏と霊（タマ）の人類学――仏教文化の深層構造. Tokyo: Shunjūsha.

Schattschneider, Ellen, 2003. *Immortal Wishes: Labor and Transcendence on a Japanese Sacred Mountain*. Durham: Duke University Press.

SCHNELL, Scott, 1999. *The Rousing Drum: Ritual Practice in a Japanese Community*. Honolulu: University of Hawai'i Press.

SCHOPEN, Gregory, 1997. *Bones, Stones, and Buddhist Monks: Collected Papers on the Archaeology, Epigraphy, and Texts of Monastic Buddhism in India*. Honolulu: University of Hawai'i Press.

SHINNO Toshikazu 真野俊和, 1991a. *Nihon yugyō shūkyōron* 日本遊行宗教論. Tokyo: Yoshikawa Kōbunkan.

———, 1991b. *Sei naru tabi* 聖なる旅. Tokyo: Tōkyōdō Shuppan.

———, 1993. From *minkan shinkō* to *minzoku shūkyō*: Reflections on the Study of Folk Buddhism. Tr. Paul L. Swanson. *Japanese Journal of Religious Studies* 20: 187–206.

SHINNO Toshikazu, ed., 1996. *Kōza Nihon no junrei* 講座日本の巡礼. 3 vols. Tokyo: Yūzankaku. (vol. 1 *Honzon junrei* 本尊巡礼; vol. 2 *Seiseki junrei* 聖跡巡礼; vol. 3 *Junrei no kōzō to chihō junrei* 巡礼の構造と地方巡礼)

SHŪKYŌ SHAKAIGAKU NO KAI 宗教社会学の会, ed., 1985. *Ikoma no kamigami: Gendai toshi no minzoku shūkyō* 生駒の神々——現代都市の民俗宗教. Osaka: Sōgensha.

———, 1987. *Nihon shūkyō no fukugōteki kōzō to toshi jūmin no shūkyō kōdō ni kansuru jisshōteki kenkyū: Ikoma shūkyō chōsa* 日本宗教の複合的構造と都市住民の宗教行動に関する実証的研究——生駒宗教調査. Osaka: Kagaku Kenkyūshi Seika Hōkokusho.

———, 1999. *Kamigami yadorishi machi: Sezoku toshi no shūkyō shakaigaku* 神々宿りし都市——世俗都市の宗教社会学. Osaka: Sōgensha.

———, 2002. *Shinseiki no shūkyō: "Sei naru mono" no gendaiteki shosō* 新世紀の宗教——「聖なるもの」の現代的諸相. Osaka: Sōgensha.

SMITH, Bardwell, 2000. Review of READER and TANABE 1998. *Journal of Japanese Studies* 26: 452–56.

SMITH, Robert J., 1974. *Ancestor Worship in Contemporary Japan*. Stanford: Stanford University Press.

SMYERS, Karen A., 1999. *The Fox and the Jewel: Shared and Private Meanings in Contemporary Japanese Inari Worship*. Honolulu: University of Hawai'i Press.

TAKEDA Akira 武田 明, 1972. *Junrei no minzoku* 巡礼の民俗. Tokyo: Iwasaki Bijitsusha.

———, 1987. *Nihonjin no shireikan: Shikoku minzokushi* 日本人の死霊観——四国民俗史. Tokyo: San'ichi Shobō.

TAKEDA Chōshū 竹田聴洲, 1971. *Minzoku Bukkyō to sosen shinkō* 民俗仏教と祖先信仰. Tokyo: Tōkyō Daigaku Shuppan.

TSURUMURA Shōichi 鶴村松一, 1978. *Shikoku henro: 280-kai Nakatsuka Mohei gikyō* 四国遍路——二百八十回中務茂兵衛義教. Matsuyama: Matsuyama Furusatoshi Bungaku Kenkyūkai.

TSURUMURA Shōichi, ed., 1979. *Shikoku reijō ryaku engi dōchūki taisei* 四国霊場略縁起道中記大成. Matsuyama: Matsuyama Furusatoshi Bungaku Kenkyūkai.

UENO Kazuo 上野和男 et al., 1978. *Minzoku kenkyū handobukku* 民俗研究ハンドブック. Tokyo: Yoshikawa Kōbunkan.

YANAGAWA Keiichi 柳川啓一, 1987. *Matsuri to girei no shūkyōgaku* 祭と儀礼の宗教学. Tokyo: Chikuma Shobō.

YANAGITA Kunio 柳田國男, 1962–1963. *Teihon Yanagita Kunio shū* 定本柳田國男集. Tokyo: Chikuma Shobō.

Trevor ASTLEY

New Religions

The study of "new religions" provides us with the opportunity of viewing a group in what is arguably the most interesting stage in its development. The proximity to the present of the founding of such groups allows for eyewitness accounts of the characters involved and of events taking place during the crucial initial stages of a group's history. The appeal of a new religious group, often centered on the personal attraction of a charismatic leader, is immediate. New religious groups or movements are vitalistic; they are dynamic; and their scope for creativity is perhaps only limited by the extent of the human imagination (NELSON 1987). Essentially, they concern themselves with the here and now, with this very existence. People can relate to them because they are contemporary and deal with the problems facing people in the world as they perceive it. They provide alternative means of making sense of human experience amidst the social change that accompanies advances in scientific and technological knowledge. They also may provide hope for the future, or direction in people's lives, and invariably offer people some form of control over their destiny. And yet, so many of these movements also provide a link to the past. These are indeed powerful forces in the everyday lives of ordinary people.

Answering the needs of the time in a vital form while retaining a familiarity of mode is indeed a potent formula. Arguably, this formula may be more potent in times when a society is undergoing rapid change or transformation or is perceived to be in a state of crisis (BECKFORD 1986; MORIOKA 1978; McFARLAND 1967). In addition, one must take into consideration the potential for new religious movements to transform themselves radically in a relatively short space of time, such that they may have a different appeal, carry a different message, and respond to different problems of human existence in different ways at different times (cf. ASTLEY 1995). The immense scope, the incredible diversity, and the rapid development of the so-called Japanese "New Religions" in the postwar era are such that these points need to be kept in mind when embarking on a study of the phenomenon of new religious movements in Japan.

PROBLEMS

The study of the Japanese New Religions leads to a somewhat broader and indeed more complicated field than one might anticipate. The initial task of identifying and defining these New Religions and placing them in context is in itself problematic, while the scale of the New Religions—in terms of their number, the size of their combined membership figures, and the extent of their penetration—means that any broad assessment of modern Japanese society remains incomplete without taking this phenomenon into consideration. The diversity and complexity of religious life in Japan historically derives from the elaborate relationship formed between Japanese Buddhism, Shinto practices, Confucian thought, the native folk religious tradition, and other elements borrowed from Continental Asia or from the West. Combining elements from the native religious traditions with those from other religious traditions to form new modes of religious expression and faith is part of a tradition of religious creativity that characterizes Japanese religious history (KITAGAWA 1966, 1987; EARHART 1982, 1984). Thus, the contemporary religious landscape in Japan is a product of such a fusion of ideas and practices, which requires an integrated, holistic approach rather than a linear, monolithic approach that seeks to treat the Buddhist, Shinto, Confucian, folk, and other traditions as disparate, unrelated elements. An understanding of the historical and doctrinal aspects of the individual traditions and the symbiotic relationship between them therefore becomes a prerequisite to an appreciation of the contemporary religious scene in Japan rather than an explicit understanding of it.

In setting out to try and identify a common core at the heart of the religious activities of the Japanese in terms of how the people interact with religion in different social and cultural contexts, scholars such as Pye and Swyngedouw have challenged the more conservative approach of treating each tradition as a distinct entity, allowing for a more lateral approach to the subject, whereby the religious behavior or religiosity of the Japanese could be understood not so much in terms of metaphysical and doctrinal concerns but rather

TRADITIONS

in terms of social function and social, cultural, and psychological needs. PYE (1987) refers to this common core as "a common language of minimal religiosity," while SWYNGEDOUW (1976), in his contribution to the debate on Bryan Wilson's theory of secularization, uses the term "religiosity of Japanese-ness" to describe this phenomenon and discusses the complex nature of contemporary Japanese religiosity in a later paper (1986), and READER and TANABE (1998) formulated this expression of religiosity in terms of a "common religion" (see also Reader's essay in this *Guide*). Heuristically, this approach allows a far more dynamic means of analyzing religious behavior in modern Japan, enabling us to treat the subject matter in terms of themes, socio-cultural functions, and social scientific theory. This holds true not only for broader studies of the role of religion in contemporary Japan (READER 1991a; DAVIS 1992) but also for thematic-based studies (READER and TANABE 1998) as well as more specific studies in the field of Japanese New Religions (HARDACRE 1986).

In the case of the Japanese New Religions, there are a number of issues that the researcher ought to be aware of when approaching the subject. First of all, there is the question of *terminology* and what is understood by the term "Japanese New Religions." Secondly, it is important to understand that the historical development of the New Religions traces back to the mid-nineteenth century and that there have been *phases* during that period, each with its own socio-cultural and political context, that need to be identified in order to allow us to categorize the groups in terms of their characteristics for analytical purposes. Thirdly, the sheer number alone of newly founded religious groups that fall under the rubric of New Religions in modern and contemporary Japan represents a major task in setting out to analyze them. The difficulty of the task is exacerbated by a confusing and contradictory mass of *statistics* pertaining to the subject, which makes it difficult to discern precise figures: firstly, as to how many there are of these groups, and then as to how many adherents there are within each of these groups. Finally, there is the issue of *affiliation*: firstly, in terms of how the authorities categorize groups for official purposes; and, secondly, in terms of how individual groups locate themselves within the respective religious traditions. After discussing some of the key points of the above issues in brief, I shall provide an overview of the background to the development of the New Religions in contemporary Japan and an outline of work carried out in the field, before indicating some of the areas that have aroused interest in the field as issues of concern to the research community.

TERMINOLOGY

The terms most commonly used in Japanese to describe the New Religions are *shinkō shūkyō* 新興宗教 and *shinshūkyō* 新宗教, with the latter being the term of preference among scholars in the field. *Shūkyō* is the standard term for "religion" or "religions" (Japanese does not differentiate between singular and plural) and in both of these compounds it is the religious groups (or a specific group) rather than religion per se that is being referred to. The term *shinshūkyō* thus translates as "new religions," while *shinkō shūkyō* has been rendered variously in Western literature as "newly-arisen religions," "newly-established religions," "newly-born religions," "newly-arisen religious groups or movements," "new religious sects or groups," as well as the more mundane "new religions."

In the 1950s and 1960s, *shinshūkyō* was used by some Japanese scholars to refer to those new religious groups that had appeared during the nineteenth century, while *shinkō shūkyō* was used to refer to the groups that had risen to prominence during the interwar and the postwar periods. The term *shinkō shūkyō* has, however, somewhat derogatory overtones: although *shinkō* 新興 (newly arisen) is neutral per se, it is found in compounds such as *shinkō narikin* 新興成金 and *shinkō kaikyū* 新興階級, referring to the "nouveau riche" and "new social classes" respectively, with the implication of "arriviste" or "upstart." According to Murakami (1980, p. 83), the term *shinkō* was fashionable in the 1920s or so, attached indiscriminately in such phrases as "newly arisen" *or* "newly developed" housing or literature. Today, the most common contexts in which the term is used are in the compounds *shinkō narikin* and *shinkō shūkyō*. Because of the negative implications of the term *shinkō*, the leaders and members of new religious groups have distanced themselves from this term (see also Hayashi's essay in this *Guide*). Since the 1970s, the term *shinshūkyō* 新宗教 has been adopted by scholars in the field to refer to the Japanese New Religions in general, although it should be noted that the term *shinkō shūkyō* is still in use not only in popular circles but also among scholars who are either not familiar with the field or who choose to refer to new religious groups disparagingly.

Similarly, the term "New Religions" is problematic in Western academic circles. Above all, the concept of *religion* itself is open to discussion, while the question as to whether a given body of thought and practices may constitute a religion in its own right is equally contestable. With regard to a group that considers itself religious, or is labeled in such a way, discussion revolves around the issues of whether the group is a religion in its own right—rather than a branch, sub-sect, or sub-division of an established religion—and whether a group's teachings or doctrines are original enough, or a sufficient departure from those of the established religion from which it claims authority, to warrant the appellation "new" (cf. Beckford 1976; Werblowsky 1980). The preference among those involved in the field is to use such terms as "new religious sects," "new religious groups," or "new religious movements," with the latter term widely favored, notably so in sociology of religion, where the acronym "NRM" is employed extensively.

In Western literature within Japanese studies, the term *shinkō shūkyō* has been used somewhat indiscriminately and usually in the generic sense, particularly in literature dating from the 1960s and 1970s. This is also true of more recent work found mainly in nonspecialist literature, which presumably has adopted the term from the now rather outdated studies carried out during the 1960s. The norm among students of Japanese religious studies is to use the term *shinshūkyō*. This may be rendered in English as "(Japanese) New Religions" when taken collectively as a phenomenon or as "new religious group(s)," "new religious movement(s)," or "new sect(s)" when referring to a specific group or groups, although it must be pointed out that there is no consensus on the issue of usage or conventions such as capitalization, italicization, and the use of quotation marks. Certainly when dealing with individual groups, however, the term New Religions has to be used with caution on the grounds that the vast majority of the main groups do not break with Japanese religious tradition (cf. Oishi 1964, pp. 47–49). Usage in this paper, it may be noted, limits the term New Religions to denote the collective phenomenon particular to the Japanese religious historical context, with capitalization indicating that it is being treated as a technical term.

A further development is that the emergence of a new breed of religious movements in the latter half of the 1970s led to the coining of the term *shin-shinshūkyō* 新新宗教 (that is, "*new* new religions"), the best-known example of this genre being the now infamous Aum Shinrikyō. The term appears in 1979 in a paper by Nishiyama Shigeru 西山 茂 (reproduced in MIYAKE et al. 1986, pp. 198–204) in which he argues a significant point of departure from previous group characteristics among the emerging new groups, identifying two broad types of groups: namely, (1) those with eschatological fundamentalistic tendencies, and (2) those that enveloped themselves in a thick veil of magical mysticism (pp. 202–203). The irony of the term *shin-shinshūkyō* is not lost in translation, but does result once again in the unfortunate proliferation of terminology to denote the same phenomenon: new new religions; "new" new religions; *new* new religions; new, new religions; neo-new religions; and so on. Here the term New New Religions is employed to provide a parallel to its counterpart, New Religions.

PHASES

Occasionally when the New Religions have received attention in the public arena in Japan—be it through the mass media or popular writers—a simplified prewar/postwar form of categorization is employed to serve rather rudimentary analytical purposes. Other times, commentators—not only in the Japanese media but also in academia—declare the onset of a "religious boom." This was an issue prior to the Aum Affair in 1995, with the more recent developments of the 1980s and 1990s frequently referred to as either the third or the fourth "religious boom." Such talk of religious booms or revivals is often of a trivial nature, and the phenomenon of religious activity itself is often trivialized; yet for students in the field it is essential that we construct these invisible markers and plant them on the historical backcloth in order to allow us to identify discrete phases in the development of the New Religions and thus categorize the groups and apply the analytical tools of our respective disciplines. As long as the essentially artificial nature of the exercise is kept firmly in mind and the task of periodization is treated as a means of providing us with a heuristic tool, then it should allow us to accept a multiple number of possibilities for dividing their development into phases in accordance with the stated objectives of a given study, as each has its relative worth.

As previously indicated, what are referred to as the New Religions are not purely a product of the postwar era, but have their roots in the nineteenth century. The problem of whether one can refer to these as *new*, thus remaining faithful to the Japanese nomenclature, is acknowledged in the first extensive treatments of the subject in the English language. THOMSEN (1963), for example, chooses the term "Old" New Religions to refer to the early groups that developed from the mid-nineteenth to the late nineteenth century on, such as Tenrikyō 天理教, Kurozumikyō 黒住教, and Konkōkyō 金光教. Meanwhile, OFFNER and VAN STRAELEN (1963) make a point of circumventing the issue by declaring their interest in "Modern Japanese Religions," yet include in their study all the major religious groups that had been founded since the nineteenth century and that were being referred to as *shinkō shūkyō* in the contemporary Japanese literature. McFarland, in his attempt to organize the array of opinions on the division of the periods, put forward the following five periods:

1. The declining years of the Tokugawa shogunate in the mid-nineteenth century
2. The middle years of the Meiji period, about 1880–1900
3. The end of the Meiji period and the Taishō period, from the Russo-Japanese War (1904–1905) to about 1925
4. The early Shōwa period, about 1930–1935
5. The post-World War II period, since 1945   (McFarland 1967, p. 54)

The above assessments, however, only take account of the situation in response to the rapid spread of new religious movements in the 1950s and 1960s, and, with the subsequent developments in the 1970s and 1980s when the newer breed of New New Religions were emerging, a review of the division of the periods became necessary. Taking these later developments into account, Hardacre (1986), Shimazono (1992a), and Ōmura and Nishiyama (1988), among others, posited their respective views on the division of the periods, with the "oil shock" of 1973 remaining the most frequent point of reference, especially among Japanese commentators, as the defining watershed in the impact of the postwar socio-economic development of Japan on religious behavior and attitudes. The emergence of the New New Religions is regularly interpreted in Japan as a reaction to the new social milieu resulting from the event of the oil shock and is identified as a new phase in the history of the New Religions, distinguished by the characteristics noted above by Nishiyama (1986; see also Ōmura and Nishiyama 1988). This phase or period then comes to an abrupt end with the sarin gas attack on the Japanese subway by Aum Shinrikyō in March 1995, after which we are left with a post-Aum era that continues to the present.

To summarize the above discussion, the history of the New Religions may be broadly divided according to the following periods of activity:

1. The latter part of the nineteenth century
2. The 1920s and 1930s
3. The immediate postwar period, especially the 1950s and 1960s
4. Post-"oil shock" (1973), especially 1980s on
5. Post-Aum Affair (1995)

STATISTICS

The idea often portrayed in non-specialist accounts and in the media that Japan is teeming with new religious "cults" and that this is evidence that the Japanese are a deeply religious people is most misleading. Underpinning such a view are the raw, unprocessed statistics on the New Religions: this applies not only to the matter of how many such groups there are but also to the numerical strength of the individual groups. The official number of recognized religious organizations in Japan is somewhere in the region of 200,000 (Agency for Cultural Affairs 1978), while the number of adherents, according

TRADITIONS

to official statistics—that is to say, government statistics, as responsibility for their colla-tion lies with the Agency for Cultural Affairs (Bunkachō 文化庁) within the Ministry of Education, Culture, Sports, Science and Technology 文部科学省 (formerly the Ministry of Education 文部省)—consistently outstrips the actual population figures.

These are indeed startling statistics, but really need to be treated with utmost care. Firstly, the vast majority of the large number of religious organizations can be accounted for by groups representing traditional Buddhism and traditional Shinto, to the numerous sects and sub-sects of which we must also add the many individual temples and shrines throughout the country that see fit to register as independent bodies. Secondly, researchers have to deal with the legacy of the lax legal provisions for attaining status as a recognized religious organization, which guaranteed significant benefits in terms of tax exemption under the Religious Juridical Persons Law (*shūkyō hōjin hō* 宗教法人法), also referred to as the Religious Corporations Law. Although there was a recent revision of this law in April 1995, the repercussions of which are discussed in DORMAN 1996, the conditions for being granted official recognition as a religious organization had hitherto been relatively easy. Thus, we have to take into consideration not only the local temples or shrines gaining legal status through declaring their institutional independence but also a host of diverse organizations, including groups created by individual priests with their own following, devotional or cultic associations, and numerous lay groups, many of which are somewhat artificial and have been inspired more by the tax breaks afforded legally recognized reli-gious organizations than by ostensibly religious considerations.

Having taken these matters into account, however, one is still left with a remarkable ar-ray of religious groups that have come into being in the postwar era and that stand outside the authority of the established traditions. Such "New Religions" number in the hundreds at a conservative estimate, and even discounting the many smaller and localized groups that have little or no significance or influence beyond their very minimal membership, there are still a considerable number of groups that have sizeable followings and consider-able influence in people's lives.

The numerical size of the groups also ranges from a few hundred to a few thousand to several million adherents. Here again, the statistics are highly speculative as the Agency for Cultural Affairs has relied since the Occupation solely on the voluntary cooperation of religious organizations.[1] OFFNER and VAN STRAELEN point out that:

> Denominations and their constituent bodies prepare their statistics according to their own standards, which are usually quite different from those of other denominations, especially those of other religions. (1963, pp. 18–19)

With regard to the figures referred to above concerning the total number of adherents of religious groups in Japan, this can be accounted for partly by the interesting phenomenon of multiple affiliation—whereby one can be counted as being both Shinto and Buddhist (local shrines and temples often include members of the local population or "parish" in

---

1. See Part III (Statistics) in HORI et al. 1972, especially the section on "Problems of Com-pilation and Interpretation," pp. 233–34.

their figures by default)—and partly by the often rather arbitrary means of collating statistics by both the authorities and the groups themselves. In the case of the New Religions, each group will have its own means of calculating its membership. This may or may not take account of active and non-active members; this may be based on sales or distribution figures of the group's publications; this may be based on the traditional method of treating the *ie* or household as the unit, whereby the membership of the head of the household implicitly denotes the membership of the entire household, meaning that figures may be subjected to multiplication by a factor of between two and four, on average; or this may be based on something as trivial as having visited the group headquarters or another center of the organization and signed one's name in the guestbook. Thus, it is necessary when researching a given group to try and establish the precise means by which it calculates its membership, bearing in mind that the group may have one method for official purposes for reporting to the authorities and another for internal purposes. Moreover, it is also important to realize that the actual means of calculation may not be divulged by the group as a matter of internal policy. This issue is discussed by READER (1988; 1991a), HARDACRE (1984; 1986), and also by ASTLEY (1995).

AFFILIATION

Finally, there are further problems to be encountered in the definition of the groups themselves—not that these are as such insurmountable, but merely that they demand a great deal of care on the part of the researcher. Sects may change their names, and they may appear to change their "affiliation," if that is the right expression. In the prewar era in Japan, religious groups had to subscribe to one of the established religions by way of protocol in order to gain official recognition, the benefit of which for new religious groups was that they would thereby avoid the attention of, or even persecution by, the authorities. NEWELL and DOBASHI (1968) discuss the problem of classifying groups, pointing to the case of Tenrikyō, which has been through various stages of affiliation by way of convenience, connecting itself at one stage with Buddhism and later with Shinto in order to gain official recognition. Under the freedom afforded in the postwar period, however, Tenrikyō was asserting that it was entirely different from Shinto (OFFNER and VAN STRAELEN 1963, p. 58). PL (Perfect Liberty) Kyōdan, meanwhile, started off in 1912 as a group within Mitakekyō 御嶽教—one of the thirteen sects of Sect Shinto—and was originally known as Tokumitsukyō 徳光教. Later it was registered under another of the Sect Shinto sects, Fusōkyō 扶桑教, when it was known first as Jindō Tokumitsukyō 人道徳光教 and later as Hito no Michi ひとのみち. During the war the group was suppressed and then disbanded, and after the war it was re-formed as PL Kyōdan. Similarly, Ōmoto's 大本 history in the interwar years is also fraught with conflict with the authorities (NADOLSKI 1980). Further, in common with several other significant groups, Ōmoto provided the breeding ground for a number of other new groups. One of these splinter groups, founded by Okada Mokichi 岡田茂吉, provides us with an apt illustration of the fortunes of the new religious groups. Originally formed around 1936 as the Dainihon Kannonkai 大日本観音会 and subsequently abandoned the following year (under charges of fraud), it was resurrected after the war as Nihon Kannon Kyōdan 日本観音教団 in 1947. The following year, Okada also formed the Nihon Miroku Kyōkai 日本弥勒教会 and then in 1950 disbanded them both to establish Sekai Kyūseikyō 世界救世教, one of the main postwar new religious groups.

BACKGROUND TO THE DEVELOPMENT OF
THE NEW RELIGIONS IN CONTEMPORARY JAPAN

Some treatments of the Japanese New Religions portray them as a remarkable phenomenon exclusive to the postwar era and point to postwar conditions to explain their rise. The impression is often given that hundreds of New Religions suddenly sprang from nowhere in the aftermath of the war. While there *was* a tremendous growth in the number of officially recognized groups in that immediate postwar period, such accounts tend to preclude a broader understanding of the context of the growth, and this is also misleading for the purposes of analyzing this phenomenon. The idea that the government-controlled thirteen sects of Sect Shinto up to 1945 gave rise to several hundred new sects due to the granting of religious freedom and the prevailing socio-economic conditions of a devastated people is—while providing a rather neat and seemingly self-explanatory account of the rise of the New Religions—quite simplistic.

The religious scene of the last century and a half has been extremely complex, however, involving as it does the interaction of the various religious traditions that go together to make up that which we know as "Japanese religions." A consideration of some points from the pre-1945 situation to afford us an overview are in order here.

The roots of the new religious groups that have arisen to date lie in the religious developments of the Bakumatsu or Late Tokugawa period (roughly the 1820s to 1868). Of the thirty or so "Major New Religions" for which MURAKAMI (1980, pp. 170–71) provides data, ten had been founded by 1873 and the remainder by 1951.[2] What are considered the oldest of the New Religions have thus now been established for over a century, their initial founding or founder's initiatory religious experiences having taken place as long ago as nearly two centuries; Tenrikyō 天理教, Kurozumikyō 黒住教, and Konkōkyō 金光教 are the main representatives of this era, though by no means the only ones. To these ought to be added the rest of the sects that together made up the thirteen sects of Sect Shinto during the Meiji period, a classification that was to be valid until the end of the Second World War as an administrative measure essentially as part of a means of, on the one hand, exerting control over religious groups and, on the other, of substantiating the government's philosophy of the state in the form of the *kokutai* 国体 (National Polity) cult. Reports dealing with the latter half of the nineteenth century suggest that a considerable amount of energy was expended as a means of alleviating the pitiful state of the peasant masses through the expression of religious activity. The *okage mairi* おかげ参り (return of divine favor pilgrimage) pilgrimages to the Ise Shrine, and the somewhat eccentric *ee ja nai ka* ええじゃな

2. See Appendix II of MURAKAMI 1980, pp. 170–71. Eleven of the thirty-one groups were formed by 1892, all of them by 1951. Murakami's data is based on the 1978 almanac of religious affairs (*Shūkyō nenkan* 宗教年鑑), an annual publication of the Agency for Cultural Affairs.

いか and *yo-naoshi* 世直し (world renewal) dances are oft-cited examples of such activity. KITAGAWA (1966) relates them closely to the peasant uprisings (*ikki* 一揆), while socialist writers such as TAKAGI (cf. 1959; 1964) ruefully view these activities as a misguided waste of potential revolutionary spirit on the part of the masses.

The restoration of the Imperial household during the Meiji period wrought tremendous upheaval amidst the religious world, to have repercussions that are still felt today (cf. HARD-ACRE 1989a). The elevation of Shinto to a state cult (*kokka Shintō* 国家神道), the separation of Shinto and Buddhism and the subsequent suppression of Buddhism (*haibutsu kishaku* 廃仏毀釈), and the coercive measures taken by the Meiji government towards conformity of all other religious groups to the state ethos ridicule the nominal assertion of religious freedom for all guaranteed by Article 28 of the Meiji Constitution, which reads as follows:

> Japanese subjects shall, within limits not prejudicial to peace and order, and not antagonistic to their duties as subjects, enjoy freedom of religious belief. (BUNCE 1955, pp. 170–71)

Laws passed during the period up to 1900 (cf. CREEMERS 1968, p. 31; HORI 1972, pp. 162–63) provided the framework for the regulation of religious groups and their activities by subjecting them to persistent superveillance by the police and to official scrutiny prior to the granting of legal status, which required doctrines to be in line with the state cult regarding the status and worship of the emperor and the veneration of the Sun Goddess, Amaterasu Ōmikami 天照大神. The government had accepted the existence of *kyōha Shintō* 教派神道 or Sectarian/Sect Shinto, formally separating this from State Shinto early in the Meiji period and, in due course, the formation of new sects was forbidden. There were, thus, thirteen legally approved sects (known as the thirteen Sect Shinto sects), and any new group forming subsequently and right up to the end of the war was obliged to become a sub-sect of one of the thirteen sects or, alternatively, exist as a non-officially recognized organization, in which case it was treated as a semi-religious organization (*shūkyō ruiji dantai* 宗教類似団体) or quasi-religious organization (*giji shūkyō dantai* 疑似宗教団体). Groups falling under the latter category were treated with even greater suspicion and contempt by the authorities, thus limiting their chances of expanding. Moreover, they came under the inspection and control of the Home Ministry rather than the Bureau of Religion within the Ministry of Education (MURAKAMI 1980, p. 83).

The problems that the authorities encountered with the New Religions escalated after the First World War and throughout the 1920s and 1930s, the numerous cases of police investigations against them bearing testimony to this. The Peace Preservation Law (*chian iji hō* 治安維持法) of 1925, whose primary intended target was actually socialism, was also implemented in respect to new religious groups on the pretext of countering "dangerous thoughts"—Ōmoto as early as 1921 and then again in 1935 and Honmichi 本道 in 1938 providing us with examples of such groups targeted by the authorities for suppression. The Religious Organizations Law (*shūkyō dantai hō* 宗教団体法) of 1940 was the final nail in the coffin for many New Religions, many of their number being dissolved, with some of the groups' leaders and activist members spending the war years imprisoned on charges of lèse majesté. The law stated its objective as constituting "the control of religion and mobilization of religion for the war effort" (MURAKAMI 1980, p. 95). To illustrate how widespread these movements had become during this later period, some 400 New Religions were accounted for in 1930 and just over 1000 in 1935.[3] In addition to these there were, comparatively (speaking), relatively few yet very significant sects that hid under the organizational umbrellas of the thirteen sects. It is important to bear this point in mind when assessing the growth of the New Religions in the postwar period as it shows the widespread scale of these groups prior to the declaration of religious freedom by the Allied Powers at the end of the war.

This prewar situation is also a source of difficulty for the researcher concerned with the development of such sects in terms of classification and simply tracing them. As discussed above, groups were often wont to change their names as well as their affiliations. Further, in the postwar era the sects were allowed complete freedom to assert themselves and espouse their doctrines as they wished, which meant that the prewar classifications were no longer necessarily valid (in terms of the Buddhist, Shinto, or Other categories), while the postwar classification in many respects constitutes an almost arbitrary exercise.

A useful starting-point for a study of the development of new religious movements in the postwar era is the declaration of religious freedom guaranteed by the 1947 Constitution. The articles most pertinent to this important landmark in Japanese religious history are articles 20 and 89, reproduced here from HARDACRE (1989, pp. 137–39).[4]

Article 20 states:

Freedom of religion is guaranteed to all. No religious organization shall receive any privileges from the state, nor exercise any political authority. No person shall be compelled to take part in any religious act, celebration, rite or practice. The state and its organs shall refrain from religious education or any other religious activity.

Article 89 states:

No public money or other property shall be expended or appropriated for the use, benefit or maintenance of any religious institution or association, or for any charitable, educational or benevolent enterprises not under the control of public authority.

Thus, these two articles at once provided for the freedom of religion to be enjoyed by the individual, the separation of state and religion, and, significantly, the curtailing of any state sponsoring of religion. Further, article 14 forbade "discrimination in political, economic, or social relations because of ... creed," while article 19 provided that "freedom of thought and conscience shall not be violated" (HARDACRE 1989, pp. 137–39).

In contradistinction to the declaration of religious freedom in the Meiji Constitution, the 1947 Constitution prepared the way for an unconditional approval of religious freedom uninhibited by the state. The guarantee of religious freedom is arguably the greatest factor in the initial development of the new religious movements: many groups and sects

---

3. This was according to a Ministry of Education survey, the cited figures being 414 for 1930 and 1029 for 1935 (MURAKAMI 1980, p. 85). Compare this also with an earlier survey for 1924 that gave 98 organizations, the breakdown for which was 65 Shinto, 29 Buddhist, and 4 Christian groups, these all being distinct from the officially recognized religions (p. 83).

4. See Chapter 7 of HARDACRE 1989 for postwar developments.

that had previously been forced to exist under the umbrella of one of the thirteen Sect Shinto sects in the prewar era were suddenly allowed to declare their independence from the parent-sect. Precise details as to the exact number of sects that seceded from the Sect Shinto sects are difficult to ascertain, but, as of 1959, 59 of the 129 Shinto sects recognized by the government were secessions from the original thirteen, only two of which were true splinter sects (NORBECK 1970, p. 11). Such sects or groups combined with the numerous movements that had been suppressed pre-1945 must account for a significant proportion of the incredibly large number of new religious movements that appeared immediately after the war and then during the 1950s following the enactment of the Religious Juridical Persons Law of 3 April 1951, which enabled religious organizations to acquire legal capacity. The law also, as has been noted, granted tax-exempt status to religious organizations.

The reaction of the newly formed (15 October 1951) Union of New Religions (*Shin Nippon shūkyō dantai rengōkai* 新日本宗教団体連合会 or, as it is more commonly known, *Shinshūren* 新宗連) was very favorable toward this new found freedom. Understandably the reaction from the established religions—Buddhism and Shinto—was tempered by concern for their very own future survival. Shinto had lost not only much of its credibility among a very disillusioned populace but, moreover, its whole financial basis, which had previously been guaranteed through the sponsorship of the prewar government. The subsequent breakdown of the power base of the established religions caused by extreme demographic changes beginning in the early 1950s meant that rural depopulation was depriving the tradition-bound rural areas of its financial base and leaving behind the imbalance of an aging rural society. This mobility was to have far-reaching consequences for the established religions, not only in the rural but also in the urban areas. The static community-based temples and shrines suffered and have continued to do so as a consequence of these changes (MCFARLAND 1967, p. 50).[5]

The new religious groups of the early postwar period prospered amidst the impoverished conditions that faced the Japanese people. They provided members with a sense of community and identity, which was of especial significance in the rapidly urbanizing areas where social dislocation was most in evidence, and they also offered ontological assurances in the wake of the collapse of State Shinto as well as a common goal in the form of an "ideal" future. Poverty, sickness, and the search for comfort in times of hardship are often cited in the early literature on the postwar New Religions as being fundamental to their growth and success, and it is difficult to deny the historical reality of the prevailing conditions in Japan in the wake of defeat in the war. The fact that most of the major groups continue to exist until today (and many even prosper)—despite the stability and prosperity

5. In his footnote on the issue (p. 240, fn. 22), McFarland cites the 26 July 1964 edition of the *Japan Times*, which reports Japanese Agriculture and Foresty Ministry figures indicating that rural depopulation was still continuing into the 1960s on a large scale: 600,000 in 1961, 524,000 in 1962, and 710,000 in 1963. The majority of the displacement was reported as being accounted for by young people under the age of twenty and what are termed as middle-aged breadwinners. For more detailed, specialist analysis of postwar changes in the rural population, see FUKUTAKE 1980, especially the section on the "Impact of Rapid Economic Growth" for a breakdown of the figures from 1950 to 1975 (pp. 11–14).

provided by the socio-economic circumstances of the 1970s and 1980s as Japan established itself as a world economic and industrial superpower—would suggest that many groups had managed to adapt themselves to the newly acquired prosperity and the benefits of a fledgling state welfare system. In other words, their appeal had been transformed as doctrinal matters took root and highly efficient organizational structures emerged.

The appeal of the newer movements that started in the 1970s and emerged as discrete and identifiable entities in the 1980s, however, was different. As noted above, the oil shock of 1973 is frequently referred to as the key event in the development of a new breed of new religious groups in the postwar era. By this time, the abating of the shift away from rural areas towards the cities had given rise to an increase in social stability, while the rapid economic growth that Japan experienced from the 1950s onwards had rewarded the general population with unprecedented prosperity. So while the 1950s and 1960s had seen the rapid rise of such groups as Sōka Gakkai 創価学会, Risshō Kōseikai 立正佼成会, Seichō no Ie 生長の家, Sekai Kyūseikyō, and Reiyūkai 霊友会, along with the consolidation of the older groups such as Tenrikyō, Konkōkyō, and Ōmoto, the 1970s marked something of a transition period. The groups that had either emerged from their prewar roots or had formed in the aftermath of the war were already well beyond the formative stage by the time of the oil shock and were by and large "established" organizationally as well as doctrinally.

Although many of the groups continued to prosper after 1973, it was less in terms of increases in membership and more in terms of organizational consolidation. Concerning membership issues, the majority of groups had reached the stage where they were contracting or, at best, stagnating—often with membership losses offset by natural cumulation through the offspring of members. With regard to organizational matters, in addition to the construction of buildings that would both satisfy the spiritual needs of the adherents and serve the needs of their community, the establishing of administrative structures that borrowed heavily from the successful business enterprises in Japan was equally important. It was already being noted in the early 1960s that the construction of lavish headquarters to provide the focal point of religious activities was a key feature among contemporary groups, but it was also quite common for a group to establish a range of facilities for its own purposes as well as for use by the wider community. These included educational facilities from pre-school to higher education as well as other facilities including hospitals and libraries, in keeping with a vibrant spirit of world renewal that complemented the postwar spirit of reconstruction and revival.

In contrast to their predecessors, the New New Religions—groups that either came into being or experienced their most significant period of development in the 1970s and 1980s—were not offering a way out of poverty, relief from common ailments, or precious "hope," but were appealing more specifically to the spiritual needs of the people as an antidote to the increase in prosperity, the increasing marginalization of the traditional *ie* (household) as the basis of social order, and the advances in science and technology, which offered a challenge to traditional worldviews. Many of those attracted to these groups can be viewed as having sought recourse to magical, mystical practices, and experiences in response to their perceived needs, while the apocalyptic elements implicit in many of the groups' teachings appealed to a sense of uncertainty and unease over the future of Japan as they started to reflect on a certain meaninglessness in Japan's postwar materialistic quest for economic supremacy and on their own impotency. Representative of the New New Religions are GLA (God Light Association), Agonshū 阿含宗, Gedatsukai 解脱会, Sūkyō Mahikari 崇教真光, Shinnyoen 真如苑, Kōfuku no Kagaku 幸福の科学, and Aum Shinrikyō オーム真理教.

A feature of the late 1980s and early 1990s was the appeal of New New Religions or new religious or spiritualist movements among the more affluent and more highly educated Japanese. This is particularly true of Kōfuku no Kagaku and Aum Shinrikyō and it contrasts starkly with the popular image of the New Religions as being a refuge for lower-class, poorly educated people—a stigma that, while true to a large degree up to the 1960s and, perhaps, early 1970s, was no longer a fair reflection of the composition of the New Religions as a whole by the 1990s. While several groups, such as Agonshū and Kōfuku no Kagaku, have become widespread movements and were very prominent publicly at the end of the 1980s and beginning of the 1990s, the New New Religions have not emulated the groups of the 1950s and 1960s in becoming truly mass movements. Social change since 1945 has meant that the social networks are different, while technological advances have meant that the spread of new movements is not restricted to dissemination by word-of-mouth and printed materials. More traditional social networks are still important and the printed materials are now of significantly higher quality and are easier to produce and distribute than thirty or forty years ago, but the religious and spiritualist movements of the 1980s and 1990s were also able to make use of audio-visual aids, provided primarily by the widespread adoption of the video cassette recorder and by the implementation of communications technology to transmit live images of festivals and events via satellite. A more dispersed system of social networks has also been able to take advantage of the Internet, which has expanded the potential to disseminate information beyond the "traditional" social networks. While many new religious groups have a presence on the World Wide Web, perhaps more important are the bulletin boards, newsgroups, chat sites, and individually maintained Web sites in terms of creating a new form of "religious" activity. If the potential for new mass religious movements was already being regarded as unlikely before the sarin gas attack on the Tokyo underground railway in 1995 by Aum Shinrikyō members, then certainly that potential has become even more of an unlikelihood in the post-Aum world of Japanese new religious movements.

OUTLINE OF WORK DONE ON THE JAPANESE NEW RELIGIONS

Study of the Japanese New Religions has been pursued by scholars from across the social sciences as one might expect in a field dealing with any contemporary interaction with society. It is interesting to note, however, the development of research on this area, for it reflects on the one hand the development of such areas as anthropology, sociology, and psychology since the war and, on the other, offers a broad scope of interpretation to the researcher.

Reports from Japan of the rich pickings to be made in the study of New Religions through journals diverse as *American Anthropologist, Numen, Ethnology, History of Religion,*

Journal of Asian and African Studies, Social Compass, in addition to the specialist journals dealing with Japan itself, as well as through books dealing specifically with this "new" phenomenon, saw a rise in consciousness of these New Religions and a considerable amount of literature produced on the subject during the 1960s and early 1970s. As an indication of the *reported* scale of these New Religions, it has been claimed that 171 such groups existed in 1958, with a total membership of over 18 million, and it has also been suggested as many as a fifth, third, or even half (cf. NORBECK 1970, p. 3) of the population of Japan was involved in the New Religions. The largest group, Sōka Gakkai, was claiming more than fifteen million adherents by the mid-1960s and, according to its own reckoning, was the fastest growing religion in the world with a monthly increase of some 100,000 members in the late 1950s and early 1960s. All this from apparently nothing in the wake of the war: New Religions became a new object of study. It is perhaps significant to observe that since Thomsen and Offner and van Straelen published their books on New Religions in Japan and Modern Religions in Japan respectively, over forty years have passed in which no single volume has been published in the English language that deals exhaustively with the wider spectrum of the New Religions in Japan. This reflects more the size of the task facing the researcher than a lack of work done in the area as such. Even now, half a century after the declaration of religious freedom, new groups are emerging, the older groups are evolving, and the even older groups are established within the mainstream of religious tradition.

Daniel C. Holtom was one of the leading foreign scholars of Japanese religions in the period immediately prior to the war, and his works on the Shinto faith and political implications of State Shinto in the prewar and immediate postwar period still provide invaluable and reliable sources of information. His knowledge was called upon by the Supreme Commander of the Allied Powers (SCAP)—this refers to the whole administrative organ, not only to MacArthur himself—although due to ill health he was unable to take an active part in the Religions (and Cultural Resources) Division of the CIE (Civil Information and Education Section). William Bunce was the Chief of the Religions (and Cultural Resources) Division and in that capacity acted as editor of a report by the Division on Religions in Japan in March 1948. The report on the New Sects and developments in Sectarian Shinto are interesting if for no other reason than the fact that it shows the immediacy of interest in them in the first years of the Occupation. The statistics of religious sects and denominations for 1946 are also a valuable source. Also, William P. Woodard, who worked under Bunce as expert advisor on Japanese Religions and was later Director of the Institute for the Study of Religions in Tokyo (and was also later editor of *Contemporary Religions in Japan* from 1964), produced *The Allied Occupation of Japan 1945–1952 and Japanese Religions,* an invaluable source of information on this critical period, drawing on his experience and first-hand contact with the various religious leaders and Japanese scholars of religion of the time. This volume, incidentally, was not in fact published until 1972, some twenty years after the Occupation. In the meantime, Christian missionary scholars had been working hard to produce work on the contemporary religious situation, much of which, one might add, was quite sympathetic towards the New Religions. Thomsen, Offner, van Straelen, Spae, and Hammer were all of the Christian clergy. This sympathetic approach was in some part at least due to the optimistic outlook of the Christian church with respect to its prospects of making inroads into Japanese society, not to mention also in part due to the fascination with the moribund activity within the religious sphere. Moreover, the question of religiosity of the Japanese people seems to have preoccupied many such a scholar. Thomsen's *The New Religions of Japan* (1963)[6] and Offner and van Straelen's *Modern Japanese Religions* (also 1963) were certainly bold attempts to bring knowledge of this field to a wider audience in spite of their respective shortcomings. A critical review of these works, principally the former, by Ōishi Shūten 大石秀典 and others in the March 1964 issue of *Contemporary Religions in Japan* manages to run to no less than thirty-five pages (pp. 45–80).

Ōishi (1964, p. 45) describes Thomsen's work as follows:

[It is] an unusually attractive, splendidly illustrated, and very interesting presentation of a subject about which there is a great deal of interest but very little factual knowledge.... Since this is only the second volume in English to deal with the total situation, the book is certain to be read widely, and it will give the general reader a reasonably satisfactory overall picture of these modern sects. It is extremely unfortunate, however, that it is not as accurate and thoroughly reliable as it should be.

And he continues:

Had the manuscript been submitted to any one of a number of competent scholars in the field before publication, some of the more serious errors at least could have been eliminated.

Indeed Ōishi's worst fears seem to have been justified to some extent at least by the appearance later in the 1960s and 1970s of articles in non-specialist journals (i.e., outside the area of Japanese religious studies) quoting misinformation on the number of sects, membership numbers, etc., and incorporating tenuous classifications of groups and perpetuating an interpretative methodology of characterizing that lacked analytical integrity and a tendency to account for the development of the New Religions principally in terms of a spiritual crisis, which later crystalized as crisis or anomie theory.

It was in the late 1960s and early 1970s that the influence of sociology made an impact on the study of New Religions in Japan. The New Religions in Japan now attracted a good number of Japanese scholars from this field who were interested in the interaction between religion and society. *Social Compass* in 1968 and the *Journal of Asian and African Studies* in 1972 devoted whole issues to monographs on the Sociology of Religion in Japan, the con-

---

6. Thomsen's "shopping" list:
     1. They center around a religious Mecca
     2. They are easy to enter, understand, and follow
     3. They are based on optimism
     4. They want to establish the Kingdom of God on earth, here and now
     5. They emphasize that religion and life are one
     6. They rely upon a strong leader
     7. They give man a sense of importance and dignity
     8. They teach the relativity of all religions
Listed in ŌISHI 1964, p. 54; taken from THOMSEN, pp. 21–31.

tributors being predominantly Japanese. Edward Norbeck's *Religion and Society in Modern Japan* (1970) also gave a commendable and reliable account of the relationship between religion and society in terms of tradition and change and is arguably one of the best general introductions to the New Religions in Japan during the immediate postwar period.

Meanwhile a trend toward studies of individual groups was in progress—mainly by American researchers—with articles appearing on the Japanese New Religions in which the data was taken from perhaps only one or two of the new groups. Observation of and participation in these groups during this period has given us the monographic accounts of individual new groups or single locations that have appeared during the 1980s. Winston Davis's *Dojo* (1980) is a study of Sūkyō Mahikari, and, as the title suggests, the book is the result of six months' participation at one of the branches. This is perhaps rather typical of the approach to the more recent study of the New Religions in Japan, an admixture of anthropological techniques of observation and the application of analytical techniques from sociology based on the collation of substantive and statistical data through interviews and questionnaires. It also raises the problem that many of these studies do tend very much to be highly localized and intensive, which means that the group under study is not treated to an exhaustive accounting and therefore we have the situation whereby a new religious group has been dealt with, but perhaps only in a micro sense. As to whether we can apply the information and data to the rest of the group, for instance rural versus urban characteristics of the group or large versus small churches or regional differences, is somewhat debatable. It is almost as if once a particular group has been "done" then it is struck off the list of things-to-do: the number of groups of diversity is such that it is easier to pick a group as yet untreated by other Western scholars and make it your own than to undertake in-depth research into a group already covered. Especially since the description and conclusions will have sufficient validity on a general basis due to the overall nature of the New Religions in any case. However, it is another matter as to whether or not one might be able to adopt and apply their data universally. Stewart Guthrie's *A Japanese New Religion* (1988) is an example of one of a few anthropological accounts, his dealing with the Nichiren Buddhist-derived group, Risshō Kōseikai, in a remote mountain village.

Helen Hardacre produced two works in the 1980s on different new religious groups; namely, the Nichiren Buddhist-derived Reiyūkai in *Lay Buddhism in Contemporary Japan* (1984), and Kurozumikyō in *Kurozumikyō and the New Religions of Japan* (1986). It is perhaps toward Hardacre's work that one might look to define the latest trends in research by non-Japanese on the new religious movements in Japan. Not only does Hardacre criticize and challenge the crisis theory put forward by various writers since the 1960s—especially by McFarland's *The Rush Hour of the Gods* (1967)—but she puts forward a theory to replace it, which seeks to explain the New Religions in terms of a common worldview:

> This study has identified a vitalist, spiritualist world view as the most fundamental factor unifying the new religions. Whereas prior studies have recognized a rather standardized list of traits as shared by a number of the new religions, this study has tried to show how those traits are unified in originating from a particular conceptualization of self in relation to other levels of existence coupled with regular patterns of thought, action and

emotion. The kingpin of the system is the idea that the self-cultivation of the individual determines destiny. (HARDACRE 1986, p. 188)

As far as future research in the field is concerned, one must wonder whether an overview of the New Religions will soon be forthcoming or not. Already there are a number of such works in the Japanese language that have been recently published, among whose number there are a few rather interesting encyclopedic volumes: namely, *Shinshūkyō gaido bukku* 新宗教ガイドブック (Guidebook to the New Religions) (1987), which poses the question "*Kimi wa dono shūkyō to kyōso o erabu no ka* 君はどの宗教と教祖を選ぶのか" (Which religion and which founder will *you* choose?!) on the cover, contains information on seventy new religious movements. Of these, fewer than twenty have actually been dealt with in any detail by Western scholars, roughly half of that number being only in the most cursory fashion. When one considers that this guidebook does not attempt to cover anything more than the most well-known and popular groups, the extent of the uncovered ground to date is even more marked. Furthermore, there is *Shinshūkyō jiten* 新宗教辞典 (Dictionary of the New Religions) published in 1984 and edited by Matsuno Junkō 松野純孝, who had gathered the information for this dictionary through his work at the Religious Affairs Section of the Ministry of Education. He speculates in his foreword as to whether there might not be as many as two or three thousand new religious groups and restricts his volume to a brief outline of some 200 of the main groups that are registered as religious juridical bodies. The latest of these encyclopedic reference books is also titled *Shinshūkyō jiten* 新宗教事典 (Dictionary of the New Religions), published in 1990 as an update of *Shinshūkyō kenkyū chōsa handobukku* 新宗教研究調査ハンドブック (Handbook of studies on the New Religions) (1981). This is a comprehensive guide to the subject and it deals not only with details of some 300 groups but also consists of a section on "themes," which are summarized by TAMARU (1990, p. 16) as follows:

1. The appearance and development of new religions, their branches, and sub-sects
2. Founders, their associates, and successors
3. Organization, including leaders and followers
4. Teachings, objects of worship, and symbols
5. Practices such as proselytization, training, and ritual
6. Holy places and other facilities
7. Changes in such areas as national law, religious control, friction over religion, and the tone of media commentary
8. Internationalization, overseas proselytization, and import of religious movements originating in the US, Europe, India, South Korea, etc.

This thematic approach seeks to present a picture of the New Religions from a broad perspective, an aspect that has not been dealt with as effectively in the English-language works so far and is becoming more and more pressing not only on account of the fact that there is already sufficient information available to produce such studies but also because there is the need to progress beyond the descriptive toward analysis and interpretation, as Winston DAVIS (1992) was indicating over a decade ago.

TRADITIONS

CURRENT ISSUES

Recent studies on Japanese new religions have helped to locate some of the more recent groups within broader trends in religion worldwide. For example, HAGA and KISALA (1995) explore the relationship of the so-called New New Religions in Japan to new age movements in the West. SHIMAZONO (1993, 2004) has introduced the term "new spirituality movements," drawing attention to the fact that much current religiosity cannot be contained within traditional concepts of "religion" and individual religious institutions.

Another topic currently receiving increasing attention in the study of Japanese New Religions is the role of women in these groups. OOMS (1993) has done work on a woman founder, while NAKAMURA (1997) and USUI (2003) have focused more broadly on the experience of women in the New Religions.

In the wake of the Aum Affair, violence has been a major focus of research, with READER (1996, 2000a, 2000b) producing the most comprehensive studies on Aum itself. Work on violence in new religions, and Japanese religions in general, precedes Aum's attacks, as illustrated by READER and TANABE (1994). Millennial concepts as a contributor to violence also received much attention as the second millennium came to a close (BLACKER 1971; SHIMAZONO 1986; MULLINS 1997; KISALA 1998; OOMS 1993; ROBBINS and PALMER 1997).

Japanese New Religions overseas is another current topic in this field of research. YANAGAWA (1983), INOUE (1985), and NAKAMAKI (1986; 1989; 2003) were early leaders in this area, and MULLINS and YOUNG (1991) and Peter CLARKE (1999a 1999b; CLARKE and SOMERS 1994) have made significant contributions. Two important studies of Soka Gakkai in the West, WILSON and DOBBELAERE 1994, and HAMMOND and MACHACEK 1999, are also worth mentioning in this context.

BIBLIOGRAPHY

AGENCY FOR CULTURAL AFFAIRS 文化庁, 1978. *Shūkyō nenkan* 宗教年鑑. Tokyo: Bunkachō.

ANDERSON, Richard W., 1991. What Constitutes Religious Activity? *Japanese Journal of Religious Studies* 18: 369–72.

ARAKI Michio 荒木美智雄, ŌHAMA Tetsuya 大濱徹也, ŌMURA Eishō 大村英昭, NISHIYAMA Shigeru 西山 茂, and INOUE Nobutaka 井上順孝, eds., 1990. *Kindaika to shūkyō būmu* 近代化と宗教ブーム. Kyoto: Dōhōsha Shuppan.

ASTLEY, Trevor, 1995. The Transformation of a Recent Japanese New Religion: Ōkawa Ryūhō and Kōfuku no Kagaku. *Japanese Journal of Religious Studies* 22: 343–80.

BARKER, Eileen, 1989. *New Religious Movements: A Practical Introduction*. London: HMSO.

BECKFORD, James A., 1976. New Wine in New Bottles: A Departure from Church-Sect Conceptual Tradition. *Social Compass* 23: 71–85.

BECKFORD, James A., ed., 1986. *New Religious Movements and Rapid Social Change*. London: SAGE Publications.

BLACKER, Carmen, 1971. Millenarian Aspects of the New Religions in Japan. In *Tradition and Modernization in Japanese Culture*, ed. Donald H. Shively, pp. 563–600. Princeton: Princeton University Press.

BUNCE, William K., 1955. *Religions in Japan.* Tokyo: Tuttle.

CLARKE, Peter B., 1999a. Japanese New Religious Movements in Brazil: From Ethnic to "Universal Religions." In WILSON and CRESSWELL 1999, pp. 197–210.

CLARKE, Peter B., ed., 1999b. *Bibliography of Japanese New Religions: With Annotations and an Introduction to Japanese New Religions at Home and Abroad.* Richmond, UK: Japan Library.

CLARKE, Peter B., and Jeffrey SOMERS, eds., 1994. *Japanese New Religions in the West.* Folkestone, UK: Japan Library.

CREEMERS, Wilhelmus H. M., 1968. *Shrine Shinto after World War II.* Leiden: E. J. Brill.

DAVIS, Winston B., 1977. *Toward Modernity: A Developmental Typology of Popular Religious Affiliations in Japan.* Cornell University East Asia Papers 12. Ithaca: Cornell University.

———, 1980. *Dojo: Magic and Exorcism in Modern Japan.* Stanford: Stanford University Press.

———, 1992. *Japanese Religion and Society: Paradigms of Structure and Change.* Albany: SUNY Press.

DORMAN, Benjamin, 1996. The Revisions of the Religious Corporations Law in 1995: Perspectives on the Soka Gakkai through the Print Media. B.A. (Honours) dissertation, Australian National University.

———, 2004. SCAP's Scapegoat? The Authorities, New Religions, and a Postwar Taboo. *Japanese Journal of Religious Studies* 31: 105–40.

EARHART, H. Byron, 1982. *Japanese Religion: Unity and Diversity.* 3rd ed. Belmont: Wadsworth Publishing.

———, 1983. *The New Religions of Japan: A Bibliography of Western-Language Materials.* Michigan Papers in Japanese Studies 9. Ann Arbor: Center for Japanese Studies, University of Michigan. (updated and expanded version of 1970 edition published by Sophia University, Tokyo)

———, 1984. *Religions of Japan.* New York: Harper & Row.

———, 1989. *Gedatsu-kai and Religion in Contemporary Japan.* Bloomington: Indiana University Press.

FUKUTAKE, Tadashi, 1980. *Rural Society in Japan.* Tokyo: University of Tokyo Press.

GUTHRIE, Stewart, 1988. *A Japanese New Religion: Risshō Kōsei-kai in a Mountain Hamlet.* Ann Arbor: University of Michigan.

HAGA Manabu and Robert J. KISALA, eds., 1995. *The New Age in Japan.* Special issue, *Japanese Journal of Religious Studies* 22/3–4.

HAMMER, Raymond, 1961. *Japan's Religious Ferment.* London: SCM Press.

HAMMOND, Phillip E., and David W. MACHACEK 1999. *Soka Gakkai in America: Accommodation and Conversion.* Oxford: Oxford University Press.

HARDACRE, Helen, 1984. *Lay Buddhism in Contemporary Japan: Reiyūkai Kyōdan.* Princeton: Princeton University Press.

———, 1986. *Kurozumikyō and the New Religions of Japan.* Princeton: Princeton University Press.

———, 1989a. *Shintō and the State, 1868–1988.* Princeton: Princeton University Press.

———, 1989b. The *Lotus Sutra* in Modern Japan. In *The Lotus Sutra in Japanese Culture,* ed.

George J. Tanabe, Jr., and Willa J. Tanabe, pp. 209–24. Honolulu: University of Hawai'i Press.

HOLTOM, Daniel C., 1938. *The National Faith of Japan: A Study in Modern Shintō*. London: Kegan Paul, Trench, Trubner & Co.

_____, 1943. *Modern Japan and Shinto Nationalism: A Study of Present-Day Trends in Japanese Religions*. Chicago: University of Chicago Press.

HORI Ichiro et al., eds., 1972. *Japanese Religion: A Survey by the Agency for Cultural Affairs*. Tokyo: Kodansha International.

INOUE Nobutaka 井上順孝, 1985. *Umi o watatta Nihon shūkyō* 海を渡った日本宗教. Tokyo: Kōbundō.

_____, 1991. *New Religions*. Contemporary Papers in Japanese Religion 2. Tokyo: Institute for Japanese Culture and Classics, Kokugakuin University.

_____, 1992. *Shinshūkyō no kaidoku* 新宗教の解読. Tokyo: Chikuma Shobō.

INOUE Nobutaka, KŌMOTO Mitsugi 孝本 貢, SHIOYA Masanori 塩谷政憲, SHIMAZONO Susumu 島薗 進, TSUSHIMA Michihito 対馬路人, NISHIYAMA Shigeru 西山 茂, YOSHIHARA Kazuo 吉原和男, and WATANABE Masako 渡辺雅子, eds., 1987. *Shinshūkyō kenkyū chōsa handobukku* 新宗教研究調査ハンドブック. 3rd ed. Tokyo: Yūzankaku.

INOUE Nobutaka, KŌMOTO Mitsugi, TSUSHIMA Michihito, NAKAMAKI Hirochika 中牧弘允, and NISHIYAMA Shigeru, eds., 1990. *Shinshūkyō jiten* 新宗教事典. Tokyo: Kōbundō.

KAWAHASHI Noriko and KUROKI Masako, eds., 2003. *Feminism and Religion in Contemporary Japan*. Special issue, *Japanese Journal of Religious Studies* 30/3–4.

KISALA, Robert, 1998. 1999 and Beyond: The Use of Nostradamus' Prophecies by Japanese Religions. *Japanese Religions* 23: 143–57. (special issue on millennial movements in East and Southeast Asia)

_____, 1999. *Prophets of Peace: Pacifism and Cultural Identity in Japan's New Religions*. Honolulu: University of Hawai'i Press.

KISALA, Robert J., and Mark R. MULLINS, eds., 2001. *Religion and Social Crisis in Japan: Understanding Japanese Society through the Aum Affair*. New York: Palgrave.

KITAGAWA, Joseph M., 1966. *Religion in Japanese History*. New York: Columbia University Press.

_____, 1971. New Religions in Japan: A Historical Perspective. In *Religion and Change in Contemporary Asia*, ed. Robert F. Spencer, pp. 27–43. Minneapolis: University of Minnesota Press.

_____, 1987. *On Understanding Japanese Religion*. Princeton: Princeton University Press.

MATSUNO Junkō 松野純孝, ed., 1984. *Shinshūkyō jiten* 新宗教辞典. Tokyo: Tōkyōdō Shuppan.

MCFARLAND, H. Neill, 1967. *The Rush Hour of the Gods: A Study of New Religious Movements in Japan*. New York: Macmillan.

MIYAKE Hitoshi 宮家 準, KŌMOTO Mitsugi, and NISHIYAMA Shigeru, eds., 1986. *Shūkyō* 宗教. Rīdingusu: Nihon no Shakaigaku リーディングス 日本の社会学 19. Tokyo: Tōkyō Daigaku Shuppankai.

MORIOKA Kiyomi, 1975. *Religion in Changing Japanese Society*. Tokyo: University of Tokyo Press.

MORIOKA Kiyomi 森岡清美, ed., 1978. *Hendōki no ningen to shukyō* 変動期の人間と宗教. Tokyo: Miraisha.

MULLINS, Mark R., 1992. Japan's New Age and Neo-New Religions: Sociological Interpretations. In *Perspectives on the New Age*, ed. James R. Lewis and J. Gordon Melton, pp. 232–46; 339–46. Albany: SUNY Press.

_____, 1997. Aum Shinrikyō as an Apocalyptic Movement. In ROBBINS and PALMER 1997, pp. 313–24.

MULLINS, Mark R., SHIMAZONO Susumu, and Paul L. SWANSON, eds., 1993. *Religion and Society in Modern Japan: Selected Readings*. Berkeley: Asian Humanities Press.

MULLINS, Mark R., and Richard Fox YOUNG, eds., 1991. *Japanese New Religions Abroad*. Special issue, *Japanese Journal of Religious Studies* 18/2–3.

MURAKAMI Shigeyoshi, 1980. *Japanese Religion in the Modern Century*. Tr. Byron H. Earhart. Tokyo: University of Tokyo Press. (originally published 1968 by Kōdansha as *Nihon hyakunen no shūkyō* 日本百年の宗教)

MURATA Kiyoaki, 1969. *Japan's New Buddhism: An Objective Account of Soka Gakkai*. New York: Weatherhill.

NADOLSKI, Thomas P., 1980. The Socio-Political Background of the 1921 and 1935 Omoto Suppressions in Japan. Ph.D. dissertation, University of Pennsylvania.

NAKAMAKI Hirochika 中牧弘允, 1986. *Shin-sekai no Nihon shūkyō: Nihon no kamigami to ibunmei* 新世界の日本宗教——日本の神々と異文明. Tokyo: Heibonsha.

_____, 1989. *Nihon shūkyō to nikkei shūkyō no kenkyū: Nihon, Amerika, Burajiru* 日本宗教と日系宗教の研究——日本・アメリカ・ブラジル. Tokyo: Tōsui Shobō.

_____, 1990. *Shūkyō ni nani ga okiteiru ka* 宗教に何がおきているか. Tokyo: Heibonsha.

_____, 2003. *Japanese Religions at Home and Abroad: Anthropological Perspectives*. New York: RoutledgeCurzon.

NAKAMURA Kyōko, 1997. The Religious Consciousness and Activities of Contemporary Japanese Women. *Japanese Journal of Religious Studies* 24: 87–120.

NELSON, Geoffrey K., 1987. *Cults, New Religions and Religious Creativity*. London: Routledge & Kegan Paul.

NEWELL, William H., and DOBASHI Fumiko, 1968. Some Problems of Classification in Religious Sociology as Shown in the History of *Tenri Kyokai*. *Journal of Asian and African Studies* 3: 84–100.

NEWELL, William H., and MORIOKA Kiyomi, eds., 1968. *The Sociology of Japanese Religion*. Leiden: E. J. Brill. (reprint from special issue on contemporary Japanese religions in *Journal of Asian and African Studies* 3/1–2, 1968)

NISHIJIMA Takeo 西島建男, 1988. *Shinshūkyō no kamigami: Chiisana ōkoku no genzai* 新宗教の神々——小さな王国の現在. Tokyo: Kōdansha.

NISHIYAMA Shigeru 西山 茂, 1986. *Shin-shinshūkyō no shutsugen* 新新宗教の出現. In MIYAKE et al., 1986, pp. 198–204.

_____, 1991. Youth, Deprivation, and New Religions: A Sociological Perspective. Tr. Mark R. Mullins. *Japan Christian Quarterly* 57: 4–11. (special issue on new religions and indigenous Christianity)

NORBECK, Edward, 1970. *Religion and Society in Modern Japan: Continuity and Change*. Houston: Tourmaline Press.

NUMATA Kenya 沼田健哉, 1988. *Gendai Nihon no shinshūkyō* 現代日本の新宗教. Tokyo: Sōgensha.

OFFNER, Clark B., and Henry van STRAELEN, 1963. *Modern Japanese Religions: With Special Emphasis Upon Their Doctrines of Healing.* Leiden: E. J. Brill.

ŌISHI Shūten, 1964. The New Religious Sects of Japan. *Contemporary Religions in Japan* 5: 45–67.

ŌMURA Eishō 大村英昭 and NISHIYAMA Shigeru 西山 茂, eds., 1988. *Gendaijin no shūkyō* 現代人の宗教. Tokyo: Yūhikaku.

OOMS, Emily G., 1993. *Women and Millenarian Protest in Meiji Japan: Deguchi Nao and Ōmotokyō.* Ithaca: Cornell University East Asia Program.

PYE, Michael, 1987. A Common Language of Minimal Religiosity. *The Journal of Oriental Studies* 26: 21–27.

READER, Ian, 1988. The Rise of a Japanese "New New Religion": Themes in the Development of Agonshū. *Japanese Journal of Religious Studies* 15: 235–61.

_____, 1990. Returning to Respectability: A Religious Revival in Japan? *Japan Forum* 2: 57–67.

_____, 1991a. *Religion in Contemporary Japan.* London: Macmillan.

_____, 1991b. What Constitutes Religious Activity? *Japanese Journal of Religious Studies* 18: 373–76.

_____, 1996. *A Poisonous Cocktail? Aum Shinrikyō's Path to Violence.* Copenhagen: NIAS Publications.

_____, 2000a. *Religious Violence in Contemporary Japan: The Case of Aum Shinrikyō.* Honolulu: University of Hawai'i Press.

_____, 2000b. Imagined Persecution: Aum Shinrikyō, Millennialism, and the Legitimation of Violence. In *Millennialism, Persecution, and Violence: Historical Cases,* ed. Catherine Wessinger, pp. 158–82. Syracuse: Syracuse University Press.

READER, Ian, with Esben ANDREASEN and Finn STEFÁNSSON, 1993. *Japanese Religions: Past and Present.* Folkestone, UK: Japan Library.

READER, Ian, and George J. TANABE, Jr., 1998. *Practically Religious: Worldly Benefits and the Common Religion of Japan.* Honolulu: University of Hawai'i Press.

READER, Ian, and George J. TANABE, Jr., eds., 1994. *Conflict and Religion in Japan.* Special issue, *Japanese Journal of Religious Studies* 21/2–3.

REID, David, 1991. *New Wine: The Cultural Shaping of Japanese Christianity.* Berkeley: Asian Humanities Press.

ROBBINS, Thomas, and Susan J. PALMER, eds., 1997. *Millennium, Messiahs, and Mayhem: Contemporary Apocalyptic Movements.* New York: Routledge.

SHIMADA Hiromi 島田裕巳, 1991. *Ima shūkyō ni nani ga okotteiru no ka* いま宗教に何が起こっているのか. Tokyo: Kōdansha.

_____, 1992. *Kamisama no tsugō: Shūmatsu no firudowāku* 神サマのつごう──終末のフィールドワーク. Tokyo: Hōzōkan.

SHIMAZONO Susumu, 1986. The Development of Millennialistic Thought in Japan's New Religions: From Tenrikyō to Honmichi. In BECKFORD 1986, pp. 55–86.

_____ 島薗 進, 1992a. *Gendai kyūsai shūkyō ron* 現代救済宗教論. Tokyo: Seikyūsha.

_____, 1992b. *Shin-shinshūkyō to shūkyō būmu* 新新宗教と宗教ブーム. Tokyo: Iwanami Shoten.

_____, 1993. New Age and New Spiritual Movements: The Role of Spiritual Intellectuals. *Syzygy* 2: 9–22.

_____, 1995. In the Wake of Aum: The Formation and Transformation of a Universe of Belief. *Japanese Journal of Religious Studies* 22: 381–415.

_____, 2004. *From Salvation to Spirituality: Popular Religious Movements in Japan*. Melbourne: TransPacific Publishers.

Shimizu Masato 清水雅人, ed., 1994–1997. *Shinshūkyō jidai* 新宗教時代. 5 vols. Tokyo: Daizō Shuppan.

Shimizu Masato et al., eds., 1978–1979. *Shinshūkyō no sekai* 新宗教の世界. 5 vols. Tokyo: Daizō Shuppan.

Shinshūkyō Kenkyūkai 新宗教研究会, ed., 1987. *Shinshūkyō gaidobukku* 新宗教ガイドブック. Tokyo: KK Besuto Bukku.

Spae, Joseph J., 1971. *Japanese Religiosity*. Tokyo: Oriens Institute for Religious Research.

Swyngedouw, Jan, 1976. Secularization in a Japanese Context. *Japanese Journal of Religious Studies* 3: 283–306.

_____, 1986. Religion in Contemporary Japanese Society. *The Japan Foundation Newsletter* 13/4: 1–14. (reprinted in Mullins, Shimazono, and Swanson, 1993, pp. 49–72)

Takagi Hiroo 高木宏夫, 1959. *Nihon no shinkō shūkyō* 日本の新興宗教. Tokyo: Iwanami Shoten.

_____, 1964. The Rise of the New Religions. *Japan Quarterly* 11: 285–92.

Tamaru Noriyoshi, 1990. Review of *Shinshūkyō jiten*, ed. Inoue Nobutaka et al. *Japan Foundation Newsletter* 17/5–6: 15–17.

Tamaru Noriyoshi and David Reid, eds., 1996. *Religion in Japanese Culture: Where Living Traditions Meet a Changing World*. New York: Kodansha International.

Thomsen, Harry, 1963. *The New Religions of Japan*. Tokyo: Tuttle.

Usui Atsuko, 2003. Women's "Experience" in New Religious Movements: The Case of Shinnyoen. In Kawahashi and Kuroki 2003, pp. 217–41.

Werblowsky, R. J. Z., 1980. "Religions New and Not So New." Review article. *Numen* 27: 155–66.

White, James W., 1970. *The Sokagakkai and Mass Society*. Stanford: Stanford University Press.

Wilson, Bryan, and Jamie Cresswell, eds., 1999. *New Religious Movements: Challenge and Response*. New York: Routledge.

Wilson, Bryan, and Karel Dobbelaere, 1994. *A Time to Chant: The Soka Gakkai Buddhists in Britain*. New York: Clarendon Press.

Woodard, William P., 1972. *The Allied Occupation of Japan 1945–1952 and Japanese Religions*. Leiden: E. J. Brill.

Yamaori Tetsuo, 2000. Aum Shinrikyō Sounds the Death Knell of Japanese Religion. In *Years of Trial: Japan in the 1990s*, ed. Masuzoe Yōichi. Tokyo: Japan Echo. (originally published 1995 in *Japan Echo* 22/3: 48–53)

Yanagawa, Keiichi 柳川啓一, ed., 1983. *Japanese Religions in California. A Report on Research Within and Without the Japanese American Community*. Tokyo: Dept. of Religious Studies, University of Tokyo.

Yanagawa Keiichi and Anzai Shin 安齋 伸, eds., 1979. *Shūkyō to shakaihendō* 宗教と社会変動. Tokyo: Tōkyō Daigaku Shuppankai.

TRADITIONS

Mark R. Mullins

Japanese Christianity

Readers may be surprised to find a chapter on Christianity in a handbook on Japanese religions, since it is so often referred to as a "Western" or "foreign" religion in this context. Christianity, however, is hardly the only foreign-born religion in Japan. Buddhism, Confucianism, and, over the past century, scores of new religious movements have similarly been transplanted from abroad. Without disregarding the importance of various indigenous folk and Shinto traditions, the larger and fascinating story of religion in Japan is one of the reception and adaptation of foreign-born religions in relation to native traditions and cultural concerns.

Christianity in Japan consists of a wide range of phenomena. It includes the most obvious mission churches, denominations, and related institutions established by Western missionaries, numerous indigenous movements (churches or sects established by Japanese which are organizationally independent of Western churches), as well as the personal beliefs and ritual practices of Japanese influenced by Christianity but unaffiliated with any of its organizational forms. The challenge of studying Christianity in this context is how to make sense of these diverse expressions of what began as a transplanted foreign religion. Following a brief historical sketch, this essay will consider the main lines of research on Christianity in Japan in terms of *impacts* and *responses*.[1] In order to understand the significance of this religious tradition in Japan, the study of Christianity must include both the transplanted Christian traditions and their impact on Japanese society as well as the diverse Japanese responses to and appropriations of Christianity that fall outside the framework of the Western churches. A review of the literature to date indicates that the first part of this equation—the history and impact of the mission churches—has received the overwhelming attention and efforts of scholars, but that in recent decades there has been a broadening of research interests and increasing attention given to the study of more diverse responses among Japanese.

HISTORICAL ORIENTATION

Although there is some evidence that Nestorian Christianity may have reached Japan as early as the thirteenth century, the first well-documented encounter between Christianity and Japanese culture began in the mid-sixteenth century with the Roman Catholic mission to Japan. Accompanying the colonial expansion of the Portuguese and Spanish into Asia, the first Jesuit missionaries arrived in Japan in 1549. Missionaries from several other Catholic orders arrived later in the century. The Catholic mission to Japan met with considerable success, so much so that this period has been referred to as "the Christian century in Japan," with the Christian percentage of the population reaching a proportion several times higher than what it is today. This first encounter between Christianity and Japan "officially" ended by the mid-seventeenth century after the country was unified by the Tokugawa authorities. Government decrees prohibited Christianity as an evil religion (*jakyō* 邪教), ordered the expulsion of European missionaries, and mandated the systematic persecution of Japanese converts. In spite of the widespread persecution, arrest, and execution of Christians, as well as effective methods of social control instituted by the *bakufu* government (the *danka seido* 檀家制度 and *terauke seido* 寺請制度, for example), pockets of Christians managed to survive and transmit the tradition to successive generations. Although the Christian success story was thereby brought to an abrupt end, the encounter with Christianity continued "unofficially" for the next two centuries as the "hidden Christians" (Kakure Kirishitan) sought to survive in the hostile environment and secretly carry on the faith they had received.[2] At the end of the Tokugawa period,

1. Here I am borrowing the subtitle of the volume by BREEN and WILLIAMS 1995. In preparing this essay, I have drawn on material and the approach advanced in my earlier work, *Christianity Made in Japan* (MULLINS 1998).

2. For helpful studies of this first phase of Christian mission to Japan, see BOXER 1951, HIGASHIBABA 2001, and Miyazaki Kentarō, "Roman Catholic Mission in Pre-Modern Japan," in MULLINS 2003.

when Westerners were once again admitted to the country and Catholic missionaries were able to resume their activities and hold religious services, a number of these Christians rejoined the Roman Catholic Church. A number of others, however, felt that they could not abandon the Kakure Kirishitan tradition which had been passed down to them directly from their ancestors.

The second encounter between Christianity and Japan began in 1859 (only six years after Commodore Perry persuaded Japan to open its doors to the West) with the return of the Roman Catholics and the arrival of the first Protestant and Orthodox missionaries. This was a time of widespread confusion and chaos. The feudal order was disintegrating rapidly by the end of the Tokugawa period (1600–1868) and the new Meiji government had not yet begun to build the new social order. It was during this difficult transition period that this second phase of mission began. Since the mid-nineteenth century, over two hundred mission societies, representing scores of churches and denominations as well as numerous national cultures, have been transplanted to Japanese soil. The missionary impulse has been especially strong in North America, with the United States and Canada being the home base for approximately one-third of all missionary societies that have been active in Japan.[3]

Christian missionary efforts in Japan finally began to meet with some success after the Japanese government rescinded the edict prohibiting Christianity in 1873. After two long decades of anti-Christian sentiment and resistance, Japan entered a brief period of *seiyō-sūhai* 西洋崇拝, or "worship of the West." The persistent efforts of missionaries suddenly began to pay off in this new social climate of openness. Even missionaries were overwhelmed by the positive response and rapid growth of mission churches and institutions in the 1880s. The optimism was so great that at the second Conference of Protestant Missionaries of Japan held in 1883 it was almost taken for granted that Japan would become a Christian nation in the near future. As Otis Cary observed in his history of this early period, "Some went so far as to say that if the call sent out by the Conference asking for reinforcements was heeded by the churches at home, the work of evangelizing Japan could be accomplished within ten years, or at least before the close of the century."[4] Even some non-Christian Japanese leaders and politicians were advocating that Christianity be adopted as the state religion of Japan. This was understood as an effective strategy for making Japan a recognized member of the international community as quickly as possible.

The "honeymoon" was not to last. As the Meiji government stabilized and began to recast a national identity based upon State Shinto and the emperor system, the initial growth period for Christian churches and institutions came to an end. The leaders of the Meiji government established an alternative ideology to control the process of Japan's modernization: Western technology and learning would be adopted without Christianity. As the strong arm of the state took control of Japan's modernization, an environment was created

3. The literature and major developments of this period are reviewed by Helen J. Ballhatchet in "The Modern Missionary Movement in Japan: Roman Catholic, Protestant, Orthodox," in MULLINS 2003.

4. This is reported in Cary's summary of the Conference in his *A History of Christianity* (CARY 1976, Vol. 2, p. 166).

which put a damper on the growth of Christianity. This is not to say that Christian churches did not record modest growth from time to time over the next century, but the "success" of missionary efforts and the Christianization of Japan anticipated in the 1880s turned out to be a mirage and a case of wishful thinking.

The development of Christianity in postwar Japan has been framed by the fundamental changes in the political and legal system that resulted from Japan's defeat on 15 August 1945 and the arrival of the Occupation Forces. The postwar Constitution of Japan (1847), with its principle of religious freedom and separation of religion and state, led to the disestablishment of State Shinto and created a free-market religious economy for the first time in Japanese history. These legal and political changes, accompanied by demographic changes related to postwar industrialization, helped to create a more favorable environment for Christian missionary activities. Responding to General MacArthur's call for missionary reinforcements to join in building a new Japan, over fifteen hundred new missionaries arrived in Japan between 1949 and 1953.

While churches have continued to report baptisms and membership increases throughout the postwar period, for decades annual statistics have indicated that less than one percent of the Japanese are church members. As a relatively late-arrival Christianity has perhaps had more difficulty in shedding its "foreign" images and associations than has Buddhism and hence has remained a minority religion throughout its history in Japan. Even today, less that one percent of the Japanese population belongs to a Christian church of any kind. While Christian churches have had a difficult time attracting new members, there has been a gradual increase in membership and in the percentage of the Japanese population during the postwar period. In 1948, for example, the total Protestant, Catholic, and Orthodox membership was 331,087, which constituted 0.423 percent of the population. This number had tripled by 1995 and remained rather steady until now. The latest statistics for 2002 indicate a total membership of 1,098,730 (Protestant, Catholic, and Orthodox combined), which represents 0.864 of the total population (KIRISUTOKYŌ NEN-KAN HENSHŪBU [*Christian Yearbook*] 2002). The hard reality is that the rate of defections and the increase in the Japanese population have kept Christian churches from gaining a larger share of the market in Japan's religious economy. Although missionary efforts have only achieved minimal success when measured in terms of converts or church membership, Christianity has nevertheless been a highly influential minority religious tradition that has had a significant impact on Japanese history, institutions, and even other religious traditions.

TRANSPLANTED CHRISTIAN TRADITIONS
AND THEIR IMPACT ON JAPANESE SOCIETY

The study of Christianity in most cultural contexts begins with the documentation of the missionary enterprise—the transplantation of mission churches, biographies of early missionary pioneers, and early "native" leaders. This has also been the case in Japan. In fact, much scholarship has been based in institutions related to the mission churches and focused on the preservation and study of the early history of their respective traditions in Japan. Given the investment in education by the mission churches, we should not be surprised to find that Christianity in Japan has been the focus of considerable scholarly attention and research, in spite of its minority status. The image and reputation of Christianity as a religion for "intellectuals" has been created in part by this emphasis on education and research. Many Christian universities in Japan maintain research institutes, departments of theology or Christian studies, and special library collections and archives, which preserve many of the documents of various transplanted mission churches. Sophia (Jōchi) University, for example, maintains the Kirishitan Bunko, which focuses on the collection of materials related to the Jesuit mission in the sixteenth century. Similarly, Dōshisha University, an institution with roots in the Congregational Protestant tradition, has collected and published many important materials documenting the Protestant mission churches and denominations. The list could go on.[5]

As a review of extensive bibliographies will reveal, Christianity is probably the most documented and studied minority religion in Japan.[6] The scope and range of scholarship is apparent in the massive reference work, *Nihon Kirisutokyō rekishi daijiten* (Historical Dictionary of Christianity in Japan), a volume of over 1,700 pages, which draws on the expertise of some 1,300-plus scholars and writers from diverse denominational traditions, movements, Christian institutions, as well as scholars working outside of Christian churches and institutions (EBISAWA 1988). In the context of these denominational histories and collections, considerable attention has been given to the study of "great figures," the significant missionary pioneers and Japanese Christian leaders who played central roles in the transplantation and development of various Christian traditions in Japan. In a review of the literature one will quickly come across studies of such prominent figures as Xavier, Valignano, Janes, Clark, Hepburn, Verbeck, Nikolai, Williams, Uchimura, Uemura, Niijima, Yamamuro, and Kagawa. These figures continue to attract attention and research.[7]

A great deal of research has also considered the impact of the "missionary carriers" of Christianity on the receiving society—giving attention to evangelistic work, church planting, contributions in the fields of education and social welfare. Important studies in this regard include SUMIYA 1961, MORIOKA 1976, and IKADO 1972, which consider the social background and class connections of early converts to the Protestant missionary movement, the formation of churches in Japan, conflict between Christians and local communities, and the contribution of the Christian missionary movement to the modernization of Japan. A useful sociological and comparative study of variations in church growth is YAMAMORI Tetsunao's *Church Growth in Japan: A Study in the Development of Eight Denominations, 1859–1939*, which examines contextual and institutional factors related to growth.

The formation of new religious communities or groups is only one aspect of the impact of Christianity in Japan. The disproportionate role of Christians in the field of education,

---

5. For an overview of the archival resources on Christianity in Japan, see Yoshida Ryō, "Archival Collections in Japanese Institutions," in MULLINS 2003.

6. See, for example, EBISAWA 1960; IKADO and McGOVERN 1966; and TERAO 2001.

7. Relatively recent studies of these key figures include MORAN 1993, RIGHTMIRE 1997, and ŌE 2000.

for example, is readily apparent when one compares the number of private schools associated with the major religious traditions in Japan. By the early 1960s, the number of Christian schools exceeded the number of Buddhist- and Shinto-related institutions combined. While there were 652 Buddhist-related schools, and only 92 Shinto-related schools, there were 840 Christian-related educational institutions (the numbers for each religious tradition include universities, junior colleges, high schools, junior high schools, elementary schools, and kindergartens).[8] The significance of mission schools, particularly in pioneering in education for women, has been widely noted. In addition to the field of education, there are many studies documenting the impact of Christians in medical work, in social reform movements and the development of labor unions, in social welfare, and politics.[9]

ALTERNATIVE JAPANESE RESPONSES AND PATTERNS OF APPROPRIATION

It is undeniable that Christianity has had a significant impact in various spheres of Japanese society. The encounter between cultures and religious traditions, however, results in change in more than one direction. Christianity has also been transformed through its encounter with Japanese society and culture. The study of the transmission and cultural diffusion of Christianity in Japan requires that we give attention to a wide range of responses and patterns of appropriation; in short, we cannot confine our concerns to the history and documentation of its most obvious organizational forms (that is, the churches and institutions established by Western mission societies). Japanese were not passive recipients of transplanted Christianity, but active agents who reinterpreted and reconstructed the faith in terms that made sense to them.

Here the focus of our concern shifts from the intentions of the "missionary carriers" to the perception and reception of the "natives" and the impact of the receiving culture and society on the imported religion. In other words, we must consider how Christianity—its beliefs, rituals, and institutions—has been appropriated and transformed through its encounter with Japanese culture and religious traditions. The process whereby "foreign" and seemingly irrelevant religions become meaningful and rooted in local culture is referred to by such terms as indigenization, inculturation, contextualization, or syncretism (choice of nomenclature largely depending on one's academic reference group or theological commitments).[10] In the social sciences, indigenization has been defined as the process whereby foreign-born religions are transformed through contact with native religion and culture. Notwithstanding the popular image of the homogenous Japanese, Miyazaki Akira reminded us many years ago that "Japanese culture is not a single unified culture, but a complex of cultures." Given this pluralism, Miyazaki argued that we should expect Christianity in

8. Based on a report on "the current state of education in Christian schools in Japan," KIRISUTOKYŌ GAKKŌ KYŌIKU DŌMEI 1961–1966, p. 133.

9. See, for example, the contributions of Hastings, Endō, Seat, and Steele in the *Handbook on Christianity in Japan* (MULLINS 2003).

10. Roman Catholics tend to use the term "inculturation" while Protestants usually prefer "contextualization."

Japan to appear in diverse forms as a result of its dynamic encounter with the native traditions of Shinto, Shugendō, Bushidō, Confucianism, and Buddhism (MIYAZAKI 1965, p. 62). Any simple caricature of "a Japanese Christianity" is quickly confounded by the diverse patterns of appropriation that have appeared over the course of Japan's modern century.

Numerous studies have appeared in recent years that shift attention away from the efforts and intentions of the missionary carriers and focus more on the Japanese perceptions and appropriation of Christianity. A recent study of the earliest period of Roman Catholic mission in Japan along these lines is Ikuo HIGASHIBABA's *Christianity in Early Modern Japan: Kirishitan Belief and Practice* (2001). The author notes that most studies of this period have either focused on the political and economic dimensions of Christian mission or have been detailed studies of the well-known Jesuit missionary leaders, such as Francis Xavier or Alessandro Valignano. HIGASHIBABA's study, however, explores the "popular religious life and culture of ordinary Japanese followers … whose existence has been so often ignored in the traditional histories of the Christian century" (2001, p. xiv).

Another area that has received particular attention is the study of the *Kakure Kirishitan*, those Japanese who continued to practice Christianity after it became a proscribed religion in the early seventeenth century. The "hidden Christians" denied their faith in public by stepping on a *fumie*, but continued to practice their Christian religion in private. This indigenous tradition of Christianity evolved during the Tokugawa period as Japanese struggled to preserve their faith without the continued support and guidance of the Jesuit missionaries. Much to the surprise of both Japanese officials and Western Church representatives, a sizable Kakure Kirishitan community reappeared in 1865, some meeting with the Roman Catholic missionaries who had returned to Nagasaki. Many of these Kirishitan rejoined the Catholic Church, but others continued to practice the religious tradition as it had been handed down to them. When the notice boards proscribing Christianity were removed by the government in 1873, the *raison d'être* for the Kakure Kirishitan was essentially eliminated. Over the past century, their history has been one of steady decline. Miyazaki, the foremost researcher in this field, estimates that today only 1,000 to 1,500 followers remain. This fascinating indigenous tradition of Christianity has attracted considerable research attention in recent years—perhaps, in part, because the Kakure Kirishitan represent an "endangered species," and many are concerned to document this phenomenon before it disappears entirely. Historical and anthropological studies have analyzed their social organization, considered how the transplanted Christian tradition was reshaped by Japanese cut off from the control and ongoing instruction of the Jesuit missionaries, and analyzed to what extent the Kakure actually preserved elements of sixteenth-century folk Catholicism transmitted along with orthodox Christian teaching (what Turnbull compares to a "time capsule"). The sacred text of the Kakure, *Tenchi hajimari no koto* (The Beginning of Heaven and Earth) has been helpfully introduced and translated into English by Christal WHELAN (1996).[11]

Considerable research has also been devoted to the study of indigenization within the

---

11. On the Kakure Kirishitan, see HARRINGTON 1993; MIYAZAKI 1996; TURNBULL 1998; and WHELAN 1996.

transplanted mission churches in the modern period, particularly in relation to the needs of many Japanese to show special care and respect for the ancestors. In the Japanese context, proper care and respect for the dead involved not only taking part in a number of rituals surrounding the funeral itself, but also the performance of annual festivals and memorial rites over the course of many years. It is well known that most mission churches regarded the Japanese ancestral cult as something incompatible with the Christian faith and ritual care of the dead beyond the funeral was clearly not a part of the Protestant tradition transplanted to Japan in the late nineteenth century.

In spite of their early stance, many of the Christian churches in Japan related to denominations from Europe and North America have instituted a wide range of post-funerary rites over the course of the past century. There are a number of helpful studies documenting these ritual developments and the Japanese Christian understanding of the place of the ancestors in religious life. David REID (1991) has analyzed the manner in which members of the United Church of Christ in Japan (Nihon Kirisuto Kyōdan) have adapted Christian practices to indigenous ancestral rituals. Similarly, NISHIYAMA Shigeru's (1985) study of the Anglican-Episcopal Church in Japan (Nippon Seikōkai) revealed that the ancestral cult has significantly transformed the practice of Christianity within this denomination. David DOERNER's (1977) survey of a Roman Catholic parish likewise showed that numerous accommodations have been made to indigenous beliefs and practices related to the dead. As J. M. Berentsen notes, the Roman Catholic tradition has a more natural affinity to the ancestral cult than Protestant forms of Christianity because of its long practice of "offering liturgical prayers for the dead" (BERENTSEN 1985, pp. 196–98). More recently, Mark LUTTIO (1996) has shown how the Lutheran Church has created a funeral rite that is more compatible with Japanese sensibilities and concerns. Luttio also provides a helpful analysis of the funeral rite developed by the Japan Evangelical Lutheran Church (JELC) in 1993, comparing this ritual not only with the JELC's first funeral rite of 1897 but also with traditional Buddhist rites for the dead. Faithful to the early missionary tradition, the 1897 rite consisted of only a funeral and burial (on the same day). The 1993 rite has adapted and incorporated many elements found in the protracted process of ritual care provided by the Japanese Buddhist tradition.

The process of indigenization is even more apparent in the independent Christian movements that have appeared over the past century in response to the mission churches. These movements are indigenous not only in terms of the minimum conditions of "self-support, self-control, and self-propagation," but illustrate that Japanese have found new ways to interpret, organize, and practice the Christian faith. For many years the independent indigenous Christian movements were largely ignored in the study of Japanese Christianity because established churches considered many of these movements as heretical. The Spirit of Jesus Church (Iesu no Mitama Kyōkai イエス之御霊教会), a Japanese pentecostal movement with some twenty thousand members, for example, was not considered a legitimate research topic for decades because of its rejection of trinitarian formulations of the Christian faith. In my view, however, it is important to examine all groups that define themselves as Christian, then document what they do with the Christian faith when free of the control of the Western churches, rather than exclude them prematurely on the basis of theological criteria.

Carlo CALDAROLA's *Christianity: The Japanese Way* (1979) represents a pioneering work in the study of independent and indigenous forms of Christianity in Japan. This book focused on Uchimura Kanzō and the Nonchurch movement (Mukyōkai 無教会), the first independent expression of Japanese Christianity founded in 1901, which subsequently functioned as the fountainhead of indigenous Christian movements in Japan. Uchimura's version of Christianity was a Confucian one, grafted on to Bushido, and had particular appeal to educated members from the samurai class. While Caldarola's monograph provided an important beginning in the study of indigenous Christian movements, his misleading subtitle—*The Japanese Way*—implied that there was one authentic Japanese version of Christianity. The successive appearance of indigenous movements over the past century, however, indicates that there are other *ways* to be both Japanese and Christian.

In *Christianity Made in Japan* (MULLINS 1998) I attempted to provide some basic documentation of some of these alternative movements, which were also founded by charismatic individuals who accepted the Christian faith (on their own terms) but rejected the missionary carriers and their particular "Western" and "denominational" understanding of religion.[12] The prominent role of charismatic leaders and the manifestation of various charismatic phenomena are important features of these movements, which distinguish them from most transplanted churches as well as Uchimura's Nonchurch movement. The religious experiences of indigenous leaders and their unique combination of foreign (reformed theology, pentecostalism, Unitarianism, dispensationalism) and native religious and cultural elements (Confucianism, shamanism, Bushido, ancestral cult) have produced a number of alternative Japanese Christian traditions.

An important treatment of a new charismatic expression of Japanese Christianity is provided by IKEGAMI Yoshimasa (1991). This in-depth case study of an indigenous church founded in the 1970s—which grew rapidly into a movement of over one thousand members—indicated that the success of charismatic Christianity in Okinawa was related to the effective reinterpretation of the traditional shamanistic spirit world and the stress upon healing, exorcism, and speaking in tongues. Just as Europeans and North Americans require diverse cultural expressions of Christianity, the Japanese also have different tastes and dispositions. It is hardly surprising that, alongside a variety of denominations and sects of Western origins, an equal variety of indigenous Christian groups—high church, low church, evangelical, pentecostal, shamanistic, and so on—should flourish in Japan. In this sense, microsociological studies of new indigenous movements as well as the Japanese reshaping of transplanted Christian traditions can contribute to a more accurate macrosociological understanding of Japan as a more heterogeneous society than is often recognized in many popular characterizations.

In addition to studies of cultural adaptation in institutions and movements, it is also important to give attention to the selective appropriation of elements from Christianity

---

12. See the Appendix of MULLINS 1998 for a "Bibliographical Guide to Indigenous Christian Movements."

in popular religious culture. While less than one percent of the Japanese have chosen to affiliate with any organized expression of Christianity, a much higher percentage have appropriated elements of Christianity or tried to make sense of Jesus on their own terms. It is here that the study of Christianity in Japan overlaps with the field of *minzoku shūkyō* 民俗宗教 (see Ian Reader's chapter on "folk religion" in this *Guide*)—popular religious phenomena that have been drawn from or influenced by Christianity, but clearly diverge from the "official" or "church-defined" understanding of normative religion. This can be seen in recent trends in the rites of passage as well as in some Japanese new religions.

A change in attitudes toward Christianity among the postwar generations provides important background for understanding significant developments in ritual behavior. The "NHK Survey of Japanese Religious Consciousness" conducted almost two decades ago provided helpful information for understanding how Japanese perceptions of Christianity had changed in the postwar environment (NHK HŌSŌ YORON CHŌSASHO 1984). Although exclusive commitment to an organized form of Christianity is still rare among Japanese, the survey discovered that some 12 percent feel a certain empathy (*shitashimi*) for Christianity. While empathy for Buddhism and Shinto increase with age, Jan Swyngedouw has noted that "Christianity shows a completely reverse trend. In the 16–19 age bracket, it reaches a favorable claim of 29.7 percent to go gradually down to 4.5 percent and 5.4 percent for, respectively, the 60–69 and the over-70 age brackets" (SWYNGEDOUW 1985, pp. 5–6). My guess is that this trend has continued with the decrease in the percentage of the population socialized in prewar Japan, but I am unaware of any other surveys that provide a follow-up to the NHK findings.

Although exclusive commitment to a Christian church or any religious organization (Buddhist or Shinto) is still rare among Japanese, many have begun to accept the ritual contribution of Christianity (on their own terms) into the religious division of labor. Just as Shinto has traditionally dominated the rituals associated with birth and Buddhism has monopolized rituals connected to death, Christian churches and schools, as well as hotel chapels, are becoming significant competitors in the sacralization of weddings. In 1982 most weddings (90 percent) were still conducted by Shinto priests, and only 5.1 percent were performed with a Christian service. A 1991 survey discovered that the percentage of Christian or church-related weddings had increased to 35.9 percent in the Kantō region and 23.8 percent in the Kansai region. According to the most recent study by Michael FISCH, by 1998 the percentage of Christian weddings had increased to 53.1 percent, while Shinto weddings had declined to 32.3 percent (see FISCH 2001 and MULLINS 1998, p. 192). This trend of "Christian" weddings represents a natural Japanese appropriation of another religious tradition into the rites of passage in contemporary society.

For a variety of reasons, Christianity seems to be finding a niche for itself in the complex of Japanese folk religion by performing this fashionable, yet compartmentalized role. Prewar generations were socialized in an environment that tended to reinforce negative images of Christianity as *jakyō*, the evil religion from abroad. Today over 300,000 Japanese are enrolled in Christian schools from kindergarten through university. While not all encounters with Christianity in these institutions are positive by any means, it is apparent that many Japanese develop some empathy (or *shitashimi*, as the NHK survey put it) toward

Christianity, which was rare for previous generations. The fact that young Japanese are choosing Christian weddings—and their parents are permitting them—is one manifestation of this shift of consciousness with regard to Christian images and associations. While many church representatives are critical of the "wedding business" both within churches and those conducted in major hotel wedding chapels, it can be argued that wedding services provide one of the few positive points of contact between churches and younger Japanese. Whether or not this will eventually translate into higher numbers actually making a commitment to organized Christianity through baptism and church membership remains to be seen. The dropout rate for membership in both Christian churches and new religious movements remains extremely high.

The selective appropriation of elements from the Christian tradition is also a prominent feature of a number of Japanese new religions and deserves more serious consideration. The founders of many new religions have felt compelled to find some place for the Christ figure in their mythologies and incorporated various ideas from the biblical tradition into their own scriptures.[13] Tensokōkyō 天祖光教, a messianic movement based in Nagoya, for example, draws on both Buddhist and Christian traditions. It does not use the Bible in worship or teaching, but its sacred text, *La Voco de Sfinkso* (*The Voice of the Sphinx*, written by the founder), is permeated by biblical themes and ideas, particularly from Genesis and Revelation. The founder is understood to be a manifestation of the second coming of Christ and the future Buddha (Maitreya), thus superseding both Buddhism and Christianity.

A more recent and notorious example is provided by Asahara Shōkō, the founder of Aum Shinrikyō, who initially focused his movement on Buddhist teachings and ascetic practices aimed at personal liberation and enlightenment. To this he added apocalyptic ideas from the Bible and came to understand himself in messianic terms as the second coming of Christ who would lead his followers in the establishment of an ideal society referred to as the Kingdom of Shambhala. Asahara's character became increasingly authoritarian as he elaborated an apocalyptic vision with himself as a central character in the unfolding drama, and the loose association of yoga practitioners evolved into a movement of mass destruction.[14] Ōkawa Ryūhō, the founder of Kōfuku no Kagaku, one of the most prominent new religions in contemporary Japan, has also drawn on Christianity in the development of his eclectic movement. Ōkawa claims to communicate in trance with spirits from the "other world" and writes down the messages he receives. These have been published as spirit revelations and consist of messages from many luminaries, including Buddha and Jesus Christ. Jesus Christ is clearly a significant figure, but just one of the many spirits sending messages to this world.[15] The place and influence of Jesus Christ and

13. For additional observations on the relationship between Christianity and Japanese new religions, see YOUNG 1989, and "The 'Christ' of the Japanese New Religions" in MULLINS and YOUNG 1995; also Shimazono Susumu, "New Religions and Christianity," in MULLINS 2003.

14. See my essay, "Aum Shinrikyō as an Apocalyptic Movement," in ROBBINS and PALMER 1997, pp. 313–24.

15. The English translation of Ōkawa's work on Christ was published as *The Spiritual Guidance of Jesus Christ: Speaking on the Resurrection of Love and the Spirit of the New Age* (Tokyo: IRH Press, 1991).

the Christian tradition on Japanese new religions clearly needs more systematic study. These few examples, in any case, illustrate that ideas from the biblical tradition and interest in Jesus (or even Christianity) in Japan extends far beyond the boundaries of established churches and indigenous movements.

CONCLUSION

In spite of its minority status, Christianity in Japan has been a relatively well-studied and documented religious tradition. As has been the case in other non-Western contexts, research was initially burdened by a Eurocentric and North American orientation, and studies tended to focus on transplanted mission churches, missionary leaders, and institutions. Over the past three decades a growing number of scholars have begun to seriously consider some additional ways in which Japanese have engaged and appropriated the transplanted Christian traditions. The study of these "missing persons"—marginal Christian groups outside of the established "mainline" denominations and issues related to the actual practice of Christianity in everyday life—is being undertaken by a number of scholars with a social science research orientation. In addition to drawing on archival resources, this research involves the collection of new data through field studies, participant observation, and interviews.[16] These studies reveal that *what happens to a world religion as it moves from one culture to another is beyond the control of its initial missionary carriers.* As Wendy James and Douglas Johnson explain: "Christianity does not necessarily spread as an organic entity; partial elements, themes, and practices, are characteristically taken up by a particular culture or civilization, ethnic, class, or interest group, at a particular time" (JAMES and JOHNSON 1985, p. 5). Established churches in the West cannot control how the Christian tradition will be appropriated in other times and places. The transmission and cultural diffusion of world religions is clearly not a tidy affair that can be categorized simply in terms of acceptance versus rejection. In order to understand the place and significance of Christianity in Japan, in any case, we need to consider the diverse reactions and patterns of appropriation that have appeared in response to this cross-cultural religious encounter.

BIBLIOGRAPHY

BERENTSEN, J. M., 1985. *Grave and Gospel.* Leiden: E. J. Brill.

BOXER, Charles Ralph, 1951. *The Christian Century in Japan, 1549–1650.* Berkeley: University of California Press.

16. Several years ago a research group was formed within the Association for the Study of Religion and Society ("*Shūkyō to Shakai*" *Gakkai* 「宗教と社会」学会) to give more attention to the study of some of these neglected groups and issues. For a guide to the growing social science literature on the study of Christianity in Japan, see the very useful "*Nihon shakai to kirisutokyō" ni kansuru shakaigakuteki kenkyū no bunken mokuroku* 「日本社会とキリスト教」に関する社会学的研究の文献目録 [Bibliography of sociological studies on Christianity and Japanese society], provided by Kawamata Toshinori online at http://toshi-k.net/booklist/JC.htm.

BREEN, John, and Mark WILLIAMS, eds., 1995. *Japan and Christianity: Impacts and Responses.* London: Macmillan.

CALDAROLA, Carlo, 1979. *Christianity: The Japanese Way.* Leiden: E. J. Brill.

CARY, Otis, 1976. *A History of Christianity in Japan.* Tokyo: Charles E. Tuttle. (reprint of 1909 edition)

DOERNER, David L., 1977. Comparative Analysis of Life after Death in Folk Shinto and Christianity. *Japanese Journal of Religious Studies* 4: 151–82.

DOHI Akio 土肥昭夫, 1980. *Nihon Purotesutanto shi* 日本プロテスタント史. Tokyo: Shinkyō Shuppansha.

DŌSHISHA UNIVERSITY HUMANITIES RESEARCH INSTITUTE, ed., 1997. *Nihon Purotesutanto shokyōha-shi no kenkyū* 日本プロテスタント諸教派史の研究. Tokyo: Kyōbunkan.

DRUMMOND, Richard H., 1971. *A History of Christianity in Japan.* Grand Rapids: Eerdmans.

EBISAWA Arimichi 海老沢有道, comp., 1960. *Christianity in Japan: A Bibliography of Japanese and Chinese Sources (1543–1858).* Tokyo: Committee on Asian Cultural Studies, International Christian University.

_____, 1988. *Nihon Kirisutokyō rekishi daijiten* 日本キリスト教歴史大事典. Tokyo: Kyōbunkan.

FISCH, Michael, 2001. The Rise of the Chapel Wedding in Japan. *Japanese Journal of Religious Studies* 28: 57–76.

FURUYA, Yasuo, ed. and tr., 1997. *A History of Japanese Theology.* Grand Rapids: Eerdmans.

HARRINGTON, Ann M., 1993. *Japan's Hidden Christians.* Chicago: Loyola University Press.

HIGASHIBABA Ikuo, 2001. *Christianity in Early Modern Japan: Kirishitan Belief and Practice.* Leiden: E. J. Brill.

IGLEHART, Charles W., 1959. *A Century of Protestant Christianity in Japan.* Tokyo: Charles E. Tuttle.

IKADO Fujio 井門冨二夫, 1972. *Sezoku shakai to shūkyō* 世俗社会と宗教. Tokyo: Nihon Kirisuto Kyōdan Shuppankyoku.

IKADO Fujio and James R. MCGOVERN, comps., 1966. *A Bibliography of Christianity: Protestantism in English Sources (1859–1959).* Tokyo: Committee on Asian Cultural Studies, International Christian University.

IKEGAMI Yoshimasa 池上良正, 1991. *Akurei to seirei no butai: Okinawa no minshū Kirisutokyō ni miru kyūsaikai* 悪霊と聖霊の舞台——沖縄の民衆キリスト教に見る救済世界. Tokyo: Dōbutsusha.

JAMES, Wendy, and Douglas H. JOHNSON, eds., 1985. *Vernacular Christianity.* JASO Occasional Papers 7. Oxford: JASO.

KIRISUTOKYŌ GAKKŌ KYŌIKU DŌMEI, ed., 1961–1966. *Nihon ni okeru Kirisutokyō gakkō kyōiku no genjō* 日本におけるキリスト教学校教育の現状. Tokyo: Education Association of Christian Schools.

KIRISUTOKYŌ NENKAN HENSHŪBU キリスト教年鑑編集部, ed., 2002. *Kirisutokyō nenkan* キリスト教年鑑. Tokyo: Kirisutokyō Shinbunsha.

KUMAZAWA Yoshinobu and David L. SWAIN, eds., 1991. *Christianity in Japan, 1971–1990.* Tokyo: Kyo Bun Kwan.

LUTTIO, Mark D., 1996. The Passage of Death in the Japanese Context: In Pursuit of an Inculturated Lutheran Funeral Rite. *The Japan Christian Review* 62: 18–29.

MIYAZAKI Akira 宮崎 彰, 1965. *Genshi fukuin kenkyū* 原始福音研究. Tokyo: Nihon Kirisuto Kyōdan Senkyō Kenkyūjo.

MIYAZAKI Kentarō 宮崎賢太郎, 1996. かくれキリシタンの信仰世界 *Kakure Kirishitan no shinkō sekai*. Tokyo: Tōkyō Daigaku Shuppankai.

MORAN, J. F., 1993. *The Japanese and the Jesuits: Alessandro Valignano in Sixteenth-Century Japan*. New York: Routledge.

MORIOKA Kiyomi 森岡清美, 1976. *Nihon no kindaishakai to Kirisutokyō* 日本の近代社会とキリスト教. Tokyo: Hyōronsha.

MULLINS, Mark R., 1997. Aum Shinrikyō as an Apocalyptic Movement. In ROBBINS and PALMER 1997, pp. 313–24.

———, 1998. *Christianity Made in Japan: A Study of Indigenous Movements*. Honolulu: University of Hawai'i Press.

———, ed., 2003. *Handbook of Christianity in Japan*. Leiden: E. J. Brill.

MULLINS, Mark R., and Richard Fox YOUNG, eds., 1995. *Perspectives on Christianity in Korea and Japan: The Gospel and Culture in East Asia*. Lewiston: Edwin Mellen Press.

NHK Hōsō Yoron Chōsasho NHK 放送世論調査所, ed., 1984. *Nihonjin no shūkyō ishiki* 日本人の宗教意識. Tokyo: Nihon Hōsō Shuppan Kyōkai.

NISHIYAMA Shigeru, 1985. Indigenization and Transformation of Christianity in a Japanese Community. *Japanese Journal of Religious Studies* 12: 17–61.

ŌE Mitsuru 大江 満, 2000. *Senkyōshi Uiriamuzu no dendō to shōgai: Bakumatsu, Meiji no Beikoku Seikōkai no kiseki* 宣教師ウイリアムズの伝道と生涯──幕末・明治米国聖公会の軌跡. Tokyo: Tōsui Shobō.

PHILLIPS, James M., 1981. *From the Rising of the Sun: Christians and Society in Contemporary Japan*. Maryknoll: Orbis Books.

REID, David, 1991. *New Wine: The Cultural Shaping of Japanese Christianity*. Berkeley: Asian Humanities Press.

RIGHTMIRE, R. David, 1997. *Salvationist Samurai: Gunpei Yamamuro and the Rise of the Salvation Army in Japan*. Lanham: Scarecrow Press.

ROBBINS, Thomas, and Susan J. PALMER, eds., 1997. *Millennium, Messiahs, and Mayhem*. New York: Routledge.

SUMIYA Mikio 隅谷三喜男, 1961. *Kindai Nihon no keisei to Kirisutokyō* 近代日本の形成とキリスト教. Tokyo: Shinkyō Shuppansha.

SWYNGEDOUW, Jan, 1985. The Quiet Reversal: A Few Notes on the NHK Survey of Japanese Religiosity. *Japan Missionary Bulletin* 39: 4–13.

TERAO Kazuyoshi 寺尾寿芳, 2001. *Nihon Kirisutokyō kankei bunken shūsei* 日本キリスト教関係文献集成. *Nanzan Shūkyō Bunka Kenkyūsho kenkyū shohō* 11: 14–45.

TURNBULL, Stephen, 1998. *The Kakure Kirishitan of Japan: A Study of their Development, Beliefs and Rituals to the Present Day*. Richmond, UK: Japan Library.

WHELAN, Christal, 1996. *The Beginning of Heaven and Earth: The Sacred Book of Japan's Hidden Christians*. Honolulu: University of Hawai'i Press.

YAMAMORI Tetsunao, 1974. *Church Growth in Japan: A Study in the Development of Eight Denominations, 1859–1939*. South Pasadena: William Carey Library.

YOUNG, Richard Fox, 1989. Jesus, the "Christ," and Deguchi Onisaburō: A Study of Adversarial Syncretism in a Japanese World-Renewal Religion, *Japanese Religions* 15: 26–49.

History

Matsumura Kazuo 松村一男

Ancient Japan and Religion

Traditionally, views of "this world" and "the other world" are generally divided into two parts, the temporal and the spatial (Miyake 1989, pp. 373–83). Traditional worldviews can also be divided vertically and horizontally. The vertical worldview has a cultural connection to the Altaic language groups of the northern regions, and the horizontal worldview to the southern regions of Oceania and Southeast Asia.

There are the northern Altaic types of myth, such as the myth of advent of the grandson of the Sun Goddess *Tenson kōrin shinwa* 天孫降臨神話 in which Hononinigi, the descendant of the supreme goddess Amaterasu, descends from Takamagahara (the "Plain of High Heaven") onto Ashihara no nakatsukuni wrapped in a sacred robe to become the earthly ruler. This is similar to the legend of Tan'gun of Ancient Korea and the Shuro myth 首露神話 of Kaya. On the other hand, there is the myth of the lost fishing hook, whereby Hononinigi's son, Howori (also

Yamasachihiko 山幸彦) visits the palace of the underwater kami and marries his daughter Toyotamabime in order to retrieve the hook he lost. In this myth the descendant of Howori becomes the emperor. There is a similar lost fishhook myth in Indonesia. While the vertical worldview of the northern regions and the horizontal worldview of the southern regions exist in both the *Kojiki* and *Nihon shoki*, they are not always distinguished from each other and, in many cases, they converge.

VARIETIES OF WORLDVIEWS

The Vertical Worldview

Myths that include a three-layered structure of the upper, middle, and lower worlds—Takamagahara, Ashihara no nakatsukuni, and Yomi no kuni (also known as Ne no kuni) respectively—can be found in the *Kojiki* and *Nihon shoki*. These three worlds are not isolated from each other but are connected through the universal axis (axis mundi). In the opening of the myths, this axis, called Ame no mihashira 天之御柱, was placed on the island of Onokoro. After the parents of the world, Izanagi and Izanami, circulated around the axis, they had sexual intercourse and gave birth to the lands and various kami. In other words, this is the origin from which all things are born. The central pillar, Shin no mihashira 心御柱, of the main shrine at the Grand Shrine of Ise, might be modeled on Ami no mihashira.

The Horizontal Worldview

Together with the vertical view, there is a horizontal worldview that focuses on the revolutions of the sun from east to west. At Miwayama (in Sakurai-shi, Nara Prefecture) there are shrines in various places, from the summit to its foothills, dedicated to the worship of sunrise and sunset at times of seasonal change. In addition, there are sacred sites along the 34°32' north latitude line where Miwayama lies that are connected to rites for Amaterasu from the east at Ise's Saigu Palace to Kamishima, to the west at the Hibara Shrine 檜原神社, Nijō mountain, and Awaji Island. This east-west axis is known as "the way of the sun" (*taiyō no michi* 太陽の道) (OGAWA 1973; MIZUTANI 1980). By the time the capital of Japan became modeled on the Chinese capital, whose direction was based on the Northern Star, this horizontal worldview, which focused on the east-west axis, was replaced by a view that focused on the north-south axis. For instance, the emperor and imperial princes were called Hi no miko 日の御子, and the emperor's residence is called Hi no mikado 日の御門, the word *hi* being a term for sun. These are examples of how the east-west axis took precedence. On the other hand, the term *tennō* 天皇 (emperor), which seems to have been used from the Asuka period (583–710), originated from the term *tennōtaitei* 天皇大帝 (great emperor), who was the deification of the Northern Star and the ultimate god of Daoism in China.

The Temporal Worldview

The standard view held by many is that there are three worlds: the past life, the present life,

HISTORY

and life after death. It appears, however, that it was once thought to be possible to move from one life to another to some extent. In folk beliefs spirits of the dead are often called upon by mediums. In Shinto, however, there is no clear concept of past and future lives. Therefore the notion of retribution based on cause and effect, as in a judgment after death, is not very prominent.

The Other World

Space is divided into two worlds: This (real) World and the Other World. It seems that it was assumed that the Other World Above Ground and the Other World Below Ground were vertical to This World, whereas the Other World in the Mountains and the Other World Above the Seas were horizontal. It was believed that existences other than normal humans, such as supernatural beings like kami, dead people, and non-human beings (birds, animals, and fish, and so on) lived in these worlds.

The boundaries between the worlds were not strict and movement between the worlds was considered possible to a certain extent. For this reason, kami and dead people and beings from other worlds appeared in this world, and people held rituals for kami, made offerings to the dead, and hunted and fished at the boundary between the worlds. Generally the boundaries were marked by trees for the Other World Above Ground, caves and wells for the Other World Below Ground, by graves in mountain passes, hills, and foothills for the Other World in the Mountains, and graves at beaches, capes, and seashores for the Other World of the Sea. However, there also was a merging of the vertical Other World and the horizontal Other World. So, the Other World Above Heaven and the Other World in the Middle of the Mountains merged to become the Other World Above the Mountains, and the Other World Above the Sea; the Other World Below the Earth merged to form the Other World in the Sea (see MIYAKE 1989, pp. 373–83).

RELIGION OF THE JŌMON PERIOD

The Jōmon Period

The Jōmon period began around twelve thousand years ago when the Ice Age ended, marking the start of climatic conditions of the contemporary age. The clues to learning about religion of this period lie in pit cave dwellings and the ruins of villages, and also in excavated earthenware implements, clay figurines, masks, and stone poles.

Despite the term "pit cave dwellings," these seem to have not been dwellings as such, and everyday earthenware items were not excavated from them. It appears that they were not used as spaces for everyday life. The only things that were excavated from the pit cave dwellings were specially shaped items such as earthenware vases and objects that are thought to have been used in special types of religious rituals. The villages were comprised of houses that were built in a circle. Furthermore, graves were dug in spaces not taken up by houses. Thus public space was surrounded by houses and graves. It could be said that villages included both the living and the dead (KOBAYASHI 1999, pp. 13–19). Apart from this, manmade memorials evoke the spiritual world of the time. Stone circles, huge wooden poles, and great structures, like the Sannai Maruyama ruins in Aomori Prefecture, are presumed to have been community memorials of some sort that people created together. In other words, "society" itself was viewed as sacred.

Clay Figurines

Clay figurines were also used for rites. Many of the figurines are female, and the religious significance is often discussed in relation to goddess beliefs (YOSHIDA 1986; 1987; 1993). Among the earthenware implements, there are some vases that have female faces and are shaped like pregnant women. It is possible that these were used as lamps, and if that is the case, it is conceivable that there was a belief in a goddess who had fire burning inside her body (IDOJIRI KŌKOKAN 1988, pp. 110–11). According to Japanese myth, Izanami gave birth to the fire god Kagutsuchi, whose fire came from the body of a goddess. These earthenware vases suggest the possibility that this type of myth may have appeared as far back as the Jōmon period. Myths about fire originating from a woman's body are found in many places around the world, including Oceania and South America (FRAZER 1930).

It is rare for clay figurines to be excavated in their complete form, and often the figurines have been found broken in pieces. There are also cases where the figurines were purposely made so that they would separate into parts when broken. In addition, broken clay figurines were tossed away casually in various places, such as areas surrounding the living quarters, rubbish dumps, and in shell heaps (ESAKA 1990, p. 172). It was not rare for different pieces of one figurine to be thrown away in completely different places.

Concerning this treatment of the figurines, it is presumed that they were buried in the hope that grains would grow from the pieces, which were believed to be the corpse of a grain goddess. There are two factors leading to this hypothesis. Firstly, there is the myth of the origin of grains in the *Kojiki* and *Nihon shoki* whereby the goddess Ohogetsuhime (*Kojiki*) or Ukemochi (*Nihon shoki*) is killed and grains develop from her body. Secondly, there is the possibility that the clay figurines were believed to be not only a goddess but also a murdered maiden goddess (Hainuwele type, or Dema type) whom the tuber-cultivating people of Melanesia worshipped (JENSEN 1963 and 1966). Considering these factors together, a picture can be formed in which the figurines were purposely broken, thus symbolizing the killing of a goddess in a sacrificial rite (YOSHIDA 1993, pp. 136–58).

This interpretation has been criticized on the grounds that the possibility of accidental breakage has not been given enough consideration and thus is based on insufficient evidence (WATANABE 2001, p. 277). Furthermore, some insist that Jōmon clay figurines are the same type as Ongon or even Oshira. Ongon is a human/god statue worshipped by people of the present-day Amur and Obi river basins in Siberia. When Ongon's powers are believed to be ineffective, the statues are destroyed. In some cases Ongon are buried outside as a cure for sickness, and there are also female Ongon that women worship (ŌBAYASHI 1997, pp. 129–30). It is said that the practice of destroying clay figurines, which began in the highlands of the Chūbu region, became a general practice after the middle Jōmon period and was widely accepted by the end of the period (HARADA 1995, 17). There are thus two contrasting views on this issue. One view, promoted by YOSHIDA, is that clay figurines are related to the Hainuwele type of "murdered maiden goddess" found among the tuber-cultivating people of Melanesia. In contrast, the other view is that clay figurines came to Japan from the Baikal region of Siberia via the Amur River, and that they were family goddesses that were used for private rites that originated in female goddess beliefs in the later Stone Age in northern Eurasia. However, it is possible to consider that although the characteristics of the figurines of the early Jōmon period were influenced by the hunting culture of the north, after the middle Jōmon period these characteristics came to be influenced by the tuber-cultivating culture of Melanesia which appeared at that time.

Masks

Compared to clay figurines, only a small number of masks have been excavated. We can surmise a variety of reasons for this, such as the possibility that rites were not conducted very often, or there was no need to make many masks, or many of them were made with materials that deteriorated easily. Considering the fact that masks were used, although not widely, during different periods and in different regions, we can not say that it was unusual to use masks for rites. Rather, we can assume that the use of only a small number of masks was intentional. Also, as a number of masks found show that they were broken on purpose, as in the case of clay figurines, it has been suggested that they were used in rituals and embodied the death and rebirth of gods (ISOMAE 1994, pp. 72–77). However, there is a view that this use of the Jōmon mask is connected to a type of "new-skin ceremony" that occurred in places such as ancient China, New Guinea, and Mexico (HENZE 1989, pp. 10–29; NAUMANN 2000).

Stone Pillars

Stone pillars shaped like penises appeared in the middle of the Jōmon period. Clay figurines symbolizing women and stone pillars symbolizing men seem to have been a visualization of the principle of harmony and cooperation between men and women. Although the stone pillars were initially made as small objects that could be held in the hand, by the middle period they gradually grew in size to 1 meter, and even as large as 2.5 meters. MIZUNO (1986, pp. 58–62) assumes that the small ones were enshrined in pit cave dwellings and the large-scale ones were placed in circular public areas of villages. KOBAYASHI (1996, pp. 217–24) argues that the pillars in the stone circles found in Kazuno City in Akita Prefecture served as sundials. The fact that religions in later periods were concerned with the sun, as expressed in terms such as sun goddess Amaterasu, the emperor (*hi no miko*), or the "way of the sun" shows a continued interest in the sun from the Jōmon period.

RELIGION IN THE YAYOI PERIOD

The Yayoi Period

Yayoi culture, which was characterized by rice growing and bronze and iron implements, flourished from around the middle of the fourth century BCE to the third century CE. Before the nation formed, a class structure was established. A giant pillar-like monument (19.7 meters in height, 6.9 meters in width), which was excavated from the Ikegami ruins in Ikegami, Izumi City, in the southern part of Osaka Prefecture in 1994, indicates that there was a great concentration of wealth in one area (HIROSE 1998, pp. 121–34).

Yamatai and Himiko

The growth in rice production intensified wars of conquest and integration between clans of small countries. It is said that the queen Himiko, ruler of Yamatai in the third century, seized power and quelled these internal disturbances. The following is recorded in the Wei dynastic history *Wei Zhi*, which is part of the histories of the Three Kingdom Period (220–280 CE) in China:

> The country formerly had a man as ruler. For some seventy or eighty years after that there were disturbances and warfare. Thereupon the people agreed upon a woman for their ruler. Her name was Pimiko [Himiko]. She occupied herself with magic and sorcery, bewitching the people. Though mature in age, she remained unmarried. She had a younger brother who assisted her in ruling the country. After she became ruler, there were only a few who saw her. She had a thousand women as attendants, but only one man. He served her food and drink and acted as a medium of communication.
> (TSUNODA and GOODRICH 1951)

Himiko is said to have appeared between the reigns of Huan-di 桓帝 (147–168 CE) and Ling-di 靈帝 (168–189 CE) in the Later Han period. Also, she is said to have died after 247 CE, which means that she ruled from between the second and third centuries CE. It appears that the temperatures were low and crops suffered severe damage due to the cold during this period. Thus, it is assumed that the countries ceased fighting temporarily to avoid the risk of collapsing together, and installed a queen as a temporary measure (KUDŌ 1999, p. 103).

Yamatai was a strong country that controlled about thirty countries including Itokoku 伊都国 and Nakoku 奴国. Various theories have been offered regarding the location of these countries since the research of the Arai Hakuseki 新井白石 (1657–1725) in the Edo period. The "Northern Kyushu" theory and the "Yamato" theory have been debated for many years. The giant circular settlements containing castles discovered in 1989 at the Yoshinagari ruins in Kanzaki, Saga Prefecture, were touted at the time as being Yamatai. However, this does not seem to be the case as this particular area reached its height of prosperity around the middle of the first century and began to decline in the third century. Burial mounds (*kofun* 古墳) were first constructed in the Yamato area around 220 CE. At this stage, the oldest recognized burial mounds were the tombs of Makimuku Ishizuka 纏向石塚 in Sakurai City, Nara Prefecture. Although recent excavations reveal that there was a high level of culture in Yamato in the third century, these are not enough to prove the "Yamato theory" conclusively. Therefore, neither the "Northern Kyushu" nor "Yamato" theories have been conclusively proven (TAKEMITSU 2000, pp. 90 and 206).

Magic and Shamanism

The terms "shaman" or "shamanism" are often used to describe characteristics of Japan's indigenous beliefs (KITAGAWA 1987 pp. 34–5; EBERSOLE 1989 pp. 171, 187; KAWAMURA 1992; OKABE et al. 2001). Originally shamanism meant an ecstatic type of practice conducted mainly by men in Siberia whereby souls float away from the body to the Other World (ŌBAYASHI 1991, pp. 123–70). However, many examples of shamanism in Japan are of the female-possession type, such as Himiko who practiced magic and sorcery, Amaterasu who hid in a cave, Amenouzume who became intoxicated through dance, Jingū Kōgō who became possessed at the sound of a *koto* (a Japanese harp), and folk mediums such as shrine mediums, *itako* of the Tōhoku region, and the *yuta* of Okinawa. Originally, shamanism that dates back to the hunting culture of Siberia was dominated mainly by ecstatic male shamans. In Japan, however, the possessed-female type of shaman become predominant. This difference can be explained by looking at the situation on the Korean peninsula, which lies between these countries. In the Korean peninsula, there are male shamans called *pakusū* and female ones called *mudang*. Both names originate in the language of the Ural Altaic region. There are more female shamans than male ones, and in modern times, females comprise about 80% of all shamans (LEE 1977, p. 121). This is very similar to Japan.

In any case, if the *Wei Zhi* is correct, it means that Himiko stayed in the position of queen for nearly seventy years. The reason why she was able to rule for such a long time was probably because, as the *Wei Zhi* says, "she occupied herself with magic and sorcery, bewitching the people." Considering the above, it is appropriate to view the magic of Himiko as shamanism.

Female Spiritual Power and the Himehiko System

If the situation was just as the *Wei Zhi* describes, however, then Himiko did not appear in public and the important role of delivering her speeches and preparing her food was dominated by one man. This person should be recognized as Himiko's brother, who was "assisting her in ruling the country," as is written in the chronicle. Himiko's magic could be considered as one part of a form of governance divided between male and female: Himiko—female—inner [*uchi* 内]—sacred ←→ brother—male—outer [*soto* 外]—secular (ŌBAYASHI 1977, p. 99).

Some insist that rites were controlled by women in ancient times, citing Yanagita Kunio's *Imo no chikara* 妹の力 [The Power of Sisters] and the examples of Saigū 斎宮, Saiin 斎院, the Ise Shrine Virgin, the medium of Jingikan 神祇官 (the Department of Divinity, a government office in charge of Shinto rituals), and the girl who produces sake for the Daijōsai 大嘗祭 rites, the first ceremony performed by a newly crowned emperor.[1] As previously mentioned, Himiko's magic is often seen as a part of such rites. However, as YOSHIE Akiko (1996, p. 250) has pointed out, the relation between women and rites is often seen not so much as being based on female spiritual power but rather as indicating day-to-day cooperation between men and women, which is reflected in rites as well. This type of management, where an organization is led by a male/female couple, can be seen in today's organizations of new religions as well. Thus the Himehiko system, as well as

---

1. Young females served at Shinto shrines and performed various functions, including presiding over festivals, acting as mediums, and interpreting divinations from the gods. Saiin were female high priests of Kamo Shrine, and Saigō were female high priests of Ise Shrine.

the *wonarigami* belief in Okinawa, whereby sisters protect brothers spiritually, should be understood as the sacralization of cooperation between the sexes, rather than as belief in female spiritual power (Matsumura 1999, pp. 119–49).

MYTHS IN THE *KOJIKI* AND *NIHON SHOKI* AND RELIGION

The Kofun Period

The Kofun period (from the latter half of the third century to around the seventh century) was a time when unified rule in Yamato was being established. The building of keyhole-shaped burial mounds, which were the visible expression of political power in the Kinai region, spread throughout the country in the fourth century, and in the fourth and the sixth centuries, the giant burial mounds known as the *kofun* of Emperor Ōjin (the *Kondayama kofun* 誉田山古墳) and the *kofun* of Emperor Nintoku (the *Daisen kofun* 大山古墳) were built in the Kawachi plains of southern Osaka. In 2000, during an excavation conducted next to the shrine of Izumo Taisha, the base of a pillar was discovered. This pillar consisted of three pillars bound together and its diameter measured more than three meters. It is said that the shrine was an extremely high building that reached sixteen *jō* (about forty-eight meters) in height. Items that were used for rites, such as *magatama* 勾玉 (comma-shaped beads) have also been excavated from the site (Amano 2001, p. 96). Thus, there is a possibility that kami were also worshipped in the high-rise shrines of the Kofun period (Matsumura 1991, pp. 208–9). Some deny the connection between ancient buildings and worship, on the grounds that shrines were not for worship originally, but the natural objects such as mountains, giant trees, or rocks were worshiped (Hirose 1998, pp. 158–64). However, if we take the view that worship of natural objects began from the Jōmon period and the worship of man-made objects began after the Yayoi period, it is conceivable that both types of worship co-existed, thus showing the multi-structured character of the culture at the time.

Kofun Rituals

Kofun were the graves of the powerful, and the rituals of succession were held at the same time as the burial. Moats created a sacred space that separated *kofun* from the outside world. Three levels of upper, middle, and lower steps were carved into the burial mound, and clay figurines, shaped vessels, and jar pots were placed at each level. It appears that these were installed in order to prevent the entry of evil forces from the outer world. The slope of the upper level was covered by slate tiles, so that when the sun shines it is conspicuous, indicating that it was meant to be seen as a man-made monument. There was a stone burial chamber placed at the back part of the top of the mound. Shield and quiver figurines were placed in the corners of the chamber expressing authority and force, and a mansion-shaped figurine was place in the center.

In some cases chair-and-serving-table figurines were placed in front of the mansion figurine and these are thought to have been used for ritual feasts for the dead. Also, there are many cases where a platform was built at the top of the front part of the mound and clay figurines were placed there. When we consider this, it seems that the back part of the mounds were the domain of the dead and the front part the domain of the living, the back part being the place of succession and the front part being that of ascension (MIZUNO 1986, pp. 74–83; KOKUGAKUIN DAIGAKU NIHON BUNKA KENKYŪJO 1999, pp. 67–130).

The Differences between the "Kojiki" and "Nihon shoki"

It appears that once Emperor Tenmu (Prince Ōama) ascended to the throne by defeating his relative Prince Ōmoto (Emperor Kōbun) at the battle of the year of Jinshin (672 CE), he felt the need to prove his legitimacy to imperial power. Thus the *Kojiki* was published in 712 and the *Nihon shoki* in 720. There are very few records in the *Kojiki* related to negotiations between Japan and China and there is no reference to Buddhism, which was transmitted to Japan in the sixth century. Yet by the beginning of the eighth century when both books were compiled, even the emperor had Buddhist funeral rites. Therefore we must conclude that this was a conscious choice to omit the reference to Buddhism. Texts using *man'yōgana* (the earliest form of written Japanese) also showed this tendency. In contrast, the *Nihon shoki* is written in classical Chinese and shows dates and events in chronological order. In other words, it can be considered that the *Kojiki* was compiled to preserve the indigenous elements at a time when continental Chinese culture was becoming accepted. As opposed to this, the *Nihon shoki* shows the acceptance of foreign influence. It is composed with a historical framework (and therefore records things differently) whereas the *Kojiki* is composed using a mythological framework. However, this mythological framework, that is, the systemization of mythological thought, developed from desperation to save indigenous tradition in the face of the shock of encroaching Chinese culture. In other words, the *Kojiki* was like a storehouse of tradition. Therefore, the *Kojiki* was relatively little known (and no one saw the need to promote it) and it did not influence later Japanese culture at all, unlike the *Nihon shoki*, which was influential even up to the Edo period (MACÉ 1992; pp. 60, 65). Within the field of Japanese literature, the difference between the *Kojiki* and the *Nihon shoki* is described as that of "two kinds of cosmology" (KŌNOSHI 1986, 1999).

Trends in Research on the Myths of the "Kojiki" and "Nihon shoki"

Myths recorded in the *Kojiki* and *Nihon shoki* show the influence of various cultures from the countries surrounding Japan. The origins of these myths have been clarified through ethnological research, which has discovered and analyzed the similarities among the myths in various countries of the world and rediscovered the process of transmission of these myths. Although there are mainly only two types of myths, namely, the northern type and of southern type (ŌBAYASHI 1986, 1995), there are many cultures found in them, including those from Oceania, Southeast Asia, minority groups in southern China, China, the Korean peninsula, and Altaic language types such as Mongolian and Turkish, as well as Indo-European influences (MATSUMURA 1996).

Certainly the myths described in the *Kojiki* and the *Nihon shoki* have political aspects as they assert the legitimacy of imperial rule and authority on the grounds that the emperor is a descendant of Amatsukami of Takamagahara (UENO 1985; YAMAGUCHI 1989;

TAKEZAWA 1992; MIZUBAYASHI 2001). However, even though these myths were born from political intentions, their elements came from myths that described the worldview in the culture of the Jōmon, Yayoi, and Kofun periods. Current research is investigating these factors. Considering the issues of the Jōmon period, there is a view that the myth of the murder of the food goddess is reflected in the custom of destroying clay figurines. Also, the myths relating to rice farming and agricultural techniques, which were brought into Japan from the end of the Jōmon period through the Yayoi periods, reveal another layer of influence to the myths in the *Kojiki* and *Nihon shoki* (SHIMADA 1998). Deer and birds were important in myths of the Yayoi period (HIROSE 1998, pp. 173–76). This can also be seen in examples of pottery from the period (HIRABAYASHI 1992).

The unification of the Yamato government advanced as clans from various regions submitted to its power. Myths from these areas are recorded in works such as the *Fudoki* 風土記 (MATSUMURA 1998, 240–45) and also in the *Kojiki* and *Nihon shoki*, although the format of the myths were modified to fit with the demands of the Yamato government. These include the Izumo myth, which centers on the establishment of the country of Izumo, and the Hyuga myth, which is about the Hayato tribe in southern Kyushu. Also, powerful clans which followed the imperial house, especially the Nakatomi clan, recorded their achievements in the *Kojiki* and *Nihon shoki*. In contrast, some of the clans who felt that their achievements were not valued enough compiled their own histories. For instance, the Inbe clan compiled the *Kogoshūi* 古語拾遺 and the Mononobe clan the *Sendai kuji hongi* 先代旧事本記. Although the sun goddess Amaterasu is the goddess of supremacy and imperial origin in the *Kojiki* and *Nihon shoki*, originally the supreme god was Takamimusuhi. The most widely accepted theory at the moment is that at some point the supreme deity was exchanged (MIZOGUCHI 2000, pp. 241–77). Amaterasu used to be a local god in Ise. However, Ise became an important place as a military base for the eastern province of Tōgoku 東国, thus elevating the status of Ise. It seems that after the Jinshin disturbance (*jinshin no ran*), the goddess Amaterasu was chosen as a new symbol for the new national system and became the goddess of imperial ancestors. This change occurred around the seventh or eighth centuries, just before the *Kojiki* and *Nihon shoki* were compiled, during the reigns of Emperor Tenmu or Empress Jitō. This is not unconnected with the worldview that concentrates on the east-west axis known as the "way of the sun." However, at present there is no consensus as to why Amaterasu had to be a female goddess (MATSUMURA 1999, pp. 93–118).

The Concept of Kami

Japan's traditional concept of kami incorporates nature, living and dead humans, animals, and even the temporary condition of spiritual possession. It is not easy to have a definition of kami that will inclusively explain all these things. For instance, if we define the concept of kami in broad terms as something sacred with a supernatural existence, then phenomena such as natural objects that are considered special (for example, mountains), entities that are invisible yet are believed to exist, living people who are seen to be unique (living gods *arahito gami* 現人神), and people who become gods after death (*so rei* 祖霊) can be explained without too much trouble. Also animals that are considered to be special (e.g., foxes, snakes) and auspicious beings (e.g., white deer, white snakes), and even those whose minds are not normal can be considered as possessing a form of kami nature. Kami is a category that is not judged by an objective standard but is determined by sensory and subjective standards (KOKUGAKUIN DAIGAKU NIHON BUNKA KENKYŪJO 1999, pp. 37-38).

BIBLIOGRAPHY

AMANO Yukihiro 天野幸弘, 2001. *Hakkutsu Nihon no genzō: Kyūsekki kara Yayoi jidai made* 発掘日本の原像—旧石器から弥生時代まで. Tokyo: Asahi Shimbunsha.

EBERSOLE, Gary L., 1989. *Ritual Poetry and the Politics of Death in Early Japan.* Princeton: Princeton University Press.

ESAKA Teruya 江坂輝弥, 1990. *Nihon no dogū* 日本の土偶. Tokyo: Rokkō Shuppan.

FRAZER, J. G., 1930. *Myths of the Origin of Fire.* London: Macmillan.

HARADA Masayuki 原田昌幸, 1995. *Dogū* 土偶. Nihon no Bijutsu 日本の美術 345. Tokyo: Shinbundō.

HENZE, Carl, 1989. "Atarashii hifu" ni yoru saisei saishiki 「新しい皮膚」による再生祭式. In *Jōmon zuzōgaku: Kamen to shintaizō* 縄文図像学——仮面と身体像, ed. Jōmon Zōkei Kenkyūin, pp. 9-29. Tokyo: Gensōsha.

HIRABAYASHI Akihito 平林章仁, 1992. *Shika to tori no bunkashi: Kodai Nihon no girei to jujutsu* 鹿と鳥の文化史——古代日本の儀礼と呪術. Tokyo: Hakusuisha.

HIROSE Kazuo 広瀬和雄, ed., 1998. *Toshi to shinden no tanjō: Nihon kodaishi* 都市と神殿の誕生——日本古代史. Tokyo: Shinjinbutsu Ōraisha.

IDOJIRI KŌKOKAN 井戸尻考古館, 1988. *Yatsugatake jōmun sekai saigen* 八ヶ岳縄文世界再現. Tokyo: Shinchōsha.

ISOMAE Jun'ichi 磯前順一, 1994. *Dogū to kamen: Jōmon shakai no shūkyō kōzō* 土偶と仮面——縄文社会の宗教構造. Tokyo: Azekura Shobō.

JENSEN, Ad. E., 1963. *Myth and Cult among Primitive Peoples.* Chicago: University of Chicago Press.

_____, 1966. *Die getötete Gottheit.* Stuttgart: W. Kohlhammer.

KAWAMURA Kunimitsu 川村邦光, 1992. Kidō (shāmanizumu) to sōsai 鬼道（シャーマニズム）と葬制. In *Himiko no jidai: Koko made wakatta "Yamatai koku"* 卑弥呼の時代——ここまでわかった「邪馬台国」, ed. Ōmi Shōji 近江昌司 et al., pp. 169-202. Tokyo: Gakuseisha.

KITAGAWA, Joseph M., 1987. *On Understanding Japanese Religion.* Princeton: Princeton University Press.

KOBAYASHI Tatsuo 小林達雄, 1996. *Jōmon jin no sekai* 縄文人の世界. Tokyo: Asahi Shinbunsha.

_____, 1999. Jōmon sekai ni okeru kūkan ninshiki 縄文世界における空間認識. In KOKUGAKUIN DAIGAKU NIHON BUNKA KENKYŪJO 1999, pp. 1-32.

KOKUGAKUIN DAIGAKU NIHON BUNKA KENKYŪJO 國學院大學日本文化研究所, ed., 1994. *Shintō jiten* 神道事典. Tokyo: Kōbundō.

_____, 1999. *Saishi kūkan, girei kūkan* 祭祀空間・儀礼空間. Tokyo: Yūzankaku.

KŌNOSHI Takamitsu 神野志隆光, 1986. *Kojiki no sekaikan* 古事記の世界観. Tokyo: Yoshikawa Kōbunkan.

KŌNOSHI Takamitsu, ed., 1999. *Kojiki no genzai* 古事記の現在. Tokyo: Kasama Shoin.

KUDŌ Takashi 工藤 隆, 1999. *Yamato shōsū minzoku bunkaron* ヤマト少数民族文化論. Tokyo: Taishūkan Shoten.

LEE Togen 李 杜鉉 et al., eds., 1977. *Kankoku minzokugaku gaisetsu* 韓国民俗学概説. Tr. Ch'oe Kil Song 崔吉城. Tokyo: Gakuseisha.

MACÉ, François, 1992. Nihon no denshō kijutsu ni miru futatsu no ekurichūru 日本の伝承記述に見る二つのエクリチュール. *Gendai shisō* 現代思想 20: 58-67.

MATSUMURA Kazuo 松村一男, 1991. Taikoku shudensetsu to Izumo shinwa 大国主伝説と出雲神話. In *Nihonkai to Izumo sekai* 日本海と出雲世界, ed. Mori Kōichi 森 浩一 et al., pp. 199-228. Umi to Rettō Bunka 海と列島文化 2. Tokyo: Shōgakkan.

———, 1996. Shinwa 神話. In *Nihon minzokugaku no genzai: 1980-nendai kara 90-nendai e* 日本民族学の現在――1980年代から90年代へ, ed. Yōzefu Kurainā [Josef Kreiner], pp. 120-27. Tokyo: Shin'yōsha.

———, 1998. "Fudoki" ni tōjō suru shinwa no tokuchō 「風土記」に登場する神話の特徴. In *Nihon kodaishi "Kiki, Fudoki" sōran: Kojiki, Nihon shoki, kaku Fudoki kara saguru janru betsu kodaishi jiten.* 日本古代史「記紀・風土記」総覧――古事記・日本書紀・各風土記から探るジャンル別古代史事典, pp. 178-79. Tokyo: Shinjinbutsu Ōraisha.

———, 1999. *Megami no shinwagaku: Shojo boshin no tanjō* 女神の神話学――処女母神の誕生. Tokyo: Heibonsha.

MIYAKE Hitoshi 宮家 準, 1989. *Shūkyō minzokugaku* 宗教民俗学. Tokyo: Tōkyō Daigaku Shuppankai.

MIZOGUCHI Mutsuko 溝口睦子, 2000. *Ōken shinwa no nigen kōzō: Takamimusuhi to Amaterasu* 王権神話の二元構造――タカミムスヒとアマテラス. Tokyo: Yoshikawa Kōbunkan.

MIZUBAYASHI Takeshi 水林 彪, 2001. *Kiki shinwa to ōken no matsuri* 記紀神話と王権の祭り. Revised edition. Tokyo: Iwanami Shoten.

MIZUNO Masayoshi 水野正好, 1986. Seisha to shisha no nurinasu sekai 生者と死者の織りなす世界. In *Uchū e no inori: Kodaijin no kokoro o yomu* 宇宙への祈り――古代人の心を読む, ed. Kanaseki Hiroshi 金関 恕, pp. 49-100. Tokyo: Shūeisha.

MIZUTANI Keiichi 水谷慶一, 1980. *Shirarezaru kodai* 知られざる古代. Tokyo: Nihon Hōsō Shuppan Kyōkai.

NAUMANN, Nelly, 2000. *Japanese Prehistory: The Material and Spiritual Culture of the Jomon Period.* Wiesbaden: Harrassowitz.

ŌBAYASHI Taryo 大林太良, 1977. *Yamataikoku* 邪馬台国. Tokyo: Chūō Kōronsha.

———, 1986. *Shinwa no keifu* 神話の系譜. Tokyo: Seidosha.

———, 1991. *Hokubō no minzoku to bunka* 北方の民族と文化. Tokyo: Yamakawa Shuppan.

———, 1995. *Kita no kamigami: Minami no eiyū* 北の神々――南の英雄. Tokyo: Shōgakkan.

———, 1997. *Kita no hito: Bunka to shūkyō* 北の人――文化と宗教. Tokyo: Daiichi Shobō.

OGAWA Kōzō 小川光三, 1973. *Yamato no genzō: Kodai saishi to sujin ōchō* 大和の原像――古代祭祀と崇神王朝. Tokyo: Yamato Shobō.

OKABE Takashi 岡部隆志 et al., 2001. *Shāmanizumu no bunkagaku: Nihon bunka no kakureta suimyaku* シャーマニズムの文化学――日本文化の隠れた水脈. Tokyo: Shinwasha.

SHIMADA Yoshihito 嶋田義仁, 1998. *Inasaku bunka no sekaikan: "Kojiki" jindai shinwa o yomu* 稲作文化の世界観――『古事記』神代神話を読む. Tokyo: Heibonsha.

HISTORY

TAKEMITSU Makoto 武光 誠、2000. *Yamataikoku ga miete kita* 邪馬台国がみえてきた. Tokyo: Chikuma Shobō.

TAKEZAWA Shōichirō 竹沢尚一郎, 1992. *Shūkyō to iu gihō: Monogatari-ronteki apurōchi* 宗教という技法——物語論的アプローチ. Tokyo: Keisō Shobō.

TSUNODA, Ryusaku, and L. Carrington GOODRICH, tr. and eds., 1951. *Japan in the Chinese Dynasties Histories: Later Han through Ming Dynasties*. South Pasadena: P. D. and Ione Perkins.

UENO Chizuko 上野千鶴子, 1985. "Gaibu" no bunsetsu: Kiki no shinwa ronrigaku 「外部」の分節——記紀の神話論理学. In *Kami to hotoke: Bukkyō juyō to shinbutsu shūgō no sekai* 神と仏——仏教受容と神仏習合の世界, ed. Sakurai Yoshirō, pp. 261–310. Taikei Bukkyō to Nihonjin 大系仏教と日本人 1. Tokyo: Shunjūsha.

YAMAGUCHI Masao 山口昌男, 1989. *Tennōsei no bunka-jinruigaku* 天皇制の文化人類学. Tokyo: Rippū Shobō.

YOSHIDA Atsuhiko 吉田敦彦, 1986. *Jōmon dogū no shinwagaku: Satsugai to saisei no ākeorojī* 縄文土偶の神話学——殺害と再生のアーケオロジー. Tokyo: Meicho Kankōkai.

_____, 1987. *Jōmon no shinwa* 縄文の神話. Tokyo: Seidosha.

_____, 1993. *Jōmon shūkyō no nazo* 縄文宗教の謎. Tokyo: Yamato Shobō.

YOSHIE Akiko 義江明子, 1996. *Kodai Nihon no saishi to josei* 古代日本の祭祀と女性. Tokyo: Yoshikawa Kōbunkan.

WATANABE Hitoshi 渡辺 仁, 2001. *Jōmon dogū to josei shinkō* 縄文土偶と女神信仰. Tokyo: Dōseisha.

[Translated by Benjamin Dorman]

YOSHIDA Kazuhiko 吉田一彦

Religion in the Classical Period

Archaeological surveys and research have made great strides in Japan recently, and the remains of what are believed to be the performance of religious rituals have been identified in archaeological sites from the Jōmon, Yayoi, and Kofun periods. As might be expected, these findings indicate that there were beliefs in gods (kami) in the country of Wa 倭 (ancient Japan) before the introduction of Buddhism. Without any textual evidence, however, we have no concrete idea as to how these kami were perceived, the contents of the beliefs in kami, or how the kami were worshipped. It is presumed that these were relatively simple beliefs, and probably there were no systematic doctrines, nor any religious structures that correspond to the shrines (*jinja* 神社) of later times. One could classify these phenomena as one type of the common beliefs in gods that were to be found across the East Asian world of ancient times. These beliefs in gods/kami in ancient Japan were, in later times, taken to be the original form of "Shinto." At present, however, these phenomena are considered to be different from what we now call "Shinto." The view that "Shinto" existed as an independent entity before the introduction of Buddhism in the sixth century is untenable today (see TAKATORI 1979; KURODA 1995; TEEUWEN and SCHEID 2002; and the essay by Norman Havens in this *Guide*).

THE INTRODUCTION OF BUDDHISM

Buddhism was introduced to the land of Wa in about the middle of the sixth century CE. Buddhism, mostly of the Mahāyāna tradition, was transmitted to China in about the first century CE. At first Buddhism did not fit well into Chinese society, but from around the fourth century many of the Buddhist scriptures were translated into Chinese, and gradually a Chinese form of Buddhism developed. The countries surrounding China were strongly influenced by Chinese culture, including Chinese writing, Confucian teachings, Buddhism, and legal codes. Buddhism was transmitted to the kingdoms on the Korean peninsula at around the fourth or fifth century, and then was transmitted in turn from the Korean kingdom of Paekche to Japan around the middle of the sixth century.

It is important to consider the official records as well as the results of archaeological research when examining the transmission of Buddhism to Japan. The remains of the earliest temples are distributed throughout the Asuka and wider Yamato area in central Japan. The official records from this period, such as the *Nihon shoki* 日本書紀 compiled in 720, state that Buddhism was introduced in 552. The passage that reports the transmission of Buddhism, however, refers to a version of the *Suvarṇaprabhāsa-sūtra* 金光明最勝王経 (T. no. 665) which was not translated into Chinese until 703, reflecting the fact that much of the information in this record was composed by its editors (see FUJII 1925; INOUE 1961). The year 552 was chosen on the basis of the belief that, according to some calculations, this was the beginning of *mappō* 末法, the degenerate age. In any case it is difficult to accept this dating as a historical fact. On the other hand, a number of records point to the year 538 as the date of transmission. One of these texts, the *Gangōji garan engi narabini ruki shizaichō* 元興寺伽藍縁起并流記資財帳 (part of the *Gangōji engi* manuscripts kept at Daigoji) claims to have been compiled in Tenpyō 19 (747) but is probably a much later forgery of the later Heian period, and thus is not a reliable source for the date of transmission (see KITA 1980). The *Jōgū Shōtoku Hōōteisetsu* 上宮聖徳法王帝説 (extant at Chion'in) also posits the year 538, but this text probably was not compiled until the early Heian period. The oldest document using the date 538 is the *Gangōji engi* 元興寺縁起 quoted by Saichō in his *Kenkairon* 顕戒論. This is a different text than the *Gangōji garan engi* referred to above, and is not extant. All we know about it is the short part quoted in the *Kenkairon*, and it is presumed to be a history of Gangōji from the mid- to late eighth century. Thus it appears that the 538 dating is later even than the *Nihon shoki*, being proposed around the end of the eighth century; this dating also is most likely a hypothesis presented at a later period, and cannot be accepted as historical fact (see YOSHIDA 2001). All that we can say for certain is that the story that Buddhism was transmitted from Paekche during the time of Kinmei was in circulation from around the end of the seventh and into the eighth century, and we have no basis for pinning down a specific date. Though the exact date for the transmission of Buddhism is not clear, it may be admitted that it most likely occurred during the time of Kinmei (539–571).

ASUKA BUDDHISM

The Buddhism of Wa from the period after the official transmission until the early mid-seventh century is now referred to as "Asuka Buddhism" 飛鳥仏教. This was a time when Buddhism was sustained by the political powers of the Wa state, such as the powerful aristocratic families (*ujizoku* 氏族)—especially the Soga 蘇我 family—and influential visitors and naturalized immigrants from abroad. The Asukadera, built by the Soga family, was the first full-scale temple in Japan (see Tsuboi 1985). The imperial family was more apprehensive about embracing Buddhism, but there were some members—such as Umayado no miko 厩戸王, who established Hōryūji—who were exceptions and were active in promoting it. A number of families of immigrant origin, such as the Hata 秦 family, also built Buddhist temples. There are about fifty temple ruins from this period known to us today; these were located around Asuka in Yamato and mostly in the Kinai (Kansai) area. It is believed that most of these were family temples of the *ujizoku*. For the most part, Asuka Buddhism could be described as the Buddhism of the *ujizoku*. Another characteristic of this period is that many nuns were active during the early days of Buddhism in Wa, and many temples (*amadera* 尼寺) were built for nuns.

WHO WAS "SHŌTOKU TAISHI"?

Any discussion of Asuka Buddhism in the past focused on the figure of Shōtoku Taishi 聖徳太子, who was presented as an outstanding politician as well as a man of culture, who fully understood sophisticated Chinese thought and Buddhist philosophy, created the "Seventeen-article constitution" 憲法十七条, and composed commentaries on three major Buddhist sutras. Contemporary Japanese historians, however, have looked closely at the evidence for these claims, veiled in the mists of legend, and discredited them one after the other as a later product of the Shōtoku Taishi cult. Kume Kunitake (1988) has claimed that the various stories recorded in the *Shōtoku Taishi denryaku* 聖徳太子伝暦 are not historical facts, and the basic records in the *Nihon shoki*—that he was born in a stable, could predict the future, and so forth—are nothing more than creative fiction. Tsuda Sōkichi (1950) also claimed that many of the accounts in the *Nihon shoki* are not historically accurate, and argued convincingly that the so-called "Seventeen-article constitution" was composed at the time the *Nihon shoki* was compiled. Fujieda Akira (1975) compared the commentaries attributed to Shōtoku Taishi with texts discovered at Tunhuang and concluded that these commentaries were composed in China, not by Shōtoku Taishi in Japan. On the basis of these studies, Ōyama Seiichi (1998; 1999; 2003) has argued that the figure we know of as "Shōtoku Taishi" was created at the time of the compilation of the *Nihon shoki*. Ōyama acknowledges the historical existence of Umayado no miko, but recognizes the historicity of only three facts associated with him: his family lineage,

HISTORY

date of birth, and his involvement in the construction of the Ikaruga 斑鳩 palace and establishment of the Ikaruga temple (later to become Hōryūji). He does not recognize the
historicity of any other events associated with Shōtoku Taishi recorded in the *Nihon shoki*,
and concludes that they were produced by the editors of this compilation. He also argues
that the historical materials at Hōryūji—such as the famous inscription on the halo of the
Śākyamuni triad in the Kondō of Hōryūji, and the inscription on the *Tenjukoku shūchō* 天
寿国繡帳 embroidery ("this world is an illusion; only the Buddha is real")—were not composed in the time of Suiko 推古 (592–628) but after the compilation of the *Nihon shoki*,
probably by those involved in the Shōtoku Taishi cult around the middle of the eighth
century. Ōyama argues that the image we know of as "Shōtoku Taishi" was created in the
Nihon shoki on the basis of the idealized image of a Chinese sage who combines the three
"ways" of Confucius, Buddha, and the Tao. Thus we should consider "Shōtoku Taishi" as a
figure created at a later date, and it is a mistake to try to understand the Buddhism of this
period in terms of his life and activities.

HAKUHŌ BUDDHISM

        The Buddhism in Japan from the later half of the seventh century to around
the time of the transfer of the capital to Heijōkyō/Nara (710) is called "Hakuhō Buddhism"
白鳳仏教. Buddhism infiltrated rapidly throughout Japan during this period, which began
about a century after its official transmission. In contrast to Asuka Buddhism, which was
based on an axis of powerful families (*ujizoku*) in the Yamato region, Hakuhō Buddhism
developed among a greater variety of social classes and geographical regions. The Buddhism of the *ujizoku* continued to prosper, and at the same time became actively involved
with Buddhism and its promotion, thus laying the foundation for "state Buddhism." In
the outlying regions we find Buddhism promoted by powerful regional clans, as well as
the beginnings of Buddhism among the common people, with many temples being built
throughout the Japanese archipelago.

    "State Buddhism" began under the ruler Jomei; that is, he established the Kudara ōdera
百済大寺—the first royal, or "national," temple in Wa—in 639. The ruins of this temple
were excavated in 1997 and 1998, revealing a very large site with buildings that must have
taken many years to construct. "National" temples were then built one after the other:
Kawaradera 川原寺 and Sūfukuji 崇福寺 by Tenji 天智, and the construction of Yakushiji 薬
師寺, begun by Tenmu and completed under Jitō. The nation's name was changed from Wa
to Nippon at the end of the seventh century, and the ruler took on the title of *tennō* ("emperor"). Jitō could thus be considered the first Japanese *tennō*, and she also was the first to
complete a Chinese-style capital—Fujiwara-kyō in Asuka. Kudara ōdera was transferred
to Fujiwara-kyō as a national temple and renamed Daikan daiji 大官大寺; this was joined
by Kawaradera 川原寺 (Gufukuji 弘福寺), Yakushiji, and the Asukadera 飛鳥寺 confiscated
from the Soga family (which became Gangōji 元興寺).

    As for the temples of the *ujizoku*, Soga no Kuranoyamada no Ishikawa no Maro estab-
lished the Yamadadera 山田寺, and the Nakatomi (Fujiwara) family the Yamashina-dera
山科寺 (later Kōfukuji 興福寺). Excavations on the site of Yamadadera show that the cor-

ridors of the temple building had fallen to the side and remained preserved in the ground. Thus a building constructed in the second half of the seventh century—having collapsed in the first half of the eleventh century—was preserved for us to see. This important discovery revealed much about the temples of the *ujizoku*.

The most important aspect of Buddhism in this period, however, was the construction of many temples in local areas throughout Japan. Over seven hundred sites have been excavated, and further excavations promise to yield even more results. The existence of so many temples from this time period indicate that this was the first construction boom in temples for the Japanese archipelago. The concrete characteristics of these temples can be viewed in local museums around the country, and are available in catalogues published at the time of various exhibitions (e.g., RITTŌ REKISHI MINZOKU HAKUBUTSUKAN 1991; NAGOYA-SHI HAKUBUTSUKAN 1994; GIFU-KEN HAKUBUTSUKAN 1995). The people who constructed these temples were powerful local clan families. Stories concerning the Buddhist faith of these local families and the construction of these temples can be found in collections such as the *Nihon ryōiki* 日本霊異記 (see NAKAMURA 1973) and *Izumo no kuni fudoki* 出雲国風土記 (see the essay by Morrell in this *Guide*).

This period also saw the spread of Buddhism among the "common people." An entry in the oldest extant handwritten copy of a sutra in Japan (the 金剛場陀羅尼経 [*Vajramaṇḍā-dhāraṇī*], T no. 1345) reports that a certain preacher-monk named Hōrin 宝林 was active in Shiki no kōri 志貴評 in the land of Kawachi in 686, and that he had organized a group of "friends" (*chishiki* 知識) to practice the copying of sutras. Shiki no kōri was a progressive area and still within the Kinai area, but this entry indicates that monks were active in propagating Buddhism in such local areas, and that Buddhism had begun to spread among the common people.

THE ISSUE OF "STATE BUDDHISM"

Buddhism in ancient Japan is often explained in terms of "state Buddhism." This concept has been in use by many for a long time, including scholars such as TAMAMURO Taijō (1940) and HORI Ichirō (1977), and was a mainstay of postwar scholarship from the 1950s to the 1970s. TAMURA Enchō (1982) argued that state Buddhism began in the Hakuhō period and characterized the developments from Asuka Buddhism to Hakuhō Buddhism as a shift from "*ujizoku* Buddhism to state Buddhism." According to this theory, the state played a central role in the acceptance of Buddhism into Japan, and such a state system was formed by the second half of the seventh century. INOUE Mitsusada (1971), on the other hand, argued that the state Buddhism of ancient Japan should be understood in terms of the legal structure (such as the *ritsuryō* 律令 regulations) that regulated such matters. From this perspective, the basic character of state Buddhism can be seen in the laws and regulations promulgated in the legal codes such as the *sōniryō* 僧尼令 (regulations for monks and nuns), *kandosei* 官度制 (regulations for bureaucrats), and *sōgōsei* 僧綱制 (see YOSHIDA 1995).

Beginning in the 1980s, however, the theories on "state Buddhism" began to be criticized from many different angles, so that they are no longer tenable on their own. In the first place, the term "state Buddhism" itself is too ambiguous, and a close examination of its various aspects reveal numerous problems. The regulations of the *sōniryō*, for example, were mostly disfunctional, so any theory based on the assumption that the letter of the law was reflected in actual practice is untenable. Again, "privately ordained" monks and nuns (*shido sōni* 私度僧尼) were indeed proscribed by law, but in fact they were widely accepted, and were very active in all areas, including the Buddhism of local clan families, among the common people, and even within "state Buddhism" (consider, for example, the case of Kūkai).

What is required is a relativization of "state Buddhism." There is no doubt that in ancient Japan there was a form of "state Buddhism" (see the following section). This was not, however, the total sum of Buddhism during this period. "State Buddhism" was only a part of a greater array of Buddhist activity that included the Buddhism of the imperial court and the aristocratic families, that of the local clan families, and that of the common people, as well as the interaction between these aspects. The shift from Asuka Buddhism to Hakuhō Buddhism, therefore, is not a simple development from "aristocratic *ujizoku* Buddhism" to "state Buddhism," but a more complicated development from "aristocratic Buddhism" to a variety of "Buddhisms" including aristocratic Buddhism, state Buddhism, the Buddhism of the local clan families, and that of the common people (see YOSHIDA 1995).

The view of Buddhism in ancient Japan as merely "state Buddhism" has also served as a basis for presenting a contrast with the new Buddhist movements of the Kamakura era and the medieval period, which are then explained as "Buddhism for the masses" (*minshū bukkyō* 民衆仏教; see, for example, HARA 1929; IENAGA 1947). In this view, the history of Buddhism from ancient to medieval Japan is explained in terms of a shift "from state Buddhism to Buddhism for the masses." The *kenmitsu-taisei* 顕密体制 theory of KURODA Toshio (1975, 1990, and 1994; DOBBINS 1996), however, presents a convincing argument that the real axis of medieval Buddhism was formed by the "old" Buddhist schools of the "exoteric and esoteric" schools (*kenmitsu bukkyō*), so that there was also a mixture of various "Buddhisms" in medieval times as well. In any case, the *kenmitsu-taisei* theory requires a wholesale reevaluation of ancient Japanese Buddhism, not just Buddhism in the medieval period.

BUDDHISM AND THE STATE IN ANCIENT JAPAN

From the later half of the seventh century, the state adopted policies to actively promote Buddhism, such as the construction of temples and statues, the sponsorship of rituals (*hōe* 法会) and the copying of sutras, and the promotion of monks and nuns. The era of empress Jitō 持統 (690?–697) was a turning point. Jitō sought to establish a state based on Chinese models of legal codes, the construction of a capital, and the compilation of a national history. Religious policy called for a dual religious foundation for a newly reborn Japanese state based on both *jingi*/kami rituals (*jingi saishi* 神祇祭祀) and Buddhism. Japanese myths were created, providing a literary expression for the imperial transmission through a single family lineage. Buddhism was tapped for state rituals based on the *Suvarṇaprabhāsa-sūtra* to be performed across the country. The state also provided regulations for the ordination of monks and nuns, borrowing the Chinese system for state recognition of ordinands. The number of annual official ordinations (*nenbundosha* 年分度者)

was set at ten. The empress established a capital (Fujiwara-kyō) that was lined with splendid state-supported temples such as Yakushiji, and she was cremated after her death.

The imperial line of Jitō, continuing with Monmu 文武, Genmei 元明, Genshō 元正, and so forth, all attached great importance to Buddhism. The next emperor, Shōmu 聖武 (724–749), in accordance with the wishes of the empress Kōmyō 光明, established Kokubunji 国分寺 and Kokubun-niji 国分尼寺 around the country (see Tsunoda 1986–1997), and built the "big Buddha" (*daibutsu* 大仏) of Tōdaiji (see Inoue 1966; Horiike 1980–1982). The Kokubunji series of temples was modeled on the Chinese system and built with the advice of Dōji 道慈, a monk who had traveled to China. When the capital was moved from Fujiwara-kyō to Heijō-kyō (Nara) in 710, major temples such as Daianji 大安寺, Yakushiji, and Gangōji were transferred to the new capital, the temple housing the *daibutsu* was renamed "Tōdaiji" 東大寺, and the residence of empress Kōmyō was made into a nunnery and named "Hokkeji" 法華寺. The empress's daughter, who became the next *tennō* Kōken/Shōtoku 孝謙・称徳 (749–758 and 764–770), established the temple Saidaiji 西大寺. In this way the new capital was filled with large state temples. The copying of the Buddhist canon also was a large-scale state-supported project. The details of this project are recorded in the Shōsō'in documents 正倉院文書, which have received close scrutiny recently (see Yamashita 1999). It should also be noted that Shōmu himself was ordained as a monk, the first case of an ordained *tennō* in Japanese history. Shōmu abdicated at around the same time he was ordained, and his daughter Kōken/Shōtoku also abdicated once before becoming a nun, and then later ascended the throne again. This is notable as the only case in Japanese history where a *tennō* reigned while ordained a Buddhist monk/nun (see Katsuura 2000). The system for regulating the sangha was gradually institutionalized, and in 734 (Tenpyō 6) it was required that anyone to be ordained as an official monk or nun must master two texts: the *Lotus Sūtra* and *Suvarṇaprabhāsa-sūtra*. It is presumed that this requirement was also influenced by the advice of Dōji.

The imperial line of Jitō came to an end with Kōken/Shōtoku, and shifted to the line of Kōnin 光仁 (770–781) and Kanmu 桓武 (781–806), and the capital also shifted first to Nagaoka and then to Heian (Kyoto). It is often said that the capital was moved in order to avoid the political meddling of the Buddhist establishment, but this theory is no longer accepted. The capital was moved because there was a change in the imperial line. Kanmu performed a *kōten* ritual 郊天祭祀 and announced the change in imperial lines. This Kōnin imperial line also followed a policy promoting Buddhism, establishing major temples in the new capital such as Tōji 東寺 and Saiji 西寺. Kanmu was a strong supporter of Saichō, and Saga 嵯峨 (809–823) supported Kūkai (see below).

JINGI RITUALS AND THE STATE IN ANCIENT JAPAN

At the time of Tenmu and Jitō at the end of the seventh century, the Japanese state developed a series of state religious rituals (*jingi saishi*) that were modified but based on such religious rituals current at the time in T'ang China. The Japanese regulations (*ritsuryō*) from this time include a section on "kami-related" matters (*jingiryō* 神祇令), but the contents were prepared on the basis of the T'ang ritual regulations (*shirei* 祠

令). The contents of these two codes are identical in many respects, but there are some crucial differences. The twin pillars of the imperial rites in China were the rituals for honoring "heaven" (kōshi 郊祀) and the rituals for honoring the imperial ancestors (sōbyō 宗廟), and the regulations in general were based on this structure. A comparison of the T'ang regulations and the Japanese jingiryō show that the regulations for ritual sacrifices (shakuten 釈奠) in the T'ang regulations are covered under the "scholarly regulations" (gakuryō 学令) in Japan; that the Japanese regulations do not make a distinction between the ritual honoring of the heavenly deities (shi 祠) and the ritual honoring of earthly deities (sai 祭); that the jingiryō includes instructions of imperial ascension rituals not included in the Chinese regulations; and that the jingiryō includes descriptions of ōharai 大祓, a matter that did not exist in the Chinese regulations.

The idea of the "mandate of heaven" 天命, that the person who has the favor of "heaven" ascends the imperial throne, developed early in China. In ancient Japan, however, the acceptance of this idea was shunned because of the implication that the imperial line could be overthrown and replaced. Instead, the idea was produced that the imperial family was in a blood relationship and descended from the gods, and this idea was expressed through the creation of myths. This significant difference was reflected in the respective codes, such as the inclusion of imperial ascension rituals in the jingiryō. These imperial ascension rituals consisted of the sensoshiki 践祚式 and the daijōsai 大嘗祭 accession ceremonies. It was also at this time that Ise Shrine was identified as the place that enshrines the ancestral deities of the imperial family (see HAYAKAWA 1986).

The jingiryō prescribed thirteen types of state rituals to be carried out nineteen times in a year. The most important were the rituals of praying for and blessing the crops in the spring, and the rituals for celebrating the harvest in the fall. The first consisted of an annual festival of prayers (kinensai/toshigoi no matsuri 祈年祭), and the latter included the three celebrations of offering fruits from the new harvest: the shinjōsai/kanname no matsuri 神嘗祭,[1] ainamesai/ainie no matsuri 相嘗祭,[2] and the niinamesai 新嘗祭.[3] The four celebrations (three types) of the kinensai, niinamesai, and the tsukinamisai 月次祭[4] (twice, once each in the sixth and twelfth months) were called "the four festivals" (shikasai 四箇祭), and were considered the most important rituals. All of the most important shrine officials from around the country would gather for a hanpei 班幣 offering[5] on these occasions. Also, the jingiryō included provisions for the ōharai purification ritual which is not found in the T'ang regulations, indicating that state rituals for removing impurity were considered important in Japan (see YAMAMOTO 1992).

1. An annual festival during which the emperor offers, at Ise Shrine, sake and food made with rice from the new harvest.

2. The offering of fresh grain from the new harvest at specifically designated shrines.

3. The harvest festival and offering of grain from the new harvest at the imperial palace and at shrines throughout Japan. The first niinamesai after the ascension of a new emperor is the daijōsai.

4. A festival celebrated twice a year, on the eleventh day of the sixth and twelfth months, bringing together state officials for prayers.

5. An offering of nusa 幣 (zig-zag shaped paper) by state officials during state-supported ritual.

It was only a few decades after the promulgation of the *jingiryō*, however, that it was necessary to revise these state rituals. As Okada Shōji (1994) has shown, new official rituals were introduced one after the other from the last half of the eighth century into the ninth century. These new rituals were lined up along with the *jingiryō* rituals to form the core of state *jingi* rituals. These included local festivals such as the Kasuga *matsuri* 春日祭, Hirano *matsuri* 平野祭, Sonokarakami *matsuri* 園韓神祭, Kamo *matsuri* 賀茂祭, Matsuo *matsuri* 松尾祭、Umemiya *matsuri* 梅宮祭, Ōharano *matsuri* 大原野祭, Ōmiwa *matsuri* 大神祭, Taima *matsuri* 当麻祭, Hiraoka *matsuri* 平岡祭, Isakawa *matsuri* 率川祭, and the Yamashina *matsuri* 山科祭. Eventually the ceremony of the *hanpei* offering was not performed during *jingiryō* rituals, and the significance of this ceremony changed. The newly established official rituals merged with the evolving *jingiryō* rituals to form the system of state rituals, forming the core of Japanese *jingi* rituals from the beginning of the Heian period to the end of the Muromachi period.

THE REJECTION OF TAOISM

Taoism, along with Confucianism and Buddhism, is one of the representative religious traditions of China. Eventually Taoist culture—not just Buddhism—was transmitted to Japan. Many aspects of Taoist culture were accepted into Japan and flourished especially during the reign of Tenmu, in the second half of the seventh century. "Mahito" 真人, one of the so-called "eight-colored titles" (*yakusa no kabane* 八色の姓) established during this period, and the posthumous title of Tenmu (天渟中瀛真人天皇) are examples of Taoist influence. By the eighth century, however, the situation began to change, and there was a sharp difference of opinion among those at the center of political power as to whether or not Taoism should be accepted. Eventually, after the revolt of Nagaya ō (*Nagaya ō no hen* 長屋王の変) in 729, when the Fujiwara family took the reigns of power, state policy tightened against the acceptance of Taoism, and envoys to T'ang China were instructed not to bring back any documents related to Taoism. As a result there were no examples of Taoist religious specialists in Japan, and a specifically Taoist worldview did not take root. Japan chose a policy to develop its own religious *jingi* rituals and practices that were different from the Taoist tradition in China (see Noguchi 1996, 1997; Shinkawa 1999).

DŌJI AND GYŌKI

The two monks who best represent the Nara period are Dōji 道慈 (?–744) and Gyōki 行基 (668–749) (see Inoue 1961 and Sakuma 1983). Dōji was a monk who supported state Buddhism during the first half of the Nara period. Upon returning to Japan after studying Buddhism in T'ang China, he received the confidence and support of the Fujiwara family and Nagaya ō. He was involved in the compilation of the *Nihon shoki*, and wrote many of the entries related to Buddhism, such as the entries on the official transmission of Buddhism, on the early conflict between those who supported and those who rejected the acceptance of Buddhism, on Shōtoku Taishi, on Sōmin 僧旻, and so forth (see Yoshida 2002). In addition, his advice was probably crucial in the development of state policies such as the emphasis on the *Lotus Sūtra* and *Suvarṇaprabhāsa-sūtra*, the construction of the Kokubunji temple network, and the invitation of vinaya-precept monks from China.

Gyōki, on the other hand, was supported by local clans and the focus of the fervent support of the masses (INOUE 1959 and 1997). He was at first criticized by the central government, but later his social work—such as his role in the construction of bridges, shelters, and lakes—won the trust and support of the government. He cooperated in raising funds for constructing the "big Buddha," and was eventually given the high rank of *daisōjō* 大僧正. Gyōki traveled from town to town spreading the Buddhist teachings, and it is said that he was beloved by the people and was called a bodhisattva. It is also said that he established forty-nine centers of worship in the Kinai area alone (the "forty-nine temples" *shijūku'in* 四十九院). Finally, there were many women included among his disciples.

ARISTOCRATIC BUDDHISM, LOCAL CLAN BUDDHISM, AND THE BUDDHISM OF THE MASSES

The powerful clan families (*ujizoku*) were gradually incorporated as state officials from the end of the seventh and into the eighth century, until they became "aristocrats." Many of them were enthusiastic supporters of Buddhism, but the focus of their activities was the family temple or their own homes. As KATSUURA (2000) has recently clarified, monks and nuns were frequent guests at the homes of the aristocrats, sometime for a short period but often for a much longer period. Those who stayed for a long period took on the character of "family" monks or nuns. Although it was known that such "family monks" 家僧 (or "family teachers" 家師, 門師) existed in China, but it is only recently discovered that such figures were also active in Japan in the homes of the aristocrats. It is possible to characterize such famous monks as Genbō 玄昉, Ganjin 鑑真, and Dōkyō 道鏡 as the "family monks" of the imperial family, and it is known that Dōji began his career as a family monk for the Nagaya family. Katsuura argues that Buddhist activity in ancient Japan was not limited to temples, but also had private homes as one of its foundations. This is an important point that has been overlooked by those who would understand the Buddhism of this time only in terms of "official monks" (*kansō* 官僧) and "privately ordained monks" (*shidosō* 私度僧). The homes of the aristocrats often included Buddhist facilities, were adorned with Buddhist images, were the site of Buddhist ceremonies, and were often used for the practice of sutra-copying. The sutra-copying of the Nagaya family, for example, resulted in two famous collections—the Wadōkyō 和銅経 and the Jinkikyō 神亀経—both large-scale copies of the Buddhist canon.

At the local level the clan families, as in previous times, continued to build temples and Buddhist images, welcomed monks and nuns, and sponsored Buddhist ceremonies (see SUZUKI 1994). It is probably safe to assume that, like the aristocratic families of the capital, the local clan families also sponsored and invited monks and nuns to stay at their homes. When a monk from a major temple in the capital would visit a local area, he would often give a lecture on Buddhist teachings. Buddhist activities in local areas are vividly described in collections of tales such as the *Nihon ryōiki* (see NAKAMURA 1973). One of the fascinating aspects of this collection is that it reveals the Buddhist faith not only of the local clan families but also of the common people, including, for example, stories of how people of a certain village cooperated in constructing a Buddhist place of worship, how two poor fishermen were lost at sea but were saved by chanting "Namu Shakamuni-butsu," how a miner was accidentally caught underground but was saved through his Buddhist faith, how Buddhist ceremonies and sutra-copying were performed in a local setting, and so forth. Buddhist customs, such as performing memorial services a week or seven weeks after a person's death, were widespread among the common people by around the middle of the eighth century. The tales include scenes of the major temples in the capital (such as Daianji) as well, such as that of a poor woman making a visit to a temple, indicating that the state temples were open also to the common people.

It is often said that Buddhism spread to the masses during the Kamakura period, and that the birth of so-called "new Kamakura Buddhism" was the first appearance of "Buddhism for the masses" in Japan. This view, however, is no longer tenable. Buddhism had spread among the masses to a great extent already by the Nara and Heian periods, and can be traced as far back as the Hakuhō period (see YOSHIDA 1995).

CHARACTERISTICS OF BUDDHIST FAITH IN ANCIENT JAPAN

The characteristics of Buddhist faith in ancient Japan can be known through collections of Buddhist stories such as the *Nihon ryōiki* and *Nihon kanryōroku* 日本感霊録, inscriptions on Buddhist images (see MŌRI 1985), postscripts on copies of sutras,[6] temple histories (*engi*) and registers, biographies of monks such as the *Enryaku sōroku* 延暦僧録 and *Gyōki nenpu* 行基年譜, and various state documents, histories, and other historical materials.[7] One is struck by how different these practices were from the so-called "orthodox" Buddhism of India. In the past these differences have been explained or understood as the result of the mixture of Buddhism with indigenous religious elements in Japan, or as an expression of a unique Japanese spirituality. If we compare the Buddhist faith of ancient Japan with the contemporaneous situation in China and Korea, however, it is clear that the Buddhist faith of ancient Japan was a direct import from China and Korea. An important task for the future is to scrutinize the historical materials on Buddhism in ancient Japan and compare them carefully with related historical materials from that time in China and Korea, in order to clarify which elements were held in common, as well as identify any differences.

WOMEN AND BUDDHISM

One of the characteristics of Buddhism in ancient Japan is the prominent role of women. The *Nihon shoki* records that the first person in Yamato to take ordination was the daughter of Shiba Tatto 司馬達等, and that she was named Zenshin'ni 善信尼. This

6. Important studies on the copying of sutras and the contents of their postscripts include TANAKA 1973 and 1974, and NARA KOKURITSU HAKUBUTSUKAN 1983.
7. On stone monument inscriptions see KOKURITSU REKISHI MINZOKU HAKUBUTSUKAN 1997 and ATARASHII KODAISHI NO KAI 1999.

passage in the *Nihon shoki* shows indications of embellishment by the editors, but there is no good reason to doubt that her ordination was a historical fact. And in the following years nuns were very active in the Yamato of the seventh century, with the construction of many nunneries such as Sakatadera 坂田寺 and Toyouradera 豊浦寺.

Even after the incorporation of the official regulations concerning Buddhist monks and nuns in the eighth century, the number of nuns continued to be significantly large, and nuns also participated in the official Buddhist ceremonies in the imperial palace. The imperial line at this time consisted of Jitō,* Monmu, Genmei,* Genshō,* Shōmu, and Kōken,* of which the four marked with an asterisk were women.

Another important point is that there were also a large number of women among the lay supporters of Buddhism. In the world of state Buddhism and the Buddhism of the imperial court, there were many women emperors and empresses, as well as other women at the court, who pursued policies that strongly supported Buddhism. Many women in aristocratic circles also supported Buddhism, and historical records reveal that they were active in the production of Buddhist images and paintings, and in sutra copying. The same could be said for local clan families. Stories such as those in the *Nihon ryōiki* show that women were deeply involved in Buddhism. Many women among the common people were also involved in a variety of Buddhist activities (see NISHIGUCHI 1987, TAKAGI Yutaka 1988).

This situation began to gradually change from the later part of the Nara period and into the early Heian period. With the shift in imperial line to that of Kōnin and Kanmu, the *Naikubu jūzenji* 内供奉十禅師 regulations were introduced in 772 by Kōnin, after which Buddhist affairs at the court were managed by the *jūzenji*, or ten male monks. Later, under Kanmu, a new system of annual ordinands was introduced in 806 on the advice of Saichō. This proved to be a crucial change of policy that established the longterm framework for Buddhism in Japan (see below). This change in policy meant that henceforth the annual ordinands would be assigned according to "school/sect" (*shūha* 宗派), laying the foundation for the sectarianism of Japanese Buddhism. USHIYAMA (1990) argues that this was a turning point in Japanese Buddhism, after which only male ordinands were trained to run the various Buddhist sects. As a result women, for the most part, lost the opportunity to be ordained, and the number of officially ordained women decreased drastically. Many nunneries lost support and were abandoned, and some became temples for male monks. Nuns were thus forced out of involvement in state and court Buddhist affairs, and the focus of their activities shifted to other areas (see KATSUURA 1995 and 2000; YOSHIDA et al., 1999).

THE AMALGAMATION OF KAMI AND BUDDHAS

The mixture and amalgamation of indigenous deities (kami) and "foreign" buddhas has often been explained and understood in terms of a unique development within the Japanese archipelago as a "Japanese" phenomenon. The usual explanation was that there was conflict between Buddhism and the indigenous kami beliefs and practices (*kami shinkō* 神信仰) in Wa when Buddhism was first transmitted to Japan, but eventually the supporters of Buddhism won the day. After this there was a gradual merging of Buddhism and local spirituality, leading eventually to the religious culture known as the "amalgamation of kami and buddhas" (*shinbutsu shūgō* 神仏習合). Tsuji Zennosuke was the first to put together this theory academically; in an article on "the origin of the *honji-suijaku* theory," first published in 1907 (see Tsuji 1983), he presented an outline of the route supposedly taken by which the idea of the amalgamation of kami and buddhas originated and developed in Japan, eventually giving rise to the theory of the relationship between buddhas and kami as that of "basis" and "traces" (*honji suijaku* 本地垂迹). Tsuji's theory has long been accepted as standard. This theory of "internal origin," however, came in for early criticism by Tsuda Sōkichi, who pointed out that the same phenomena explained as a Japanese amalgamation of kami and buddhas can also be found in the early Chinese biographies of monks 高僧伝 (see reprint in Tsuda 1964). I have followed up on Tsuda's suggestion and concluded that the amalgamation of kami and buddhas in ancient Japan developed through the acceptance of such ideas that were already present in Chinese Buddhism (see Yoshida 1996).

The historical documents relating to the amalgamation of kami and buddhas in ancient Japan often state that the kami suffer from "*shintō* recompense" 神道報 due to their heavy "karmic offenses" 罪業, or the kami confess that they became such due to their "karmic destiny" 宿業, or say that they want to escape from the "kami way" (*shintō*) because of the deep suffering that accompanies having a "kami body" 神身, or plead to take refuge in the "three treasures" or "Buddha dharma" of Buddhism in order to be saved from their current suffering and karmic path 業道, reflecting an attitude of wanting to be liberated from being kami (神身離脱). Stories with these elements can be found in the historical documents of shrine-temples (*jingūji* 神宮寺) such as Kehi Jingūji 気比神宮寺, Wakasa 若狭 Jingūji, Tado 多度 Jingūji, and Kaharu 香春 Jingūji, as well as in the *Nihon ryōiki*. These stories were understood in the past as indicating that such ideas were unique to Japan. The same type of stories, logic, and vocabulary, however, are also found in Chinese texts such as the *Biographies of Eminent Monks* 高僧伝 (T. no. 2059) and *Further Biographies of Eminent Monks* 続高僧伝 (T. no. 2060). These ideas, and even the vocabulary, were imported into Japan as the result of influence from Chinese Buddhism.

Thus it is proper to say that the concepts underlying the amalgamation of kami and buddhas in Japan were introduced and implanted from Chinese Buddhism. It is likely that monks who had traveled to and studied in China, and had a good understanding of the amalgamation of deities and buddhas in China—such as Dōji, Saichō, and Kūkai—transmitted this way of thinking to Japan.

SAICHŌ AND KŪKAI

The monks who best represent Buddhism in the early Heian period are Saichō 最澄 (767–822), transmitter of the Chinese T'ien-t'ai/Tendai 天台 tradition, and Kūkai 空海 (774–835), transmitter of the Shingon 真言 tradition. These two were deeply involved in the management of state Buddhism and made important contributions in this regard, but in addition had a definitive influence on the later development of Buddhism in Japan (see Stone's essay in this *Guide*). The new Buddhist system that was formed around them defined the Buddhism of the Heian and Kamakura periods (for details see GRONER 1984; ABÉ 1999; ANDŌ and SONODA 1974; SONODA 1981; and TAKAGI 1997).

THE FORMATION OF SECTARIANISM—THE "EIGHT SCHOOLS" SYSTEM

Sectarianism in Japanese Buddhism, as mentioned above, received a major impetus in Enryaku 25 (806) with the implementation of a new ordination system. This revised system was proposed by Saichō, with the endorsement of Nara monks such as Gomyō 護命, and approved by the government. The revision called for assigning a specific number of annual ordinands to each of the seven schools of Buddhism: the "six schools" (but actually only four schools) in Nara and the new Tendai school. This system of annual ordinands began in the tenth year of Jitō (696) by officially sanctioning ten annual ordinands. At this early date there were no distinct "schools," and thus the ordinands were not assigned to any specific tradition. The Enryaku-period revision, however, incorporated the concept of "schools" (shūha) and assigned three ordinands to each of the Hossō 法相 and Sanron 三論 (which included the Kusha 倶舎 and Jōjitsu 成実) schools, and two each to the Kegon 華厳, Ritsu 律, and Tendai 天台 schools, increasing the total annual ordinands to twelve. As a result, the state officially recognized seven independent "schools," leading to the development of sectarianism. A bit later, on the twenty-third day of the first month in Jōwa 2 (835), the government approved an additional three ordinands to be assigned annually to the Shingon school, thus raising to eight the number of officially recognized schools. Thus arose the system of "eight schools" (hasshū 八宗) which dominated the religious world of the Heian and Kamakura periods.

The early sprouts of this sectarianism actually began to germinate a bit earlier. Documents in the Shōsō'in documents from the middle of the eighth century already contain references to groups with the term shū (衆 or 宗). In this context, however, as SONODA Kōyū (1981) and SONE Masato (2000) have pointed out, these terms refer to academic schools or groups that were quite different from the sectarian "schools" of the Heian and Kamakura periods and continuing to our contemporary times. During the Nara period, monks of different "schools" lived in the same temple, worshipped the same buddha, and chanted the same sutras. There was little sense of doctrinal or exclusivist sectarianism. The term shū began to take on sectarian connotations from the middle of the eighth century, but these were preliminary developments, and the definitive point in the birth of true sectarianism was the new system of ordinands introduced in 806. After this point, anyone who took the path of an official monk had to follow this system and become ordained as a monk of one of the officially recognized "schools," at the ordination platform associated with that school. The phrase "the six schools of Nara" (nanto rokushū 南都六宗) is often used; however, this is not a phrase from the Nara period but has real referents only with the adoption of this revised system in 806. SONE (2000) argues that it was only after this time that each "school" decided on identifying their own "orthodox" Chinese founder and their basic texts, leading to the formation of sectarian doctrine (shugi 宗義) and sectarian studies (shūgaku 宗学). Eventually sectarian temples were also founded.

In Tenchō 7 (830), emperor Junna 淳和 decreed that each school submit a description of their teachings (*Tenchō roppon shūsho* 天長六本宗書), and a representative of each school prepared a report on the doctrinal characteristics and historical development of their own tradition. The six documents that were submitted were the *Daijō Hossō kenshin shō* 大乗法相研神章 by Gomyō 護命, the *Daijō Sanron daigi shō* 大乗三論大義鈔 by Gen'ei 玄叡, the *Kegon-shū ichijō kaishin ron* 華厳宗一乗開心論 by Fuki 普機, the *Kairitsu denrai ki* 戒律伝来記 by Buan 豊安, the *Tendai hokkeshūgi shū* 天台法華宗義集 by Gishin 義真, and the *Himitsu mandara jūjūshin ron* 秘密曼荼羅十住心論 by Kūkai. There was little of what could be called "Buddhist doctrinal studies" (*bukkyō kyōgaku* 仏教教学) in Japan in the sixth and seventh centuries, and it was only in the middle of the eighth century that doctrinal studies by some scholar-monks begin to appear, but they were few and far between, and their arguments still not mature. Once we get into the ninth century, however, doctrinal studies were promoted and kept pace with the formation of sectarianism, and the study and debate of Buddhist thought, as well as the production of doctrinal treatises, became prominent.

THE PERIODIZATION OF JAPANESE RELIGIOUS HISTORY

In dividing the history of Japanese religion into periods, the rise of the new Buddhist movements in the Kamakura period is often presented as a epochal development. The figures who appeared in the Kamakura period—Hōnen 法然, Shinran 親鸞, Eisai 栄西, Dōgen 道元, Nichiren 日蓮, Ippen 一遍—are considered to be different from those who came before, presenting teachings that were selective and easy to understand and practice, and that Buddhism spread among the common people and the warrior caste as never before. In contrast to the Buddhism of the state and the aristocrats, it was said, this new Buddhism offered salvation for the common people. This was called a "new Buddhism" that reformed the Buddhism of old. Today, however, this interpretation should be called "the theory on Kamakura new Buddhism" (*Kamakura shin-bukkyō ron* 鎌倉新仏教論), a theory that began among intellectuals of the Meiji period and the early scholars of modern historiography. As ŌSUMI Kazuo (1975) has pointed out, the theories of Hara Katsurō 原 勝郎 (the founder of the study of medieval history in Japan) compared the formation of new movements in the Kamakura period with the European Protestant reformation (see HARA 1929), and subsequent studies in this area were greatly influenced by this idea. The discussion of Kamakura new Buddhism in terms of a "religious reformation" was standard for most historians almost to the end of the twentieth century, and the history of medieval Japanese Buddhism was usually presented with the new Kamakura movements at the center of discussion.

This interpretation, however, is more and more perceived by Japanese historians as a theory of the past. KURODA Toshio proposed his theory of the "system of exoteric and esoteric [Buddhist power structures]" (*kenmitsu taisei ron* 顕密体制論) in 1975, and this theory has had a decisive influence on our view of medieval history, society, and religion (see the essay by Bodiford in this *Guide*). The most important point of Kuroda's theory is that the "new" Kamakura movements had not spread very much at all during the Kamakura period, and it was still the "old" Buddhism of the exoteric/esoteric schools (*kenmitsu bukkyō* 顕密仏教) that were the dominant influence on the state and society in general. Scholars of the later medieval and modern period have also proposed that the "new" Buddhist movements were not very influential during the Kamakura period but only began to spread and permeate society in the later medieval and early modern period. This "new Buddhism" began to permeate society and the common people along with the formation of the *ie* 家 as a dominant social unit around the fifteenth century, along with the development of "funerary Buddhism" (*sōshiki [sōsai] bukkyō* 葬式[葬祭]仏教). At the same time, studies of ancient Buddhism (as discussed above) have shown that Buddhism had already spread to a great extent in local areas and among the common people from ancient times. Thus it must be said that the "theory on Kamakura new Buddhism," as understood for many years, is no longer tenable.

If we were to summarize the findings of recent scholarship, it must be said that the two major times of epochal change for Japanese Buddhism occurred in the ninth century and in the fifteenth century. As explained above, the ninth century saw the development of sectarianism in Japanese Buddhism, and was the time in which the structure of the "eight schools system" was developed. It was also at this time that the system of regulations for official monks and religious ranks was established. Again, the incorporation of Buddhist rituals—such as the Gosai-e 御斎会, the Yuima-e 維摩会, and Saishō-e 最勝会— as state ceremonies was established at this time, and were managed and performed by the monks of the eight exoteric-esoteric schools. The amalgamation of kami and buddhas also began at around the middle of the eighth century, and permeated society in the Heian period. At first the idea of the kami wanting to escape their current state, and then the idea of the buddhas as the "basic ground" with the kami as their "phenomenal traces," were imported from China, and eventually evolved into the *honji-suijaku* theory, which functioned as a way to combine the kami with the buddhas and bodhisattvas of Buddhism. As a result, temples and shrines were established together, or next to each other, and functioned as a unit in providing religious services. Thus it was during the ninth century that the basic structure was created for religion in Japan, continuing through the Heian and Kamakura periods and up to the fifteenth century (see YOSHIDA 2003a).

BIBLIOGRAPHY

ABÉ Ryūichi, 1999. *The Weaving of Mantra: Kūkai and the Construction of Esoteric Buddhist Doctrine*. New York: Columbia University Press.

ANDŌ Toshio 安藤俊雄 and SONODA Kōyū 薗田香融, eds., 1974. Saichō 最澄. Nihon Shisō Taikei 日本思想大系 4. Tokyo: Iwanami Shoten.

ATARASHII KODAISHI NO KAI 新しい古代史の会, 1999. *Tōgoku sekibun no kodaishi* 東国石文の古代史. Tokyo: Yoshikawa Kōbunkan.

DOBBINS, James C., ed., 1996. *The Legacy of Kuroda Toshio*. Special issue, *Japanese Journal of Religious Studies* 23/3–4.

FUJIEDA Akira 藤枝 晃, 1975. *Kaisetsu: Shōmangyō gisho* 解説・勝鬘経義疏, *Shōtoku Taishi shū* 聖徳太子集, ed. Ienaga Saburō 家永三郎 et al., pp. 484–544. Nihon Shisō Taikei 2. Tokyo: Iwanami Shoten.

FUJII Kenkō 藤井顕孝, 1925. Kinmei-ki no Bukkyō denrai no kiji ni tsuite 欽明紀の仏教伝来の記事について. *Shigaku zasshi* 38/8: 71–74.

FUKUYAMA Toshio 福山敏男, 1968. *Nihon kenchiku-shi kenkyū* 日本建築史研究. Tokyo: Bokusui Shobō.

GIFU-KEN HAKUBUTSUKAN 岐阜県博物館, 1995. *Mino, Hida no kodaishi hakkutsu: Ritsuryō kokka no jidai* 美濃・飛騨の古代史発掘――律令国家の時代. Gifu: Gifu-ken Hakubutsukan.

GRONER, Paul, 1984. *Saichō: The Establishment of the Japanese Tendai School.* Berkeley Buddhist Studies Series 7. University of Hawai'i Press. (reprint 2000)

HARA Katsurō 原 勝郎, 1929. Tōzai no shūkyō kaikaku 東西の宗教改革. In *Nihon chūseishi no kenkyū* 日本中世史の研究, Hara Katsurō, pp. 304–21. Tokyo: Dōbunkan.

HAYAKAWA Shōhachi 早川庄八, 1986. Ritsuryōsei to tennō 律令制と天皇. In *Nihon kodai kanryōsei no kenkyū* 日本古代官僚制の研究, Hayakawa Shōhachi, pp. 1–31. Tokyo: Iwanami Shoten.

HORI Ichirō 堀 一郎, 1977. *Kodai bunka to Bukkyō* 古代文化と仏教. *Hori Ichirō chosakushū* 堀一郎著作集 1, ed. Kusunoki Masahiro 楠 正弘. Tokyo: Miraisha.

HORIIKE Shunpō 堀池春峰, 1980–1982. *Nanto Bukkyōshi no kenkyū* 南都仏教史の研究. 2 vols. Kyoto: Hōzōkan.

IENAGA Saburō 家永三郎, 1947. *Chūsei Bukkyō shisōshi kenkyū* 中世仏教思想史研究. Kyoto: Hōzōkan.

INOUE Kaoru 井上 薫, 1959. *Gyōki* 行基. Tokyo: Yoshikawa Kōbunkan.

_____, 1961. *Nihon kodai no seiji to shūkyō* 日本古代の政治と宗教. Tokyo: Yoshikawa Kōbunkan.

_____, 1966. *Nara-chō Bukkyōshi no kenkyū* 奈良朝仏教史の研究. Tokyo: Yoshikawa Kōbunkan.

INOUE Kaoru, ed., 1997. *Gyōki jiten* 行基事典. Tokyo: Kokusho Kankōkai.

INOUE Mitsusada 井上光貞, 1971. *Nihon kodai no kokka to Bukkyō* 日本古代の国家と仏教. Tokyo: Iwanami Shoten.

KATSUURA Noriko 勝浦令子, 1995. *Onna no shinjin: Tsuma ga shukke shita jidai* 女の信心――妻が出家した時代. Tokyo: Heibonsha.

_____, 2000. *Nihon kodai no sōni to shakai* 日本古代の僧尼と社会. Tokyo: Yoshikawa Kōbunkan.

KITA Sadakichi 喜田貞吉, 1980. Daigoji-bon *Shoji engishū* shoshū "Gangōji engi" ni tsuite 醍醐寺本『諸寺縁起集』所収「元興寺縁起」について. In *Kita Sadakichi chosakushū* 喜田貞吉著作集 6, *Nara jidai no jiin* 奈良時代の寺院, ed. Itō Nobuo 伊東信雄, pp. 90–126. Tokyo: Heibonsha.

KOKURITSU REKISHI MINZOKU HAKUBUTSUKAN 国立歴史民俗博物館, ed., 1997. *Kodai no ishibumi: Ishi ni kizamareta messēji* 古代の碑――石に刻まれたメッセージ. Chiba: Kokuritsu Rekishi Minzoku Hakubutsukan.

KUME Kunitake 久米邦武, 1988. *Shōtoku Taishi no kenkyū* 聖徳太子の研究. *Kume Kunitake Rekishi chosakushū* 久米邦武歴史著作集 1. Tokyo: Yoshikawa Kōbunkan.

KURODA Toshio 黒田俊雄, 1975. *Nihon chūsei no kokka to shūkyō* 日本中世の国家と宗教. Tokyo: Iwanami Shoten.

_____, 1990. *Nihon chūsei no shakai to shūkyō* 日本中世の社会と宗教. Tokyo: Iwanami Shoten.

_____, 1994. *Kenmitsu taiseiron* 顕密体制論. *Kuroda Toshio chosakushū* 黒田俊雄著作集 2. Kyoto: Hōzōkan.

_____, 1995. *Shinkoku shisō to senju nenbutsu* 神国思想と専修念仏. *Kuroda Toshio chosakushū* 4. Kyoto: Hōzōkan.

Mōri Hisashi 毛利 久, ed., 1985. *Zōzō meiki shūsei* 造像銘記集成. Tokyo: Tōkyōdō Shuppan.

Nagoya-shi Hakubutsukan 名古屋市博物館, ed., 1994. *Hakkutsu sareta Tōkai no kodai: Ritsuryō seika no kuniguni* 発掘された東海の古代——律令制下の国々. Nagoya: Nagoya-shi Hakubutsukan.

Nakamura, Kyoko Motomochi, tr., 1973. *Miraculous Stories from the Japanese Buddhist Tradition: The Nihon ryōiki of the Monk Kyōkai.* Cambridge: Harvard University Press.

Nara Kokuritsu Hakubutsukan 奈良国立博物館, ed., 1983. *Nara-chō shakyō* 奈良朝写経. Tokyo: Tōkyō Bijutsu.

Nishiguchi Junko 西口順子, 1987. *Onna no chikara: Kodai no josei to Bukkyō* 女の力——古代女性と仏教. Tokyo: Heibonsha.

Noguchi Tetsurō 野口鐵郎, ed., 1996. *Dōkyō no denpa to kodai kokka* 道教の伝播と古代国家. Senshū: Dōkyō to Nihonjin 選集——道教と日本人 1. Tokyo: Yūzankaku.

_____, 1997. *Kodai bunka no tenkai to dōkyō* 古代文化の展開と道教. Senshū: Dōkyō to Nihonjin 選集——道教と日本人 2, Tokyo: Yūzankaku.

Okada Shōji 岡田莊司, 1994. *Heian jidai no kokka to saishi* 平安時代の国家と祭祀. Tokyo: Zoku Gunsho Ruijū Kanseikai.

Ōsumi Kazuo 大隅和雄, 1975. *Kamakura Bukkyō to sono kakushin undō* 鎌倉仏教とその革新運動. Iwanami Kōza Nihon Rekishi 岩波講座日本歴史 5, pp. 211–49. Tokyo: Iwanami Shoten.

Ōyama Seiichi 大山誠一, 1998. *Nagaya ōke mokkan to kinsekibun* 長屋王家木簡と金石文. Tokyo: Yoshikawa Kōbunkan.

_____, 1999. *"Shōtoku Taishi" no tanjō* ＜聖徳太子＞の誕生. Tokyo: Yoshikawa Kōbunkan.

Ōyama Seiichi, ed., 2003. *Shōtoku Taishi no shinjitsu* 聖徳太子の真実. Tokyo: Heibonsha.

Rittō Rekishi Minzoku Hakubutsukan 栗東歴史民俗博物館, 1991. *Konan no kodai jiin: Kurita-gun no Hakuhō ji'in o chūshin ni* 湖南の古代寺院——栗太郡の白鳳寺院を中心に. Rittō: Rittō Rekishi Minzoku Hakubutsukan.

Ruch, Barbara, ed., 2002. *Engendering Faith: Women and Buddhism in Premodern Japan.* Ann Arbor: Center for Japanese Studies, University of Michigan.

Saeki Arikiyo 佐伯有清, 1992. *Dengyō Daishi den no kenkyū* 伝教大師伝の研究. Tokyo: Yoshikawa Kōbunkan.

Sakuma Ryū 佐久間竜, 1983. *Nihon kodai sōden no kenkyū* 日本古代僧伝の研究. Tokyo: Yoshikawa Kōbunkan.

Shinkawa Tokio 新川登亀男, 1999. *Dōkyō o meguru kōbō: Nihon no kunshu, dōshi no hō o agamezu* 道教をめぐる攻防——日本の君主・道士の法を崇めず. Tokyo: Daishūkan Shoten.

Sone Masato 曽根正人, 2000. *Kodai Bukkyōkai to ōchō shakai* 古代仏教界と王朝社会. Tokyo: Yoshikawa Kōbunkan.

Sonoda Kōyū 薗田香融, 1981. *Heian Bukkyō no kenkyū* 平安仏教の研究. Kyoto: Hōzōkan.

Suzuki Keiji 鈴木景二, 1994. Tohikan kōtsū to zaichi chitsujo: Nara-Heian shoki no Bukkyō o sozai toshite 都鄙間交通と在地秩序——奈良平安初期の仏教を素材として. *Nihon-shi kenkyu* 379: 34–59.

Takagi Shingen 高木訷元, 1997. *Kūkai: Shōgai to sono shūhen* 空海——生涯とその周辺. Tokyo: Yoshikawa Kōbunkan.

TAKAGI Yutaka 高木 豊, 1988. *Bukkyōshi no naka no nyonin* 仏教史のなかの女人. Tokyo: Heibonsha.

TAKATORI Masao 高取正男, 1979. *Shintō no seiritsu* 神道の成立. Tokyo: Heibonsha.

TAMAMURO Taijō 圭室諦成, 1940. *Nihon Bukkyōshi gaisetsu* 日本仏教史概説. Tokyo: Risōsha.

TAMURA Enchō 田村圓澄, 1982. *Kokka Bukkyō no seiritsu katei* 国家仏教の成立過程. In *Nihon Bukkyōshi* 日本仏教史 1, ed. Tamura Enchō, pp. 208–26. Kyoto: Hōzōkan.

TANAKA Kaidō 田中塊堂, ed., 1973. *Nihon koshakyō genzon mokuroku* 日本古写経現存目録. Kyoto: Shibunkan.

———, 1974. *Nihon shakyō sōkan* 日本写経綜鑑. Kyoto: Shibunkan.

TEEUWEN, Mark, and Bernhard SCHEID. 2002. Tracing Shinto in the History of Kami Worship: Editors' Introduction. *Japanese Journal of Religious Studies* 29: 196–207.

TSUBOI Kiyotari 坪井清足, 1985. *Asuka no tera to kokubunji* 飛鳥の寺と国分寺. In *Kodai Nihon o hakkutsu suru* 古代日本を発掘する 2. Tokyo: Iwanami Shoten.

TSUDA Sōkichi 津田左右吉, 1950. *Nihon koten no kenkyū* 日本古典の研究. Tokyo: Iwanami Shoten.

———, 1964. *Nihon no shintō* 日本の神道. *Tsuda Sōkichi chosakushū* 津田左右吉著作集 9. Tokyo: Iwanami Shoten.

TSUJI Zennosuke 辻善之助, 1983. *Nihon Bukkyōshi kenkyū* 日本仏教史研究, vol. 1. Tokyo: Iwanami Shoten. (reprint; first published in 1907)

TSUNODA Bun'ei 角田文衞, 1986–1997. *Shinshū kokubunji no kenkyū* 新修国分寺の研究. 7 vols. Tokyo: Yoshikawa Kōbunkan.

USHIYAMA Yoshiyuki 牛山佳幸, 1990. *Kodai chūsei jiin soshiki no kenkyū* 古代中世寺院組織の研究. Tokyo: Yoshikawa Kōbunkan.

YAMAMOTO Kōji 山本幸司, 1992. *Kegare to ōbarae* 穢と大祓. Tokyo: Heibonsha.

YAMASHITA Yumi 山下有美, 1999. *Shōsōin monjo to shakyōsho no kenkyū* 正倉院文書と写経所の研究. Tokyo: Yoshikawa Kōbunkan.

YOSHIDA Kazuhiko 吉田一彦, 1995. *Nihon kodai shakai to Bukkyō* 日本古代社会と仏教. Tokyo: Yoshikawa Kōbunkan.

———, 1996. Tado Jingūji to shinbutsu shūgō 多度神宮寺と神仏習合. In *Ise-wan to kodai no Tōkai* 伊勢湾と古代の東海, ed. Umemura Takashi 梅村 喬, pp. 217–57. Tokyo: Meicho Shuppan.

———, 2001. Gangōji engi" o meguru shomondai 『元興寺縁起』をめぐる諸問題. *Kodai* 110: 267–88.

———, 2002. Nihon shoki to Dōji 日本書記と道慈. In *Shōtoku Taishi no jitsuzō to genzō* 聖徳太子の実像と幻像, ed. Umehara Takeshi 梅原 猛 et al., pp. 167–86. Tokyo: Daiwa Shobō.

———, 2003a. Nihon Bukkyōshi no jiki kubun 日本仏教史の時期区分. In *Bunkashi no kōsō* 文化史の構想, ed. Ōsumi Kazuo, pp. 20–57. Tokyo: Yoshikawa Kōbunkan.

———, 2003b. Revisioning Religion in Ancient Japan. *Japanese Journal of Religious Studies* 30: 1–26.

YOSHIDA Kazuhiko, KATSUURA Noriko 勝浦令子, and NISHIGUCHI Junko 西口順子, eds., 1999. *Nihonshi no naka no josei to Bukkyō* 日本史の中の女性と仏教. Kyoto: Hōzōkan.

[Translated by Paul L. Swanson]

William M. Bodiford

The Medieval Period

Eleventh to Sixteenth Centuries

The term "medieval" generally refers to the period between "classical" and "early modern." The precise chronological dates that can be assigned to each of these periods depend on the nature of the phenomena under consideration so that scholars in different fields (such as history, art history, literature, etc.) frequently adopt different periodization schemes. Scholars of religion have not attempted to reach agreement on the dates of the medieval period or its distinguishing characteristics. The label "medieval" has been applied to phenomena dating from as early as the eleventh century, which some Japanese of that time had identified as the beginning of the age of the decline of the Dharma (*mappō* 末法), to as late as the seventeenth century, when independent Confucian academies were beginning to appear and just before reform-minded Buddhist monks (e.g., Manzan Dōhaku 卍山道白, 1636–1714; Reikū

Kōken 靈空光謙, 1652–1739; etc.) introduced new standards for doctrinal orthodoxy based on sectarian distinctions, reliance of published texts, and evidentiary learning.

This long span of time witnessed many radical transformations in all (not just religious) aspects of life in Japan. Sociologically, villagers and local landowners in rural areas developed greater wealth and importance as new agricultural technologies and intensive investments of labor enabled the cultivation of previously unproductive land. Politically, the eastern regions (Kantō 關東 and beyond) gained power as the royal court, warrior bands, and religious establishments competed to claim the economic fruits of its development. This competition resulted in successive political transformations, beginning with the formation of Japan's first warrior administration in Kamakura 鎌倉 in 1185 (identified by recent historians as the start of "late classical"), the failed struggle by Go-Daigo 後醍醐 (1288–1339) to abolish warrior rule beginning in 1333, and the founding of the powerful Ashikaga warrior government in 1336 (now identified by them as the start of "medieval"), the Ōnin 應仁 War of 1466 (which marked the rise of regional domains ruled by semi-autonomous war lords), and the re-imposition of centralized administration by the Tokugawa 德川 warrior government in 1603 (identified as the start of "early modern"). Literate culture witnessed the development of native traditions of theater (*sarugaku* 申樂 or *nōgaku* 能樂) as well as many new genres of literature (war tales, legendary accounts of cultic centers, illustrated hagiographies, linked verse, etc.). Internationally, this period witnessed the growth of overseas trade, the importation of Chinese Song-dynasty 宋 (960–1279) thought and technology (including printing, books, arts, architecture, Buddhist monks, and coins), two failed attempts (in 1274 and 1281) at military invasion by troops of the Chinese Yuan 元 dynasty (1206–1368), the arrival of European Christian missionaries in 1549 and their forced expulsion within a century, as well as military campaigns by Japanese armies to conquer Korea in 1592 and 1597.

Religion figured prominently in all of these developments. Increased rural wealth supported the construction of new regional religious institutions that cemented local societies together, linked them to centers of culture, and displayed their new identities. New warrior administrations competed culturally with the established royal court by donating lands to religious institutions formerly associated exclusively with the central authority (Ise 伊勢, Mt. Hiei 比叡山, etc.) and by sponsoring temple construction for new religious movements (Pure Land, Zen 禪, and Lotus). Theatrical performances, story telling, and recitation of verse and legends accompanied all important religious festivals as members of the religious community ritually invoked the presence of buddhas and gods, and used popular entertainment to reveal their workings in the world of humans. Renewed contacts with Song and Yuan China did more than just foster the growth of the new exclusive Zen movement. The importation of printing technology allowed temples in Kamakura and Nara 奈良 to print their own editions of imported Chinese texts, especially Chinese poetry, Zen (Chan) literature, as well as Confucian and Buddhist scriptures. In addition to Zen, these developments also exerted profound influence on other flavors of Japanese Buddhism (such as Pure Land, Vinaya, and Kegon 華嚴), and provided bases for the development of Confucianism and for new non-Buddhist cosmologies (such as those taught within Watarai 度會 and Yoshida 吉田 Shinto 神道 lineages). Military invasions by Yuan troops, though defeated, focused renewed attention on the relationship between the political realm and divine power as governing elites sought military aid from local buddhas and gods. The arrival and expulsion of Christian missionaries radically altered the social and political roles of Buddhist temples, first as the war lord Oda Nobunaga 織田信長 (1534–1582) sought to enlist Christianity in his campaign to eliminate the military power of Buddhist temples, and later as subsequent leaders enlisted Buddhist temples in their efforts to eliminate Christianity. In short, during this period religion imbued every facet of Japanese life.

Both existing and new religious organizations underwent transformations just as diverse and vast in scope. The Buddhist monasteries of central Japan attained their greatest prosperity and, at the hands of Oda Nobunaga, suffered their greatest devastation. Throughout the centuries prior to Oda, the monasteries functioned as miniature states within a state, with their own politics, privileged classes of clerics who ruled over less-privileged ones, vast land holdings, peasants and craftsmen, commercial enterprises, and militias. The militias protected monastic lands, protested government interference, and attacked rival institutions. These institutional rivalries existed not just between monasteries (Mt. Hiei versus Kōfukuji 興福寺, or Mt. Hiei versus Onjōji 園城寺), but also within them. Inside Kōfukuji, for example, Ichijōin 一乗院 competed against Daijōin 大乗院. Mt. Hiei, with its subdivisions of three pagodas and sixteen valleys (santō jūrokukoku 三塔十六谷), had the most complex internecine conflicts: the scholars (gakushō 學生) fought against the ritualists (dōshu 堂衆), Yokawa 横川 competed against Saitō 西塔, and Tōdō 東塔 was divided into its Mudōji 無動寺 valley versus its southern valley. All of these institutions, along with others such as the two shrines of Ise, competed against one another to acquire additional lands in Eastern Japan, on which they established branch temples and sub-shrines to collect offerings (i.e., taxes).

Needless to say, nothing approximating a unified Buddhism (or Buddhist church) existed. It is equally misleading to imagine a set number of Buddhist schools or denominations such as the ones that exist today. Individual clergy owed allegiance not to some larger sectarian organizations, but to the particular temple communities with whom they lived, and to the teaching lineages into which they had been initiated. These two structures (temples and lineages) could overlap in bewildering complexity. The Tendai monk Kōshū 光宗 (1276–1350), for example, received initiations from more than eighty-five different teachers on Mt. Hiei from whom he learned more than fifteen separate subjects, spanning the entire range of Buddhist and secular learning (see his Keiran shūyōshū 溪嵐拾葉集). Doctrines and practices that should be rejected according to the teachings of one lineage could be defended according to the teachings of another lineage, and monks frequently would study the teachings of both sides. Debate was more common than consensus.

Aristocrats, beginning with the sovereign (tennō 天皇, "emperor") and other members of the royal family, shrine celebrants (negi 禰宜), high-ranking warriors, and other people of status routinely entered Buddhist orders when their secular careers ended. Acceptance or rejection by members of these eminent households constituted the nearest equivalent to designations of orthodoxy or heterodoxy. Teachings and teachers once rejected, however, frequently could find protection from a rival patron, as happened to the Tendai monk Eisai (Yōsai) 榮西 (1141–1215). In 1194 the court in Kyoto banned Eisai's exclusive Zen, but within a decade he was constructing his own monastery in Kyoto under the protection of the new warrior administration in Kamakura. For these reasons, both doctrinally and institutionally the religious scene became ever more diverse. It is impossible to reduce this doctrinal and institutional diversity to a few general characteristics or trends.

MAIN DEVELOPMENTS

Within this complexity, three sets of developments have received the most attention from previous scholars of religion: 1) an awakening of historical self-consciousness; 2) the maturation of previously established Buddhist organizations; and 3) the appearance of new religious organizations.

Historical Self-consciousness

Renewed contact with the continent seems to have awakened in medieval Japanese a self-consciousness of the distinctiveness of their own historical circumstances. Pre-1945 scholars identified this self-consciousness with a burgeoning nationalism because some medieval texts seem to assert that Japan is a "divine land" (*shinkoku* 神國). Both the interpretation of this term and its purported link to nationalism, however, now are regarded as being very problematic (RAMBELLI 1996).

Nonetheless, it is true that for the first time numerous hagiographies, lineage histories, and religious gazetteers were written to locate Japanese traditions vis-à-vis China and India. Collected hagiographies like *Nihon kōsō den yōmonshō* 日本高僧傳要文抄 (3 fascicles; ca. 1251) and *Nihon kōsō den shijishō* 日本高僧傳指示抄 (1 fasc.; ca. 1251) along with lineage histories like *Sangoku dentōki* 三國傳燈記 (originally 3 fasc.; 1173), *Sangoku buppō denzū engi* 三國佛法傳通緣起 (3 fasc.; 1311; see BLUM 2002), *Shōmyō genruki* 聲明源流記, (1 fasc.), *Jōdo hōmon genrushō* 淨土法門源流章 (1 fasc.; 1311)—the last three all by the Tōdaiji 東大寺 monk Gyōnen 凝然 (1240–1321)—*Shingon den* 眞言傳 (7 fasc.; ca. 1325), and *Kegon soshi eden* 華嚴祖師繪傳 (6 fasc.; ca. 13th or 14th cent.) present a narrative of doctrinal orthodoxy resting on the transmission of lineages from India to China to Japan. Gazetteers like *Sangoku meishō ryakki* 三國名匠略記 (1 fasc.; 1275) and the aforementioned *Keiran shūyōshū* (originally 300 fasc.; 1348) ground this orthodoxy in concrete historical precedents (*kojitsu* 故實).

The most important historical work of this period is *Genkō shakusho* 元亨釋書 (30 fasc.; 1322) by the Tōfukuji 東福寺 Zen monk Kokan Shiren 虎關師鍊 (1278–1346). *Genkō shakusho* emulates the format of Chinese dynastic histories (hence the word *sho* 書, Chinese *shu*, in its title) by combining biographies (*den* 傳), chronological history (*hyō* 表), and gazetteers (*shi* 志) to produce the first comprehensive account of religion in Japan. To a large degree the above texts still shape the way that Japanese view their Buddhist past.

Maturation of Established Buddhism

Established Buddhism refers both to doctrinal practices and to the institutions (monasteries, temples, shrines, chapels, etc.) where initiates in those practices lived. During the medieval period many ritual practices, doctrinal interpretations, and institutional relationships assumed the format that they would retain until the middle of the nineteenth century, if not longer. The importation of new Chinese scriptures fostered a flourishing of doctrinal studies—especially among the previously established Hossō 法相, Sanron 三論, Kegon, Tendai, and Shingon 眞言 lineages. Together these lineages (along with Mahāyāna precept lineages) constituted what Buddhists of that time frequently referred to as the exoteric-esoteric teachings and practices (*kenmitsu hōmon* 顯密法門). During the medieval period, texts associated with these lineages shared certain characteristics.

First, the one vehicle (*ichijō* 一乘) doctrine (universal salvation and universal buddha nature) came to be affirmed within all of these lineages, including the Hossō and Sanron which traditionally had rejected it. Second, all of these lineages likewise affirmed the supremacy of esoteric tantric ritual practices with their promises of immediate benefits in this world (*genze riyaku* 現世利益) and of the embodiment of buddhahood in this lifetime (*sokushin jōbutsu* 即身成佛). Third, texts associated with these lineages generally tend to affirm a vertical cosmology consisting, from top to bottom, of timeless cosmic buddhas (the tathāgatas depicted in Mahāyāna scriptures) who provide the vehicle of salvation, the god Brahmā (Bonten 梵天) who rules our world system, the god Śakra (Taishaku 帝釋; Indra) who promotes Buddhism among humans, the four heavenly kings (*shitennō* 四天王, gods of the four directions) who protect Buddhist kingdoms, the minor gods who control the fates of men, the gods of Japan's ruling houses, local buddhas (enshrined in local temples) who grant blessings, and local gods (likewise enshrined in the local Buddhist temples or in their neighboring shrines) who protect the property of the local buddhas and who punish wrongdoers. Knowledge concerning each lineage's history, its doctrines, its esoteric rituals, its buddhas, and its gods tended to be organized according to the same systems of associations also used to describe the layout of maṇḍala (see below), and these associations usually were explained via secret oral initiations (*kuden* 口傳).

During this same period, the religious institutions of central Japan gradually developed networks of branch temples and shrines in rural areas, especially Eastern Japan. These branch temples and shrines served to legitimate control over plots of land (and over the peasants who worked those plots) that had been donated to the central institutions. The Tendai monasteries of Mt. Hiei and Onjōji outside of Kyoto, the Shingon monasteries on Mt. Kōya 高野山, the Kōfukuji and Tōdaiji monasteries in Nara, as well as the two shrines in Ise were especially active in recruiting donations of land, but they also competed with countless lesser institutions. Regardless of institutional affiliation, the local buddhas and gods (enshrined in the branch temples and shrines) threatened divine retribution for anyone who transgressed the land, accepted the fruits of the land as offerings, and promised blessings to local patrons. The people in most of these localities never before had access to a properly constituted temple or shrine. The acquisition of rural estates by central religious institutions, therefore, occasioned the popularization of organized religion among ordinary people in the countryside.

After the Ōnin War many of these branch temples were taken over by groups affiliated with the new religious organizations described below. Even after conversions to different doctrinal lineages, the local temples frequently continued to provide their local patrons with the same types of ritual services as they had under their previous affiliation. In some cases, rural patrons supported multiple institutions, each one with a specialized role: an esoteric temple for military power, a Pure Land (Jōdo 淨土) temple for the salvation of people killed in warfare, an Ise-type shrine (*kandachi* 峙 or *shinmeisha* 神明社) for bountiful harvests, a Confucian temple (*seidō* 聖堂) to teach loyalty, and a Zen temple for funerals and ancestor memorial rites (BODIFORD 1993, pp. 124–25). Even in these cases, though, only rarely were explicit relationships between sectarian affiliation and ritual functions specified.

New Religious Organizations

While the above six lineages (Hossō, Sanron, Kegon, Tendai, Shingon, Mahāyāna precept) and their sub-branches constituted the mainstream of Buddhist learning down to the time of the Ōnin War, by no means did they represent the full range of organized medieval religion. Today most textbooks identify this period primarily with the emergence and establishment of new categories of lineages, of which six were most prominent: Pure Land, Zen, Vinaya (Ritsu 律), Lotus (Hokke 法華), Shinto, and Shugendō 修驗道. All of these lineages developed in close relationship to, and sometimes in tension against, the previously established forms of Buddhism. Although scholars frequently write about them as if each one were a unified organization or movement, each category actually encompasses distinct entities. There was no Pure Land School, no Zen School, no Vinaya School, no Lotus School. The major groups (ignoring numerous subdivisions) within each category can be summarized as follows.

The exclusive (*senshu* 專修) Pure Land movement began with Hōnen 法然 (Genkū 源空; 1133–1212) and his numerous disciples, three of whose lineages attracted the most adherents: the Chinzei 鎮西 lineage of Benchō 辨長 (1162–1238), the Seizan 西山 lineage of Shōkū 證空 (1177–1247), and the so-called Ikkō 一向 (or, more properly, Shinshū 眞宗) lineage of Shinran 親鸞 (1173–1263). The most widespread Pure Land group during the fourteenth and early fifteenth centuries, though, probably was the Jishū 時宗—a completely unrelated lineage deriving from Ippen 一遍 (Chishin 智眞; 1239–1289)—but it declined after the Ōnin War.

Zen is traditionally said to consist of twenty-four separate lineages introduced from China during the medieval period. These individual lineages can be conveniently divided into two main groups: those affiliated with the Five Mountain (*gozan* 五山) system of temples (which were dominant prior to the Ōnin War) and those not (i.e., the so-called rural, *rinka* 林下, lineages which became dominant after the Ōnin War). Note that the distinction between Sōtō 曹洞 and Rinzai 臨濟, the two main Zen denominations of modern Japan, was not yet significant. Both the Five Mountain and the Rinka temples included lineages affiliated with Sōtō and with Rinzai factions.

Two distinct Vinaya lineages were established, one by Shunjō 俊芿 (1166–1227) who founded Sennyūji 泉涌寺 temple in Kyoto, and another by Eison 叡尊 (1201–1290) who founded Saidaiji 西大寺 temple near Nara. The exclusive Lotus movement began with Nichiren 日蓮 (1222–1282) and eventually coalesced into five separate lineages associated with his disciples Nisshō 日昭 (1221–1323), Nichirō 日朗 (1245–1320), Nikkō 日興 (1246–1333), Nikō 日向 (1253–1314), and Nichijō 日常 (1216–1299). Two distinct Shinto lineages appeared. First, Watarai Yukitada 度會行忠 (1236–1305) and Watarai Ieyuki 家行 (1256–1362) compiled oracles, gazetteers, and precedents to justify use of the "imperial" (*kōtai* 皇太) title by the Watarai Shrine at Ise. About two hundred years later, Yoshida Kanetomo 吉田兼倶 (1435–1511) formulated Yuiitsu 唯一 Shinto teachings.

Medieval Shugendō lacked any distinctive organizational structure, and its practitioners were for most purposes indistinguishable from other lower-level members of Tendai, Shingon, Hossō, Zen, or Jishū lineages with which they were affiliated. This unity can still be seen today at Mt. Hiei where Tendai training includes one traditional form of Shugendō, called mountain circumambulation (*kaihōgyō* 回峰行). As powerful temples in remote areas (first at Ise, Kumano 熊野, Katsuragi 葛城, Kinpusen 金峰山, and later at Haguro 羽黒, Hakusan 白山, Hiko 英彦, Ishizuchi 石鎚, etc.) acquired ever more distant land holdings, the people (typically low-ranking priests and land managers) who traveled between those lands and the temples founded trails through the mountains. Shugendō organizations appeared when the branch temples along many of these routes formed associations of guides (called *sendatsu* 先達 or *ajari* 阿闍梨) to lead pilgrims, a trend that accelerated after the Ōnin War when temples lost most of their distant land holdings. During the 1480s the Tendai monk Dōkō 道興 (1465–1501), in particular, worked to affiliate organizations of guides from across Japan with Kumano and place them under the protection of Shōgoin 聖護院, a royal (*monzeki* 門跡) Tendai temple in Kyoto, to form the Honzanha 本山派 branch. By this time many organizations of guides in the central Kinki 近畿 region already had become affiliated with Ichijōin, a royal Hossō temple within Kōfukuji, to form the Tōzanha 當山派 branch. In 1613 the Tokugawa warrior administration officially recognized Shōgoin as the head temple of the Honzanha, appointed Sanbōin 三寶院 (a royal Shingon temple in Kyoto) as the head temple of the Tōzanha, and ordered all minor Shugendō groups to become affiliated with one or the other. At the same time, they placed Kinpusen and Haguro under the control of Rinnōji 輪王寺, a royal Tendai temple administered directly from the Tokugawa capital city of Edo 江戸 (modern Tokyo), and allowed certain other Shugendō groups (such as those at Mt. Hiko) to remain independent.

INTERPRETIVE ISSUES

No consensus exists regarding how to study the aforementioned religious developments. Speaking generally, academic works by Japanese scholars reveal more about the trees than the forest. Specialists in Buddhism have focused on hagiography and narrow textual or doctrinal issues associated with the emergence and development of the aforementioned sectarian lineages. Their scholarship ignores the shared religious landscape of beliefs and practices unrelated to sectarian affiliations. Specialists in intellectual history have focused on features they identify as modern in the teachings of Shinran, Nichiren, and the Zen monk Dōgen 道元 (1200–1253), but have ignored their medieval context. Specialists in Shinto, trying to avoid anything related to Buddhism (which formed the heart of medieval Shinto), have examined only a very narrow range of rather unrepresentative texts. Social historians, beginning with the late Kuroda Toshio 黒田俊雄 (1926–1993), have begun to explore the economic, political, geographic, and military power of mainstream

Buddhist monastic institutions (see below). In spite of the accomplishments of Kuroda and his successors, very little has been revealed regarding how those monasteries functioned as institutional settings for religious life and learning. By default, the task of explaining medieval religious beliefs and practices has largely fallen to scholars of literature and art history. Every work of literature or piece of art they describe is embedded within a densely rich religious context that demands explanation. With only a few exceptions, however, in their publications this religious context rarely receives sustained description and analysis. In short, the field of medieval Japanese religion is wide open. A comprehensive study (along the lines proposed by Ronald M. DAVIDSON's 2002 social history of esoteric Buddhism in India) has yet to be attempted.

For all forms of scholarship the most important development of this period was the spread of literacy. Each subsequent decade produced increasing numbers of surviving written sources that can be used to document religious life beyond the confines of the urban elites. Many religious ideas and practices are mentioned in writing for the first time during this period. Without earlier records for comparison, however, frequently no decisive evidence dictates whether these early mentions should be interpreted as accounts of existing traditions that survived from earlier ages or as signs of new developments. Fabricated accounts, backdated documents, and false attribution of authorship to earlier generations frequently add to our chronological confusion. Even when accurate dates and authorship can be ascertained, one must guard against the tendency to automatically interpret earlier texts in accordance with the sectarian commentaries (and dogmas) from subsequent periods. Faced with these difficulties, it is only natural (though no less regrettable) that anachronisms abound in the existing scholarship. For this reason, assertions about the origins, transformations, implications, or prevalence of beliefs, customs, and institutional interests must be entertained with extreme caution.

Although rarely noted by scholars, the spread of literacy produced a proportionate spread of illiteracy or semi-literacy. In other words, increasing numbers of surviving texts contain illogical or ungrammatical Chinese, Japanese, or a mixture of the two. Grammatical violations were not necessarily mistakes. Sometimes they were deliberate strategies for revealing the esoteric truth hidden behind the literal meaning of the text. Important medieval religious figures, such as Hōnen, Shinran, Dōgen, and Nichiren, all have been celebrated (and attacked) for their "innovative" (i.e., wrong) readings of Chinese Buddhist scriptures. Nonetheless, there exist only a few studies of their individual linguistic particularities, and not a single comprehensive guide to the specialized varieties of language used in medieval religious texts. In many cases we cannot know with certainty if the ways that modern scholars punctuate sentences, pronounce vocabulary, or render Chinese passages into Japanese word order resemble how these acts were done prior to the seventeenth century. Hand-copied manuscripts frequently contain marginalia, rarely reproduced in published editions, that can provide important clues. The standard published editions of most medieval religious texts, moreover, are based on late (18th- and 19th-cent.) woodblock editions that suffered extensive "correcting" at the hands of their more literate editors. Therefore, scholars and translators always should work from holographs or their facsimiles when possible.

HISTORY

We know the least, probably, about those aspects of religious life that mattered the most to the people of medieval Japan: their ceremonies. They devoted prodigious recourses (of labor, time, and produce) to ceremonies that publicly displayed and thereby confirmed social status, familial obligations, geographical alliances, economic prerogatives, and political authority. Religious ceremonies not only imbued events with meaning, but also provided entertainment. Costumes, decorations, parades, dance, music, poetry, theater, sports, bonfires, and feasts linked cultic practices to all modes of cultural production. They reconfigured physical space, transformed geographic landforms, required new architectural structures, and filled the air with sounds. These ceremonies and their diffusion, both socially (from high court aristocrats down to military rulers, land-owning military governors, regional landowners, villagers) and geographically (from main monasteries, to regional temples, to village temples), and their adaptation to local social conditions demands much more scrutiny than they heretofore have received. They draw our attention to the heart of Japanese religious life, namely, village, professional, and family relationships.

Another major weakness of current scholarship results from the teleological tendency to interpret earlier data in terms of subsequent developments. As outlying regions generated economies of surplus wealth they began to support their own religious specialists who could supervise and develop local ceremonial traditions. Eventually (or retrospectively) many of these new regional developments became identified with narrowly defined religious traditions (the previously established Buddhist lineages or new organizations). Nonetheless, we must be alert to the possibility that such identifications originally were less rigid than they later became. Comparative reading of medieval texts now associated with separate lineage traditions reveals many similarities (shared vocabulary, rites, and initiations), suggesting that each of these narrow traditions functioned within a shared religious milieu. Within this larger milieu participation in multiple religious roles—such as performing in esoteric (established) Buddhist rituals, acting as celebrants at a shrine to a local (Shinto) god, practicing asceticism in mountains (Shugendō), chanting or sitting in meditation at a Zen (new lineage) chapel—produced no incongruity. The practitioners themselves might have been oblivious to the sectarian labels imposed by subsequent scholarship. Or, their sectarian sensibilities might have reconciled ritual differences within an exclusive vision of religious truth. Either way, competing doctrinal systems appropriated similar forms of ceremonial practices. The same ritual sites accommodated people devoted to different buddhas or gods. This flexibility allowed religious institutions to mediate between the conflicting demands of different patrons and audiences. Scholarship that too quickly identifies people, ceremonies, or institutions exclusively with one religious identity or another risks overlooking the rich intertextuality, multiplicity of religious referents, and fluidity of identities that constitute one of the prominent features of medieval culture.

Likewise, the appearance of Shinto lineages did not yet constitute the full emergence of an autonomous Shinto religion independent from Buddhism. Despite the fact that most of our current books, articles, and reference works anachronistically draw, or use language that implies, a clear distinction between Buddhism and Shinto, in reality that kind of obvious separation did not exist prior to 1868. Many authors (including me) commonly use the word "shrine" to imply a structure for worshiping gods (i.e., Shinto) and use the words "temple" or "monastery" to imply a structure for performing Buddhist rituals. This usage does not accord with the reality of medieval Japan. Shrines were used for worshiping both buddhas and gods. Temples and monasteries enshrined both buddhas and gods. The main social distinction was that the position of shrine celebrant (*negi*) could be hereditary, whereas the position of Buddhist monk (in theory at least) could not. (In reality, the abbotship at many temples, especially royal ones, was reserved for the children of their main patrons.) The main religious distinction was that rituals for gods, while important for a wide variety of immediate (familial, geographic, economic, agricultural, political, etc.) purposes, generally did not address the ultimate soteriological vehicle of the buddhas. Despite these minor differences, buddhas and gods inhabited the same cosmological space and revealed the same religious teachings.

Scholars are not in agreement as to how far back in time one can detect signs of tension or antagonism that might have prefigured the emergence of an independent Shinto. During the thirteenth and fourteenth centuries, at least, members of the Watarai family (and of the Arakida 荒木田 family, the hereditary celebrants of the other shrine at Ise) were devout Buddhists who supported many Buddhist temples (*bodaiji* 菩提寺). Like celebrants at other independent shrines, aside from performing their shrine rituals they also worshiped buddhas, copied Buddhist scriptures, swore Buddhist vows, and received Buddhist funerals. Tokugawa-period (1603–1868) Confucians interpreted certain phrases (such as *hei buppō soku* 屏佛法息) in medieval Watarai texts as expressions of anti-Buddhist sentiments. Those interpretations, however, are no longer accepted. Even if such sentiments had existed, the destruction of the Watarai Shrine by warfare in 1486 and the long seventy-year period before it could be rebuilt severely limited any influence Watarai family teachings might have exerted during the medieval period. Many scholars also question whether or not the epistemological framework of medieval Japan could have admitted a non-Buddhist cosmology. Even the Yuiitsu Shinto teachings of Yoshida Kanetomo, which self-consciously distinguished themselves from Buddhism, exhibit many structural parallels with Buddhism. Just like the mainstream Buddhism of that time, they consisted of both exoteric (*kenro* 顯露) and esoteric (*on'yū* 隠幽) doctrines, and they included as one of their most important rituals the Buddhist fire invocation (*goma* 護摩; Sanskrit *homa*). This Buddhist cosmological framework was not fully rejected until the Tokugawa period when Watarai and Yoshida texts were reinterpreted by Confucian scholars.

The 1868 government-mandated separation of buddhas and gods helped create not just a false image of Shinto as inherently different from Buddhism, but also an equally false representation of a Buddhism without gods. Nothing could be further from the truth. Gods play prominent roles in Buddhist scriptures and they have been worshiped by Buddhists in all parts of Asia. Japan was no exception. Almost all medieval Japanese Buddhist lineages (with the noteworthy exception of those deriving from Hōnen) taught initiations regarding Buddhist rituals for worshiping gods. Many figures now regarded as major Shinto gods (Hachiman 八幡, Hakusan, Nachi 那智, etc.) previously were worshiped as Buddhist bodhisattvas or buddhas in local guise (*gongen* 權現). They were enshrined at Buddhist monasteries where Buddhist monks performed Buddhist rituals in their names. Religious sites now regarded as Shinto shrines (e.g., Tsurugaoka 鶴岡 in Kamakura, Kumano,

Tōnomine 多武峰 near Nara; see GRAPARD 1984) had been Buddhist monasteries with all that entailed: Buddhist libraries, Buddhist bells, and Buddhist icons, etc. Texts written by Buddhist monks—for example, Kōshū's *Keiran shūyōshū*, Kokan Shiren's *Genkō shakusho*, Mujū Dōgyō's 無住道暁 (1226–1312) *Shasekishū* 沙石集 (10 fasc.; 1283; see MORRELL 1985), or the *Shintōshū* 神道集 (10 fasc.; a late 14th-cent. collection of legends compiled on Mt. Hiei)—provide some of our most detailed accounts of the roles of the gods now identified with Shinto and their rituals in medieval religious life.

INTERPRETIVE MODELS

During the twentieth century Japanese scholars developed three main conceptual models for interpreting the overall significance of religion in medieval Japan. These models have been extremely influential. To some extent, all extant monographs, textbooks, and reference works present medieval religion according to one or another of these three approaches. Rarely, though, is the model explicitly acknowledged. Evidence is cited as if its interpretation is self-evident and vocabulary is used without distinguishing between its possible variant senses as historical terms, as analytic concepts, or as theoretical explanations (HALL 1983). As a result, the distinction easily becomes lost between what we know and what we think it means. Readers, therefore, must learn to recognize these interpretive models and to detect the analytical strategies upon which they rest. The models, in chronological order, are: original awakening thought, religious reformation, and exoteric-esoteric establishment.

Original Awakening Thought

Original awakening thought (*hongaku shisō* 本覺思想; also translated as "original enlightenment thought") was first identified as an analytic model by SHIMAJI Daitō 島地大等 (1875–1927), one of the founding fathers of modern Japanese Buddhist studies, in his 1906 essay titled "Original Awakening Faith" ("Hongaku no shinkō" 本覺の信仰). He returned to this topic repeatedly in essays and lectures, published posthumously in books such as *Thought and Faith* (*Shisō to shinkō* 思想と信仰, 1928), *Outline of Buddhism* (*Bukkyō taikō* 佛教大綱, 1931), and *Doctrinal History of Japanese Buddhism* (*Nihon Bukkyō kyōgaku shi* 日本佛教教學史, 1933). For Shimaji, original awakening thought represented a broad interpretive rubric for medieval Buddhist doctrinal developments concerning not just the nature of religious awakening, but also faith, human nature, evil, the relationship of nirvāṇa (salvation) to secular life, and links between buddhas and gods. Collectively these developments constituted the "climax" of Buddhist philosophy, which resolved all the contradictions that had propelled the Buddhist dialectic ever since its beginnings in ancient India, and they gave birth to Japan's medieval culture, especially its new religious organizations. In this way, Shimaji portrayed Japanese Buddhism as the ultimate culmination and conclusion of Asian Buddhist history. His interpretations dominated pre-1945 scholarship on medieval religion.

Since 1945 other interpretive models have appeared, but they build upon rather than replace original awakening thought as an analytic category. After the religious reformation model became normative, for example, TAMURA Yoshirō 田村芳朗 (1921–1989), in his *Study of the Thought Underlying Kamakura New Buddhism* (*Kamakura shin-Bukkyō shisō no kenkyū* 鎌倉新仏教思想の研究, 1965), skillfully reworked Shimaji's model to argue that reformed Buddhism represented a synthesis of the philosophical sublimity of original awakening thought and of the practical need for an accessible method of religious practice (STONE 1999, pp. 85–92). More recently, as the exoteric-esoteric establishment model (and its critique of institutional abuses of power) has become influential, advocates of "Critical Buddhism" (*hihan Bukkyō* 批判仏教) have argued that original awakening thought represents false Buddhist doctrines that the founders of reformed Buddhism rightfully had rejected. Because their successors did not fully appreciate this rejection, though, the influence of original awakening thought was not fully eliminated. Ultimately this incomplete rejection allowed Buddhist institutions to justify participation in many social ills (HUBBARD and SWANSON 1997).

Regardless of the validity of these value judgments, one cannot deny the fact that religious vocabulary related to original awakening pervades all aspects of traditional Japanese culture, its treatises on poetry, flower arranging, theater performance, music, and so forth. Therefore, familiarity with the basic contours of original awakening thought is essential for all students of premodern Japan. Original awakening thought, however, is the most difficult of the interpretive models to summarize briefly. Even if we ignore the different ways scholars after Shimaji have used this model, the basic phenomena it addresses are exceedingly complex. One way to reduce its complexity is to first explain its underlying logical structure, and then to discuss how these various phenomena fit into that structure.

Its logic consists of a system of associations, or resemblances similar to what Michel FOUCAULT (1973, p. 30), in his analysis of the role of resemblances in Western knowledge up to the end of the sixteenth century, characterized as an "infinite accumulation of confirmations all dependent on one another." In the case of medieval Japan, knowledge of the precise associations was secret, accessible only to properly initiated disciples of a teacher. Typically, each separate lineage of transmission explained the associations in its own way and criticized the teachings of rival lineages. The overall system of associations was the same, regardless of lineage. It rests on the ritual structure of the esoteric Buddhist maṇḍala with its multiple layers of meaning, each one of which is simultaneously represented by certain divinities, Sanskrit sounds, Chinese glyphs, Japanese words, colors, ritual implements, abstract symbols, bodily postures, directions, and so forth. Any one of these representations immediately entails all of its associated equivalent meanings and representations.

A Buddhist maṇḍala is a two- or three-dimensional map that depicts simultaneously the layout of the cosmos, of the buddha, and of the true human self. Like all maps, it is designed to show us where we are, where we want to go, and the route that takes us there. Maṇḍalas can have many different formats, but a very generic one would be as follows. It consists of an outer boundary in the shape of a large circle or square and of a central object that marks its spiritual focal point. In between these two extremes (periphery and center) there are many other objects arrayed in a series of concentric circles or courtyards. Typically, the central object is (or represents) the buddha as the fundamental nature of the cosmos itself. The objects arrayed around the center, going outward to the periphery, depict (or symbolize) the myriad individual appearances that make up the diversity of the world: lesser buddhas, bodhisattvas, gods and goddesses (in both beautiful and demonic forms), men and women, animals, celestial and terrestrial natural objects, sounds and speech, movements and gestures, as well as man-made tools, implements, and buildings.

This layout depicts the spiritual structure of the cosmos. The center point, where the buddha sits, is salvation (nirvāṇa). From here, one experiences a 360-degree perspective and experiences the bliss of unity, for all the phenomena of existence to the outermost boundary are emanations (constructions) of the buddha's own self-nature (*jishō shojō* 自性所成). From the periphery, however, one can attain only a very narrow perspective and, consequently, experiences the suffering of diversity (such as individual alienation). This peripheral realm of suffering (saṃsāra) is where humans, gods, and animals dwell.

The maṇḍala is not static, however; it also depicts activity. Directionally, humans strive to ascend (*kōjō* 向上) inward. From the moment of their initial spiritual aspirations (seeds) they progress toward the goal (fruit) of buddhahood (*jūin kōka* 從因向果). This pursuit of wisdom (*chie* 智慧) for one's own benefit (*jiri* 自利) is called acquiring awakening (*shikaku* 始覺). Although this ascending direction seems normative, in reality the most important movement is in the reverse direction (*jūka kōin* 從果向因) from the position of buddha (fruit) toward humanity (seeds). The buddha descends (*kōge* 向下) outward, appearing as the diverse phenomena of the world so as to save humans. This compassionate (*jihi* 慈悲) movement for the purpose of benefiting others (*rita* 利他) is called original awakening (*hongaku* 本覺). It is the inherent buddhahood without which acquiring awakening would be impossible to achieve.

A maṇḍala with this structure exhibits several interesting features. First, seen from the periphery, nirvāṇa and saṃsāra clearly are two separate realms. Seen from the center, however, they are one and the same. The entire maṇḍala is the buddha realm and everything in it is buddha. Humans, just as they are in the human realm, are buddhas. Animals, just as they are in the animal realm, are buddhas. The human and animal realms never diminish in size no matter how many beings are saved. Second, we (each one of us) already are buddhas. For us to authenticate (*shō* 證) our buddhahood, we merely must have faith that it is so. Third, Mahāyāna scriptures teach that the highest goal of Buddhism should not be escaping into nirvāṇa, but compassionately appearing in the world to save (i.e., benefit) others. If this is so, then who among the beings depicted in the maṇḍala is pursuing this highest goal? Certainly it is not the buddha sitting in nirvāṇa. Instead, the highest Buddhism is exemplified by the gods who appear in the world of saṃsāra to reveal the buddha's teachings. The Japanese verses (*waka* 和歌) inspired by these gods are equivalent to the Sanskrit spells (*dhāraṇī*) of the buddhas. Fourth, therefore, the true goal of Buddhism lies not in becoming a buddha (and thereby abandoning our humanity), but is achieved by moving in the reverse direction and expressing buddhahood in our everyday human activities.

Medieval texts repeatedly identify these kinds of assertions as the doctrines of original awakening (*hongaku hōmon* 本覺法門). Shimaji (and his followers) identified their logic of reversal (from buddha to human) as one of the hallmarks of original awakening thought, and said that this reversal is evident in two sets of historical developments, one negative and one positive. On the one hand, for monks in the established Buddhist monasteries of central Japan (e.g., Mt. Hiei), the affirmation of human activities degenerated into antinomianism, widespread abandonment of traditional Buddhist discipline, hedonistic involvement in secular affairs, and renewed interest in gods (i.e., Shinto). The leaders of new Buddhist organizations, on the other hand, purified original awakening thought by grounding it in an ethical worldview (i.e., we must express buddhahood in our human lives) and by providing people with new means (i.e., simplified forms of practice) of actualizing it. In short, the restructuring (or, reorienting) of all knowledge according to the reverse direction of the maṇḍala marks a turning point in the doctrinal, institutional, and social history of Japanese Buddhism.

Shimaji's model is breathtaking in its scope and in its ability to provide seemingly reasonable explanations for so many different (even contradictory) developments. On closer examination, however, the evidence is not nearly as tidy as Shimaji suggests. Texts from different lineages present and organize original awakening doctrines in different ways. Their interpretations do not agree with one another. There are no clear criteria for determining which sets of doctrines are or are not identifiable as original awakening thought. Moreover, many of the so-called reversed assertions merely restate normative Mahāyāna theoretical doctrines (*ri* 理) concerning awakening. They (and the medieval texts in which they appear) do not necessarily imply a different approach to the concrete ritual practices (*ji* 事) required for achieving it. Examinations of the actual historical circumstances of specific monastic lineages who transmitted some of these doctrines fail to reveal the kinds of correlations suggested by Shimaji's model. (For a masterful analysis of original awakening doctrines, of Japanese scholarship on original awakening, and of medieval Buddhist scholastics in general, see Stone 1999.)

Religious Reformation

The religious reformation (*shūkyō kaikaku* 宗教改革) model was first coined by Hara Katsurō 原勝郎 (1871–1924), a historian of European modernization, in his 1911 essay "Religious Reformations East and West" ("Tōzai no shūkyō kaikaku" 東西の宗教改革), which explicitly compares the social effects of Martin Luther's (1483–1546) Protestant Reformation with certain features of the new Buddhist lineages of medieval Japan. Hara's approach was not fully fleshed out, however, until the postwar period when Ienaga Saburō 家永三郎 (1913–2002) published his extremely influential *Studies in the Intellectual History of Medieval Buddhism* (*Chūsei Bukkyō shisōshi kenkyū* 中世仏教思想史研究, 1948). After Ienaga, the reformation model dominated scholarship for the next thirty-five years, and its influence is still felt today.

In brief, the reformation model exalts the so-called Kamakura New Buddhism (*Kamakura shin Bukkyō* 鎌倉新仏教) as being representative of a new spiritual culture that first appeared in the thirteenth century, took root in subsequent centuries, and eventually became the mainstream Japanese spirituality. Specifically, it identifies Kamakura New Buddhism as the Pure Land, Zen, and Lotus teachings—especially as expressed in the Japanese-language writings of Shinran, Dōgen, and Nichiren—and asserts that they all shared certain key characteristics in rejecting the previously existing Buddhist institutions as being corrupt and in advocating a new reformed vision of Buddhism that would change the course of Japanese history. This new religious vision rejected the obscure metaphysics and complex ritual practices of previous Buddhism for a radically simplified approach to religion that is accessible to all people—monastic and lay, male and female. The keys to this simplified Buddhism are individual faith (instead of clerical status), a single practice (e.g., calling the buddha's name, sitting in meditation, or chanting the title of the *Lotus*) that excludes all other rituals, and an emphasis on religion as a means of personal salvation (instead of as an institution of state power).

The reformation model presented an interpretation of medieval Buddhism ideally suited to the new political climate of postwar Japan. The Kamakura reformers were seen as popularizers whose teachings promoted social progress, institutional reforms, individualism, egalitarianism, inclusion of women, democratization of (religious) power—all the social values that intellectuals wanted for postwar Japanese society. This interpretation allowed postwar Japanese to identify their own situation and concerns with the historical roots of their contemporary religious denominations. Moreover, it is compatible with the proselytizing strategies of those denominations, for whom veneration of their founders exerts as strong a tie on the hearts and minds of their parishioners as does the founder's purported teachings. In short, it is a model that makes the Kamakura founders relevant to modern life.

The reformation model's emphasis on the roots of modern Buddhism explains why its rubric of Kamakura New Buddhism does not include the Vinaya, Shinto, and Shugendō lineages which also appeared during the medieval period. None of them constitute large Buddhist denominations today. The Jishū branch of Pure Land is slighted for the same reason. Similarly, the writings of Shinran, Dōgen, and Nichiren are interpreted through the eyes of Tokugawa-period commentaries in terms of how they address modern concerns and forms of religious practice. Their possible meanings for medieval audiences—as well as other writings and practices that might have been even more important for the medieval period—are ignored. (For a more detailed overview of the reformation model, see DOBBINS 1999.)

Exoteric-Esoteric Establishment

The exoteric-esoteric establishment (*kenmitsu taisei* 顕密体制) model was advocated as a more historically accurate alternative to the reformation model by the historian Kuroda Toshio (mentioned above). KURODA explained the exoteric-esoteric establishment in numerous ground-breaking essays and books, especially *The State and Religion in Medieval Japan* (*Nihon chūsei no kokka to shūkyō* 日本中世の国家と宗教, 1975) and *Dominion by Temples and Shrines: Another Side of Medieval Society* (*Jisha no seiryoku: Mō hitotsu no chūsei shakai* 寺社勢力——もう一つの中世社会, 1980). Since the publication of these works, most cutting-edge scholarship on medieval religion has adopted, in broad strokes at least, Kuroda's model.

Kuroda rejected the religious reformation model for two main reasons. First, it cannot adequately explain the role of religious institutions in medieval society, which Kuroda saw as being dominated by three wealthy power blocs (*kenmon* 権門): aristocratic houses (*kuge* 公家), warrior houses (*buke* 武家), and temple-shrine institutions (*jisha* 寺社). The most powerful religious institutions were the ones of central Japan (Nara, Kyoto, and Mt. Hiei) where (according to Kuroda) orthodox religion consisted of the exoteric-esoteric teachings and practices (*kenmitsu hōmon*), especially ones associated with original awakening. The Kamakura reformers (Shinran, Dōgen, Nichiren, etc.) were peripheral figures whose heterodox teachings had been suppressed by those dominant institutions. Those peripheral figures are unimportant for Kuroda's Marxist historiography, which seeks to explicate how the powerful central religious institutions exerted power. Second, the reform model fails to provide an adequate corrective to the mistaken nationalistic historiography of pre-1945 State Shinto. The reform model presents medieval Buddhism separately from the worship of gods, and thereby allows those gods to be interpreted solely in nativistic terms as expressions of a uniquely ethnic Japanese spirituality (i.e., Shinto). Kuroda was the first major scholar to argue persuasively that a separate religion identifiable as "Shinto" did not always exist throughout Japanese history (for a sample in English, see KURODA 1981). This is the significance of the fact that Kuroda used the words "religion" (not "Buddhism") and "temples and shrines" (not "temples" alone) in the titles of his books and in his scholarship.

Kuroda was a social historian, not a scholar of religion. The religious features of the exoteric-esoteric establishment were never his main concern. It is only natural, therefore, that from a religious studies standpoint his model exhibits many inadequacies. The term "exoteric-esoteric establishment" implies an institutional and doctrinal unity that did not exist. While the phrase "exoteric-esoteric" (*kenmitsu*) appears repeatedly in medieval texts, there is no evidence that it implied any particular unified system of teachings and practices. Attempts to identify such a system have embroiled scholars of religion in many irresolvable disputes (e.g., as to what was or was not religious orthodoxy). Nonetheless, the strengths of Kuroda's model outweigh its weaknesses. It reminds us that the previously established religious institutions remained socially and historically important for far longer than previously acknowledged. It focuses our attention on the practical role of religion as it was actually lived in medieval society. It forces us to confront the economic and political power of religious institutions. And, it counters our tendency to project back onto earlier history the modern configurations of Japanese religion, especially the tendency to imagine Shinto as having always existed. (For a more detailed overview, see ADOLPHSON 2000; DOBBINS 1996).

FUTURE PROSPECTS

It is important to be well read in secondary scholarship, but scholars of medieval Japanese religion need not be bound by existing scholarly models. Knowledge of models cannot substitute for extensive reading in primary sources (Buddhist scriptures, commentaries, treatises, ritual manuals, regulations, diaries, letters, etc.), for first-hand examination of physical evidence (art, geography, architecture, etc.), and for imagination. In interpreting these sources, scholars writing in Japanese must address the concerns of a Japanese audience, many of whom live with the modern legacy of medieval religions. Their concerns are not necessarily the same as (nor necessarily different from) the concerns of an English-language audience. When writing in English, scholars must strive to make the fruits of their research accessible not just to other specialists in medieval Japanese religion, but also to colleagues who are not interested in Japan and to ones who are not interested in religion. In other words, medieval Japanese religion should be explained in ways relevant to scholars of religion outside of Japan (who study Asian religions, or Buddhism, or medieval religion in Europe, etc.) and to specialists in other areas of Japanese studies (history, art, literature, etc.). The inadequacies of our expositions must not provide scholars in these other fields with an excuse to ignore the religious doctrines, cosmological structures, sectarian organizations, or ritual practices of medieval Japan.

The vocabulary of medieval religion requires more careful examination. Reference works usually gloss religious terminology in accordance either with its established usage in Chinese religious texts or according to the explanations of Tokugawa-period scholars, many of whom consciously rejected previous medieval interpretations in favor of their own linguistic or religious reforms. These interpretations must be verified against actual usage in a variety of medieval contexts, especially ritual manuals. Today the word *zenji* 禪師, for example, usually implies "Zen teachers" (members of Zen lineages), but for centuries it served as a generic designation for "meditators" (any common practitioner of Buddhist austerities). Although transcribing terms according to modern pronunciations is less burdensome for readers and authors alike, medieval pronunciations also should be provided if significant. The medieval "Tenshō Daijin" 天照大神, for example, conveys none of the nativist connotations of the post-1868 standardized pronunciation "Amaterasu Ōkami." Likewise, care should be exercised to convey the rich complexity of social and divine hierarchies. Too often people are reduced to generic status as plain aristocrats, warriors, or monks—and divinities are merely buddhas, bodhisattvas, or gods. And, the complex variety of gods become just *kami* 神 (instead of *chinju* 鎮守, *dakini* 荼吉尼, *dōsojin* 道祖神, *eirei* 英靈, *fukujin* 福神, *gongen* 權現, *goryō* 御靈, *hotoke* 佛, *jinmyō* 神明, *kishin* 鬼神, *kō* 公, *ma* 魔, *marebito* 客, *mikoto* 命, *mitama* 魂, *mono* 物, *myōō* 明王, *oni* 鬼, *ryūō* 龍王, *ryūten* 龍天, *ten* 天, *tengu* 天狗, *tenjin* 天神, *shinshō* 神將, *shoson* 諸尊, *sorei* 祖靈, etc.). Of course, many of the categories of gods just named actually are Buddhist divinities, but our distinction between native and foreign gods was meaningless in medieval Japan. This Buddhist identity, however, must not pass unnoted. Sanskrit vocabulary (which is familiar to scholars of Buddhism regardless of geographic region) always should be included alongside English equivalents or transliterated Japanese (which is recognizable only by Japan specialists).

The range of topics that cry out for more sustained scholarly attention is limited only by the available evidence and by our imagination. Innovative studies of medieval material culture, social practices, healing rituals, monastic education, initiation rituals, etc., currently underway bode well for the future. I also would like to see more studies of the following traditional topics, which have been unduly neglected in English-language publications. (1) Medieval Hossō represented an innovative tradition of Buddhist Yogācāra learning that is all but unknown today even among scholars of Japanese religion, not to mention students of Buddhism outside of Japan. Its philosophical richness, however, certainly is not less significant than other currents of medieval thought (e.g., Dōgen) that have generated comparative studies in recent years. (2) The royal family and their *monzeki* temples played a central role in Buddhist affairs from the thirteenth century until 1868. Today, though, the average person both inside and outside Japan hardly knows that the royal family once relied on Buddhism to consecrate its status. (3) Nuns played crucial roles in every aspect of medieval religion. Studying nuns in any one of these aspects will reveal much of significance not only about the religious lives of Japanese women, but also about medieval society in general. (4) Mt. Hiei with its power, its complexity, its glory, and its perversity remains unrivalled as a crucial component of medieval religion. Understanding even a little more about Mt. Hiei would tell us much more about medieval Japan. And finally, (5) a broad survey history of medieval esoteric teachings and practices, covering doctrines, rituals, gods, associations, institutions, and social relationships would benefit the field immensely.

BIBLIOGRAPHY

The works listed below were selected as a minimal list of monographs (with a few key articles) that should be read by anyone interested in medieval Japanese religion.

ABÉ, Ryuichi, 1999. *The Weaving of Mantra: Kūkai and the Construction of Esoteric Buddhist Discourse.* New York: Columbia University Press.

ADOLPHSON, Mikael S., 2000. *The Gates of Power: Monks, Courtiers, and Warriors in Premodern Japan.* Honolulu: University of Hawai'i Press.

AVERBUCH, Irit, 1995. *The Gods Come Dancing: A Study of the Ritual Dance of Yamabushi Kagura.* Ithaca: Cornell University East Asia Program.

BERRY, Mary Elizabeth, 1982. *Hideyoshi.* Cambridge: Harvard University Press.

_____, 1994. *The Culture of Civil War in Kyoto.* Berkeley: University of California Press.

BIELEFELDT, Carl, 1988. *Dōgen's Manuals of Zen Meditation.* Berkeley: University of California Press.

BLUM, Mark L., 2002. *The Origins and Development of Pure Land Buddhism: A Study and Translation of Gyōnen's Jōdo Hōmon Genrushō.* New York: Oxford University Press.

BODIFORD, William, 1993. *Sōtō Zen in Medieval Japan.* Honolulu: University of Hawai'i Press.

BOXER, C. R., 1974. *The Christian Century in Japan, 1549–1650.* Berkeley: University of California Press.

BREEN, John, and Mark TEEUWEN, eds., 2000. *Shintō in History: Ways of the Kami.* Honolulu: University of Hawai'i Press.

COLLCUTT, Martin, 1981. *Five Mountains: The Rinzai Zen Monastic Institution in Medieval Japan.* Cambridge: Harvard University Press.

DAVIDSON, Ronald M., 2002. *Indian Esoteric Buddhism: A Social History of the Tantric Movement.* New York: Columbia University Press.

DE BARY, Wm. Theodore et al., eds., 2001. *Sources of Japanese Tradition.* Second edition. Volume 1, *From Earliest Times to 1600.* New York: Columbia University Press.

DOBBINS, James C., ed., 1996. *The Legacy of Kuroda Toshio.* Special issue, *Japanese Journal of Religious Studies* 23/3–4.

_____, 1999. Envisioning Kamakura Buddhism. In PAYNE 1999, pp. 24–42.

HISTORY

_____, 2002 (1989). *Jōdo Shinshū: Shin Buddhism in Medieval Japan*. Honolulu: University of Hawai'i Press.

_____, 2004. *Letters of the Nun Eshinni: Images of Pure Land Buddhism Medieval Japan*. Honolulu: University of Hawai'i Press.

ELISON, George, and Bardwell L. SMITH, eds., 1981. *Warlords, Artists, and Commoners: Japan in the Sixteenth Century*. Honolulu: University of Hawai'i Press.

FAURE, Bernard, 1991. *The Rhetoric of Immediacy: A Cultural Critique of Chan/Zen Buddhism*. Princeton: Princeton University Press.

_____, 1993. *Chan Insights and Oversights: An Epistemological Critique of the Chan Tradition*. Princeton: Princeton University Press.

_____, 1996. *Visions of Power: Imagining Medieval Japanese Buddhism*. Princeton: Princeton University Press.

_____, 1998. *The Red Thread: Buddhist Approaches to Sexuality*. Princeton: Princeton University Press.

_____, 2003. *The Power of Denial: Buddhism, Purity, and Gender*. Princeton: Princeton University Press.

FOUCAULT, Michel, 1973 (1966). *The Order of Things: An Archaeology of the Human Sciences*. New York: Vintage Books.

GAY, Suzanne M., 2001. *The Moneylenders of Late Medieval Kyoto*. Honolulu: University of Hawai'i Press.

GOBLE, Andrew E., 1996. *Kenmu: Go-Daigo's Revolution*. Cambridge: Harvard University Press.

GOODWIN, Janet R., 1994. *Alms and Vagabonds: Buddhist Temples and Popular Patronage in Medieval Japan*. Honolulu: University of Hawai'i Press.

GRAPARD, Allan G., 1984. Japan's Ignored Cultural Revolution. *History of Religions* 23: 240–65.

_____, 1992. *The Protocol of the Gods: A Study of the Kasuga Cult in Japanese History*. Berkeley: University of California Press.

GRONER, Paul, 2000. *Ryōgen: The Restoration and Transformation of the Tendai School*. Honolulu: University of Hawai'i Press.

HALL, John W., 1983. Terms and Concepts in Japanese Medieval History: An Inquiry into the Problems of Translation. *Journal of Japanese Studies* 9: 1–32.

HALL, John W., and TOYODA Takeshi, eds., 1977. *Japan in the Muromachi Age*. Berkeley: University of California Press.

HALL, John W. et al., eds., 1981. *Japan before Tokugawa: Political Consolidation and Economic Growth, 1500–1650*. Princeton: Princeton University Press.

HIROTA, Dennis, 1995. *Wind in the Pines: Classic Writings of the Way of Tea as a Buddhist Path*. Fremont: Asian Humanities Press.

HUBBARD, Jamie, and Paul L. SWANSON, eds., 1997. *Pruning the Bodhi Tree: The Storm over Critical Buddhism*. Honolulu: University of Hawai'i Press.

HURST, G. Cameron, III, 1976. *Insei: Abdicated Sovereigns in the Politics of Late Heian Japan, 1086–1185*. New York: Columbia University Press.

KLEIN, Susan B., 2002. *Allegories of Desire: Esoteric Commentaries of Medieval Japan.* Cambridge: Harvard University Press.

KURODA Toshio, 1981. Shinto in the History of Japanese Religions. Tr. James C. Dobbins and Suzanne M. Gay. *Journal of Japanese Studies* 7: 1–21.

LAFLEUR, William R., 1983. *The Karma of Words: Buddhism and the Literary Arts in Medieval Japan.* Berkeley: University of California Press.

LAFLEUR, William R. et al., eds., 1992. *Flowing Traces: Buddhism in the Literary and Visual Arts of Japan.* Princeton: Princeton University Press.

MACHIDA, Soho, 1999. *Renegade Monk: Hōnen and Japanese Pure Land Buddhism.* Berkeley: University of California Press.

MASS, Jeffrey P., 1992. *Antiquity and Anachronism in Japanese History.* Stanford: Stanford University Press.

_____, 1999. *Yoritomo and the Founding of the First Bakufu: The Origins of Dual Government in Japan.* Stanford: Stanford University Press.

MASS, Jeffrey P., ed., 1997. *The Origins of Japan's Medieval World: Courtiers, Clerics, Warriors, and Peasants in the Fourteenth Century.* Stanford: Stanford University Press.

McCALLUM, Donald F., 1994. *Zenkōji and Its Icon: A Study in Medieval Japanese Religious Art.* Princeton: Princeton University Press.

McMULLIN, Neil, 1984. *Buddhism and the State in Sixteenth-Century Japan.* Princeton: Princeton University Press.

_____, 1989. Historical and Historiographical Issues in the Study of Pre-Modern Japanese Religions. *Japanese Journal of Religious Studies* 16: 3–40.

MIYAKE Hitoshi, 2001. *Shugendō: Essays on the Structure of Japanese Folk Religion.* Edited with an Introduction by H. Byron Earhart. Ann Arbor: University of Michigan Press.

MORRELL, Robert E., tr., 1985. *Sand and Pebbles (Shasekishū): The Tales of Mujū Ichien, A Voice for Pluralism in Kamakura Buddhism.* Albany: SUNY Press.

_____, 1987. *Early Kamakura Buddhism: A Minority Report.* Berkeley: Asian Humanities Press.

PARKER, Joseph D., 1999. *Zen Buddhist Landscape Arts of Early Muromachi Japan (1336–1573).* Albany: SUNY Press.

PAYNE, Richard, ed., 1999. *Re-Visioning Kamakura Buddhism.* Honolulu: University of Hawai'i Press.

RAMBELLI, Fabio, 1996. Religion, Ideology of Domination, and Nationalism: Kuroda Toshio on the Discourse of "Shinkoku." In DOBBINS 1996, pp. 387–426.

RAMBELLI, Fabio, and Mark TEEUWEN, eds., 2003. *Buddhas and Kami in Japan: Honji Suijaku as a Combinatory Paradigm.* New York: Routledge.

ROGERS, Minor L., and Ann T. ROGERS, 1991. *Rennyo: The Second Founder of Shin Buddhism.* Berkeley: Asian Humanities Press.

RUCH, Barbara, ed., 2002. *Engendering Faith: Women and Buddhism in Premodern Japan.* Ann Arbor: Center for Japanese Studies, University of Michigan.

RUPPERT, Brian D., 2000. *Jewel in the Ashes: Buddha Relics and Power in Early Medieval Japan.* Cambridge: Harvard University Press.

HISTORY

SHIVELY, Donald H., and William H. McCULLOUGH, eds., 1999. *Heian Japan. The Cambridge History of Japan*, vol. 2, ed. John W. Hall et al. New York: Cambridge University Press.

STONE, Jacqueline, 1999. *Original Enlightenment and the Transformation of Medieval Japanese Buddhism*. Honolulu: University of Hawai'i Press.

TANABE, George J., Jr., 1992. *Myōe the Dreamkeeper: Fantasy and Knowledge in Early Kamakura Buddhism*. Cambridge: Harvard University Press.

TANABE, George J., Jr., ed., 1999. *Religions of Japan in Practice*. Princeton: Princeton University Press.

TANABE, George J., Jr., and Willa J. TANABE, eds., 1989. *The Lotus Sutra in Japanese Culture*. Honolulu: University of Hawai'i Press.

TEEUWEN, Mark, 1966. *Watarai Shintō: An Intellectual History of the Outer Shrine in Ise*. Leiden: Research School CNWS.

TEN GROTENHUIS, Elizabeth, 1999. *Japanese Mandalas: Representations of Sacred Geography*. Honolulu: University of Hawai'i Press.

THORNHILL, Arthur H., III, 1993. *Six Circles, One Dewdrop: The Religio-Aesthetic World of Komparu Zenchiku*. Princeton: University of Princeton Press.

TYLER, Royall, 1990. *The Miracles of the Kasuga Deity*. New York: Columbia University Press.

TYLER, Susan, 1992. *The Cult of Kasuga Seen through Its Art*. Ann Arbor: Center for Japanese Studies, The University of Michigan.

VEERE, H. van der, 2000. *A Study into the Thought of Kōgyō Daishi Kakuban*. Amsterdam: Hotei Publishing.

YAMAMURA, Kōzō, ed., 1999. *Medieval Japan. The Cambridge History of Japan*, vol. 3, ed. John W. Hall et al. New York: Cambridge University Press.

YIENGPRUKSAWAN, Mimi H., 1988. *Hiraizumi: Buddhist Art and Regional Politics in Twelfth-Century Japan*. Cambridge: Harvard University Press.

Duncan Ryūken WILLIAMS

Religion in Early Modern Japan

Robert Bellah's 1957 *Tokugawa Religion* begins, "We have valuable studies of many aspects of Japanese religion in the Tokugawa period (1600–1868) without which this book could not have been written. We do not have, however, any study in English of what the whole of Japanese religion in this period meant in the lives of the Japanese people" (BELLAH 1957, p. 1). Although Bellah's groundbreaking work on the role of early modern religion in the rise of Japan's political and economic modernity sought to fill this vacuum, nearly fifty years later it would still be hard to say that any one book in Japanese or a Western language has managed to accomplish that lofty goal. Despite this lacunae, the study of early modern (also known as the Tokugawa or Edo period) Japanese religions has become increasingly sophisticated and diverse, particularly since the 1980s, in terms of the traditions and themes covered by scholars both in Japan and the West. Increasingly, the Tokugawa period is being recognized as a crucial link between the medieval and modern forms of religious practice in Japan, both in terms of popular religious cults and the institutional structures of mainstream Buddhism, Shugendō, and "Shinto" organizanizations.

One major obstacle to a comprehensive survey of the religious life in this period is the sheer volume of primary materials from the period. Unlike medieval religious history, the numbers of significant discoveries of new early modern texts in village house attics or temple-shrine archives continues to grow exponentially every year. Vast numbers of new materials related to a shrine or temple's founding (patronage or legends), ritual activity (manuals or logbooks), economics (landholdings or fund-raising drives), relationships with its parishioners (parishioner registers or letters regarding legal disputes), as well as popular literature and art (miracle tales of Buddhist deities or mandalas) have been dis-covered and catalogued by local history archives and religious institutions since the mid-1980s. While temple fires, time, and weather-damaged paper, the nature of record keeping, and other factors have contributed to the relative paucity of extant medieval sources, early modern manuscripts are readily available, especially the later one goes in the period. Nathalie Kouamé's introduction and workbook on how to read handwritten religious documents from the period is the only guidebook of the sort that helps Western researchers navigate these manuscripts (KOUAMÉ 2000).

While the study of medieval Japanese religions suffers in part because of a lack of quan-tity and variety of sources, the study of early modern religion is, at times, made difficult simply by the sheer number of manuscripts available. What Robert Bellah had available to him on the topic in the late 1950s has multiplied, in the order of thousands, new pri-mary material as well as the more recent Japanese secondary literature on these materials. Even in Western-language scholarship, recent research has highlighted the value of these new local history sources for the study of early modern religion (AMBROS and WILLIAMS 2001; HARDACRE 2002). These works focused on early modern religiosity as it appeared in local contexts, the "lived religion" as practiced in local settings, with regions, villages, towns, and cities as socially significant units to understand religion. A more detailed pic-ture has emerged of the comparative strengths of religious traditions in each region, how the Tokugawa government's religious policies were implemented on the ground, and how religious specialists and laypeople participated in religious life.

Although the early modern period boasts a large number of extant religious textual and non-textual sources for researchers, scholars working on the history of Japanese religions, especially Buddhist studies scholars, have generally ignored the early modern period in favor of medieval religion until quite recently. This can be attributed, in part, to "the the-ory of Edo Buddhist degeneration" (*Edo Bukkyō darakuron* 江戸仏教堕落論) advanced by the influential historian of Japanese Buddhism, Tsuji Zennosuke, who viewed the Edo or Tokugawa period as one of corruption and decline of Buddhism and thus unworthy of se-rious scholarly attention. Despite this view, a wide range of studies have emerged on prom-inent Buddhist priests of the period. Just in the Western-language literature, one can find book-length studies on the following religious figures: Bankei (1622–1693, HASKEL 1984; WADDELL 1984); Chōon Dōkai (1628–1695, SCHWALLER 1996); Enkū (ca. 1632–1695, TANA-HASHI 1982); Gensei (1623–1668, WATSON 1983); Hakuin Ekaku (1686–1768, ARAKAWA 1956;

CLEARY 2000; SEO 1997; SHAW 1963; STEVENS 1993b; TANAHASHI 1984; WADDELL 1994, 1996, 1999; YAMPOLSKY 1971); Jiun Sonja (1718–1804, WATT 1978); Manzan Dōhaku (1638–1714, GROSS 1998); Menzan Zuihō (1683–1769, RIGGS 2002); Ryōkan (1758–1831, HASKEL and ABÉ 1996; KODAMA 1969, 1999; STEVENS 1977, 1993a, 1993b; WATSON 1974; YUASA 1981); Sengai Gibon (1750–1837, FURUTA 2000; SUZUKI 1971); Suzuki Shōsan (1579–1655, BRAVER-MAN 1994; TYLER 1977; KING 1986); Tenkei Denson (1648–1735, CLEARY 2000); Tetsugen Dōkō (1630–1682, SCHWALLER 1989); Takuan Sōhō (1573–1645, HIROSE 1992; LISHKA 1976; WILSON 1986); Tōrei Enji (1721–1792, MOHR 1997; OKUDA 1996); and Tōsui Unkei (d. 1683, HASKEL 2001).

From the perspective of the degeneration of Buddhism theory, the medieval period was seen as the golden age of Buddhism not only in terms of doctrinal innovation and eminent monks, but also regarding the place of Buddhism in medieval society as a powerful institution. Seen as a force equal in stature to the court and the new warrior class, medieval Buddhism was the conceptual resource for the political ideology of the co-dependency of the ruler and the Buddhist Dharma (*ōbō-buppō*王法仏法). In the eyes of earlier scholars, some of the shifts in political ideologies during the early modern period which favored Neo-Confucianism over Buddhism supported the contention that early modern religion could be studied without Buddhism.

Bellah's book reflected this idea that Japan's emergence as a modern political and economic nation had its roots in Neo-Confucian ideology among the elites and a corresponding popular version of it among merchants and others. Until the 1970s, most scholars of Japanese Buddhism also accepted this contention, resulting in very few studies of early modern Buddhism. Instead of Buddhism, the field of early modern religions was dominated by intellectual historians of Neo-Confucianism and the nativist reaction to Chinese learning, the Kokugaku 国学 (National Learning) movement.

In Western-language scholarship, after Bellah's work, studies blossomed on individual figures in these movements as well as the movements in general. The English translation of MARUYAMA Masao's seminal essays on early modern intellectual history, *Studies in the Intellectual History of Tokugawa Japan* (1974), became a classic in the field against which subsequent researchers measured their work and theories. In Neo-Confucian studies, most research has centered on the Chinese philosophical bases for political ideology as articulated by individuals such as Fujiwara Seika (1561–1619), Hayashi Razan (1583–1657), and Yamazaki Ansai (1618–1682) in the early years of the *bakufu* (BOOT 1982; OOMS 1985). Other eminent Chu Hsi, Wang Yang-ming, and Kōgaku school Confucian scholars and advisors to *bakufu* and domainal authorities, such as Arai Hakuseki (1657–1725), Dazai Shundai (1680–1747), Itō Jinsai (1627–1705), Kaibara Ekiken [Ekken] (1630–1714), Kumazawa Banzan (1619–1691), and Ogyū Sorai (1666–1728), have received sustained attention as dissertations and monographs (ACKROYD 1979, 1982; ANSART 1998; HLAWATSCH 1985; KRACHT 1986; LEINSS 1995; LIDIN 1970, 1973, 1983, 1999; McMULLEN 1991; NAJITA 1978, 1998; NAKAI 1988; PFULB 1993; TUCKER [J.] 1998; TUCKER [M.] 1989; VAN BREMEN 1984; YAMASHITA 1981, 1994).

Broader studies on the place of Confucianism and Chinese learning include a landmark volume on Confucianism and Tokugawa culture (NOSCO 1984), an exploration of Confu-

HISTORY

cianism and education (KASSEL 1996), an analysis of the synthetic Shingaku 心学 move-ment that tied Neo-Confucian values to the contemplative techniques of Zen (SAWADA 1993), and a study of the influence of the I-ching on early modern society (NG 2000).

This line of religious and intellectual history and the Tokugawa state and society also informed studies of nativist reactions to Chinese thought in impressive book-length re-search on the Kokugaku movement, including works on figures such as Motoori Nori-naga (1730–1801) and Hirata Atsutane (1776–1843) (HAROOTUNIAN 1988; MCNALLY 1998; MATSUMOTO 1970; NOSCO 1990; WEHMEYER 1996). The reaction to the "foreign religions" of Buddhism and Confucianism and a search for Japanese roots marked a moment in Japanese history that Kokugaku or National Learning scholars considered "disordered." The eighteenth-century interest in what was "purely" Japanese, in both literary and reli-gious terms, helped later attempts to define "Shinto" as a national religion as well as pro-vide ideological support for those dissatisfied with the Tokugawa regime in the nineteenth century. In addition, the heterogenous philosophical tradition of the Mito school 水戸学, centered in the early period on the compilation of the *Dai Nihonshi* 大日本史 and later on Mito samurai nationalism, developed as another significant religio-philosophical school interested in the true nature of the Japanese nation (*kokutai* 国体) and its identity as a "country of the gods" (*shinkoku* 神国). The writings of its leaders were also instrumental at the end of the Tokugawa period in influencing the proimperial movement that would soon come to power (KOSCHMANN 1987).

Though these studies of Neo-Confucianism and nativism have helped build an im-pressive literature in early modern intellectual history, it is not until very recently that researchers have collaborated to go beyond the traditional divisions between Confucian, nativist, and Buddhist studies and the divides between intellectual, political, and scientific history (GIRARD et al. 2002; SAWADA 2004). In addition to the trend of contextualizing early modern intellectual history, studies on the institutional and social history of main-line Buddhist sects as well as Shugendō and Shinto organizations have also developed exponentially in recent years. Japanese historians, Buddhist and Shinto studies specialists, and folklorists have accomplished much to cover the broader terrain of the early modern Japanese religious landscape as a lived practice. In the past five years, Western scholars have also contributed to the study of both popular religiosity as well as the social and institutional structures of religious traditions other than Neo-Confucianism and nativ-ism. For instance, the Tokugawa Religions Seminar (a five-year project at the American Academy of Religion, 1997–2001) has provided a forum for much of the new research on this period.

This recent trend in the study of early modern Japanese religions has centered on two major themes: the institutional structures of religion under the Tokugawa regime's policy to control religion and the popular religious practices of the period. While it is impos-sible to chronicle the entire span and history of recent Japanese and Western-language scholarship, this essay will highlight the key issues of religion-state relations and popular religiosity.

THE TOKUGAWA *BAKUFU* AND
NEW STRUCTURES FOR RELIGIOUS INSTITUTIONS

The Tokugawa *bakufu*, upon assuming power, created a new legal framework for governance through directives (*hatto* 法度 or *gohatto* 御法度), including the regulation of religious institutions. The state control, or attempt at control, over religion is the primary theme in the study of institutional mainline Buddhism, Shugendō, and Shinto. Tamamuro Taijō and his son Tamamuro Fumio have long been the central Japanese scholars to articulate this vision of an early modern shift in the institutional place of Buddhist and Shinto institutions. Tamamuro Taijō's 1967 *Nihon Bukkyōshi 3: Kinsei kindaihen* and his son's 1971 co-edited volume with Ōkuwa Hitoshi, *Edo bakufu no shūkyō tōsei*, began an impressive array of monographs and edited volumes by leading historians and scholars of Buddhism (FUTABA 1980–1981, 1990a, 1990b; IMATANI and TAKANO 1998; TAKANO 1989; TAMAMURO Fumio 1971, 1985–1986, 1986, 1987, 1996; TAMAMURO Taijō 1967; UDAKA 1987a, 1987b; for more on the impact of Tamamuro Fumio's scholarship on the study of early modern religious history, see AMBROS and WILLIAMS 2001, pp. 210–25).

In the new Tokugawa order, potential rival sources of power and authority (local lords, the imperial court and aristocrats in Kyoto, and religious institutions) would be awarded a certain level of autonomous decision-making authority, but only under the ultimate control of the regime. The first shogun, Tokugawa Ieyasu (1542–1616), followed the model established by earlier warlords (*sengoku daimyo* 戦国大名) who tried to unify the Japanese provinces under their control, such as Oda Nobunaga (1532–1582) and Toyotomi Hideyoshi (1536–1598). They had used a double-pronged strategy of destroying, or at least weakening, any religious institution that posed a potential threat to their control on the one hand, and on the other, provided patronage to temples to help solidify their hegemony over this powerful institution (McMULLIN 1985).

The earliest directives were generally limited to a single Buddhist temple or a particular region. It was not until 1615 that the *bakufu*'s key advisors on religious affairs such as Konchiin Sūden (a Rinzai Zen priest, 1549–1633) and Tenkai (a Tendai priest, 1536–1643), were able to issue more broad-based rules that covered all sects and regions of Japan (NOSCO 1996; TAMAMURO 1987). These directives clarified the organizational structure primarily of Buddhist institutions and the hierarchy of priestly ranks so that such institutional matters would come under the purview of the *bakufu*, rather than be left completely up to the discretion of each sect. Although the rules for each sect differed in specific details, in the main, the *bakufu* decreed the following for each sect: a supreme head temple (*honzan* 本山) for Buddhist training, a system of head and branch temple relations enabling each head temple to have authority over its branch temples; a standard for priestly qualifications or regulations (e.g., the length of training to become a fully fledged priest, robe colors for each rank, and standards of moral discipline); and prohibitions on warrior monks and the buying or selling of temple abbotships.

While the medieval period was characterized by a fairly flexible, and at times tumultuous, relationship between the established temples and the fast-growing, more recently erected temples, the Tokugawa *bakufu* hoped to establish a stable system of head and branch temples in which the head temple had absolute legal authority over the branch temples. The basic administrative shape of all Tokugawa-period religious institutions was a pyramid. The *bakufu*, or more precisely, the institution set up in 1635 to oversee religious institutions—the Office of Temples and Shrines (*jisha bugyō* 寺社奉行)—sat at the top of the pyramid. With the headquarter temple at the next level of the pyramid, all religious institutions in Japan were linked through a hierarchical network of head and branch temples to the sectarian headquarter. Originally formed by links between a Buddhist teacher's temple (head temple) and his disciples' temples (branch temples), a head temple often had a number of affiliated lineage branch temples. This linkage between two generations of temples formed the basis for the concept that a particular temple was hierarchically superior to another. Under the Tokugawa regime, informal lineage-based ties became formalized and even temples that had no lineage ties were sometimes arbitrarily placed in head and branch temple relationships. During the first half of the early modern period, the *bakufu* transformed the medieval structures of religious institutions with new political imperatives. This was to provide, for the first time, an early modern pyramidal structure of authority and a legal framework for religious traditions which resulted in unified sects that transcended regional and lineage boundaries to encompass the whole of Japan. This system of head and branch temple relations (*honmatsu seido* 本末制度), which formed the organizational and sectarian basis of religious institutions into the modern period, has been the subject of study for many scholars of Tokugawa religious history including a special issue of *Rekishi kōron* edited by Chiba Jōryū, Fujii Manabu, and Tamamuro Fumio in 1985 (CHIBA 1985) and collections of primary manuscripts on these relationships for different sects (JIIN HONMATSUCHŌ KENKYŪKAI 1981; KAGAMISHIMA 1980; TAKENUKI 1990).

The formation of clearly distinct sectarian organizations in legal terms did not mean that trans-sectarian religious life disappeared; both ideologically and structurally sect distinction began to gained increased currency. Book-length studies of Buddhist sects attest to the sectarian legacy of Tokugawa Buddhism: Ji sect (NISHIGAI 1984; TAMAMURO et al. 1977–1979, 1982); Jōdo sect (HASEGAWA 1980, 1985); Jōdo Shin sect (KASAHARA 1978; KASHIWARA 1996; KODAMA 1976; MORIOKA 1981; UEBA 1999); Nichiren sect (AIBA 1975; ANDŌ 1976; FUJII 1957; FUJITA 1996; KAGEYAMA 1956; MIYAZAKI 1959, 1969, 1978; NAGAMITSU and TSUGAMA 1978); Shugendō sects (FUJITA 1996); Ōbaku Zen sect (BARONI 2000; TAKENUKI 1990); Rinzai Zen sect (FURUTA 1956; MORI 1977); Sōtō Zen sect (TAMAMURO 1999a; TSUTSUMI 1999; WILLIAMS 2005a). In terms of this type of institutional history and Buddhist-state relations, research on the Tendai and Shingon schools deserve further attention in the future. On the development of "Shinto" institutional history, particularly the rise of the Ise shrines as well as the Yoshida吉田 and Shirakawa 白川 schools, much work is still to be done. Recent studies on Watarai 渡会 Shinto at the Ise Shrine (TEEUWEN 1996), the Austrian Academy of Science's Yoshida Shinto project (an initial study from the institute can be found in SCHEID 2001), and a forthcoming Harvard dissertation on Yoshida Shinto (MAEDA 2003) will likely provide the benchmark studies for Tokugawa institutional Shinto studies.

It was within the structure of state-religion relations that the physical structures of religious institutions also emerged. For example, the late 16th and early 17th centuries was the peak of temple construction or reestablishment for all the larger sects of Buddhism. The vast majority of these new temples were so-called "parish temples" (alternately *dannadera* 檀那寺, *dankadera* 檀家寺, or *bodaiji* 菩提寺), which by the middle of the early modern period became the predominant locus for lay Buddhist temple affiliation. Indeed, far from the notion of a "Buddhist degeneration," for ordinary Japanese, the emergence of the parish temple as a religious establishment meant that for the first time in Japanese history, all Japanese became Buddhists. The Japanese scholarship on the early modern parish system (*danka seido* 檀家制度) has increased in recent years (HUR 2005; KOBAYASHI 1991; MARCURE 1985; ŌKUWA 1979; TAMAMURO 1999b; WILLIAMS 2005a).

Organizing Buddhist adherents into parishes stems from the Tokugawa government's anti-Christian (Kirishitan) campaigns and ordinances of 1613–1614. Christianity, which had achieved a foothold in certain regions during the sixteenth century through the efforts of Portuguese and Spanish missionaries, was increasingly seen by the new Tokugawa regime as a subversive force and a threat to their hegemony. The threat of Christianity, as seen from the perspective of government officials, lay less with its Biblical teachings and doctrines, than with the issue of Christian loyalty to God and the Pope, rather than to the Tokugawa government's secular authority. This led to a ban on Christianity in 1614.

To check that no Japanese remained a Christian, the government ordered "Investigations of Christians" (*Kirishitan aratame* キリシタン改め) to be conducted by each domain. Former Christians were certified by the local Buddhist temple and village officials as no longer Christians, but as parish members of a Buddhist temple. Beginning in 1614, the first surveys of Christians were followed by more extensive ones ordered by the government in 1659 in which not only the parish temple but also the village *goningumi* 五人組 (a unit of five households sharing mutual responsibility) were required to attest to the fact that no one in their group was a Christian (CIESLIK 1951). By 1670 the practice of temple investigation and registration (*terauke seido* 寺請制度) had become near universal when a standardized temple registration certificate was adopted by Buddhist temples across all regions of Japan, certified that their parishioners were neither Christians nor Nichiren Fuju-fuse members (a sect of Nichiren Buddhism banned by the government in 1669). Although the Buddhist temple held primary responsibility for monitoring and reporting on its parishioners to the village head, each village head had to gather these certificates so that reports, called the Registry of Religious Affiliation (*shūmon aratamechō* 宗門改帳) and also known as the *shūmon ninbetsuchō* 宗門人別帳 or the *shūshi aratamechō* 宗旨改帳, could be compiled (TAMAMURO 1999b).

These religious registries helped the authorities to monitor and control the populace at large by using Buddhist temples and local authorities to maintain detailed records of the populace while weeding out any persons who might be a potential threat to the government. From the perspective of the average parishioner, however, this practice of temple registration legally obligated them both ritually and economically to their parish temple under the threat of being branded a "heretic," which continued to have meaning even as the possibility of Christian subversion of the government disappeared. Even though overt Christian affiliation became impossible, Christian faith endured underground as the extensive Western-language literature on the "hidden Christians" (Kakure Kirishitan) attests (HARRINGTON 1993; TURNBULL 1993, 1998; WHELAN 1996).

Buddhist temple membership was not an individual affair, rather the unit of religious affiliation was the emergent unit of social organization, the "household" (*ie* 家) (MORIOKA 1981; NAGATA and YONEMURA 1998). Thus from the mid-Tokugawa period onwards, the term *danka* 檀家 (though used interchangeably with *danna* 檀那)—which includes the Chinese character for "household"—became the dominant term for parish households and was passed on from generation to generation. For each household, the main benefit of membership was the funerary and on-going memorial services that temples provided for all the members of their household. Parish temples also were the location for the family gravestones. Thus once a family registered as a member of a particular temple, that affiliation continued for successive generations during which sect changes were virtually impossible.

What parish temples emphasized to parishioners was their obligations for ritual attendance (funerals and ancestral rites) and financial support. Whether it be to pay for rituals or temple construction, it is clear that parishioners were not simply being asked, but were obligated to support their parish temple. The consequences of not doing so resulting in being branded a heretic. In ritual terms, the parish temple also became virtually synonymous with "funerary Buddhism," where death rituals, as opposed to meditation, sutra study, or prayers for worldly benefits, became the main ritual practice. The term "funerary Buddhism" (or *sōshiki Bukkyō* 葬式仏教) was coined by TAMAMURO Taijō in his classic work by the same title (1963) and refined by FUJII Masao and ITŌ Yuishin's *Sōsai Bukkyō* (1997) and TAMAMURO Fumio's *Sōshiki to danka* (1999b).

Beyond the funeral proper, Buddhist parish priests performed death rites throughout the year. Memorial services were routinely performed for a period of thirty-three years following a death. Services were also performed for various classes of people such as "hungry ghosts," "the ancestors," and women and children who had died during childbirth. Large festivals for the dead, such as the summer Obon Festival for the ancestors or the Segaki Festival for hungry ghosts, marked important moments in the temple's annual ritual calendar. This preoccupation with ritualizing death was intimately tied to the emergence of the Buddhist parish temples during the Tokugawa period. Hereditary parishioners, who associated the parish temple with the proper maintenance of funerary rites and family customs, provided the ritual and economic backbone of Buddhist temples. This parish system, originally established as a method to monitor Christians, ended up as the basic organizational structure for Japanese Buddhism into the contemporary period.

POPULAR RELIGIOSITY

The second dimension of recent Western-language research on early modern religiosity has been focused on the spread of popular religion at the local and translocal levels. At the most local level, the role of religious institutions in the social life of the village can be found in studies such as VESEY's work on the role of Buddhist priests in mediating village disputes (2002) or HARADA's work on the role of "shrine guild" organizations and their members in the organization of local festivals (1988). Furthermore, in the increasingly urban centers such as Edo, Nam-lin HUR's work (2000) on Sensōji 浅草寺 and its relationship to the surrounding Asakusa district represents a new direction in urban temple life studies, while WRIGHT's study (1996) on the "divorce temple" Mantokuji 満徳寺 highlights highly specialized functions of certain temples.

Most of the new research on popular religiosity is characterized by two dimensions of religious life that functioned outside of the *bakufu*-mandated Buddhist temple registration and parish systems: (1) faith in deities and sacred sites that transcend both locality and sectarian organizations and (2) a focus on deriving this-world benefits (*genze riyaku* 現世 利益) such as healing, rain-making, or business prosperity.

Although one's religious affiliation for legal and funerary purposes may have belonged to the sect of one's Buddhist parish temple, other forms of religious affiliation based on faith in particular deities or sacred sites developed to form multiple religious affiliations. Rather than concern simply with the other-world, this-worldly or "practical benefits," as READER and TANABE (1998) put it, played a major role in attracting the faith and economic support for temples and shrines that featured the transference of miraculous powers of the enshrined deity to the faithful through prayers (*kitō* 祈祷) or amulets and talismans. Whether it be bringing good luck and fortune or warding off or protecting against misfortune, various deities came to be known as having special abilities to, for example, ensure safe childbirth, promise large catches of fish, or guard against theft and disease. Foremost among the practical benefits sought in these popular cults was healing and Hartmut ROTERMUND's work (1991) on the vast range of healing deities is probably the best treatment of this subject.

Popular syncretic deities such as Konpira (DEVI 1986; THAL 2005) as well as Buddhist deities such as Fudō (AMBROS 2002), Jizō (MIYAZAKI and WILLIAMS 2001; WILLIAMS 2005b), Kannon (MACWILLIAMS 1990), or Miroku (COLLCUTT 1988) became linked to certain cultic centers. Pilgrims seeking talismans and travel participated in a Tokugawa period "boom" in pilgrimage as sacred mountains, such as Mt. Fuji 富士 (COLLCUTT 1988; EARHART 1989; TYLER 1981, 1984), Ōyama 大山 (AMBROS 2002), and Tateyama立山 (FORMANEK 1993), and temples and shrines such as the Ise 伊勢 shrines or Zenkōji 善光寺 began to enjoy increased popularity. As overland and sea travel became increasingly developed during the Tokugawa period, even peripheral locations such as the 88-temples pilgrimage of Shikoku dedicated to Kōbō Daishi came to prosper (KOUAMÉ 2000, 2001; PAYNE 1999). Such pilgrimages became a part of both highly organized pilgrimage confraternities (*kō* 講) lodged by lay proselytizers or *oshi* 御師 (AMBROS 2001) as well as mass pilgrimages, especially to Ise, in which millions of people absconded from their village and towns in what some scholars have interpreted as forms of social protest (BOHNER 1941; DAVIS 1983–1984; WILSON 1988).

Just as pilgrimages came to be represented in travel books and guidebooks, the powers of deities to save believers from hells or a raging sea, to heal incurable diseases, or to bring forth bountiful crops were represented in popular plays and sermons by traveling priests and performers. FISH's study of "Shinto theatricals" (1994), HARRISON's research on Jōdo Shin preachers (1992) or MATISOFF on "sermon-ballads" (1992), ROTERMUND's (1983) and BOUCHY's (1983) books on religious itinerants, and GROEMER's study on popular religious performers or *gannin* 願人 (2000), are all examples of this interest in public representations and performances of religion in an itinerant mode. An important Japanese study of such religious professionals as performers is TAKANO 2000.

By the end of the Tokugawa period, new apocalyptic and healing movements, which would later be known as the first wave of Japanese new religions, also emerged as movements that would operate outside the boundaries of the temple parish system. Although they often had initial associations with established religious institutions—for example, founders such as Kurozumi Munetada (1780–1850) and Nakayama Miki (1787–1856) received certification from the Yoshida house—they would soon come to form independent organizations such as Kurozumikyō 黒住教 (HARDACRE 1986), Tenrikyō 天理教 (ELLWOOD 1973), Konkōkyō 金光教, Misogikyō 禊教, and Maruyamakyō 丸山教 (SAWADA 1998), or Nyoraikyō 如来教 (PARKER 1983). Hardacre's study on conflict between three of the newly emergent movements and Shugendō in terms of healing practices and gender is a good example of how these "new religions" came to differentiate themselves ideologically and organizationally (HARDACRE 1994). In terms of characterizing these new movements, some scholars have pointed to the influence of Neo-Confucian values and mind-cultivation as the basis for new visions of social relations or of Shintō and Buddhist teachings on purification or karma, but all illustrate the movements' vision for an alternative to the established institutions. Many of the charismatic founders also drew on folk traditions of shamanistic possession by deities and several scholars have noted the predominance of women as founders, such as Nakayama Miki of Tenrikyō (PEREIRA 1992; WÖHR 1989).

These so-called new religions represented new forms of organized religiosity that marked the end of a certain formation of Tokugawa religion. The Meiji Restoration ushered in new orders, both political and religious, that would also contain this tension among the state-regulated organizations as popular religiosity at times circumvented the established institutions. While this essay surveyed the growing interest in early modern religions as a crucial link between the medieval and modern forms of religious practice in Japan, it is also suggested there are numerous discrete topics that deserve book-length studies as well as synthetic works that go across the boundaries of sect, region, time, and methodology.

BIBLIOGRAPHY

ACKROYD, Joyce, 1979. *Told Round a Brushwood Fire: The Autobiography of Arai Hakuseki*. Tokyo: University of Tokyo Press.

———, 1982. *Lessons from History: Arai Hakuseki's Tokushi Yoron*. St. Lucia: University of Queensland Press.

AIBA Shin 相葉 伸, 1975. *Fuju-fuseha junkyō no rekishi* 不受不施派殉教の歴史. Tokyo: Daizō Shuppan.

AMBROS, Barbara, 2001. Localized Religious Specialists in Early Modern Japan: The Development of the Ōyama Oshi System. *Japanese Journal of Religious Studies* 28: 329–72.

———, 2002. The Mountain of Great Prosperity: The Cult of Ōyama in Early Modern Japan. Ph.D. dissertation, Harvard University.

AMBROS, Barbara, and Duncan WILLIAMS, eds., 2001. *Local Religion in Tokugawa History*. Special issue, *Japanese Journal of Religious Studies* 28/3–4.

ANDŌ Seiichi 安藤精一, 1976. *Fuju-fuseha nōmin no teikō* 不受不施派農民の抵抗. Osaka: Seibundō.

ANSART, Olivier. 1998. *L'empire du rite: la pensée politique d'Ogyū Sorai, Japon, 1666–1728*. Geneva: Librairie Droz.

ARAKAWA Yasuichi, 1956. *Master Hakuin and His Art*. Kyoto: Maria Gobo.

BARONI, Helen J., 2000. *Ōbaku Zen: The Emergence of the Third Sect of Zen in Tokugawa Japan*. Honolulu: University of Hawai'i Press.

BELLAH, Robert N., 1957. *Tokugawa Religion: The Values of Pre-Industrial Japan*. Glencoe: The Free Press.

BOHNER, Hermann, 1941. Massen-Nukemairi. *Monumenta Nipponica* 4: 160–70.

BOOT, Willem Jan, 1982. The Adoption and Adaptation of Neo-Confucianism in Japan: The Role of Fujiwara Seika and Hayashi Razan. Ph.D. dissertation, University of Leiden.

BOUCHY, Anne-Marie, 1983. Tokuhon, ascète du nenbutsu: Dans le cadre d'une Étude sur les religieux errants de l'Époche Edo. *Cahiers d'Études et de documents sur les religions du Japon* 5. Paris: E.P.H.E.

BRAVERMAN, Arthur, 1994. *Warrior of Zen: The Diamond-Hard Wisdom Mind of Suzuki Shōsan*. Tokyo: Kodansha International.

CHIBA Jōryū 千葉乗隆, FUJII Manabu 藤井 学, and TAMAMURO Fumio 圭室文雄, eds. 1985. *Rekishi kōron* 歴史公論 2: *Kinsei no Bukkyō* 近世の仏教. Tokyo: Yūzankaku.

CIESLIK, Hubert, 1951. Die Goningumi im Dienste der Christenüberwachung. *Monumenta Nipponica* 7: 102–55.

CLEARY, Thomas, 2000. *Secrets of the Blue Cliff Record: Zen Comments by Hakuin and Tenkei*. Boston: Shambhala.

COLLCUTT, Martin, 1988. Mt. Fuji as the Realm of Miroku: The Transformation of Maitreya in the Cult of Mt. Fuji in Early Modern Japan. In *Maitreya, the Future Buddha*, ed. Alan Sponberg and Helen Hardacre, pp. 248–69. Cambridge: Cambridge University Press.

DAVIS, Winston, 1983–1984. Pilgrimage and World Renewal: A Study of Religion and Social Values in Tokugawa Japan. *History of Religions* 23: 97–116.

DEVI, Shanti, 1986. Hospitality for the Gods: Popular Religion in Edo, Japan: An Example. Ph.D. dissertation, University of Hawai'i.

EARHART, H. Byron, 1989. Mount Fuji and Shugendō. *Japanese Journal of Religious Studies* 16: 205–26.

ELLWOOD, Robert, 1973. *Tenrikyo: A Pilgrimage Faith*. Tenri: Oyasato Research Institute, Tenri University.

FISH, David Lee, 1994. "Edo Sato Kagura": Ritual, Drama, Farce, and Music in a Pre-Modern Shinto Theatrical. Ph.D. dissertation, University of Michigan.

FORMANEK, Susanne, 1993. Pilgrimage in the Edo Period: Forerunner of Medieval Domestic Pilgrimage? The Example of the Pilgrimage to Mt. Tateyama. In *The Culture of Japan as Seen through Its Leisure*, ed. Sepp Linhart and Sabine Frühstück, pp. 165–94. Albany: SUNY Press.

FUJII Masao 藤井正雄 and ITŌ Yuishin 伊藤唯真, 1997. *Sōsai Bukkyō: Sono rekishi to gendaiteki kadai* 葬祭仏教——その歴史と現代的課題. Tokyo: Jōdoshū Sōgō Kenkyūjo.

FUJII Shun 藤井 駿, 1957. *Nichirenshū Fuju-fuseha shiryō* 日蓮宗不受不施派史料. Okayama-ken: Risshō Gohōkai.

FUJITA Teikō 藤田定興, 1996. *Kinsei Shugendō no chiikiteki tenkai* 近世修験道の地域的展開. Tokyo: Iwata Shoin.

FURUTA Shōkin 古田紹欽, 1956. *Kinsei no Zensha tachi* 近世の禅者達. Kyoto: Heirakuji Shoten.

———, 2000. *Sengai: Master Zen Painter*. Tokyo: Kodansha International.

FUTABA Kenkō 二葉憲香, ed., 1980–1981. *Nihon Bukkyōshi kenkyū: Kokka to Bukkyō, kinsei, kindaihen* 日本仏教史研究——国家と仏教、近世、近代篇. 2 vols. Kyōto: Nagata Bunshōdō.

FUTABA Kenkō, 1990a. *Nihon Bukkyōshi: Chū* 日本仏教史・中. Kyōto: Nagata Bunshōdō.

———, 1990b. *Shiryō Nihon Bukkyōshi kenkyū: Chū* 史料日本仏教史研究・中, rev. ed. Kyōto: Nagata Bunshōdō. Rev. ed.

GIRARD, Frederic, Annick HORIUCHI, and Mieko MACÉ, eds., 2002. *Repenser l'ordre, repenser l'heritage: paysage intellectuel du Japon (XVIIe–XIXe siècles)*. Paris: École Pratique des Hautes Études/Droz.

GROEMER, Gerald, 2000. A Short History of Gannin: Popular Religious Performers in Tokugawa Japan. *Japanese Journal of Religious Studies* 27: 41–72.

GROSS, Lawrence, 1998. Manzan Dōhaku and the Transmission of the Teaching. Ph.D. dissertation, Stanford University.

HARADA Toshiaki, 1988. The Origin of Rites of Worship within the Local Community. In *Matsuri: Festival and Rite in Japanese Life*, ed. Inoue Nobutaka, pp. 20–32. Tokyo: Institute for Japanese Culture and Classics, Kokugakuin University.

HARDACRE, Helen, 1986. *Kurozumikyō and the New Religions of Japan*. Princeton: Princeton University Press.

———, 1994. Conflict Between Shugendō and the New Religions of Bakumatsu Japan. *Japanese Journal of Religious Studies* 21: 137–67.

———, 2002. *Religion and Society in Nineteenth-Century Japan: A Study of the Southern Kanto Region, Using Late Edo and Early Meiji Gazeeters*. Ann Arbor: Michigan Center for Japanese Studies.

HAROOTUNIAN, Harry D., 1988. *Things Seen and Unseen: Discourse and Ideology in Tokugawa Nativism*. Chicago: University of Chicago Press.

HARRINGTON, Ann, 1993. *Japan's Hidden Christians*. Chicago: Loyola University Press.

HARRISON, Elizabeth G., 1992. Encountering Amida: Jōdo Shinshū Sermons in Eighteenth-Century Japan. Ph.D. dissertation, University of Chicago.

HASEGAWA Masatoshi 長谷川匡俊, 1980. *Kinsei nenbutsusha shūdan no kōdō to shisō: Jōdoshū no baai* 近世念仏者集団の行動と思想——浄土宗の場合. Tokyo: Hyōronsha.

———, 1985. *Kinsei Jōdoshū no shinkō to kyōka* 近世浄土宗の信仰と教化. Tokyo: Keisuisha.

HASKEL, Peter, 1984. *Bankei Zen: Translations from the Record of Bankei*. New York: Grove Weidenfeld Press.

———, 2001. *Letting Go: The Story of Zen Master Tōsui (Tōsui oshō densan)*. Honolulu: University of Hawai'i Press.

HASKEL, Peter, and Ryūichi ABÉ, 1996. *Great Fool: Zen Master Ryōkan: Poems, Letters, and Other Writings*. Honolulu: University of Hawai'i Press.

HIROSE Nobuko, 1992. *Immovable Wisdom: The Art of Zen Strategy, The Teachings of Takuan Soho*. Shaftesbury: Element.

HLAWATSCH, George O., 1985. The Life of Dazai Shundai, 1680–1747. Ph.D. dissertation, University of Hawai'i.

HUR, Nam-Lin, 2000. *Prayer and Play in Late Tokugawa Japan: Asakusa Sensōji and Edo Society*. Cambridge: Harvard University Asia Center.

_____, 2005. *Death and Social Order in Tokugawa Japan: Buddhism, Anti-Christianity, and the Danka System*. Cambridge: Harvard University Asia Center.

IMATANI Akira 今谷 明 and TAKANO Toshihiko 高埜利彦, eds., 1998. *Chūkinsei no shūkyō to kokka* 中近世の宗教と国家. Tokyo: Iwata Shoin.

JIIN HONMATSUCHŌ KENKYŪKAI 寺院本末帳研究会, ed., 1981. *Edo bakufu jiin honmatsuchō shūsei* 江戸幕府寺院本末帳集成. 3 vols. Tokyo: Yūzankaku.

KAGAMISHIMA Sōjun 鏡島宗純, 1944 [1980]. *Enkyō do Sōtōshū jiin honmatsuchō* 延享度曹洞宗寺院本末帳. Tsurumi: Daihonzan Sōjiji. (reprint, Tokyo: Meicho Fukyūkai)

KAGEYAMA Gyōō 影山堯雄, ed., 1956. *Nichirenshū Fuju-fuseha no kenkyū* 日蓮宗不受不施派の研究. Kyoto: Heirakuji Shoten. (expanded edition reprinted 1972)

KASAHARA Kazuo 笠原一男, 1978. *Kinsei ōjōden no sekai: Seiji kenryoku to shūkyō to minshū* 近世往生伝の世界――政治権力と宗教と民衆. Tokyo: Kyōikusha.

KASHIWAHARA Yūsen 柏原祐泉, 1971. *Kinsei shomin Bukkyō no kenkyū* 近世庶民仏教の研究. Kyoto: Hōzōkan.

_____, 1996. *Shinshūshi Bukkyōshi no kenkyū 2: Kinsei* 真宗史仏教史の研究 2――近世. Kyoto: Heirakuji Shoten.

KASHIWAHARA Yūsen and FUJII Manabu 藤井 学, 1973. *Kinsei Bukkyō no shisō* 近世仏教の思想. Zoku Nihon Shisō Taikei 5. Tokyo: Iwanami Shoten.

KASSEL, Marleen R., 1996. *Tokugawa Confucian Education: The Kangien Academy of Hirose Tansō (1782–1856)*. Albany: SUNY Press.

KING, Winston, 1986. *Death Was His Kōan: The Samurai Zen of Suzuki Shōsan*. Berkeley: Asian Humanities Press.

KOBAYASHI Masahiro 小林正博, 1991. *Shūmon mondai o kangaeru: Danka seido to sōzoku no kankei* 宗門問題を考える――檀家制度と僧俗の関係. Tokyo: Daisan Bunmei.

KODAMA Misao 児玉 操, 1969. *Ryōkan the Great Fool*. Kyoto: Kyoto Seika Junior College Press.

_____, 1999. *The Zen Fool Ryōkan*. Rutland: Charles E. Tuttle.

KODAMA Satoru 児玉 識, 1976. *Kinsei Shinshū no tenkai katei: Nishi Nihon o chūshin to shite* 近世真宗の展開過程――西日本を中心として. Tokyo: Yoshikawa Kōbunkan.

KOSCHMANN, J. Victor, 1987. *The Mito Ideology: Discourse, Reform, and Insurrection in Late Tokugawa Japan, 1790–1864*. Berkeley: University of California Press.

KOUAMÉ, Nathalie, 2000. *Initiation à la paléographie japonaise: à travers les manuscrits du pèlerinage de Shikoku*. Paris: Langues & Mondes–L'Asiathèque.

_____, 2001. *Pèlerinage et société dans le Japon des Tokugawa: Le pèlerinage de Shikoku entre 1598 et 1868*. Paris: École Française d'Extrême-Orient.

KRACHT, Klaus, 1986. *Studien zur Geschichte des Denkens im Japan des 17. bis 19. Jahrhunderts: Chu-Hsi-Konfuzianische Geist-Diskurse.* Wiesbaden: Harrassowitz.

LEINSS, Gerhard, 1995. *Japanische Anthropologie: Die Natur des Menschen in der Konfuzianischen Neoklassik am Anfang des 18. Jahrhunderts — Jinsai und Sorai.* Wiesbaden: Harrassowitz.

LIDIN, Olof G., 1970. *Bendō: Distinguishing the Way.* Tokyo: Sophia University Press.

———, 1973. *The Life of Ogyū Sorai: A Tokugawa Confucian Philosopher.* Lund: Studentlitt.

———, 1983. *Ogyū Sorai's Journey to Kai in 1706: With a Translation of the Kyōchūkikō.* London: Curzon Press.

———, 1999. *Ogyū Sorai's Discourse on Government (Seidan): An Annotated Translation.* Wiesbaden: Harrassowitz.

LISHKA, Dennis, 1976. Buddhist Wisdom and Its Expression as Art: The Dharma of the Zen Master Takuan. Ph.D. dissertation, University of Wisconsin.

MACWILLIAMS, Mark, 1990. Kannon Engi: Strategies of Indigenization in Kannon Temple Myths of the Saikoku Sanjūsansho Kannon Reijōki and the Sanjūsansho Bandō Kannon Reijōki. Ph.D. dissertation, University of Chicago.

MAEDA Hiromi, 2003. Imperial Authority and Local Shrines: Yoshida Shinto and Its Influence on the Development of Local Shrines. Ph.D. dissertation, Harvard University.

MARCURE, Kenneth, 1985. The Danka System. *Monumenta Nipponica* 40: 39–67.

MARUYAMA Masao, 1974. *Studies in the Intellectual History of Tokugawa Japan.* Princeton: Princeton University Press.

MATISOFF, Susan, 1992. Holy Horrors: The Sermon-Ballads of Medieval and Early Modern Japan. In *Flowing Traces: Buddhism in the Literary and Visual Arts of Japan*, ed. William LaFleur, James Sanford, and Masatoshi Nagatomi, pp. 234–61. Princeton: Princeton University Press.

MATSUMOTO Shigeru, 1970. *Motoori Norinaga, 1730–1801.* Cambridge: Harvard University Press.

MCMULLEN, Ian James, 1991. *Genji gaiden: The Origins of Kumazawa Banzan's Commentary on The Tale of Genji.* Oxford/Ithaca: Oxford Oriental Institute Monographs 13/Ithaca Press for the Board of the Faculty of Oriental Studies.

MCMULLIN, Neil. 1985. *Buddhism and the State in Sixteenth-Century Japan.* Princeton: Princeton University Press.

MCNALLY, Mark Thomas, 1998. Phantom History: Hirata Atsutane and Tokugawa Nativism. Ph.D. dissertation, University of California, Los Angeles.

MIYAZAKI Eishū 宮崎英修, 1959. *Kinsei Fuju-fuseha no kenkyū* 近世不受不施派の研究. Kyoto: Heirakuji Shoten.

———, 1969. *Fuju-fuseha no genryū to tenkai* 不受不施派の源流と展開. Kyoto: Heirakuji Shoten.

MIYAZAKI Eishū, ed., 1978. *Hokekyō kenkyū 7: Kinsei Hokke Bukkyō no tenkai* 法華経研究 7——近世法華仏教の展開. Kyoto: Heirakuji Shoten.

MIYAZAKI Fumiko and Duncan WILLIAMS, 2001. The Intersection of the Local and Translocal at a Sacred Site: The Case of Osorezan in Tokugawa Japan. *Japanese Journal of Religious Studies* 28: 399–440.

MOHR, Michel, 1997. *Traité sur l'inépuisable Lampe du Zen: Tōrei et sa vision de l'éveil*, 2 vols. Brussels: Institute Belge des Hautes Études Chinoises.

MORI Keizō 森 慶造, ed., 1977. *Kinsei Zenrin genkōroku* 近世禅林言行録. Tokyo: Nihon Tosho Sentā.

MORIOKA Kiyomi 森岡清美, 1981. *Shinshū kyōdan ni okeru 'ie' seido* 真宗教団における「家」制度. Osaka: Sōbunsha.

NAGAMITSU Norikazu 長光徳和 and TSUMAGA Junko 妻鹿淳子, eds., 1978. *Nichirenshū Fuju-fuseha dokushi nenpyō* 日蓮宗不受不施派読史年表. Tokyo: Kaimei Shoin.

NAGATA, Mary, and Chiyo YONEMURA, 1998. Continuity, Solidarity, Family and Enterprise: What is an *ie*? In *House and Stem Family in Eurasian Perspective*, ed. Antoinette Fauve-Chamoux and Emiko Ochiai, pp. 193–214. France: Proceedings of the C18 Session Twelfth International Economic History Congress.

NAJITA, Tetsuo, ed., with Irwin Scheiner, 1978. *Japanese Thought in the Tokugawa Period: Methods and Metaphors*. Chicago: University of Chicago Press.

———, 1998. *Tokugawa Political Writings*. Cambridge: Cambridge University Press.

NAKAI, Kate Wildman, 1988. *Shogunal Politics: Arai Hakuseki and the Premises of Tokugawa Rule*. Cambridge: Harvard East Asian Monographs 134, Harvard University Press.

NG, Wai-ming, 2000. *The I Ching in Tokugawa Thought and Culture*. Honolulu: University of Hawai'i Press.

NISHIGAI Kenji 西海賢二, 1984. *Kinsei yugyō hijiri no kenkyū* 近世遊行聖の研究. Tokyo: San'ichi Shobō.

NOSCO, Peter, 1990. *Remembering Paradise: Nativism and Nostalgia in Eighteenth-Century Japan*. Cambridge: Council on East Asian Studies, Harvard University.

———, 1996. Keeping the Faith: Bakuhan Policy Towards Religions in Seventeenth-Century Japan. In *Religion in Japan: Arrows to Heaven and Earth*, ed. Peter Kornicki and Ian McMullen, pp. 136–55. Cambridge: Cambridge University Press.

NOSCO, Peter, ed., 1984. *Confucianism and Tokugawa Culture*. Princeton: Princeton University Press. (reprinted Honolulu: University of Hawai'i Press, 1996)

OKUDA Yōko, 1989. *The Discourse on the Inexhaustible Lamp of the Zen School By Zen Master Torei Enji*. London: The Zen Centre. (reprinted Rutland: Charles E. Tuttle, 1996)

ŌKUWA Hitoshi 大桑 斉, 1979. *Jidan no shisō* 寺檀の思想. Tokyo: Kyōikusha.

OOMS, Herman, 1985. *Tokugawa Ideology: Early Constructs, 1570–1680*. Princeton: Princeton University Press.

PARKER, Kenneth, 1983. Okyōsama: Documentation of the Founding of Nyorai-kyō, Japan's First New Religion. Ph.D. dissertation, University of Pennsylvania.

PAYNE, Richard, 1999. Reflections on the Shikoku Pilgrimage: Theoretical and Historical Considerations. *Kōyasan Daigaku Mikkyō Bunka Kenkyūjo kenkyū kiyō* 12: 94–114.

PEREIRA, Ronan Alves, 1992. *Possessão por Espírito e Inovação Cultural: A Experiência Religiosa das Japonesas Miki Nakayama e Nao Deguchi*. São Paulo: Alian a Cultural Brasil-Japão/Massao Ohno.

PFULB, Gerhard, 1993. *Soziale Ordnung als Problem: Auffassungen über soziale Ordnung im japanischen Konfuzianismus, 1660–1750*. Bochum: Dr. N. Brockmeyer.

READER, Ian, and George J. TANABE, Jr., 1998. *Practically Religious: Worldly Benefits and the Common Religion of Japan*. Honolulu: University of Hawai'i Press.

HISTORY

RIGGS, David, 2002. Menzan Zuihō and the Reform of Japanese Sōtō Zen Buddhism. Ph.D. dissertation, University of California, Los Angeles.

ROTERMUND, Hartmut O., 1983. *Pèlerinage aux Neuf Sommets: carnet de route d'un religieux itinérant dans le Japon du XIXe siècle*. Paris: Centre National de la Recherche Scientifique.

_____, 1991. *Hōsōgami ou la Petite Vérole Aisément: matériaux pour l'étude des épidémies dans le Japon des XVIIIe, XIXe siècles*. Paris: Maisonneuve & Larose.

SAWADA, Janine Anderson, 1993. *Confucian Values and Popular Zen: Sekimon Shingaku in Eighteenth-Century Japan*. Honolulu: University of Hawai'i Press.

_____, 1998. Mind and Morality in Nineteenth-Century Japanese Religions: Misogi-kyō and Maruyama-kyō. *Philosophy East and West* 48: 108–41.

_____, 2004. *Practical Pursuits: Religion, Politics, and Personal Cultivation in Nineteenth-Century Japan*. Honolulu: University of Hawai'i Press.

SCHEID, Bernhard, 2001. *Der eine und einzige Weg der Götter. Yoshida Kanetomo und die Erfindung des Shinto*. Vienna: Austrian Academy of Sciences.

SCHWALLER, Dieter, 1989. *Der japanische Ōbaku-Mönch Tetsugen Dōkō: Leben, Denken, Schriften*. Bern: Peter Lang.

_____, 1996. *Unreiner Zen? Zwei Texte des Ōbaku-Mönchs Chōon Dōkai (1628–1695)*. Bern: Peter Lang.

SEO, Audrey, 1997. Painting-Calligraphy Interactions in the Zen Art of Hakuin Ekaku (1685–1768). Ph.D. dissertation, University of Kansas,.

SHAW, R. D. M., 1963. *The Embossed Tea Kettle: Orate Gama and Other Works of Hakuin Zenji*. London: George Allen and Unwin.

STEVENS, John, 1977. *One Robe, One Bowl: The Zen Poetry of Ryōkan*. New York: Weatherhill.

_____, 1993a. *Dewdrops on a Lotus Leaf: Zen Poems of Ryōkan*. Boston: Shambhala.

_____, 1993b. *Three Zen Masters: Ikkyu, Hakuin, Ryokan*. Tokyo: Kodansha.

SUZUKI Daisetsu T., 1971. *Sengai: The Zen Master*. London: Faber and Faber.

TAKANO Toshihiko 高埜利彦, 1989. *Kinsei Nihon no kokka kenryoku to shūkyō* 近世日本の国家権力と宗教. Tokyo: Tōkyō Daigaku Shuppankai.

_____, 2000. *Minkan ni ikiru shūkyōsha: Shirīzu kinsei no mibunteki shūen 1* 民間に生きる宗教者——シリーズ近世の身分的周縁 1. Tokyo: Yoshikawa Kōbunkan.

TAKENUKI Genshō 竹貫元勝, 1990. *Kinsei Ōbakushū matsujichō shūsei* 近世黄檗宗末寺帳集成. Tokyo: Yūzankaku Shuppan.

TAMAMURO Fumio 圭室文雄, 1985–1986. *Edoki no shūkyō tōsei* 江戸期の宗教統制. 2 vols. Tokyo: Sōtōshu Shūmuchō.

_____, 1986. *Ronshū Nihon Bukkyōshi 7: Edo jidai* 論集日本仏教史 7——江戸時代. Tokyo: Yūzankaku.

_____, 1987. *Nihon Bukkyōshi: Kinsei* 日本仏教史—近世. Tokyo: Yoshikawa Kōbunkan.

_____, 1999a. *Edo jidai no Sōtōshū no tenkai* 江戸時代の曹洞宗の展開. *Shūkyō to sabetsu* 宗教と差別 11. Tokyo: Sōtōshū Shūmuchō. (Sōtōshū booklet)

_____, 1999b. *Sōshiki to danka* 葬式と檀家. Tokyo: Yoshikawa Kobunkan.

TAMAMURO Fumio, ed., 1996. *Nihon Bukkyō no rekishi: Edo jidai* 日本仏教の歴史——江戸時代. Tokyo: Kōsei Shuppansha.

TAMAMURO Fumio, with ŌKUWA Hitoshi 大桑 斉, eds., 1971. *Edo bakufu no shūkyō tōsei* 江戸幕府の宗教統制. Tokyo: Hyōronsha.

TAMAMURO Fumio et al., eds., 1977–1979. *Yugyō nikkan* 遊行日鑑. 3 vols. Tokyo: Kadokawa Shoten.

_____ et al., eds., 1978–1980. *Kinsei ōjōden shūsei* 近世往生伝集成. 3 vols. Tokyo: Yamakawa Shuppansha.

_____ et al., eds., 1982. *Zenkoku Jishū shiryō shozai mokuroku* 全国時宗史料所在目録. Tokyo: Daigaku Kyōikusha.

TAMAMURO Taijō 圭室諦成, 1967. *Nihon Bukkyōshi 3: Kinsei kindaihen* 日本仏教史 3——近世近代篇. Kyōto: Hōzōkan.

TAMAMURO Taijō, ed., 1963. *Sōshiki Bukkyō* 葬式仏教. Tokyo: Daihōrinkaku.

TANAHASHI Kazuaki, 1982. *Enku: Sculptor of a Hundred Thousand Buddhas*. Boston: Shambhala.

_____, 1984. *Penetrating Laughter: Hakuin's Zen and Art*. Woodstock: Overlook Press.

TEEUWEN, Mark, 1996. *Watarai Shintō: An Intellectual History of the Outer Shrine in Ise*. Leiden: Research School CNWS.

THAL, Sarah E., 2005. *Rearranging the Landscape of the Gods: The Politics of a Pilgrimage Site in Japan 1573–1912*. Chicago: University of Chicago Press.

TSUTSUMI Kunihiko 堤 邦彦, 1996. *Kinsei Bukkyō setsuwa no kenkyū* 近世仏教説話の研究. Tokyo: Kanrin Shobō.

_____, 1999. *Kinsei setsuwa to zensō* 近世説話と禅僧. Osaka: Izumi Shoin.

TUCKER, John Allen, 1998. *Itō Jinsai's Gomō Jigi and the Philosophical Definition of Early Modern Japan*. Leiden: E. J. Brill.

TUCKER, Mary Evelyn, 1989. *Moral and Spiritual Cultivation in Japanese Neo-Confucianism: The Life and Thought of Kaibara Ekken (1630–1714)*. Albany: SUNY Press.

TURNBULL, Stephen R., 1993. *Devotion to Mary among the Hidden Christians of Japan*. Wallingford, UK: Ecumenical Society of the Blessed Virgin Mary.

_____, 1998. *The Kakure Kirishitan of Japan: A Study of Their Development, Beliefs and Rituals to the Present Day*. Richmond, UK: Japan Library/Curzon Press.

TYLER, Royall, 1977. *Selected Writings of Suzuki Shōsan*. Ithaca: China-Japan Program, Cornell University.

_____, 1981. A Glimpse of Mt. Fuji in Legend and Cult. *Journal of the Association of Teachers of Japanese* 16: 140–65.

_____, 1984. The Tokugawa Peace and Popular Religion: Suzuki Shōsan, Kakugyō Tōbutsu, and Jikigyō Miroku. In *Confucianism and Tokugawa Culture*, ed. Peter Nosco, pp. 92–119. Princeton: Princeton University Press.

UDAKA Ryōtetsu 宇高良哲, ed., 1979. *Edo Jōdoshū jiin shiryō shūsei* 江戸浄土宗史料集成. Tokyo: Daitō Shuppansha.

_____, 1987a. *Edo bakufu no Bukkyō kyōdan tōsei* 江戸幕府の仏教教団統制. Tokyo: Tōyō Bunka.

_____, 1987b. *Tokugawa Ieyasu to Kantō Bukkyō kyōdan* 徳川家康と関東仏教教団. Tokyo: Tōyō Bunka.

UEBA Akio 上場賢雄, 1999. *Kinsei Shinshū kyōdan to toshi jiin* 近世真宗教団と都市寺院. Kyoto: Hōzōkan.

VAN BREMEN, Jan Gerhard, 1984. The Moral Imperative and Leverage for Rebellion: An Anthro-

HISTORY

pological Study of Wang Yang-Ming Doctrine in Japan. Ph.D. dissertation, University of California, Berkeley.

VESEY, Alexander M., 2002. The Buddhist Clergy and Village Society in Early Modern Japan. Ph.D. dissertation, Princeton University.

WADDELL, Norman A., 1984. The Unborn: The Life and Teaching of Zen Master Bankei, 1622–1693. San Francisco: North Point Press.

———, 1994. The Essential Teachings of Zen Master Hakuin: A Translation of the Sokkō-roku Kaien-fusetsu. Boston: Shambhala.

———, 1996. Zen Words from the Heart: Hakuin's Commentary on the Heart Sutra. Boston: Shambhala.

———, 1999. Wild Ivy: The Spiritual Autobiography of Zen Master Hakuin. Boston: Shambhala.

WATSON, Burton, 1974. Ryōkan: The Zen Monk-Poet of Japan. New York: Columbia University Press.

———, 1983. Grass Hill: Poems and Prose by the Japanese Monk Gensei. New York: Columbia University Press.

WATT, Paul B., 1978. The Life and Thought of Jiun Sonja (1718–1804). Ph.D. dissertation, Columbia University.

WEHMEYER, Ann, tr., 1996. Kojiki-den. Book 1. Ithaca: Cornell East Asia Series.

WHELAN, Christal, tr., 1996. The Beginning of Heaven and Earth: The Sacred Book of Japan's Hidden Christians. Honolulu: University of Hawai'i Press.

WILLIAMS, Duncan, 2005a. The Other Side of Zen: A Social History of Sōtō Zen Buddhism in Tokugawa Japan. "Buddhisms" Series. Princeton: Princeton University Press.

———, 2005b. The Healing Jizō Bodhisattva in Tokugawa Japan: The 1822 Enmei Jizōson inkō riyakuki. Monumenta Nipponica 60: 493–524.

WILSON, George M., 1988. "Ee ja nai ka" on the Eve of the Meiji Restoration in Japan. Semiotica 70: 301–19.

WILSON, William Scott, 1986. The Unfettered Mind: Writings of the Zen Master to the Sword Master. Tokyo: Kodansha International.

WÖHR, Ulrike, 1989. Frauen and Neue Religionen: Die Religionsgründerinnen Nakayama Miki und Deguchi Nao. Vienna: Wiens Institut für Japanologie, Universität Wien.

WRIGHT, Diana E., 1996. The Power of Religion/The Religion of Power: Religious Activities as Upaya for Women of the Edo Period. The Case of Mantokuji. Ph.D. dissertation, University of Toronto.

YAMASHITA, Samuel Hideo, 1981. Compasses and Carpenter's Squares: A Study of Itō Jinsai (1627–1705) and Ogyū Sorai (1666–1728). Ph.D. dissertation, University of Michigan.

———, 1994. Master Sōrai's Responsals: An Annotated Translation of 'Sorai Sensei Tomonsho'. Honolulu: University of Hawai'i Press.

YAMPOLSKY, Philip B., 1971. The Zen Master Hakuin: Selected Writings. New York: Columbia University Press.

YUASA, Nobuyuki, 1981. The Zen Poems of Ryōkan. Princeton: Princeton University Press.

Hᴀʏᴀsʜɪ Makoto 林淳

Religion in the Modern Period

Tracing the research history of modern religion in Japan is a more difficult task than one may imagine. If we were tracing the history of religion in the ancient or medieval period, we could consult a mass of information because reviews of the research history for those periods are numerous. Reviews of the research history for modern religion, however, are scant.

Why is this the case? Here I would like to highlight just two reasons. First, the ancient and medieval periods are golden ages for the history of both Buddhism and Shinto, and thus have attracted the interest of many researchers. In modern Buddhism and Shinto, however, there is no such golden age. Furthermore, it is not easy to perceive long-term trends and currents in the research history of modern religion because few scholars specialize on religion in the modern period and, as a result, there are few research articles on it. Even if we were to take the research articles that exist here and there and link them together, we would still not get a clear idea of general trends.

Second, studies on modern history have almost never taken up religion as a subject for research. The reputable historical journal *Shigaku zasshi* 史学雑誌 includes a section called "Retrospect and Prospect," which has a selective list of works that command esteem among historians. In the sections on ancient, medieval, and early modern (*kinsei* 近世) history, religion is one of the items covered; but religion is not covered in the part on modern (*kindai* 近代) history. In the study of modern history, "religion" has been neglected to such a degree that it is as if it did not exist as an area of research. Today this continues to be the case. In the study of modern history, in both Marxist and positivist historiography, research on economics and politics has taken precedence, while religion and culture have been virtually ignored. In short, one can not expect to get support from historians for the study of modern religions.

The reader can probably imagine other reasons in addition to the two given here. Whatever the reasons, however, the fact is that there have been few attempts to reflect on the history of research on religion in the modern period.[1] There is no choice but to make my own judgments and evaluations of the field. I will start with a discussion of research on modern Buddhism and then proceed to do the same for research on State Shinto and new religions before ending with an examination of the concept of *shūkyō* (religion).

FROM "MEIJI BUDDHISM" TO "MODERN BUDDHISM"

For those who lived in the Taishō and Shōwa periods, "Meiji" became a historical period worthy of study soon after it ended. The research that began on "Meiji Buddhism" in the Taishō period is a good example. For those whose lives overlapped the Meiji and Taishō periods, there was a large gap separating the two. Tokushige Asakichi, who edited *Meiji Bukkyō kenkyū shiryō*, stated the following:

> Meiji culture was political and nationalistic with hardly a tinge of anything representative of the ordinary people or society at large. These two characteristics were also historical conceptual words of the Meiji period and were part of the Meiji period's distinctiveness. In the Buddhist teachings that transcend these individual characteristics, there should be variants of meaning and form depending on factors such as the country and historical time. What is called "Meiji Buddhism" is one such variant. (TOKUSHIGE 1933)

Here it is pointed out that the culture of the Meiji period was political and nationalistic, in contrast to the culture of the Taishō period, which was characterized by that of the ordinary people and society. In other words, there was a shift from the Meiji culture that focused on the nation-state and politics, to the Taishō culture that was based on humanism and democracy. Consequently, Meiji Buddhism came to be depicted as serving the state and as political in character.

---

1. Nitta Hitoshi's two articles about research on State Shinto, published in 1999, are very informative, and among the few articles that reflect on the research history of State Shinto.

Tomomatsu Entai, the founder of the Meiji Bukkyōshi Hensanjo 明治仏教史編纂所 (Institute for the Historical Study of Meiji Buddhism), began to collect historical documents relevant to the study of Meiji Buddhism as a result of the encouragement he received from Sylvain Lévi (IKEDA 2004). Tomomatsu established the Institute in Kanda (Tokyo) and collected books, magazines, and newspapers on Buddhism in the Meiji period. He also was the founder and leader of the Meiji Bukkyō-kai 明治仏教会 (Association for the Study of Meiji Buddhism), which published a journal entitled *Meiji Bukkyō*. Other works that were published on Meiji Buddhism include *Meiji Ishin shinbutsu bunri shiryō* (TSUJI 1926–1929), *Ishin seiji shūkyōshi kenkyū* (TOKUSHIGE 1934), and *Meiji Bukkyō shi* (TSUCHIYA 1939). The compilation of documents entitled *Meiji Ishin shinbutsu bunri shiryō* was the result of concern that sources on the Meiji period would be scattered and lost. Although scholars of history—particularly those who knew Buddhist history—took an interest in collecting documents and studying Meiji Buddhism, research on the Buddhist thought of the Meiji period was rare in mainstream Buddhist studies, which focused on the origins of Buddhism in India and on philological studies of sutras and their commentaries.

Research on modern Buddhism has its beginning after World War II. The research topic known as "Meiji Buddhism" before the war was reformulated as "modern Buddhism." This was not just a change of wording. For the Japanese who conceived of the period from the Meiji Restoration to the end of the war as one era, the experience of losing the war could not be avoided. The first scholar to give an account of the history of modern Buddhism was Yoshida Kyūichi, a leading historian of social work, who based his research of modern Buddhism on his extensive collection of documents and his study of historical accounts produced after the war. YOSHIDA's book *Nihon kindai Bukkyōshi kenkyū* is a study that "seeks to find the relationship between modern Japanese history and Buddhism as an independent entity" (1959, p. 2) by being cognizant of postwar historical studies, and yet distancing himself from modern historical studies that take a completely economic and political approach. As topics for his study, he discussed in meticulous detail the religious riots in Mikawa in the first years of Meiji, the movement by Buddhist priests to separate from the Great Teaching Academy (Daikyōin 大教院) that was fostering a closer relationship between Buddhism and the state, the clash between Christianity and Buddhism, spiritualist movements, new Buddhist movements, and the incident that led to the execution of the leftist activist Kōtoku Shūsui in 1911 for conspiring to assassinate the emperor. He says, however, that he "chose only topics that I think are part of modern Buddhism and have a place in modern Japanese history." Yoshida intended his research on modern Buddhism to follow the criteria of research for modern history so specialists of modern history who read it would find value in it. Yoshida's research is important in that it creates, with reference to historical studies, separate historical periods in modern Buddhist history. The first period, according to Yoshida, is from the first year of Meiji (1868) to 1885. This is the time when the conditions were set to create a modern, unified nation state. The second period is mid-Meiji, from 1886 to 1899, when the process of establishing absolutism through the promulgation of the Imperial Rescript on Education and the Constitution of the Empire of Japan set the context for the rise of ultranationalism and the start of Buddhism's clash with Christianity. It was also a time when Buddhist reforms were being proposed. The

HISTORY

third period is the end of Meiji (1900–1912), which was the formative period for Japanese imperialism and when Buddhism began to separate itself from state power and to confront it. During this third period there was a rise of Buddhist movements, and Buddhists began to address social problems. Yoshida later published *Kingendai Bukkyō no rekishi* (1998) in which he kept his historical divisions and added to them the period of "Taishō democracy," which together he saw as forming the period of "modern Buddhism." It is due to Yoshida's continual research that the study of modern Buddhism has achieved a level that has met the standards of historians.

Kashiwahara Yūsen, who is known for his research on the history of Shinshū in the medieval, early modern, and modern periods, distanced himself from an apologetic stance for understanding Shinshū and strived to clarify our understanding of Buddhism in the early modern and modern periods. KASHIWAHARA (1969), while looking at the popularization of Buddhism and responses to anti-Buddhist arguments, attempted to view modern Buddhism on the basis of early modern Buddhism. Kashiwahara's *Nihon Bukkyōshi: Kindai* (1990) is an excellent and balanced overview of the history of Buddhism from the Meiji Restoration to the contemporary period. As a leading scholar of Shinshū history, he focuses on Shinshū in his depictions of modern Buddhist history, devoting many pages to Kiyozawa Manshi's spiritualism movement and closely analyzing activities from the same era, including the movement to have Buddhism recognized as the official religion of the country, the opposition to the religion bill (*shūkyō hōan* 宗教法案), and the 1912 "Meeting of the Three Religions [Buddhism, Shinto and Christianity]" (*sankyō kaidō* 三教会同). Compared with Yoshida, however, Kashiwahara pays little attention to how modern Buddhist history fits in with historical studies of the modern period; he attempts instead to place modern Buddhism in the larger context of Buddhism's long history.[2]

We have learned much from the historical studies of pioneering scholars such as Yoshida and Kashiwahara, but they are limited in a number of ways. Yoshida regretted that there was not a "spiritual revolution" in Japanese Buddhism, while KASHIWAHARA (2004, p. 429) was disappointed that the nature of modern Buddhist institutions was one of conformity with the political establishment. Although they used the term "modern Buddhism" (*kindai Bukkyō* 近代仏教), they were skeptical about whether Japanese Buddhism has ever modernized. That is why Yoshida and Kashiwahara praised reform movements; it is also why they did not investigate the historical process of the government's policy toward Buddhist sects. Perhaps they did not see the significance of understanding issues such as the process by which Buddhism came to comply with the government.

Succeeding Yoshida and Kashiwahara is Ikeda Eishun, who is one of the few researchers to specialize in modern Buddhism. Unlike Yoshida and Kashiwahara, who considered Shinshū to be the model of modern Buddhism, IKEDA (1994) focused on collecting Sōtō documents, and investigated the Buddhist precepts movement (*kairitsu undō* 戒律運動) as well as the teaching assemblies (*kyōkai* 教会) and lay societies (*kessha* 結社) of the early Meiji period. How teaching assemblies and lay societies reconfigured religious orders is

2. See KASHIWAHARA 1995, 1996, and 2000, whose research is clearly based on Buddhist historical ideas that permeated the medieval period and existed up to the modern period.

without doubt an important problem, and Ikeda's research as a whole has been significant for revising the Shinshū-centric view of modern Buddhism.

Yoshida, Kashiwahara, and Ikeda were pioneering scholars who, despite the different directions in which they pursued their interests, were all implicitly interested in how Buddhists engaged with and responded to modernity. This interest is what fascinated and motivated them. It was thus inevitable that their research should focus on Buddhist reform movements. YOSHIDA wrote of the new Buddhist movement of 1880 as "the formation of modern Buddhism" (1998, p. 123), while KASHIWAHARA referred to the spiritualism of Kiyozawa Manshi as "a development in the modernization of Buddhism" (1990, p. 112). In retrospect, the theory that modern Buddhism was formed 30 years after the Meiji Restoration is questionable. We might regard Buddhism after the Meiji Restoration as submissive to the state or as revivalistic, but should we not think of those in their own way as being forms of modern Buddhism? Many issues still need to be examined, including the religious policy of the government, the widening social networks of Buddhist leaders, and the political activities of the leaders of each Buddhist organization in response to the government's policy.

The Nihon Kindai Bukkyōshi Kenkyūkai 日本近代仏教史研究会 (Society for the Study of Modern Japanese Buddhist History), which was proposed by Ikeda and established in 1992, operates as a forum for scholars of different generations and fields.[3] The study of modern Buddhism has certainly not been a bright shining light in the academy, but it has plodded along with some endeavor. In comparison with other periods, there is an inexhaustible amount of documents, but it is not clear what kind of research we can use them for, or in what direction our research should progress. One of the weak points in the study of modern Buddhism is that, since Yoshida, there has been little conscious effort made to link it with historical studies. In recent years, however, we have seen some encouraging trends quietly emerge, four of which I would like to mention here.

First, there is the recognized need to investigate Buddhist history in the modern period as part of the relationship between religion and the state. The study of modern Buddhism lacks basic historical research on institutions, and thus lags behind the study of State Shinto. Paradoxically, the study of modern Buddhism should use historical documents not related to Buddhism in order to depict Buddhism. Haga Shōji's work, for example, not only depicts the government's policy toward religion and the establishment of the autonomy of Buddhist orders, but also astutely observes that the change from a head-temple system to a system of superintendent priests was indicative of modern Buddhist organizations.[4]

Second, some recent research deals directly with the problem of Buddhism and nationalism. The larger framework of modern nationalism cannot be properly understood from the earlier studies that just examined movements that proposed a modern establishment of the self, such as the spiritualism movement. Even after the Sino-Japanese War (1894–1895)

---

3. The annual journal of this association, *Kindai Bukkyō,* has been published every year since 1994. The contents of this journal reveals how the interests of researchers have changed with each new generation.

4. See HAGA 1994, especially the section "Kyōdō shokusei to seikyō kankei."

and Russo-Japanese War (1904–1905), all the Buddhist sects felt they had a positive national mission and became deliberate promoters of nationalism. Ōtani Eiichi's *Kindai Nihon no Nichirenshugi undō* (2001), which carefully traces the Nichiren-based movements of Tanaka Chigaku and Honda Nisshō and places them within the context of modern history, shows how this occurred. Sueki Fumihiko's *Kindai Nihon no shisō: Saikō* (2004) reexamines the internal pursuit of consciousness among those such as Kiyozawa Manshi, Takayama Chogyū, and Tsunajima Ryōsen, who were all prominent during the time between the Sino-Japanese and Russo-Japanese wars. Sueki perceptively notes that Kiyozawa Manshi's movement easily transcended secular morality and, even worse, lacked the basis for an ethical relationship with others; it thus became in part uncritically wrapped up with government policy and secular ethics.

Third, there is the relationship between Buddhism in Japan and in other countries. Proselytization outside Japan by Japanese Buddhist organizations is not a minor topic of study in modern Buddhism, and there is a widespread awareness that it can offer important clues for reevaluating modern Japanese international politics and Japan's management of its colonies. Since the publication of Kojima Masaru and Kiba Akeshi's *Ajia no kaikyō to kyōiku* (1992) many studies have taken up this topic. Another study of modern Buddhism from a new perspective is Moriya Tomoe's *Amerika Bukkyō no tanjō* (2001), which deals with proselytization among ethnic Japanese in the USA and the Americanization of Buddhism.

Fourth, there is the greatly increased number of contributions by scholars outside Japan. By taking modern Buddhism as their topic of research, non-Japanese scholars can dig into both the problem of Buddhism and modernity. Western scholars have shown, for example, that modern Japanese Buddhist intellectuals created things that did not historically exist; they appear like magic by using Western Orientalism to present Japanese culture to the West. These Buddhist intellectuals depicted non-Western Buddhism and Zen in a way that idealized the two and made them appealing to Western religious intellectuals (SHARF 1993 and 1994, SWANSON 2004). This response by Japanese Buddhists became ubiquitous at a time when Western modernity was being forced upon them. The most idealized form of Buddhism among Western religious scholars was "Zen," and as a result it has now become an object for criticism. The critical studies of Robert Sharf and Brian Victoria in particular challenged the image of Zen. Victoria's *Zen and War* (1997) exposes how Zen priests actively supported and participated in WWII. For Japanese readers, the fact that Zen priests supported the war—just like civilians and priests of other sects—is not surprising. In fact, it would probably come as a shock to Japanese that Western readers were shocked by the idea that Zen priests supported the war—such is the gap between the understanding of Zen in the West and Japan.

Among Western contributions there are also important empirical studies such as James Ketelaar's *On Heretics and Martyrs in Meiji Japan* (1990), Richard Jaffe's *Neither Monk nor Layman* (2001), and the special issue of the *Japanese Journal of Religious Studies* on "Meiji Zen" (1998). Ketelaar's book traces how Buddhism, which was for a time treated as a heresy due to anti-Buddhist ideas and the movement to abolish Buddhism and destroy all its images (*haibutsu kishaku* 廃仏毀釈), was reborn as a modern religion. He takes up

Gyōnen's *Hasshū kōyō* 八宗綱要 and the World's Parliament of Religions in Chicago to examine the birthing process of modern Buddhism, which was radically transformed as nonsectarian through evolutionary theory. Jaffe challenges the widely held view that the marriage of priests began as a result of the promulgation of a law in 1872 that permitted priest to marry and eat meat (*nikujiki saitai* 肉食妻帯) by revealing the complications that existed within the Sōtōshū and the history of its acceptance of married priests at the end of the Meiji period.

Among the four recent trends I have pointed out here, the last one, which highlights the contributions of scholars outside Japan, is particularly noteworthy. Research on modern Buddhism by non-Japanese scholars is being imported into Japan and has the potential to stimulate Japanese scholars. What is fascinating about modern Buddhism as an object of study is that it can suggest comparative topics for research that transcend national borders, such as "Buddhism and modernity" and "Buddhism and colonization" in Asian countries.

THE REVIVAL OF STATE SHINTO

The pioneer of State Shinto research was Murakami Shigeyoshi. Murakami's *Kokka Shintō* 国家神道 (1970) was the first study to comprehensively pursue the topic and was a mass-market paperback published by Iwanami Shinsho that netted a wide readership. As can be seen in the conclusion of the book, MURAKAMI announced to his fellow Japanese the dangers of a revival of State Shinto and, for the advancement of democracy, called on them to oppose such a revival (1970, pp. 226–27). At a time when a movement had arisen for making Yasukuni a state-protected shrine, MURAKAMI took up the study State Shinto as empirical research necessary to prevent its resurgence (see 1970, preface). After Murakami, studies of State Shinto accumulated various empirical results, but at times their political connotations interfered. People who made left-wing assertions that were in agreement with Murakami criticized his theory from an empirical perspective and revised it, but they continued to proceed along the same track of study that was intent on preventing the resurgence of State Shinto. Conversely, those who took a right-wing perspective attempted to completely revise Murakami's theory. They claimed that his theory was empirically incorrect and that his political assertions were mistaken. Despite the conflict of political assertions, which existed on one level, empirical studies of State Shinto produced remarkable results. The dismantling of State Shinto, which supported the ideology of the national polity (*kokutai* 国体), was mandated by the Shinto Directive of 1945 and carried out shortly thereafter. At that time, State Shinto (as well as Shrine Shinto) was regarded as an ideological pillar of prewar ultranationalism. Among Shintoists, the term "State Shinto" has been criticized as not being a solid academic term because it is thoroughly tainted by the political policy and ideology of the GHQ of the postwar occupational forces.[5] The objectification of State Shinto that started with Murakami was a postwar phenomenon.

5. See the symposium discussion in "Kindai seikyō kankei no wakugumi o megutte" in *Kōgakkan Daigaku Shintō Kenkyūsho Kiyō*, volume 15 (1994), for an insight into how scholars have understood the term "*kokka Shintō*."

Murakami was a scholar of religion who was also a famous economic historian of the Kōza-ha and an admirer of the Marxist historian Hattori Shisō.[6] We can see that Murakami, with his unique academic background, made the study of State Shinto possible. Murakami's theory is formed by joining a structural theory of State Shinto with a theory of periodization. MURAKAMI claims that State Shinto was "a unique ethnic religion that was formed by directly connecting Shrine Shinto to the Shinto of the Imperial Household" (1970, p. 78) and that this "officially recognized religion based on kami and buddhas reigned as national rites that were suprareligious" (1970, p. 79). This situation MURAKAMI called the "State Shinto system," a system supported by the Constitution of the Empire of Japan and the Imperial Rescript on Education. Although the terms "ethnic religion" and "suprareligious" are vocabulary used by scholars of religion, Murakami as a historian of religion concludes that "State Shinto is a peculiar national religion for which there is almost nothing comparable even in the history of the world's religions" (1970, preface).

Murakami also produced a clear periodization for State Shinto that divided it into four distinct periods. The first was the formative period from the Meiji Restoration to Meiji 20 (1887). Second was the doctrinal-completion period that lasted from the promulgation of the Constitution of the Empire of Japan until the Russo-Japanese War. Third was the systematic-completion period that went from the 1900s until the beginning of the Shōwa period or late 1920s. This was State Shinto during the imperialistic era. Fourth was the fascist, national-religion period that started at the time of the Manchurian Incident (1931) and ended with the defeat of Japan in World War II. State Shinto developed a militaristic, aggressive doctrine and was complicit with aggression. This periodization is based on generally accepted periods in studies of modern history. Murakami's research describes the establishment and development of State Shinto, linking it with the periods used in studies of modern history. Because of this, it has been widely accepted among historians and also welcomed by general readers.

The strength of Murakami's theory lay in two constructions that were the axis of his argument, namely, a religious studies' structural theory and a historical periodization theory. It can be said that later State Shinto studies pursued the direction of these two constructions. His book *Kokka Shintō* consists of clear, straightforward logic, but when viewed by specialists, criticisms are made of it as an over-simplification that disregards the vicissitudes and setbacks that are a part of the historical process. YASUMARU Yoshio expresses as follows the vital problematic point in Murakami's theory that many readers were vaguely aware of but were unable to articulate:

> [Murakami's] view is somewhat persuasive when we reflect on the 15-year period of war, during which ultranationalism and coercive Shinto were important historical experiences. In modern Japan, while there were many changes, it can reasonably be said that widespread support was attained for the emperor's and the state's power. According to this view, however, the "State Shinto system" in effect completely overturned the history

---

6. Translator's note: The Kōza-ha was a faction in historical studies that analyzed the history of Japanese capitalism and emphasized the survival of feudalistic elements in it.

of modern Japanese religion, and one gets the impression of an impatience that drove diverse religious phenomena into a cage. When you think about it, it is quite strange that State Shinto, while the national religion, became established as rites devoid of doctrine. I think that while pursuing how this puzzling result came about we need to go beyond Murakami's theory. (YASUMARU 1992, p. 194)

Murakami's theory directly links the early Meiji period, when there was a policy to make Shinto the state religion, with the fifteen-year war period, and depicts the in-between periods, which he labels as the "formative period" and "establishment period," as progressing along a straight line from coalescence, to development, to establishment. Much time, however, elapsed between the early Meiji and the fifteen-year war period that must be meticulously reexamined. Just as Marxist historical studies in the past depicted state power as having a magnificently large presence, Murakami's depiction of State Shinto exaggerated it as a huge, coercive force. Did State Shinto actually have that much power? Within it was there no disaccord, no powerlessness, no fragility? These questions have been raised, at least among scholars who recognize the necessity of very carefully tracing the trial-and-error and the contradictions that are inherent to complex historical processes. After Murakami, Nakajima Michio, Miyachi Masato, and Sakamoto Koremaru have all taken to heart Yasumaru's suggestion and have reexamined Murakami's theory on the basis of historical documents.

Nakajima Michio points out that for a period of time the Meiji government ignored Shinto shrines. He places the establishment of State Shinto between Meiji 27 (1894) and Meiji 45 (1912), in other words, during the age of Japanese imperialism (NAKAJIMA 1977a), which is later than the establishment period postulated in Murakami's theory. State Shinto was established after the Russo-Japanese War and the revision of treaties, when the imperialistic modern state artificially incorporated the principles of religious freedom and the separation of religion and government. Nakajima clearly departs from Murakami by claiming that the regulation and persecution of various religions that occurred during the fascist period was not so much the culmination of State Shinto as it was its collapse.

Miyachi has taken issue with Nakajima regarding the time when State Shinto was established, placing it in Meiji 15 (1882) when the government abolished religious instruction by shrine priests.[7] Miyachi is a leading political historian of the *bakumatsu* and Meiji periods who has illuminated political history by clarifying how the idea of the state held by village teachers of the Hirata Kokugaku School was completely eradicated while the bureaucratic state, with its centralized authoritarian rule, pressed forward with modernization. While Shinto was expanding, the state, in order to avoid the crisis of a unified Shinto breaking up, abolished religious instruction by shrine priests and defined Shinto-shrine worship as a nonreligious civic virtue.

Yasumaru did not attempt to create a periodization. Instead, he attempted to surpass Murakami's structural theory by critically evaluating it. Yasumaru, from his unique per-

---

7. A debate between Nakajima Michio and Miyachi Masato's is published in MIYACHI 1977 and NAKAJIMA 1977b.

spective, reveals the historical processes that occurred from the separation of the buddhas and kami and the *haibutsu kishaku,* to the policy for the nationalization of Shinto (a
state policy that was thwarted by Shinshū), and then to the establishment of the Japanese-
style separation of religion and government (YASUMARU 1979, pp. 208–9). The "Japanese-
style separation of religion and government" (*Nihon-teki seikyō bunri* 日本的政教分離) is a
phrase coined by Yasumaru that refers to the free competition among religious sects to prove
their effectiveness in responding to the ideological demands of the state, a phenomenon that
began around 1873 when Shinshū split from the Great Teaching Academy. From Yasumaru's
perspective, some researchers are overly concerned with the history of institutions and do
not try to see things from the perspective of the lives of people living in society (YASUMARU
1988). Yasumaru looks at the psychological ethos and power of the people who endeavored
to carry forward the national ideology. The weakness of Yasumaru's theory, however, is that
it does not provide a set time for the establishment of the Japanese style of separation of religion and government, nor does it discuss its changes and disappearance.

State Shinto studies since Murakami have been conducted and promoted by Marxist
historians, but those in the Shinto shrine world have responded with empirical rebuttals.
The scholarship of Sakamoto Koremaru has greatly reconfigured traditional research on
the topic. Sakamoto had an advantage over pervious scholars in that he was the first to use
the now publicly available records from the cabinet of the Meiji government (*dajōruiten* 太
政類典) that are housed in the National Archives of Japan. The administration of religion
by the government in the early Meiji period was meticulously inspected by Sakamoto. He
proved that there was not, as Murakami had imagined, consistently strong protection by
the administration of the government's Shinto shrines. The establishment of State Shinto
was not something that was planned or formed in the early Meiji period. After many twists
and turns, the state founded the Shinto Shrine Bureau (Jinjakyoku 神社局) in 1900. It was
at this point that the government set out to regulate shrines. According to Sakamoto's theory, the government's policy for shrines before 1900 preceded the establishment of State
Shinto. Sakamoto, who was familiar with what was happening within Shinto shrine circles,
pioneered a method of research that lined up the tendencies in the policy-making process
with those of Shintoists. He showed to what extent politicians and bureaucrats were unconcerned with shrines, and how policy was carried out in a way that differed from the
intentions of Shintoists. We learn from Sakamoto's research that the situation in the shrine
world was not monolithic. Sakamoto's research took the points made by Nakajima and
Yasumaru and provided empirical evidence.

As mentioned above, studies of State Shinto include both theories of structure and periodization. Murakami's arguments about the structure of State Shinto were grappled with
and rewritten by Yasumaru. In addition to Yasumaru, a number of other scholars suggested their own theories of periodization. The work of all of these scholars contributed
to State Shinto studies being debated on a historical level. Although the debates increased,
a general consensus on State Shinto did not emerge and the individuality and the gaps
between the debates were conspicuous. Originally, State Shinto was not an historical term,
but after the war the term was recognized among scholars as historical. The image of State
Shinto was very wide and elastic; the expressions "the narrow meaning of State Shinto"

and "the broad meaning of State Shinto" were often used. Some have called for it not to be used at all, but until a better term is created to replace it, I think we should continue to use the term for expressing the totality of state-religion relations in Japan from the time of the Meiji period to the end of the war in 1945.

It is worth adding that although Nakajima, Miyachi, and Sakamoto all endeavored to clarify the establishment of State Shinto in the Meiji period, they did not carry out in-depth research on State Shinto in the Taishō and Shōwa periods. This gap in research has been somewhat filled by Akazawa Shirō's *Kindai Nihon no shisō dōin to shūkyō tōsei* (1985). Focusing on the period between the First and Second World War, this book carefully traces activities in the shrine world, the movement to establish the Jingi-in (Board of Shinto), the second bill for the religion law (*dainiji shūkyō hōan* 第二次宗教法案), the first bill for the Religious Organizations Law, General Mobilization for Educating the Citizenry (*kyōka sōdōin* 教化総動員), persecutions of religions, and the Peace Preservation Law (*chian ijihō* 治安維持法). Akazawa's approach was to look at the relationship between the state's political policies and the social bases for those policies. With regards to shrine administration in the fascist period, Akazawa points out that it severed the roots of the State Shinto system. Akazawa's arguments deserve consideration in conjunction with those of Nakajima. The debate over State Shinto in the fascist period is split over whether it was "manifesting its essence" (Murakami) or was collapsing (Nakajima and Akazawa). Murakami's image of State Shinto is based on actual experience of the fascist period; moreover, he believed that the evaluation of State Shinto in this period was definitively important, as did other scholars. With the exception of the research of Akazawa, however, research on religion and the state during the fifteen-year war period is insufficient in terms of both the history of shrines and Buddhism.

The history of modern shrines is not, of course, confined to State Shinto. Morioka Kiyomi's *Kindai no shūraku jinja to kokka tōsei* (1987) and Sakurai Haruo's *Yomigaeru mura no kamigami* (1992) both use the situation in Mie Prefecture to grapple with the interactions of the government's administration with local shrines. Sakurai analyzes cases of shrines and their rites that were revitalized after being destroyed when shrines were arranged by the government into a system. Nitta Hitoshi's work *Kindai seikyō kankei no kibanteki kenkyū* (1997) claims that "State Shinto" is an inappropriate term and questions the relationship between religion and the state. Yamaguchi Teruomi's *Meiji kokka to shūkyō* (1999) deals with the relationship of the state with religion during the formative years of the Meiji state, while being cognizant of the correspondence between the formative period of the Meiji state and the formation of the concept of religion (*shūkyō*).

POPULAR RELIGION AND NEW RELIGIONS

The term *shinkō shūkyō* 新興宗教 was used for a while after the war, but since *shinkō* ("newly arisen") has slightly pejorative connotations in Japanese, today the neutral term *shin shūkyō* 新宗教 is used (INOUE 1981, p. 208). After World War II the study of new religions developed in earnest, but before the war studies on Sect Shinto included studies of new religions. The terms "Sect Shinto" (*kyōha Shintō* 教派神道) and "pseudo religions" (*ruiji shūkyō* 類似宗教) ceased being used and were replaced by *shin shūkyō*. In the study of new religions, Murakami Shigeyoshi's *Kindai minshū shūkyōshi no kenkyū* (1958) is a classic research monograph, for which Murakami used his in-depth knowledge of the relevant documents to trace historical currents in modern popular religion from the time of Tenrikyō and Konkōkyō to Ōmotokyō. Murakami, influenced by the Marxist historian Hattori Shisō, contrasted the state with popular religions and depicted the latter as persecuted resistance movements that were antagonistic toward the state's power in the emperor system. Seventeen years later, the leading scholar in the study of popular religions, Yasumaru Yoshio, in his books *Nihon no kindaika to minshū shisō* (1974) and *Deguchi Nao* (1977) brought together topics of interest from unique theories of common morality and heretical cosmologies to Fujikō and Ōmotokyō. These books also gave sympathetic portrayals of the ways in which founders of new religions deviated from the ideology of the emperor system. Yasumaru investigated and sympathetically reported on the place of the spirit among the masses who fell outside the civilization-and-enlightenment track. Kozawa Hiroshi described the point of contention between popular religions, such as Konkōkyō, and the state's emperor system that they relentlessly confronted.

The study of popular religions started by Murakami and Yasumaru, which might be seen as the religious edition of the history of the general populace, has continued in Katsurajima Nobuhiro's *Bakumatsu minshū shisō no kenkyū* (1992) and Kanda Hideo's *Nyoraikyō no shisō to shinkō* (1990). From an ethnological perspective, we have works by Miyata Noboru on Miroku (1970) and millenarianism (1987), which attempted to demonstrate Japanese millenarianism and "world-renewal" (*yo-naoshi* 世直し) thought by researching early modern Fujikō and Ontakekō. Scholars of popular religion have clarified the cosmology and thought of popular religion during periods of transition in the modern and early modern period, while taking into consideration issues in ethnology and thought in the latter part of the early modern period (KANDA 1995).

In the latter half of the 1970s, new religions were of interest not only to ethnologists and historians but also attracted the attention of a new generation of sociologists. Before the late 1970s there were studies by Oguchi Iichi, Morioka Kiyomi, and Ikeda Akira, but these were critiques of secular matters or individual case studies. The new generation of sociologists was influenced by scholarly trends outside Japan—research on "sects" by Bryan Wilson; secularization theories by Thomas Luckmann, David Martin, and Eileen Barker; studies of new religions by Robert Bellah and Phillip Hammond—which they used to try to understand new religions in Japan in their entirety. It soon became clear that religious consciousness in modern Japan could not be grasped merely in terms of religious consciousness in the West. Younger Japanese sociologists also sought to advance beyond secularization theory by pointing out the persistence of new religions and their contemporary development (YAMANAKA and HAYASHI 1995). The study of popular religion in the tradition of Murakami and Yasumaru, carried on by Katsurajima Nobuhiro and Kanda Hideo, has been squeezed into a restrictive time frame that ranges from the *bakumatsu* period to the end of the Meiji period. In contrast, scholars such as Shimazono Susumu, Nishiyama Shigeru, and Tsushima Michihito have taken a wide scope that ranges from the *bakumatsu* to the present-day and have tried to grasp the thought structures of new religions as containing unique characteristics of modern religion. In the historical study of popular religions, the central issue has been the authority of the state and the resistance of popular religions to that authority. The focus is less clear in the study of new religions, but sociological ideas that have tried to draw out underlying similarities in the soteriologies of each new religion have been influential. The so-called "vitalistic conception of salvation" (*seimei shūgiteki kyūsaikan* 生命主義的救済観) is a sociological term used by these scholars to describe both the activities for this-worldly benefits in Japanese new religions and the mind set that holds more interest in this world than the next (Tsushima 1979).

Shimazono and Nishiyama, who have made great advances in the study of new religions, turned to the contemporary period and gradually shifted interest in the field of new religions to the study of religious consciousness after the 1970s. To understand new religions after the 1970s and how they were essentially different from the older new religions, Shimazono created the neologism "new spirituality movements" (*shin reisei undō* 新霊性運動) and Nishiyama coined the phrase "new-new religions" (*shin shin shūkyō* 新々宗教) (see Shimazono 1996 and Nishiyama 1979). With the term "new spirituality movements," Shimanozo attempts to act in concert with the interest in the West in New Age spirituality. While creating an image from a very broad perspective in the history of religions that consists of traditional religions, new religions, and new spirituality movements, Shimazono tries to locate new spirituality movements in the history of civilization. In comparison, the phrase "new-new religions," while frequently used in the mass media, was not widely debated in the academic world.

The sociology of religion is a part of sociology and as such it has the tendency to sharply question phenomena that are fundamentally contemporary, especially those that are topical, and which can be traced back into history. The Aum incident that occurred in 1995 was a shocking event that demanded comment from every sociologist of religion. In addition to Aum, topics that had never been dealt with up to that point—the ways scholars interact with religious organizations; the relationship between violence and religion, between cults and the anti-cult movement, and between the courts and research—suddenly came flooding to the forefront and led to questions about the way new religions were studied (see Nanzan Shūkyō Bunka Kenkyūjo 2002). These topics continue to be debated. As with the concept "vitalistic conception of salvation," studies that delineate a complete image of new religions using the early new religions as models have receded. Since the latter half of the 1980s, sociologists of religion have been drawn to the contemporary period, and their gaze has remained fixed there mostly as a result of the Aum incident.

The sociological study of religions jumped from studying new religions in the early part of the modern period to the present, and as a result few studies have dealt with new religions during the interim periods of Taishō and the earlier half of Shōwa. These periods remain blanks in the study of new religions because scholars of popular religion did not write about new religions beyond Ōmotokyō and sociologists of religion abruptly shifted their research area to the present. This left the new religions from the 1910s to the 1960s largely unexamined, including the many religions that were the foundations for today's large new religions. The study of modern new religions as a whole has passionately discussed the "beginning" and the "end" of the history of new religions, but it would be fair to say that it has neglected serious research on the interim periods spanning the two (HAYASHI 2002).

ON THE CONCEPT OF *SHŪKYŌ*

Finally, I would like to introduce the problems surrounding the concept of *shūkyō* 宗教. It is well known that the term *shūkyō* was created and gained popularity in the early Meiji period as a translation for "religion." Before then, the words *shūshi* 宗旨 and *shūmon* 宗門 were used, but in the modern period the term *shūkyō*, which was associated with the Western concept of religion, started to be used.

The concept of "religion" in Western religious studies and anthropology is not a neutral term, as scholars in religious studies once believed. Scholars are now aware that it is a concept that thoroughly reflects its Western origins and Western values, and that when modernization brought the concept to non-Western areas it had the power to change indigenous cultures and the perceptions of indigenous peoples. The problem with the concept of religion, which has become a popular topic also among Western academics, has caused new problems to emerge, such as what type of epistemological changes were brought by the introduction and formation of the concept of religion in Japan and its political effects. Naturally, religious studies as an academic discipline that takes religion as its object of study was also not neutral. This realization has led to the examination of the historical and political contexts in which religious studies formed, as well as the social functions it has served. ISOMAE Jun'ichi (2003) has digested the recent debates in the West and concisely clarifies the appearance of the concept of religion within the context of modern Japan, and the origins of Shinto studies and religious studies. Other important works include SHIMAZONO Susumu and TSURUOKA Yoshio's work on "rethinking *shūkyō*" (2004), and the collection *Shūkyō to wa nanika*, which starts with an interpretive preface by SEKI Kazutoshi (2003), one of the book's editors, and then expands into a debate among religious studies scholars and anthropologists on the concept of religion.

It is important for the problem of the concept of religion to be approached as one example of the many concepts that were imported in the modern period and recreated in modern law. Modern concepts such as "the state," "freedom," "human rights," and "society" are concepts that have much more significance, and it is only in connection with them that we should try to surmise the function and location of "religion." We should also examine the formation of religious studies as linked with the formative process of research in the humanities and social sciences. We will not perceive the impact of religion if we isolate the formation of religious studies from these areas.

SUMMARY

In this essay I have attempted to give a research history of religion in the modern period. I would like to highlight three points from among the four parts into which the essay is divided.

First is the reliance on postwar historical conceptions in the study of modern religion to gain a general understanding of the period from the Meiji Restoration to the end of the war as modern history. The term *kindai* (modern) had been used before the war, but it did not become an established part of Japanese historical understanding until after the war. Moreover, the key words that express certain areas of study, such as "modern Buddhism," "State Shinto," and "new religions," were also not widely used until after the war.

Second is the general trend in which the Meiji period was widely taken up in each area of the study of modern religion, while, by comparison, there was a decreasing level of interest in the Taishō and Shōwa periods (especially the fifteen-year war period). The Meiji period, as a time when the founders of Tenrikyō and Konkōkyō lived and the standard-bearers of Buddhist reform movements appeared, seems to have been a particularly interesting period for researchers, but the attention given to periods after it is seriously insufficient. Even in the study of State Shinto, the Meiji period was usually at the center of debate. The precedence given to the Meiji period, which continues today with the use of categories such as "Meiji Buddhist history" and "Meiji Shinto history," is a weakness in the study of modern religion.

Third is the relationship of the study of new religions and history with sociology. There is a need to compare historical methods and results with the interpretations of historical documents and theories of periodization. It is also necessary to look at the questions asked in sociology about modernity and modernization from the standpoint of our understanding of modern religions. The study of State Shinto has produced a mass of empirical studies that are similar to historical studies in that they have concentrated on political history and the process in which policies were made. The study of new religions has been perceived as an important subject of study for sociologists of religion and there is a large amount of research and investigations on new religions from a sociological perspective. The study of modern Buddhism, however, has not been a part of either sociology or history and only rarely is it linked with either. To vitalize the study of modern Buddhism, its connection to history needs to be strengthened, as does cooperative efforts with research being done outside Japan.

BIBILIOGRAHY

AKAZAWA Shirō 赤澤史郎, 1985. *Kindai Nihon no shisō dōin to shūkyō tōsei* 近代日本の思想動員と宗教統制. Tokyo: Azekura Shobō.

HAGA Shōji 羽賀祥二, 1994. *Meiji ishin to shūkyō* 明治維新と宗教. Tokyo: Chikuma Shobō.

HAYASHI Makoto 林 淳, 2002. Shimazono Susumu no kindai shūkyōshi kenkyū ni yosete 島薗進の近代宗教史研究に寄せて. *Nanzan Shūkyō Bunka Kenkyūjo Kenkyū Shohō* 12: 42–43.

IKEDA Eishun 池田英俊, 1994. *Meiji Bukkyō kyōkai kesshashi no kenkyū* 明治仏教教会・結社史の研究. Tokyo: Tōsui Shobō.

_____, 2004. Aratanaru hishō no ba o kizuku tameni 新たなる飛翔の場をきづくために. *Kindai Bukkyō* 11: pp. 1–13.

INOUE Nobutaka 井上順孝, et al., eds., 1981. *Shinshūkyō kenkyū chōsa handobukku* 新宗教研究調査ハンドブック. Tokyo: Yūzankaku.

ISOMAE Jun'ichi 磯前順一, 2003. *Kindai Nihon no shūkyō gensetsu to sono keifu* 近代日本の宗教言説とその系譜. Tokyo: Iwanami Shoten.

JAFFE, Richard, 2001. *Neither Monk nor Layman: Clerical Marriage in Modern Japanese Buddhism*. Princeton: Princeton University Press.

JAFFE, Richard, and Michel MOHR, eds., 1998. "Meiji Zen." Special issue, *Japanese Journal of Religious Studies* 25/1–2.

KANDA Hideo 神田秀雄, 1990. *Nyoraikyō no shisō to shinkō* 如来教の思想と信仰. Tenri: Tenri Daigaku Oyasato Kenkyūjo.

_____, 1995. Kokumin tōgo to minshū shūkyō 国民統合と民衆宗教. In *Kinsei shisōshi kenkyū no genzai* 近世思想史研究の現在, ed. Kinugasa Yasuki 衣笠安喜, pp. 381–400. Kyoto: Shibunkaku.

KASHIWAHARA Yūsen 柏原祐泉, 1969. *Nihon kinsei kindai Bukkyōshi no kenkyū* 日本近世近代仏教史の研究. Kyoto: Heirakuji Shoten.

_____, 1990. *Nihon Bukkyōshi: Kindai* 日本仏教史——近代. Tokyo: Yoshikawa Kōbunkan.

_____, 1995–2000. *Shinshūshi Bukkyōshi no kenkyū* 真宗史仏教史の研究, 3 vols. (*Shinran: chūseihen* 親鸞・中世篇, 1995; *Kinseihen* 近世篇, 1996; *Kindaihen* 近代篇, 2000). Kyoto: Heirakuji Shoten.

KATSURAJIMA Nobuhiro 桂島宣弘, 1992. *Bakumatsu minshū shisō no kenkyū* 幕末民衆思想の研究. Tokyo: Bun'rikaku.

KETELAAR, James Edward, 1990. *Of Heretics and Martyrs in Meiji Japan: Buddhism and Its Persecution*. Princeton: Princeton University Press.

KOJIMA Masaru 小島 勝 and KIBA Akeshi 木場明志, 1992. *Ajia no kaikyō to kyōiku* アジアの開教と教育. Kyoto: Ryūkoku Daigaku Bukkyō Bunka Kenkyūjo.

MIYACHI Masato 宮地正人, 1977. Kindaishi bukai hōkoku hihan 近代史部会報告批判. *Nihonshi kenkyū* 178: 53–56.

MIYATA Noboru 宮田 登, 1970. *Miroku shinkō no kenkyū* ミロク信仰の研究. Tokyo: Miraisha.

_____, 1987. *Shūmatsukan no minzokugaku* 終末観の民俗学. Tokyo: Kōbundō.

MORIOKA Kiyomi 森岡清美, 1987. *Kindai no shūraku jinja to kokka tōsei* 近代の集落神社と国家統制. Tokyo: Yoshikawa Kōbunkan.

MORIYA Tomoe 守屋友江, 2001. *Amerika Bukkyō no tanjō* アメリカ仏教の誕生. Tokyo: Gendai Shiryō Shuppan.

MURAKAMI Shigeyoshi 村上重良, 1958. *Kindai minshū shūkyō shi no kenkyū* 近代民衆宗教史の研究. Kyoto: Hōzōkan.

_____, 1970. *Kokka Shintō* 国家神道. Tokyo: Iwanami Shoten.

NAKAJIMA Michio 中島三千男, 1977a. "Meiji kenpō taisei" no kakuritsu to kokka ideorogī seisaku 「明治憲法体制」の確立と国家イデオロギー政策. *Nihonshi kenkyū* 176: 166–91.

_____, 1977b. "Kokka Shintō taisei" kenkyū hatten no tame ni 「国家神道体制」研究の発展のために. *Nihonshi kenkyū* 178: 48–63.

NANZAN SHŪKYŌ BUNKA KENKYŪJO 南山宗教文化研究所, ed., 2002. *Shūkyō to shakai mondai no "aida"* 宗教と社会問題の＜あいだ＞. Tokyo: Seikyūsha.

NISHIYAMA Shigeru 西山 茂, 1979. Shinshūkyō no genkyō 新宗教の現況. *Rekishi kōron* 517: 33–37.

NITTA Hitoshi 新田 均, 1997. *Kindai seikyō kankei no kisoteki kenkyū* 近代政教関係の基礎的研究. Tokyo: Taimeidō.

———, 1999a. "Kokka Shintō" ron no keifu (jō) 「国家神道」論の系譜 (上). *Kōgakkan Ronsō* 31/1: 1–36.

———, 1999b. "Kokka Shintō" ron no keifu (ge) 「国家神道」論の系譜 (下). *Kōgakkan Ronsō* 31/2: 23–59.

ŌISHI Makoto 大石 真, HIRANO Takeshi 平野 武, and MOMOCHI Akira 百地 章, eds., 1999. *Kindai seikyō kankei no wakugumi o megutte* 近代政教関係の枠組みをめぐって. *Kōgakkan Daigaku Shintō Kenkyūjo kiyō* 15: 1–53.

ŌTANI Eiichi 大谷栄一, 2001. *Kindai Nihon no Nichirenshugi undō* 近代日本の日蓮主義運動. Kyoto: Hōzōkan.

SAKURAI Haruo 櫻井治男, 1992. *Yomigaeru mura no kamigami* 蘇るムラの神々. Tokyo: Taimeidō.

SEKI Kazutoshi 関 一敏, IKEGAMI Yoshimasu 池上良正, ODA Yoshiko 小田淑子, SHIMAZONO Susumu 島薗 進, SUEKI Fumihiko 末木文美士, and TSURUOKA Yoshio 鶴岡賀雄, eds., 2003. *Shūkyō to wa nanika* 宗教とはなにか. Iwanami Kōza: Shūkyō 岩波講座 宗教 1. Tokyo: Iwanami Shoten.

SHARF, Robert H., 1993. The Zen of Japanese Nationalism, *History of Religions* 33: 1–43.

———, 1994. Whose Zen? Zen Nationalism Revisited. In *Rude Awakenings: Zen, the Kyoto School & the Question of Nationalism*, ed. James W. Heisig and John C. Maraldo, pp. 40–51. Honolulu: University of Hawai'i Press.

SHIMAZONO Susumu 島薗 進, 1996. *Seishin sekai no yukue* 精神世界のゆくえ. Tokyo: Tōkyōdō.

SHIMAZONO Susumu and TSURUOKA Yoshio 鶴岡賀雄, eds., 2004. *"Shūkyō" saikō* ＜宗教＞再考. Tokyo: Pelican.

SUEKI Fumihiko 末木文美士, 2004. *Kindai Nihon no shisō: Saikō* 近代日本の思想・再考, 2 vols. Tokyo: Transview.

SWANSON, Paul, 2004. *Zen hihan no shosō* 禅批判の諸相. In special issue on "Zen Studies Today" 禅研究の現在. *Shisō* 960: 124–34.

TOKUSHIGE Asakichi 徳重浅吉, 1933. *Meiji Bukkyō kenkyū shiryō* 明治仏教研究資料. *Shūkyō Kenkyū* 10/1: 308–32. (reprinted in *Ishin seiji shūkyōshi kenkyū* 維新政治宗教史研究, Tokyo: Meguro Shoten, 1934, and by Kyoto: Ritsumeikan Shuppanbu, 1941)

TSUCHIYA Senkyō 土屋詮教, 1939. *Meiji Bukkyō shi* 明治仏教史. Tokyo: Sanseidō.

TSUJI Zennosuke 辻善之助, MURAKAMI Senshō 村上専精, and WASHIO Junkyo 鷲尾順敬, eds., 1926–1929. *Meiji Ishin shinbutsu bunri shiryō* 明治維新神仏分離史料. Tokyo: Tōhō Shoin. (reprinted Tokyo: Meicho Shuppan, 1970)

TSUSHIMA Michihito 対馬路人, NISHIYAMA Shigeru 西山 茂, SHIMAZONO Susumu 島薗 進, and SHIRAMIZU Hiroko 白水寛子, eds., 1979. *Shinshūkyō ni okeru seimei-shūgiteki kyūzaikan* 新宗教における生命主義的救済観. *Shisō* 665: 95–115. (published 1979 in English translation: "The Vitalistic Conception of Salvation in Japanese New Religions," *Japanese Journal of Religious Studies* 6: 139–61)

VICTORIA, Brian (Daizen) A., 1997. *Zen at War*. New York: Weatherhill.

YAMAGUCHI Teruomi 山口輝臣, 1999. *Meiji kokka to shūkyō* 明治国家と宗教. Tokyo: Tōkyō Daigaku Shuppankai.

YAMANAKA Hiroshi 山中 弘 and HAYASHI Makoto 林 淳, 1995. Nihon ni okeru shūkyō shakaigaku no tenkai 日本における宗教社会学の展開. *Aichi Gakuin Daigaku Bungakubu kiyō* 25: 67–82.

YASUMARU Yoshio 安丸良夫, 1974. *Nihon no kindaika to minshū shisō* 日本の近代化と民衆思想. Tokyo: Aoki Shoten. (reprinted Tokyo: Heibonsha, 1999)

———, 1977. *Deguchi Nao* 出口なお. Tokyo: Asahi Shinbunsha.

———, 1979. *Kamigami no Meiji ishin* 神々の明治維新. Tokyo: Iwanami Shoten.

———, 1988. Kindai tenkanki ni okeru shūkyō to kokka 近代転換期における宗教と国家. In *Shūkyō to kokka* 宗教と国家 (Nihon Kindai Shisō Taikei 日本近代思想大系 5), ed. Yasumaru Yoshio and Miyachi Masato, pp. 490–564. Tokyo: Iwanami Shoten.

———, 1992. *Kindai tennōzō no keisei* 近代天皇像の形成. Tokyo: Iwanami Shoten.

YOSHIDA Kyūichi 吉田久一, 1959. *Nihon kindai Bukkyōshi kenkyū* 日本近代仏教史研究. Tokyo: Yoshikawa Kyōbunkan.

———, 1964. *Nihon kindai Bukkyō shakai shi kenkyū* 日本近代仏教社会史研究. Tokyo: Yoshikawa Kōbunkan.

———, 1998. *Kingendai Bukkyō no reikishi* 近現代仏教の歴史. Tokyo: Chikuma Shobō.

[Translated by Clark Chilson]

SHIMAZONO Susumu 島薗 進

Contemporary Japanese Religions

Following the end of the Second World War on 15 August 1945, the institutions related to religion in Japan underwent tremendous change. The framework for this change was determined by the so-called Shinto Directive (October 1945) and the Emperor's Declaration of Humanity (1 January 1946)—formally titled "Directive on the Abolition of Governmental Sponsorship, Support, Perpetuation, Control, and Dissemination of State Shinto or Shrine Shinto," and the "Proclamation at the Beginning of the Year," respectively. Both of these were proposed by the Allied General Headquarters and were based on the fundamental policy laid out in the postwar American occupation strategy. Finally, the directions given in these documents were given legal expression in the provisions in the Japanese Constitution (promulgated in November 1946) related to the emperor and religion, the Religious Corporations Directive (December 1945), and its revision as the Religious Corporations Law (April 1951) (INOUE 1969; WOODARD 1972; ABE 1989; ŌHARA 1993; ŌISHI 1996).

THE DISMANTLING OF STATE SHINTO
AND THE ESTABLISHMENT OF RELIGIOUS FREEDOM

The institutional reformation promoted by these documents has been summarized as the dismantling of State Shinto and the establishment of religious freedom. However, there is not necessarily a clear agreement regarding the content of that reformation, because the meaning of State Shinto is not always clear (NIITA 1997). In its narrow meaning, it indicates Shrine Shinto given a special position by the state. Here it is distinguished from Sect Shinto, given a position equal to other religions, and it indicates facilities, organizations, and personnel recognized as having a special connection with the state through the performance of specific rituals. However, the term is also given a broader meaning (MURAKAMI 1970), and I believe that this broader meaning is more appropriate (SHIMAZONO 2001a, 2001b). Here, State Shinto indicates a system of worship of the gods, who are seen as having a special relationship with the Japanese state and people, as well as worship of the emperor as a holy presence in the divine lineage of Amaterasu Omikami, the main divinity.

In this understanding of State Shinto, not only court rituals, but also rituals related to the Imperial Rescript on Education and the Imperial Portrait, as well as moral training and education in national history are seen as serving an important function of State Shinto. Here the system of national holidays and many of the official state activities can be taken as rituals of State Shinto. Furthermore, the relations between the state and the shrines were varied, and not all of Shrine Shinto can be subsumed under State Shinto. Although some shrines functioned as central State Shinto facilities—such as Ise Shrine, Yasukuni Shrine, and the *gokoku jinja* 護国神社, as well as the shrines in colonial countries—among the local shrines there were some that had, at best, tenuous connections with the state.

When State Shinto is understood in the wider sense, its dismantling must be seen as something that transcended the narrow meaning of religious institutions. Educational reform was an important part of the dismantling of State Shinto, and postwar thought control also played an important role in this dismantling. Therefore, it is inadequate to focus merely on the Shinto Directive and the Declaration of Humanity in order to understand the full framework of postwar Japanese religion. However, on the other hand, there is no need to argue with the assumption that the framework of this new Japanese religious structure can be described in terms of the dismantling of State Shinto and the establishment of religious freedom (IKADO 1993).

The question comes down to the extent of the dismantling of State Shinto. The imperial system has been preserved in the emperor as a symbol of the state, and although Yasukuni Shrine and the *gokoku jinja* are now considered private shrines, they are supported as facilities for the enshrinement of the spirits of national military forces. Shrines built since the Meiji era, such as Meiji Jingū 明治神宮 and Kashihara Jingū 橿原神宮, which were deeply related to domestic State Shinto, have not been abolished, and the sentiment toward emperor worship remains strong in Shinto shrine, Shinto thought, and Shinto studies circles. So we see that State Shinto has not completely disappeared, and although its extent may have been greatly reduced in comparison to prewar practices, it continues to garner some degree of support. And occasionally the reemergence of State Shinto becomes a topic of controversy.

Supporters of Yasukuni Shrine and government participation in imperial accession rites are many, causing long-standing political problems (NAKAJIMA 1990; HIRANO 1995; KOBORI 1998). The movement to make Yasukuni Shrine a national facility began in the 1950s, and since the latter half of the 1970s the appropriateness of official visits to the shrine by the prime minister have become a matter of controversy. In addition to the domestic opposition that rests on the constitutional prohibition of state support of a specific religious group, there has also been an increasing opposition from China and Korea because of the internment of the spirits of Class A war criminals in 1979. In the latter half of the 1990s a movement to give greater weight to the role of the emperor in history textbooks gained strength, leading to the publication of a "new history textbook" in 2001. Along with the problem of official visits by the prime minister to Yasukuni Shrine, this development has led to an increase in domestic opposition, as well as in concern expressed by neighboring countries.

Under the principle of religious freedom, control of, or interference in religious groups by the state is prohibited, and the freedom to establish a religious group has been enhanced. Along with a strengthening of the power of self-governance of religious groups, it has also become easy to establish new religions as well as to break off from established religious groups. It goes without saying that the explosive expansion in the number of new religions in the postwar period is deeply related to this institutional reform.

THE DEVELOPMENT OF NEW RELIGIOUS MOVEMENTS

The development of new religious movements in the postwar period has been remarkable, leading to expressions such as "they appear like bamboo shoots after the rain," and the "rush hour of the gods" (MCFARLAND 1967). Research on such groups has also flourished since the 1950s (TAKAGI 1959; SAKI 1960). If we consider as new religions those groups that have been established since the nineteenth century, in the Taishō period only the sects of Sect Shinto and groups such as Honmon Butsuryūkō 本門佛立講 would have been included in this category. However, by the 1980s researchers speculate that new religions number "more than two or three thousand" (MATSUNO 1984).

It would not be correct to see this as merely a post–World War II development, however. Among the groups that developed rapidly until the 1960s, Reiyūkai 霊友会, Seichō no Ie 生長の家, and Sekai Kyūseikyō 世界救世教 had already built up quite a following in the 1930s. Other groups, such as Sōka Gakkai 創価学会 and PL Kyōdan PL教団, had a considerable following before the war (when they were known as Sōka Kyōiku Gakkai 創価教育学会 and Hito no Michi Kyōdan ひとのみち教団 respectively), were disbanded as a result of government interference, and reemerged in the postwar period. Still other groups, such as Risshō Kōseikai 立正佼成会, Gedatsukai 解脱会, Ennōkyō 円応教, Zenrinkyō 善隣教, and Shinnyoen 真如苑, had to some extent established a base in the prewar period (INOUE et al. 1989; SHIMAZONO 1992).

Although there were groups that grew rapidly in the postwar period that trace their foundation to the time just after the war, such as Jiu 璽宇 and Tenshōkō Daijingūkyō 天照皇大神宮教, many of the groups that developed into major players in this period were founded prewar or during the war. Historically, therefore, new religions can be divided into three groups, with the period until the 1880s as the first period, from that point until around 1920 as the second period, and from the 1920s until the 1970s as the third period (SHIMAZONO 2001a and 2001b). Even those that were established in the mid-nineteenth century, such as Tenrikyō, Konkōkyō, and Honmon Butsuryūkō, grew rapidly in the postwar period, and in this way the period from the end of the war until the 1960s was a good time for Japanese new religions as a whole.

Among the new religions, the growth of Sōka Gakkai has been particularly noteworthy, increasing from a membership of around five thousand in 1951 to 50,000 households in 1957, and claiming 7,500,000 households in 1971. This denomination started as a lay movement within the traditional Nishiren Shōshū sect, and under the direction of Toda Jōsei 戸田城聖 and Ikeda Daisaku 池田大作 it developed strong local organizations centered on devout believers who venerate (gongyō 勤行) the gohonzon ご本尊 and gather as local groups of believers for the zadankai 座談会. Incorporating scientific rhetoric and at the same time engaging in a fierce type of proselytization critical of other religions, namely shakubuku 折伏, it attracted large numbers of followers and in a short time developed into a major organization. Because of its aggressive proselytization and rejection of other religions it became the object of severe criticism from several quarters and found itself in a relationship of animosity with many other religious groups. From an early stage Sōka Gakkai also made forays into the world of politics. Starting with the sponsoring of candidates in the unified local elections of 1955, its candidates were elected to the Upper House of Parliament in the following year, and in 1964 its own political party, the Kōmeitō 公明党, was formed. From the 1970s the Kōmeitō would regularly attract more than ten percent of the vote in nationwide proportional voting for the Upper House of Parliament, becoming a major political power (MURAKAMI 1967).

In addition to Sōka Gakkai, groups within the Reiyūkai lineage also are lay groups within the tradition of the Lotus Sūtra and Nichiren Buddhism. Reiyūkai, founded by Kubo Kakutarō 久保角太郎 and Kotani Kimi 小谷喜美, spawned many other groups, including Risshō Kōseikai, founded by Niwano Nikkyō 庭野日敬 and Naganuma Myōkō 長沼妙佼, and if we add up the membership claimed by all the groups in the Reiyūkai lineage it amounts to more than ten million believers. Like Sōka Gakkai, groups within the Reiyūkai lineage do not rely on temples and monks for their practice; rather they encourage their lay believers to engage in independent Buddhist practice based on the Lotus Sūtra, especially highlighting ancestor veneration. They have developed the unique practice of venerating not only the ancestors of the husband's family but of the wife's family as well, and neighborhood gatherings that focus on the sharing of experiences—called hōza 法座, among other names—and omichibiki お導き, or inviting one's neighbors to join the faith, have been quite effective in drawing others to the group.

Among the Shinto-based new religions, Sekai Kyūseikyō and Seichō no Ie—both in the Ōmotokyō 大本教 lineage—have shown remarkable growth. In Sekai Kyūseikyō, founded by Okada Mokichi 岡田茂吉, healing through the practice of *tekazashi* 手かざし (*gojōrei* ご淨霊) is practiced, whereas in Seichō no Ie, healing through a unique form of prayer called *shinsōkan* 神想観, as well as through the learning of the concept of a pervading "life force" promoted in their magazines, has become a major tool for proselytization. Within the Hito no Michi lineage, in addition to PL Kyōdan, founded by Miki Tokuchika 御木徳近 and preaching healing through the practice of an ethic of daily life, groups that do not call themselves a religion, such as Jissen Rinri Kōseikai 実践倫理宏正会 and Rinri Kenkyūjo 倫理研究所, have also appeared and have gathered a considerable following. Whether they be Buddhist-based or Shinto-based, these new religious movements all emphasize this-worldly benefits such as healing as the expression of salvation, as well as the practice of *kokoro naoshi* 心なおし—the healing of the spirit—that aims toward harmonious human relationships within the family and those that one lives and works with daily. In this way, these new religions can be said to be generally this-worldly focused, directed toward salvation in the present world.

Although the primary aim of these new religious movements is to lead individuals toward salvation and create a warm community of believers, many of them are also actively involved more broadly in society. In addition to political activities, Sōka Gakkai has been engaged in its own independent support of the United Nations and international friendship activities. A federation of denominations called the Federation of New Religious Organizations of Japan (Shin Nihon Shūkyō Dantai Rengōkai 新日本宗教団体連合会, abbreviated as Shinshūren 新宗連) was formed in 1951 to promote common social activities. Some of the major members of the Shinshūren, such as Risshō Kōseikai and Myōchikai Kyōdan 妙智會教団, have also been involved in interreligious cooperation through organizations such as the World Conference on Peace and Religion (WCRP, Kisala 1999).

Many of the new religious movements have also been engaged in proselytization outside of Japan. New religious groups engaged in foreign missionary work that showed some success in attracting non-Japanese members, such as Tenrikyō and Honmon Butsuryūkō in Korea, are limited in number, but since the 1960s Sōka Gakkai, Seichō no Ie, Sekai Kyūseikyō, and others have been successful in attracting members in Korea, Brazil, the United States, and other countries throughout the world (Maeyama 1997; Watanabe 2001). However, since the 1970s, as these major new religions of the third period increased in size abroad, they also entered a period of stagnation domestically. New religious groups that have developed since the 1970s can be described as belonging to the fourth period in the history of new religions in Japan. In this period groups such as GLA, Mahikari 真光, and Agonshū 阿含宗, along with the Jehovah's Witnesses from the United States and the Unification Church (Tōitsu Kyōkai 統一教会, more formally The Holy Spirit Association for the Unification of Christianity, Sekai Kirisutokyō Tōitsu Shinrei Kyōkai 世界基督教統一神霊協会) from Korea experienced rapid growth. In addition, groups such as Aum Shinrikyō オウム真理教, Kōfuku no Kagaku 幸福の科学, Worldmate ワールドメイト, and Hō no Hana Sanpōgyō 法の華三法行 are remarkable for their development since the mid-1980s (Numata 1995; Shimazono 2001a).

These groups are often called "new new religions," and they are characterized by their attraction to a younger age of believer as well as a more negative attitude toward the present world than previous groups. Among them, one group that has attracted attention is the Unification Church, based on Christianity but developing its own unique idea of the family and emphasizing veneration of its founder, Sun Myung Moon 文鮮明. This group has been criticized for offering young believers a communal lifestyle while cutting them off from their families and forcing them to participate in rather extreme proselytization practices, but at the same time, because of its anti-communist political activities it has received some degree of protection from the LDP (Liberal Democratic Party) and has been successful in obtaining the cooperation of right-wing academics. Since the 1980s it has been accused of fraudulently obtaining large donations through the practice of *reikan shōhō* 霊感商法, and has become the target of lawsuits by former members who have accused it of fraudulent proselytization practices. Since the end of the 1980s we have seen an increase in groups that have been accused of causing harm, such as Aum Shinrikyō, and several have become objects of continuing criticism by being identified as "cults."

It goes without saying that no new religious group has posed more of a threat to society than Asahara Shōkō's 麻原彰晃 Aum Shinrikyō. Drawing influence from Agonshū and Tibetan Buddhism, Aum Shinrikyō started to proselytize actively around the mid-1980s, attracting some popularity as a group that practiced meditation for the purpose of attaining "final liberation" and gathering a following among young people in their 20s and 30s, including some who were highly educated. However, following the abuse of some members by forcing them to participate in extreme practices, it developed a doctrine that justified the use of violence, eventually engaging in attacks that included the murder of those who criticized the group. In the early 1990s it proclaimed that the final battle with the forces of evil—Armageddon—was near, and began developing biological and chemical weapons, eventually engaging in indiscriminate acts of terrorism through the release of sarin gas in Matsumoto in 1994 and on the Tokyo subways in March 1995. Following this attack, criticism of new religions by society increased, leading to a revision of the Religious Corporations Law that made it easier to strip religious groups of their legal standing and requiring stricter accounting by these groups.

CHANGES IN TRADITIONAL RELIGION

It would be hard to describe the religious policies of the occupation period as being particularly beneficial to the traditional Buddhist sects. Although there was greater freedom of thought, many temples lost their land as a result of the land reform, and it was mainly the new religions that were able to gain a greater following through free competition among religious groups. However, even more than these institutional problems, the decline in local communities and family relationships that temples had relied on in the past dealt a serious blow to these traditional religious groups. The status of the monk as one held in high esteem gradually declined. Typical of those who cut their ties with the temples were immigrants to the cities. This "floating religious population" (Fujii 1974) that left the countryside and moved to the cities was seen as a major source of recruits for the new religious movements (Suzuki 1963–1964). If not a few immigrants to the city were able to find a refuge in the new religions, it is easy to assume in return that the temples lost many of them as parishioners.

It is true that many of the new religious movements—excluding Sōka Gakkai—allowed their believers to maintain their ties with the temples and call on the monks to perform funerals and memorial rites, and so the damage to the Buddhist sects was limited. The relationship between the temples and parishioners, however, gradually became formalistic, and the tendency toward estrangement between the temple and its parishioners increased. "Funeral Buddhism" was proposed as an academic term around 1960 (TAMAMURO 1963), and from the 1980s funeral services and cemeteries were increasingly a topic of conversation. Doubts were raised regarding the practice of offering a donation for a *kaimyō*, or posthumous name, and there were exposés on the profitable funeral industry and suppliers of *butsudan*. Meanwhile, so-called "natural funerals" (*shizen-sō* 自然葬), or the scattering of the ashes of the dead, and the use of common graves attracted interest. It became apparent that the foundations of temple Buddhism, based on the family unit and rites of ancestor veneration, were crumbling (ITO and FUJII 1997).

How about Buddhism as part of the culture? Through the popularization of high school and university education, basic knowledge of Japanese religion became widespread, and the possibility of access to knowledge of Buddhism, although fragmentary, increased. Newspapers, magazines, books, movies, and radio were popularized from the Taishō period, and in the postwar period tape recorders, TV, and video were added to these, increasing tremendously the influence of the media. In addition, the 1990s saw the rapid popularization of digital media. Although the proliferation and diversification of media had a considerable influence on Japanese religion in general, in the case of Buddhism, with its rich resources in the printed word and iconography, opportunities to make these available to ordinary people increased greatly. Among scholars of literature and philosophers Shinran 親鸞 and Dōgen 道元 have always been popular. The manga artist Tezuka Osamu 手塚治虫 drew his "Buddha" series in the 1970s (1972–1979), and the increase in works and texts drawing on Buddhist themes—tapes of the sutras and sermons of respected monks from Nara and Kyoto to videos offering instruction in esoteric Tibetan meditation—was remarkable.

Let us take a look at Christianity. Japanese Christianity's characteristic foundation on the intellectual class—descendents of the samurai—continued in the postwar period. Although Christianity had some appeal in the immediate postwar period as the religion of the conqueror, it did not show a corresponding increase in membership. In the United States in the 1960s we see an increase in evangelists and their penetration among the well educated, and in Korea until the 1980s, along with the well-educated Christians, we see the development of a popular Christianity. In Japan, aside from Okinawa, popular Christianity remains a small-scale affair (IKEGAMI 1991; MULLINS 1998). Among the well educated as well, there was nothing to compare with the powerful movements of the Meiji period. By the 1990s the Non-Church Movement, comprising the disciples of Uchimura Kanzō 内村 鑑三, was clearly failing. It is true, however, that since the 1970s the Unification Church and Jehovah's Witnesses have exhibited remarkable growth, and if one considers these groups Christian, then we can speak of the development of popular Christianity in Japan as well.

Although Christianity has not made significant inroads as a religious organization,

Christianity as culture has had a measure of success. Christianity enjoys a rather high status in literary works, and a number of famous Christian writers, such as Shiina Rinzō 椎名麟三, Endō Shūsaku 遠藤周作, and Miura Ayako 三浦綾子, have appeared. Opportunities to become acquainted with Christianity through the study of Western culture, music, and art have increased among those pursuing higher education, and among ordinary people as well the celebration of Christmas and the use of Christian wedding ceremonies have become commonplace (ISHII 1993).

It goes without saying that Shrine Shinto and Shinto culture have suffered a serious blow through the dismantling of State Shinto. In addition, small local shrines, linked closely to the local community, have suffered considerably due to the scattering of that community. In the popular culture, however, a revitalization of Shinto rites and Shinto culture has emerged. Shinto weddings, *shichi-go-san* 七五三 (a festival on 15 November for five-year-old boys, and three- and seven-year-old girls), *hatsu mairi* 初参り, and *hatsu mōde* 初詣 (New Year's visit to a shrine) all have become homogenous rites performed in much the same way throughout the country in the postwar period. For example, *hatsu mōde* is a custom that emerged in the Meiji period (TAKAKI 1997), and although only 56% of the population said that they participated in the rite in 1979, by 1994 this had increased to 62% (ISHII 1993). This would seem to indicate a long-term trend toward increasing participation.

Since the 1980s, an increasing interest in "Early Shinto" and "animism," with ties to cultural nationalism and a growing ecological awareness, also indicate the rising influence of Shinto culture in a broad sense. This is related to the popularity of Japanese culturalism (Nihonjinron 日本人論). Although there has been a constant interest in Japanese culturalism since the end of World War II, since the late 1970s this has taken on a self-assertive character emphasizing its religious aspect. For example, UMEHARA Takeshi has attracted considerable support to his ideas, presented in *Nihonjin no "ano yo" kan* (Japanese view of the Other World, 1989) and *Mori no shisō ga jinrui o sukuu* (The forest-concept will save humankind, 1991), that the human-centered worldview of Christianity and the other world religions has contributed to ecological destruction, and that we need to return to the animistic culture that is at the foundation of Japanese culture—that is, the sensibilities of the hunter-gatherers of Jōmon culture preserved more in the Okinawa and Ainu cultures than in mainstream Japanese culture. At about the same time there was an increase in discourse supporting official visits to Yasukuni Shrine and state participation in imperial succession rites, but for our present purpose discourse in support of early Shinto and discourse on political Shintoism should be considered separately. It cannot be denied, however, that the two are related on some level (SHIMAZONO 1996, 2001a).

BEYOND ANY SPECIFIC RELIGION

The fact that the number of people who place their hope in "animism" has increased reflects the heightened interest in "spirituality" that we see broadly in the developed world. The idea that one should seek after a "spirituality" that can only be obtained through each individual's direct experience and sensitivity, rather than an organized religion with some doctrine, has increased in influence in Japan as well since around the mid-1970s (SHIMAZONO 1996). This spiritual culture, often called New Age in the West, is usually called the "spiritual world" in Japan. The increasing interest in *qigong* (*kikō* 気功) that we see in the 1980s is also part of this spiritual culture. In contrast to the value put on animism, which is self-consciously in solidarity with Native American culture and the cultures of the Pacific islands and Southeast Asia, the interest in *qigong* draws its influence from China and is oriented toward a cultural solidarity with East Asia. Although the new spiritual culture shows influence from the United States and India, it is also related to the urge to seek a new regional identity against the backdrop of renewed interest in national culture as one result of globalization.

The idea that there is a basic religion with its roots in the life of the common people, distinct from religion with doctrine and denominational organization, has had strong influence on the study of religion in Japan. Postwar folk religious studies prospered based on this idea, traced to Yanagita Kunio 柳田国男 and Orikuchi Shinobu 折口信夫, paying special attention to ancestor veneration, shamanism, and Shugendō 修験道 and other mountain beliefs. All of these traditional forms of folk religion have been in decline since the end of the war, giving rise to speculation as to how these folk religious beliefs might transform themselves. With regard to the tendency for magico-religious elements to play an increasingly prominent role in contemporary popular culture, while inquires into its relationship with the occult boom continue (ŌMURA and NISHIYAMA 1988), new investigations into the domain of faith of the individual are also being pursued.

Much interest has been paid to *mizuko kuyō* 水子供養, in connection with this practice as a social problem. In contrast to the United States, where abortion has been the object of heated debate, in Japan there has been little debate on the subject, and instead since around the 1970s *mizuko kuyō* has quietly become widespread, with much research devoted to its development and spread (LAFLEUR 1992; HARDACRE 1997). *Mizuko kuyō* has become an object of debate because of the possibility that it might promote discrimination against women, but beyond this particular practice, criticism of religious support of discrimination generally has increased, particularly since the 1980s, and religious denominations have promoted studies of their doctrine and past practices and discourse in order to reform themselves. Likewise, similar criticism and study has been devoted to the issue of religious cooperation in the war effort.

With regard to shamanism, in addition to studies of its traditional forms in Okinawa and northeastern Japan, research into its new contemporary urban forms has begun (SASAKI 1989; IKEGAMI 1999). Regarding pilgrimage, studies have shown that the number of participants in the Shikoku pilgrimage has increased three-fold between 1970 and 1988. Research has also progressed on the popularity of the Shikoku pilgrimage and the new meanings given it (HOSHINO 2001, READER 2005). And with regard to ancestor veneration, efforts have been made to explore changes in contemporary attitudes through studies of *ihai* 位牌 practices, cemeteries, and changes in funeral rites (SMITH 1974; MORIOKA 1984; KŌMOTO 2001).

Additionally, the change in attitudes toward death and the afterlife has also emerged as an object of study. Everyone in contemporary society must face death, and this is rarely done without some connection with religion or spirituality in its broad sense. As more and more people search for their own way of understanding life and death, interest has been paid not only to understandings offered by denominational doctrine and folk religion, but also to that reflected in literary works such as *tanka* 短歌 and haiku, as well as other traditional art forms (TATSUKAWA 2000). The increase in interest in life ethics as a result of the question of brain death has also contributed considerably to this increasing interest in the understanding of life and death (NAMIHIRA 1996).

In a somewhat different area, the question of religiosity in corporate culture presents itself as another field of study. Following WWII, in addition to his corporate activities, the founder of Panasonic, Matsushita Kōnosuke 松下幸之助, also started a spiritual movement for the promotion of a meaningful life under the title of PHP, and that movement continues today. In addition, many corporations hold company funerals for their owners and top management, and have established corporate gravesites. These, and the new corporate culture being pursued through them, which builds on the attitude of the household company that has existed from the Edo period, have been the object of research (NAKAMAKI 1999). The idea that contemporary religiosity and spirituality cannot be captured with an understanding of religion centered on religious denominations has become widespread, and the proliferation of research based on this idea characterizes the situation of religious research in Japan at the start of the twenty-first century.

BIBLIOGRAPHY

ABE Yoshiya 阿部美哉, 1989. *Seikyō bunri: Nihon to Amerika ni miru shūkyō no seijisei* 政教分離——日本とアメリカにみる宗教の政治性. Tokyo: Saimaru Shuppankai.

FUJII Masao 藤井正雄, 1974. *Gendaijin no shinkō kōzō: Shūkyō fudō jinkō no kōdō to shisō* 現代人の信仰構造——宗教浮動人口の行動と思想. Tokyo: Hyōronsha.

HARDACRE, Helen, 1984. *Lay Buddhism in Contemporary Japan*. Princeton: Princeton University Press.

_____, 1997. *Marketing the Menacing Fetus in Japan*. Berkeley: University of California Press.

HIRANO Takeshi 平野　武, 1995. *Seikyō bunri saiban to kokka shintō* 政教分離裁判と国家神道. Kyoto: Hōritsu Bunkasha.

HOSHINO Eiki 星野英紀, 2001. *Shikoku henro no shūkyōgakuteki kenkyū: Sono kōzō to kingendai no tenkai* 四国遍路の宗教学的研究——その構造と近現代の展開. Kyoto: Hōzōkan.

IKADO Fujio 井門富二夫, 1993. *Senryō to Nihon shūkyō* 占領と日本宗教. Tokyo: Miraisha.

IKEGAMI Yoshimasa 池上良正, 1993. *Akurei to seirei no butai: Okinawa no minshū Kirisutokyō ni miru kyūsai sekai* 悪霊と聖霊の舞台——沖縄の民衆キリスト教に見る救済世界. Tokyo: Dōbutsusha.

_____, 1999. *Minkan fusha shinkō no kenkyū: Shūkyōgaku no shiten kara* 民間巫者信仰の研究——宗教学の視点から. Tokyo: Miraisha.

INOUE Egyō 井上恵行, 1969. *Shūkyō hōjin hō no kisoteki kenkyū* 宗教法人法の基礎的研究. Tokyo: Daiichi Shobō.

INOUE Nobutaka 井上順孝, et al., 1989. *Shinshūkyo jiten* 新宗教事典. Tokyo: Kōbundō.

ISHII Kenji 石井研士, 1993. *Toshi no nenjū gyōji: Henyō suru Nihonjin no shinsei* 都市の年中行事——変容する日本人の心性. Tokyo: Shunjūsha.

_____, 1997. *Dētabukku gendai Nihonjin no shūkyō: Sengo gojūnen no shūkyō ishiki to shūkyō kōdō* データブック現代日本人の宗教――戦後五〇年の宗教意識と宗教行動. Tokyo: Shin'yōsha.

Itō Yuishin 伊藤唯真 and Fujii Masao 藤井正雄, eds., 1969. *Sōsai Bukkyō: Sono rekishi to gendaiteki kadai* 葬祭仏教――その歴史と現代的課題. Tokyo: Nonburusha.

Kisala, Robert, 1999. *Prophets of Peace: Pacifism and Cultural Identity in Japan's New Religions.* Honolulu: University of Hawai'i Press.

Kobori Keiichirō 小堀桂一郎, 1998. *Yasukuni jinja to Nihonjin* 靖国神社と日本人. Tokyo: PHP Kenkyūjo.

Kōmoto Mitsugi 孝本 貢, 2001. *Gendai Nihon ni okeru senzo saishi* 現代日本における先祖祭祀. Tokyo: Ochanomizu Shobō.

LaFleur, William, 1992. *Liquid Life: Abortion and Buddhism in Japan.* Princeton: Princeton University Press.

Maeyama Takashi 前山 隆, 1997. *Ihō ni "Nihon" o matsuru: Burajiru Nikkeijin no shūkyō to esunishiti* 異邦に「日本」を祀る――ブラジル日系人の宗教とエスニシティ. Tokyo: Ochanomizu Shobō.

Matsuno Junkō 松野純孝, ed., 1984. *Shinshūkyō jiten* 新宗教辞典. Tokyo: Tōkyōdō Shuppan.

McFarland, H. Neill, 1967. *The Rush Hour of the Gods: A Study of New Religious Movements in Japan.* New York: Macmillan.

Morioka Kiyomi 森岡清美, 1984. *Ie no henbō to senzo no matsuri* 家の変貌と先祖の祭. Tokyo: Nihon Kirisutokyōdan Shuppankyoku.

Mullins, Mark R., 1998. *Christianity Made in Japan: A Study of Indigenous Movements.* Honolulu: University of Hawai'i Press.

Murakami Shigeyoshi 村上重良, 1967. *Sōka Gakkai=Kōmeitō* 創価学会=公明党. Tokyo: Aoki Shoten.

_____, 1970. *Kokka Shintō* 国家神道. Tokyo: Iwanami Shoten.

Nakajima Michio 中島三千男, 1990. *Tennō no daigawari to kokumin* 天皇の代替わりと国民. Tokyo: Aoki Shoten.

Nakamaki Hirochika 中牧弘允, ed., 1999. *Shasō no keiei jinruigaku* 社葬の経営人類学. Osaka: Tōhō Shuppan.

Namihira Emiko 波平恵美子, 1996. *Inochi no bunka jinruigaku* いのちの文化人類学. Tokyo: Shinchōsha.

Nitta Hitoshi 新田 均, 1997. *Kindai seikyō kankei no kisoteki kenkyū* 近代政教関係の基礎的研究. Tokyo: Taimeidō.

Numata Kenya 沼田健哉, 1995. *Shūkyō to kagaku no neoparadaimu* 宗教と科学のネオパラダイム. Osaka: Sōgensha.

Ōhara Yasuo 大原康男, 1991. *Shintō shirei no kenkyū* 神道指令の研究. Tokyo: Hara Shobō.

Ōishi Makoto 大石 真, 1993. *Kenpō to shūkyō seido* 憲法と宗教制度. Tokyo: Yūhikaku.

Ōmura Eishō 大村英昭 and Nishiyama Shigeru 西山 茂, eds., 1998. *Gendaijin no shūkyō* 現代人の宗教. Tokyo: Yūhikaku.

Reader, Ian, 2005. *Making Pilgrimages: Meaning and Practice in Shikoku.* Honolulu: University of Hawai'i Press.

HISTORY

SAKI Akio 佐木秋夫, 1960. *Shinkō shūkyō: Sore o meguru gendai no jōken* 新興宗教——それをめぐる現代の条件. Tokyo: Aoki Shoten.

SASAKI Kōkan 佐々木宏幹, 1989. *Sei to juryoku: Nihon shūkyō no jinruigaku josetsu* 聖と呪力——日本宗教の人類学序説. Tokyo: Seikyūsha.

SHIMADA Hiromi 島田裕巳, 2001. *Oumu: Naze shūkyō wa terorizumu o unda no ka* オウム——なぜ宗教はテロリズムを生んだのか. Tokyo: Transview.

SHIMAZONO Susumu 島薗 進, 1992. *Gendai kyūsai shūkyō ron* 現代救済宗教論. Tokyo: Seikyūsha.

———, 1996. *Seishin sekai no yukue: Gendai sekai to shin reisei undō* 精神世界のゆくえ——現代世界と新霊性運動. Tokyo: Tōkyōdō Shuppan.

———, 2001a. *Posutomodan no shin shūkyō: Gendai Nihon no seishin jōkyō no teiryū* ポストモダンの新宗教——現代日本の精神状況の底流. Tokyo: Tōkyōdō Shuppan.

———, 2001b. Jūkyū seiki Nihon no shūkyō kōzō no henyo 一九世紀日本の宗教構造の変容. In *Kosumorojii no kinsei* コスモロジーの近世, ed. KOMORI Yōichi 小森陽一 et al. Tokyo: Iwanami Shoten.

SMITH, Robert J., 1974. *Ancestor Worship in Contemporary Japan*. Stanford: Stanford University Press.

SUZUKI Hiroshi 鈴木 広, 1963–1964. *Toshi kasō no shūkyō shūdan* 都市下層の宗教集団. *Shakaigaku kenkyū* 社会学研究 vols. 22, 24, 25.

TAKAGI Hiroo 高木宏夫, 1989. *Nihon no shinkō shūkyō: Taishū shisō undō no rekishi to ronri* 日本の新興宗教——大衆思想運動の歴史と論理. Tokyo: Iwanami Shoten.

TAKAGI Hiroshi 高木博志, 1997. *Kindai tennōsei no bunkashiteki kenkyū: Tennō shūnin girei, nenjū girei, bunkazai* 近代天皇制の文化史的研究——天皇就任儀礼・年中儀礼・文化財. Tokyo: Azekura Shobō.

TAMAMURO Taijō 圭室諦成, 1963. *Sōshiki Bukkyō* 葬式仏教. Tokyo: Daihōrinkaku.

TATSUKAWA Shōji 立川昭二, 2000. *Inochi no bunkashi* いのちの文化史. Tokyo: Shinchōsha.

UMEHARA Takeshi 梅原 猛, 1989. *Nihonjin no "ano yo" kan* 日本人の「あの世」観. Tokyo: Chūōkōronsha.

———, 1991. *"Mori no shisō" ga jinrui o sukuu* 「森の思想」が人類を救う. Tokyo: Shōgakkan.

WATANABE Masako 渡辺雅子, 2001. *Burajiru Nikkei shinshūkyō no tenkai: Ibunka fukyō no jissen to kadai* ブラジル日系新宗教の展開——異文化布教の実践と課題. Tokyo: Tōshindō.

WOODARD, William P., 1972. *The Allied Occupation of Japan 1945–1952 and Japanese Religions*. Leiden: E. J. Brill.

[Translated by Robert Kisala]

Themes

Richard K. Payne

The Ritual Culture of Japan

Symbolism, Ritual, and the Arts

The term "ritual culture" is used here to encompass the full range of ritualized practices, both social and religious. Ritual culture provides a unifying category that allows for considering the interrelations between ritual practices, and religious art and symbol in ways that considering them as three separate categories does not. From the perspective of the study of Japanese religion, not only ritual practices but also religious art and symbolism must first be contextualized within the ritual culture before being interpreted from other theoretical perspectives, such as aesthetics, art history, or psychology. The ritual culture is also of primary importance to our understanding of the actualities of Japanese religion as it is practiced by the vast majority of people (READER and TANABE 1998). As Frits STAAL has pointed out for Asian religions generally, the religious culture of Japan gives greater importance to ritual practice than to doctrine (1989, pp. 387–406). It is practice which makes it possible for one to attain one's goals, whether those be defined as liberation, awakening, harmony, prosperity, longevity, purification, or protection. Contrary to the intellectualist presumptions of probably the vast majority of Western language treatments of Asian religions, doctrine is the least important element according to Staal's analysis.[1] Proper belief—orthodoxy—is only very rarely considered to have any direct efficacy in attaining the goal sought. Further indication of the primacy of practice over doctrine is the way in which ritual practices persevere over time and across cultural boundaries, even while the doctrinal rationales for their efficacy changes.[2]

In contemporary Japan the relative ease with which people participate in rituals, ceremonies, and festivals conducted by Shinto shrines, Buddhist temples, folk practitioners, or new religions also evidences the greater concern for practical efficacy than for doctrinal purity. Much less casually, women who were raised in a Buddhist family feel no particular compunction about changing their religious practices upon marrying into the family of a Shinto priest. The new religious practices are seen as simply a matter of family custom (KENNEY 1996–1997, p. 400).

This analysis also applies historically. It was, for example, the similarity between existing ritual practices and those performed by Roman Catholic missionaries that was essential to the introduction of Christianity to Japan in the sixteenth century. Specifically, baptism became culturally accessible because of its similarity with both purification by water (Jpn. *misogi* 禊), and Shingon initiation (Jpn. *kanjō* 灌頂, Skt. *abhiṣeka*) which also includes unction with water as part of the ritual. According to Ikuo HIGASHIBABA, this indicates the "primacy of practice over doctrine" (2001, p. 201). Consistent with this symbolic interplay between baptism and other, more familiar practices is the way in which the ritual practices of contemporary "hidden Christians" (Kakure Kirishitan 隠れ切支丹) show a convergence of the Eucharist and indigenous *matsuri* (TURNBULL 1995 and 1998).

The concept of ritual culture is also a way of identifying the fact that rituals do not exist in isolation, but rather are embedded in a network of practices. For example, one of the most enduring practices in Japanese ritual culture is the complex of possession and exorcism. It is dramatically recorded in the *Genji monogatari* written by Murasaki Shikibu at the beginning of the eleventh century. Two centuries later, possession played a pivotal role in the life of Myōe Kōben, who, upon the advice of a trance medium possessed by the Kasuga deity, changed his plans to go to India (GIRARD 1990, p. 84). Possession

1. Just one example which happens to be ready at hand is PAINE and SOPER 1981, p. 27. The reader may examine for him/herself almost any of the standard textbooks on Asian religions for evidence of the presumption of the centrality of doctrine on the part of the text's author.

2. Similar to the presumption in Western treatments of the primacy of doctrine is the distinction between ritual and meditation. This distinction is at best a rhetorical one, despite its being virtually foundational to contemporary Western religious culture. This is not a natural distinction, but rather one which has arisen out of the history of the polemics between Protestant and Catholic since the Reformation. Particularly in the Anglophone world, meditation is in general positively valued, while ritual is negatively valued. Neither the distinction nor the values are transferable to Japan. What is called Zen meditation is highly ritualized, while the ritual practices of the Shingon tradition are meditative.

continues right into the present day as part of the practices of new religions—for example, Shinnyoen and Mahikari (see DAVIS 1980)—and in the trance oracles of village shrines. It has also been identified as the historical background of the dances performed by female shrine attendants (*miko*) in contemporary Shinto shrines (see BLACKER 1975). Possession by fox spirits, traditionally evidenced by "unusual eating habits, inappropriate use of language, inability to follow social norms, …newfound abilities in literacy" (SMYERS 1999, p. 178) and other asocial and eccentric behaviors (see also HEINE 1999), forms a particularly long-standing religious practice and literary theme. In the Meiji era, treatment of fox possession by female shamans was displaced by Western, and male-dominated, medicine and psychiatry (see FIGEL 1999, p. 99). Despite the increasing likelihood of such behaviors being treated as medical or psychological problems, exorcism of fox spirits continues in contemporary Japan.

A structurally similar network of practices is based on fear of the threat posed by those dead who, lacking any family connections by which they will be transformed into ancestors, become hungry ghosts (Jpn. *gaki* 餓鬼, Skt. *preta*; see PAYNE 1999). Likewise, there is the danger that one's own ancestors are for one reason or another dissatisfied and causing afflictions among their living heirs. Such concerns about the threats posed by hungry ghosts and dissatisfied ancestors are similar to concern about the fate of aborted fetuses, and the threat they can pose for spirit attacks (Jpn. *tatari* 祟り), leading to the recent creation of memorial rituals for the spirit of the aborted fetus (Jpn. *mizuko kuyō* 水子供養).[3] These rituals are part of the general category of memorial rituals (Jpn. *kuyō* 供養, Skt. *pūjā*) which have been performed for both living beings and the products of material culture. According to Fabio Rambelli, "Traditionally, *kuyō* refers to an ambiguous set of rituals dealing either with the end of beings (death) or with the inauguration of sacred objects. Concerning the former, we find prayers and rites for the happiness in the afterlife of the dead members of the family (*tsuizen* 追善 *kuyō*), but also rites for those dead who because they have not been taken care of by their bereaved have turned into 'hungry ghosts' (*segaki* 施餓鬼 *kuyō*). Among the rituals for the inauguration of sacred objects, there are rituals celebrating new statues (*kaigen* 開眼 *kuyō*), copies of the scriptures (*kyō* 経 *kuyō*), temple bells (*kane* 金 *kuyō*). In other words, an important aspect of *kuyō* rituals consisted in giving offerings to beings and things that could affect the salvation of the donor" (RAMBELLI 1998, p. 6). Thus, although the ritual practice as such has retained its own identifiable character, its doctrinal explanation has been extended from the generation of merit to include protection from spirit attacks and possession by the threatening dead.

Possession is perhaps most frequently considered in contemporary religious studies literature to be a category of religious experience. However, because it exists within a network of interrelated practices, beliefs, and experiences,[4] it is more appropriate to consider it as

---

3. See UNDERWOOD, 1990, in an issue of the *Journal of the American Academy of Religion* devoted to the topic of *mizuko kuyō*, with additional articles by Elizabeth G. Harrison, William R. LaFleur, and Ronald M. Green. See also HARDACRE 1997 and STEFÁNSSON 1995.

4. The concept of network of practices is borrowed from Bruno LATOUR's work (1993) in science studies. See also COLE and ENGESTRÖM 1993. The concept of network should not be

part of the ritual culture. The category of religious experience almost invariably perpetuates nineteenth-century conceptions of the mind as the passive recipient of experiences, i.e., a patient (WRIGHT 1998, p. x). In this conception the source of experience is an active agent external to the mind. In the case of religious experience the metaphysical status of the agent is most commonly thought of as one that is autonomous, and superhuman, extraordinary or supernatural. The intentional character of human consciousness, however, identifies the role of the mind as actively engaged in the process by which experience is created. To identify possession as part of the ritual culture is not to deny that it has experiential qualities, but rather to deny the theoretical view that the source of those experiences is an external agent acting on a patient who is the passive recipient of the experiences.

Further, it is to deny that experiences exist autonomously rather than as part of a network of practices, beliefs, and experiences. That network of practices is socially sustained[5] and is learned in the course of socialization. Socialization extends to meditative practice as well (see SHARF 1995, p. 418). The belief systems, which are an integral part of the network of practices, serve not only to interpret the experience, but they also serve to create the context for possession experiences to occur, molding them and defining them as possession experiences. Thus, possession is not separable from the diagnostic rituals, including trance possession, in which the source of the spirit attack or possession is determined, and ritual procedures for its relief are prescribed.

Possession is also marked by gender. While there are cases in which men are possessed (for example, by female fox spirits), the majority of those who either suffer from possession or engage in possession professionally have been women (see BLACKER 1975). The case of the *Genji monogatari* is particularly informative in this connection (see BARGEN 1997).

Ritual culture provides a heuristically valuable perspective on the study of ritual practice, and symbolic and artistic representations in Japan for several reasons. First is the priority of ritual practice over doctrine. Second, as an inclusive category, ritual culture allows for seeing the interrelations between ritual practice and religious art and symbol more clearly than if the three were considered as existing in isolation from one another. And third, ritual practices and religious art and symbols necessarily exist within socially maintained networks of practices, beliefs, and experiences.

FIXED AND PORTABLE

Ritual cultures combine elements which are fixed and elements which are portable.[6] Fixed elements are those which are not only in some way unique, but more

taken as implying a stable, consistent, orderly social system, i.e., in the way functionalism classically would have. As I am trying to formulate the concept of networks of practices here for use in the study of ritual cultures, they can be unstable and far from logically coherent, perhaps closer to Levi-Strauss's *bricolage*. See, for example, TAUSSIG 1987.

5. A classic study of the social character of possession is LEWIS 1971.

6. The terminology of "fixed and portable" draws on the work of Lionel ROTHKRUG (1980) on the patterns of Reformation allegiances.

importantly are only relevant to a particular locale. For example, the Sannō cult of Mt. Hiei is only relevant to the locale of Mt. Hiei (see GRAPARD 1987 and 1998). Both the cult of Ōmiwa and that of Mt. Iwaki are additional examples of networks of ritual practices, beliefs and experiences fixed on a specific location (see LISCUTIN 2000). Among the new religions, a particularly clear instance of a fixed element in the ritual culture is Tenrikyō's emphasis on returning "home to the Jiba, the site of humankind's original home marked by the Kanrodai pillar" (see ELLWOOD 1982, p. 52). In contrast, some elements of a religious tradition are portable: they can be relocated from one place to another. For example, many of the Vedic deities were incorporated into the tantric Buddhist pantheon, and were brought to Japan together with cultic practices devoted to them (see LUDVIK 1999–2000; FRANK 1991, 2000a, and 2000b).

However, the categories of fixed and portable are not mutually exclusive, but rather form a range with many intermediate instances. For example, some of the Kasuga deities are believed to have been relocated from their original shrines in Kashima and Katori (GRAPARD 1992, p. 31). The very possibility that such movement could have occurred suggests that there was fluidity between an identification with a particular territory and their role as clan deities (*ujigami* 氏神). Similarly, it seems likely that Mt. Fuji was originally a fixed cult, but having become a symbol of the entire nation, Mt. Fuji is not only worshipped locally, but also from afar.[7] At least equally ambiguous is the creation of miniature replicas of the Shikoku pilgrimage, each of the eighty-eight stations of which would traditionally require some of the soil from the corresponding temple on the island circuit.[8]

Allan Grapard has argued forcefully for attention to the unique local character of religious practice and symbol. For example, in his discussion of the *honji suijaku* 本地垂迹 theory, he says:

> The crucial point is that these systematic associations were always established at the level of particular shrines and temples, and not at an abstract, national level. In other words Shinto-Buddhist syncretism remained grounded in each particular religious community, thereby retaining original Shinto characteristics. This is why studies of these systems of communication between cultures must be made *in situ* before any general conclusions may be drawn: the syncretism found at the Hie shrines is characteristically different from that found at the Kasuga shrines, Kumano shrines, Hachiman shrines, and so on. (Kodansha Encyclopedia, vol. 7, p. 127)

At the same time, the "persisting practices"[9] of Japan's ritual culture are not purely local, but are also interconnected with global histories of the movement of religions across cultural

---

7. For brief discussion of the social and political dimensions of the Fuji sect per se, see DAVIS 1992.

8. See READER 1988; for a fuller discussion of pilgrimage, see Barbara Ambros's essay on "Geography, Environment, Pilgrimage" in this *Guide*.

9. The phrase is from KEIRSTEAD 1992, p. 98, who in turn has borrowed it from CORRIGAN and SAYER 1985.

boundaries.[10] The apparent opposition between local and global perspectives on religion is reconciled by the categories of fixed and portable. In many cases the unique character of the local results from its being the point of intersection between the fixed and portable.[11]

That religious elements are fixed does not mean that they are invariant. Some, such as the "Oracles of the Three Shrines" may be of long duration, though undergoing gradual, almost imperceptible changes (see BOCKING 2001). In other cases, claims of invariance and long duration are made for recently created ritual practices (see RANGER and HOBSBAWM 1992). In the same way, the portability of some religious elements does not mean that there is some eternal, timeless, unchanging essence that is manifest in each of these times and places, but rather that there is a historical continuity across the cultural boundaries.

Mandalas, the *goma* 護摩 ritual and recitation practices provide three different examples of how portable religious elements have interacted with the local ritual culture of Japan, to create unique forms. While much of Western scholarship usually engages mandalas as paintings, that is, as a form of art, they originate in India as representations of the cosmic court of a deity surrounded by his retinue. The complexity of mandalas is famous and has led to several extensive studies devoted solely to the details of which deities are represented in what form and in what location (TOGANOO 1932; SNODGRASS 1988; MAMMITZSCH 1991). In some cases, mandalas are formed of sculptures rather than painted. Two particularly important examples are the main hall at Tōji in Kyoto and the Eastern Pagoda at the Garan in Kōyasan (see FRANK 1991, pp. 163–85). Interpretations of mandalas need to give primacy to the fact that the context in which mandalas are created is ritual and symbolic, rather than simply viewing mandalas as artistic creations.

The cosmic symbolism of the mandala makes it a very potent organizing image, one which was extended into a wide variety of different realms. As discussed by Barbara Ambros in this collection, the geography of Japan was frequently seen as a kind of mandala, as for example, in the mountain pilgrimages of Shugendō practitioners (see TEN GROTENHUIS 1999; MIYAKE 2001). Conversely, specific shrine-temple complexes such as Kasuga were represented as mandalas, indicating "that the sacred space of cultic centers was associated with the transcendental space of the cosmos of buddhas and bodhisattvas" (GRAPARD 1992, p. 91). These often show the equations between kami and buddhas or bodhisattvas. Not only do these give some intimate glimpses of medieval religious life in Japan, but they also reveal the cultic organization of the shrine-temple portrayed. Even the robe of Buddhist monks (Jpn. *kesa* 袈裟, Skt. *kāṣāya*) was interpreted as a mandala, portraying the Buddhist cosmos, while also being homologized with the seat of enlightenment (Skt. *bodhimaṇḍa*) of the buddhas (FAURE 1995, p. 357).

Frequently seen in Shingon temples are a pair of mandalas. These are the *kongōkai* 金剛界 and *taizōkai* 胎藏界 mandalas, representing the compassion and wisdom of Dainichi (Skt. Mahāvairocana), the chief deity (*honzon* 本尊) of the Shingon tradition. This

---

10. With what appears to be the same idea in mind, Robert S. CORRINGTON (2000) employs the terminology of "regional and generic."

11. For a more general discussion of the same issues in contemporary historiography, see IGGERS 1997, esp. Chapter 9: "From Macro- to Microhistory: The History of Everyday Life."

pairing of the two mandalas coincides with the integration in Shingon of two ritual traditions—the deities arrayed in the two mandalas being the deities evoked in the course of performing the rituals of each lineage of ritual practice.[12]

One of the most famous of the Japanese mandalas is the Taima mandala, a representation of the Pure Land of Amida as described in the *Visualization Sūtra*. Medieval legends tell of the miraculous creation of the Taima mandala in response to the prayers of the devout nun Chūjōhime (see TEN GROTENHUIS 1992). However, as a result of examinations of wall paintings at Dunhuang it is now evident that the format of the Taima mandala originated in western China (TEN GROTENHUIS 1999, pp. 28–32). The gradations between ritual and drama, and the highly performative character of Japan's ritual culture are evidenced by the legend of Chūjōhime, graphic representations of which were employed in proselytizing performances recounting the legend (see GLASSMAN 2004). Even these quasi-dramatic performances combine global and local dimensions. Victor MAIR (1988) has shown that such picture storytelling can not only be traced back to China, but that it has its origins in India.

The *goma* (Skt. *homa*) also evidences the way in which a ritual can be portable across cultural boundaries. The history of the *goma* can be traced back through China to the medieval development of tantra (or *mikkyō* 密教) in India, and even further to the fire rituals of Vedic practice. In its classic form the *goma* is a rite of votive offering, or sacrifice, in which the offerings are made into a fire. Though other groupings are known, the Shingon tradition (along with other tantric Buddhist traditions) categorizes its *goma*s and other rituals into five categories (Jpn. *goshuhō* 五種法) according to function: protection (Jpn. *sokusai* 息災, Skt. *śāntika*), increase (Jpn. *sōyaku* 増益, Skt. *pauṣṭika*), subjugation (Jpn. *jōbuku* 調伏, Skt. *abhicāraka*), subordination (Jpn. *keiai* 敬愛, Skt. *vaśīkaraṇa*), and acquisition (Jpn. *kōchō* 鈎召, Skt. *aṅkuśa*). Additionally, there are *goma*s devoted to a wide variety of different buddhas, bodhisattvas, dharma protectors, and other deities (see PAYNE 2000). In contemporary Japan, the *goma* is known in a variety of related forms. It is performed in both Tendai and Shingon temples, where the tantric form of Buddhism has been particularly important. There are discernible differences between the Shingon and Tendai forms of the *goma*. These are in large part attributable to the fact that the Tendai tradition, in addition to the *Dainichi-kyō* 大日経 (Skt. *Vairocanābhisaṃbodhi-sūtra*) and *Kongōchō-kyō* 金剛頂経 (Skt. *Vajraśekhara-sūtra*), also draws upon the *Soshitsuji-kyō* 蘇悉地経 (Skt. *Susiddhikaramahātantra*). This latter text became increasingly popular in Chinese esoteric Buddhism after the time of Saichō and Kūkai, when Tendai prelates such as Ennin traveled to China in search of additional esoteric materials needed to complete the Tendai esoteric teachings.

While in Buddhist settings the *goma* is generally performed inside a temple building,

12. The direct involvement of mandalas in ritual performances is to be distinguished from the idea that the practitioner is to form a complete mental image of the entirety of the mandala. Although this latter idea has become part of the common understanding of mandalas, Robert Sharf has recently demonstrated that they do not function that way in Japanese ritual culture (see SHARF 2001).

another form identified with Shugendō is performed outside. This is known as the *saitō goma* 柴燈護摩, and can be found being performed on the grounds of Buddhist temples, at Shugendō sites, and at Shinto shrines. In the medieval period traditions which identified themselves as Shinto, such as Ōmiwa and Yuiitsu (or Yoshida), created their own *goma* ceremonies. Practice of such hybrid forms was completely suppressed during the Meiji period.

Just as the *goma* was imported from India, recitation practices of various kinds current in Japan can also be traced back to India. Indic ritual culture is largely motivated by an understanding of the Vedas as the eternal vibratory foundation of the phenomenal world. The power of the Vedas could then be drawn upon in ritual performances through the recitation of pieces of the Vedic texts, that is, mantra. Mantra (*shingon* 真言) and *dhāraṇī* (*darani* 陀羅尼) were introduced as part of Shingon and the esoteric tradition within Tendai. Most commonly known today are those forms of recitation found in the "new" Buddhisms established in the Kamakura era. The history of these practices indicates the complex ways in which relatively simple ritual practices come into the popular ritual culture.

One example is the "Clear Light Mantra" (*kōmyō shingon* 光明真言), which has several benefits attributed to it. As pronounced in Japanese, the mantra is *on abogya beiroshanō makabodara mani handoma jimbara harabaritaya un* (Skt. *oṃ amogha vairocana mahāmudrā maṇi padma jvāla pravarttaya hūṃ*). It is perhaps a comment on the difficulties faced by those living in the Kamakura era that one of its most popular uses was the empowerment of common dirt. This dirt could then be sprinkled on a dying person, a corpse, or a grave, purifying the karma of the deceased and assuring birth in the Pure Land of Amida. The Clear Light Mantra was promoted by many practitioners, perhaps the best known of whom is Myōe Kōben (see UNNO 1998).

Nichiren is associated with the recitation of the title of the *Lotus Sūtra* (*daimoku* 題目), familiar in the form of the phrase *namu myōhō renge kyō*, 南無妙法蓮華経 or "praise the scripture of the lotus blossom of the wonderful Dharma." Despite the common assumption that Nichiren initiated this practice, it is part of a series of almost identical invocations of the power of the *Lotus Sūtra*. These earlier forms include expressions such as *namu ichijō myōhō renge kyō* 南無一乗妙法蓮華経 and *namu gokuraku nan chigū myōhō renge kyō* 南無極楽難値遇妙法蓮華経, as well as combinations such as invoking both the *Lotus Sūtra* and a buddha (such as Amida; see STONE 1998).

Similarly, although the contemporary practice in the Pure Land schools is of the six-character invocation *namu Amida butsu* 南無阿弥陀仏, this only became the standard version around the time of Rennyo, considered the second founder of the Shin tradition of Pure Land (ROGERS and ROGERS 1991; ROGERS 1996). Earlier, other forms of the *nenbutsu* had been used, including a ten-character version: *kimyō jin jippō muge kō nyorai* 歸命盡十方無礙光如來. The combination of artistic, symbolic, and ritual practice is exemplified by the many scrolls on which Rennyo inscribed the name of Amida (*myōgō* 名号). Other scrolls were more fully illustrated, the aesthetic representation becoming even more complexly saturated with symbolic and performative significance, blurring the lines we draw between written and visual representations (see BLUM 2001).

These three examples—mandalas, *goma,* and recitation—all exemplify the unique, local character of Japanese ritual culture. The unique character arises out of the intersection of portable and fixed elements. Thus, while one dimension of research needs to attend to the global movement of ritual elements across cultural boundaries, another dimension needs to attend to fixed and local aspects. These two interact dialectically, new forms being given to the local by imported practices, while portable elements are themselves molded as they are integrated into the ritual culture of Japan.

Local ritual cultures, however, have come under increasing pressure toward uniformity as a result of Japan's modernization over the last century and a half. Two interrelated kinds of pressures toward uniformity are at work. The first of these is the homogenization of Japanese culture by mass media. The second is the commodification of local customs, including revivals of local customs for the sake of tourism. The latter may have the appearance of supporting locally unique customs, but the process of commodification for the tourist trade itself imposes uniformity. This homogenization and commodification continues the Meiji-period neo-romantic nostalgia for local culture and belief in the authenticity and wisdom of "das Volk."[13] Thus, the historical processes by which fixed and portable elements interact can lead not only to a unique local form, but also move toward convergence across a wider ritual culture.

RITUAL AND SYMBOL AS NATURALIZED CATEGORIES

As an interpretive category, the concept of ritual culture includes the idea that it is a social creation. This is a way of treating the elements of the ritual culture—ritual practice, and religious symbol and art—naturalistically.[14] Such a naturalistic view of ritual culture entails that it be understood as existing in a variety of relations to other dimensions of the social reality; for example, history, economics, politics, culture, and religion.[15] In other words, these other dimensions are aspects of the social context within which Japanese ritual culture exists. The inclusion of religion as one of the contextualizing

---

[13] On the relation between folklore studies and modernization in Japan, see FIGAL 1999.

[14] In contemporary scholarly discourse the term "naturalize" and its cognates are employed in oddly antithetical ways. On the one hand it is used to mean something like "subject to treatment as an object of inquiry on a par with any other natural object or social practice." On the other it is taken to mean something like "simply a given which, therefore, cannot be questioned or examined." Those who employ the latter meaning often resort to the expression "denaturalize" when they wish to call something into question—in other words when under the first meaning they want to naturalize it. How this strange situation came about is not at all clear to this author. However, what he does wish to make clear is that he is talking about naturalizing ritual in the former sense. In other words treating ritual as part of the human repertoire of actions and behaviors, comparable, for example, to shopping, and subject therefore to a number of inquiries—economic, social, psychological, political, and so on. This is in opposition to the implicit exceptionalism found frequently in religious studies, such as the Eliadean interpretation of ritual as making sacred time and space present in the midst of the mundane.

[15] This also implies that religion is understood as a social creation, that is, it is not sui generis.

dimensions indicates that ritual culture itself is not simply a subset of religion, but rather has its own social function.[16]

At the same time, the category of ritual culture is used here in order to include a wide range of activities which "ritual"— understood more narrowly as a genre distinct from other genres such as ceremony, festival, pageant, and drama—might be thought to exclude. Use of a wider, more inclusive category is necessitated by the "conspicuously performative nature of Japanese religious thought and practice" (AVERBUCH 1995, p. 258; see also LAW 1997).

As part of the ritual culture, the symbolic lexicon of Japanese religion is also considered here to be a social creation. In other words, it is not—as is so often thought to be the case—that symbols are autonomous, ahistoric representations of some timeless and universal religious meaning. This is important to clarify, since in the Western academic study of religion the intellectual apprehension of symbol differs from the apprehension of ritual. The historical character of ritual has long been recognized in Christian religious culture, due, no doubt, to the concerns with the historical establishment of the sacraments by Jesus. This was the central concern in the debates of the Reformation era. This attention to the historicity of ritual has not been obscured by the neo-Romantics, despite the universalizing of an ahistorical view of ritual by, for example, Mircea Eliade. Symbol, however, is still largely approached ahistorically. The neo-Platonic tendency of Western religious culture, reinforced by the neo-Romantic character of influential strains within the psychology of religion have obscured the historical character of symbols.

One of the consequences of treating symbol as autonomous and ahistoric is that it contributes to an understanding of symbols as having a meaning separate from the specific, local religious setting in which the symbol actually exists. This is found in the work of any of those in the comparative study of religions who implicitly accept a view of symbols that assumes what may be called a "universal hermeneutics," that is, this idea that the meaning of a symbol is the same everywhere and at all times. The corollary of this is that the meaning can be understood without reference to its historical, cultural, religious, political, or economic context.

Sometimes this view is explicated by distinguishing between symbols and signs. The assertion made in support of this distinction is that while signs are arbitrary social conventions, symbols are in some sense natural, and do not depend upon culture for their meaning. Frequently, the idea of a universal hermeneutic is itself based upon a metaphysical preconception in which the source of religious symbols is a transcendent reality, a "timeless realm," from which the symbols are derivative. Frequently, this metaphysic is left implicit, and the Platonic roots of Western intellectual culture make it difficult to even

[16] While the discussion in this essay focuses primarily on the political function of religion, it is also important to note that the Western academic study of religion seems to systemically obscure the economic function of religion. This probably is the result of a generalized aversion to any reductive approach, and a specific aversion to Marxist theory. Yet, without attention to this dimension the motivation behind civic and other institutional support for a wide variety of rituals, ceremonies, and festivals cannot be understood. Why bother organizing a pilgrimage route if not to attract pilgrims and the economic benefits they bring?

explicate, much less call into question. Such a set of assumptions, however, makes it all too easy to presume an equivalence between a symbol whose meaning is known and one whose meaning is unknown simply on the basis of analogy. These presumptions may result in both reading onto the unfamiliar symbol a set of meanings not part of the Japanese understanding, and at the same time obscuring the actual significance the symbol has as part of the ritual culture of Japan.

An example of this is the imposition of the dualistic division of the world into sacred and profane realms onto the religious landscape of Japan. This symbolic division is very widely employed because of the influential role of Eliade, and because his dualistic worldview builds on dualistic religious assumptions implicit in Western understanding of religion (see ELIADE 1959). In contrast, however, Edmund GILDAY (1987 and 1990) has demonstrated that the Japanese religious worldview comprises three parts. The three different realms that Gilday identifies are the mountain, the fields, and the village. The mountain is the realm of the kami, the village the realm of humans, and the fields the realm of contestation between the two: the kami residing in the fields in the winter and moving to the mountains during the summer when humans take over the fields for agricultural purposes. GILDAY suggests that "*pacification* may be one way to characterize the objective of all *matsuri*, insofar as every *matsuri* is marked by an effort to enforce a particular articulation of order" (1990, p. 264).

Not only is there a problem with the idea of a universal hermeneutic or a universal symbolic typology, but symbols do not have any unchanging permanent significance. Any treatment of symbols that decontextualizes them from their social and historical location is fundamentally inaccurate. For example, the symbol of Shōtoku Taishi has been employed in a variety of different rhetorical strategies, and hence has carried different meanings according to the context. Both Buddhist adherents and Buddhist scholars have felt the urgency for the control of representation, because such representations serve in "legitimizing doctrinal interpretations and practices, promoting a particular socio-political agenda, or advancing a scholarly methodology or interpretation."[17] Another instance is the "Oracles of the Three Shrines" (*sanja takusen* 三社託宣), which exemplify the historical and political character of symbols. The oracles originated as political propaganda during the period of conflict between the Northern and Southern courts. Go-Daigo Tennō, head of the Southern court, is portrayed as the rightful ruler, bringing together the religious authority of his Buddhist identity (he is portrayed as a Shingon priest), and the endorsement of the three most important shrine deities, Ise, Hachiman, and Kasuga (BOCKING 2001, p. 34).

Another fundamental difference between Japanese and Western religious cultures important to an understanding of the function of symbols is the absence in Japan of any concern about idolatry. Thus, there is less of the sense that everything religious is solely referentially symbolic, that is, representing something else, some other, "higher" reality.

---

[17] See Mark Dennis, "Shifting Images of Prince Shōtoku: The Urgency for the Control of Representation," paper presented at the 2001 conference of the International Association of Shin Buddhist Studies, 2–5 August 2001; Ōtani Daigaku, Kyoto, Japan, p. 3. For the phrase "the urgency of the control of representation," Dennis cites LOPEZ 1995, p. 251.

This does not mean that there are not symbolic associations, but rather that it is possible for the actual object and its symbolic significance to be homologized, that is, treated as identical. Thus, Dōgen can assert that any *kesa* sewn by a newly ordained Zen monk, does not symbolically represent, but simply is the robe of the Buddha Śākyamuni (FAURE 1995, p. 349). Likewise in contemporary Zen in its export form, the meditation cushion (*zafu* 坐蒲) is homologized to Mt. Meru, the cosmic mountain at the center of the Indian universe. Bernard FAURE points out that far from diminishing the value of the object, such ritual reproduction sustains the full potency of the original (1995, p. 352). Indeed, one might suspect that the potency of such objects is created exactly through their being infinitely reproducible.

While these examples are found in the portable aspects of Japanese religion, the absence of referential symbolism is found in the fixed aspects as well. For example, Mt. Fuji does not stand for or represent anything. It is just what it is, and as such is sacred in the sense of being a place of great power. There is an "intimate relationship among the gods (*kami*), the land, and its inhabitants.... The ordinary world is explained as an arena of divine activity" (TANABE 1999, p. 8). Exposure to the West may have degraded this cognitive culture over the last hundred fifty years, so that one may find discussions about such things as if they were representatively, or referentially, meaningful. However, this would appear to be an adaptation to the assumptions and expectations of Western religious culture. Japanese religious culture prior to the modern era consistently employs homologies, that is, assertions of an identity which goes beyond a referentially symbolic "standing for," as a primary rhetorical strategy. Such homologies also had hierarchical implications, as in the theory of "true nature and manifestation" (*honji suijaku*), and informed the deification of political leaders as kami (see SUGAHARA 1996).

As mentioned by many other authors in this *Guide*, the distinction between Shinto and Buddhism as we know them today is a modern one. Motivated by nationalist responses to European imperialism in East Asia, and informed by Romantic conceptions of religion and its search for the authentic in the indigenous, the institutional separation of the two traditions was enforced by a series of imperial edicts issued in 1868 (see KETELAAR 1990; BREEN 2000). This distinction is reflected in the modern institutional terms employed, that is, the distinction between Shinto "shrines" (*jingū* 神宮 or *jinja* 神社) and Buddhist "temples" (*tera* or *ji* 寺). As a result the term Shinto must be used with proper attention to sociohistorical context, appropriate only to the rise of self-consciously Shinto movements such as Ōmiwa and Yuiitsu in the late medieval and early premodern periods, and the subsequent separation in Meiji (see, for example, ANTONI 1995). The importance of keeping such contextual concerns in mind in studying ritual culture is the need to avoid anachronisms, which can only be accomplished by clarity about the historical location of the ritual, artwork, or symbol being examined.

Part of the religious recreation of Shinto as an autonomous and indigenous tradition was the creation of a ritual culture, much of which since that time has taken on the patina of "ancient Shinto rites." For example, the Shinto wedding ceremony[18] that is familiar

---

[18] See SMITH 1995, p. 28. For a study of recent changes in wedding practices, see FISCH 2001.

today and commonly thought of as an ancient custom was newly created in 1900 for the wedding of the Crown Prince (later, the Taishō Emperor). Such recency emphasizes how powerful the Meiji-period rhetoric was that instituted emperor-centered Shinto as a matter of "clarification of what had previously been obscure and a restoration of what had earlier been displaced" (BOCKING 2001, p. 96).

One of the assumptions inherited from functionalist theory in the anthropological study of religion is that ritual is basically conservative of the social order, that it reinforces the existing social order, conveys an understanding of that social order to younger members of that society, and is itself unchanging. The study of the creation of tradition, however, discloses first that rituals, whether conservative or not, are not themselves unchanging, though they often are seen as such very quickly. Also, there are many rituals, both in Japan and elsewhere, which are actively expressive of social tensions. The case of the Furukawa *matsuri* called *okoshi daiko* 起し太鼓 or "rousing drum" evidences both the changing character of ritual and its use as a subversive activity.[19] Prior to the push to modernize Japan in the late nineteenth century, the "rousing drum" was a very peaceful announcement of a Shinto rite to be performed later that same day. In its much more raucous contemporary forms, the wealthy and greedy may be physically assaulted and their property damaged in the course of the ritual. The functionalist explanation of such apparently antisocial behaviors, deriving perhaps ultimately from Aristotelian theories of the social function of drama, but more recently from Turner, is that these are cathartic, that is, they are relatively safe expressions of social tensions, which if not allowed expression under these constrained circumstances might lead to real social change and disruption.[20] However, as Scott SCHNELL suggests, the "instrumental value of religious ritual as a means of adapting to—or perhaps even introducing—changes in the sociopolitical order remains largely unexplored" (1999, p. 4).

The political function of ritual, ceremony, and pageant[21] is evident throughout Japanese history. The ritual power of relics and political control of rituals for their display began in the Heian and continued through the Ashikaga. According to Brian RUPPERT (2000), the "court's appropriation of Buddha relics reflected its view that such public performances represented the largess of the emperor vis-à-vis major shrines and displayed the power of

---

[19] See SCHNELL 1999; see also Schnell's essay in this *Guide*. Similar festivals are known in India and Europe. The potentially deadly character of what are sometimes called "rituals of inversion" is evidenced in LADURIE 1979. For an important series of discussions of these issues, see LINCOLN 1989, esp. Part II: Ritual.

[20] The functionalist presumption that stability is the norm for society runs the risk of creating a petitio principii fallacy in which because stability is assumed, activities counter to that stability are simply interpreted as ultimately supportive of the social order through the cathartic release of tensions. On the basis of this presumption then, more extreme disruptions are categorized as something else—rebellions—and explained by reference to a different set of dynamics.

[21] Philippe BUC (2001) has recently critiqued the undiscriminating use of the term "ritual" as a category encompassing too many different political events, and indeed, the events described by T. Fujitani discussed here include several different kinds of activities. Hence, the more comprehensive list of "ritual, ceremony, and pageant."

the central government throughout the countryside."[22] Political functions at times also merged with economic ones: "Temples, and the collections of sculptures, paintings, and sutras they housed, were used by members of the imperial household and their associates as tax shelters through the commendation of lands to their upkeep" (YIENGPRUKSAWAN 1998, p. 92).

The Meiji period saw an equally effective use of ritual, ceremony, and pageantry in the assertion of a new, unified Japan, taking its proper place on the world stage under the guidance of the Meiji emperor. These productions combined "ancient-looking rites performed within the innermost sanctuary of the Imperial Palace" with Western-style parades of Japan's modern, that is, Westernized, military and civil authority (FUJITANI 1996, p. 106).

The Meiji emperor also engaged in military reviews, including a review celebrating Japan's success against Russia. This was a review of the ships of the Imperial Navy, and of ships captured from Japan's enemies. The purpose of this review was "to display the enormous spectacle of men and ships, an incredible mass of volatile military power, transformed into docile objects of the emperor's gaze" (FUJITANI 1996, p. 131). This function is reminiscent of one of the earliest recorded political rites, the ritual viewing of the land (*kunimi* 国見) by the Heavenly Sovereign[23] (*tennō* 天皇), recorded in *Nihon shoki* 日本書紀 and *Man'yōshū* 万葉集. Also similar is the goal of "creating the illusion of permanence and unbroken continuity. By simultaneously presenting the new human order and aligning it with the divine order, each ritual performance sought to win the public's acceptance of the legitimacy of the socio-political order" (EBERSOLE 1989, p. 25). The political importance of such rituals, ceremonies, and pageants is found even in cases where the events did not actually occur, as in the funeral services planned for Hideyoshi (see MACÉ 1996–1997).

Detailed information about the festivals and kami worship conducted by the nobility of the court at the transition from the tenth to eleventh centuries is found in the administrative procedures compiled during the Engi era (901 to 922), known as the *Engi shiki* 延喜式 (BOCK 1970 and 1972). This included worship at the Ise Shrine, as well as the procedures for the Bureau of the Consecrated Imperial Princess who represented the sovereign at the Ise Shrine. The fourth book, devoted to the Ise Shrine, includes information on the names of deities in the various shrines in the area as well as the number of attendants (*uchindo*, or *uchibito* 内人) in service at each one. The offerings for each of the annual cycle of rituals is given in great detail. For example, for the Festival of Deity Raiment the list of offerings includes the exact measurements of the silk to be offered, the exact number of strands of silk for jewelry and for sewing, as well as such details as one long knife and sixteen short knives (BOCK 1970, p. 126).

In the eighth book, the liturgies (*norito* 祝詞) of the rituals and festivals are given, many of which correlate with the myths of the *Kojiki* 古事記 and *Nihon shoki*. This connection between the ritual practices detailed in the *Engi shiki* and the myths of the *Kojiki* and *Nihon shoki* is important in giving a larger context to the rituals, as the myths primarily

---

[22] RUPPERT 2000, p. 262. For information regarding relic veneration in South Asian Buddhism, see TRAINOR 1997.

[23] This usage follows PIGGOTT's discussion of the proper terminology (1997, pp. 8–9). In the Meiji period, however, the term "emperor" does seem appropriate, and hence is used here as well.

function as charter myths, that is, justification for the political dominance of the imperial clan (MATSUMAE 1993, p. 323).

That the myths and rituals have a socio-political function does not mean that they are not religious. The naturalistic view of ritual and symbol being employed here avoids the presumption that religion is sui generis and that religious experience, or religious emotion, is irreducible and the single defining characteristic of religion. Such a conception of religion originates in attempts by Western scholars of religion in the late nineteenth century and early twentieth century to protect religion from what were seen as destructive reductionist inquiries. These authors created a rhetoric that makes religion something which cannot be explained, and which, therefore, is not to be explained. Not only does such a view of religion preclude serious research, but it is based on theological conceptions originating from the Western monotheisms, and are therefore inappropriate to the study of Japanese ritual culture. At the same time, it is anachronistic to impose onto the early Japanese situation the idea that for religion to be religious it needs to not have social and political functions. At that time the political and religious realms were less clearly divided than we consider them to be today: "The sovereign was simultaneously the ritual and political head of the nation" (EBERSOLE 1989, p. 24; see also PIGGOTT 1997, pp. 208–26). State control of religion is one manifestation of this, and in one form or another the Japanese state attempted to control religion right up to the declaration of religious freedom in the twentieth century.

THE INFLUENCE OF BUDDHIST TANTRA, AND BUDDHIST RITUAL STRUCTURES

As the frequent references in the preceding indicate, esoteric Buddhism, introduced by Kūkai and Saichō at the beginning of the ninth century, deeply pervades Japanese religion. A familiar example is the presence of Fudō Myōō (Skt. Acalanatha Vidyarājā, also known as Caṇḍamahāroṣaṇa) in many locations where cold water austerities (Jpn. misogi 禊) are practiced. Wrapped in flames generated by his own concentrative power, Fudō ensymbols the generation of inner heat. One of the classic records of this is found in the Heike monogatari 平家物語. In chapter five the warrior Mongaku engages in cold water austerities under the Nachi falls at Kumano in midwinter, vowing to stay there for twenty-one days while reciting the Fudō mantra three hundred thousand times. He stayed in the freezing water below the falls until he was on the edge of death. At that point two of Fudō's eight attendant youths revived him, and assured him that Fudō knew of his vow. Renewed in his confidence, Mongaku "returned to the pool and stood under the waterfall again. Thanks to the divine protection, the blowing gales no longer pierced his flesh; the descending waters felt warm" (McCULLOUGH 1988, p. 179).

The pervasion of esoteric Buddhism is also evident in the area of ritual practice, esoteric ritual having been appropriated not only by other Buddhist sects, but also in the formation of sects which specifically identified themselves as Shinto. As mentioned above, both Ōmiwa Shinto and Yuiitsu (or Yoshida) Shinto developed their own version of the goma. Yuiitsu also borrowed the Eighteen Stages ritual (Jūhachidō 十八道) from Shingon, where today it is the first ritual in the training of a Shingon priest (*ajari* 阿闍梨, Skt. *acarya*), re-naming it the Eighteen Kami. The third of the three rituals that formed the core of Yuiitsu liturgy is devoted to the Northern Dipper, apparently also borrowed from Shingon. Here we see an instance of the need for attention to the portability of ritual practices, as esoteric Buddhist rituals devoted to the Northern Dipper were composed in China, in response to the important role of the Northern Dipper in Taoism.

Buddhist liturgical practice, the kinds of rites one can observe in temples all over Japan today, may initially appear to be very diverse, and unique to each particular sect (*shū* 宗) and even lineage (*ryū* 流) within the sect. Beneath the variety, however, certain consistent elements and patterns can be seen.[24] These originate in the Indian Mahāyāna, where it is known as the "supreme worship" (or "supreme offering," Skt. *anuttara-pūjā*).[25] While most frequently comprising seven elements, other groupings of from three to nine are also found. At the same time, different specific liturgies employ various elements, so that the total pool of actions is larger. The most commonly occurring are eleven ritual actions: praise, veneration, confession of faults, rejoicing in the merits of others, requesting the teaching, begging the buddhas not to abandon living beings, going for refuge, vows, sacrifice of oneself, arousal of bodhicitta, and transfer of merit.[26] The ritual tradition of Buddhism, however, has not been attended to in Western scholarship until relatively recently.

The neo-romanticism which permeates Western religious studies emphasizes mystical experience as the most important aspect of religion. This contributed to raising of the "sudden enlightenment" teaching of Zen, what Bernard Faure (1991) has called "the rhetoric of immediacy," together with its portrayal of Zen meditation as entrée to a condition of pure spontaneity, to normative status. Doing so obscured the ritualistic character of some aspects of Japanese religion, such as Zen meditation itself which is highly ritualized. At the same time it marginalized those aspects for which ritual could not be obscured, such as

---

[24] Morse and Morse 1995, p. 8. This exhibition catalogue also includes valuable essays by James H. Foard, "Ritual in the Buddhist Temples of Japan," Samuel Crowell Morse, "Space and Ritual: The Evolution of the Image Hall in Japan," and Kawada Sadamu with Anne Nishimura Morse, "Japanese Buddhist Decorative Arts: The Formative Period, 552–794."

[25] See Śāntideva 1995; I am indebted to Bruce Williams for his assistance with this section.

[26] The terminology varies between sources:
      praise (*vandanā*),
      worship/offering/veneration (*pūjā, pūjanā*),
      confession/confession of faults (*deśana, pāpa-deśana*),
      rejoicing/rejoicing in merits/rejoicing in the merits of others (*modanā,*
       anumodanā, puṇyānumdodanā),
      requesting the teaching (*adhyeṣaṣā*),
      begging (*yācanā*, i.e., begging the buddhas not to abandon living beings),
      going for refuge (*śaraṇa-gamana*),
      vows (*praṇidāna*),
      sacrifice of oneself (*atmatyāga, ātmabhāvananiryātana*),
      arousal of bodhicitta (*bodhicittotpāda*), and
      transfer of merit (*pariṇāmanā*).

THEMES

the ongoing role of esoteric Buddhism in Japan after the Heian, the point at which it disappears from most Western language books on the history of Japanese religion.

For related reasons, Western scholarship has also overlooked the scholastic character of Japanese Buddhism such as the traditions of debates in Shingon and Shin, which continue into the present. Such debates are both highly ritualized and scholastic, rather than aesthetic and mystical. This may explain why, although we read about the debate in literature and biographies of monks, they are almost entirely neglected in the study of Japanese Buddhism. There is, for example, a monthly debate conducted in the Sannōin on Kōyasan.[27] As one might expect, the topics are related to the *Lotus Sūtra*, and the debate exchange is placed within a very ritualized setting. The entire ritual takes place over a two-hour period, of which about the last forty-five minutes are devoted to the debate per se. Its location in the Sannōin indicates that it is conducted for the edification and amusement of the deities who protect the mountain, who would conventionally be identified as Shinto.

CONCLUSION

The study of Japan's ritual culture requires a series of integrative perspectives. One is the view of ritual culture as incorporating not only ritual practices, but symbolic and artistic representations as well. Similarly, ritual culture includes military pageants and political ceremonies as well as religious rituals per se. This points toward a wide range of contextualizing factors that may be investigated when ritual culture is naturalized, that is, seen as a social product. Another perspective is that of ritual culture as a network involving ritual practices, beliefs, and experiences, which are socially maintained and integrated through a variety of socialization processes.

Japan's ritual culture is both a challenge and an opportunity, as it is based on assumptions and beliefs which are radically at variance with those of Western religious studies. To the extent that the latter grows out of the Western religious tradition it tends to a set of implicit assumptions, for example, that ritual derives from doctrine, that are not appropriate to the study of the religious culture of Japan.

BIBLIOGRAPHY

ANTONI, Klaus, 1995. The "Separation of Gods and Buddhas" at Ōmiwa Shrine in Meiji Japan. *Japanese Journal of Religious Studies* 22: 139–59.

AVERBUCH, Irit, 1995. *The Gods Come Dancing: A Study of the Japanese Ritual Dance of Yamabushi Kagura*. Ithaca: East Asia Program, Cornell University.

BARGEN, Doris G., 1997. *A Woman's Weapon: Spirit Possession in The Tale of Genji*. Honolulu: University of Hawai'i Press.

BLACKER, Carmen, 1975. *The Catalpa Bow: A Study of Shamanistic Practices in Japan*, London: George Allen and Unwin.

[27] I was privileged to attend one of these sessions in August 2001, through the generous invitation of the late Rev. Chisei Aratano, whom I wish to thank publicly.

BLUM, Mark, 2001. Illuminated Honzon: Ekphrasis and Intermediality in Medieval Jōdoshin-shū. Paper presented to The Seventh International Conference on the Lotus Sutra: The Lotus Sutra and Pure Land Buddhism, Chuo Academic Research Institute, August 2001.

BOCK, Felicia, tr., 1970 and 1972. *Engi-Shiki: Procedures of the Engi Era.* 2 vols. Tokyo: *Monumenta Nipponica*, Sophia University.

BOCKING, Brian, 2001. *The Oracles of the Three Shrines: Windows on Japanese Religion.* Richmond, UK: Curzon Press.

BREEN, John, 2000. Ideologues, Bureaucrats and Priests: On "Shinto" and "Buddhism" in Early Meiji Japan. In *Shinto in History: Ways of the Kami*, ed. John Breen and Mark Teeuwen, pp. 230–51. Honolulu: University of Hawai'i Press.

BUC, Philippe, 2001. *The Dangers of Ritual: Between Early Medieval Texts and Social Scientific Theory.* Princeton: Princeton University Press.

COLE, Michael, and Yrjö ENGESTRÖM, 1993. A Cultural-Historical Approach to Distributed Cognition. In *Distributed Cognitions: Psychological and Educational Considerations*, ed. Gavriel Salomon. Cambridge: Cambridge University Press.

CORRIGAN, Philip, and David SAYER, 1985. *The Great Arch: English State Formation as Cultural Revolution.* Oxford: Basil Blackwell.

CORRINGTON, Robert S., 2000. *A Semiotic Theory of Theology and Philosophy.* Cambridge: Cambridge University Press.

DAVIS, Winston, 1980. *Dojo: Magic and Exorcism in Modern Japan.* Stanford: Stanford University Press.

_____, 1992. *Japanese Religion and Society: Paradigms of Structure and Change.* Albany: SUNY Press.

EBERSOLE, Gary L., 1989. *Ritual Poetry and the Politics of Death in Early Japan.* Princeton: Princeton University Press.

ELIADE, Mircea, 1959. *The Sacred and the Profane: The Nature of Religion.* Tr. Willard R. Trask. New York: Harcourt, Brace and World.

ELLWOOD, Robert S., Jr., 1982. *Tenrikyo, A Pilgrimage Faith: The Structure and Meanings of a Modern Japanese Religion.* Tenri: Oyasato Research Institute, Tenri University.

FAURE, Bernard, 1991. *The Rhetoric of Immediacy: A Cultural Critique of Chan/Zen Buddhism.* Princeton: Princeton University Press.

_____, 1995. Quand l'habit fait le moine: The Symbolism of the *kāṣāya* in Sōtō Zen. *Cahiers d'Extrême-Asie* 8: 335–69.

FIGAL, Gerald, 1999. *Civilization and Monsters: Spirits of Modernity in Meiji Japan.* Durham: Duke University Press.

FISCH, Michael, 2001. The Rise of the Chapel Wedding in Japan: Simulation and Performance. *Japanese Journal of Religious Studies* 28: 57–76.

FRANK, Bernard, 1991. *Le panthéon bouddhique au Japon: Collections d'Emile Guimet.* Paris: Éditions de la Réunion des Musées Nationaux.

_____, 2000a. Les *deva* de la tradition bouddhique et la société japonaise: l'exemple d'Indra Taishaku-ten. In *Amour, colère, couleur: essais sur le bouddhisme au Japon*, by Bernard Frank. Paris: Institut des Hautes Études Japonaises, Collège de France.

_____, 2000b. *Dieux et Bouddhas au Japon.* Paris: Odile Jacob.

FUJITANI Takashi, 1996. *Splendid Monarchy: Power and Pageantry in Modern Japan.* Berkeley: University of California Press.

GILDAY, Edmund T., 1987. The Pattern of *Matsuri:* Cosmic Schemes and Ritual Illusion in Japanese Festivals. Ph.D. dissertation, University of Chicago.

———, 1990. Power Plays: An Introduction to Japanese Festivals. *Journal of Ritual Studies* 4: 263–95.

GIRARD, Frédéric, 1990. *Un moine de la secte Kegon a l'Époque de Kamakura, Myōe (1173–1232) et le "Journal de ses Rêves."* Paris: École Française d'Extrême-Orient.

GLASSMAN, Hank, 2004. "Show me the place where my mother is!": The Chūjōhime Legend and Religious Performance in Late Medieval and Early Modern Japan. In *Approaching the Pure Land: Religious Praxis in the Cult of Amitābha,* ed. Richard K. Payne and Kenneth K. Tanaka. Kuroda Institute Studies in East Asian Buddhism. Honolulu: University of Hawai'i Press.

GRAPARD, Allan G., 1987. Linguistic Cubism: A Singularity of Pluralism in the Sannō Cult. *Japanese Journal of Religious Studies* 14: 211–34.

———, 1992. *The Protocol of the Gods: A Study of the Kasuga Cult in Japanese History.* Berkeley: University of California Press.

———, 1998. *Keiranshūyōshū*: A Different Perspective on Mt. Hiei in the Medieval Period. In PAYNE 1998, pp. 55–69.

———, s.v. "Honji suijaku," *Kodansha Encyclopedia*, vol. 7, p. 127. Tokyo: Kodansha.

HARDACRE, Helen, 1997. *Marketing the Menacing Fetus in Japan.* Berkeley: University of California Press.

HEINE, Steven, 1999. *Shifting Shape, Shaping Text: Philosophy and Folklore in the Fox Kōan.* Honolulu: University of Hawai'i Press.

HIGASHIBABA Ikuo, 2001. *Christianity in Early Modern Japan: Kirishitan Belief and Practice.* Leiden: E. J. Brill.

IGGERS, Georg G., 1997. *Historiography in the Twentieth Century: From Scientific Objectivity to the Postmodern Challenge.* Hanover: Wesleyan University Press, University Press of New England.

KEIRSTEAD, Thomas, 1992. *The Geography of Power in Medieval Japan.* Princeton: Princeton University Press.

KENNEY, Elizabeth, 1996–1997. Shintō Mortuary Rites in Contemporary Japan. *Cahiers d'Extrême-Asie* 9: 397–440.

KETELAAR, James Edward, 1990. *Of Heretics and Martyrs in Meiji Japan: Buddhism and Its Persecution.* Princeton: Princeton University Press.

LADURIE, Emmanuel LeRoy, 1979. *Carnival in Romans.* Tr. Mary Feeney. New York: George Braziller.

LATOUR, Bruno, 1993. *We Have Never Been Modern.* Tr. Catherine Porter. Cambridge: Harvard University Press.

LAW, Jane Marie, 1997. *Puppets of Nostalgia: The Life, Death, and Rebirth of the Japanese Awaji Ningyō Tradition.* Princeton: Princeton University Press.

LEWIS, I. M., 1971. *Ecstatic Religion: An Anthropological Study of Spirit Possession and Shamanism.* Harmondsworth, UK: Penguin Books.

LINCOLN, Bruce, 1989. *Discourse and the Construction of Society: Comparative Studies of Myth, Ritual, and Classification.* Oxford: Oxford University Press.

LISCUTIN, Nicola, 2000. Mapping the Sacred Body: Shinto versus Popular Beliefs at Mt. Iwaki in Tsugaru. In *Shinto in History: Ways of the Kami*, ed. John Breen and Mark Teeuwen. Honolulu: University of Hawai'i Press.

LOPEZ, Donald S., Jr., 1995. Foreigner at the Lama's Feet. In *Curators of the Buddha: The Study of Buddhism under Colonialism*, ed. Donald S. Lopez, Jr. Chicago: University of Chicago Press.

LUDVIK, Catherine, 1999–2000. La Benzaiten à huit bras: Durgā déesse guerrière sous l'apparence de Sarasvatī. *Cahiers d'Extrême-Asie* 11: 292–338.

MACÉ, François, 1996–1997. Le cortège fantôme: Les funérailles et la déification de Toyotomi Hideyoshi. *Cahiers d'Extême-Asie* 9: 441–62.

MAIR, Victor H., 1988. *Painting and Performance: Chinese Picture Recitation and Its Indian Genesis.* Honolulu: University of Hawai'i Press.

MAMMITZSCH, Ulrich, 1991. *Evolution of the Garbhadhātu Maṇḍala.* Śata-Piṭaka Series, Indo-Asian Literature, no. 363. New Delhi: International Academy of Indian Culture and Aditya Prakashan.

MATSUMAE Takeshi, 1993. Early kami worship. Tr. Janet Goodwin. In *The Cambridge History of Japan*, vol. 1: *Ancient Japan*, ed. Delmer M. Brown. Cambridge: Cambridge University Press.

MCCULLOUGH, Helen Craig, tr., 1988. *The Tale of the Heike.* Stanford: Stanford University Press.

MIYAKE Hitoshi, 2001. *Shugendō: Essays on the Structure of Japanese Folk Religion*, ed. and intr. H. Byron Earhart. Ann Arbor: Center for Japanese Studies, The University of Michigan.

MORSE, Anne Nishimura, and Samuel Crowell MORSE, eds., 1995. *Object as Insight: Japanese Buddhist Art and Ritual.* Katonah: Katonah Museum of Art.

PAINE, Robert Treat, and Alexander SOPER, 1981. *The Art and Architecture of Japan.* 3rd ed. New Haven: Yale University Press.

PAYNE, Richard Karl, 1999. Shingon Services for the Dead. In *Religions of Japan in Practice*, ed. George J. Tanabe, Jr., pp. 159–65. Princeton: Princeton University Press.

———, 2000. Ritual Manual for the Protective Fire Offering Devoted to Mañjuśrī, Chuin Lineage. In *Tantra in Practice*, ed. David Gordon White. Princeton: Princeton University Press.

PAYNE, Richard, ed., 1998. *Re-Visioning "Kamakura" Buddhism.* Kuroda Institute Studies in East Asian Buddhism 11. Honolulu: University of Hawai'i Press.

PIGGOTT, Joan R., 1997. *The Emergence of Japanese Kingship.* Stanford: Stanford University Press.

RAMBELLI, Fabio, 1998. Objects, Rituals, Tradition: A Genealogy of the Memorial Services (Kuyō) for Objects in Japan. Paper presented to the Tantric Studies Consultation, annual meeting of the American Academy of Religion, Orlando.

RANGER, Terence, and Eric J. HOBSBAWM, eds., 1992. *The Invention of Tradition.* Cambridge: Cambridge University Press.

READER, Ian, 1988. Miniaturization and Proliferation: A Study of Small-Scale Pilgrimages in Japan. *Studies in Central and East Asian Religions* 1: 50–66.

READER, Ian, and George J. TANABE, Jr., 1998. *Practically Religious: Worldly Benefits and the Common Religion of Japan*. Honolulu: University of Hawai'i Press.

ROGERS, Minor L., 1996. Rennyo's *Ofumi* and the Shinshū in Pure Land Tradition. In *The Pure Land Tradition: History and Development*, ed. James Foard, Michael Solomon, and Richard K. Payne. Berkeley Buddhist Studies Series 3. Berkeley: Berkeley Buddhist Studies Series.

ROGERS, Minor L., and Ann T. ROGERS, 1991. *Rennyo: The Second Founder of Shin Buddhism*. Nanzan Studies in Asian Religions 3. Berkeley: Asian Humanities Press.

ROTHKRUG, Lionel, 1980. Religious Practices and Collective Perceptions: Hidden Homologies in the Renaissance and Reformation. *Historical Reflections/Réflexions Historiques* 7: 1–251.

RUPPERT, Brian, 2000. *Jewel in the Ashes: Buddha Relics and Power in Early Medieval Japan*. Harvard East Asian Monographs 188. Cambridge and London: Harvard University Asia Center, Harvard University Press.

ŚĀNTIDEVA, 1995. *The Bodhicaravatara*. Tr. Kate Crosby and Andrew Skilton. Oxford: Oxford University Press.

SCHNELL, Scott, 1999. *The Rousing Drum: Ritual Practice in a Japanese Community*. Honolulu: University of Hawai'i Press.

SHARF, Robert H., 1995. Sanbōkyōdan: Zen and the Way of the New Religions. *Japanese Journal of Religious Studies* 22: 417–58.

―――, 2001. Visualization and Mandala in Shingon Buddhism. In *Living Images: Japanese Buddhist Icons in Context*, ed. Robert H. Sharf and Elizabeth Horton Sharf, pp. 151–97. Stanford: Stanford University Press.

SMITH, Robert J., 1995. Wedding and Funeral Ritual: Analysing a Moving Target. In VAN BREMEN and MARTINEZ 1995, pp. 25–37.

SMYERS, Karen A., 1999. *The Fox and the Jewel: Shared and Private Meanings in Contemporary Japanese Inari Worship*. Honolulu: University of Hawai'i Press.

SNODGRASS, Adrian, 1988. *The Matrix and Diamond World Mandalas in Shingon Buddhism*. 2 vols. Śata-Piṭaka Series, Indo-Asian Literatures, nos. 354 & 355. New Delhi: Aditya Prakashan.

STAAL, Frits, 1989. *Rules without Meaning: Ritual, Mantras and the Human Sciences*. New York: Peter Lang.

STEFÁNSSON, Halldór, 1995. On Structural Duality in Japanese Conceptions of Death: Collective Forms of Death Rituals in Morimachi. In VAN BREMEN and MARTINEZ 1995, pp. 83–107.

STONE, Jacqueline I., 1998. Chanting the August Title of the *Lotus Sutra*: *Daimoku* Practices in Classical and Medieval Japan. In PAYNE 1998, pp. 116–66.

SUGAHARA Shinkai, 1996. The Distinctive Features of Sannō Ichijitsu Shinto. *Japanese Journal of Religious Studies* 23: 61–84.

TANABE, George J., Jr., 1999. Introduction. In *Religions of Japan in Practice*, ed. George J. Tanabe, Jr., pp. 3–20. Princeton: Princeton University Press.

TAUSSIG, Michael, 1987. *Shamanism, Colonialism, and the Wild Man: A Study in Terror and Healing*. Chicago: University of Chicago Press.

TEN GROTENHUIS, Elizabeth, 1992. Chūjōhime: The Weaving of Her Legend. In *Flowing Traces:*

Buddhism in the Literary and Visual Arts of Japan, ed. James H. Sanford, William R. LaFleur, and Masatoshi Nagatomi. Princeton: Princeton University Press.

———, 1999. *Japanese Mandalas: Representations of Sacred Geography*. Honolulu: University of Hawai'i Press.

TOGANOO Shōun 栂尾祥雲, 1932. *Mandara no kenkyū* 曼荼羅の研究. Koyasan: Kōyasan Daigaku Shuppanbu.

TRAINOR, Kevin, 1997. *Relics, Ritual, and Representation in Buddhism: Rematerializing the Sri Lankan Theravāda Tradition*. Cambridge Studies in Religious Traditions 10. Cambridge: Cambridge University Press.

TURNBULL, Stephen, 1995. Mass or Matsuri? The Oyashiki-sama Ceremony on Ikitsuki. *Monumenta Nipponica* 50: 171–88.

———, 1998. *The Kakure Kirishitan of Japan: A Study of their Development, Beliefs and Rituals to the Present Day*. Richmond, UK: Japan Library, Curzon Press.

TYLER, Royall, 1990. *The Miracles of the Kasuga Deity*. New York: Columbia University Press.

TYLER, Susan C., 1992. *The Cult of Kasuga Seen through Its Art*. Michigan Monograph Series in Japanese Studies 8. Ann Arbor: Center for Japanese Studies, University of Michigan.

UNDERWOOD, Meredith, 1999. Strategies of Survival: Women, Abortion, and Popular Religion in Contemporary Japan. *Journal of the American Academy of Religion* 67: 739–68.

UNNO, Mark, 1998. Recommending Faith in the Sand of the Mantra of Light: Myōe Kōben's *Kōmyō Shingon Dosha Kanjinki*. In PAYNE 1998, pp. 167–218.

———, 2004. *Shingon Refractions: Myōe and the Mantra of Light*. Boston: Wisdom.

VAN BREMEN, Jan, and D. P. MARTINEZ, eds., 1995. *Ceremony and Ritual in Japan: Religious Practices in an Industrialized Society*. London: Routledge.

WRIGHT, Dale S., 1998. *Philosophical Meditations on Zen Buddhism*. Cambridge: Cambridge University Press.

YIENGPRUKSAWAN, Mimi Hall, 1998. *Hiraizumi: Buddhist Art and Regional Politics in Twelfth-Century Japan*. Cambridge: Harvard University Asia Center, Harvard University Press.

THEMES

Robert E. MORRELL

Literature and Scripture

Few would deny, in so many words, that the past is influenced by its own past, and that both underlie their future; that literature of an earlier time inevitably reveals its own underpinning of traditional values and ideas, however puzzling to later generations, whose own creations cannot escape their continuing presence. But what cannot be denied can easily enough be overlooked, consciously ignored, or glibly interpreted with values, preconceptions, and critical notions compatible with later times and places.

Our focus here is on these underpinnings of Japanese literature—many elusive, but some with convenient, though debatable, labels: Shinto, Buddhist, Confucian, Christian, etc. Such labels also describe long-established areas of scholarship to mark the broader areas of literature, history, "modern" philosophy (*tetsugaku* 哲学), traditional thought (*shisō* 思想), sociology, economics, etc., often with their narrowly established procedures for investigation. Specialists in these areas of learning often have little knowledge or interest in what their colleagues in other disciplines may be doing. Thus, students of Japanese literature are often content to analyze their materials solely in terms of the current literary vocabulary, while students of religion pursue their research in their own proprietary terminology—both with little knowledge or interest beyond their own delimited specialties. But an interdisciplinary approach can often reveal mutually useful insights unseen when the focus is too narrow. For example, to see the interaction of "literature and scripture" is to show not only the influence of the ideological underpinning on the literary product but also the extent and perception of particular aspects of the ideological ground at different times and places. Thus, a reference to Chuang Tzu's dreaming butterfly in a literary work is more than an allusion to a flying insect; and, at the same time, the frequency and treatment in Japanese literary works of certain Taoist ideas (and the neglect of others) can clearly show us their extent and importance in the Japanese literary imagination.

The issue of ideological underpinnings can be controversial, beginning with what we even mean by our broad categories. Does an indigenous system of rituals and beliefs called Shinto actually exist? If so, how and among what elements of the population does it manifest itself? Is Japanese Buddhism really Buddhism, if judged by the standards of China or India (see HUBBARD and SWANSON 1997)? And what do we mean by Japanese Confucianism, which is not identical to its parent in China?

If we could arrive at a consensus on these issues, we would then have to make allowance for specific time periods. How much Buddhist influence could we expect to find in, say, the *Man'yōshū* (ca. 759)? Probably very little…. Should we continue to expect significant "Shinto" influence on the literature and behavior of the post-1945 Japanese? Dare we even ask the question?…There are those who apparently believe that these so-called traditional underpinnings magically vanished with the Meiji Restoration in 1868. In short, the "scripture" part of our "literature and scripture" topic is sure to raise questions.

Let us assume that we can agree on some basic definitions. Then, where an obvious, explicit reference to a specific "scripture" occurs, we can speak of influence. Questions only arise when it may be necessary to guess what was in the mind of a writer, albeit unconsciously, to give rise to a particular configuration of words and ideas. We are always in danger of reading in too much or too little—and the choice cannot be avoided. Was an apparent connotation intended, or entirely fortuitous? Consider, for example, Brower and Miner's translation and discussion of a famous *waka* by Fujiwara Teika (BROWER and MINER 1961, 262-63):

Haru no yo no	The bridge of dreams
Yume no ukihashi	Floating on the brief spring night
Todae shite	Soon breaks off:
Mine ni wakaruru	Now from the mountaintop a cloud
Yokogumo no sora.	Takes leave into the open sky.

The translators discuss this verse at some length, rightly noting that it is basically a "Spring" poem about love, with myriad implications, including overtones from the *Genji*, and possibly the *Heike monogatari*. They then suggest that the poem could also be inter-preted as a "symbolic depiction of the life of man," with the "open sky" (*sora*) suggesting "the Buddhist 'emptiness' (*kū* 空), to the realization of which we awaken when enlighten-ment ends the illusory dream of the reality of the phenomenal world."

But does the verse really support a religious interpretation? I am sure that many mod-ern Western interpreters will dismiss the notion out of hand, looking instead, perhaps, for some reflection of feudal reactionary social values, or whatever. However, some will not—although they must be prepared for some resistance from the trend setters. The issue, then, is how far we can and should go in trying to uncover the sense of a tradition whose sources often differ greatly from those in the West; and, if we do try, how much can we afford to ignore?

In any case, established academic disciplines generally rigidly define—by means of degree requirements, permitted courses and topics of research, and the subsequent covert influence of these on the control of professional panels and meetings, as well as tenure and hiring expectations—the acceptable limits and procedures of research, in spite of vehe-ment denials of coercion.

SHINTO AND LITERATURE

Since Shinto has always been a more baffling puzzle for Western rationalists than either Buddhism or Confucianism, its influence in secular literature is probably the most difficult to demonstrate. Some would say that it is not even a religion or ideology, but merely a grab-bag of folk beliefs and practices which have been given a name and virtual reality to distinguish it from its continental competitors. To make matters worse, it is tainted by the reputation of its association with pre-WWII nationalism and even lacks a clearly defined body of scriptures, such as we expect of any self-respecting ideology.

Recently there has been a revival of interest in Shinto, predictably following the same shift away from earlier approaches "emphasizing philological, textual, and doctrinal stud-ies" toward "specific historical, social, and institutional contexts" which Professor Stone has noted with respect to Buddhism. We can see recent examples of this shift in many of the essays in *Shinto in History* (BREEN and TEEUWEN 2000), in *Shintō and the State, 1868–1988* (HARDACRE 1989), and, to a lesser extent, in some of the items in *Sources of Japanese Tradition, Second Edition: Volume One: From Earliest Times to 1600* (DE BARY 2001), the earlier *Sources of Japanese Tradition, Volume II* (TSUNODA 1964), *Religions of Japan in Practice* (TANABE 1999), and in *Ritual Poetry and the Politics of Death in Early Japan* (EBERSOLE 1989).

Elsewhere in this *Guide*, the essay by Norman Havens on Shinto provides us with a detailed description of the issues and current *socio-historical* attempts to define this amor-phous object of study. The issues are highly controversial. And yet, however we classify it, or by whatever name we call it, this clearly observable Japanese phenomenon persists. Since our *literary* approach is among those "emphasizing philological, textual and doctri-nal studies," we will refer to it here, for the sake of convenience, as "Shinto"—*pace* to those early Meiji revivalists by whom "the very name of Shiñ-tau [*sic*] is repudiated" (SATOW

1882, p. 165), and their modern successors. Literature and the other arts are concerned with Shinto as a repository of traditional modes of feeling and behavior, rather than as a socio-political phenomenon. In addition to the name, it is probably also useful for the student of literature not to discard, quite yet, the traditional three defining characteristics of Shinto: belief in pantheistic *kami*, ritual purity (rather than moral righteousness), and—most problematic of all for contemporary logolators—the inability of reason to grasp the ineffable (MOTOORI 1780, pp. 19–22, "Wonder").

While both approaches have their uses and limitations, literature stresses the perceived presence of Shinto notions in the mindset of those for whom they have immediate aesthetic recognition as literature. Thus, for example, in addition to seeing the *Kojiki* (712) as quasi-history or possibly as political propaganda, we can also approach it as a work to be read *as literature* (see KEENE 1983). The same can be said for the *Nihon shoki* (720), for which, after a century, we should probably have an updated translation to complement Aston's amazing accomplishment (ASTON 1896)—and any number of other writings.

Although Shinto lacks a single book or books revered as Holy Scripture, as are certain texts in Western traditions, we can identify a collection of respected writings which can qualify as "divine texts" (*shinten* 神典): the *Kojiki* 古事記, *Nihon shoki* 日本書紀 , *Kujiki* 舊 事記 (or *Sendai kuji hongi* 先代旧事本記), *Kogoshūi* 古語拾遺 , *norito* 祝詞, etc. (*Shintō Daijiten* 1969, p. 785). One can find a nice overview of such material in *Shintō: At the Fountainhead of Japan* (HERBERT 1967, pp. 34–41). When such works are cited in secular literature, this might well qualify as Shinto *influence*.

The reader might also note old and new translations of Shinto items in recent anthologies which will become basic references for students of Japanese for several decades: *Religions of Japan in Practice* (TANABE 1999) and *Sources of Japanese Tradition, Second Edition, Volume One: From Earliest Times to 1600* (DE BARY 2001). It is particularly gratifying to see so many new translations at a time when translation is discouraged in some academic circles even partially to fulfill the requirements for the M.A. or Ph.D., not to mention consideration for tenure.

Teasing out Shinto influence on Japanese literary aesthetics will eventually become possible after we have surveyed its obvious items of concrete influence from the histories, poetry collections, *monogatari*, *setsuwa*, *noh*, *otogizōshi*, *kabuki*—everything. For starters, for example, what can the 33 items comprising the first book (*jingi* 神祇, "gods, shrines, [and rituals]") of the *setsuwa* collection, *Kokonchomonjū* 古今著聞集 (1254), tell us about Shinto as it was actually apprehended by the Kamakura general public not versed in its arcane details of thought and practice?

Among the *Collections of Twenty-one Reigns* [or "Imperial Anthologies"] (*nijūichidaishū* 二十一代集), compiled between 905 and 1439, the eighteen collections beginning with the fourth, the *Goshūishū* 後拾遺集 (1086), included a genre of poems known as *jingika*. Of course, we also find Shinto-inspired poems in earlier compendia, but under different labels: "Poems of Divine Music and Dance" *kamiasobi no uta* 神遊びの歌, *kagurauta* 神楽歌, etc. The affinity which the *kami* were seen to have with *waka* is implied by the designation of the "Three Gods of Poetry" (*waka sanjin* 和歌三神: Sumiyoshi 住吉, Tamatsushima 玉津 島, and Hitomaro Myōjin 人麿明神. See *Nihon Koten Bungaku Daijiten* 1985, vol. 3, pp. 455–

56). *Jingika* have a family resemblance to "Poems on Śākyamuni's Teachings" (*shakkyōka* 釈教歌) with whom they often appear side by side in poetry collections (e.g., see Morrell, "The *Shinkokinshū*...," in Hare 1996, pp. 281–320). From the late Heian period they sometimes reflect Shinto-Buddhist syncretism (*honji suijaku* 本地垂迹).

In short, Shinto influences here and elsewhere in early poetry are clearly evident, but mostly ignored. A student of Japanese literature searching for a lifetime research topic could do worse than translating and explicating the *jingika* of the medieval collections. This would not be as easy as it might seem. Surprisingly, among the *Collections of Twenty-One Reigns*, only two are to be found in modern annotated editions—the well-known *Kokinshū* 古今集 (ca. 905–920) and *Shinkokinshū* 新古今集 (1216). The rest can be found, minimally annotated, within the 28 volumes of *Kōchū Kokka Taikei* 1930–1931; for the first eight, Yamagishi 1960 (based on Kitamura Kigin's [1624–1705] *Notes*) may be of some limited help.

BUDDHISM AND LITERATURE

In its appeal to the Western student of Japanese institutions Buddhism has always had an advantage over Shinto, Confucianism, and (Japanese) Christianity. It is perceived by some—justifiably or not—to provide not just clues for understanding Japanese society, but for providing viable answers to universal philosophical and religious questions. This interest has generated a substantial body of research and literary production over the years, from Ernest Fenollosa and Lafcadio Hearn, through involvement with the Beat Generation, to conscientious religious practice, and also serious scholarship. This, in turn, has made available a wealth of resources at the fingertips of the student interested in pursuing any of a million leads. Of course, the flip side of this marvel was the inevitable appearance of kitsch Buddhism, with everything from Samsara perfume to Zen underwear and microbiotic therapy—more than a passing annoyance, but the reinforcement of an inhibiting academic disdain for religion in general and "oriental mysticism" in particular.

Nevertheless, the current state of interest and research in Buddhism seems (at least to this observer) never to have been healthier, and this can be said as well of Buddhism *and literature*. The lively debates over Critical Buddhism (see Hubbard and Swanson 1997), the disaffection of some earlier enthusiasts, the reevaluation of old sectarian boundaries and self-serving apologetics, are surely signs that Japanese Buddhism continues to make progress toward being taken seriously as religion and philosophy on equal terms with the West. Yes, departments of philosophy or literature in many Western universities continue to be as smugly self-centered as they have been for decades, or even centuries, but exclusiveness now can be maintained only at the cost of civilization itself.

Research on Japanese religions can be approached in a variety of ways, and limiting our focus to literary matters raises additional concerns. The various perspectives, however, can be classified into two major groups: those which approach a topic from the outside, as it were, through an analysis of social, political, or economic conditions; and those which attempt to reach the aesthetic experience intended by the artist and enjoyed by those who participate in the project—from the inside, as it were. It is a distinction which reflects a basic polarity in ways of reasoning, and since the two approaches cannot be rationally reconciled, the easy solution to the problem is simply to ignore it. Easy perhaps, but dangerous.

The implications are widespread in all the arts and ethical practices in every society, which are constant prey to rational schemes which attempt to explain rather than to experience them. Experience of the poem, the graphic image, the musical configuration, the religious mythology, etc., is rarely enhanced (and more often obscured) by external analysis of the conditions which surround the event, but which ultimately can never satisfactorily explain it. Frustrating as this may be to the stubborn rationalist, the aesthetic experience may be suggested, but never captured, by fingers pointing at the moon.

Ideally, both of these general perspectives have some merit in the discussion of literature and the other arts, however incidental the "definable" features of an analysis may be to an item's aesthetic understanding. I am concerned, however, that the renewed emphasis on the "historical bases," and such, may be to project an air of "scientific objectivity" that will overpower other avenues of research that are, in my opinion, equally, and even more, legitimate. Graduate students will be "advised" to follow paths that lead to financial support, and may even be reminded of the nail that sticks out. Mammon is alive and well in academe.

In addressing the problem of "providing an overview of key issues and important topics of research with regard to Japanese religions" as expressed in literature, I would like to focus on the question of the mindset which the investigator brings to his project, because the attitude of the worker is the common ingredient of what he produces, whatever it may be. Perhaps the best example to illustrate some of the issues involved in research is the great Heian classic, the *Tale of Genji*. We now have three complete translations of Lady Murasaki's novel into English—by Arthur WALEY (1935), Edward SEIDENSTICKER (1976), and Royall TYLER (2001)—each skillfully rendered and each with its own unavoidable strengths and weaknesses, depending on the expectations of their critics. Fortunately, it is not my business here to attempt an evaluation of relative worth. In one conspicuous instance, however, it is possible to suggest that the author and her translator may not have shared the same take on the text. Or did they?

I hope the reader will excuse my recycling some comments from a decade-old review which still expresses my firm conviction and for which I cannot today find clearer words or a better example. Arthur Waley's introduction to his partial translation of Sei Shōnagon's *Pillow Book* can be read today as defining the basic agenda for at least a generation of Western scholars of Japanese literature. Since his *Genji* first appeared in 1925–1933 in six installments, the 1928 *Pillow Book* can reasonably be expected to represent his thinking at the time:

> It is, then, not only their complete absorption in the passing moment, but more generally the entire absence of intellectual background that makes the ancient Japanese so different from us.... Again, the purely aesthetic approach to religion, which was the rule in Heian, has often been fostered in Europe by cliques of exceptional people. At first sight, indeed, Buddhism (with its rosaries, baptism, tonsured monks, and nuns; its Heaven, Purgatory, and Hell) appears to have many points of resemblance to Catholic Christianity. But I fancy, all the same, that the fundamental difference between the Japanese (or, for that matter,

any Far Eastern nation) and us is the fact, obvious indeed yet constantly overlooked, that they were not Christians.   (WALEY 1928, pp. 12, 14–15)

As long as Heian society could be seen as subordinating every activity to "the Rule of Taste" (in George Sansom's phrase), there was no need to come to terms with the ideological bases of a society characterized by "the entire absence of intellectual background." Buddhism, Shinto, and Confucianism might occasionally provide topical color to a scene in the form of "rosaries, baptism, tonsured monks, and nuns," but they were not to be engaged seriously as, say, Christianity would be for providing not only content, but the basis for formal assumptions of medieval, Renaissance, and even modern literature in the West. Surface was all that mattered—much to the relief of translators and critics. A self-confident Waley can even decline to translate a short chapter which he sees as so much religious flummery—#38, "The Bell Cricket" (*Suzumushi*). That is his right as a translator, just as it is our right as readers to question his judgment in the matter.

But the many heirs of nineteenth-century positivism have even more reason to be thankful for his guidance than those with a conscious Judeo-Christian commitment. For the positivist, all religion is mere proto-science, whose ideas may be of interest to the cultural antiquarian; but those who pretend to view the statements of the traditional Japanese ideologies as serious philosophy are, at best, hopeless romantics. Of course, our positivists are never as objective as they imagine themselves to be, even today. The covert values they bring to their understanding of Japanese literature are inevitably reflected in what they choose to translate, in what they choose to ignore, and in how they present their translations and explanations—highlighting here, suppressing there—and in the subsequent analyses of what they produce as representative of that literature.

Our three translators have provided us with three elegant and careful translations. But what are we to make of them? Most of us probably already at least partly subscribe to Motoori Norinaga's (1730–1801) characterization of the whole of the *Genji* as a novel of *mono no aware*, a phrase which has sometimes been translated as "the sadness of things." Motoori, however, may have meant by it something closer to a "sensitivity to things"—sensitivity to the fall of a flower or to an unwept tear (DE BARY 2001, p. 198). See also Makoto UEDA's *Literary and Art Theories in Japan* (1967, pp. 196–213: "Shintoism and the Theory of Literature"). In any case, Motoori seems not to be saying that it is simply a "novel of manners." And Professor Konishi does not agree that *mono no aware* is enough to define the *Genji*.

> Motoori Norinaga asserts that the *Genji* should be read in terms of deep human emotion (*mono no aware*) rather than from a Buddhist standpoint. This was an outstanding view in its day and is generally accepted even now. It cannot be seen, however, as the only valid interpretation. My reading is based on Kamakura period theories, which I have recast in modern terms. I believe that a perceptive stance more proximate to that taken in Murasaki Shikibu's time is likely to yield a more accurate reading. (KONISHI 1986, p. 333, n. 130)

The passage in the "Hotaru" chapter in which Murasaki defends the use of "fabrications" in the novel and the inclusion of both good and bad elements is closely tied to her insistence that it describes, just as they are, things in the world that are intrinsically interesting.

[In the *monogatari*] we are not told of things that happened to specific people exactly as they happened; but the beginning is when there are good things and bad things, things that happen in this life which one never tires of seeing and hearing about, things which one cannot bear not to tell of and pass on for all generations.... Good things and bad things alike, they are things of this world and no other. [The editors of Konishi's *History* have borrowed the translation, with minor changes, from SEIDENSTICKER 1976, 1:437. Cf., MORRIS 1964, pp. 309–10.]

Genji next explains that fabrication in *monogatari* serves the same purpose as the Buddhist expedients (*hōben*) that explicate the Dharma; and that the relation between fiction and fact is similar to that between delusion and enlightenment.... It is an outstanding passage.   (KONISHI 1986, p. 319)

An outstanding passage which provides Lady Murasaki with a solid rationale, based on Buddhist principles, for even composing "fiction," in disagreement with traditional moralists who disapproved of this as simply lying. Elsewhere, Professor Konishi distinguishes three parts and three defining themes of the *Genji*:

Part One [Chapters 1–33] of the *Genji* may have been written with a realistic theme in mind—a just royal succession, for example. Murasaki Shikibu certainly did not intend it to have a Buddhist theme like karma. Karma is the impetus of Part Two [Ch. 34–41], however, and it comes to encompass Part One as well: the lives and actions of all the characters in Part One are seen to originate in acts committed in previous lives.   (Ibid., p. 328)

.... The characters in Part Three [Ch. 42–54] wander lost in the midst of endless change. If Part Two is a world of suffering, Part Three is one of illusion. Illusion signifies uncertainty as to the truth, an aspect of *avidyā* (J. *mumyō*), spiritual blindness. The theme of Part Three is "piety and spiritual blindness."   (Ibid., p. 333)

The three themes of the *Genji*—reality and clear insight, karma and predetermined suffering, piety and spiritual blindness—are not simply contiguous elements. When the *Genji* consisted of only Part One, its theme was reality and clear insight. When Part Two appeared, the theme of Part One was enveloped by Part Two, karma and predetermined suffering.... The completion of Part Three led to its theme, piety and spiritual blindness, enveloping the earlier themes, which become elements of a theme for the entire *Tale of Genji*.   (Ibid., p. 333)

In comparing the concept of time often suggested between that of Murasaki's *Genji* and Marcel Proust's *À la recherche du temps perdu* (Remembrance of Things Past, 1913–1927), we have this comment:

... If Murasaki Shikibu can be said to have a philosophical view of time, it is that embodied by Tendai Buddhism, and particularly by the sixteenth chapter of the *Lotus Sūtra*, "The Life-Span of the Thus Come One." Time, as it appears in the *Genji*, is based on a concept well known to Murasaki Shikibu's contemporaries, that of karma (*sukuse*, lit. previous existences). This pertains to past time, before one's birth into the present life. Karma involves the acts committed in a past existence, and is not erased by death but influences one's next life.... The cause-and-effect relationship continues through countless rebirths

THEMES

[until one at last achieves enlightenment]. Proust envisions time rather differently: his past serves as a source of influence on present existence alone.   (Ibid., p. 327)

In short, Murasaki Shikibu does not appear to live in either Proust's or Jane Austen's world. And we cannot expect even the most skillful translator to capture its endless nuances, with Shinto, Confucian, Buddhist, or whatever, antecedents.

We are, however, blessed with an abundance of resources not available just a few decades ago, including five complete English translations of Kumārajīva's Chinese translation (406) of the *Lotus Sūtra* (T. 262), which was wildly influential in Japan (WATSON 1993, KUBO and YUYAMA 1993, HURVITZ 1976, KATŌ 1975, and MURANO 1974), as well as a reliable, inexpensive, annotated, pocket edition in three volumes, with the original Chinese and modern Japanese translations (SAKAMOTO and IWAMOTO 1962, 1964, 1967). Stone's landmark study *Original Enlightenment and the Transformation of Medieval Japanese Buddhism* (1999) should be on the bookshelves of anyone interested in the religion and/or literature of the premodern period beside Swanson's *Foundations of T'ien-t'ai Philosophy* (1989), LaFleur's *The Karma of Words: Buddhism and the Literary Arts in Medieval Japan* (1983), and (especially for those who may have lingering doubts about Heian religious commitment) Kamens's *The Buddhist Poetry of the Great Kamo Priestess: Daisaiin Senshi and Hosshin Wakashū* (1990).

Also relevant to *Genji* studies (among others) is ISHIDA Mizumaro's handy two-volume colloquial translation of Genshin's *Ōjōyōshū* 往生要集 (1996), and *Jōdo sanbukyō* (NAKAMURA 1963–1964): Chinese originals, translations, and notes to the [*Dai*]*muryōjukyō* (T. 276), the *Kanmuryōjukyō* (T. 365), and the *Amidakyō* (T. 366). It is sometimes suggested that the model for "the bishop of Yokawa" who appears in the "Tenarai" (#53) chapter of the *Genji* is none other than Genshin 源信 (Eshin 恵心, 942–1017). Be that as it may, his *Ōjōyōshū* (985) defined the Pure Land thought of Murasaki's day and should not be confused with the Kamakura movements of Hōnen and Shinran (see MORRELL 1987, 13–22, for a discussion of Tendai Amidism, including a translation of Genshin's "Yokawa Tract"). We cannot expect translators to pursue such details—but they do matter. And the *Genji* provides us with a good example of some of the problems of translation, analysis, and interpretation which apply to all literature with non-Western ideological underpinnings.

The aesthetics of *mono no aware* lead us inevitably to the related ideal of *yūgen* 幽玄 ("mystery and depth"), of major importance to the poetry of the *Shinkokinshū*, linked verse (*renga* 連歌), and the *nō* 能 theater (DE BARY 2001, pp. 364–98). I am pleased to note that the revised *Sources I* includes the lucid comments from the *Mumyōshō* 無名抄 of Kamo no Chōmei 鴨長明 (1153–1216) (DE BARY 2001, p. 387; cf. BROWER and MINOR 1961, pp. 387–88). Cranston's "'Mystery and Depth' in Japanese Court Poetry" (HARE 1996, pp. 65–104), LaFleur's "Symbol and *Yūgen*: Shunzei's Use of Tendai Buddhism," (in SANFORD 1992, pp. 16–46), and Makoto UEDA's "Imitation, *Yūgen*, and Sublimity: Zeami on the Art of the Nō Drama" (1967, pp. 55–71), are all important voices in this discussion.

We have time only to call attention to the voluminous Muromachi "Five Mountains" literature (*gozan* 五山)—yes, with a clear "*sā*." (See the multi-volume Shogakkan dictionary for *Nippo jisho* and *Dainihon bunten* examples.) Also, among the period's short stories (*otogizōshi* 御伽草子) we should note CHILDS's *Rethinking Sorrow: Revelatory Tales of Late Medieval Japan* (1991) and MULHERN's "Cinderella and the Jesuits" (1979, see below)—both with obvious ideological ancestries.

CONFUCIANISM, INDEPENDENT THINKERS, AND LITERATURE

The influence of Confucianism, or at least of indigenous patterns of social behavior rationalized or reinforced by the Chinese import, is apparent from the earliest accounts in the *Record of Ancient Matters* (*Kojiki*, 712) to the present day. Scholarly interest has naturally focused on the Edo period (1600–1868), when the Tokugawa military government officially supported Hayashi Razan's version of Chu Hsi's Neo-Confucianism as its social philosophy, and a variety of alternatives flourished. The revised *Sources of Japanese Tradition, Second Edition: Volume One: From Earliest Times to 1600* (DE BARY 2001) upgrades the 1958 edition to 1600, and we can assume that the succeeding volume will do the same for the Edo and later periods (TSUNODA 1958).

New translations of primary materials such as the *Jikkinshō* 十訓抄 (1252) *setsuwa* collection [GEDDES], Kaibara Ekiken's (1630–1714) *Kadōkun* 家道訓 [TUCKER], and Nakazawa Dōni's (1725-1803) *Dōni-ō dōwa* 道二翁道話 [SAWADA] are to be found in *Religions of Japan in Practice* (TANABE 1999). For various articles and discussions see *Confucianism and Tokugawa Culture* (NOSCO 1984), and *Tokugawa Ideology: Early Constructs, 1570–1680* (OOMS 1985).

We can easily enough point to obvious literary instances of Confucianism in, say, the *Jikkinshō*, in the plays of Chikamatsu (1653–1725; see TSUNODA 1958, pp. 443–49), in the *Hakkenden* of Takizawa Bakin (1767–1848), and perhaps the *ninjōbon* of Tamenaga Shunsui (1790–1843)—but we await a champion to step forward in its defense.

CHRISTIANITY/WESTERN IDEOLOGIES AND LITERATURE

In dealing with literary, in contrast to socio-political-historical, impressions on Japanese literature, we should also include non-"religious" influences: Graeco-Roman, Marxist, etc.—if only to mention them in passing in this overview.

A minor, but intriguing, example of possible Graeco-Roman influence—perhaps introduced by Christian missionaries, but possibly by the Silk Route trade between Rome and Han China and thence to Japan—is the appearance of phrases and axioms in the language which are so close in structure to possible antecedents that they are unlikely to have evolved spontaneously. For example, the authoritative *Nihon Kokugo Daijiten* (vol. 12, p. 552) discusses the familiar proverb *taizan meidō shite nezumi ippiki* 大山鳴動して鼠一匹 ["The great mountain trembles and a tiny mouse comes forth"], prints the Latin parallel—*Parturiunt montes, nascetur ridiculus mus*—and even attributes it to Horace, but without specifying the source (*Ars poetica*, ca. 19 BCE, 139). So how did Horace get to Japan?

We know that Aesop arrived with the Portuguese Jesuit missionaries, and his *Fables* are thought to be the first Japanese translation of a Western work, the *Esopo no fabulas*, published by the Amakusa press in 1593. A later, more elegant version appeared ca. 1620 as

Isoho monogatari 伊曽保物語. Was this an influence on *kanazōshi* or other Edo literature? And what about *otogizōshi*—for example, "Cinderella and the Jesuits: An Otogizōshi Cycle as Christian Literature" (MULHERN 1979, pp. 409–47)?

The history of the missions during the "Christian Century" are peripheral to our literary concerns, and are discussed in the writings of COOPER 1973, BOXER 1951, ELISON 1973, SANSOM 1950, 1961, and others. However, a number of writings are still of considerable interest to the student of Japanese literature: João Rodrigues'*História da Igreja do Japão* (Part I, Books 1 & 2) (COOPER 1973 and 1974), his *Arte da Lingoa de Iapam* (ca. 1608) [his account of Japanese Poetry] (COOPER 1971), and, of course, the still widely cited Portuguese-Japanese dictionary, *Vocabulario da Lingoa da Iapam* (*Nippo jisho* 日葡辞書, published in 1603–1604 (see COOPER 1976).

In short, if one accepts the proposition that Japanese literature should be explored first and foremost through an examination of its own underlying national sentiments, ideals, and thought processes, there will be no end to our labors—fortunately. I ask those who may twinge at my using such a phrase as Japanese "national sentiments, ideals, and thought processes" whether Japan is the only nation under the sun which is not permitted to take pride in some kind of national identity? The citizens of the United States, Great Britain, France, Russia, mainland China, and so forth, certainly have no qualms about flaunting their flags and anthems whenever they wish—and why should they not? And why should not everyone?

To understand the aesthetics of a society's literature we must first search for its sources on its own terms, in the thought and behavior of those who actually composed it and were moved by it, rather than with theoretical models developed out of the experience of alien cultures. Still, those who favor a Gallic twist to their aesthetic ruminations could certainly do no harm by returning to an ideal of "clear and distinct ideas" by which Descartes hoped to dispel the theoretic miasma of his own day.

ANNOTATED REFERENCES

ABÉ, Ryūchi, 1999. *The Weaving of Mantra: Kūkai and the Construction of Esoteric Buddhist Discourse.* New York: Columbia University Press.

AKIYAMA Ken 秋山 虔, ed., 2000. *Ōchōgo jiten* 王朝語辞典. Tokyo: University of Tokyo Press. Subtitled: "A Dictionary of Heian Literary Vocabulary."

500 selected items each discussed on a single page.

ASTON, William G., 1896. *Nihongi, chronicles of Japan from the earliest times to A.D. 607. Transactions and Proceedings of the Japan Society London*, Supplement I, 2 vols. London: The Japan Society.

Many reprints. Surely an updated translation is long overdue.

BOXER, C. R., 1951. *The Christian Century in Japan, 1549–1650.* Berkeley: University of California Press.

BREEN, John, and Mark TEEUWEN, eds., 2000. *Shinto in History: Ways of the Kami.* Honolulu: University of Hawai'i Press.

BROWER, Robert H., and Earl MINER, 1961. *Japanese Court Poetry*. Stanford: Stanford University Press.

CHILDS, Margaret Helen, 1991. *Rethinking Sorrow: Revelatory Tales of Late Medieval Japan*. Ann Arbor: University of Michigan.

COOPER, Michael, 1971. The Muse Described: João Rodrigues' Account of Japanese Poetry. *Monumenta Nipponica* 26: 55–75.

Translation from Rodrigues' *Arte da Lingoa de Iapam* (ca. 1608).

_____, 1973. *This Island of Japon: João Rodrigues' Account of 16th-Century Japan*. Tokyo: Kodansha International. Selected, annotated translation of Rodrigues' (ca. 1561–1633) *História da Igreja do Japão*, Part I, Books 1 & 2.

_____, 1974. *Rodrigues the Interpreter: An Early Jesuit in Japan and China*. New York and Tokyo: Weatherhill. (paperback, 1994)

_____, 1976. "The *Nippo Jisho*," review article in *Monumenta Nipponica* 31: 417-30.

Basically a detailed discussion of Benseisha's facsimile of the original Portuguese dictionary–*Vocabulario da Lingoa da Iapam* [*Nippo jisho*日葡辞書], published in 1603–1604. The popular edition of this famous work is actually a translation of this work into French by Léon Pagés as *Dictionnaire Japonais-Français* (1868), and therefore sometimes more properly referred to as the *Nichifutsu jisho* 日仏辞書, printed by Sanseidō, 1953; Hakuteisha, 1968.

COPELAND, Rebecca L., 1997. *Translators are actors/ yakusha wa yakusha*. In *Currents in Japanese Culture: Translations and Transformations*, ed. Amy Vladeck Heinrich. New York: Columbia University Press.

CRANSTON, Edwin A., 1993. *A Waka Anthology, Volume One: The Gem-Glistening Cup*. Stanford: Stanford University Press.

990 solid pages without critical flim-flam.

DE BARY, Wm. Theodore, Donald KEENE, George J. TANABE, Jr., and Paul VARLEY, eds., 2001. *Sources of Japanese Tradition, Second Edition: Volume One: From Earliest Times to 1600*. New York: Columbia University Press.

Revised and enlarged edition of material to 1600 published by Columbia University Press in 1958.

EBERSOLE, Gary L., 1989. *Ritual Poetry and the Politics of Death in Early Japan*. Princeton: Princeton University Press.

ELISON, George, 1973. *Deus Destroyed: The Image of Christianity in Early Modern Japan*. Cambridge: Harvard University Press.

Includes four basic translations: the Japanese apostate Fabian FUCAN's *Deus Destroyed* (Ha Daiusu, 1620), the apostate Christovão FERREIRA's *Kengiroku* (Deceit Disclosed, 1636), the anonymous *Kirishitan Monogatari* (1639), and SUZUKI Shōsan's *Christians Countered* (Ha Kirishitan, 1642).

FUJIMURA Tsukuru 藤村 作, 1952. *Nihon bungaku daijiten* 日本文学大辞典. Tokyo: Shinchōsha.

Title sometimes preceded by the characters *zōho kaitei* 増補改訂 since this early post-WWII edition is somewhat "enlarged and revised." See HALL 1954, # 331 (entry somewhat muddled). Although the dictionary's pre-Meiji materials are updated by Iwanami Shoten's *Nihon koten bungaku daijiten* 1985, the earlier work cannot be said to be superseded. For example, FUJIMURA, vol. 4, 192–94, devotes two full pages of illustrations and almost two pages of text, to the curious nationalistic notion of an indigenous Japanese script during the Age of the Gods (*jindai moji* 神代文字). *Nihon koten bungaku daijiten* 1985, III:492, disposes of the issue in a quarter of a page.

FUKUDA, Naomi, ed., 1979. *Bibliography of Reference Works for Japanese Studies*. Ann Arbor: University of Michigan Center for Japanese Studies.

An updating of Hall 1954 with reference to the 1962 *Nihon no sankōtosho* 日本の参考図書——人文・社会編, and complemented by the following two items.

_____ , 1984, 1986. *Japanese History: A Guide to Survey Histories, Part I by Period, Part II Literature*. Ann Arbor: University of Michigan Center for Japanese Studies.

Volume II (of particular importance to students of literature) includes a breakdown of contents in such popular multi-volume sets as Iwanami Shoten's *Nihon koten bungaku taikei* 日本古典文学大系 (1957–1968, 100 v.) and its *Nihon shisō taikei* 日本思想大系 (1970–1982).

Gunsho kaidai 群書解題, 1960–1967. Tokyo: Zoku Gunsho Ruijū Kanseikai. 31 vols.

The 23 *kan* of the original compilation are printed in 31 modern volumes, grouped generally according to the pattern of items in the *Gunsho ruijū* 群書類従 and the *Zoku Gunsho ruijū* 続群書類従. For example, the first 4+ volumes include commentaries and indices on items relating to *jingi* 神祇, "gods and shrines," while volumes numbered 7 through 10 refer to *waka* items.

HALL, John W. 1954. *Japanese History: A Guide to Japanese Reference and Research Materials*. University of Michigan Center for Japanese Studies Bibliographical Series Number 4. Ann Arbor: University of Michigan Press.

A valuable obsolescent tool, complemented but not replaced by the recent work of Naomi FUKUDA 1979. See also HOLZMAN and MOTOYAMA 1959.

HANAWA Hokiichi 塙保己一 (1746–1821), 1931. *Gunsho ruijū* 群書類従. Naigai Shoseki Kaisha, 1928–1931. 39 vols. (FUKUDA 1979, A64; HALL 1954, #384).

The work in this and the 72-vol. continuation, the *Zoku Gunsho ruijū* 続群書類従 (1931–1933), are discussed and indexed in the 31-vol. *Gunsho kaidai*, q.v. And the subsequent three compendia (FUKUDA 1979, A66–A68) also contain a mountain of information yet to be explored.

HARDACRE, Helen, 1989. *Shintō and the State 1868–1988*. Princeton: Princeton University Press.

HARE, Thomas, Robert BORGEN, and Sharalyn ORBAUGH, eds., 1996. *The Distant Isle: Studies and Translations of Japanese Literature in Honor of Robert H. Brower*. Ann Arbor: University of Michigan.

Among fifteen articles in the collection, I mention only two which have particular relevance to this article: Edwin A. Cranston's "'Mystery and Depth' in Japanese Court Poetry," pp. 65–104, and Robert E. Morrell's "The *Shinkokinshū*: Poems on Śākyamuni's Teachings (*Shakkyōka*)," pp. 281–320. I am certain that the remaining thirteen articles will be of equal interest to others, but the *festschrift* format has a reputation for mislaying many fine compositions.

HERBERT, Jean, 1967. *Shintō: At the Fountain-Head of Japan*. London: George Allen & Unwin.

HOLZMAN, Donald, and MOTOYAMA Yukihiko, et al., 1959. *Japanese Religion and Philosophy: A Guide to Japanese Reference and Research Materials*. University of Michigan Center for Japanese Studies Bibliographical Series Number 7. Ann Arbor: University of Michigan Press.

Annotated survey of materials on Shinto, Buddhism, Confucianism, Christianity, etc. Obsolescent but still useful. Cf. HALL 1954.

HUBBARD, Jamie, and Paul L. SWANSON, eds., 1997. *Pruning the Bodhi Tree: The Storm over Critical Buddhism*. Honolulu: University of Hawai'i Press.

Or tempest in a teapot?—you be the judge.

HURVITZ, Leon, tr., 1976. *Scripture of the Lotus Blossom of the Fine Dharma (The Lotus Sūtra)*. New York: Columbia University Press.

ISHIDA Mizumaro 石田瑞麿, tr., 1996 [1992]. *Ōjōyōshū* 往生要集. Tokyo: Iwanami Shoten. Iwanami Bunko paperback.

Complete annotated translation but without the *kanbun* original which can be found in *Nihon shisō taikei* 6.

ITŌ Sei 伊藤 整, 1965. Modes of Thought in Contemporary Japan. *Japan Quarterly* 12: 501–14.

Itō Sei (1905–1969) built his reputation as a novelist and literary critic, but is probably best known for his seven-year court case over publishing an unexpurgated translation of *Lady Chatterley's Lover*. Since *JQ* indicates neither source nor translator and the survey seems directed at a Western audience, I am assuming that this is an original piece by Itō, who died just four years after its publication.

KAMATA Shigeo 鎌田茂雄 and TANAKA Hisao 田中久夫, eds., 1971. *Kamakura kyū-Bukkyō* 鎌倉旧仏教. *Nihon shisō taikei* 日本思想大系 15. Tokyo: Iwanami Shoten.

KAMENS, Edward, 1990. *The Buddhist Poetry of the Great Kamo Priestess: Daisaiin Senshi and Hosshin Wakashū*. Michigan Monograph Series in Japanese Studies 5. Center for Japanese Studies, University of Michigan. Ann Arbor: University of Michigan Press.

KATŌ Bunnō, TAMURA Yoshirō, MIYASAKA Kōjirō, et al., 1975. *The Threefold Lotus Sutra: Innumerable Meanings, The Lotus Flower of the Wonderful Law, and Meditation on the Bodhisattva Universal Buddha*. New York: Weatherhill-Kosei.

Translations of the *Muryōgikyō* (T. 276) and *Fugengyō* (T. 177), the "opening" and "closing" items of the "Threefold Lotus Sutra" (*Hokke sambukyō*), in addition to the *Hokekyō* (T. 262). See MINER et al. 1985, pp. 376–93.

KEENE, Donald, 1967. *Essays in Idleness: The Tsurezuregusa of Kenkō*. New York: Columbia University Press.

_____, 1983. The *Kojiki* as Literature. In *The Transactions of the Asiatic Society of Japan*, Third Series, Vol. 18, pp. 99–132, including 2-page bibliography.

KERN, H., 1909. *The Saddharma-Pundarîka, or the Lotus of the True Law*. Oxford: Clarendon Press.

Twenty-seven chapter translation from a Sanskrit manuscript rather than Kumārajīva's 28-chapter Chinese version (T. 262) of 406 CE.

KITAGAWA, Hiroshi S., and Bruce T. TSUCHIDA, trs., 1975. *The Tale of the Heike (Heike Monogatari)*. Tokyo: University of Tokyo Press.

Kōchū Kokka Taikei 校註国歌大系, 1930–1931, ed. Kokumin Tosho Kabushiki Kaisha 国民図書株式会社, 28 vols. Tokyo: Kokumin Tosho K.K.

See HALL 1954, #505; FUKUDA 1979, E100, E96.

Koji ruien 古事類苑 1931–1936, ed. Jingū Shichō 神宮司庁, 60 vols. Tokyo: Naigai Shoseki.

FUKUDA 1979, A80; HALL 1954, #207. Indispensible encyclopedia of pre-modern materials.

KONISHI, Jin'ichi, 1986. *A History of Japanese Literature—Volume Two: The Early Middle Ages*, tr. Aileen Gatten, ed. Earl Miner. Princeton: Princeton University Press.

KUBO Tsugunari and YUYAMA Akira, trs., 1993. *The Lotus Sutra*. BDK English Tripitaka 13-I. Berkeley: Numata Center for Buddhist Translation and Research.

LaFLEUR, William R., 1983. *The Karma of Words: Buddhism and the Literary Arts in Medieval Japan*. Berkeley: University of California Press.

MAKINO, Yasuko, and SAITŌ, Masaei, 1994. *A Student Guide to Japanese Sources in the Humanities*. Michigan Papers in Japanese Studies 24. Center for Japanese Studies, University of Michigan. Ann Arbor: University of Michigan Press.

McCULLOUGH, Helen Craig, 1988. *The Tale of the Heike*. Stanford: Stanford University Press.

MINER, Earl, Hiroko ODAGIRI, and Robert E. MORRELL, eds., 1985. *The Princeton Companion to Classical Japanese Literature*. Princeton: Princeton University Press.

The emphasis is on literature, of course, but with special overviews of materials on pre-modern Japanese criticism, Buddhist sects, and a survey of sutras (especially the *Lotus* and its parables) and secondary works prominent in medieval Japan, pp. 364–93.

MORRELL, Robert E., 1987. *Kamakura Buddhism: A Minority Report*. Berkeley: Asian Humanities Press.

MORRIS, Ivan, 1964. *The World of the Shining Prince: Court Life in Ancient Japan*. London: Oxford University Press.

MOTOORI Norinaga, 1780. *Kuzubana* くず花 (Arrowroot), tr. in TSUNODA et al., eds., 1964, pp. 19–22 ("Wonder").

Hopefully to be included in the forthcoming second edition of DE BARY et al., eds., *Sources of Japanese Tradition, Second Edition: Volume Two*.

MULHERN, Chieko Irie, 1979. Cinderella and the Jesuits: An Otogizōshi Cycle as Christian Literature. *Monumenta Nipponica* 34: 409–47.

Hanayo no Hime ("Princess Blossom"), *Hachikazuki* ("The Bowl Bearer"), and *Ubakawa* ("The Bark Gown").

MURANO Senchū, tr., 1974. *The Sutra of the Lotus Flower of the Wonderful Law*. Tokyo: Nichiren Shu Headquarters.

NAKAMURA Hajime 中村 元, 1981. *Bukkyōgo daijiten* 仏教語大辞典. Tokyo: Tokyo Shoseki. 3-volume edition, 1975.

FUKUDA 1979, B82. Note that this is a dictionary of "terms," with examples not only from Buddhist scripture but from current editions (e.g., *Nihon koten bungaku taikei*) of "literary" works.

NAKAMURA Hajime 中村 元, HAYASHIMA Kyōshō 早島鏡正, and KINO Kazuyoshi 紀野一義, eds., 1963–1964. *Jōdo sanbukyō* 浄土三部経. Tokyo: Iwanami Bunko.

Chinese originals, translations, and notes to the [*Dai*]*muryōjukyō* 大無量寿経 (T. 276), the *Kanmuryōjukyō* 観無量寿経 (T. 365), and the *Amidakyō* 阿弥陀経 (T. 366).

NAKAMURA Hajime 中村 元 and KINO Kazuyoshi 紀野一義, eds., 1996 [1960]. *Hannya shingyō, Kongō hannyakyō* 般若心経・金剛般若経. Tokyo: Iwanami Bunko.

> Chinese originals, translations, and notes to the *Heart* and *Diamond* sutras.

Nihon Bukkyō jinmei jiten 日本仏教人名辞典, 1992, ed. Nihon Bukkyō Jinmei Jiten Hensan Iinkai. Kyoto: Hōzōkan.

> Emphasis on important non-clerical Buddhists, with pointers to Washio Junkei's land-mark compilation (1903, 1911) and other dictionaries as appropriate. (Students of literature might be pleased to compare, say, the entry on Saigyō with what appears elsewhere.)

Nihon kokugo daijiten 日本国語大辞典 1976. Tokyo: Shōgakkan. 20 vols. (FUKUDA 1979, D38).

Nihon koten bungaku daijiten 日本古典文学大辞典 1985. Tokyo: Iwanami Koten. 6 vols.

> See MAKINO and SAITO 1994; FUJIMURA 1952.

NOSCO, Peter, ed., 1984. *Confucianism and Tokugawa Culture.* Princeton: Princeton University Press. 1989 paperback.

OOMS, Herman, 1985. *Tokugawa Ideology: Early Constructs, 1570-1680.* Princeton: Princeton University Press. 1989 paperback.

PAYNE, Richard, ed., 1998. *Re-Visioning "Kamakura" Buddhism.* Honolulu: University of Hawai'i Press.

READER, Ian, and George J. TANABE, Jr., 1998. *Practically Religious: Worldly Benefits and the Common Religion of Japan.* Honolulu: University of Hawai'i Press.

SADLER, A. L., tr., 1918, 1921. Heike Monogatari. *Transactions of the Asiatic Society of Japan* 46, 2; 49, 1.

> Complete translation, with annotations. Obsolescent, perhaps; but compare the opening "*Gion shōja…*" translation with its successors.

SAKAMOTO Yukio 坂本幸男 and IWAMOTO Yutaka 岩本裕, eds., 1962, 1964, 1967. *Hokekyō* 法華経. 3 vols. Tokyo: Iwanami Bunko.

SANFORD, James H., William R. LAFLEUR, and Masatoshi NAGATOMI, eds., 1992. *Flowing Traces: Buddhism in the Literary and Visual Arts of Japan.* Princeton: Princeton University Press.

SANSOM, George, 1950. *The Western World and Japan: A Study in the Interaction of European and Asiatic Cultures.* New York: Alfred A. Knopf; fifth printing, 1965.

_____, 1961. *A History of Japan, 1334–1615.* Stanford: Stanford University Press.

SATOW, Ernest, 1882. The Revival of Pure Shiñ-tau. *The Transactions of the Asiatic Society of Japan*, Reprints Vol. II (December 1927), p. 165. Original in *TASJ* First Series, Vol. III.

> This reprint volume also contains extensive, annotated translations of *norito*, pp. 6–164.

SEIDENSTICKER, Edward G., tr., 1976. *The Tale of Genji*, by Murasaki Shikibu. New York: Alfred A. Knopf.

Shintō daijiten 神道大辞典, 1969. Kyoto: Rinsen Shoten.

> One-volume reprint of 3-vol. edition published by Heibonsha, 1937–1940. Pre-WWII, but the best in its day and currently available.

STONE, Jacqueline I., 1999. *Original Enlightenment and the Transformation of Medieval Japanese Buddhism.* Honolulu: University of Hawai'i Press.

> Landmark study on a basic concept of Japanese Buddhism and literature.

THEMES

SWANSON, Paul L., 1989. *Foundations of T'ien-t'ai Philosophy: The Flowering of the Two Truths Theory in Chinese Buddhism.* Berkeley: Asian Humanities Press.

Too important for Japanese Tendai to be overlooked.

TANABE, George J., Jr., 1992. *Myōe the Dreamkeeper: Fantasy and Knowledge in Early Kamakura Buddhism.* Cambridge: Council on East Asian Studies, Harvard University.

TANABE, George J., Jr., ed., 1999. *Religions of Japan in Practice.* Princeton: Princeton University Press.

TSUNODA, Ryusaku, Wm. Theodore DE BARY, and Donald KEENE, eds., 1964 [1958]. *Sources of Japanese Tradition, Volume II.* New York: Columbia University Press.

TYLER, Royall, tr., 2001. *The Tale of Genji.* 2 vols. New York: Viking Penguin.

UEDA, Makoto, 1967. *Literary and Art Theories in Japan.* Cleveland: The Press of Western Reserve University.

WALEY, Arthur, tr., 1928. *The Pillow-Book of Sei Shōnagon.* London: George Allen & Unwin.

_____, tr., 1935. *The Tale of Genji.* London: Allen and Unwin.

Originally published separately in 6 volumes, 1925–1933.

WASHIO Junkyo 鷲尾順敬, ed., 1925–1927; 1927–1933. *Kokubun tōhō Bukkyō sōsho* 国文東方仏教叢書, Series One, 10 vols. Tokyo: Kokubun Tōhō Bukkyō Sōsho Kankōkai; Series Two, 8 vols. Tokyo: Tōhō Shoin.

FUKUDA 1979, B128 (only Series One noted); HALL 1954, #485: "…281 works by pre-Meiji Japanese Buddhists written in Japanese." Sparsely annotated. Reprinted 1978, 1992, Tokyo: Meicho Fukyūkai.

WATSON, Burton, tr., 1993. *The Lotus Sutra.* New York: Columbia University Press.

WEBB, Herschel, 1965. *Research in Japanese Sources: A Guide.* New York and London: Columbia University Press [reprint 1994]. Michigan Papers in Japanese Studies 11. Center for Japanese Studies, University of Michigan. Ann Arbor: University of Michigan Press.

YAMAGISHI Tokuhei 山岸徳平, ed., 1960. *Hachidaishūshō* 八代集抄. 3 vols. Tokyo: Yūseidō.

Update of Kitamura Kigin's (1624–1705) *Notes on the Collections of Eight Eras.* See BROWER and MINER 1961.

Helen HARDACRE

State and Religion in Japan

A close relation between state and religion has frequently been identified as a distinctive feature of Japanese religions. This relation has assumed a variety of forms in different eras and with respect to Japan's major religious traditions: Shinto, Buddhism, Christianity, and new religions. Throughout history we can observe a dynamic in which the state draws upon the ideas and symbols of religion as part of its legitimation, while religions seek connection with the state in order to elevate their prestige. Until modern times, the state patronized Buddhism and Shinto (usually in combination), and religions competed in promoting themselves as possessing magical powers to protect the state and to strengthen its reign. In ancient Japan emperors performed ritual aiming to regulate the cosmos in communion with their divine ancestors. Religious advisors served Japanese political rulers, and powerful Buddhist clerics promoted their sects through court connections. Large temples and shrines sometimes intimidated the court through the manipulation of religious symbols and deployment of their own armies. Provincial overlords were generally free to regulate the religious practice of the populace under their control, and religious institutions controlling large estates enjoyed powers of the police and courts over their tenants. During the Edo period a national system for the administration of religious institutions was instituted. Buddhist clerics exercised functions of social control at the local level, while the shogunate both regulated the sects and effectively guaranteed their economic support. In modern times the state has regulated religious organizations, whose material resources and ability to influence public debate or to restrain the state has largely declined, relative to premodern eras.

Researchers investigating the relation of religion and state in any period will find it necessary to understand the legal framework of the subject, which requires a grasp of the laws governing the practice of religion, the ability to identify and cite such laws correctly, and to relate them to the flow of religious history. Several research tools are available. For quick reference, Kasahara Kazuo's *Nihon shūkyōshi nenpyō* can aid in acquiring a grasp of the timing of the issuance of particular provisions in relation to other historical events. Date Mitsuyoshi's *Nihon shūkyō seido shiryō ruijū kō* provides the texts and proper citation for laws relating to religion from earliest times through the Meiji period. Umeda Yoshihiko's *Nihon shūkyō seido shi* provides detailed historical analysis of major legal provisions regarding religion through the Meiji period, with abbreviated treatment of a few later laws. For religious law since Meiji, see MONBUSHŌ BUNKAKYOKU SHŪMUKA (1968). The journals *Shūkyō hō* 宗教法 and *Shūkyō gyōsei* 宗教行政 publish essays on religious law, with an emphasis on contemporary issues. *Shūkyō kankei hanrei shūsei*, edited by Ōie Shigeo, is a ten-volume comprehensive collection of legal cases involving religion from the Meiji period to about 1980.

PREHISTORY AND ANCIENT JAPAN

The earliest indications of sacral rulership in Japan come from the *Records of Wei (Wei chih)*, a fifth-century Chinese dynastic history which states that in the third century the island country of Wa (Japan) was ruled by a woman named Himiko, who ruled through magic, remained unmarried, and was assisted by a younger brother. Nearly every detail of the Chinese account has been investigated by historians, archaeologists, and scholars of religion, but almost no aspect has been finally resolved. The location of Himiko's polity, its political structure, the extent and nature of its tributary connections with China, and the character of theurgy all remain topics of intense scholarly concern. Contemporary accounts of similar regimes in Chinese and Korean records suggest that similar rulers were "sacrificing to ghosts and spirits, holding communal planting and harvest festivals, and worshipping in shrine-like holy places" in "rites directed to the sun, moon, and stars; the cardinal directions; mountains and rivers; and heroes of the past," as well as rites of healing, exorcism, and oracles (PIGGOTT 1997, p. 26). In Japan the chieftain's charisma expressed itself principally in the fertility of the rice fields.

The *Kojiki* 古事記 (712) and the *Nihon shoki* 日本書紀 (720) are collections of the oral literature of the ancient period compiled into a continuous historical narrative for the purpose of establishing the legitimacy of the Yamato clan. The main narrative of these texts, into which a variety of myths from other clans are woven, identifies the Yamato clan as descended from the sun goddess Amaterasu. The early chapters explain the creation of the Japanese islands and people by two primal deities (called "kami") named Izanagi and Izanami, who produce Amaterasu and her brother Susanoo, the founding ancestor of the Izumo clan, the Yamato's main rival. After overcoming the opposition of Susanoo and his allies, Amaterasu sends her grandson Ninigi from the High Fields of Heaven to the Land of the Heavenly Reed Plains (the Japanese islands), to rule as the first emperor. Thus establishing the divine origins of the Yamato clan, the narrative implies that usurpation of rule by any other clan would be a violation of divine plan.

Recent research strives to overcome the ahistoricity of these mythic texts by combining textual analysis with evidence from archaeology, continental history, and comparative ethnohistorical research to produce a clearer understanding of the historical processes by which the Japanese state evolved from the chieftainship model seen in Himiko's case to the more extensive rule characteristic of the Yamato court (PIGGOTT 1997, p. 3). The construction of monumental *kofun* 古墳 (tumuli, or mounds over a grave) for each deceased sovereign is a central focus of such research. The construction materials and grave goods were assembled from a wide territorial extent, presumably indicating the geographical boundaries of the sovereign's rule. Concurrently, the ancestral gods of the Yamato clan began to be venerated at Ise (in what is now Mie Prefecture) in the third century, eventually resulting in a great complex of shrines known as the Ise Grand Shrines. Other powerful clans also built their own shrines and tumuli.

INTRODUCTION OF BUDDHISM

A great many advisers, technicians, and artisans from China and Korea came into Japan beginning in the late fourth century, and many of them practiced Buddhism. The concentration of immigrant clans under the wing of the Yamato clan tended to weaken the old system of rule by clan federation and to aid the Yamato in establishing a bureaucratic state as an alternative. Both Buddhism and Chinese statecraft provided invaluable aids to the Yamato in transforming a clan-based system of rule into a bureaucratic state on a Chinese model. Buddhism's universalism provided a symbolic representation of national unity under Yamato rule, supplanting the particularistic myths of various clans.

Hoping for Japanese military assistance in a war against his neighboring states, in 538 or 552 the king of Paekche, on the Korean peninsula, presented a gold and copper image of the Buddha Shakyamuni and some scriptures to the Yamato court. The powerful clans around the Yamato throne quarreled as to whether these gifts should be accepted. The Soga argued that Buddhism should be accepted because all the neighboring countries had accepted it, and Japan should not be left behind. The Mononobe and Nakatomi clans involved in the performance of ritual for the native kami violently opposed the Soga position. The decision for Japan in the eyes of all the political players was about which type of kami, the foreign or the indigenous, was most likely to benefit the people and be most helpful to the political regime. The theological subtleties distinguishing the kami from the buddhas were not yet apparent. Eventually, the pro-Buddhist faction prevailed.

A religious system emerged in which Buddhism and Shinto, or, more accurately, Buddhism in the form it took under state patronage, and the cults of kami in the analogous form, were all called upon to provide essential parts of political rule. The term used for the rule of the state was *matsurigoto*, a word that does not distinguish between religious ritual (*matsuri*) and affairs of state. The Seventeen Article of Prince Shōtoku expressed respect for the kami, the buddhas, and for Confucianism. The role of the emperor was constructed along the lines of a cosmic ruler who, because of his divine descent, communed with or was inspired by the kami. If he performed rites for his divine ancestors regularly, sincerely, and correctly, he could be assured that his rule would go smoothly and that the country would prosper, free of famine, disease, and natural disaster. Conversely, if he or his officials failed in ritual performance, misfortune would be visited upon the people. They must then atone for those offenses in order to reinstate the beneficence of the kami. The court commissioned local gazetteers (*fudoki* 風土記) of the provinces, of which several are extant. These records list all temples and shrines, providing the central government with a wealth of information about religious institutions (Aoki 1997).

THE RITSURYŌ SYSTEM

The Ritsuryō system was a centralized state based upon a penal code (*ritsu* 律) and an administrative code (*ryō* 令), lasting from the Taika Reform of 645 to the end of the Heian Period.[1] It represented a pinnacle in the relation between religion and state, an ideal in which the emperor and his ministers performed rites according to a centralized liturgical calendar coordinating ritual at the palace and in the provinces to uphold and sustain the realm. Contemporary research seeks to understand the political processes by which this system came into being, the Chinese sources that served as a model, the degree to which its ideals were realized, and the geographical extent of its sway.

The imperial court began conducting an elaborate annual calendar of rites derived from Buddhism, Taoism, and Shinto, without declaring exclusive allegiance to a single tradition. In effect, all these traditions, as well as Confucianism, found a place in a multifaceted ritual, symbolic, and philosophical legitimation of the political order. Shinto's distinctive contribution lay in its symbolism based on agriculture, and the kami were regarded as divine protectors of the state. Provincial governors paid tribute at the major shrines of

---

1. As a political organization, the Council of Divinity (Jingikan) was the highest branch of government, above the Council of State (Dajōkan), while the country was divided into provinces, districts, and villages. The bureaucracy was ranked according to a hierarchy of titles and functions corresponding closely to a Chinese prototype. The land was minutely alloted to each man, woman, and child corresponding to tax assessments, and the people were divided into several estates, including a slave class, all accounted for in central census records. A national taxation system was established to support the state, and military corps were established around the country.

each province, in microcosmic imitation of the emperor's worship of the imperial ancestors. Shrines were recorded in the *Engi shiki* of 927.

Buddhism offered a more universal framework than the native tradition. The *cakravar-
tin*, or "Wheel Turning King" provided a model of the universal Buddhist king. To sponsor Buddhism was to promote a single standard of faith, ethics, and allegiance among the
people, undercutting primordial ties based on kinship or territory. Buddhist deities were
also regarded as supernatural protectors of the realm. An edict of 741 established in each
province a pair of temples (called *kokubunsōji* 国分僧寺 and *kokubuniji* 国分尼寺, "provincial monks' temple" and "provincial nuns' temple"). The monks and nuns of the provincial
temples were charged to study Buddhist teachings, copy scriptures, and perform rites on
a set schedule. Many of these rites—praying for rain, or apologizing for errors by the emperor, which might be responsible for crop failures, eclipses, and natural disasters—were
supposed to protect the state. Provincial temples were constructed throughout the country, as pairs on the same or adjacent sites. They were given special grants of land, and the
clerics were excused from the duties of taxation, corvée labor, and military service. The
state regulated the conduct of clerics through the twenty-seven-article Regulations for
Monks and Nuns (*Sōniryō*), instituted in 701 and reissued several times. At the apex of this
network stood the mammoth Tōdaiji temple, built at Nara by Emperor Shōmu to house a
monumental statue of Vairocana Buddha and to serve as "head temple" to the provincial
temples. Shōmu received the precepts in a spectacular ceremony consecrating the temple
in 752 (INOUE Mitsusada 1971).

Buddhism's influence upon the state expanded until the Dōkyō affair (764-770), involving a monk of the Hosso sect named Dōkyō, advisor to Empress Kōken, a post he achieved
after supposedly curing the empress of an illness. Over the next few years, Dōkyō enjoyed
a meteoric rise and was appointed to a new post almost equal to the empress herself. As
his political influence soared, he attempted to be made emperor, but with the death of
the empress, he was punished with banishment, and women were thereafter barred from
ascending the throne.

HEIAN PERIOD (794–1185)

After the Dōkyō affair, the capital was moved from Nara to Kyoto to remove
the court from the power of great temples and Buddhist sects. The understanding that Buddhism "protects the state" persisted, however, and temples continued to be much occupied
with ritual for that purpose. During the Heian period (794–1185), great monastic centers
for the Tendai and Shingon sects were founded with state support, and state-sponsored
ordination continued. The court sent noted monks to China to study and to retrieve new
scriptures and commentaries. Toward the end of the Heian period, however, the Ritsuryō
system broke down and was replaced by a semifeudal system based on local military
warlords. Such temples as Enryakuji (center of the Tendai sect), Kōfukuji (Hossō), and
Kōyasan (Shingon) grew exceedingly rich and powerful through the donation to them of
landed estates (*shōen*). These temples ruled their lands with a free hand over their resident
peasantry, exercising police, judicial, and taxation powers without intervention by civil

authorities, enjoying a kind of "extraterritoriality." Kōfukuji alone is thought to have had no less than 300 such estates (ADOLPHSON 2000, p. 6).

"GATES OF POWER"
THE KENMON TAISEI IN THE MEDIEVAL PERIOD (1185–1600)

Traditional periodization in Japanese religious history followed the practice of political history, dividing discussion of the relation of religion and state into distinctly demarcated Heian, Kamakura, and Muromachi eras (KITAGAWA 1966). In recent years, however, the influential *kenmon taisei* 権門体制 ("gates of authority system") theory of KURODA Toshio (1975, 1980, 1994) has significantly recast this received historiography.[2] This theory is closely related to the idea that medieval Japan was characterized by an "exoteric-esoteric system" (*kenmitsu taisei* 顕密体制) of ideology. Briefly, the *kenmon taisei* theory describes Japan from the eleventh to the fifteenth century as a system of rulership shared by three power blocs (*kenmon* 権門, literally "gates of power"): the court nobility, the warrior aristocracy, and the great temples and shrines. The power blocs were mutually dependent, and they supplanted the old Ritsuryō state through the accumulation of land, which became the basis of their wealth and power as the state lost the capacity to monopolize allotment of land. Although significant new schools of Buddhist thought arose in the Kamakura period based on the thought of Hōnen, Shinran, Nichiren, Dōgen, Ippen, and others,[3] in Kuroda's view the medieval period was shaped far more powerfully by the continuing influence of the six Nara Buddhist schools plus Tendai and Shingon. Kuroda referred to the ideological framework provided by these schools collectively as the "exoteric-esoteric system." The *kenmitsu taisei* has been examined extensively and in depth in a memorial issue of the *Japanese Journal of Japanese Studies*, edited by James DOBBINS (1996). One hallmark of that system of particular significance for the relation of religion and state was the idea of the interdependence of imperial rule and Buddhist law (*ōbō buppō* 王法仏法). This idea incorporated the notion of kami as protectors of the Buddhist law and institutions; political rule and Buddhism were said to depend on each other like the two wheels of a cart or the wings of a bird.

Through the 1990s Kuroda's formulation prevailed, with some important revisions. TAIRA Masayuki (1992) has questioned whether the temples were ever so powerful as the aristocracy and the warriors, and this raises the further question of the degree of interdependence that could have existed with the two other blocs. It can also be pointed out, as Adolphson has done, that since the great temples competed with each other for court patronage, it hardly makes sense to think of them as a unified bloc. And if that is so, it would be misleading to think of them as a body capable of taking collective action (ADOLPHSON 2000, p. 16).

2. See ADOLPHSON 2000, "Introduction" for a lucid summary of Kuroda's theory, developed by Kuroda over a period of years.

3. The clerics of these sects were ordained outside the Ritsuryō framework of state ordination and patronage and hence had primary loyalty to their respective sects.

For Kuroda, medieval Shinto did not exist independent of Buddhism, but was institutionally dependent upon and philosophically largely derivative of Buddhism. Nevertheless, its philosophers made important contributions to a theory of state. Fourteenth-century statesman Kitabatake Chikafusa 北畠親房 (1293–1354) in his treatise *Jinnōshōtōki* 神皇正統記 (1339), held that Japan must always be ruled by an "unbroken line" of sovereigns. In this way, Japan would always be divinely guided, and imperial rule would always rest on a sacred foundation. Shinto theologians sought to establish a new preeminence for the kami by claiming that the kami were original divinities while the buddhas were merely secondary. Their writings circulated mainly within shrine lineages and were submitted as court memorials. Recent research on the history of Shinto in this era is beginning to explore a greater variety of Shinto thinkers and their views on religion's proper relation to the state (BREEN and TEEUWEN 2000).

The period of political disunity in the sixteenth century paralleled the spread through the countryside of temples of all the new Kamakura sects, as well as branches of the major shrines. As before, the cults of kami and buddhas continued to coexist, sometimes within a single temple-shrine complex, but religious institutions increasingly became caught up in protracted warfare. The warlord Oda Nobunaga *(1534–1582)* burned the monastery called Enryakuji in 1571 after it gave shelter to Nobunaga's fleeing enemies. But a much longer campaign was needed to defeat the Honganji, the primary temple of the True Pure Land sect, which by this time had adherents throughout central Japan. They fought Nobunaga from 1570 to 1580, and he was able to defeat them only by slaughtering great numbers of both lay people and monks (MCMULLIN 1984).

CHRISTIANITY

For a period of about a century, Roman Catholic missionaries were active in medieval Japan, beginning with Francis Xavier, who arrived in Japan in 1549. Missionaries accompanied Portuguese (and later, Spanish) traders, who introduced the warlords to many aspects of European culture and technology, especially firearms. As the dominant local warlords (daimyō) entered alliances with the traders, they gave missionaries free rein in large areas of Kyushu and also around Kyoto. Whole domains were converted by fiat, and by 1579, it is estimated that there were 100,000 Christians in Japan. The so-called Christian daimyō were largely defeated during sixteenth-century warfare, however, and the existence of Christianity was increasingly viewed as a threat by Japan's new rulers. As they saw it, Japanese Christians worshiped a foreign deity and owed allegiance not to themselves, but to the pope, whom they perceived to be a close ally of European traders in the materiel of advanced warfare. The potential for Christianity to become a fifth column and a source of domestic rebellion posed so significant a threat as to warrant the religion's complete extermination. Spectacular mass, public crucifixions of missionaries and their followers began in earnest in the 1580s, to accompany prohibitions of the religion. By the 1630s Christians numbered around 300,000. In 1637 a group of peasant Christians fought to the last man, woman, and child in the Shimabara Rebellion. After that, all remaining Christian stalwarts practiced in secret, known as Hidden Christians (Kakure Kirishitan).

A surprising number managed to perpetuate their religion in secret, finally to reemerge in the 1870s. Meanwhile, much of the Edo period's framework of religious control was constructed to enforce the ban on Christianity.

THE EDO PERIOD (1600–1868)

Originating with policies of domains that demanded certification of suspected Christians' renunciation of their faith, a universal requirement was established by the state that all subjects become parishioners of a Buddhist temple. Temples then were authorized to issue certificates authenticating each person as a Buddhist in annual sectarian investigations (*shūmon aratame* 宗門改め). Without certification, a person suspected as a Christian could be arrested, interrogated, and executed, with the entire family subjected to the same treatment. In that sense, the Buddhist clergy had great power over the population. In turn, parishioners were required to support the temples and priests economically (this system is called the *danka seido* 檀家制度). Temple records functioned like census data, and the Buddhist priesthood began to be perceived as similar to village officials. The Buddhists amassed great wealth through this state-sponsored system of temple registration (*terauke seido* 寺請制度), and as a result Buddhism penetrated the lives of individuals and communities with a new intensity (TAMAMURO 1980).

It was in this period that the practice of Buddhist funerals and ancestral ritual was virtually universalized, each aspect of ceremony commodified. Buddhist scholarship and learning advanced greatly when formal seminary training was mandated by shogunal decrees issued to each sect. Decrees from the shogun set out a model for the priesthood as learned moral exemplars and teachers of virtue. Simultaneously, the state initiated intensified control of Buddhism, limiting the construction of new temples and requiring existing temples to accept supervision by a pyramidal chain of head and branch temples in each sect. This system of head and branch temples (called the *honmatsu seido* 本末制度) accentuated the sectarian character of Japanese Buddhism and greatly concentrated the power of the head temples of each sect over the branch temples. The "extraterritoriality" that temples had in the medieval period was abolished, but both temples and shrines retained significant landholdings. The affairs of temples and shrines were put under a shogunal magistrate of temples and shrines (Jisha Bugyō 寺社奉行), one of the highest offices in the shogunate. Priests of significant shrines were expected to affiliate with one of two court lineages, the Shirakawa (mainly associated with imperial ritual) or the Yoshida. By making payments to these lineages, provincial shrines and priests could advance in rank, receive periodic audiences with the shogun in some cases, or in other ways draw nearer to the state.

Shinto philosophy during the Edo period was revitalized by the Shinto scholar Motoori Norinaga's great study of the *Kojiki,* titled *Kojikiden.* In this work, completed in 1798, Motoori mined the ancient myths to discover the life of the ancient Japanese before the advent of Buddhism. His thesis was that the spiritual life of the people and their original unity with the kami had been distorted and undermined by Buddhism. Nativist philosophy stemming from Motoori's work was known as Kokugaku 国学, or National Learning. Although it began as a kind of historical-philological scholarship, during the nineteenth century, under the stimulus of the scholar Hirata Atsutane and his followers, it developed into a philosophy and a religious movement within the Shinto priesthood closely associated with the desire to rid shrines of all Buddhist elements and to reestablish the Ritsuryō-era Council of Divinities (Jingikan 神祇官) as the highest branch of government. The cluster of ideas and sentiments associated with *kokugaku* came to inform new ideals of the proper relation between religion and state that emerged in the Meiji period.

Like previous regimes, the Edo shogunate maintained a liturgical schedule as part of its symbolic legitimation. The provinces were drawn into this by the custom of gift exchange and offerings of special provincial products to the shogun, by shogunal audiences granted to temple and shrine priests above a certain rank (ŌTOMO 1999). In the early to mid-nineteenth century, the shogunate carried out an extensive survey of the Kantō region which provided a great quantity of information on area temples and shrines; the gazetteers that resulted constitute one type of monitoring of religious affairs that is continuous with the *fudoki* of the ancient period (ASHIDA 1996, 1998).

MODERN JAPAN (1868–1945)

Japan's modern period in the relation between religion and state was initiated with the Meiji Restoration of 1868. One faction of Restoration leaders was devoted to Shinto nativism, which blamed many of Japan's problems on Buddhism and issued an order for the "separation of Buddhism and Shinto" (*shinbutsu bunri rei* 神仏分離令) in 1868. But where nativist Shinto priests were strong, and in areas ruled by anti-Buddhist daimyō, the official call for "separation" was taken as a tacit call for destruction, leading to the "movement to destroy Buddhism" (*haibutsu kishaku* 廃仏毀釈). Although short-lived, in some areas the great majority of temples were destroyed, with many priests killed or forcibly laicized. Thus the modern period began with the abolition of state patronage of Buddhism (TSUJI 1983; MURATA 1999).

The Edo-period's requirement of temple affiliation came to an end, and while most of the populace in fact remained parishioners of a temple, the priesthood's economic security was imperiled by the loss of its former state authorization. The priesthood's social position had rested in part upon that authorization, and also upon a perception of its members as living a "pure" life characterized by celibacy, a vegetarian diet, and adherence to many other religious precepts. This image of purity was undercut by Meiji law permitting priests to marry and eat meat. The law relieved the state of responsibility to monitor clerical adherence to sectarian precepts, touching off heated debate, both within Buddhism and in the wider society, about the compatibility of monasticism with a modern society (JAFFE 2001).

The end of state support of Buddhism set the stage for a fundamental renovation of the state's relation to Shinto. Edicts described the new state's foundation as a "restoration of imperial rule" (*ōsei fukkō* 王政復興) based on "unity of government and ritual" (*saisei itchi* 祭政一致). For a brief time, Shinto leaders steeped in Kokugaku thought held influence in the early Meiji government, where they championed the re-establishment of the Jingikan as the highest branch of government.[4] Throughout its modern history, Shinto theologians have argued that Shinto is not a religion, but instead the source of the rites and

THEMES

creed of the Japanese nation (*kokka no sōshi* 国家の宗祀). This interpretation has made it possible to argue that, unlike religion, which is based on individual conviction, Shinto is a suprareligious entity whose practice is among the duties of all Japanese, who thus can be compelled to support shrines, participate in their rites, and observe worship practices in the home (SAKAMOTO 1983; FUJII 1977; MUTA 1996).

The term "State Shinto" is used to describe systemic state support for Shinto from the beginning of the Meiji period to the end of World War II. It encompassed government support for and regulation of shrines and priests, the emperor's priestly roles, state creation of Shinto doctrine and ritual, construction of shrines in imperial Japan's colonies, compulsory participation in shrine rites, teaching Shinto myth as history, and suppression of other religions that contradicted some aspect of Shinto. Between 1870 and 1884, Shinto bureaucrats attempted to make a state religion out of Shinto, through the Great Promulgation Campaign. Bureaucrats composed an official creed loosely based on Shinto, and authorized Shinto priests to create a network of preachers to spread it to the populace. But because the creed had no basis whatever in popular religiosity, and because it mostly consisted of platitudinous injunctions to obey civil authority and revere the emperor (who previously had played no role in popular religious life), the people found it incomprehensible and the priests ludicrous. When the campaign failed, Shinto bureaucrats fell out of favor, and state support for Shinto declined (HOLTOM 1963, 1995, 1996; LOKOWANDT 1978, 1981; HARDACRE 1989).

Recent research by Shinto scholars seeks to clarify the extent of government support for Shinto during this period, arguing that from the viewpoint of the priesthood, Shinto never received sufficient monetary or political support to justify a systemic concept like "State Shinto" (SAKAMOTO 1994). Other scholars question whether Western ideas of "religion" capture the reality of Shinto, which has historically been less preoccupied with theological subtleties and individual faith and more focused on communal attitudes and practices (SUZUKI 1979). Other researchers stress the relative recency of Shinto's emergence from institutional and intellectual dependence upon Buddhism, and the use of Shinto in unifying the people behind the modernizing agenda of the Meiji government (AKAZAWA 1985).

During the Meiji period, shrines were drawn into a national hierarchy and into a unified annual ritual calendar centering on imperial ritual and observances on new, national holidays, with newly created national symbols, such as a flag and an anthem (GLUCK 1985; FUJITANI 1996). This gave the shrines a national focus for the first time. The cult of the war dead was institutionalized with the construction of the Yasukuni Shrine (1879) in Tokyo

---

4. Much contemporary Shinto historical scholarship has focused on the influence of Shinto figures in the Meiji government. The Jingikan was revived briefly, beginning in 1868. In the following year it was elevated as the highest branch of government. But in 1871 it was downgraded to a ministry within the Dajōkan, and in the following year it was abolished outright. Some of its functions were continued within the Kyōbushō until 1877, when that branch was abolished and its oversight of the building of temples and shrines and the appointment of monks and nuns were absorbed within the Home Ministry.

and an associated network of provincial shrines for the war dead, the Nation-Protecting Shrines (*gokoku jinja* 護国神社). The fate of dying in battle was upheld as the highest possible honor for a Japanese subject, since the emperor personally visited the Yasukuni Shrine to pay tribute to the spirits enshrined there. The Meiji constitution of 1889 described the emperor as "sacred and inviolable," in other words, as divine, and gave the Japanese people limited freedom of religion, "to the extent that it does not interfere with their duties as subjects." From about 1880 to 1905 the Shinto priests gradually organized themselves, forming a national association of priests in 1900.

Japan's victory in the Russo-Japanese War in 1905 stimulated an expansion of Shinto's influence. The dead from this war were enshrined at Yasukuni (as those from the Sino-Japanese War of 1894–1895 had been), bringing many ordinary people to Tokyo to pay respect to their loved ones (ŌE 1984). The annexation of Korea in 1910 and the colonization of Manchuria led to a heightened mood of patriotism and to energetic shrine construction in the colonies. The state increased its support of Shinto and financed the training of shrine priests; priests of a certain rank were automatically certified as teachers in the public schools, where they promoted the teaching of mythology as history. Rites to revere the imperial portrait and ceremonial recitations of the Imperial Rescript on Education were established as regular school observances, along with pilgrimages to shrines for school pupils. Observance of shrine rites in local communities began to assume a semiobligatory character, and local administrations routinely assessed residents for the support of shrines.

Shinto theology describes Japan as "the land of the gods." Popular religious life was influenced by Shinto ideas in the curriculum of compulsory education, and by state suppression of religious organizations seen to contravene Shinto doctrine. Most striking were the refusal of Christian school teacher Uchimura Kanzō to bow sufficiently low for a reading of the Imperial Rescript on Education, and the suppression in 1921 and again in 1935 of the rapidly growing new religion Ōmoto, which had been founded in 1892. Other religions were suppressed on charges of *lèse majesté* if their doctrines conflicted with Shinto mythology. In 1932 Christian students of Sophia University refused to pay tribute at the Yasukuni Shrine, and a national outcry arose accusing Christianity of being unpatriotic. In 1940 a Board of Rites was established within the state government, marking a further expansion of Shinto's influence. State appropriations for priests' training and for shrines continued at a high level. Shinto exerted great influence on popular religious life as more households enshrined talismans from the Ise shrines in their homes. During World War II Shinto priests served as chaplains, and local shrine parishes were mobilized to support the war effort (MURAKAMI 1982).

CONTEMPORARY JAPAN (1945 TO THE PRESENT)

State Shinto came to an end with the Shinto Directive of 1945, which prohibited all state support for and patronage of Shinto and required that all Shinto influence be removed from the public schools. The postwar constitution of 1947 grants freedom of religion and mandates separation of religion from state (article 20) and prohibits state patronage of any religion (article 89). Prewar bureaucracy for the administration of shrines

THEMES

was dismantled, and many Shinto figures were purged. Meanwhile, the Supreme Court has gradually expanded the scope of religious activity deemed permissible to the state (O'BRIEN and OHKOSHI 1996). While the general populace remains unaware of, and unconcerned with, these postwar developments for the most part, a minority, mainly Christians and members of those religious movements persecuted before 1945, closely monitors the state's actions in this area and protests vigorously. The academic community has consistently opposed all state efforts to revive Shinto symbolism, whether it be state support for the Yasukuni Shrine or the attempt to give legal status to the national flag, anthem, or names of reigns of the emperors as the official form of dating. Because of the postwar era's open and pluralistic political culture, the state must answer these vocal critics and is not free to reestablish its former patronage of Shinto without debate, although the priesthood overwhelmingly favors a return to the prewar situation.

In addition to constitutional provisions, religious organizations are considered "public service corporations" (*kōeki hōjin* 公益法人), with the right to incorporate under the Religious Corporations Law of 1951 (INOUE Egyō 1969). Incorporation offers significant tax advantages and provides religions the capacity to operate for-profit businesses. In reaction to heavy-handed state regulation of religion during the prewar period, the postwar framework incorporated the assumption that the state must be restrained from undue interference in religious affairs. Religious bodies' status as *kōeki hōjin* led to the general presumption that religions are a positive force in society. Until 1995 no functioning religious body was deprived of its status as a religious corporation, and law enforcement generally took a "hands off" attitude to complaints about religious organizations.

Contemporary relations between religion and state have centered on litigation to test and interpret the 1947 constitution's article 20 and article 89. The issue of state support for the Yasukuni Shrine was repeatedly taken up by the Liberal Democratic Party until 1988, apparently as a sop to their hard-line conservative supporters. Lawsuits have repeatedly sought to prohibit public expenditure by local administrations on Shinto ground-breaking rites for public buildings, or on the installation of memorials for the war dead. The result has been mixed. Shinto ground-breaking rituals were eventually declared "customary" rather than religious in nature (thus allowing expenditure of public funds), while publicly constructed war memorials have frequently been disallowed.

The largest of Japan's new religions, the Buddhist group Sōka Gakkai, formed a political party in 1964 called Kōmeitō, "Clean Government Party." While in the opposition, it acted as a swing party capable of determining the outcome in issues pitting (usually) the Liberal Democratic Party against the Socialist Party. Its tight-knit organization has allowed it to be extremely effective, especially in prefectural elections. It is a party of the center that favors the expansion of social welfare and restriction of the defense budget. When Kōmeitō entered a coalition with the LDP in the 1990s and thus became part of the government, renewed debate about the proper relation between religion and state arose.

The poison gas attack on the Tokyo subway in March 1995 by the religious group Aum Shinrikyō provoked widespread questioning of the postwar relation between religion and state. Aum's case has been highly controversial, pitting those who see great danger in allowing the religion to continue to proselytize against those who see a violation of religious freedom in any attempt to muzzle the group or restrict its rebuilding. The Aum Shinrikyō incident seems likely to stimulate the state to strengthen its oversight of religious organizations. Laws passed in the immediate aftermath resemble the prewar relation between religion and state in seeming to assume a responsibility for the state to monitor religious organizations to protect society and a presumption that religion is an appropriate object of state oversight (see KISALA and MULLINS 2001).

BIBLIOGRAPHY

ADOLPHSEN, Mikael, 2000. *Gates of Power: Monks, Courtiers, and Warriors in Premodern Japan.* Honolulu: University of Hawai'i Press.

AKAZAWA Shirō 赤澤史郎, 1958. *Kindai Nihon no shisō dōin to shūkyō tōsei* 近代日本の思想動員と宗教統制. Tokyo: Kōsō Shobō.

AOKI Michiko, 1997. *Records of Wind and Earth: A Translation of Fudoki, with Introduction and Commentaries.* Monograph and Occasional Paper Series 53. Ann Arbor: USA Association for Asian Studies.

ASHIDA Koreto 蘆田伊人, 1996. *Shinpen Musashi fudoki kō* 新編武蔵風土記稿. 12 vols. Dai Nihon Chishi Taikei. Tokyo: Yūzankaku.

———, 1998. *Shinpen Sagami kuni fudoki kō* 新編相模国風土記稿. 7 vols. Dai Nihon Chishi Taikei. Tokyo: Yūzankaku.

BREEN, John, and Mark TEEUWEN, eds., 2000. *Shinto in History: Ways of the Kami.* London: Curzon.

DATE Mitsuyoshi 伊達光美, 1981. *Nihon shūkyō seido shiryō ruijū kō* 日本宗教制度史料類聚考. Kyoto: Rinsen Shoten.

DOBBINS, James C., ed., 1996. *The Legacy of Kuroda Toshio.* Special issue, *Japanese Journal of Religious Studies* 23/3–4.

EBERSOLE, Gary L., 1989. *Ritual Poetry and the Politics of Death in Early Japan.* Princeton: Princeton University Press.

FRIDELL, Wilbur M., 1973. *Japanese Shrine Mergers, 1906-12: State Shinto Moves to the Grassroots.* Tokyo: Sophia University.

FUJII Sadafumi 藤井貞文, 1977. *Meiji Kokugaku hassei shi no kenkyū* 明治国学発生史の研究. Tokyo: Yoshikawa Kōbunkan.

FUJITANI Takashi, 1996. *Splendid Monarchy: Power and Pageantry in Modern Japan.* Twentieth-Century Japan 6. Berkeley: University of California Press.

GLUCK, Carol, 1985. *Japan's Modern Myths: Ideology in the Late Meiji Period.* Princeton: Princeton University Press.

HARDACRE, Helen, 1989. *Shintō and the State, 1868–1988.* Princeton: Princeton University Press.

HOLTOM, Daniel Clarence, 1963. *Modern Japan and Shinto Nationalism: A Study of Present-Day Trends in Japanese Religions.* New York: Paragon Book Reprint Corp.

———, 1995. *The National Faith of Japan: A Study in Modern Shintō.* London: Kegan Paul International. (reprint of 1938 edition)

———, 1996. *The Japanese Enthronement Ceremonies.* London: Kegan Paul International.

(reprint of 1972 edition, Sophia University: Monumenta Nipponica Monographs; original 1928 edition, Tokyo: Kyo Bun Kwan)

IKADO Fujio 井門富二夫, 1993. *Senryō to Nihon shūkyō* 占領と日本宗教. Tokyo: Miraisha.

INOUE Egyō 井上恵行, 1972. *Shūkyō hōjinhō no kisoteki kenkyū* 宗教法人法の基礎的研究. Tokyo: Daiichi Shobō.

INOUE Mitsusada 井上光貞, 1971. *Nihon kodai no kokka to Bukkyō* 日本古代の国家と仏教. Nihon Rekishi Sōsho 5. Tokyo: Iwanami Shoten.

JAFFE, Richard, 2001. *Neither Monk Nor Layman: Clerical Marriage in Modern Japanese Buddhism.* Princeton: Princeton University Press.

KASAHARA Kazuo 笠原一男, 1974. *Nihon shūkyōshi nenpyō* 日本宗教史年表. Nihonjin no Kōdō to Shisō Bekkan 2. Tokyo: Hyōronsha.

KETELAAR, James Edward, 1990. *Of Heretics and Martyrs in Meiji Japan: Buddhism and Its Persecution.* Princeton: Princeton University Press.

KISALA, Robert, and Mark R. MULLINS, eds., 2001. *Religion and Social Crisis in Japan: Understanding Japanese Society Through the Aum Affair.* New York: Palgrave.

KITAGAWA, Joseph Mitsuo, 1966. *Religion in Japanese History.* New York: Columbia University Press.

KURODA Toshio 黒田俊雄, 1975. *Nihon chūsei no kokka to shūkyō* 日本中世の国家と宗教 Tokyo: Iwanami Shoten.

———, 1980. *Jisha seiryoku* 寺社勢力. Tokyo: Iwanami Shoten.

———, 1994. *Kenmitsu taisei ron* 顕密体制論. *Kuroda Toshio chosakushū* 2. Kyoto: Hōzōkan.

LOKOWANDR, Ernst, 1978. *Die rechtliche Entwicklung des Staats—Shintō in der ersten Hälfte der Meiji-Zeit (1868–1890).* Wiesbaden: Harrassowitz.

———, 1981. *Zum Verhältnis von Staat und Shinto im heutigen Japan: Eine Materialsammlung.* Wiesbaden: Harrassowitz.

MAYUMI Tsunetada 真弓常忠, 1997. *Kodai saishi no kōzō to hattatsu* 古代祭祀の構造と発達. Kyoto: Rinsen Shoten.

McMULLIN, Neil, 1984. *Buddhism and the State in Sixteenth-Century Japan.* Princeton: Princeton University Press.

MONBUSHŌ BUNKAKYOKU SHŪMUKA 文部省文化局宗務課, 1968. *Meiji igo shūkyō kankei hōrei ruisan* 明治以後宗教関係法令類纂. Tokyo: Daiichi Hōki Shuppan.

MURAKAMI Shigeyoshi 村上重良, 1982. *Kokka Shintō to minshū shūkyō* 国家神道と民衆宗教. Tokyo: Yoshikawa Kōbunkan.

MURATA Yasuo 村田安穂, 1999. *Shinbutsu bunri no chihōteki tenkai* 神仏分離の地方的展開. Tokyo: Yoshikawa Kōbunkan.

O'BRIEN, David M., with Yasuo OHKOSHI, 1996. *To Dream of Dreams: Religious Freedom and Constitutional Politics in Postwar Japan.* Honolulu: University of Hawai'i Press.

ŌE Shinobu 大江志乃夫, 1984. *Yasukuni Jinja* 靖国神社. Tokyo: Iwanami Shoten.

ŌIE Shigeo 大家重夫, ed., 1984. *Shūkyō kankei hanrei shūsei* 宗教関係判例集成. 10 vols. Tokyo: Daiichi Shobō.

ŌTOMO Kazuo 大友一雄, 1999. *Nihon kinsei kokka no ken'i to girei* 日本近世国家の権威と儀礼. Tokyo: Yoshikawa Kōbunkan.

PIGGOTT, Joan, 1997. *The Emergence of Japanese Kingship*. Stanford: Stanford University Press.

RUOFF, Kenneth James, 2001. *The People's Emperor: Democracy and the Japanese Monarchy, 1945–1995*. Harvard University Asia Monographs 211. Cambridge: Harvard University Press.

RUPPERT, Brian, 2000. *Jewel in the Ashes: Buddha Relics and Power in Early Medieval Japan*. Harvard University Asia Center. Cambridge: Harvard University Press.

SAKAMOTO Ken'ichi 阪本健一, 1983. *Meiji Shintōshi no kenkyū* 明治神道史の研究. Tokyo: Kokusho Kankōkai.

SAKAMOTO Koremaru 阪本是丸, 1994. *Kokka Shintō keisei katei no kenkyū* 国家神道形成過程の研究. Tokyo: Iwanami Shoten.

SUZUKI Norihisa 鈴木範久, 1979. *Meiji shūkyō shichō no kenkyū* 明治宗教思潮の研究. Tokyo: Tōkyō Daigaku Shuppankai.

TAIRA Masayuki 平 雅行, 1992. *Nihon chūsei no shakai to Bukkyō* 日本中世の社会と仏教. Tokyo: Hanawa Shobō.

TAKEDA Hideaki 武田秀章, 1996. *Ishinki tennō saishi no kenkyū* 維新期天皇祭祀の研究. Tokyo: Daimeidō.

TAMAMURO Fumio 圭室文雄, 1980. *Edo bakufu no shūkyō tōsei* 江戸幕府の宗教統制. Nihonjin no Kōdō to Shisō 16. Tokyo: Hyōronsha.

TSUJI Zennosuke 辻善之助, MURAKAMI Senshō 村上専精, and WASHIO Junkyo 鷲尾順敬, eds., 1983. *Shinpen Meiji ishin shinbutsu bunri shiryo* 新編明治維新神仏分離史料. Tokyo: Meicho Shuppan.

UMEDA Yoshihiko 梅田義彦, 1971. *Nihon shūkyō seido shi* 日本宗教制度史. 4 vols. Tokyo: Tōsen Shuppan.

WOODARD, William P., 1972. *The Allied Occupation of Japan 1945–1952 and Japanese Religions*. Leiden: E. J. Brill.

THEMES

Barbara AMBROS

Geography, Environment, Pilgrimage

T he field of geography and the environment in Japanese religions covers a broad range of diverse topics. In the context of environmentalism and ecology, the first studies in English had a textual and literary orientation (BLOOM 1972; EARHART 1970b; LAFLEUR 1973; SHIVELY 1957; WATANABE 1987). With the growing interest in ecology and environmental movements in the 1990s, the number of academic studies on geography and the environment in Japan and Asia as a whole has also expanded tremendously. Arne KALLAND's work has been the most prolific in the field (KALLAND and MOERAN 1993; KALLAND 1995; BRUUN and KALLAND 1995; ASQUITH and KALLAND 1997; KALLAND and PERSOON 1998; KALLAND and SELIN 2003). These environmental studies include research on the connection between Japanese religious traditions and ecology. While in many early studies Buddhist influences on Japanese views of the natural environment took precedence over other religious traditions, more recent studies have also examined Confucianism and Shinto. In the 1990s the Harvard University Center for the Study of World Religions hosted a series of symposia on ecology and specific religious traditions, including Buddhism, Confucianism, and Shinto. The conference proceedings on Buddhism and Confucianism have been published and contain valuable material on Japanese religions and the environment (TUCKER and WILLIAMS 1997; BERTHRONG and TUCKER 1998). Even though the corresponding volume on Shinto and ecology has not yet been published, SONODA Minoru's classic article on the subject has recently been translated into English (2000).

Japanese attitudes toward the relationship between religion and geography perhaps find their most concrete expression in religious travel. In the second half of the twentieth century, the Japanese have become renowned worldwide not only for their economic and technological achievements but also for their love of travel. At almost any destination of some renown, one is bound to encounter Japanese tourists. Travel has in fact been a favorite and celebrated pastime of the Japanese for centuries. In the past, travel often took the form of religious travel, or pilgrimage, which we might define as a journey to a sacred site or through a sacred landscape. As an important and integral part of Japanese culture, the topic of pilgrimage reveals a great deal about Japanese attitudes toward cosmology, sacred geography, and their physical environment in general as pilgrimages are often symbolic journeys to other worlds.

PILGRIMAGE TERMINOLOGY

While the Western term "pilgrimage" covers a wide range of types of religious journeys, the Japanese language has distinct terms that distinguish between two broad types of journeys: linear and circular. In the case of a linear journey, one whose primary destination is a particular sacred site, the Japanese use terms such as *mairi* 参り, *mōde* 詣, or combination of the two forming the more academic term *sankei* 参詣, each conveying the notion that one is on a journey to a site held in high esteem. For example, pilgrims will call their journey to the Ise shrines "Ise *mairi*," to Mt. Fuji "Fuji *mairi*," to the shrines at Kumano "Kumano *mōde*," to the Buddhist temple Zenkōji "Zenkōji *mairi*," while SHINJŌ Tsunezō, a well-known scholar of pilgrimage, uses the term *shaji sankei* 社寺参詣 to refer to pilgrimage to shrines and temples in general (SHINJŌ 1982).[1]

In the case of a circular pilgrimage—a journey on which the pilgrim travels along a circuit of multiple, equally important sacred sites—terms such as *meguri* 巡り, *junrei* 巡礼, and *junpai* 巡拝 are used to indicate a circular motion or circumambulation in order to worship at several sacred sites. Whereas pilgrims on linear pilgrimages may elect to visit additional sacred sites along the way but ultimately work toward a single destination, pilgrimage circuits have no central destination but pilgrims are obligated to visit multiple clearly specified sites en route. The ultimate objective is to complete the circuit rather than

1. People also refer to their first visit to their local Buddhist temple or Shinto shrine in the new year as *hatsu mōde* 初詣 (the first visit) or to a more general visit to a local temple as *sanpai* 参拝 (going to worship).

THEMES

to reach a central destination. *Junrei* or *meguri* are used, for example, to designate the pilgrimage circuits of thirty-three temples dedicated to the bodhisattva Kannon that exist all across Japan, the most famous of which is found in the Kyoto-Nara region. They also apply to the famous pilgrimage circuit of the eighty-eight stations on the island of Shikoku, a pilgrimage dedicated to the memory of Kōbō Daishi, the founder of Shingon Buddhism in Japan. In case of the latter, a more specialized term, *henro* 遍路, is used to designate the pilgrimage, which implies that the traveler is wandering about on a long journey. Even the practice of Tendai monks, who circumambulate Mt. Hiei—the headquarters of the Tendai sect—following a circuit of sacred sites on the mountain side in a practice called *kaihōgyō* 回峯行 (ascetic practice of circumambulating the peak), could be considered under this category though it is also related to the terms *nyūbu* 入峰 or *mineiri* 峰入 (entering the peaks), a term used to refer to the practice of *yamabushi* 山伏 (mountain ascetic) of entering and wandering through the mountains for ascetic exercises. The mountain ascetics follow a prescribed route that takes them through the mountains from one sacred place to the next, usually without retracing their ascending route on the descent.[2]

STUDIES OF JAPANESE PILGRIMAGE

Japanese scholars have produced a vast secondary literature on pilgrimage in Japan, especially since the explosion of the local history field in the 1980s and 1990s. It is impossible to do all their works justice in an article of such limited scope. Therefore, only the most fundamental studies shall be mentioned here. The most important works in the field are perhaps SHINJŌ Tsunezō's *Shaji to kōtsū* (1960), *Shomin no tabi no rekishi* (1971), and *Shaji sankei no shakai keizaishiteki kenkyū* (1982), three studies of the historical development of travel and pilgrimage in Japan. In his works, SHINJŌ traces the beginnings of pilgrimage with the religious journeys of aristocrats in the Heian period, to the more widespread appeal of pilgrimage in the Kamakura and Muromachi periods and the apex of the popularity of pilgrimage in the Edo period. He also outlines the development of social structures that supported the growing pilgrimage business such as the development of professional innkeeper proselytizers (*oshi* 御師) at many sacred sites as well as pilgrimage guides (*sendatsu* 先達) and pilgrimage associations (*kō* 講). Another scholar who has covered a wide variety of pilgrimages is GORAI Shigeru, whose works range from research on itinerant monks (1975) and on the broader topic of itinerancy (1989) to studies of specific pilgrimages (1988 and 1995). Other important scholars of Japanese pilgrimage are MAEDA Takashi (1971), HOSHINO Eiki (1981 and 2001), and more recently SHINNO Toshikazu (1980; 1991a; 1991b). These studies as well as countless others tend to be historical or ethnographic in orientation.[3]

2. READER and SWANSON present a useful overview of the terminology and the distinction between single- and multiple-site pilgrimages in their introduction to a special issue of the *Japanese Journal of Religious Studies* dedicated to the topic of pilgrimage (1997, pp. 232–37).
    3. For a more detailed overview of the field in Japan, see READER and SWANSON 1997.

Scholars of Japanese religions have also found ways to distinguish thematically between different types of pilgrimage. An early noteworthy attempt was made by Joseph KITAGAWA (1967), who distinguished three types of pilgrimage according to what attracted pilgrims: pilgrimage to sacred mountains, pilgrimage based on faith in a divinity, and pilgrimage based on faith in a charismatic holy person. While these categories are not mutually exclusive but often overlap in reality, they provide a useful typology.

SACRED MOUNTAINS

Mountains have been regarded as sacred for various reasons throughout Japanese history. They appear in the ancient national chronicles, the *Kojiki* (712) and the *Nihongi* (720), as places where heavenly *kami* 神 were said to have descended onto earth, where human beings could encounter supernatural beings, and where sovereigns went to view their land. In the medieval period, as Buddhism became increasingly indigenized, Buddhist deities were often said to have manifested themselves on mountain peaks, which themselves were said to have flown to Japan from other Buddhist countries such as India or China. In an animistic culture like Japan, in which natural phenomena like rocks, trees, waterfalls, the sun, and the moon all have been considered manifestations of the divine or the seat of spirits, it is not surprising that mountains, majestic and ever present in the Japanese islands, have been regarded likewise.

Relying heavily on the research of the folklorist Yanagita Kunio (1875–1962), Hori Ichirō (1911–1975) has pointed out that there are three basic types of mountain veneration. One is the veneration of volcanoes such as Mt. Fuji[4] and other conically shaped mountains. Renowned for their awesome destructive as well as creative powers, such mountains were regarded as the residence or even the embodiment of the divine and in some cases even took the place of the object of worship instead of a man-made shrine building on the mountain side.[5] Often fishermen prayed to mountain deities to grant them a bountiful catch. The second type is the veneration of mountains as watersheds and sources of water. The mountain deity (*yama no kami* 山の神) was believed to descend to the rice paddies in the spring and become the nurturing deity of the field (*ta no kami* 田の神) until the fall. Thus mountains played a seminal role in an agricultural society that was heavily dependent on a steady water supply for rice cultivation in paddy fields. The third type casts mountains as the realm of spirits and the dead, perhaps reflecting the function of mountains as burial grounds and the existence of ancient hill-shaped tombs (*kofun* 古墳). As an extension of the belief that mountains were the abode of divinities, spirits, and the dead, mountains were regarded as the portal to other worlds or took on the function of an axis mundi, the embodiment of the entire universe akin to the mythical Buddhist peak Mt. Sumeru (HORI 1966).

As the embodiment of other worlds ranging from hell to paradise, mountains were

---

4. For studies on Mt. Fuji, see COLLCUTT 1988, EARHART 1989, and TYLER 1981 and 1984.

5. For a study on man-made mountains ranging from burial to ceremonial mountain-like objects, see NITSCHKE 1995.

regarded as highly suited for religious, especially monastic and ascetic, training. Mountains were used as sites for Buddhist temples in the late Nara and Heian periods. The most famous instances are perhaps Mt. Kōya, a center of monastic training of the Shingon school, and Mt. Hiei, its Tendai equivalent. Studies by Robert RHODES, John STEVENS, and Steve COVELL of the practice of *kaihōgyō* on Mt. Hiei shed light on an extreme case of mountain asceticism imbedded in monastic training until this day. A Tendai monk practicing *kaihōgyō* circumambulates Mt. Hiei on a course between 20 and 25 miles long either one hundred times over one year or one thousand times over seven years (RHODES 1987; STEVENS 1980, 1988, 1995).

There is an extensive body of scholarship on the tradition of mountain asceticism in Japan (Shugendō 修験道), whose practitioners are called *shugenja* or *yamabushi*. The Japanese scholars GORAI Shigeru, who edited eight volumes in the eighteen-part series *Sangaku shūkyōshi kenkyū shōsho* and whose other works on Shugendō and pilgrimage have all become classics, and MIYAKE Hitoshi, perhaps the most prolific scholar working on Shugendō, have pioneered the field. Their research has provided the basis for the work of many Western scholars. Since the early studies by Gorai and Miyake focused primarily on the Kumano-Ōmine region, much of the Western scholarship likewise has concentrated on this region. The first Western study of Shugendō, which appeared in German in 1922, was by Georg SCHURHAMMER. Gaston RENONDAUE's *Le Shugendō* (1965) and Carmen BLACKER's *Catalpa Bow* (1975) have become classics in the field as have studies by Byron EARHART (1970a) on Shugendō at Mt. Haguro, and Hartmut ROTERMUND (1968) on medieval Shugendō.

Research on Shugendō and sacred mountains has made important contributions to the topic of pilgrimage and cosmology. In her study entitled "Initiation in the Shugendō: The Passage through the Ten Stages of Existence," Carmen Blacker discusses how the ascetic practices of the *yamabushi* in the mountains enact a journey through other worlds, namely the ten realms of existence: the realms of hell, hungry ghosts, animals, humans, the war-like Asura, heavenly beings, sravakas, pratyeka buddhas, bodhisattvas, and the Buddha. The journey through the mountain was a physical journey toward enlightenment and often featured motifs of birth and rebirth (BLACKER 1965), a topic also discussed by HARDACRE (1983) and SEIDEL (1992–1993). These studies imply the notion that mountains and mountain ranges have often been regarded as physical embodiments of esoteric mandalas such as the Womb and Diamond World mandalas, a theme discussed at length in the work of Allan GRAPARD (1982, 1986, 1987a, 1998) and raised also by Elizabeth TEN GROTENHUIS (1999). Pilgrims and mountain ascetics therefore traveled physically through a mandala that had been superimposed onto the mountain landscape.

FAITH IN DIVINITY

Pilgrimage to mountains often overlaps with another type of pilgrimage: pilgrimage inspired by faith in a divinity or a group of divinities. For example, *kaihōgyō* practitioners identify themselves with the fierce wisdom king Fudō Myōō 不動明王, a central deity for mountain ascetics, while those on the Saikoku pilgrimage identify the thirty-three sacred places of Kumano (*Saikogu sanjūsan reijō* 西国三十三霊場) with Kannon because they associate Kumano Nachi Falls with the bodhisattva Kannon. The area near the falls is identified with Kannon's Pure Land Fudarakusen 補陀落山. In the past, for example, corpses and determined believers willing to commit suicide were placed in boats that were released off the seacoast of the Kumano region in hopes that they would drift toward Kannon's pure land (TEN GROTENHUIS 1999, pp. 163–82; MOERMAN 2000, pp. 71–109).[6]

The thirty-three sacred places of Kannon constitute a pilgrimage of great importance. In addition to the Kumano shrines, the circuit comprises some the most famous temples in western Japan, which have been the destinations for pilgrimage since the Heian period (MOERMAN 1997 and 2000; AMBROS 1997): Hasedera, Ishiyamadera, and Kiyomizudera. All these sites, whether in the mountains or in urban areas, are connected by their association with Kannon, which is the main image of worship at most sites. Other regions in Japan have similar thirty-three Kannon circuits. According to the founding legend of the Bandō thirty-three Kannon route, Kannon appeared to the retired emperor Kazan (968–1008), informing him that he, Kannon, had manifested himself in thirty-three places in the Kantō region. Like Kumano on the Saikoku route, some of the temples on the Bandō route were associated with Kannon's paradise Fudarakusen. For example, the founding legends of Ōyaji, one of the temples on the route, which features a Kannon relief carved into a cliff, clearly identify the topography of the temple with Kannon's Pure Land (MACWILLIAMS 1997, pp. 376 and 387).

In addition to HAYAMI Tasuku's seminal study on the Kannon cult (1970) and countless other Japanese works, the pilgrimage has been covered extensively in English, with studies ranging from its art (RUGOLA 1986) to its early modern contribution to a national identity (FOARD 1982). The popularity of the pilgrimage inspired the creation of similar circuits throughout Japan, an example of which is the thirty-three sacred places of Kannon of eastern Japan (*Bandō sanjūsansho* 坂東三十三所) (MACWILLIAMS 1990a, 1990b, and 1997).

An important issue that has surfaced in these studies is whether Victor and Edith Turner's hypothesis that pilgrimage is a liminal experience—borrowing VAN GENNEP's terminology (1960)—and inspires communitas among the pilgrims (TURNER and TURNER 1978) is applicable to Japanese pilgrimage. LAFLEUR (1979) and FOARD (1982) consider this approach useful, whereas SMYERS (1997) and AMBROS (1997)—while retaining the concept of liminality—are critical of the concept of communitas and suggest that Japanese pilgrimages have the potential to heighten individualism and social distinctions.

Another famous pilgrimage that has been the focus of much scholarship is the pilgrimage to the Ise shrines, Ise *mairi* (also *sangū* 参宮). Its two primary shrines are dedicated to Amaterasu Ōmikami, the sun goddess and mythical imperial ancestor, and Toyoukehime, an agricultural deity. Even though its roots lie in the Kamakura and Muromachi periods, the pilgrimage became particularly famous during the Edo period (1600–1867) for attracting periodic waves of mass pilgrimage (*okagemairi* 御蔭参 or *nukemairi* 抜け参り) in 1650, 1705, 1771, and 1830, during which millions of people absconded from their villages and

---

6. The ocean as another locus for other worlds is a motif that appears as early as the *Kojiki*, the *Nihongi*, and the *Man'yōshū*.

urban neighborhoods to journey to the Ise shrines. Eager to explain the phenomenon as a challenge to *bakufu* authority, scholars used to emphasized the subversive potential of the pilgrimage as a means of social protest against poverty and oppression. Focusing on the Edo period, Blacker, for example, argues that the archetypal religious traveler is the mendicant (*yugyōsha* 遊行者), a wandering ascetic, who appeared time after time in Japanese history. She holds that temporary pilgrims absconding to Ise or traveling along the long circuit in Shikoku emulated the ideal of the solitary mendicant and turned to pilgrimage as a means to escape from the confines of the ordinary world, forsaking their community for an individualistic journey. During the Edo period such religious travel was regarded as antisocial and disruptive by domainal authorities, who tried to impose legal limitations on it (BLACKER 1984). This interpretation has since been challenged by scholars in Japan and the West. In the West, for example, Winston DAVIS (1984) has described the role of the pilgrimage as a safety valve to relieve built-up tension in a structured manner. Moreover, it is important to note that pilgrimages to Ise, apart from years of mass pilgrimage, occurred in a very orderly fashion: pilgrims traveled in village-, or neighborhood-based pilgrimage associations (*kō*) and were housed by innkeepers (*oshi* 御師) at their destination with whom they and their villages had cultivated ties for generations. While the mendicant is truly an important figure in Japanese religious lore and is often revered as the founder of temples or pilgrimage circuits, he is an ideal type, who does not serve as a role model for all religious travel in Japan, particularly those occurring in community-based confraternities. Just as there is a dual tendency in Buddhism allowing believers the option of emulating the Buddha or worshiping him, pilgrims might either emulate or venerate such charismatic figures.

Zenkōji, a temple in central Japan famous for its statue of Amida, had a system that was similar to the one at Ise. In the Edo period, the temple not only developed a temple town (*monzenmachi* 門前町) to house the great numbers of pilgrims but also featured forty-six temples incorporated into its institutional structures that specialized in housing pilgrims and proselytizing in villages in specific regions of central Japan. Zenkōji was able to attract a strong following despite its remote location through the careful management of access to its main image of worship, an Amida triad. The statue was considered so sacred that it was never revealed to the eyes of the faithful, but a copy of the image was periodically displayed at six-year intervals at Zenkōji itself and on occasion sent to urban areas such as Edo, Osaka, and Kyoto for display (*kaichō* 開帳). At other times, pilgrims could circumambulate the main altar with the concealed image, through a pitch-black underground corridor (*kaidan meguri*) symbolizing a journey through hell, only to reemerge from the passage in the main sanctuary, whose gilded ornaments shimmering in the soft light of lanterns gave it a semblance of paradise. Having touched a lock hidden in the passage underneath the altar and thereby having established a karmic connection with the main image, the pilgrims could thus dramatically reenact their own salvation (McCALLUM 1994; GRUMBACH 1995). During the Edo period, similar strategies of site management were found at many other sacred sites or sacred mountains such as Ōyama, Mt. Fuji, or Dewa Sanzan, which also had hereditary innkeeper/proselytizers (*oshi*) and only opened their summits for brief periods in the summer, drawing large crowds of pilgrims traveling in associations (*kō*). AKAIKE (1981), BOUCHY (1987), and AMBROS (2001) are studies of such pilgrimage confraternities associated with sacred mountains.

FAITH IN A CHARISMATIC HOLY PERSON

The connection with a charismatic holy person is what draws many pilgrims to temples and shrines. That is why many religious institutions hoping to attract pilgrims claim to have been founded or visited by famous historical persons. The legends of the founding (*engi* 縁起) of temples and shrines often feature mendicants like Gyōgi (668–749) and Ippen (1239–1289), the retired emperor Kazan (968–1008)—legendary revitalizer of the thirty-three Kannon pilgrimage (MACWILLIAMS 1995)—or famous monks such as the Kegon monk Rōben (689-773)—known as the founder of Ishiyamadera in Shiga Prefecture and Ōyamadera in Kanagawa Prefecture—or the Tendai monk Ennin (792–862). There are even entire pilgrimage circuits connecting temples associated with the founders of several schools of Kamakura Buddhism such as Hōnen (1133–1212), Shinran (1173–1262), and Nichiren (1222–1282). New religions have also been able to turn sites associated with their founders into pilgrimage centers. The Tenrikyō headquarters in Nara Prefecture attracts pilgrims not only because followers consider the Tenri City the center of the universe and spiritual home of mankind (Ojiba おじば) but also because of its history as former residence of the foundress Nakayama Miki (1798–1887). Since they consider it the place of their origin, followers do not use the ordinary pilgrimage terminology *mairi* or *mōde* (visiting) but use *kaeru* かえる (to return) instead, calling the pilgrimage Ojiba-gaeri.[7] Like most of the pilgrimages dedicated to founders of a particular Buddhist school, the pilgrimage to the Tenrikyō headquarters is usually not transsectarian.

Attracting pilgrims from all Buddhist schools, the most famous pilgrimage associated with a charismatic figure is undoubtedly the circuit of the eighty-eight sacred places of Shikoku, which all claim a connection to Kōbō Daishi, or Kūkai (774–835), the founder of Shingon Buddhism in Japan. The pilgrimage route of about one thousand miles encircles the island of Shikoku running through its mountains and along its sea coast, through remote wilderness and through urban areas. The number of eighty-eight temples distributed over four provinces or prefectures has been variously explained as (1) a physical representation of a four-fold mandala with eighty worlds to which eight sites were added, (2) a representation of eighty-eight illusions expounded upon by Kōbō Daishi, (3) a representation of the eighty-eight buddhas of the present and past worlds, and (4) a representation of eight countries and eight stupas in India among which the ashes of the historical Buddha, Shakyamuni, were distributed (TANAKA 1980b, p. 126).

Both in Japan and the West the Shikoku pilgrimage has generated a large body of scholarship. In the West, Alfred BOHNER published the first study of this pilgrimage in German in 1931. TANAKA Hiroshi completed a doctoral dissertation in English on the geographical aspects of the pilgrimage in 1975, but it was Oliver STATLER's popular book, *Japanese*

---

7. For more on the pilgrimage to the Tenrikyō headquarters, see KANEKO 1967, ELLWOOD 1982, and MORI 1986.

Pilgrimage (1983), that made the circuit emblematic of pilgrimage in Japan in general. The most prolific Western scholar studying the Shikoku pilgrimage is Ian Reader, who has published a variety of articles on the subject since 1984. Most recently, Nathalie Kouamé (1997, 2000, and 2001), who unlike the aforementioned scholars does not focus on the contemporary Shikoku pilgrimage but its history during the Edo period, has made important contributions to the field.

Despite its status as a representative example of pilgrimage in Japan, the circuit in Shikoku features several aspects that are highly distinctive. The pilgrimage is known by the special name *henro*, which is related to the term *henreki* 遍歴 (itinerancy) and is also used to designate the pilgrim on the journey. Pilgrims on the Shikoku circuit have traditionally relied on the charity of residents along the route, whose donations are called *settai* 接待 (alms). The most distinctive element is of course the focus on Kōbō Daishi. Even though the eighty-eight temples on the circuit enshrine a variety of Buddhist deities in their main halls[8] and belong to various Buddhist schools,[9] all have a small side hall dedicated to Kōbō Daishi (Daishidō 大師堂), elsewhere in Japan a common feature only found at Shingon temples. While pilgrims tend to recite prayers at the main hall, they offer special prayers addressed to Kōbō Daishi at the Daishidō. Many temples also feature a cave within their precinct, where Kōbō Daishi is said to have trained (Tanaka 1977 and 1997, pp. 289–91).[10] Another distinctive element, which highlights the importance of Kōbō Daishi, is the motto of the pilgrimage, *dōgyō ninin* 同行二人 (walking together as a pair), indicating that the pilgrim is thought to be accompanied by Kōbō Daishi himself, who is represented by the pilgrim's staff. Traditional miracle tales associated with the pilgrimage often describe miraculous encounters with Kōbō Daishi, who is often disguised as a pilgrim himself (Reader 1999).

Even though the Shikoku pilgrimage is unique in various ways, the circuit also exemplifies many typical elements of pilgrimage in Japan. The pilgrims traditionally dress in white robes, which are said to represent their willingness to die due to their similarity to traditional shrouds. After all, as Ian Reader writes, the "symbolism was particularly potent with regard to Shikoku [四国]: the ideograms used to write the name Shikoku refer to the fact that the island consisted of four (*shi*) provinces (*koku*) but a punning alternative ideo-

8. According to Tanaka, the main images of the eighty-eight temples comprise 30 Kannon images, 24 Yakushi images, 10 Amida images, 6 Dainichi images, 6 Jizō images, 5 Shakamuni images, 4 Fudō Myōō images, 3 Kokuzō images, and 1 Miroku, Monju, Daitsuchishō, and Bishamonten each. One temple has a group of five images as the main foci of worship (Tanaka 1997, p. 274).

9. The route currently comprises 80 Shingon temples, 4 Tendai temples, 2 Rinzai temples, 1 Sōtō temple, and 1 Ji temple.

10. According to Tanaka 1997, the physical focus on Kōbō Daishi through a Daishidō at all eighty-eight temples has grown over time. In the seventeenth century, only about 40% of the temples had a Daishidō, whereas the number of temples with main halls enshrining a main image of worship has remained virtually unchanged. Nowadays, these two places are the two foci of worship for pilgrims, indicating that in the past the main attraction regarding pilgrimage rituals may have been the main hall while the connection with Kōbō Daishi was primarily through legend rather than through physical representation.

gram *shi* [死] (death) was at times used to imply that it was the land of the dead. In former times the return of a pilgrim from Shikoku was seen to be something akin to a return from a journey to the world of the dead, a renewal and reawakening of life" (1987b, pp. 133–34). At other sites, pilgrims often dress in similar robes but the rationale may have been different. At Ōyama, a sacred mountain in Kanagawa Prefecture, pilgrims have traditionally donned white robes called *jōe* 浄衣 (pure robes) to ensure that the pilgrims' clothing is not stained by ritual pollution. Like many travelers on pilgrimage circuits, pilgrims in Shikoku have tended to carry a pilgrimage album, in which they collect stamps from each of the temples to attest that they have completed the circuit. At singular sites like Ōyama or Mt. Fuji, the pilgrim's robe can take on a similar function as pilgrims collect stamps from the site each year that they visit until their jacket is covered with stamps.

Pilgrims in Shikoku, as at other sacred sites, have often been motivated by common reasons to make the pilgrimage: many have sought healing, material prosperity, and spiritual benefits. Miracle tales associated with pilgrimage circuits or singular destinations may attribute the sites' efficacy to different sources of power—mountain gods, Fudō, Kannon, Kōbō Daishi—but the nature of the benefits is often identical. Like a journey through a sacred mountain, the pilgrimage around Shikoku has also functioned as religious training for pilgrims. For example, the four prefectures through which the circuit runs—Tokushima, Kochi, Ehime, and Kagawa—are sometimes equated with the four stages to reach nirvana—*hosshin* 発心 (determination to reach enlightenment), *shugyō* 修行 (practice), *bodai* 菩提 (enlightenment), and *nehan* 涅槃 (nirvana) (Tanaka 1997, pp. 276–77). The same stages can also be found on a single sacred mountain; Ōminesan near Yoshino, for example, features four gates named after the same four stages.

The Shikoku pilgrimage is one of the longest popular routes, which has led to the practice of completing the circuit in stages, continuing one year what has been left unfinished in another. Hence some pilgrims may chose to visit only about twenty temples in one of the four prefectures at a time or even limit themselves to a smaller set of four to eight temples (Tanaka 1997, pp. 277–80). Similar practices are found in the case of other pilgrimage circuits but not in the case of single-site pilgrimages. The remote location of Shikoku has also led to the practice of making miniaturized copies of the pilgrimage in other places in Japan so that the devout can easily complete the route instead of embarking on a long, two-month journey. The phenomenon has been studied by Tanaka (1976, 1980b, 1997) and Reader (1988). About forty-one sites with miniature eighty-eight pilgrimages stretch from the northern tip of Kyushu along the Inland Sea to the Kantō region near Tokyo. Often soil is collected from each of the respective sites in Shikoku to consecrate the equivalent miniature circuit (Tanaka 1980a, p. 133; 1997, pp. 279–82). One example of the miniaturization is found at a Shingon temple in modern Tokyo called Tamagawa Daishi. In May, the temple celebrates a festival during which sand is brought from all eighty-eight stations in Shikoku and all thirty-three stations along the Kannon pilgrimage in western Japan so that pilgrims can walk barefoot across it on the temple grounds and thereby symbolically complete the two pilgrimages in a few minutes. In addition to the Kannon circuit, which can easily be recreated even in full scale in other regions of Japan, miniaturization and copying also occurs in the case of single-site pilgrimage destinations. Since Mt. Fuji, for example, was located at quite a distance and presented a challenging climb not easily accomplished, miniature versions of the mountain were constructed in the city of Edo. Likewise, Zenkōji in Nagano Prefecture was located in a distant mountain region. Beginning in the Kamakura period, copies of its famous main image of worship spread throughout Japan, allowing the devout to maintain contact with the image and even experience the *kaidan meguri* 戒壇巡り at a nearby temple (McCALLUM 1994).

One difficult and somewhat paradoxical issue that cuts across the scholarship of pilgrimage and Shugendō is the fact that despite the contemporary focus of many of the studies, many harken nostalgically back to a golden age of Shugendō and pilgrimage. In both cases the periodization is slightly different but the thrust of the argument is similar. The medieval period is generally regarded as the apex of Shugendō whereas the Edo period is often seen as a period of decline during which *yamabushi* settled down permanently in villages and lost their function as itinerant hermits. This historical narrative parallels the long-standing view that Buddhism in general declined during the Edo period, having reached its zenith during the Heian and Kamakura periods. Scholars of Buddhism have since tried to correct this image which appears to be largely influenced by negative views of Tokugawa Buddhism that evolved during the Meiji period. Scholars now emphasize that the Edo period actually nurtured institutional growth and stability rather than stagnation and moral corruption. A similar argument could be made regarding the tradition of Shugendō.

In the case of pilgrimage, the medieval period has been characterized as a time when pilgrimage first became popular as evidenced, for example, by numerous literary travelogues. Pilgrimage mandalas also emerged in the late medieval period to provide a guide for potential pilgrims. It was of course during the Edo period when travel and also pilgrimage gained widespread popularity. Countless travel journals and guidebooks attest to the popularity and commodification of travel and pilgrimage. Hence the period has been viewed as the golden age of pilgrimage.

Modern pilgrimage customs have often been measured against the idealized past that emerges from these travel narratives and modern means of transportation have been viewed by some as detrimental to traditional pilgrimage customs. Yet precisely these modern changes make for an interesting analysis. For example, while much of the religious travel in the Edo period occurred in pilgrimage associations, the Shikoku circuit traditionally was frequented by solitary itinerants with limited financial means, hence leading to their dependence on alms (*settai*). The majority of modern pilgrims in Shikoku might still don the traditional accoutrements, but instead of walking from temple to temple, they often rely on modern means of transportation and even prearranged package tours (READER 1987b). The ease with which many modern pilgrims travel along the circuit has altered their experience of sacred space. While pilgrims walking the circuit have traditionally viewed travel itself as an ascetic exercise and hence valued the space between the temples, modern tour groups often "swing between poles of behaviours, from the highly ludic and often irreverent outside or between sites, to the reverent and pious inside them. This suggests that pilgrims are making some differentiation between the sites themselves and the way that links them, that they are, by their actions, expressing the opinion that the sacred space of the pilgrimage is limited to the pilgrimage places themselves rather than the totality of the route" (READER 1987b, p. 143). In one sense, the pilgrimage in Shikoku has thus become more similar to other pilgrimages in Japan that have been relying on prearranged group travel in confraternities for centuries. The sense of nostalgia that deplores the apparent "decline of tradition" in itself is a notable subject of study. According to READER (1987a), nostalgia has been a valuable marketing tool for the modern tourist industry promoting travel to Shikoku by promising potential pilgrims a return to their "spiritual homeland." MacWILLIAMS (1995) has noted similar strategies in modern Japanese comic strips in his study of the changing image of retired emperor Kazan, the legendary founder of the circuit of the thirty-three sacred places of Kannon.

While pilgrimage no longer provides the sole opportunity for travel, the Japanese have become globally mobile in this past century and are traveling more than ever, both domestically and internationally. Contemporary ways of pilgrimage and the construction of sacred landscapes have the potential to provide a novel focus for the study of pilgrimage in a postmodern world similar to Bruce CARON's work on Tokyo Disneyland (1995). Contemporary visitors to Disneyland or international tourists may not be on a religious journey in the narrow sense, but they are transported into another world—be it fantastic or foreign—as much as a medieval pilgrim climbing a sacred mountain in search of paradise or a modern pilgrim nostalgically in search of an idealized past.

BIBLIOGRAPHY

AKAIKE Noriaki, 1981. The Ontake Cult Associations and Local Society: The Case of the Owari-Mikawa Region in Central Japan. *Japanese Journal of Religious Studies* 8: 51–81.

AMBROS, Barbara, 1997. Liminal Journeys: Pilgrimages of Noblewomen in Mid-Heian Japan. *Japanese Journal of Religious Studies* 24: 301–46.

_____, 2001. Localized Religious Specialists in Early Modern Japan: The Development of the Ōyama Oshi System. *Japanese Journal of Religious Studies* 28: 329–72.

AMES, Roger T., and J. Baird CALLICOTT, 1989. *Nature in Asian Traditions of Thought: Essays in Environmental Philosophy.* Albany: SUNY Press.

ASQUITH, Pamela J., and Arne KALLAND, 1997. *Japanese Images of Nature: Cultural Perspectives.* Nordic Institute of Asian Studies, Man and Nature in Asia 1. Richmond, UK: Curzon Press.

BERQUE, Augustin, 1986. *Le sauvage et l'artifice: les Japonais devant la nature.* Paris: Gallimard.

BERTHRONG, John H., and Mary Evelyn TUCKER, eds., 1998. *Confucianism and Ecology: The Interrelation of Heaven, Earth, and Humans.* Religions of the World and Ecology. Cambridge: Harvard University Press.

BING, Dov, and Kenneth HENSHALL, eds., 1992. *Japanese Perceptions of Nature and Natural Order.* Waikato: Center for Asian Studies, University of Waikato.

BLACKER, Carmen, 1965. Initiation in the Shugendō: The Passage through the Ten Stages of Existence. In *Initiations*, ed. C. J. Bleeker, pp. 96–111. Leiden: E. J. Brill.

_____, 1975. *The Catalpa Bow.* London: George Allen and Unwin. (2nd revised ed., 1986)

_____, 1984. Religious Travellers in the Edo Period. *Modern Asian Studies* 18: 593–608.

THEMES

BLOOM, Alfred, 1972. Buddhism, Nature, and the Environment. *Eastern Buddhist* 5: 115–29.

———, 1989. Buddhism and Ecological Perspective. *Ecology Center Newsletter* (December): 1–2.

BOHNER, Alfred, 1931. *Wallfahrt zu Zweien: Die 88 heiligen Stätten von Shikoku*. Supplement 12. Tokyo: MOAG.

BOHNER, Hermann, 1941. Massen-Nukemairi. *Monumenta Nipponica* 4: 160–70.

BOUCHY, Anne Marie, 1978. Jitsukaga: Yamabushi des premières années de Meiji et le Shugendō. *Revue de l'Histoire des Religions* 193: 187–211.

———, 1987. The Cult of Mt. Atago and the Atago Confraternities. *Journal of Asian Studies* 46: 255–77.

BRECHER, W. Puck, 2000. *An Investigation of Japan's Relationship to Nature and Environment*. Japanese Studies 12. Lewiston: Edwin Mellen Press.

BRUUN, Ole, and Arne KALLAND, eds., 1995. *Asian Perceptions of Nature: A Critical Approach*. Nordic Institute of Asian Studies, Studies in Asian Topics 18. Richmond, UK: Curzon Press.

CARON, Bruce, 1995. Magic Kingdom: Towards a Post-Modern Ethnography of Sacred Places. In *The Sacred Mountains of Asia*, ed. John Einarsen, pp. 125–30. Boston: Shambhala.

CASAL, U. A., 1965. *The Yamabushi*. MOAG 46: 1–45.

COLLCUTT, Martin, 1988. Mt. Fuji as the Realm of Miroku: The Transformation of Maitreya in the Cult of Mt. Fuji in Early Modern Japan. In *Maitreya*, ed. Helen Hardacre and Alan Sponberg, pp. 248–69. Cambridge: Cambridge University Press.

COLLIGAN-TAYLOR, Karen, 1991. *The Emergence of Environmental Literature in Japan*. The Environment: Problems and Solutions. New York: Garland Publishers.

COVELL, Stephen Grover, 2004. Learning to Persevere: The Popular Teachings of Tendai Ascetics. *Japanese Journal of Religious Studies* 31: 255–87.

DAVIS, Winston, 1984. Pilgrimage and World Renewal, Part 1 and Part 2. *History of Religion* 23: 97–116, 197–221. (revised and republished in Winston Davis, *Japanese Religion and Society*, pp. 45–80. Albany: SUNY Press, 1992)

DOUGLAS, Mary, 1993. À quelles conditions un ascétisme environnementaliste peut-il réussir? In *La nature en politique, ou l'enjeu philosophique de l'écologie*, ed. Dominique Bourg, pp. 96–120. Paris: L'Harmattan.

EARHART, H. Byron, 1965a. Four Ritual Periods of Haguro Shugendō. *History of Religions* 5: 93–113.

———, 1965b. Shugendō: The Tradition of En no Gyōja and Mikkyō Influence. In *Studies of Esoteric Buddhism and Tantrism*, pp. 297–317. Koyasan: Kōyasan Daigaku.

———, 1968. The Celebration of Haru Yama (Spring Mountain): An Example of Folk Religious Practice in Japan. *Asian Folklore Studies* 27: 1–18.

———, 1970a. *A Religious Study of the Mount Haguro Sect of Shugendō*. Tokyo: Sophia University.

———, 1970b. The Ideal of Nature in Japanese Religion and Its Significance for Environmental Concerns. *Contemporary Religions in Japan* 11: 1–25.

———, 1989. Mount Fuji and Shugendō. *Japanese Journal of Religious Studies* 16: 205–26.

EDWARDS, Ron, 1988. The Eighty-Eight Temples of Shikoku. *Arts of Asia* 18: 124–36.

ELLWOOD, Robert S., 1982. *Tenrikyo: A Pilgrimage Faith*. Tenri: Tenri University Press.

FOARD, James, 1982. The Boundaries of Compassion: Buddhism and the National Tradition in Japanese Pilgrimage. *Journal of Asian Studies* 41: 231–52.

FORMANEK, Susanne, 1998. Pilgrimage in the Edo Period: Forerunner of Modern Domestic Tension? The Example of Pilgrimage to Mount Tateyama. In *The Culture of Japan as Seen through Its Leisure*, ed. Sepp Linhart and Sabine Frühstück. Albany: SUNY Press.

GORAI Shigeru 五来重, 1975. *Kōya hijiri* 高野聖. Tokyo: Kadokawa Sensho.

———, 1988. *Zenkōji mairi* 善光寺まいり. Tokyo: Heibonsha.

———, 1989. *Yugyō to junrei* 遊行と巡礼. Tokyo: Kadokawa Sensho.

———, 1991. *Yama no shūkyō: Shugendō kōgi* 山の宗教——修験道講義. Tokyo: Kadokawa Sensho.

———, 1994. The Cult of Pilgrimage in Japan. *Dharma World* 21 (March/April): 19–24.

———, 1995a. *Saigoku junrei no tera* 西国巡礼の寺. Tokyo: Kadokawa Shoten.

———, 1995b. *Shugendō no rekishi to tabi* 修験道の歴史と旅. Tokyo: Kadokawa Shoten.

———, 1999. *Yama no shūkyō: Shugendō* 山の宗教——修験道. Kyoto: Tankosha.

GORAI Shigeru, ed., 1975. *Sangaku shūkyōshi kenkyū sōsho 4: Yoshino Kumano shinkō no kenkyū* 山岳宗教史研究叢書4——吉野熊野信仰の研究. Tokyo: Meicho Shuppan.

———, 1976. *Sangaku shūkyōshi kenkyū sōsho 3: Kōyasan to Shingon Mikkyō no kenkyū* 高野山と真言密教の研究. Tokyo: Meicho Shuppan.

———, 1978. *Sangaku shūkyōshi kenkyū sōsho 11: Kinki reizan to Shugendō* 近畿霊山と修験道. Tokyo: Meicho Shuppan.

———, 1980. *Sangaku shūkyōshi kenkyū sōsho 14: Shugendō no bijutsu, geinō, bungaku I.* 修験道の美術・芸能・文学. Tokyo: Meicho Shuppan.

———, 1981a. *Sangaku shūkyōshi kenkyū sōsho 15: Shugendō no bijutsu, geinō, bungaku II.* Tokyo: Meicho Shuppan.

———, 1981b. *Sangaku shūkyōshi kenkyū sōsho 16: Shugendō no denshō bunka* 修験道の伝承文化. Tokyo: Meicho Shuppan.

———, 1983. *Sangaku shūkyōshi kenkyū sōsho 17: Shugendō shiryōshū I* 修験道資料集. Tokyo: Meicho Shuppan.

———, 1884. *Sangaku shūkyōshi kenkyū sōsho 18: Shugendō shiryōshū II*. Tokyo: Meicho Shuppan.

GRAPARD, Allan, 1982. Flying Mountains and Walkers of Emptiness: Toward a Definition of Sacred Space in Japanese Religions. *History of Religions* 21: 195–221. (republished in John Einarsen, ed., 1995. *The Sacred Mountains of Asia*, pp. 36–42. Boston: Shambhala)

———, 1986. Lotus in the Mountain, Mountain in the Lotus. *Monumenta Nipponica* 41: 21–50.

———, 1987a. Enmountained Text, Textualized Mountain. In *The Lotus Sutra in Japanese Culture*, ed. George J. and Willa Tanabe, pp. 159–89. Honolulu: University of Hawai'i Press.

———, 1987b. Linguistic Cubism: A Singularity of Pluralism in the Sannō Cult. *Japanese Journal of Religious Studies* 14: 211–34.

———, 1998. Geotyping Sacred Space: The Case of Mt. Hiko in Japan. In *Sacred Space: Shrine, City, Land*, ed. Benjamin Kedar and R. J. Zwi Werblowsky, pp. 215–49. New York: New York University Press.

GREENBIE, Barrie B., 1988. *Space and Spirit in Modern Japan*. New Haven: Yale University Press.

GRUMBACH, Lisa, 1995. "Dying for Your Own Good": The *kaidan meguri* of Zenkōji. Unpublished M.A. dissertation, Graduate Theological Union.

HANLEY, Susan B., 1997. *Everyday Things in Premodern Japan: The Hidden Legacy of Material Culture*. Berkeley: University of California Press.

HARDACRE, Helen, 1983. The Cave and the Womb World. *Japanese Journal of Religious Studies* 10: 149–76.

HAYAMI Tasuku 速水 侑, 1970. *Kannon shinkō* 観音信仰. Tokyo: Hanawa Shobō.

HORI Ichirō, 1961. Self-Mummified Buddhas in Japan: An Aspect of the Shugendō (Mountain Asceticism) Sect. *History of Religions* 1: 222–42.

_____, 1966. Mountains and Their Importance for the Idea of the Other World in Japanese Folk Religion. *History of Religions* 6: 1–23.

HOSHINO Eiki 星野英紀, 1981. *Junrei: Sei to zoku no genshōgaku* 巡礼──聖と俗の現象学. Tokyo: Kōdansha.

_____, 1983. The Historical Significance of Pilgrimages in Japan, with Special Reference to the Shikoku Pilgrimage. *Young East* 9: 3–14.

_____, 1997. Pilgrimage and Peregrination: Contextualizing the Saikoku *Junrei* and the Shikoku *Henro. Japanese Journal of Religious Studies* 24: 271–300.

_____, 2001. *Shikoku henro no shūkyōgakuteki kenkyū* 四国遍路の宗教学的研究. Kyoto: Hōzōkan.

ITŌ Shuntarō and YASUDA Yoshinori, eds., 1992. *Nature and Humankind in the Age of Environmental Crisis: Proceedings of the VIth International Symposium at the International Research Center for Japanese Studies*. Kyoto: International Research Center for Japanese Studies.

KALLAND, Arne, 1995. *Fishing Villages in Tokugawa Japan*. Nordic Institute of Asian Studies Monograph Series. Richmond, UK: Curzon Press.

KALLAND, Arne, and Brian MOERAN, eds., 1993. *Japanese Whaling: End of an Era?* Nordic Institute of Asian Studies. London: Routledge/Curzon.

KALLAND, Arne, and Gerard PERSOON, eds., 1998. *Environmental Movements in Asia*. Nordic Institute of Asian Studies, Man and Nature 4. Richmond, UK: Curzon Press.

KALLAND, Arne, and Helaine SELIN, eds., 2003. *Nature across Cultures: Views of Nature and the Environment in Non-Western Cultures*. Norwell, MA: Kluwer Academic Publishers.

KANEKO, Keisuke, 1965. Pilgrimage through Shrines and Temples in Yamato Province. *Tenri Journal of Religion* 7: 36–45.

_____, 1967. On the Returning Home to "Jiba": An Aspect of the Pilgrimage through Shrines and Temples in Yamato during the Meiji Era. *Tenri Journal of Religion* 8: 14–27.

KANI, Sachiko Misawa, 1980. Development of the Kobo Daishi Cult and Beliefs in Japan and their Connection with the Shikoku Pilgrimage. *Young East* 6: 12–37.

KITAGAWA, Joseph, 1967. Three Types of Pilgrimage in Japan. In *Studies in Mysticism and Religion Presented to Gershom G. Scholem on His Seventieth Birthday by Pupils, Colleagues and Friends*, ed. E. E. Urbach, R. J. Zwi Werblowsky, and Chaim Wirszubski, pp. 155–64. Jerusalem: Magnes Press. (republished in 1987 in *On Understanding Japanese Religion*, pp. 127–36. Princeton: Princeton University Press)

KNIGHT, John, 1997. A Tale of Two Forests: Reforestation Discourse in Japan and Beyond. *Journal of the Royal Anthropological Institute* 3: 711–30.

_____, 2003. *Waiting for Wolves in Japan: An Anthropological Study of People-Wildlife Relations.* Oxford: Oxford University Press.

KOUAMÉ, Nathalie, 1997. Shikoku's Local Authorites and *Henro* during the Golden Age of the Pilgrimage. *Japanese Journal of Religious Studies* 24: 413–25.

_____, 2000. *Initiation à la paléographie japonaise: à travers les manuscrits du pèlerinage de Shikoku.* Paris: Langues & Mondes–L'Asiathèque.

_____, 2001. *Pèlerinage et société dans le Japon des Tokugawa: le pèlerinage de Shikoku entre 1598 et 1868.* Paris: École Française d'Extrême-Orient.

KUBOTA Nobuhiro, 1988. Shikoku Pilgrimage. *Japan Quarterly* 35: 171–74.

LaFLEUR, William, 1973. Saigyō and the Buddhist Value of Nature, Part 1 and Part 2. *History of Religions* 13: 93–127, 227–47.

_____, 1979. Points of Departure: Comments on Religious Pilgrimage in Sri Lanka and Japan. *Journal of Asian Studies* 38: 271–81.

_____, 1990. Sattva: Enlightenment for Plants and Trees. In *Dharma Gaia: A Harvest of Essays in Buddhism and Ecology*, ed. Allan Hunt Badiner, pp. 136–44. Berkeley: Parallax Press.

LEAVELL, J., and Ian READER, 1988. Research Report on the Saikoku Pilgrimage. *Studies in Central and East Asian Religions* 1: 116–18.

LISCUTIN, Nicola, 2000. Mapping the Sacred Body. Shinto versus Popular Beliefs at Mt. Iwaki in Tsugaru. In *Shinto in History: Ways of the Kami*, ed. John Breen and Mark Teeuwen, pp. 186–204. Honolulu: University of Hawai'i Press.

MacWILLIAMS, Mark, 1990a. Kannon-engi: The Reijō and the Concept of Kechien as Strategies of Indigenization in Buddhist Sacred Narratives. *Transactions of the Asiatic Society Japan* (4th Series) 5: 53–70.

_____, 1990b. Strategies of Indigenization in Kannon Temple Myths of the "Saikoku Sanjusansho Kannon Reijoki" and the "Sanjusansho Bando Kannon Reijoki." Ph.D. dissertation, University of Chicago.

_____, 1995. Buddhist Pilgrim/Buddhist Exile: Old and New Images of Retired Emperor Kazan in the Saigoku Kannon Temple Guidebooks. *History of Religions* 34: 303–28.

_____, 1997. Temple Myths and Popularization of Kannon Pilgrimage in Japan: A Case Study of Ōya-ji on the Bandō Route. *Japanese Journal of Religious Studies* 24: 375–412.

_____, 2004. Living Icons: Reizō Myths of the Saikoku Kannon Pilgrimage. *Monumenta Nipponica* 59: 35–82.

MAEDA Takashi 前田 卓, 1971. *Junrei no shakaigaku* 巡礼の社会学. Kyoto: Mineruba Shobō.

McCALLUM, Donald, 1994. *Zenkōji and Its Icon: A Study in Medieval Japanese Religious Art.* Princeton: Princeton University Press.

MIYAKE Hitoshi 宮家 準, 1971. *Shugendō girei no kenkyū* 修験道儀礼の研究. Tokyo: Shunjūsha. (revised edition, 1999)

_____, 1973. *Yamabushi: Sono kōdō to soshiki* 山伏──その行動と組織. Tokyo: Hyōronsha.

_____, 1978. *Shugendō: Yamabushi no rekishi to shisō* 修験道──山伏の歴史と思想. Tokyo: Kyōikusha Shuppan.

THEMES

_____, 1979. One Aspect of the Japanese Idea of God (around the Kumano Gongen). *Tenri Journal of Religion* 13: 118–37.

_____, 1985. *Shugendō shisō no kenkyū* 修験道思想の研究. Tokyo: Shunjūsha.

_____, 1987. Female Prohibition at Mt. Sanjo, the Omine Mountains. *Tenri Journal of Religion* 21: 55–68.

_____, 1988. *Ōmine shugendō no kenkyū* 大峰修験道の研究. Tokyo: Kōsei Shuppansha.

_____, 1989. Religious Rituals in Shugendō: A Summary. *Japanese Journal of Religious Studies* 16: 101–16 (reprinted in *Religion and Society in Modern Japan*, ed. Mark R. Mullins, Shimazono Susumu, and Paul L. Swanson, pp. 31–48. Berkeley: Asian Humanities Press, 1993)

_____, 1992. *Kumano shugen* 熊野修験. Tokyo: Yoshikawa Kōbunkan.

_____, 1999. *Shugendō soshiki no kenkyū* 修験道組織の研究. Tokyo: Shunjūsha.

_____, 2000. *En no Gyōja to Shugendō no rekishi* 役の行者と修験道の歴史. Tokyo: Yoshikawa Kōbunkan.

_____, 2000. *Haguro Shugen: Sono rekishi to mineiri* 羽黒修験——その歴史と峰入. Tokyo: Iwata Shoin.

_____, 2001. *Shugendō: Essays on the Structure of Japanese Folk Religion*. Edited and with an introduction by H. Byron Earhart. Ann Arbor: Center for Japanese Studies, the University of Michigan.

MIYAKE Hitoshi, ed. 1979. *Sangaku shūkyōshi kenkyū sōsho* 山岳宗教史研究叢 *12: Daisen, Ishizu-chi to Saigoku Shugendō* 大山・石鎚と西国修験道. Tokyo: Meicho Shuppan.

_____, 1981. *Shugenja to chiiki shakai: Niigata-ken Minami-uonuma no shugendō* 修験者と地域社会——新潟県南魚沼の修験道. Tokyo: Meicho Shuppan.

_____, 1984. *Yama no matsuri to geinō* 山の祭と芸能. Tokyo: Hirakawa Shuppansha.

_____, 1985. *Ontake shinkō* 御嶽信仰. Tokyo: Yūzankaku Shuppan.

_____, 1986. *Shugendō jiten* 修験道辞典. Tokyo: Tōkyōdō Shuppan.

_____, 1990. *Kumano shinkō* 熊野信仰. Tokyo: Yūzankaku Shuppan.

MOERMAN, David, 1997. The Ideology of Landscape and the Theater of State: Insei Pilgrimage to Kumano (1090–1220). *Japanese Journal of Religious Studies* 24: 347–74.

_____, 2000. Localizing Paradise: Kumano Pilgrimage in Medieval Japan. Ph.D. dissertation, Stanford University.

MORI Susumu, 1986. A Study of Three Pilgrimages in Japan. *Tenri Journal of Religion* 20: 79–166.

NENZI, Laura, 2004. Cultured Travelers and Consumer Tourists in Edo-Period Sagami. *Monumenta Nipponica* 59: 285–319.

NENZI, Laura, and SHINNO Toshikazu, 2002. Journeys, Pilgrimages, Excursions: Religious Travels in the Early Modern Period. *Monumenta Nipponica* 57: 447–71.

NITSCHKE, Günter, 1995. Building the Sacred Mountain: Tsukuriyama in Shinto Tradition. In *The Sacred Mountains of Asia*, ed. John Einarsen, pp. 110–18. Boston: Shambhala.

NODA Kesaya, 1978–1982. A Pilgrimage in Shikoku. In *Essays on Japanology,* ed. Intercultural Association of Kyoto, pp. 171–84. Kyoto: Bunrikaku.

ÖLSCHLÄGER, Hans-Dieter, 1989. *Umwelt und Wirtschaft der Ainu: Bemerkungen zur Ökologie einer Wildbeutergesellschaft*. Berlin: D. Reimer.

OLSON, Edward A., 1975. Man and Nature: East Asia and the West. *Asian Profile* 3–6, nos. 1–6: 643.

PAYNE, Richard, 1999. Reflections on the Shikoku Pilgrimage: Theoretical and Historical Considerations. *Kōyasan Daigaku Mikkyō Bunka Kenkyūjo kenkyū kiyō* 12: 94–114.

PYE, Michael, 1987. *O-meguri, Pilgerfahrt in Japan.* Marburg: Universitätsbibliothek Marburg.

READER, Ian, 1984. The Changing Nature of Japanese Pilgrimage. *Jinbun Ronshū* 20: 87–111.

———, 1987a. Back to the Future: Image and Nostalgia and Renewal in a Japanese Religious Context. *Japanese Journal of Religious Studies* 144: 287–303.

———, 1987b. From Asceticism to Package Tour: The Pilgrim's Progress in Japan. *Religion* 17: 133–48.

———, 1988. Miniaturization and Proliferation: A Study of Small-Scale Pilgrimages in Japan. *Studies in Central and East Asian Religions* 1: 50–66.

———, 1992. Dead to the World: Pilgrims in Shikoku. In *Pilgrimage in Popular Culture*, ed. Ian Reader and Tony Walter, pp. 107–36. Basingstoke, UK: Macmillan.

———, 1993. Sendatsu and the Development of Contemporary Japanese Pilgrimage. *Nissan Occasional Papers* 17. Oxford: Nissan Institute.

———, 1994a. Creating Pilgrimage: Buddhist Priests and Popular Religion in Japan. *Proceedings of the Kyoto Conference on Japanese Studies* 3: 311–24.

———, 1994b. The Shikoku Pilgrimage: An Aspect of Popular Buddhist Faith in Japan. *Interbeing* (Winter): 24–30.

———, 1996. Pilgrimage as Cult: The Shikoku Pilgrimage as a Window on Japanese Religion. In *Religion in Japan: Arrows to Heaven and Earth*, ed. Ian Reader and Peter Kornicki, pp. 267–87. Cambridge: Cambridge University Press.

———, 1999. Legends, Miracles, and Faith in Kōbō Daishi and the Shikoku Pilgrimage. In *Religions of Japan in Practice*, ed. George J. Tanabe, Jr., pp. 360–69. Princeton: Princeton University Press.

———, 2005. *Making Pilgrimages: Meaning and Practice in Shikoku.* Honolulu: University of Hawai'i Press.

READER, Ian, and Paul L. SWANSON, 1997. Editors' Introduction: Pilgrimage in the Japanese Religious Tradition. *Japanese Journal of Religious Studies* 24: 225–70.

RENONDEAU, Gaston, 1965. Le Shugendō: histoire, doctrine et rites. *Cahiers de la Societé Asiatique* 18. Paris: Societé Asiatique.

RHODES, Robert, 1987. The *Kaihōgyō* Practice of Mt. Hiei. *Japanese Journal of Religious Studies* 14: 185–202.

ROTERMUND, Hartmut O., 1965. Die Legende des En no Gyōja. *Oriens Extremus* 12: 221–24.

———, 1967. *Die Yamabushi: Aspekte ihres Glaubens, Lebens und ihrer sozialen Funktion im japanischen Mittelalter.* Hamburg: Kommissionsverlag Cram, De Gruyter & Co.

———, 1983. *Pèlerinage aux Neuf Sommets: carnet de route d'un religieux itinérant dans le Japon du XIXe siécle.* Paris: Centre National de la Recherche Scientifique.

RUGOLA, Patricia, 1986. Japanese Buddhist Art in Context: The Saikoku Kannon Pilgrimage Route. Ph.D. dissertation, The Ohio State University.

SCHMITHAUSEN, Lambert, 1991. *Buddhism and Nature: The Lecture Delivered on the Occasion of the EXPO 1990: An Enlarged Version with Notes.* Tokyo: International Institute for Buddhist Studies.

THEMES

SCHURHAMMER, Georg, 1965. *Die Yamabushis.* MOAG 46: 47–83. (first published in 1922)

SEIDEL, Anna, 1992–1993. Mountains and Hells: Religious Geography in Japanese Mandara Paintings. *Studies in Central and East Asian Religions* 5–6: 122–33.

SEKIMORI, Gaynor, 2002. Shugendō: The State of the Field. *Monumenta Nipponica* 57: 207–27.

SHIMIZU Yoshiaki, 1991. Multiple Commemorations: The Vegetable Nehan of Itō Jakuchū. In *Flowing Traces: Buddhism in the Literary and Visual Arts of Japan*, ed. James H. Sanford et al., pp. 201–33. Princeton: Princeton University Press.

SHINJŌ Tsunezō 新城常三, 1960. *Shaji to kōtsū* 社寺と交通. Tokyo: Shibundō.

_____, 1971. *Shomin no tabi no rekishi* 庶民の旅の歴史. Tokyo: NHK.

_____, 1982. *Shaji sankei no shakai keizaishiteki kenkyū* 社寺参詣の社会経済的研究. Tokyo: Hanawa Shobō.

SHINNO Toshikazu 真野俊和, 1980. *Tabi no naka no shūkyō* 旅のなかの宗教. Tokyo: NHK Books.

_____, 1991a. *Nihon yugyō shūkyōron* 日本遊行宗教論. Tokyo: Yoshikawa Kōbunkan.

_____, 1991b. *Sei naru tabi* 聖なる旅. Tokyo: Tōkyōdō Shuppan.

SHINNO Toshikazu, ed., 1996a. *Kōza Nihon no junrei* 講座日本の巡礼. 3 vols. Tokyo: Yūzankaku.

SHIVELY, Donald H., 1955. Buddhahood for the Nonsentient: A Theme in Nō Plays. *Harvard Journal of Asiatic Studies* 20: 135–61.

SMYERS, Karen, 1997. Inari Pilgrimage: Following One's Path on the Mountain. *Japanese Journal of Religious Studies* 24: 427–52.

SONODA Minoru, 2000. Shinto and the Natural Environment. In *Shinto in History: Ways of the Kami*, ed. John Breen and Mark Teeuwen, pp. 32–46. Honolulu: University of Hawai'i Press.

STATLER, Oliver, 1983. *Japanese Pilgrimage.* New York: William Morrow.

STEVENS, John, 1980. Traditional Buddhist Practice in Modern Japan: The Thousand-Day Training Period on Mt. Hiei. *Proceedings of the Second International Symposium on Asian Studies*, pp. 391–98. Hong Kong: Asian Research Service.

_____, 1982. Sennichi Kaihōgyō: The Thousand-Day Pilgrimage of Mt. Hiei. *Tōhoku Fukushi Daigaku kiyō* 6: 203–9.

_____, 1988. *The Marathon Monks of Mount Hiei.* Boston: Shambhala.

_____, 1995. The Spiritual Athlete: The Marathon Monks of Mt. Hiei. In *The Sacred Mountains of Asia*, ed. John Einarsen, pp. 60–66. Boston: Shambhala.

SWANSON, Paul L., 1981. Shugendō and the Yoshino-Kumano Pilgrimage. *Monumenta Nipponica* 36: 55–80.

_____, 1993. Tapping the Source Directly: A Japanese Shugendō Apocryphal Text. *Japanese Religions* 18: 95–112. (reprinted in *Religions of Japan in Practice*, ed. George J. Tanabe, Jr., pp. 246–53. Princeton: Princeton University Press, 1999)

TANAKA Hiroshi, 1975. Pilgrim Places: A Study of the Eighty-Eight Sacred Precincts of the Shikoku Pilgrimage, Japan. Ph.D. dissertation, Simon Fraser University.

_____, 1976. Religious Merit and Convenience: The Resolution of a Conflict within a Pilgrimage through Spatial-Temporal Adjustments. In *New Themes in Western Canadian Geography*, pp. 109–18. Vancouver: Tantalus Research Limited.

_____, 1977. Geographic Expression of Buddhist Pilgrim Places on Shikoku Island, Japan. *Canadian Geographer* 21: 111–32.

_____, 1980a. Sacredness in a Changing Buddhist Pilgrimage in Japan. *Ethnologische Zeitschrift* 2: 123–36.

_____, 1980b. Sacredness in a Changing Buddhist Pilgrimage in Japan. In *The Communication of Ideas*, pp. 189–206. New Delhi: Concept.

_____, 1981. Evolution of a Pilgrimage as a Spatial-Symbolic System. *Canadian Geographer* 25: 240–51.

_____, 1997. The Shikoku Pilgrimage: Essential Characteristics of a Japanese Buddhist Pilgrimage Complex. In *Sacred Places, Sacred Spaces: The Geography of Pilgrimages*, pp. 269–97. Baton Rouge, Louisiana State University: Geoscience Publications.

TEN GROTENHUIS, Elizabeth, 1999. *Japanese Mandalas*. Honolulu: University of Hawai'i Press.

TOTMAN, Conrad, 1989. *The Green Archipelago: Forestry in Preindustrial Japan*. Berkeley: University of California Press.

_____, 2004. *Pre-Industrial Korea and Japan in Environmental Perspective*. Handbook of Oriental Studies/Handbuch der Orientalistik. Leiden: E. J. Brill.

TUCKER, Mary Evelyn, and Duncan Ryūken WILLIAMS, eds., 1997. *Buddhism and Ecology: The Interconnection of Dharma and Deeds*. Religions of the World and Ecology. Cambridge: Harvard University Press.

TURNER, Victor, and Edith TURNER, 1978. *Image and Pilgrimage in Christian Culture*. New York: Columbia University Press.

TYLER, Royall, 1981. A Glimpse of Mt. Fuji in Legend and Cult. *Journal of the Association of Teachers of Japanese* 16: 140–65.

_____, 1984. The Tokugawa Peace and Popular Religion: Suzuki Shōsan, Kakugyō Tōbutsu, Jikigyō Miroku. In *Confucianism and Tokugawa Culture*, ed. Peter Nosco, pp. 92–119. Princeton: Princeton University Press.

_____, 1989. Kōfuku-ji and Shugendō. *Japanese Journal of Religious Studies* 16: 143–80.

VAN GENNEP, Arnold, 1960. *The Rites of Passage*, tr. M. B. Vizedom and G. L. Caffee. Chicago: University of Chicago Press.

WALKER, Brett, 2001. *The Conquest of Ainu Lands: Ecology and Culture in Japanese Expansion, 1590-1800*. Berkeley: University of California Press.

WATANABE Manabu, 1987. Religious Symbolism in Saigyō's Verses: Contribution to Discussions of His Views on Nature and Religion. *History of Religions* 26: 382–400.

YOKOYAMA, W. S., 1992. Circling the Mountain: Observations on the Japanese Way of Life. In *Buddhism and Ecology*, ed. Martine Batchelor and Kerry Brown, pp. 55–64. London: Cassell.

THEMES

Thomas P. KASULIS

History of Thought in Japan

In studying Japanese religions some students and scholars will want to focus primarily on the intellectual, doctrinal, and philosophical sides of the traditions. Others with primary interests elsewhere in the study of Japanese religions will still come across issues requiring some pointed engagement with the history of Japanese thought. This essay is written with both of those audiences in mind. To those who are novices in this area, it may be surprising that pursuing such topics is much more complicated than one might at first assume. The major reason for this is that modern Japanese scholarship has divided its fields of research in a manner that is counterintuitive for many Westerners familiar with the way other cultural traditions—Asian as well as Western—have approached their own scholarly study of the history of ideas. Of course, there is no "natural" or "right" way to divide up the study of a country's history of thought. The Japanese way, although strikingly different from the way Europeans have dealt with their own traditions, has its own advantages and disadvantages. Every system of scholarly classification will necessarily have blind spots. However, as in driving an automobile, the important point is to know where the blind spots are and how to compensate for them. One goal of this essay is to alert novice readers of what Japanese scholars (including Western scholars who adopt Japanese scholarly categories and methods) often do not see in their historical rear view mirrors.

To someone who knows a bit about Japanese academia, my opening paragraph may seem simply misinformed. After all, is there not a well-established field in Japan called "history of Japanese ideas" (*Nihon shisōshi* 日本思想史)? The problem is that, for the most part, *Nihon shisōshi* does not include all of Japanese history nor all kinds of Japanese ideas. First, scholars in this field (and there are important exceptions who will be mentioned along the way) tend to stress early modern and modern phenomena, so the "Japanese history of ideas" is often construed as mainly covering the period from 1600 up to the present. A good example of this is the scholarship of Maruyama Masao, probably the most influential Japanese intellectual historian of the postwar years. Although he certainly did not write exclusively on Tokugawa and modern phenomena, that was clearly his primary focus. Second, many issues of interest to a religion scholar—the development of some Buddhist idea or theme, for example—are left to scholars in fields like "Buddhist studies" (*Bukkyōgaku* 仏教学). The same can be said for the historical development of aesthetic ideas (often better treated in *bigaku* 美学) and ethics (often left to the field of *rinrigaku* 倫理学). Modern academic philosophical ideas are sometimes covered by scholars in *Nihon shisōshi,* but certain kinds of details are restricted to the field of *tetsugaku* 哲学. This last example suggests it might be worthwhile to pause here to review briefly how Western academics have generally divided up the study of history of Western thought. If we are to appreciate what is distinctive in the Japanese approach, it is worth bearing in mind with what it contrasts.

In studying the thought of culture historically, there are two main approaches, one centered in the discipline of history, the other in philosophy. The historian's study—intellectual history—is itself often divided into two subfields: the history of ideas and the history of intellectual institutions (academies, schools of thought, government agencies, and so forth). Although there can be considerable overlap, the difference in emphasis between the two forms of intellectual history is sometimes crucial. The history of ideas foregrounds the ways ideas shaped historical individuals and how those individuals reshaped those ideas in historically contextualized times and places. Institutional intellectual history, by contrast, highlights the social-historical institutions that, as it were, "gave" the thinkers their ideas and served as centers through which the ideas were disseminated. In extreme cases, the difference between the two forms of intellectual history can involve a difference in how to view agency. On the one hand, when identified with the history of ideas, intellectual history places the primary locus of agency in a cluster defined by historical conditions, the thinker's biography (including personality), the interpersonal exchange with contemporaneous thinkers, and the impact within a multi-generational "school of thought" consisting of mentors and disciples. On the other hand, when identified with the history of intellectual institutions, intellectual history finds the primary locus of agency in the dynamic defined by social conditions, political or economic vectors of power or authority, institutional structures, and ideologies. (It is not surprising that as a by-product of this disciplinary orientation, Marxist or leftist historical analyses in intellectual history will gravitate toward the institutional history rather than history of ideas end of the spectrum. This is as true among intellectual historians of Japan as of the West.)

The other common disciplinary approach for the Western tradition is what is usually called "the history of philosophy." Initially one might assume this field would be redundant with the history of ideas. But it is a subset of the discipline of philosophy rather than history and this lends a clue as to the difference. On the one hand, the intellectual historian focuses on *any* kind of thinker from the past, very few of whom were historians like themselves. The historian philosopher, on the other hand, focuses almost exclusively on philosophers from the past, that is, on fellow philosophers. Thus, the history of philosophy is inherently a *reflexive* aspect of philosophy as a discipline (something that happens in the field of intellectual history only in special cases, such as when a historian studies the history of historiographical theories). The assumption is usually that the historian of philosophy is doing philosophy by studying what other philosophers in the past have said and on what rationale they have argued their case. Consequently, the historian of philosophy will usually evaluate the strengths and weaknesses of the historical philosophical system being discussed. A historian of philosophy may judge a historical position to have been incoherent or probative independently from the historical impact the ideas might have had in their own time.

To make these distinctions clearer, let us consider an example. Suppose I want to find out more about the history of the Western idea of rights. If I go to the library and look at books written by intellectual historians of ideas, I will find information about which thinkers first used the term and how the idea developed over, say, the past three or four centuries of Western history. There will be in the books some important details about the social and historical context in which the ideas developed and matured. If instead I were to look at books by institutional intellectual historians, the historical story will highlight the political and social dynamics among groups contesting for power over a period of time and how this crystallized into a conception of rights: from group rights (say of the aristocrats vis-à-vis the monarch) to individual rights, and eventually to universal social rights. The narrative would be primarily one of how different groups and institutions developed the idea in the contestation over power. If we go down a few aisles in our library to the philosophy section, we will find books in the history of philosophy. Here we will find the discussion framed in terms of certain ideas about human nature and society and how a sequence of theories was developed, each having certain limitations that were critiqued and modified by subsequent philosophers. So, for example, the emergence of an idea of individual rights was predicated on an idea of "individual," which in turn was predicated upon the evolution of certain metaphysical and epistemological positions including ideas on the integrity of atomistic units and the primacy of a knowing subject. Furthermore, not too far away we would find yet another type of discussion in the philosophy section, a place where there are books by philosophers who are analyzing the nature of rights in an almost ahistorical manner, that is, the writers will be developing their own theory of rights, drawing in part on the insights of their historical predecessors but treating those predecessors almost fully outside their historical context. So, what Aristotle said about human nature and slavery, for example, will enter into the discussion to the extent it helps clarify some issue of relevance to the idea of rights today. This is the project of constructive philosophizing wherein ideas from the past are consciously stripped of their historicity and brought into the discussion for evaluation on their own terms.

Each of these four kinds of approaches to the Western idea of "rights" has its own particular virtues and blind spots. The point is not that one perspective is better or worse than the others, but only to recognize and be aware of their differences. If we can do that, we will be less likely to fall into the trap of thinking that any one kind of account can give us the whole story. Because scholarship on Japan tends to be divided up somewhat differently, however, training in the Western traditions will often not prepare us for understanding the approaches being taken by any particular book we might be reading. To make best use of Japanese books on Japanese thought, therefore, we need to reorient our expectations and to compensate for different kinds of blind spots. Perhaps the most important point to note immediately is that there is no field in Japanese scholarship equivalent to what we might call (using the Western paradigm) the "history of Japanese philosophy" (*Nihon tetsugakushi* 日本哲学史). This does not mean that no Japanese scholars undertake an enterprise like what historians of Western philosophy do for their own tradition; it only means that their work will not have a designated place in the academy—either in the libraries or in the departments of universities. That is, the historians of Japanese philosophy could just as likely be in a Buddhist studies department, a department of Japanese intellectual history, a department of philosophy, or department of ethics, a department of literature (*bungaku* 文学), or even a department of fine arts (*bigaku* 美学).

The consequence is that a Westerner may bring to her or his research a question about some idea in the history of Japanese philosophy, but will have trouble identifying where to look for the answer because the question that may seem obvious to the Westerner falls between the categorization of the disciplines in Japan. For example, over the years some of my American students in my courses have noted a similarity between Fujiwara Teika's idea of an ideal poem as having the character of *ushin* 有心 and the Zen aesthetic of a poem as expressing *mushin* 無心. What confounds the students, of course, is that the characters for the two terms would suggest contrast rather than similarity. The etymological history of the two terms accounts for the confusion. Basically, the *shin* in *ushin* has resonances with *kokoro,* a sensitivity to the way things are. It is a term with literary roots associated in part with Shinto ideals of *makoto no kokoro,* the sincere mindful heart. By contrast, the *shin* in *mushin* derives from the Sanskrit *citta* and ultimately picks up connotations of the ordinary sentient being's discrimination or deliberation as contrasted with the no-mind *(mushin)* of an enlightened being, so-called *busshin* 仏心 or "awakened mind." So, Teika and the Zen Buddhists may agree that a fine poem shows a focused sensitivity without egocentric deliberation, but the poet associates this with the term *ushin* and the Zen Buddhist with *mushin.* However, because of the way the Japanese academy divides the history of Japanese thought into disciplines, one term is in the domain of *bungaku* and the other in *Bukkyōgaku,* so the difference in terminology seldom becomes a focus of attention. If there were a recognized field in Japanese scholarship equivalent to the history of (Japanese) philosophy, the issue would likely arise there.

RESOURCES ON JAPANESE THOUGHT

With these caveats in mind, let us now turn to resources in both Japanese and Western languages that can be of use to the student of Japanese religions interested in the history of Japanese thought. Let us begin with what is probably the most common source for researchers who can read Japanese: Japanese dictionaries. For Buddhist terminology an excellent starting point is NAKAMURA 1981. This work is best used at both the beginning and the final stage in exploring the meaning of a Buddhist term or concept. The book's virtues are its large number of entries and its attempt to use ordinary, nontechnical Japanese in its definitions. So, in the beginning it will give a good fix on the word's basic meaning and if one then needs more information and further contextual citations for the use of the term, one can turn to one of the more standard Buddhist dictionaries like MOCHIZUKI's ten-volume work (1958–1963). The reason for returning to Nakamura at the end of your study of some term is that once you have a full understanding of the word, you may have to render it into English in a word or two. Nakamura's plain Japanese definition will often be helpful in suggesting to the English reader a nontechnical English rendering for the word, thereby avoiding the common malpractice of translating Buddhist technical terms into other Buddhist technical terms, introducing Sanskrit whenever possible (although most Japanese Buddhist thinkers had no idea of the Sanskrit etymologies of terms they used). Nakamura, incidentally, was a scholar of *Bukkyōgaku* who often writes from the standpoint of the historian of Japanese philosophy in the way I am using the term in this essay. This is obvious in NAKAMURA 1969, but that approach is also found in many of his other writings in both Japanese and Western languages. Tamaki Kōshirō was another prominent scholar of Buddhist studies who often took this approach (see, for example, TAMAKI 1974). Although less philosophical than his two contemporaries, TAMURA Yoshirō also sometimes wrote in that vein and his works can be of great value to religion students seeking clarification of key Buddhist ideas.

For definitions of terms from Dōgen, Nichiren, Kūkai, Saichō, Ippen, Hōnen, and Shinran, Tōkyōdō Shuppan has published a generally useful set of dictionaries (SUGANUMA 1977; MIYASAKI 1978; KANAOKA 1979; TAMURA Kōyū 1979; IMAI 1989; FUJII 1997). Many of the most common Buddhist philosophical terms are found in the two standard one-volume philosophical dictionaries (HEIBONSHA 1971 and HIROMATSU 1998). Although both dictionaries emphasize terms from modern philosophy, helpfully including their Western equivalences, they also contain references to many premodern terms. The former tends to be better nuanced in its treatment of premodern Buddhist, Confucian, and Shinto terms, whereas the latter excels in its treatment of modern philosophical terminology, especially in numerous places where the former is somewhat outdated. Both give citations for further readings related to the concept in question. Of course, there are also gaps in each work that make the two complementary. For example, unlike the former, the latter does not have an entry (not even in its index) for "cosmogony" (*uchū kaibyakusetsu* 宇宙開闢説) whereas the former naturally does not include entries for relatively new philosophical terms like "deconstruction" (*datsu kōchiku* 脱構築) There is an important lesson in that difference relevant to the study of the history of thought in Japan: philosophical terminology is not permanently fixed. Not only do terms evolve within schools of thought, but they also have different meanings across intellectual traditions (as we saw with *ushin).* Furthermore, once we get into the modern period and Japanese terms are being coined to render Western philosophical ideas, the standard renderings can vary from decade to decade. (Recently, a more common Japanese rendering for "cosmogony" seems to be *uchū kigenron* 宇宙起源論, for example.) For those studying religious philosophical works from the Taishō and early Shōwa periods, it is especially important to consult not just the post-war dictionaries mentioned, but also to look at a standard philosophical dictionary of the time (e.g., MIYAMOTO 1922). Not only will the early Iwanami edition by Miyamoto shed light on how philosophers like Nishida Kitarō and Tanabe Hajime understood the correlation between Japanese and Western philosophical vocabulary, but some of the entries are written by those major philosophers themselves.

For dealing with the vagaries of rendering Western philosophical terms into English over the past century and a half, an important new resource is ISHIZUKA and SHIBATA 2003. Although their number is more limited than in the regular dictionaries, the entries all include thorough overviews explaining the meaning of the original Western philosophical term from its inception up through cognate terms in China and finally on to Japanese translations. This may include in places even issues of translation within Western languages. In the entry on *ki/kisoku* 気・気息, for example, the entry includes discussion not only of the Chinese idea of *qi,* but also the Western terms *pneuma, spiritus, Geist, ésprit,* and the Sanskrit *ātman.* It even mentions the issue of whether to translate the German "*Geist*" into English as "mind" or "spirit." In short, the book problematizes the whole issue of translating philosophical terms interculturally and resists the naïve assumption that a simple equivalence across languages is possible. NAKAMURA and MINESHIMA 2000 work from similar assumptions. Their focus, though, is less on the problem of translation and more on the issue of cross-cultural comparative dialogue. The entries tend to be not from just philosophy but from a much more broadly construed interdisciplinary context. The book includes a large section with entries on important thinkers from the West, the Islamic world, India, China, and Japan. Nor is the book limited to East-West comparisons: there is an entry on "*zen to nenbutsu*" 禅と念仏, for example. For the key vocabulary in the history of Japanese thought itself without any special attempt at East-West comparisons, KOYASU 2001 is a good reference work that includes entries on thinkers as well as ideas. Furthermore, unlike many works in *Nihon shisōshi,* this one includes pre-Tokugawa as well as early modern and modern thinkers. Another source for understanding the development of Japanese concepts, especially from the Kokugaku type of perspective characteristic of the Meiji period, is the *Koruien* (JINGUSHICHŌ 1995). This massive 51-volume work cites Japanese texts all the way back to ancient times. Although not always reliable in its interpretations (colored as they were at times by some State Shinto ideology), it does help one track down the usage of terms through Japanese history. Furthermore, it is helpful for understanding an important perspective from late Meiji scholarship that trickled its way into school curricula and undoubtedly influenced consciously or unconsciously many Meiji and Taishō thinkers. Unfortunately, *Koruien's* idiosyncratic organizational scheme can make it difficult to find

THEMES

the information one seeks. It is worth the effort, however, to get a general understanding of how the work is structured because it contains information not found elsewhere.

For the original writings of the major thinkers in Japanese history, the best starting place is the series Nihon Shisō Taikei 日本思想大系 (IWANAMI 1970–1982) in sixty-seven volumes. The series is excellent for its selection of thinkers and for critical notes, although one could quibble over some of the writings selected or omitted in individual volumes. Another useful series is Nihon no Shisō 日本の思想 (CHIKUMA SHOBŌ 1968–1972) in twenty volumes, which focuses on premodern thinkers. In its fifty volumes, Nihon no Meicho日本の名著 (ITŌ 1971–1974) includes some important historical thinkers as well. SAGARA, BITŌ, and AKIYAMA 1983–1984 is a helpful five-volume series of essays on Japanese thought arranged by theme.

Let us turn now primarily to works in Western languages helpful to the religion student interested in the history of Japanese ideas. For an outstanding compilation and analysis of how Japanese philosophy has been studied outside Japan (including Europe and North America), see HEISIG 2004. Specialists in Japanese philosophy from around the world have contributed essays on the direction of scholarship within their own countries. Bibliographic citations to works in European languages outside English are particularly valuable. Although there is not yet a definitive history of Japanese philosophy in a Western language, some important initial attempts have been made (BLOCKER and STARLING 2001; BRÜLL 1993; GONZÁLEZ VALLES 2000; PAUL 1986). Despite the title, NAKAMURA 1969 is not really a history but a series of collected independent essays, each of which is fine in itself but the book gives no historical bridges between the chapters. All in all, for now at least, the English reader would probably be best served by beginning with the appropriate entries in the *Routledge Encyclopedia of Philosophy* (CRAIG 1998). It includes essays on many individual thinkers as well as thematic entries, including a general entry on "Japanese Philosophy" that has links to other Japanese philosophy entries in the encyclopedia. The bibliographical references at the end of each entry are up-to-date and well chosen. The online *Stanford Encyclopedia of Philosophy* promises to have similar entries (http://plato.stanford.edu/).

For Shinto dictionaries in English, consult BOCKING 1996, INTERNATIONAL CONGRESS 1958, and PICKEN 1994. KASULIS 2004 includes a historical overview of the history of Shinto thought as well as a discussion of several central ideas. For a website defining many Shinto terms, see the "Basic Terms of Shinto" site maintained by Kokugakuin (http://www2. kokugakuin.ac.jp/ijcc/wp/bts/). (There are, incidentally, numerous serviceable dictionaries of Shinto in Japanese, including ANZU 1987 and KOKUGAKUIN DAIGAKU 1994.)

The literature on Buddhist thought available in English is extensive and is covered in more detail elsewhere in this volume. However, for a general reference based on traditional Japanese scholarship, a large number of philosophical terms and Buddhist thinkers up to the end of the Kamakura period are discussed in MATSUNAGA and MATSUNAGA 1974– 1976). Later scholarship, some of it originating in the West, has brought new perspectives on many of the classical Japanese Buddhist ideas. Some of the best representatives of these new approaches include the essays found in HUBBARD and SWANSON 1997 and PAYNE 1999). MORRELL 1987 was an important corrective on what had been the usual view of Kamakura Buddhism that focused only on the "major figures" of the era. STONE 1999 enriches our understanding of that same period by focusing on the crucial idea of original enlightenment (*hongaku* 本覚). The works mentioned in this paragraph also contain good bibliographies that can guide the reader to further resources.

Tokugawa-period thought is heavily studied in the West as well as Japan, especially by intellectual historians. Here we will consider several major works available in English and most of them contain fine bibliographies that point to other works in English as well as to some of the extensive resources available in Japanese. KRACHT 2000 is the best starting point for a bibliography of Western materials. For anthologies of essays by specialists on various topics, see NOSCO 1984 or NAJITA and SCHEINER 1978. OOMS 1985 remains a ground-breaking study of early Tokugawa state ideology undermining many common assumptions about, for example, the influence of Hayashi Razan in the *bakufu* corridors of power. Some individual figures have been well treated as the topic of whole books. For example, Ogyū Sorai is the main figure studied in HIRAISHI 1988 and LIDIN 1973. TUCKER 1998 is a study in Itō Jinsai, whereas MERCER 1991 analyzes Miura Baien. MATSUMOTO 1970 deals with Motoori Norinaga. YOSHIKAWA 1983 is a classic study originally published in Japanese and it addresses the philological themes tying together Sorai, Jinsai, and Norinaga. For a broader study of the Kokugaku movement, see NOSCO 1990 for an emphasis in aesthetics and HAROOTUNIAN 1988 for a leftist political critique of the ideology within the school. KOSCHMAN 1987 remains the classic study of the Mito school and NAJITA 1998 is an English anthology of political writings from the Tokugawa period. SAWADA 1993 analyzes the interface between Confucian and Zen values on the popular level.

For the modern period, there is a rather large number of critical studies. General anthologies of original philosophical works include DILWORTH and VIGLIELMO 1998 and FRANCK 1982. HAMADA 1994, PIOVESANA 1994, and SCHINZINGER 1983 are broad overviews that discuss several figures. WAKABAYASHI 1998 is an anthology of essays by intellectual historians. Several works focus directly on Nishida Kitarō, the founder of the Kyoto School and the most prominent of twentieth-century Japanese philosophers. These include WARGO 2005, YUSA 2002, CARTER 1997, STEVENS 2000, TREMBLAY 2000, NISHITANI 1991, and JACINTO ZAVALA 1989. Other studies related to the Kyoto School beyond just Nishida include NAGATOMO 1995, ŌHASHI 1990, HEISIG 2001, HEISIG and MARALDO 1995, and UNNO and HEISIG 1990. Two Japanese works dealing with the Kyoto School are also especially noteworthy; FUJITA 1998 is a historical perspective on the development of the school and TAKEDA 1991 is exemplary of a comparative study between a modern and traditional Japanese philosophy. Two translated studies by Kyoto school thinkers on earlier Japanese thinkers are NISHITANI 1991 and TAKEUCHI 1983. For an insight into aesthetic discussions in the modern period, see MARRA 2001 and 2002. (For a discussion of several important premodern aesthetic terms with related translations from key classical texts, see IZUTSU and IZUTSU 1981.) For an overview of the development of scientific ideas in premodern Japan, see the essays collected in SUGIMOTO and SWAIN 1978.

Scholars and philosophers have also explored Japanese thought in relation to various Western thinkers and philosophical issues. The list is too extensive to cite here, so a sampling will suffice. On the philosophy of the body, the books by YUASA (1987 and 1993) are especially provocative and were influential on the somatic philosophies developed in SHANER 1985 and NAGATOMO 1992. For the topic of abortion, see LAFLEUR 1992. For Japanese Zen in relation to Western philosophical themes, see KASULIS 1981, IZUTSU 1982, and HEINE 1985. PARKES 1987 is an anthology of essays by scholars exploring the impact of Heidegger on Japanese thought and vice versa. TUCKER and WILLIAMS 1997 explores Buddhist ideas in relation to environmental issues. KOPF 2002 uses the thought of Dōgen and Nishida to development a new theory of self. For two examples of scholars who try to apply Japanese ethical values to contemporary global moral problems, see CARTER 2000 and IVES 1992.

As for future trends, the Nanzan Library of Asian Religion and Culture series (published with the University of Hawai'i Press) is in the process of developing two further books that will serve to fill some gaps still remaining in works presently available in English. The first will be a history of Japanese philosophy and the second a sourcebook of Japanese philosophy. Both will attempt to cover the range of Japanese thought from ancient up through modern times and help address the "blind spot" in Japanese scholarship of not having an independent discipline to cover "the history of Japanese philosophy."

BIBLIOGRAPHY

ANZU Motohiko 安津素彦 and UMEDA Yoshihiko 梅田義彦, eds., 1987. *Shintō jiten* 神道辞典. Tokyo: Jinja Shinpōsha.

BLOCKER, H. Gene, and Christopher L. STARLING, 2001. *Japanese Philosophy.* Albany: SUNY Press.

BOCKING, Brian, 1996. *A Popular Dictionary of Shinto.* Richmond, UK: Curzon.

BRÜLL, Lydia, 1993. *Die japanische Philosophie: Eine Einführung.* 2nd ed. Darmstadt: Wissenschaftliche Buchgesellschaft.

CARTER, Robert E., 1997. *The Nothingness Beyond God: An Introduction to the Philosophy of Nishida Kitarō.* St. Paul: Paragon House.

_____, 2000. *Encounter with Enlightenment: A Study of Japanese Ethics,* Albany: SUNY Press.

CHIKUMA SHOBŌ 筑摩書房 (editor varies by volume), 1968–1972. Nihon no Shisō 日本の思想. 20 vols. Tokyo: Chikuma Shobō.

CRAIG, Edward, ed., 1998. *Routledge Encyclopedia of Philosophy,* 10 vols. London: Routledge.

DILWORTH, David A., and Valdo H. VIGLIELMO, eds., with Agustin JACINTO ZAVALA, 1998. *Sourcebook for Modern Japanese Philosophy: Selected Documents.* Westport: Greenwood Press.

ELBERFELD, Rolf, ed., 1999. *Logic des Ortes: Der Anfang der Modernen Philosophie in Japan.* Darmstadt: Wissenschaftliche Buchgesellschaft.

FRANCK, Frederick, ed., 1982. *The Buddha Eye: An Anthology of the Kyoto School.* New York: Crossroad.

FUJII Masao 藤井正雄, ed., 1997. *Hōnen jiten* 法然辞典. Tokyo: Tōkyōdō Shuppan.

FUJITA Masakatsu 藤田正勝, 1998. *Nishida tetsugaku kenkyū no rekishi* 西田哲学研究の歴史. Kyoto: Tōeisha.

GONZÁLEZ VALLES, Jesús, 2000. *Historia de la Filosofía Japonesa.* Madrid: Tecnos.

HALL, John W. et al., eds. 1988. *Cambridge History of Japan*. 6 vols. Cambridge: Cambridge University Press.

HAMADA Junko, 1994. *Japanische Philosophie nach 1868*. Leiden: E. J. Brill.

HARUTOONIAN, Harry D., 1988. *Things Seen and Unseen: Discourse and Ideology in Tokugawa Nativism*. Chicago: University of Chicago Press.

HEIBONSHA 平凡社 (no author), 1971. *Tetsugaku jiten* 哲学事典. Tokyo: Heibonsha.

HEINE, Steven, 1985. *Existential and Ontological Dimensions of Time in Heidegger and Dōgen*. Albany: SUNY Press.

HEISIG, James W., 2001. *Philosophers of Nothingness: An Essay on the Kyoto School*. Honolulu: University of Hawai'i Press.

HEISIG, James W., ed., 2004. *Japanese Philosophy Abroad*. Nagoya: Nanzan Institute for Religion and Culture.

HEISIG, James W., and John C. MARALDO, eds., 1995. *Rude Awakenings: Zen, the Kyoto School & the Question of Nationalism*. Honolulu: University of Hawai'i Press.

HIRAISHI Naoaki, 1988. *The Classics, the Interpreter, and His World: The Case of Ogyū Sorai, a Japanese Confucianist*. London: LSE.

HIROMATSU Wataru 廣松 渉 et al., eds., 1998. *Iwanami tetsugaku/shisō jiten* 岩波哲学・思想事典. Tokyo: Iwanami Shoten.

HUBBARD, Jamie, and Paul L. SWANSON, eds., 1997. *Pruning the Bodhi Tree: The Storm over Critical Buddhism*. Honolulu: University of Hawai'i Press.

IENAGA Saburō 家永三郎, 1997–1999. *Ienaga Saburō shū* 家永三郎集. 16 vols. Tokyo: Iwanami Shoten.

IMAI Masaharu 今井雅晴, ed., 1989. *Ippen jiten* 一遍辞典. Tokyo: Tōkyōdō Shuppan.

INTERNATIONAL CONGRESS FOR THE HISTORY OF RELIGIONS (1958 Tokyo: Shintō Committee), 1958. *Basic Terms of Shinto*. Tokyo: Jinja Honchō.

ISHIZUKA Masahide 石塚正英 and SHIBATA Takayuki 柴田隆行, eds., 2003. *Tetsugaku/shisō honyakugo jiten* 哲学・思想翻訳語事典. Tokyo: Ronsōsha.

ITŌ Sei 伊藤 整, gen. ed., 1971–1974. *Nihon no meicho* 日本の名著. 50 vols. Tokyo: Chūō Kōronsha.

IVES, Christopher, 1992. *Zen Awakening and Society*. Honolulu: University of Hawai'i Press.

IWANAMI SHOTEN (editor varies by volume), 1970–1982. Nihon Shisō Taikei 日本思想大系. 67 vols. Tokyo: Iwanami Shoten.

IZUTSU Toshihiko 井筒俊彦, 1982. *Toward a Philosophy of Zen Buddhism*. 2nd ed. Boulder: Prajna Press.

_____, 1991–1993. *Izutsu Toshihiko chosakushū* 井筒俊彦著作集. Tokyo: Chūō Kōronsha.

IZUTSU Toshihiko and IZUTSU Toyoko, 1981. *The Theory of Beauty in the Classical Aesthetics of Japan*. The Hague: Martinus Nijhoff.

JACINTO ZAVALA, Agustín, 1989. *Filosofía de la Transformación del Mondo: Introducción a la Filosofía Tardía de Nishida Kitarō*. Michoacán: El Colegio de Michoacán.

JINGUSHICHŌ 神宮司庁, 1995. *Kojiruien* 古事類苑. 51 vols. Tokyo: Yoshikawa Kōbunkan. (reprint)

KANAOKA Shūyū 金岡秀友, ed., 1979. *Kūkai jiten* 空海事典. Tokyo: Tōkyōdō Shuppan.

KASULIS, Thomas P., 1981. *Zen Action/Zen Person*. Honolulu: University of Hawai'i Press.

_____, 2004. *Shinto: The Way Home*. Honolulu: University of Hawai'i Press.

KIKUMURA Norihiko 菊村紀彦, ed., 1978. *Shinran jiten* 親鸞辞典. Tokyo: Tōkyōdō Shuppan.

KOKUGAKUIN DAIGAKU NIHON BUNKA KENKYŪJO 國學院大學日本文化研究所, 1994. *Shintō jiten* 神道事典. Tokyo: Kōbundō.

KOPF, Gereon, 2002. *Beyond Personal Identity: Dogen, Nishida, and a Phenomenology of No-Self.* Richmond, UK: Curzon.

KOSCHMAN, J. Victor, 1987. *The Mito Ideology: Discourse, Reform, and Insurrection in Late Tokugawa Japan.* Berkeley: University of California Press.

KOYASU Nobukuni 子安宣邦, ed., 2001. *Nihon shisōshi jiten* 日本思想史事典. Tokyo: Pelican.

KRACHT, Klaus, 2000. *Japanese Thought in the Tokugawa Era: A Bibliography of Western Language Materials.* Wiesbaden: Harrassowitz.

LAFLEUR, William R., 1992. *Liquid Life: Abortion and Buddhism in Japan.* Princeton: Princeton University Press.

LIDIN, Olof G., 1973. *The Life of Ogyū Sorai: A Tokugawa Confucian Philosopher.* Monograph Series 19. Lund: Scandinavian Institute of Asian Studies.

MARRA, Michael F., 2001. *A History of Modern Japanese Aesthetics.* Honolulu: University of Hawai'i Press.

MARRA, Michael F., ed., 2002. *Japanese Hermeneutics: Current Debates on Aesthetics and Interpretation.* Honolulu: University of Hawai'i Press.

MARUYAMA Masao 丸山真男, 1952. *Nihon seiji shisōshi kenkyū* 日本政治思想史研究. Tokyo: Tōkyō Daigaku Shuppankai. (tr. by Mikiso Hane, *Studies in the Intellectual History of Tokugawa Japan.* Tokyo: University of Tokyo Press, 1974)

_____, 1995–1997. *Maruyama Masao shū* 丸山真男集. Tokyo: Iwanami Shoten.

MATSUMOTO Shigeru, 1970. *Motoori Norinaga: 1730–1801.* Cambridge: Harvard University Press.

MATSUNAGA, Daigan, and Alicia MATSUNAGA, 1974–1976. *Foundation of Japanese Buddhism.* 2 vols. Los Angeles: Buddhist Books International.

MERCER, Rosemary, 1991. *Deep Words: Miura Baien's System of Natural Philosophy.* Leiden: E. J. Brill.

MIYAMOTO Wakichi 宮本和吉 et al., eds., 1922. *Iwanami tetsugaku jiten* 岩波哲学辞典. Tokyo: Iwanami Shoten.

MIYASAKI Eishū 宮崎英修, ed., 1978. *Nichiren jiten* 日蓮辞典. Tokyo: Tōkyōdō Shuppan.

MOCHIZUKI Shinkō 望月信亨, ed., 1958–1963. *Bukkyō daijiten* 佛教大辞典. Rev. ed. 10 vols. Tokyo: Sekai Seiten Kankō Kyōkai.

MORRELL, Robert E., 1987. *Early Kamakura Buddhism: A Minority Report.* Berkeley: Asian Humanities Press.

NAGATOMO Shigenori, 1992. *Attunement through the Body.* Albany: SUNY Press.

_____, 1995. *A Philosophical Foundation of Miki Kiyoshi's Concept of Humanism.* Lewiston: E. Mellen Press.

NAJITA Tetsuo, 1997. *Visions of Virtue in Tokugawa Japan: The Kaitokudō Merchant Academy of Osaka.* Honolulu: University of Hawai'i Press.

_____, 1998. *Tokugawa Political Writings.* Cambridge: Cambridge University Press.

NAJITA Tetsuo and Irwin SCHEINER, eds., 1978. *Japanese Thought in the Tokugawa Period 1600–1868: Methods and Metaphors.* Chicago: University of Chicago Press.

NAKAMURA Hajime 中村 元, 1961–1977. *Nakamura Hajime senshū* 中村元選集. 23 vols. Tokyo: Shunjūsha.

———, 1969. *A History of the Development of Japanese Thought from A.D. 592 to 1868*. 2 vols. Tokyo: Kokusai Bunka Shinkōkai. (reprinted as one volume: *History of Japanese Thought: 592–1868: Japanese Philosophy before Western Culture Entered Japan*. New York: Kegan Paul; distributed by Columbia University Press, 2002)

———, 1999. *Nakamura Hajime senshū bekkan* 中村元選集別巻. Tokyo: Shunjūsha.

NAKAMURA Hajime, ed., 1981. *Kōsetsu Bukkyōgo daijiten* 広説佛教語大辞典. 3 vols. Tokyo: Tōkyō Shoseki. (revised and expanded, 4 vols., 2001)

NAKAMURA Hajime and MINESHIMA Hideo 峰島旭雄, eds., 2000. *Hikaku shisō jiten* 比較思想事典. Tokyo: Tōkyō Shoseki.

NISHITANI Keiji, 1991. *Nishida Kitarō*. Tr. James W. Heisig and Yamamoto Seisaku. Berkeley: University of California Press.

Nosco, Peter, 1990. *Remembering Paradise: Nativism and Nostalgia in Eighteenth-Century Japan*. Cambridge: Harvard University Press.

Nosco, Peter, ed., 1984. *Confucianism and Tokugawa Culture*. Princeton: Princeton University Press.

ODIN, Steve, 1996. *The Social Self in Zen and American Pragmatism*. Albany: SUNY Press.

———, 2001. *Artistic Detachment in Japan and the West: Psychic Distance in Comparative Aesthetics*. Honolulu: University of Hawai'i Press.

ŌHASHI Ryōsuke, 1990. *Die Philosophie der Kyōto Schule*. Freiburg: Karl Alber.

OOMS, Herman, 1985. *Tokugawa Ideology: Early Constructs 1570–1680*. Princeton: Princeton University Press.

PARKES, Graham, ed., 1987. *Heidegger and Asian Thought*. Honolulu: University of Hawai'i Press.

PAUL, Gregor, 1986. *Zur Geschichte der Philosophie in Japan und zu ihrer Darstellung*. Tokyo: Deutsche Gesellschaft für Natur- und Völkerkunde Ostasiens.

PAYNE, Richard, ed., 1999. *Re-Visioning Kamakura Buddhism*. Honolulu: University of Hawai'i Press.

PICKEN, Stuart D. B., 1994. *Essentials of Shinto: An Analytical Guide to Principal Teachings*. Westport: Greenwood Press.

PIOVESANA, Gino K., 1994. *Recent Japanese Philosophical Thought: 1862–1962: A Survey*. Richmond, UK: Curzon. (original edition 1963, Tokyo: Enderle)

SAGARA Tōru 相良 亨, BITŌ Masahide 尾藤正英, and AKIYAMA Ken 秋山 虔, eds., 1983–1984. *Kōza Nihon Shisō* 講座日本思想, 5 vols. Tokyo: Tōkyō Daigaku Shuppankai.

SAWADA, Janine, 1993. *Confucian Values and Popular Zen: Sekimon Shingaku in Eighteenth-Century Japan*. Honolulu: University of Hawai'i Press.

SCHINZINGER, Robert, 1983. *Japanisches Denken: Der weltanschauliche Hintergrund des heutigen Japan*. Berlin: Eric Schmidt.

SHANER, David Edward, 1985. *The Bodymind Experience in Japanese Buddhism: A Phenomenological Perspective of Kūkai and Dōgen*. Albany: SUNY Press.

STEVENS, Bernard, 2000. *Topologie du néant: une approche de l'école de Kyōto*. Paris: Éditions Peeters.

THEMES

STONE, Jacqueline I., 1999. *Original Enlightenment and the Transformation of Medieval Japanese Buddhism*. Honolulu: University of Hawai'i Press.

SUEKI Fumihiko 末木文美士, 2004. *Kindai Nihon no shisō: Saikō* 近代日本の思想・再考. 2 vols. Tokyo: Transview.

SUGANUMA Akira 菅沼 晃, 1977. *Dōgen jiten* 道元辞典. Tokyo: Tōkyōdō Shuppan.

SUGIMOTO Masayoshi and David L. SWAIN, eds., 1978. *Science and Culture in Traditional Japan AD 600–1854*. Cambridge: MIT Press.

TAKEDA Ryūsei 武田龍精, 1991. *Shinran Jōdokyō to Nishida tetsugaku* 親鸞浄土教と西田哲学. Kyoto: Nagata Bunshōdō.

TAKEUCHI Yoshinori, 1983. *The Heart of Buddhism: In Search of the Timeless Spirit of Primitive Buddhism*. Tr. James W. Heisig. New York: Crossroad.

TAMAKI Kōshirō 玉城康四郎, 1974. *Nihon Bukkyō shisōron* 日本仏教思想論. Kyoto: Heirakuji Shoten.

———, 1985. *Hikaku shisōronkyū* 比較思想論究. Tokyo: Kōdansha.

TAMURA Kōyū 田村晃祐, 1979. *Saichō jiten* 最澄辞典. Tokyo: Tōkyōdō Shuppan.

TAMURA Yoshirō 田村芳朗, 1965. *Kamakura shin-Bukkyō shisō no kenkyū* 鎌倉新仏教思想の研究. Kyoto: Heirakuji Shoten.

———, 1969. *Nihon Bukkyōshi nyūmon* 日本仏教史入門. Tokyo: Kadokawa Shoten.

———, 1990. *Hongaku shisōron* 本覚思想論. Tokyo: Shunjūsha.

TREMBLAY, Jacynthe, 2000. *Nishida Kitarō: le jeu de l'individuel et de l'universel*. Paris: CNRS Éditions.

TUCKER, John Allen, 1998. *Itō Jinsai's Gomō jigi and the Philosophical Definition of Early Modern Japan*. Boston: E. J. Brill.

TUCKER, Mary Evelyn, and Duncan Ryūken WILLIAMS, 1997. *Buddhism and Ecology: The Interconnection of Dharma and Deeds*. Cambridge: Harvard University Center for the Study of World Religions, Harvard University Press.

UNNO, Taitetsu, ed., 1989. *The Religious Philosophy of Nishitani Keiji: The Encounter with Emptiness*. Berkeley: Asian Humanities Press.

UNNO, Taitetsu, and James W. HEISIG, eds., 1990. *The Religious Philosophy of Tanabe Hajime: The Metanoetic Imperative*. Berkeley: Asian Humanities Press.

WAKABAYASHI, Bob Tadashi, ed., 1998. *Modern Japanese Thought*. Cambridge: Cambridge University Press.

WALDENSFELS, Hans, 1980. *Absolute Nothingness: Foundations for a Buddhist-Christian Dialogue*. Tr. James W. Heisig. New York: Paulist Press.

WARGO, Robert J. J., 2005. *The Logic of Nothingness*. Honolulu: University of Hawai'i Press.

YOSHIKAWA Kōjirō, 1983. *Jinsai, Sorai, Norinaga: Three Classical Philologists of Mid-Tokugawa Japan*. Tokyo: Tōhō Gakkai.

YUASA Yasuo 湯浅泰雄, 1970. *Kindai Nihon no tetsugaku to jitsuzonshisō* 近代日本の哲学と実存思想. Tokyo: Sōbunsha.

———, 1987. *The Body: Toward an Eastern Mind-Body Theory*, ed. Thomas P. Kasulis, tr. Nagatomo Shigenori and Thomas P. Kasulis. Albany: SUNY Press.

_____, 1993. *The Body, Self-Cultivation, and Ki-Energy*. Tr. Nagatomo Shigenori and Monte S. Hull. Albany: SUNY Press.

_____, 1997. *Shūkyō keiken to shintai* 宗教経験と身体. Tokyo: Iwanami Shoten.

_____, 2002. *Yuasa Yasuo zenshū* 湯浅泰雄全集. 18 vols. Tokyo: Hakua Shobō.

YUSA, Michiko, 2002. *Zen and Philosophy: An Intellectual Biography of Nishida Kitarō*. Honolulu: University of Hawai'i Press.

KAWAHASHI Noriko 川橋範子

Gender Issues in Japanese Religions

Gender is an inclusive concept that crisscrosses a variety of different fields, and it seems virtually certain that other articles in this *Guide* will touch on matters of gender as well. Given the extremely limited space available here, my aim is to give an overview of gender in Japanese religious studies, where it has been a controversial subject in recent years, and to perform a thematic survey of debates that have received widespread attention. Along the way, I will introduce important works and identify points needing further research in terms of both theoretical perspectives and empirical research.[1]

The state of research on gender in Japanese religious studies is similar to its state in this field in Europe and America. Ursula KING finds that religious studies still gives "little explicit recognition to profound epistemological and disciplinary changes brought about by contemporary gender studies" (2002, p. 372). The *Japanese Journal of Religious Studies*

(*JJRS*) made a pioneering effort in 1983 with publication of a special issue on women and religion in Japan. The late NAKAMURA Kyōko, guest editor for that issue, pointed out that women researchers were no more than marginal presences in the Japanese academic field of women and religion. She remarked on the paucity of study in this field, and lamented its backwardness. Helen HARDACRE, the dominant voice in the West in gender study of Japanese religions, once suggested that these studies are still developing (1994a, pp. 119–20).

Gender studies and feminist approaches are, however, beginning to have an impact on the study of Japanese religions, as we can see in a groundbreaking work published 20 years after the *JJRS* special issue mentioned above, that is, the special issue of the *JJRS* on "Feminism and Religion in Contemporary Japan" (KAWAHASHI and KUROKI 2003). The purpose of this special issue was to examine the effects of gender studies and feminism on Japanese Buddhism, Christianity, and new religions, and to introduce feminist research on religion in Japan. It is seen, therefore, as an innovative effort in the field.

GENERAL OUTLINE OF THE STATE OF RESEARCH

One thing is certain: gender and feminist studies in Japan are in an awkward relationship with religious studies. From the scholarly perspective of religious studies in Japan, a dim view is taken of the political polemics that feminism is believed to assert. Feminist scholars, on the other hand, show a marked antagonism toward the patriarchy maintained by religions, and display a consequent coolness toward religion (KAWAHASHI and NOMURA 2001; KAWAHASHI and KUROKI 2003, p. 209).[2] Ōgoshi Aiko, said to be the premier feminist critic of religion in Japan, has maintained that religions themselves—cross-culturally—contain prejudice and violence toward women. In her writings on Buddhism, for example, ŌGOSHI (1997, pp. 113–15) finds that Shinran's view of women legitimized the sexual slavery of women, and she concludes that Japan's ingrained sexual discrimination and the traditional values brought forth by Buddhism are inseparably linked.[3]

It is also self-evident, however, that feminist studies are not monolithic. The recently published *Encyclopedia of Women and World Religions*, an important work, emphasizes that taking feminism as "any single name or movement for women" has its limits, and places importance instead on attentiveness to historical and cultural contexts (YOUNG 2002, pp. 334–35). Moreover, feminism does not just challenge the academic discourse of

* I want to express my deep gratitude to Dr. Richard Peterson for his many excellent suggestions and editorial expertise concerning this essay.

1. This essay partly overlaps with KAWAHASHI 2005.

2. The main research organizations and focal points for activity in feminism and women's studies in Japan are the *Nihon Josei Gakkai* 日本女性学会 (Women's Studies Association of Japan) and the *Nihon Joseigaku Kenkyūkai* 日本女性学研究会 (Women's Studies Society of Japan). YAMAMOTO 2001 also contains a clear overview of gender studies in Japan from the perspective of anthropology.

3. For ŌGOSHI's critique of Buddhism, see her joint work with MINAMOTO Junko (1994). ŌGOSHI's interpretation of Shinran is fundamentally different from the typical view of Shinran as a liberal thinker found among Western Shinshū scholars.

THEMES

religion. It can also influence women's religious practice itself. The religious world in Japan has been informed by feminism in recent years, and movements to reform religious organizations are emerging. These have elements in common with feminist theology in Europe and America, which seeks to use feminism as a critical leverage to reform male-centered Judeo-Christian religions. Future development of such movements in Japan is to be anticipated (see, for example, KOKUSAI SHŪKYŌ KENKYŪJO 1996; JOSEI TO BUKKYŌ TŌKAI-KANTŌ NETTOWĀKU 1999 and 2003; KINUKAWA 2002; KAWAHASHI 2000a; KAWAHASHI 2003).

WOMEN IN BUDDHIST HISTORY

Having developed out of the former focus of Japanese Buddhist history on doctrine and institutions, the study of women and Buddhist history is growing into an exciting field that concentrates instead on reevaluating the theoretical history of the discipline and making new discoveries in historical sources.[4] Much of this work was done by the scholars who were actively involved in the *Kenkyūkai: Nihon no Bukkyō to Josei* (Study Group on Buddhism and Women in Japan) over the decade starting in 1984 (see ŌSUMI and NISHIGUCHI 1989). A project to translate many of their valuable studies into English has just been made possible by the Institute of Medieval Japanese Studies. This important collaborative collection of more than twenty studies by Japanese and Western scholars has certainly shed new light on the theories of Japanese Buddhism and women that has dominated Western academic circles (see RUCH 2002). In addition, James DOBBINS (2004) has recently published a study of Eshinni, a Buddhist nun in medieval Japan, that is a solid portrayal of the lived experience of a dedicated female Buddhist.

A major characteristic of the new approach to the study of women and Buddhist history can be described in brief as a reversal in the way its questions are posed. That is, such studies used to gaze from a male perspective to ask how the "Buddhism" composed of patriarchs, orders, doctrines, and so on viewed women. Introduction of a gender viewpoint, however, has stimulated a new movement that asks, from a woman's perspective, about women's reception of Buddhism, as well as how they denied it and what kinds of roles they fulfilled and fulfillment they achieved within the various social constraints imposed on women. In other words, these questions are being approached from the actor's point of view. Yoshida Kazuhiko has written about the importance of "examining history from the different perspective of what Buddhism was *for women* in Japan" (YOSHIDA, KATSUURA, NISHIGUCHI 1999, p. 33; see also Yoshida's essay in this *Guide*).

As Nishiguchi Junko acknowledges, however, the undeniable fact still is that "No comprehensive history of women and Buddhism exists that brings the subject up to the present day. Even though women interacted with Buddhism in a variety of ways, and proved their devotion, the fact is that religious orders and teachings discriminated against women, and

---

4. This growth is also related to the remarkable development of research on women's history in Japan over recent years. See WAKITA et al., 1999, and SŌGŌ JOSEISHI KENKYŪKAI 1998.

the fact is that no women were founders of Buddhist sects." She therefore states that still more research will be required (YOSHIDA, KATSUURA, and NISHIGUCHI 1999, p. 3).[5]

MULTIPLE ASPECTS OF WOMEN'S SPIRITUAL POWER

One of the questions that has attracted considerable attention in recent years has to do with the interpretation of the "spiritual power of women" that is widely evident in Japan, particularly in Okinawa. Many instances can be found of women performing religious roles conditioned by the view of women as possessors of a mystical spiritual power. In some cases, conversely, women are viewed not as divine but as polluted, so that they are excluded from sacred sites and important ritual observances.

As to the former, approaches from the gender perspective have begun to point out the dangers of perceiving that spiritual power as being innate to women rather than as a cultural, social, historical construct. Such questions have become linked with Japanese folklore studies, the primary field in which women's power has been made a subject of inquiry, and this field itself is being reexamined in that connection.[6]

The spiritual power of women came to attention in the first place with the publication of *Imo no chikara* (Women's Power) in 1940 by Yanagita Kunio, the founding father of Japanese folklore studies. Yanagita viewed women as innately possessing this women's power, a mystical spiritual power that originates in women's reproductive capability, and that is expressed in such phenomena as menstruation and childbearing. By virtue of this special physiology and emotional nature, Yanagita thought, women possessed various religious abilities. Recent criticism points out, however, that this notion of women as sacred beings because of their reproductive function has actually acted to cover up folk practices that discriminated against women in various ways (see KAWAHASHI forthcoming). Such criticism is directed against Yanagita and many other Japanese scholars of folklore (most of whom are men) for imposing the view, based on biological essentialism, that women's spiritual power is something inherent, natural, and universal in women. KANDA Yoriko, a woman scholar of folklore, has countered this view by pointing out that conventional approaches were overly fixated on analysis that imposed the specific frame of women's spiritual power on individual cases, and consequently overlooked concrete religious phenomena. She observes that it is crucial to create thorough ethnographies of the societies in question (KANDA 2000, pp. 81–82).[7]

I should also attempt a brief explanation of the view that women are polluted and must

---

5. For English-language studies on Buddhism and sexuality, see FAURE 1998, and in particular on Zen priests, priest's wives, and nuns, see KAWAHASHI 1995, ARAI 1999, and JAFFE 2001. See KING 1987 and KUROKI (forthcoming) for information on life histories of nuns.

6. Details of the debate on the spiritual power of women below can be found in KAWAHASHI (forthcoming). Concerning Yanagita Kunio and folk religion, see the essay by Ian Reader in this *Guide*.

7. For specific examples of the religious roles of women, in addition to the classic work by BLACKER (1975), see, for instance, IKEGAMI 1999, KAWAMURA 1991, KANDA 1992, and SMYERS 1999.

be held apart from whatever is holy or sacred. This view underlies the phenomenon of *nyonin kinsei* 女人禁制 (also referred to as *nyonin kekkai* 女人結界). *Nyonin kinsei* is the practice of forbidding women to live in shrines, temples, sacred mountains, and ritual sites, to perform religious practice at them, or even to enter them. *Nyonin kekkai* is the establishment of a ritual space that demarcates the boundary beyond which women cannot enter. Some sacred mountains that traditionally upheld *nyonin kekkai* have recently been opened to women, while others, such as Mt. Ōmine in Nara, continue to maintain the exclusion, and this is the subject of ongoing dispute.

SUZUKI Masataka, in one of the recent overviews on this topic, acknowledges the criticism of *nyonin kinsei* as a discriminatory practice in terms of the human rights of women, but with the reservation that his purpose is not to criticize the practice but to clarify the processes whereby it came into being and has been maintained even while it was undergoing change (2002, p. 4). Suzuki's stance appears to reflect the present polarization in accounts of *nyonin kinsei* as either a discriminatory practice or as something religiously significant. Kanda Yoriko, for instance, cites the arguments made by ABE (1989) and others in suggesting that for male religious practitioners, *nyonin kinsei* "was an intellectual foundation for a faith aimed at the acquisition of spiritual power, and was a mechanism of religious culture" (KANDA 2000, p. 91).

However, the argument that sacred mountains had to be sealed off from women in order that male practitioners could obtain spiritual power then naturally raises the question of why the system gave priority to those men. USHIYAMA Yoshiyuki, a historian of Buddhism, identifies four basic reasons for the origination of *nyonin kinsei*: 1) the notion of women's blood pollution; 2) the Buddhist precepts; 3) the disdain shown women in Buddhist scriptures; and 4) the fundamental reality of Japanese folk practices. USHIYAMA points out that while conventional accounts overemphasize the first reason, the focus should instead be on the second, the Buddhist precept against sexual indulgence, and suggests that the notion of blood pollution was a later development (1996, pp. 75–78).[8]

In any event, important work remains to be done in uncovering what is actually involved when women are viewed as sacred or subjected to discriminatory treatment. What is the logic that operates, what historical changes have taken place, how did women themselves perceive their treatment, and how are such religious practices implicated in the situations of women today?[9]

---

8. YUSA 1994 presents a cogent summary of women's pollution and Shinto.

9. Space constraints do not allow discussion of the women and religion of Okinawa, where the notion of women's blood pollution is rarely if ever encountered. Another distinctive feature of Okinawan culture is *onarigami* オナリ神 belief, according to which sisters act as spiritual guardians who protect their male siblings (LEBRA 1966; MABUCHI 1964; RØKKUM 1998; WACKER 2001a). The active religious participation by women found in Okinawa has attracted many researchers. One recent ethnography that has received considerable attention is Susan Sered's *Women of the Sacred Groves* (1999), which contains a number of problems and must be read critically. For details see KAWAHASHI 2000b, WACKER 2001b, and KAWAHASHI (forthcoming). *The Ryukyuanist* (54, 2001–2002), a newsletter of Okinawa studies, contains a critique of Sered by a group of concerned scholars, and the following issue (55) contains Sered's response.

WOMEN AND NEW RELIGIONS

A great deal of research has been done on the new religions of Japan (see the essay on "new religions" in this *Guide*), and the *Shūkyō to Shakai Gakkai* (Japanese Association for the Study of Religion and Society) in particular has been central to research in this area in Japan.[10] The proportion of women in the memberships of new religions is so high that these religions are said to be supported by women. The most vocal Western scholar of women in the Japanese new religions is Helen Hardacre, who wrote as follows on Kurozumikyō:

> Restricted for the most part to the least interesting and least remunerative forms of employment, women frequently find in the new religions an extremely satisfying avenue of prestige and an outlet for talent and energy. Since there are fewer pollution restrictions to limit their participation than in established religions, women participate in great numbers and with remarkable energy. (HARDACRE 1986, p. 193)

Watanabe Masako, the foremost woman scholar of the new religions in Japan, has observed that many of these religions repeatedly attempt to inculcate in their new women members the belief that they should "awake to an understanding of the religious significance of their gender role, that they should 'lower' themselves and elevate their husbands, and that when they transform themselves, then their partners will also change in response." According to her analysis, this is "the teaching and the strategy for achievement of happiness in one's present lifetime." In short, the new religions can be said to have "provided a route by which women could achieve self-realization without amending traditional gender role assignments" (WATANABE 2002, p. 259).[11]

Much the same interpretation was expressed by Hardacre in an early study as "strategies of weakness." She explains that this technique guarantees women, who are economically dependent upon the men in their households, a way to "restructure power relations in the family" (HARDACRE 1984, pp. 208–21).

Hardacre has developed this interpretation further in her more recent work, where she seeks similarities between Japanese new religions such as Reiyūkai and Seichō no Ie, and the fundamentalism frequently found in other religions. In sum, she finds that the "characteristically conservative stance in regard to family, gender, and interpersonal relations" on the part of new religions in Japan is analogous, in its sexual discrimination, to fundamentalist religion, which places women in a subservient position to men and forces them to be self-sacrificing (HARDACRE 1994b, p. 113).[12]

10. Among recent studies of the new religions, SHIMAZONO 1999 and ASANO 2001 are particularly important.

11. INOUE Nobutaka describes this utilitarian approach with the expression いったん下がって実をとる (*ittan sagatte jitsu o toru*), meaning "take a step back (for show) but grasp the substance (of what you actually want)" (1991, p. 247). Also see NAKAMURA 1997.

12. This understanding of the involvement of women with fundamentalism, however, has also been criticized as entirely too simplistic in its equation of fundamentalism with the oppressor of women. BRINK and MENCHER 1997, for example, find the relationship between

HARDACRE also finds that new religious organizations in general are "uninterested in political action to improve society" (1986, p. 23). Those new religious organizations in turn place little value on political activity by women members. Robert KISALA, however, presenting an opposing view, affirms that practices of universal altruism that demand positive activity for the salvation and welfare of others do exist in Japanese new religions, examples being Tenrikyō and Risshō Kōseikai (1992, pp. 2–3; see also KISALA 1999).

Concerning the political activities of women in the new religions, HARDACRE concludes that, under such circumstances of male-initiated activity, they "do not seem to presage any drastic change in the stance of the organizations concerned on the family, gender, and interpersonal relations" (1994b, p. 128). Studies by Usui Atsuko and others have, however, shown the error of reaching such sweeping conclusions, that these women are blindly submitting to male-controlled programs without any political awareness or concern for justice and peace (USUI 2000 and 2003; KOMATSU 1995).

Women in the new religions definitely have adopted the strategy of working from traditional domestic roles sanctioned by their religions. This may have parallels with some kinds of fundamentalism. These women may also appear to be lacking in a critical attitude toward the oppressed positions that they have taken. It has been observed, however, that "all attempts to build a general model of women's membership in new religions have failed" (YOUNG 2002, p. 718).

As suggested above, the experiences of women in the new religions are characterized by diversity, and in this light, a fruitful direction for research would be to conduct studies based on detailed fieldwork that is attentive to the agency of women. This will also require refinement of theories relating to the religious agency of women. In connection with women's moral agency, for example, Diana MEYERS pursues the question of "how women can enact the value of care without collaborating in their own subordination" while at the same time underscoring how important it is to recognize the genuine value of women's traditional roles as mothers and caregivers (1998, p. 375). This is more than adequately suggestive of approaches for research on women in the new religions, as well.

ACCOUNTS OF *MIZUKO KUYŌ*

The past decade has seen the publication of two major studies (LAFLEUR 1992; HARDACRE 1997) of *mizuko kuyō* 水子供養 (memorial rituals for aborted fetuses and miscarried or stillborn babies), and the *Journal of the American Association of Religion* subsequently published a special issue (67/4, 1999) on "abortion and *mizuko kuyō* in Japan." *Mizuko kuyō* indeed appears to have become a perennial issue.[13]

fundamentalism and gender to be extremely complex, and they present case studies to show that the effects of fundamentalism on women are mixed (both oppressive and liberating).

13. Major reviews of LAFLEUR 1992 include READER 1995 and TANABE 1994. Positive reviews of HARDACRE 1997 are STEINHOFF 1998 and ALLISON 1999, and negative reviews are TANABE 1998 and READER 1998. GARDNER 1998 is a review article that compares these two studies. For recent studies of *mizuko kuyō* in Japan, see TAKAHASHI 1999.

It appears, moreover, that the issue of *mizuko kuyō* has extended beyond a single phenomenon in Japanese religion to become a battleground of Japanese gender issues where various scholars bring their respective political agendas into play. The best review article in this area is by Meredith Underwood, who correctly finds that the issue "stands at the intersection of several crossroads: between ancient and modern Japan, between the conflicted gender roles of Japanese men and women, between women's agency and their 'victimization,' between 'authentic' and 'inauthentic' religions" (1999, p. 739).

Although the various accounts of *mizuko kuyō* produced up to now are not necessarily in error, each one of them can be said to present a partial picture. Space considerations prevent me from taking up all the problems in these *mizuko kuyō* studies, so I shall attempt instead to identify a few possible directions for further research.

As regards the ritual itself, political agendas have ended up taking precedence over research to ascertain the realities of its practice and the actual experiences of the women concerned. We find, therefore, that data complicating those agendas has been ignored and the complexities of phenomena that should properly be differentiated for examination have instead been obfuscated. Ian Reader has pointed out, for example, that no evidence has been adduced to support the contention that fear of retribution from an aborted fetus, which would afflict women in the form of a menacing spirit, as suggested by the title of Hardacre's book, is what actually motivates women to perform *mizuko kuyō*. It is only assumed, and he finds that such generalizations "might need to be modified in the light of what participants actually say" (Reader 1998, p. 155).[14] Elizabeth Harrison, who is noted for a wealth of experience in actual fieldwork, refers to the complex picture of motivations underlying this ritual practice and explains that women "demonstrate at one and the same time both their personal sense of connection to their absent children as well as their obedience to the outside pressures of the moment to do *mizuko kuyō*" (1999, p. 791; see also Harrison 1995). Underwood, referred to earlier, criticizes *mizuko kuyō* studies by LaFleur and other men for not being attentive to the distinctive gendered experience of women, but appreciates both Hardacre and Harrison for expressing concern for women's issues.[15] Underwood then performs a comparative analysis of these two, and concludes that "what Hardacre does lose sight of in her analysis, however, is not women but women's agency" (1999, p. 751), while "Harrison provides a more complex and therefore nuanced understanding of both ritual and women's agency" (1999, p. 752). In other words, if *mizuko kuyō*

14. Hoshino Tomoko points out in her study (1999) that retribution is not involved in all *mizuko kuyō*. On this matter, Reader 1998 refers to an analysis of substantive factual information to be found in Anderson and Martin 1997.

15. Underwood describes this with the phrase "mysterious disappearing woman" (1999, pp. 750–51). The problem I find in LaFleur's study is that no fieldwork at all was conducted to uncover how the actual women concerned have expressed themselves on the subject. At the risk of oversimplification, his main point seems to be that *mizuko kuyō* is a ritual that provides women the equipment to deal with emotional issues involved in abortion. His view has been critiqued from a feminist perspective as entailing a moral danger (Green 1999, p. 817), but Ogino Miho, Japan's leading feminist historian, refers favorably to LaFleur's interpretation (2001, Ch. 6).

is taken as a misogynist ritual par excellence that stigmatizes women's non-reproductive sexual activity, as in Hardacre's work, then this effectively places many Japanese women in the position of lacking the agency to either negotiate with a male-dominant system or resist it. Consequently, Underwood and Harrison seek to challenge such orientalist representations of Japanese women.

I would like to stress the point, however, that to reinstate the agency of women in this respect is by no means to condone all *mizuko kuyō* practice. For example, some forms of *mizuko kuyō* are exploitative even when those performing the ritual are women.[16] In my own assessment of *mizuko kuyō*, I have held that the aspects of retribution and misogyny should be differentiated (KAWAHASHI 1996).

Witness the fact that fraudulent fund-raising practices by so-called cults have come under increasing criticism in recent years. As a result, few religionists in the traditional Buddhist orders are calling attention to the retribution wrought by aborted fetuses. Nevertheless, in most cases these orders do tend to take a negative view of abortion because of the Buddhist precept against taking life, and they will consequently preach guilt and repentance to women more often for that reason than on the basis of retribution.[17] In order to understand *mizuko kuyō*, therefore, it will be necessary first to highlight the distinctions between those religious groups that bring retribution to the forefront in this way from those that do not, to comprehend the actual circumstances of various specific rituals, and, above all, to hear the voices of the women who are directly involved, before privileging any specific political agenda.

In conclusion, I would like to observe again, as I did regarding the study of such subjects as *mizuko kuyō* and the new religions in a manner involving women, that research on gender and Japanese religion will have to be positioned within a dialectic between work to refine existing theories of gender and feminism on the one hand, and exhaustive fieldwork on the other. Furthermore, we must recognize that, with the emergence of Third-World and non-Western feminism, it has become necessary to consider feminisms in the plural. In other words, the statement that there is no unitary female experience is no longer a mere truism. Researchers who examine the religions and women of Japan will be called on to be reflexively aware of whether their own interpretations are imposing a Western—or some other—agenda on their subject matter.[18]

Aihwa Ong wrote as follows about the relationship between the people who are the objects of research and the people performing research: "The most critical point is not that we reap material and social benefits from their stories but that we help to disseminate their views and that we do so without betraying their political interests as narrators of their own

16. A recent case at the Nagoya temple of a Buddhist-based new religion was adjudged to constitute systematic fraud and it is possible that a prison sentence will be imposed on the priest, who happens to be a woman. She had been performing *mizuko kuyō* for large numbers of women, most of them housewives.

17. One recent example is Nakano Tōzen, a Sōtō priest who has made remarks representing traditional Buddhist circles regarding bioethics.

18. KEOWN 2001 presents excellent insights on this point.

lives" (ONG 1995, p. 354). Every student of Japanese religions and gender must learn from her words.

BIBLIOGRAPHY

ABE Yasurō 阿部泰郎, 1989. Nyonin kinsei to suisan 女人禁制と推参. In ŌSUMI and NISHIGUCHI 1989, vol. 4, pp. 153–240.

ALLISON, Anne, 1999. Review of *Marketing the Menacing Fetus in Japan*. *Journal of Asian Studies* 58: 840–43.

ANDERSON, Richard, and Elaine MARTIN, 1997. Rethinking the Practice of *Mizuko Kuyō* in Contemporary Japan. *Japanese Journal of Religious Studies* 24: 121–43.

ARAI, Paula, 1999. *Women Living Zen: Japanese Soto Buddhist Nuns*. Oxford: Oxford University Press.

ASANO Miwako 浅野美和子, 2001. *Onna kyōso no tanjō* 女教祖の誕生. Tokyo: Fujiwara Shoten.

BLACKER, Carmen, 1975. *The Catalpa Bow: A Study of Shamanistic Practices in Japan*. Richmond, UK: Curzon Press.

BRINK, Judy, and Joan MENCHER, 1997. *Mixed Blessings*. New York: Routledge.

DOBBINS, James, 2004. *Letters of the Nun Eshinni: Images of Pure Land Buddhism in Medieval Japan*. Honolulu: University of Hawai'i Press.

FAURE, Bernard, 1998. *The Red Thread: Buddhist Approaches to Sexuality*. Princeton: Princeton University Press.

GARDNER, Richard A., 1998. Matters of Life and Death. *The Eastern Buddhist* 31: 109–24.

GREEN, Ronald M., 1999. The *Mizuko Kuyō* Debate: An Ethical Assessment. *Journal of the American Academy of Religion* 67: 809–23.

HARDACRE, Helen, 1984. *Lay Buddhism in Contemporary Japan: Reiyūkai Kyōdan*. Princeton: Princeton University Press.

———, 1986. *Kurozumikyō and the New Religions of Japan*. Princeton: Princeton University Press.

———, 1994a. Shinshūkyō no josei kyōso to jendā 新宗教の女性教祖とジェンダー. In *Jendā no Nihonshi (jō)* ジェンダーの日本史(上), ed. Wakita Haruko and S. B. Hanley, pp. 119–52. Tokyo: University of Tokyo Press.

———, 1994b. Japanese New Religions: Profiles in Gender. In *Fundamentalism and Gender*, ed. John Stratton Hawley, pp. 111–33. Oxford: Oxford University Press.

———, 1997. *Marketing the Menacing Fetus in Japan*. Berkeley: University of California Press.

HARRISON, Elizabeth G., 1995. Women's Response to Child Loss in Japan: The Case of *Mizuko Kuyō*. *Journal of Feminist Studies in Religion* 11: 67–93.

———, 1999. Strands of Complexity: The Emergence of *Mizuko Kuyō* in Postwar Japan. *Journal of the American Academy of Religion* 67: 769–96.

HOSHINO Tomoko 星野智子, 1999. Kiki kanri sōchi to shite no mizuko kuyō 危機管理装置としての水子供養. In *Kamigami yadorishi machi* 神々宿りし都市, ed. Shūkyō Shakaigaku no Kai 宗教社会学の会, pp. 60–83. Osaka: Sōgensha.

IKEGAMI Yoshimasa 池上良正, 1999. *Minkan fusha shinkō no kenkyū* 民間巫者信仰の研究. Tokyo: Miraisha.

INOUE Nobutaka 井上順孝, 1991. Shinshūkyō to sei sabetsu 新宗教と性差別. *Bukkyō* 仏教 15: 244–50.

JAFFE, Richard M., 2001. *Neither Monk nor Layman*. Princeton: Princeton University Press.

JOSEI TO BUKKYŌ TŌKAI-KANTŌ NETTOWĀKU 女性と仏教 東海・関東ネットワーク, ed., 1999. *Bukkyō to jendā: Onna tachi no nyoze gamon* 仏教とジェンダー——女たちの如是我聞. Osaka: Toki Shobō.

_____, 2003. *Jendā ikōru na Bukkyō o mezashite: Zoku onna tachi no nyoze gamon* ジェンダーイコールな仏教をめざして——続女たちの如是我聞. Osaka: Toki Shobō.

KANDA Yoriko 神田より子, 1992. *Miko no ie no onna tachi* 神子の家の女たち. Tokyo: Tōkyōdō Shuppan.

_____, 2000. Minzoku shūkyō to imo no chikara 民俗宗教と妹の力. *Shūkyō kenkyū* 325: 75–96.

KAWAHASHI Noriko 川橋範子, 1995. *Jizoku* (Priests' Wives) in Sōtō Zen Buddhism: An Ambiguous Category. *Japanese Journal of Religious Studies* 22: 161–83.

_____, 1996. Mizuko kuyō: Hikaku shūkyōgakuteki kōsatsu 水子供養——比較宗教的考察. *Kyōka kenshū* 39: 226–30.

_____, 2000a. Bukkyō no saisōzō: Posuto kafuchōsei Bukkyō ni muketa josei tachi no taiwa 仏教の再創造——ポスト家父長制仏教に向けた女性たちの対話. In *Shūkyō to shūkyō no aida* 宗教と宗教の＜あいだ＞, ed. Nanzan Shūkyō Bunka Kenkyūjo 南山宗教文化研究所, pp. 302–41. Nagoya: Fūbaisha.

_____, 2000b. Review Article: Religion, Gender and Okinawan Studies. *Asian Folklore Studies* 59: 301–11.

_____, 2003. Feminist Buddhism as Praxis: Women in Traditional Buddhism. *Japanese Journal of Religious Studies* 30: 291–313.

_____, 2005. Gender and Japanese Religions. In *Encyclopedia of Religion*, 2nd ed., Lindsay Jones, ed., pp. 3345–350. New York: Macmillan Reference USA.

_____, forthcoming. Japanese Folk Religion and its Contemporary Issues. In *A Companion to the Anthropology of Japan*, ed. Jennifer Robertson. Malden: Blackwell.

KAWAHASHI Noriko and KUROKI Masako, eds., 2003. Special issue on "Feminism and Religion in Contemporary Japan." *Japanese Journal of Religious Studies* 30/3–4.

KAWAHASHI Noriko 川橋範子 and NOMURA Fumiko 野村文子, 2001. Taidan: Gendai shūkyō to josei 対談現代宗教と女性. *Gendai shūkyō* 現代宗教 2001: 123–42.

KAWAMURA Kunimitsu 川村邦光, 1991. *Miko no minzokugaku* 巫女の民俗学. Tokyo: Seikyūsha.

KEOWN, Damien, 2001. Comparative Ethics and *Mizuko Kuyō*: A Response to Ronald M. Green. *Journal of the American Academy of Religion* 69: 465–69.

KING, Sallie B., 1987. *Passionate Journey: The Spiritual Autobiography of Satomi Myodo*. Boston: Shambhala.

KING, Ursula, 2002. Is there a Future for Religious Studies as We Know it? Some Postmodern, Feminist, and Spiritual Challenges. *Journal of the American Academy of Religion* 70: 365–88.

KINUKAWA Hisako 絹川久子, 2002. *Jendā no shiten de yomu seisho* ジェンダーの視点で読む聖書. Tokyo: Nihon Kirisutokyōdan Shuppankyoku.

KISALA, Robert, 1992. *Gendai shūkyō to shakai rinri* 現代宗教と社会倫理. Tokyo: Seikyūsha.

_____, 1999. *Prophets of Peace: Pacifism and Cultural Identity in Japan's New Religions*. Honolulu: University of Hawai'i Press.

KOKUSAI SHŪKYŌ KENKYŪJO 国際宗教研究所, ed., 1996. *Josei to kyōdan* 女性と教団. Tokyo: Harvest.

KOMATSU Kayoko 小松加代子, 1995. Shūkyō katsudō to josei no yakuwari: Sekaikyūseikyō ni okeru shizenshoku undō ni kangamite 宗教活動と女性の役割——世界救世教における自然食運動にかんがみて. In *Josei to shūkyō no kindaishi* 女性と宗教の近代史, ed. Okuda Akiko 奥田暁子, pp. 79–110. Tokyo: San'ichi Publishing.

KUROKI Masako, forthcoming. Seeking a Station in Life: The Spiritual Quest of a Female Tendai Buddhist Priest. In *Memory and Imagination: Essays and Other Musings on Buddhist Thought and Culture*, ed. Ronald Y. Nakasone. (publisher to be announced)

LAFLEUR, William R., 1992. *Liquid Life: Abortion and Buddhism in Japan*. Princeton: Princeton University Press.

LEBRA, William P., 1966. *Okinawan Religion: Belief, Ritual, and Social Structure*. Honolulu: University of Hawai'i Press.

MABUCHI Toichi, 1964. Spiritual Predominance of the Sister. In *Ryukyuan Culture and Society*, ed. A. Smith. Honolulu: University of Hawai'i Press.

MEYERS, Diana T., 1998. Agency. In *A Companion to Feminine Philosophy*, ed. Alison M. Jaggar and Iris M. YOUNG, pp. 372–82. Malden: Blackwell.

NAKAMURA Kyōko, 1983. Women and Religion in Japan: Introductory Remarks. *Japanese Journal of Religious Studies* 10: 115–21.

_____, 1997. The Religious Consciousness and Activities of Contemporary Japanese Women. *Japanese Journal of Religious Studies* 24: 87–120.

OGINO Miho 荻野美穂, 2001. *Chūzetsu ronsō to Amerika shakai* 中絶論争とアメリカ社会. Tokyo: Iwanami Shoten.

ŌGOSHI Aiko 大越愛子, 1997. *Josei to shūkyō* 女性と宗教. Tokyo: Iwanami Shoten.

ŌGOSHI Aiko 大越愛子 and MINAMOTO Junko 源 淳子, 1994. *Kaitai suru Bukkyō* 解体する仏教. Tokyo: Daitō Shuppan.

ONG, Aihwa, 1995. Women out of China: Traveling Tales and Traveling Theories in Postcolonial Feminism. In *Women Writing Culture*, ed. Ruth Behar and Deborah H. Gordon, pp. 350–72. Berkeley: University of California Press.

ŌSUMI Kazuo 大隅和雄 and NISHIGUCHI Junko 西口順子, eds., 1989. *Shirīzu Josei to Bukkyō* シリーズ女性と仏教, 4 vols. Tokyo: Heibonsha.

READER, Ian, 1995. Review of *Liquid Life*. *Journal of Japanese Studies* 21: 195–200.

_____, 1998. Review of *Marketing the Menacing Fetus in Japan*. *Asian Folklore Studies* 57: 152–55.

RØKKUM, Arne, 1998. *Goddesses, Priestesses, and Sisters*. Oslo: Scandinavian University Press.

RUCH, Barbara, 2002. *Engendering Faith: Women and Buddhism in Premodern Japan*. Ann Arbor: Center for Japanese Studies, University of Michigan.

SERED, Susan, 1999. *Women of the Sacred Groves: Divine Priestesses of Okinawa*. Oxford: Oxford University Press.

SHIMAZONO Susumu 島薗 進, 1999. *Jidai no naka no shinshūkyō* 時代のなかの新宗教. Tokyo: Kōbundō.

SMYERS, Karen A., 1999. *The Fox and the Jewel*. Honolulu: University of Hawai'i Press.

THEMES

SŌGŌ Joseishi Kenkyūkai 総合女性史研究会, ed., 1998. *Josei to shūkyō* 女性と宗教. Nihon Joseishi Ronshū 日本女性史論集 5. Tokyo: Yoshikawa Kōbunkan.

Steinhoff, Patricia G., 1998. Review of *Marketing the Menacing Fetus in Japan*. *Journal of Japanese Studies* 24: 453–57.

Suzuki Masataka 鈴木正崇, 2002. *Nyonin kinsei* 女人禁制. Tokyo: Yoshikawa Kōbunkan.

Takahashi Saburō 高橋三郎, ed., 1999. *Mizuko kuyō* 水子供養. Kyoto: Kōrosha.

Tanabe, George J., Jr., 1994. Review of *Liquid Life*. *Japanese Journal of Religious Studies* 21: 437–40.

———, 1998. Review of *Marketing the Menacing Fetus in Japan*. *Japanese Journal of Religious Studies* 25: 377–80.

Underwood, Meredith, 1999. Strategies of Survival: Women, Abortion, and Popular Religion in Contemporary Japan. *Journal of the American Academy of Religion* 67: 734–68.

Ushiyama Yoshiyuki 牛山佳幸, 1996. Nyonin kinsei 女人禁制. In *Nihon no Bukkyō* 日本の仏教 6, ed. Nihon Bukkyō Kenkyūkai 日本仏教研究会, pp. 74–79. Kyoto: Hōzōkan.

Usui Atsuko, 2000. The Role of Women. In *Global Citizens: The Soka Gakkai Buddhist Movement in the World*, ed. David Machacek and Brian Wilson, pp. 153–204. Oxford: Oxford University Press.

———, 2003. Women's "Experience" in New Religious Movements: The Case of Shinnyoen. *Japanese Journal of Religious Studies* 30: 217–41.

Wacker, Monika, 2001a. Onarigami: Holy Woman in the Kingdom of Ryūkyū: A Pacific Culture with Chinese Influences. In *Ryūkyū in World History*, ed. Josef Kreiner, pp. 41–67. Bonn: Bier'sche Verlagsanstalt.

———, 2001b. Review of *Women of the Sacred Groves*. *Japanese Journal of Religious Studies* 28: 201–4.

Wakita Haruko, Anne Bouchy, and Ueno Chizuko, eds., 1999. *Gender and Japanese History*. 2 vols. Osaka: Osaka University Press.

Watanabe Masako 渡辺雅子, 2002. Shinshūkyō to josei 新宗教と女性. In *Iwanami joseigaku jiten* 岩波女性学事典, ed. Inoue Teruko 井上輝子, Ueno Chizuko 上野千鶴子, Ehara Yumiko 江原由美子, Ōsawa Mari 大沢真理, and Kanō Mikiyo 加納実紀代, pp. 259–60. Tokyo: Iwanami Shoten.

Yamamoto Matori 山本真鳥, 2001. The Anthropological Study of Gender and Sexuality in Japan. *Japanese Review of Cultural Anthropology* 2: 105–37.

Yoshida Kazuhiko 吉田一彦, Katsuura Noriko 勝浦令子, and Nishiguchi Junko 西口順子, eds., 1999. *Nihonshi no naka no josei to Bukkyō* 日本史の中の女性と仏教. Kyoto: Hōzōkan.

Young, Serinity, ed., 2002. *Encyclopedia of Women and World Religion*. New York: Macmillan Reference USA.

Yusa Michiko, 1994. Women in Shinto: Images Remembered. In *Religion and Women*, ed. Arvind Sharma, pp. 93–119. Albany: SUNY Press.

Research

Makino Yasuko 牧野康子

Japanese Reference Works, Sources, and Libraries

This essay is written for graduate students embarking on dissertation research who plan to go to Japan within a couple of years, as well as for students who are in pro-seminars on research in Japanese sources who are still undecided on their topics.

When you decide on a topic for an extensive research paper, you need, of course, to do a bibliographic search for materials written in the past, and for other research done in your field and in related fields. If you are to undertake writing a dissertation, you have to make sure you read extensively in your area of interest to conduct original research. When you do the bibliographic search, begin broadly then narrow down on the basis of your interests and what is available and manageable. In the course of your search, you should make sure your topic is broad enough to let you find enough materials.

First, you have to find out what is happening in your field, in the

Western world and in Japan. A quick way is to read through *The Introductory Bibliography for Japanese Studies* and the professional journals in your field of study. Part 2 of the Humanities volumes of *The Introductory Bibliography for Japanese Studies* contains the religion section.

If you are interested in interdisciplinary topics or comparative studies, as more and more people are these days, you need to read other sections as well. Each subject category of *The Introductory Bibliography for Japanese Studies* includes an essay describing the major research trends during the period covered and a selected bibliography with comments on important works.

GUIDE TO REFERENCE WORKS

Guides to reference works give major sources for a particular subject area and provide bibliographic information and descriptions of reference works. They explain how to find and use information contained in the sources. They are valuable as aids in identifying likely sources.

A Student Guide to Japanese Sources in the Humanities provides a guide to students who are writing papers and dissertations in the humanities based primarily on Japanese language sources as well as to be used as a textbook for Japanese bibliography courses. *Japan and the Japanese* is a guide to English-language reference materials on Japan and the Japanese, and is designed for those seeking information at all levels, and all subjects related to Japan and the Japanese. *A Guide to Reference Books for Japanese Studies* (*Nihon kenkyū no tame no sankō tosho* 日本研究のための参考図書) was started as an update of *Bibliography of Reference Works for Japanese Studies*, and it tends to include more recent publications. *A Guide to Reference Books for Japanese Studies* includes both English-language and Japanese-language materials with brief annotations. *Bibliography of Reference Works for Japanese Studies* is somewhat outdated, but it includes important monographic series (collectanea) that are not included in any of the three other guides.

Nihon no sankō tosho 日本の参考図書 covers reference works in all subjects extensively and should be consulted when you need to search broadly for specialized reference works.

SEARCHING FOR BOOKS (BIBLIOGRAPHIES)

The term "bibliography" refers to a list of works, whether comprehensive or selective, compiled upon some common principle. They are usually used to identify or verify articles or books, or used to find materials in a particular subject area. The data elements in a bibliography entry depend largely on the intent of the publication. Scope, arrangement, and coverage are very important, so make sure to read the *hanrei* 凡例, which provides instructions on how to use the book.

The following titles are called "national bibliographies," which comprehensively list the books published in Japan. *Kokusho sōmokuroku* 国書総目録 includes books that were written or translated in Japanese from the earliest times to the end of the Edo period and which are owned by various libraries. *Kotenseki sōgō mokuroku* 古典籍総合目録, which can be accessed online by going to the homepage of Kokubungaku Kenkyū Shiryōkan 国文学研

究資料館, supplements the above, so they should be used together. Since the National Diet Library (Kokuritsu Kokkai Toshokan), theoretically, owns one copy of each book published in Japan since the Meiji period, the National Diet Library's catalogs are considered to be national bibliographies, consisting of the *Kokuritsu Kokkai Toshokan shozō Meijiki kankō tosho mokuroku* 国立国会図書館所蔵明治期刊行図書目録 and the *Kokuritsu Kokkai Toshokan zōsho mokuroku* 国立国会図書館蔵書目録, which cover the Meiji period, and the Taishō, Shōwa, and Heisei periods, respectively. The records of books processed since 1948 are accessible from the homepage of the National Diet Library (www.ndl.go.jp).

The NII's (National Institute of Informatics, or Kokuritsu Jōhōgaku Kenkyūjo, formerly NACSIS) Webcat is a national union catalog of books and journals held by many colleges and universities in Japan, and can be accessed free of charge at the Institute's homepage (www.nii.ac.jp). EUREKA and WorldCat are online catalogs of books and serials (journals, magazines, and annuals), which are held in colleges and universities, and other institutions mostly in North America. Along with the following BAS (*Bibliography of Asian Studies*), your library is very likely to have a subscription to these online databases. Waseda University Scholarly Information Network (WINE) is available through the Waseda University's homepage (www.waseda.ac.jp) and has links to other libraries' online catalogs as well. *Nihon shoseki sōmokuroku* 日本書籍総目録, Japanese version of *Books in Print*, is a CD-ROM supplement to *Shuppan nenkan* 出版年鑑, an annual publication that is also available online. Its online site is the most extensive free site that lists books currently available as new books for sale, but it does not sell books directly.

For a bibliography of Western language books and journal articles, *Bibliography of Asian Studies (BAS)* is the most extensive source of information. It contains close to half a million records on all subjects pertaining to Asia published worldwide from 1971 to the present. Until 1991, BAS included individual monographs, but since 1992, newly published monographs are no longer added to the database.

There are numerous bibliographies on various subjects, small and large, so make sure to look for one in your subject area. Subject bibliographies are much more detailed and focused than general bibliographies. They can also include materials which can be easily missed by general bibliographies such as parts of books, journal articles, and papers presented at conferences. Subject bibliographies can be comprehensive or selective, and evaluative. General bibliographies are useful for bibliographic search when no subject bibliographies are available, for supplementing the outdated subject bibliographies, or for searching interdisciplinary topics you are not familiar with.

For bibliographies on the history of religions in Japan, see *Nihon shūkyōshi kenkyū bunken mokuroku* 日本宗教史研究文献目録 and *Nihon shūkyōshi kenkyū nyūmon* 日本宗教史研究入門. The latter, which uses *Nihon shūkyōshi kenkyū nenpō* 日本宗教史研究年報 as its main source, covers from 1945 to 1970, and includes both books and journal articles. *Bibliography on Buddhism, A Bibliography on Japanese Buddhism, Books on Buddhism, and Zen Buddhism* for Buddhism, *Shinto-Bibliography in Western Languages* for Shinto, *A Bibliography of Christianity in Japan, Christianity in Japan,* and *Kirishitan Bunko* for Christianity, and *The New Religions of Japan* are the standard English-language bibliographies on religions in Japan. For books written in Japanese, *Bussho kaisetsu daijiten* 仏書解説大辞

典 is an annotated bibliography of Buddhist literature covering works from earliest times to 1965. It is useful to identify readings of titles. *Nihon Bukkyō tenseki daijiten* 日本仏教典籍大辞典 is a more recent publication and an annotated bibliography of the basic Buddhist literature published before 1867. Many annotations not in *Bussho kaisetsu daijiten* are included in this work. For books on Shinto, consult *Shintō shoseki mokuroku* 神道書籍目録, *Shintō bunrui sōmokuroku* 神道分類総目録, and *Meiji Taishō Shōwa Shintō shoseki mokuroku* 明治大正昭和神道書籍目録. For works on Christianity in Japan, see *Nihon Kirisutokyō kankei bunken shūsei* 日本キリスト教関係文献集成, which is also available online. For early Christianity in Japan, *Kinsei Nihon taigai kankei bunken mokuroku* 近世日本対外関係文献目録 includes an extensive bibliography on *Kirishitan*. For new religions in Japan in English language, use *The New Religions of Japan, A Bibliography of Western-language Materials,* and *Bibliography of Japanese New Religions, with Annotations and an Introduction to Japanese New Religions at Home and Abroad.*

LOCATING INDIVIDUAL WORKS

Locating works which are included in collections or monographic series is not always clear nor easy. For locating classical works, use: *Zenshū sōsho saimoku sōran: Koten hen* 全集叢書細目総覧——古典編 and *Nihon sōsho sakuin* 日本叢書索引. For more recent publications, *Zenshū sōsho sōmokuroku* 全集叢書総目録 should be used. *Zenshū sōsho sōran* 全集叢書総覧 is a title index to collected works published between 1868 and 1981. For modern literature, *Gendai Nihon bungaku sōran shirīzu* 現代日本文学総覧シリーズ has greatly eased the task of locating individual works. *Kojin chosakushū naiyō sōran* 個人著作集内容総覧 was compiled as a sequel to the above series, and it is an index to individual works included in collected works, except those in literature, of individual authors published between 1945 and 1996. *Jinbun shakai zenshū kōza naiyō sōran* 人文社会全集講座内容総覧 is also a sequel to *Gendai Nihon bungaku sōran shirīzu.* It lists contents of monographic series other than literature, and includes books in the humanities and social sciences published between 1945 and 2001. Starting with the 1995–1999 edition, subject coverage was widened to cover all subject areas and part of the title was dropped, making its new title *Zenshū kōza naiyō sōran* 全集講座内容総覧. *Ronbunshū naiyō saimoku sōran* 論文集内容細目総覧 includes commemorative publications (Festschrift), symposium and collected papers of lectures, and so forth, published since 1945.

For works on Buddhism, *Nihon Bukkyō zenshū sōsho shiryō sōran* 日本仏教全集叢書資料総覧 includes the table of contents of approximately 400 collected works published between 1868 and 1985, so it is useful to ascertain where a particular work is reprinted. *Bukkyō sōsho (shichishu) sōsakuin* 仏教叢書 (七種) 総索引 is an author-and-title index to the seven most important Buddhist classical collections, including *Dai Nihon Bukkyō zensho* 大日本仏教全書, *Taishō shinshū daizōkyō* 大正新脩大蔵経, and *Nihon daizōkyō* 日本大蔵経. It also includes the table of contents of each collection. *Daizōkyō zenkaisetsu daijiten* 大蔵経全解説大事典 is an annotated dictionary of close to 3,000 books in *Taishō shinshū daizōkyō* arranged in the order found in the *Daizōkyō*, but includes a title index in *gojūon* order.

For Shinto, *Shintō taikei sōmokuroku* 神道大系総目録 of *Shintō taikei* lists tables of contents so it can be used as an index, although there is no easy way to locate individual works. Before looking up the titles, you have to know the correct reading of titles. The *Kokusho yomikata jiten* 国書読み方辞典 gives readings of titles that appear in the *Kokusho sōmokuroku,* using the stroke count of the first character of the title.

SEARCHING FOR JOURNAL ARTICLES (PERIODICAL INDEXES)

Journal articles are more current than books and are an essential part of research materials. *Zasshi kiji sakuin* 雑誌記事索引, the only comprehensive index to scholarly journals in Japanese, has been compiled by the National Diet Library since 1948, and it is essential for a journal article search. It is available free of charge through the Internet from their homepage. MAGAZINEPLUS, an online periodical index offered by Nichigai Associates, indexes over 8,500 journals including general magazines and academic journals in all subject areas from around 1980, depending on when each of the journals started and/or began being indexed in each of the original databases. For articles in Western-language journals, use the *Bibliography of Asian Studies*, or BAS database.

For journal articles in older journals, *Tōkyō Daigaku Hōgakubu fuzoku Meiji Shinbun Zasshi Bunko shozō zasshi mokuji sōran* 東京大学法学部付属明治新聞雑誌文庫所蔵雑誌目次総覧 is a collection of tables of contents of the journals the library owns. *Meiji Taishō Shōwa zenki zasshi kiji sakuin shūsei* 明治大正昭和前期雑誌記事索引集成 consists of *Jinbun kagaku hen* 人文科学編, *Shakai kagaku hen* 社会科学編, and *Senmon shoshi hen* 専門書誌編 and it is a reprint collection of indexes of various Japanese journals published between 1868 and 1948. This, like the above, fills the gap of journal indexes in Japan since the Meiji period to the time *Zasshi kiji sakuin* started its coverage from 1948, and later, online databases such as MAGAZINEPLUS.

Kōseisha gives free access to its online journal index database of Meiji *Taishō Shōwa zenki zasshi kiji sakuin shūsei*. It bridges the gap between NDL's *Zasshi kiji sakuin* and Ōya Sōichi Bunko's index, and it covers journal articles from the Meiji, Taishō, and early Shōwa periods. *Ōya Sōichi Bunko zasshi kiji sakuin sōmokuroku* 大宅壮一文庫雑誌記事索引総目録 is a periodical index of popular magazines collected by Ōya Sōichi. It includes more popular magazines than *Zasshi kiji sakuin* and is also available in CD-ROM format and through the Internet, making it easy to find materials published since 1988.

For English-language materials in religion, use ATLA *Religion Database*. It indexes more than 450 journals and multi-author works on religion and theology. *Bibliography of Asian Studies* (BAS) is another bibliography to books and an index to journal articles and published materials on Asian Studies in Western languages published since 1971. Prior to 1970, BAS was in paper format. As mentioned above, books published since 1992 are no longer included in BAS.

For Buddhism, *Buddhism: A Subject Index to Periodical Articles in English, Bukkyōgaku kankei zasshi bunken sōran* 仏教学関係雑誌文献総覧 and *Bukkyōgaku kankei zasshi ronbun bunrui mokuroku* 仏教学関係雑誌論文分類目録 are the standard subject bibliographies for journal articles.

For Christianity, *A Bibliography of Christianity in Japan,* and for Shinto, *Shintō ronbun sōmokuroku* 神道論文総目録 and *Zoku Shintō ronbun sōmokuroku* 続神道論文総目録 are to be used for journal articles.

NEWSPAPER INDEXES

Asahi shinbun kiji sōran 朝日新聞記事総覧 is a reprint of the table of contents printed in the reduced-size *Asahi shinbun*. Since copyrighted articles are not on CD-ASAX (*Sengo 50-nen Asahi shinbun midashi dētabēsu* 戦後50年朝日新聞見出しデータベース), CD-ROM version, it is a sure way to find what you are looking for, although it may take more time to use. *Mainichi shinbun* also has a CD-ROM version, as does *Yomiuri shinbun*. The latter covers the Meiji period through Shōwa 35 (1874–1960) and is sold as *Meiji no Yomiuri shinbun* 明治の読売新聞, *Taishō no Yomiuri shinbun* 大正の読売新聞, and *Shōwa no Yomiuri shinbun* 昭和の読売新聞.

Nikkei Telecom 21 provides access to the full text of the four daily newspapers published by the Nihon Keizai Shinbunsha and many other newspapers of various regions of Japan including *Asahi shinbun* 朝日新聞, as well as economic, corporate, and market information.

Meiji nyūsu jiten 明治ニュース事典, *Taishō nyūsu jiten* 大正ニュース事典, and *Shōwa nyūsu jiten* 昭和ニュース事典 are handy reference books to find news items.

INFORMATION ON PEOPLE

Bibliographies on People

Nihon jinbutsu bunken mokuroku 日本人物文献目録 is a biographical bibliography of books and journal articles covering from 1868 to 1966. *Nenkan jinbutsu bunken mokuroku* 年刊人物文献目録 was a biennial publication including journal articles. After the 1994 edition, it has been published as *Jinbutsu bunken mokuroku* 人物文献目録 *1995–2001*. There is a gap between *Nihon jinbutsu bunken mokuroku* and *Nenkan jinbutsu bunken mokuroku* (between 1967 and 1979). To supplement the gap of the above two titles, you have to use *Jinbutsu shoshi sakuin* 人物書誌索引, though this is much less complete. *Denki hyōden zenjōhō* 伝記評伝全情報 covers books published since 1945, so this is convenient if you are only looking for a biography in book format. *Jinbutsu kenkyū, denki hyōden tosho mokuroku* 人物研究・伝記評伝図書目録 covers books published since the Meiji period to 2000. It is divided into *Nihonjin Tōyōjin hen* 日本人東洋人編 and *Seiyōjin hen* 西洋人編, and the second set has the title *Zoku jinbutsu kenkyū, denki hyōden tosho mokuroku* 続人物研究・伝記評伝図書目録. This includes not only biographies, but diaries, study of the person's works, Festschrifts, bibliographies, photos, and so forth. *Shintō jinbutsu kenkyū bunken mokuroku* 神道人物研究文献目録 is a bio-bibliography on people related to Shinto.

Readings and Writings

Reading Japanese personal and place names correctly is a difficult and often frustrating task. *Japanese Names* is convenient for native speakers of English and includes family and given names, pseudonyms, and geographical names. For the specific reading of a name of an author of a book, consult *Kokuritsu Kokkai Toshokan choshamei tenkyoroku* 国立国会図書館著者名典拠録, and *Nihon choshamei jinmei tenkyoroku* 日本著者名人名典拠録. For checking the correct readings of historical names, *Kokusho jinmei jiten* 国書人名辞典, *Nihonshi jinmei yomikata jiten* 日本史人名よみかた辞典, and *Rekishi jinmei yomikata jiten* 歴史人名よみかた辞典 are useful for checking the correct readings of historical names. *Nihon seimei yomifuri jiten* 日本姓名よみふり辞典, *Nihon myōji daijiten* 日本苗字大辞典, and *Jinmei yomikata jiten* 人名よみかた辞典 can be used to find the readings and writings of personal names. *Nihon shinmei jiten* 日本神名辞典 for Shinto kami is arranged by reading followed by Chinese characters, but does not include a stroke-count index for Chinese characters.

Who's Who

Jinji kōshinroku 人事興信録 corresponds to *Who's Who* and is a standard work. *Nihon shinshiroku* 日本紳士録 is a similar work. *Gendai Nihon jinmeiroku* 現代日本人名録 includes Japanese people who are currently active, many of whom would not be found in the two standard *Who's Who* above. *Shintei gendai Nihon josei jinmeiroku* 新訂現代日本女性人名録 is good for finding information on women, since the standard works still tend not to include many women. *Bunkajin meiroku* 文化人名録 (*Chosakuken daichō* 著作権台帳) is a directory of copyright holders, but it can be used to verify readings of names of people who had written books. To find out who is doing what research, check READ's *Kenkyū kaihatsu shien sōgō direkutori* 研究開発支援総合ディレクトリ, which replaces NACSIS's *Kenkyūsha kenkyū kadai sōran* 研究者・研究課題総覧. Check the names of researchers in your field in NII's NACSIS-DIRR, *Kenkyūsha katsudō shigen direkutori* 研究者活動資源ディレクトリ, as well. *Shokuinroku* 職員録 is a directory of government officials. Incidentally, there is a type of reference work, which is a kind of "Who was Who," called *Bukkosha jinmei jiten* 物故者人名辞典. *Zenkoku daigaku shokuinroku* 全国大学職員録 lists names of faculty and staff of colleges and universities as well as basic information on the schools.

Directories

Nihon shinmei jiten 日本神名辞典 is a directory of Shinto kami and the enshrined people. *Shinshūkyō kyōdan, jinbutsu jiten* 新宗教教団・人物事典 is a directory and a biographical dictionary of new religions in Japan. *Kirisutokyō nenkan* キリスト教年鑑 is primarily a directory.

Biographical Dictionaries

Nihon jinmei daijiten 日本人名大事典 is the standard biographical dictionary in Japan. The earlier edition had the title *Dai jinmei jiten*. It was originally published in the 1930s and later only the Gendai section was updated to cover up to 1978. *Shinchō Nihon jinmei jiten* 新潮日本人名辞典 is a handy desktop dictionary and includes 18,000 names from ancient times to 1990, including names in mythology, fictional characters, and important foreigners who lived in Japan, as well as Japanese, in one volume. *Kōdansha Nihon jinmei daijiten* 講談社日本人名大事典, another one-volume dictionary, includes 65,000 names of people from pre-history to the end of the twentieth century, including foreigners, of all fields including mythological names and fictional characters, although the individual entries are very brief. It can also be used as a *Who's Who*. *Nihon kingendai jinmei jiten* 日本近現代人名辞典 covers 4,500 people who were active in politics, economics, foreign relations, science, and culture from 1853 and who died by 1999 (most of the people were selected from *Kokushi daijiten*); it also includes foreigners who had some relationship with Japan. *Asahi Nihon rekishi jinbutsu jiten* 朝日日本歴史人物辞典 includes 11,300 names of people who appeared in Japanese history from the ancient times to the Taishō period. Non-Japanese who contributed in Japanese history also have entries.

Namae kara hiku jinmei jiten 名前から引く人名辞典 is a first-name dictionary of Japanese from ancient times to the present who are often remembered by their given names, pseudonyms, etc. *Gō betsumei jiten* 号別名辞典 is a dictionary of pseudonyms, posthumous names, stage names, and so forth, of Japanese, with brief biographical information. *Iwanami Seiyō jinmei jiten* 岩波西洋人名辞典 includes many Westerners who resided or played active roles in the history of Japan. This is a good source of information for biographical information on missionaries or foreign teachers in Japan (*Oyatoi*), as is *Rai-Nichi Seiyō jinmei jiten* 来日西洋人名事典. *Nihon josei jinmei jiten* 日本女性人名辞典 contains profiles of 7,000 Japanese women in various fields who were deceased by 1993. For Buddhism, *Nihon Bukkyō jinmei jiten* 日本仏教人名辞典 covers not only people in the field of Buddhism, but also people in the fields of politics, literature, arts, philosophy, and so forth, who are related to Buddhism in Japan, including Chinese and Koreans. *Nihon Kirisutokyō rekishi daijiten: Jinmei hen* 日本キリスト教歴史大事典——人名編 is for people related to Christianity.

Personal Name Index

Jinbutsu refarensu jiten 人物レファレンス辞典 is useful when you are looking for biographical data. It is an extensive index to biographical information from ancient times to the present and supplies information on where you can find biographical data. It also provides brief biographical information, such as the reading of the name, dates, occupation, and birth place, and often eliminates the need to search further. Information is collected from many subject biographical dictionaries as well as standard biographical dictionaries.

Genealogies

Seishi kakei daijiten 姓氏家系大辞典 is an etymological dictionary of Japanese surnames collected from pre-1868 books, documents, and records. It explains the origins and distributions of the surnames listed. For specific prominent aristocratic families before the Meiji period, check *Sonpi bunmyaku* 尊卑分脈 (in *Shintei kokushi taikei* 新訂国史大系, which covers up to the beginning of the Muromachi period), *Gunsho keizubushū* 群書系図部集 (in *Gunsho ruijū* 群書類従 and *Zoku gunsho ruijū* 続群書類従), or *Kansei chōshū shokafu* 寛政重修諸家譜. *Nihon keifu sōran* 日本系譜総覧 is a collection of various Japanese genealogical tables, and *Keizu bunken shiryō sōran* 系図文献資料総覧 is an extensive handbook of genealogical studies.

INFORMATION ON PLACES

Kadokawa Nihon chimei daijiten 角川日本地名大辞典 is an encyclopedia of geographical names. Each volume is devoted to one prefecture and is further divided into an introduction, geographical names, gazetteers, and sources. One of the supplements to this encyclopedia is *Nihon chimei sōran* 日本地名総覧, which lists place names that appear in the main volumes. Particular attention is given to the ancient and medieval period, with historical and literary names listed in *gojūon* 五十音順 order. *Nihon rekishi chimei taikei* 日本歴史地名大系 is a similar work, but this is more convenient for checking old place names, ruins, and so forth, and each volume has an index. *Kodai chimei daijiten* 古代地名大辞典 is based on *Kadokawa Nihon chimei daijiten* and covers historical place names that appeared in sources which came into existence by 1185. *Gendai Nihon chimei yomi-kata daijiten* 現代日本地名よみかた大辞典 is a dictionary of how to pronounce and locate 310,000 place names. *Zenkoku Chimei ekimei yomikata jiten* 全国地名駅名よみかた辞典 is a spin-off of this dictionary. *Shin Nihon bunken chizu* 新日本分県地図 contains for each prefecture a detailed map, with pronunciation of geographical names to the level of *aza* 字 with various indexes for geographical names. *Nihon bunken chizu chimei sōran* 日本分県地図地名総覧 is a similar work. *Jinja jiinmei yomikata jiten* 神社寺院名よみかた辞典 gives readings for 24,000 shrines and temples arranged by stroke count of the first character.

CALENDARS AND CHRONOLOGIES

Nenpyō Nihon rekishi 年表日本歴史 gives a chronology from the birth of the islands of Japan to the Shōwa period. Each volume has a discussion of the period followed by chronological tables and various lists and an index. *Nihon shi sōgō nenpyō* 日本史総合年表 covers events from early times to 2000. *Nihon shi nenpyō* 日本史年表 compiled by Rekishigaku Kenkyūkai 歴史学研究会 is a handy chronological table with frequent revisions and a good index. *Nihon shi bunrui nenpyō* 日本史分類年表 is a chronological table separately arranged by topics, useful for quick reference and to grasp the trends and to see related matters and events. *Nihon bunka sōgō nenpyō* 日本文化総合年表 covers events that are important in the cultural history of Japan, with an extensive general index. For the modern history of Japan, use *Kindai Nihon sōgō nenpyō* 近代日本総合年表. *Bukkyō nenpyō* 仏教年表 is one example of a subject chronology. It covers from 383 BCE to 1984 for Japan, India, China, Korea, and Tibet. *Nihon Bukkyōshi nenpyō* 日本仏教史年表 in *Ronshū Nihon Bukkyōshi* 論集日本仏教史 is a small work, but coverage is longer. *Nihon Kirisutokyōshi nenpyō* 日本キリスト教史年表, the supplement of *Nihon Kirisutokyō rekishi daijiten*, is for Christianity. For the history of Japanese religions, use *Nihon shūkyōshi nenpyō* 日本宗教史年表.

For conversion of dates from traditional Japanese dates to Western calendar, use *Nihon in'yō rekijitsu taishōhyō* 日本陰陽暦日対照表. This work converts dates from 445 to 1872, the longest coverage. For quick conversion of Western years and Japanese *nengō*, you can use any *Nihonshi nenpyō* mentioned above.

DICTIONARIES AND ENCYCLOPEDIAS

Nihon kokugo daijiten 日本国語大辞典 is the most extensive and authoritative Japanese language dictionary, equivalent to the OED for the English language. There are many excellent Japanese language dictionaries of various sizes. *Dai Kan-Wa jiten* 大漢和 辞典 is the most authoritative Chinese character dictionary, which includes over 50,000 parent characters. *Hokan* 補巻, a supplement, was published in the year 2000 long after the death of the original compiler, Morohashi Tetsuji. For archaic Japanese words, use *Kado-kawa kogo daijiten* 角川古語大辞典 which is the most extensive and authoritative. *Iwanami kogo jiten* 岩波古語辞典 is an excellent pocket-size dictionary of archaic words. *Kōsetsu Bukkyōgo daijiten* 広説仏教語大辞典 is an extensive Buddhism-related word dictionary. Although in *gojūon* order, it has a stroke-count index, so the reading can be checked using that index. It also includes Tibetan, Pali, and Sanskrit. *Zusetsu Bukkyōgo daijiten* 図説仏 教語大辞典 uses illustrations to explain entries and supplements the above title. *Bukkyōgo yomikata jiten* 仏教語読み方辞典 is arranged in *gojūon* order, but also has a total stroke-count index. For Buddhist arts, *Bukkyō bijutsu jiten* 仏教美術辞典 is an excellent, extensive dictionary.

For subject dictionaries on religions in Japan, see *Nihon shūkyō jiten* 日本宗教辞典 for general information, and *Shinshūkyō jiten* 新宗教事典 for new religions. For Buddhism, there are many dictionaries based on excellent scholarship in Japanese. *Mochizuki Bukkyō daijiten* 望月佛教大辞典, *Sōgō Bukkyō daijiten* 総合佛教大辞典, and *Nihon Bukkyōshi jiten* 日本仏教史事典 are a few examples. One example of a dictionary on a specific new religion is *Tenrikyō jiten* 天理教事典. In English, *Japanese-English Buddhist Dictionary (Nichi-Ei Bukkyō jiten* 日英仏教辞典), *A Glossary of Zen Terms*, and *The Japanese-English Zen Buddhist Dictionary (Nichi-Ei Zengo jiten* 日英禅語辞典) are for Buddhism. For Shinto, *Basic Terms of Shinto* and *A Popular Dictionary of Shinto* are in English, and *Shintō daijiten* 神 道大辞典, *Shintō jiten* 神道事典, and *Shintōshi daijiten* 神道史大辞典 are in Japanese. There are various dictionaries which deal with the ethnological aspect of religions in Japan such as *Nihon minzoku shūkyō jiten* 日本民俗宗教辞典, *Nihon no shinbutsu no jiten* 日本の神仏 の辞典, and *Bukkyō bunka jiten* 仏教文化辞典. *Nihon no shinbutsu no jiten* is a dictionary of gods and related objects of worship in Japanese religions including Shinto, Buddhism, folk religions, and new religions. *Nihon Kirisutokyō rekishi daijiten* 日本キリスト教歴史大 事典 is for the history of Christianity in Japan.

As for encyclopedias, *Kodansha Encyclopedia of Japan* was completely revised into a compact two volumes: *Japan: An Illustrated Encyclopedia* with 4,000 all-color illustrations and various new features. *Sekai daihyakka jiten* 世界大百科事典 is a standard encyclopedia in Japanese, and *Nihon daihyakka zensho* 日本大百科全書 is another one. *Koji ruien* 古事類 苑 is the last of the traditional Chinese-style encyclopedias. First published between 1896 and 1914, it is a collection of primary source materials and quotations selected from books published before 1868 to preserve traditional Japanese culture with extensive indexes for ease of use. Some of the titles listed in the dictionary section are subject encyclopedias, such as *Mochizuki Bukkyō daijiten*. *Kokushi daijiten* 国史大辞典 is an important encyclo-pedic dictionary on Japanese history including many religion-related entries. For topics related to the history of religion in Japan, such as Kirishitan, *Kokushi daijiten* includes extensive information.

ACQUIRING MATERIALS FOUND THROUGH BIBLIOGRAPHIC SEARCHES

By now you should have a bibliography of the subject matter you are interested in. The next step is to find out where the materials are held. If your library does not own the items you need, you can use online databases such as EUREKA and WorldCat, which your university's library most likely subscribes to. You need to determine whether the item you are looking for is a book, a journal article, or a part of a book, since it affects your strategy for locating the actual item. If it is a book, check the title in your library's online catalog. If your library still uses a card catalog, you might have to use that, too. Attend your library's user-orientation sessions (called BI or bibliographic instruction, as well), or talk to your librarian. If it is a journal article, there is most likely no way you can find it by its author or the title of the article in your library's online catalog, which normally includes books only. Some novices make this mistake, although it seems obvious. You have to look it up under the title of the journal and its holding. If it is a part of a book, look under the title of the book. How much work you need to do yourself depends on how much help you can get from your librarian. You might have to find out for yourself which library owns the item using a national online catalog such as EUREKA and WorldCat. If you want to check individual library's holdings, the homepage of the Council on East Asian Libraries (CEAL) is a convenient place to visit. CEAL is an association to which all the East Asian libraries in North America and beyond belong. CEAL's homepage has links to individual libraries, so by going there, you can visit many Japanese collections in North America.

When you have all the necessary information, request an interlibrary loan. Many libraries now use an international interlibrary loan service. If your library is one of them, that would be handled by the librarian. The National Diet Library will accept requests from overseas and even forward the request to another library, which holds the book/journal if they don't have the item. *Kokuritsu Kokkai Toshokan shozō kokunai chikuji kankōbutsu mokuroku* 国立国会図書館所蔵国内逐次刊行物目録, *Gakujutsu zasshi sōgō mokuroku Wabun hen* 学術雑誌総合目録和文編, and NII's databases are to be consulted for journal holdings in Japan, and *National Union List of Current Japanese Serials in East Asian Libraries in North America* in North America. For holdings of each journal, you should check each library's website.

OTHER RELEVANT REFERENCE WORKS

When you are looking for statistical information, use *Nihon tōkei nenkan* 日本統計年鑑 for general statistics. This lists the source of information, so you can go back to the source for more detailed information. If you are looking for more specific statistics, check *Tōkei jōhō indekkusu* 統計情報インデックス. *Shūkyō nenkan* 宗教年鑑 lists statistics for religions in Japan and *Kirisutokyō nenkan* キリスト教年鑑 is basically a directory of groups, organizations, churches, and people, although it also has chronological description of events for the period covered. For a directory of temples and shrines, use *Jiin taikan* 寺院大鑑 and *Jinja meikan* 神社名鑑. *Nihon meisatsu daijiten* 日本名刹大事典 is a directory of famous temples.

USING JAPANESE LIBRARIES

There are over 500 college and university libraries in Japan in addition to Kokuritsu Kokkai Toshokan (The National Diet Library), the national library, municipal libraries, and numerous public and private libraries. In general, Japanese libraries are not very easy to access and still tend to be closed to outsiders. Unless you are going to be affiliated with a Japanese university, write to or access the homepage of the libraries, archives, and special collections you would like to have access to before you leave for Japan. Know what your library has in your area, and read, copy, and make a list of what will be essential to your research before you leave, so that you can make the best use of your limited time and energy in Japan.

In many cases, you can access your library's online catalog through the Internet. Be sure you bring the URL (Universal Resource Location) of your university. Also you will want to familiarize yourself with the organization of Japanese language reference sources such as library catalogs or holding lists of archival sources and bibliographies, just to get a sense of the Japanese organization of library materials. Also have a clear strategy for doing your research in Japan that suits your goals. You should have a fairly good idea as to which people and institutions to contact. Contact them before you leave the country. For researchers in your field, consult *Kenkyūsha kenkyū kadai sōran* 研究者研究課題総覧 in paper form, and check the READ online directory at http://read.jst.go.jp, which has replaced the paper format. Do the same for institutions and archives, particularly private collections and libraries as well as academic libraries. Many Japanese academic libraries limit access to the immediate student body, faculty, and staff, and require personal identification of users and some sort of introduction. You might have to get a letter of introduction from your university librarian. The letter of introduction should include that you are a Ph.D. student, and urging assistance in your research. Bring name cards (*meishi* 名刺) with your affiliated institution printed on them. Most Japanese libraries use the Nippon Decimal Classification System (*Nihon jisshin bunruihō* 日本十進分類法), although the National Diet Library has its own system that uses the alphabet. For a shortened list of the Nippon Decimal Classification System, see the appendix below. Common terms used around Japanese libraries are also appended. Many libraries still have closed stacks, which do not allow browsing, as opposed to open stacks where users can browse freely throughout the stacks.

Even romanization used in Japan is different from that commonly used outside of Japan, the Hepburn System. The one used in Japan is called *Kunreishiki* 訓令式. For example,

Hepburn system: sha shi   sho shu cha che chi   cho chu
Kunrei system: sya si   syo syu tya tye ti   tyo tyu

To find out which libraries, archives, and museums specialize in resources you need, check the following directories: *Zenkoku toshokan annai* 全国図書館案内, *Senmon jōhō kikan sōran* 専門情報機関総覧, and *Rekishi shiryō hozon kikan sōran* 歴史資料保存機関 総覧. All the information you would need to contact these places is included in these directories.

TRANSLATIONS

To find translations of Japanese works to Western languages, the following bibliographies are useful: *Bibliography of Translations from the Japanese into Western Languages, from the 16th Century to 1912* (for early translations of Japanese works); *Catalogue of Books on Japan Translated from the Japanese into English, 1945-1981*; *Japanese Publications in Foreign Languages, Social Sciences and Humanities, Science and Technology, Arts, Hobbies, Children's Books*; and *Japanese Social Science Works: A Bibliography of Translations, English, French, and German. Japanese Women Writers in English Translation: An Annotated Bibliography* includes translated works written by Japanese women for all subjects. The following two titles are for literature only: *Japanese Literature in European Languages: A Bibliography*, and *Japanese Literature in Foreign Languages 1945–1995*. There is a rather slow serial publication published by UNESCO called: *Index Translationum: International Bibliography of Translations*, which is now published electronically.

For translations from Western languages to Japanese, there are *Meiji Taishō Shōwa hon'yaku bungaku mokuroku* 明治大正昭和翻訳文学目録, *Zenshū gasshū shūsai honyaku tosho mokuroku* 全集合集収載翻訳図書目録, and *Honyaku tosho mokuroku* 翻訳図書目録. Although it is not a bibliography of translation, *Japan English Publications in Print* is a publishers' catalog of books written or translated into English and published in Japan. It has subject access.

SOURCES

A

Asahi Nihon rekishi jinbutsu jiten 朝日日本歴史人物辞典. Asahi Shinbunsha. Tokyo: Asahi Shin-
        bunsha, 1994.
Asahi shinbun kiji sōran 朝日新聞記事総覧. Asahi Shinbunsha 朝日新聞社. Tokyo: Nihon Tosho
        Sentā, 1985–.
ATLA *Religion Database.*

B

Basic Terms of Shinto. Kokugakuin Daigaku Nihon Bunka Kenkyūjo. Tokyo: Institute for Japa-
        nese Culture and Classics, Kokugakuin University, 1985.
A Bibliography of Christianity in Japan: Protestantism in English Sources (1859–1959). Ikado,
        Fujio, and James R. McGovern. Tokyo: Committee on Asian Cultural Studies, Interna-
        tional Christian University, 1966.
*Bibliography of Japanese New Religions, with Annotations and an Introduction to Japanese New
        Religions at Home and Abroad*. Peter B. Clarke. Richmand, UK: Japan Library, 1999.

Bibliography of Reference Works for Japanese Studies. Fukuda, Naomi. Ann Arbor, MI: Center for Japanese Studies, University of Michigan, 1979.

Bibliography of Shinto; see Meiji Taishō Shōwa Shintō shoseki mokuroku.

Bibliography of Translations from the Japanese into Western Languages, from the 16th Century to 1912. Inada, Hide Ikehara. Tokyo: Sophia University, 1971. (Monumenta Nipponica Monograph)

Bibliography on Buddhism. Hanayama, Shinsho. Tokyo: Hokuseido Press, 1961.

A Bibliography on Japanese Buddhism. Bando Shojun et al. Tokyo: Cultural Interchange Institute for Buddhists Press, 1958.

Books on Buddhism: An Annotated Subject Guide. Yoo, Yushin. Metuchen, NJ: Scarecrow Press, 1976.

Buddhism: A Subject Index to Periodical Articles in English, 1728–1971. Yoo, Yoshin. Metuchen, NJ: Scarecrow Press, 1973.

Bukkyō bijutsu jiten 仏教美術事典. Nakamura Hajime 中村 元, Kuno Takeshi 久野 健. Tokyo: Tokyo Shoseki, 2002.

Bukkyō bunka jiten 仏教文化辞典. Kanaoka Shūyū 金岡秀友 et al. Tokyo: Kōsei Shuppansha, 1989.

Bukkyō nanji daijiten 仏教難字大字典. Ariga Yōen 有賀要延. Tokyo: Kokusho Kankōkai, 1986.

Bukkyō nenpyō 仏教年表. Saitō Akitoshi 斉藤昭俊. Tokyo: Shinjinbutsu Ōraisha, 1994.

Bukkyō sōsho (shichishu) sōsakuin 仏教叢書 (七種) 総索引. Bukkyō Shiryō Kenkyūkai 仏教資料研究会. Tokyo: Meicho Fukyūkai, 1985.

Bukkyōgaku kankei zasshi bunken sōran 仏教学関係雑誌文献総覧. Kokusho Kankōkai 国書刊行会. Tokyo: Kokusho Kankōkai, 1983.

Bukkyōgaku kankei zasshi ronbun bunrui mokuroku 仏教学関係雑誌論文分類目録. Ryūkoku Daigaku Bukkyōgaku Kenkyūshitsu 龍谷大学仏教学研究室. Kyoto: Bukkyōgaku Kankei Zasshi Ronbun Bunrui Mokuroku Henshū Iinkai, 1931–1986.

Bukkyōgo yomikata jiten 仏教語読み方辞典. Ariga Yōen 有賀要延. Tokyo: Kokusho Kankōkai, 1989.

Bunkajin meiroku 文化人名録 (*Chosakuken daichō* 著作権台帳). Tokyo: Nihon Chosakuken Kyōgikai, 1951– .

Bussho kaisetsu daijiten 仏書解説大辞典. Ono Genmyō 小野玄妙. Tokyo: Daitō Shuppansha, 1974–1988.

C

Catalogue of Books on Japan Translated from the Japanese into English, 1945–1981. Japan Foundation. Tokyo: Japan Foundation, 1988.

Chosakken daichō; see Bunkajin meiroku.

Christianity in Japan: A Bibliography of Japanese and Chinese Sources. Ebisawa, Arimichi. Tokyo: Committee on Asian Cultural Studies, International Christian University, 1960–1969.

D

Dai Kan-Wa jiten 大漢和辞典. Morohashi Tetsuji 諸橋轍次. Tokyo: Taishūkan, 1986–2000.

Dai Nihon Bukkyo zensho 大日本仏教全書. Tokyo: Suzuki Gakujutsu Zaidan, 1970–1973.

Daizōkyō zenkaisetsu daijiten 大蔵経全解説大事典. Kamata Shigeo 鎌田茂雄 et al. Tokyo: Yūzankaku Shuppan, 1998.

Denki hyōden zenjōhō 伝記評伝全情報 45/89. Tokyo: Nichigai Asoshiētsu, 1991– .

E

EUREKA (online catalog of books and serials)

G

Gakujutsu zasshi sōgō mokuroku Wabun hen 学術雑誌総合目録 和文編. Gakujutsu Jōhō Sentā 学術情報センター. Tokyo: Maruzen, 1985–2001 (after 2001, check NACSIS Webcat).

Gendai Nihon bungaku sōran shirīzu 現代日本文学総覧シリーズ. Nichigai Asoshiētsu 日外アソシエーツ. Tokyo: Nichigai Asoshiētsu, 1982– .

Gendai Nihon chimei yomikata daijiten 現代日本地名よみかた大辞典. Tokyo: Nichigai Asoshiētsu, 1985.

Gendai Nihon jinmeiroku 現代日本人名録. Nichigai Asoshiētsu 日外アソシエーツ. Tokyo: Nichigai Asoshiētsu, 1990– .

(Shintei) Gendai Nihon josei jinmeiroku (新訂) 現代日本女性人名録. Tokyo: Nichigai Asoshiētsu, 2001.

A Glossary of Zen Terms. Inagaki Hisao. Kyoto: Nagata Bunshōdō, 1991.

Gō betsumei jiten 号別名辞典. Tokyo: Nichigai Asoshiētsu, 2003.

A Guide to Reference Books for Japanese Studies (*Nihon kenkyū no tame no sankō tosho* 日本研究のための参考図書). The International House of Japan Library. Tokyo: The International House of Japan Library, 1997.

Gunsho keizubushū 群書系図部集. Hanawa Hokiichi 塙保己一 and Ōta Tōshirō 太田藤四郎. Tokyo: Zoku Gunsho Ruijū Kanseikai, 1973.

Gunsho ruiju 群書類従. Hanawa Hokiichi 塙保己一. Tokyo: Goku Gunsho Kanseikai, 1928–1934.

H

Honyaku tosho mokuroku 翻訳図書目録 45/76- Nichigai Asoshiētsu 日外アソシエーツ. Tokyo: Nichigai Asoshiētsu, 1984– .

I

Index translationum: International Bibliography of Translations. Paris, France: UNESCO, 1932.

Introductory Bibliography for Japanese Studies. Tokyo: The Japan Foundation, 1974– .

Iwanami kogo jiten 岩波古語辞典. Ōno Susumu 大野 晋 et al. Tokyo: Iwanami Shoten, 1990.

Iwanami Seiyō jinmei jiten 岩波西洋人名辞典. Tokyo: Iwanami Shoten, 1981.

J

Japan: An Illustrated Encyclopedia. Kodansha. Tokyo: Kodansha, 1993.

Japan and the Japanese: A Bibliographic Guide to Reference Sources. Makino, Yasuko and Mihoko Miki. Westport, CT: Greenwood Press, 1996. (Bibliographies and indexes in Asian studies, no. 1)

Japan English Publications in Print. Tokyo: Japan Intercontinental Marketing Corp., 1985– .

Japanese-English Buddhist Dictionary (*Nichi-Ei Bukkyō jiten* 日英仏教辞典). Tokyo: Daitō Shuppansha, 1991.

The Japanese-English Zen Buddhist Dictionary (*Nichi-Ei Zengo jiten*日英禅語辞典). Yokoi, Yuho. Tokyo: Sankibo Buddhist Bookstore, 1991.

Japanese Literature in European Languages: A Bibliography. Tokyo: Japan P.E.N. Club, 1961 and its supplement.

Japanese Literature in Foreign Languages 1945–1995. Tokyo: Japan P.E.N. Club, 1997.

Japanese Names: A Comprehensive Index by Characters and Reading. O'Neill, P. G. New York: Weatherhill, 1972.

Japanese Publications in Foreign Languages, Social Sciences and Humanities, Science and Technology, Arts, Hobbies, Children's Books. Tokyo: Japan Book Publishers Association, 1990.

Japanese Social Science Works: A Bibliography of Translations, English, French, and German. Fujino, Yukio. Tokyo: International House of Japan Library, 1974.

Japanese Women Writers in English Translation: An Annotated Bibliography. Mamola, Claire Zebroski, 2 vols. New York: Garland, 1989–1992.

Jiin taikan 寺院大鑑. Jiin Taikan Kankōkai 寺院大鑑刊行会. Osaka: Kuon Shuppan, 1982–1983.

Jinbun shakai zenshū kōza naiyō sōran 人文社会全集講座内容総覧. Nichigai Asoshiētsu 日外ア ソシエーツ, Tokyo: Nichigai Asoshiētsu, 1995.

Jinbutsu bunken mokuroku 1995–2001 人物文献目録：1995–2001. Tokyo: Nichigai Asoshiētsu, 2004.

Jinbutsu kenkyū 人物研究, *Denki hyoden tosho mokuroku* 伝記評伝図書目録. Tokyo: Toshokan Ryūtsu Sentā, 1994–2001.

Jinbutsu refarensu jiten 人物レファレンス事典. Tokyo: Nichigai Asoshiētsu, 1996–2003.

Jinbutsu shoshi sakuin 人物書誌索引. Fukai Hitoshi 深井人詩, ed. Tokyo: Nichigai Asoshiētsu, 1979–2003.

Jinja jiinmei yomikata jiten 神社寺院名よみかた辞典. Nichigai Asoshiētsu 日外アソシエーツ, Tokyo: Nichigai Asoshiētsu, 1989.

Jinja meikan 神社名鑑. Jinja Honchō Chōsabu 神社本庁調査部, Tokyo: Jinja Honchō Jinja Meikan Kankōkai, 1962.

Jinji kōshinroku 人事興信録. Tokyo: Jinji Kōshinjo, 1903– .

Jinmei yomikata jiten 人名よみかた辞典. Tokyo: Nichigai Asoshiētsu, 2004.

K

Kadokawa kogo daijiten 角川古語大辞典. Nakamura Yukihiko 中村幸彦 et al. Tokyo: Kadokawa Shoten, 1982.

Kadokawa Nihon chimei daijiten 角川日本地名大辞典. Tokyo: Kadokawa Shoten, 1978–1990.

Kansei chōshū shokafu 寛政重修諸家譜. Hayashi Jutsusai 林述斎 et al. Tokyo: Zoku Gunsho Ruijū Kanseikai, 1964–1967.

Keizu bunken shiryō sōran 系図文献資料総覧. Maruyama Kōichi 丸山浩一. Tokyo: Ryokuin Shobō, 1992.

Kenkyūsha kenkyū kadai sōran 研究者・研究課題総覧. Monbushō Gakujutsu Jōhō Sentā 文部 省学術情報センター and Denki, Denshi Jōhō Gakujutsu Shinkō Zaidan 電気・電子情報学 術振興財団. Tokyo: Nihon Gakujutsu Shinkōkai, 1979– .

Kindai Nihon sōgō nenpyō 近代日本総合年表. Tokyo: Iwanami Shoten, 2001.

Kinsei Nihon taigai kankei bunken mokuroku 近世日本対外関係文献目録. Nakada Yasunao 中田易直. Tokyo: Tōsui Shobō, 1999.

Kirishitan Bunko: A Manual of Books and Documents on the Early Christian Mission in Japan with Special Reference to the Principal Libraries in Japan and More Particularly to the Collection at Sophia University, Tokyo, with an Appendix of Ancient Maps of the Far East, Especially Japan. Laures, Johannes. Tokyo: Sophia University, 1957. (Monumenta Nipponica Monographs, no. 5)

Kirisutokyō nenkan キリスト教年鑑. Tokyo: Kirisutokyō Shinbunsha キリスト教新聞社, 1948– .

Kodai chimei daijiten 古代地名大辞典. Tokyo: Kadokawa Bunka Shinkō Zaidan, 1999.

Kodansha encyclopedia of Japan; see *Japan: An Illustrated Encyclopedia*

Kōdansha Nihon jinmei dijiten 講談社日本人名大辞典. Ueda Masaaki 上田正昭 et al. Tokyo: Kōdansha, 2001.

Koji ruien 古事類苑. Jingū Shichō 神宮司庁. Tokyo: Yoshikawa Kōbunkan, 1967–1972.

Kojin chosakushū naiyō sōran 個人著作集内容総覧. Nichigai Asoshiētsu日外アソシエーツ. Tokyo: Nichigai Asoshiētsu, 1997–2002.

Kokuritsu Kokkai Toshokan choshamei tenkyoroku 国立国会図書館著者名典拠録. Kokuritsu Kokkai Toshokan 国立国会図書館. Tokyo: Kokuritsu Kokkai Toshokan, 1991. Updated by CD-ROM version.

Kokuritsu Kokkai Toshokan shozō kokunai chikuji kankōbutsu mokuroku 国立国会図書館所蔵国内逐次刊行物目録. Kokuritsu Kokkai Toshokan 国立国会図書館. Tokyo: Kokuritsu Kokkai Toshokan, 1987– .

Kokuritsu Kokkai Toshokan shozō Meijiki kankō tosho mokuroku 国立国会図書館所蔵明治期刊行図書目録. Kokuritsu Kokkai Toshokan. Tokyo: Iwanami Shoten, 1971–1976.

Kokuritsu Kokkai Toshokan zōsho mokuroku 国立国会図書館蔵書目録. Kokuritsu Kokkai Toshokan. Tokyo; Kokuritsu Kokkai Toshokan, 1948– .

Kokushi daijiten 国史大辞典. Kokushi Daijiten Henshū Iinkai 国史大辞典編集委員会. Tokyo: Yoshikawa Kōbunkan, 1979–1997.

Kokusho jinmei jiten 国書人名辞典. Ichiko Teiji 市古貞次 et al. Tokyo: Iwanami Shoten, 1993–1998.

Kokusho sōmokuroku 国書総目録. 8 vols. Tokyo: Iwanami Shoten, 1989–1991.

Kokusho yomikata jiten 国書読み方辞典. Uetsuki Hiroshi 植月博. Tokyo: Ōfū, 1996.

Kōsetsu Bukkyōgo daijiten 広説仏教語大辞典. Nakamura Hajime 中村元. Tokyo: Tōkyō Shoseki, 2001.

Kotenseki sōgō mokuroku 古典籍総合目録. Kokubungaku Kenkyū Shiryōkan 国文学研究資料館. Tokyo: Iwanami Shoten, 1990.

M

MAGAZINEPLUS. Tokyo: Nichigai Asoshiētsu, 2000– .

Meiji no Yomiuri Shinbun 明治の読売新聞. CD-ROM. Tokyo: Yomiuri Shinbunsha, 2002.

Meiji nyūsu jiten 明治ニュース事典. Meiji Nyūsu Jiten Henshū Iinkai & Mainichi Komyunikēshonzu. Tokyo: Mainichi Komyunikēshonzu, 1983–1986.

Meiji Taishō Shōwa hon'yaku bungaku mokuroku 明治大正昭和翻訳文学目録. Kokuritsu Kokkai Toshokan 国立国会図書館. Tokyo: Shunjūkai, 1959.

Meiji Taishō Shōwa Shintō shoseki mokuroku 明治大正昭和神道書籍目録. *A bibliography of Shinto*. Katō Genchi 加藤玄智. Tokyo: Meiji Jingū Shamusho, 1953.

Meiji Taishō Shōwa zenki zasshi kiji sakuin shūsei 明治大正昭和前期雑誌記事索引集成. Ishiyama Hiroshi 石山洋. Tokyo: Kōseisha, 1994– .

Mochizuki Bukkyō daijiten 望月佛教大辞典. Mochizuki Shinkō 望月信亨. Tokyo: Sekai Seiten Kankō Kyōkai, 1954–1963.

N

Namae kara hiku jinmei jiten 名前から引く人名辞典. Tokyo: Nichigai Asoshiētsu, 2002.

National Union List of Current Japanese Serials in East Asian Libraries in North America. Makino Yasuko et al. Los Angeles: Subcommittee on Japanese Materials, Committee on East Asian Libraries, Association for Asian Studies, 1992.

Nenkan jinbutsu bunken mokuroku 年刊人物文献目録. Tokyo: Nichigai Asoshiētsu, 1980–1994.

Nenpyō Nihon rekishi 年表日本歴史. Inoue Mitsusada 井上光貞 et al. Tokyo: Chikuma Shobō, 1980–1993.

The New Religions of Japan: A Bibliography of Western Language Materials. Earhart, H. Byron. Ann Arbor: Center for Japanese Studies, University of Michigan, 1983.

Nihon Bukkyō jinmei jiten 日本仏教人名辞典. Nihon Bukkyō Jinmei Jiten Hensan Iinkai 日本仏教人名辞典編纂委員会. Kyoto: Hōzōkan, 1992.

Nihon Bukkyōshi jiten 日本仏教史辞典. Imaizumi Yoshio 今泉淑夫. Tokyo: Yoshikawa Kōbunkan, 1999.

Nihon Bukkyōshi nenpyō 日本仏教史年表. Hiraoka Jōkai 平岡定海 et al. Tokyo: Yūzankaku Shuppan, 1999.

Nihon Bukkyō tenseki daijiten 日本仏教典籍大事典. Kanaoka Shūyū 金岡秀友 et al. Tokyo: Yūzankaku, 1986.

Nihon Bukkyō zenshū sōsho shiryō sōran 日本仏教全集叢書資料総覧. Oyamada Kazuo 小山田和雄 et al. Tokyo: Hon no Tomosha, 1986.

Nihon bunka sōgō nenpyō 日本文化総合年表. Ichiko Teiji 市古貞次 et al. Tokyo: Iwanami Shoten, 1990.

Nihon bunken chizu chimei sōran 日本分県地図地名総覧. Tokyo: Jinbunsha, annual.

Nihon choshamei jinmei tenkyoroku 日本著者名人名典拠録. Nichigai Asoshiētsu 日外アソシエーツ. Tokyo: Nichigai Asoshiētsu, 2002.

Nihon choshamei sōmokuroku 日本著者名総目録 27/44. Tokyo: Nichigai Asoshiētsu, 1991– .

Nihon daihyakka zensho 日本大百科全書 (*Encyclopedia Nipponica*). Tokyo: Shōgakkan, 1984–1994.

Nihon Daizōkyo 日本大蔵経. Suzuki Gakujutsu Zaidan 鈴木学術財団. Tokyo: Suzuki Gakujutsu Zaidan, 1973–1978.

Nihon in'yō rekijitsu taishōhyō 日本陰陽暦日対照表. Kakara Kōzaburō 加唐興三郎. Tokyo: Nittō ニットー, 1991–1993.

Nihon jinbutsu bunken mokuroku 日本人物文献目録. Hōsei Daigaku Bungakubu. Shigaku Kenkyūshitsu 法政大学文学部史学研究室. Tokyo: Heibonsha, 1974.

Nihon jinmei daijiten 日本人名大事典. Tokyo: Heibonsha, 1979.

Nihon josei jinmei jiten 日本女性人名辞典. Haga Noboru 芳賀登. Tokyo: Nihon Tosho Sentā, 1993.

Nihon keifu sōran 日本系譜総覧. Hioki Shoichi 日置昌一. Tokyo: Meicho Kankōkai, 1973.

Nihon kingendai jinmei jiten 日本近現代人名辞典. Usui Katsumi 臼井勝美. Tokyo: Yoshikawa Kōbunkan, 2001.

Nihon Kirisutokyō kankei bunken shūsei 日本キリスト教関係文献集成. In *Nanzan Shūkyō Bunka Kenkyūjo Kenkyūjo Shohō* 南山宗教文化研究所所報 11: 14–45, 2001; also available online at www.nanzan-u.ac.jp/SHUBUNKEN/publications/publications.htm.

Nihon Kirisutokyō rekishi daijiten 日本キリスト教歴史大事典. Nihon Kirisutokyō Rekishi Daijiten Henshu Iinkai 日本キリスト教歴史大事典編集委員会. Tokyo: Kyōbunkan, 1988.

Nihon Kirisutokyōshi nenpyō 日本キリスト教史年表. Nihon Kirisutokyō Rekishi Daijiten Henshū Iinkai 日本キリスト教歴史大事典編集委員会. Tokyo; Kyōbunkan, 1988.

Nihon kokugo daijiten 日本国語大辞典. Nihon Kokugo Daijiten Kankōkai 日本国語大辞典刊行会. Tokyo: Shōgakkan, 2000–2002.

Nihon meisatsu daijiten 日本名刹大事典. Tamamuro Fumio 圭室文雄. Tokyo: Yūzankaku, 1992.

Nihon minzoku shūkyō jiten 日本民俗宗教辞典. Ikegami Yoshimasa 池上良正 et al. Tokyo: Tōkyōdō Shuppan, 1998.

Nihon myōji daijiten 日本苗字大辞典. Niwa Motoji 丹羽基二. Tokyo: Hōbunkan, 1996.

Nihon no sankō tosho 日本の参考図書. 4th ed. Nihon Toshokan Kyōkai, Nihon no Sankō Tosho Henshū Iinkai. Tokyo: Nihon Toshokan Kyōkai, 2002.

Nihon no shinbutsu no jiten 日本の神仏の辞典. Ōshima Takehiko 大島建彦. Tokyo: Taishūkan Shoten, 2001.

Nihon rekishi chimei taikei 日本歴史地名大系. Tokyo: Heibonsha, 1979– .

Nihon rekishi jinbutsu jiten 日本歴史人物事典. Tokyo: Asashi Shinbunsha, 1994.

Nihon seimei yomifuri jiten 日本姓名よみふり辞典. Tokyo: Nichigai Asoshiētsu, 1990.

Nihon shi bunrui nenpyō 日本史分類年表. Kuwata Tadachika 桑田忠親. Tokyo: Tōkyō Shoseki, 1984.

Nihon shi jinmei yomikata jiten 日本史人名よみかた辞典. Tokyo: Nichigai Asoshiētsu, 1999.

Nihon shi nenpyō 日本史年表. Rekishigaku Kenkyūkai 歴史学研究会. Tokyo: Iwanami Shoten, 1995.

Nihon shi sōgō nenpyō 日本史総合年表. Katō Tomoyasu 加藤友康 et al. Tokyo: Yoshikawa Kōbunkan, 2001.

Nihon shinmei jiten 日本神名辞典. Tokyo: Jinja Shinpōsha, 1994.

Nihon shinshiroku 日本紳士録. Tokyo: Kōjunsha, 1889– .

Nihon shoseki sōmokuroku 日本書籍総目録. Tokyo: Shuppan Nyūsusha, 1977/78.

Nihon shūkyō jiten 日本宗教事典. Ono Yasuhiro 小野泰博 et al. Tokyo: Kōbundō, 1985.

Nihon shūkyōshi kenkyū bunken mokuroku 日本宗教史研究文献目録. Ōhama Tetsuya 大濱徹也 et al. Tokyo: Iwata Shoin, 1995–2000.

Nihon shūkyōshi kenkyū nenpō 日本宗教史研究年報. Tokyo: Kōsei Shuppansha, 1978–1986.

Nihon shūkyōshi kenkyū nyūmon 日本宗教史研究入門. Kasahara Kazuo 笠原一男. Tokyo: Hyōronsha, 1971.

Nihon shūkyōshi nenpyo 日本宗教史年表. Yamaori Tetsuo 山折哲雄, ed. Nihon Shūkyōshi Nenpyo Hensan Iinkai 日本宗教史年表編纂委員会. Tokyo: Kawade Shobō Shinsha, 2004.

Nihon sōsho sakuin 日本叢書索引. Hirose Toshi 広瀬 敏. Tokyo: Meicho Kankōkai, 1969.

Nihon tōkei nenkan 日本統計年鑑. Tokyo: Nihon Tōkei Kyōkai, 1949– .

Nijisseiki Nihon jinmei jiten 20世紀日本人名事典. Tokyo: Nichigai Asoshiētsu, 2004.

Nikkei Telecom 21 日経テレコム. Tokyo: Nihon Keizai Shinbun.

O

Ōya Sōichi Bunko zasshi kiji sakuin sōmokuroku 大宅壮一文庫雑誌記事索引総目録. Ōya Sōichi Bunko. Tokyō Ōya Sōichi Bunko, 1988– .

P

A Popular Dictionary of Shinto, tr. Brian Bocking. Richmond, UK: Curzon Press, 1996.

R

Rai-Nichi Seiyō jinmei jiten 来日西洋人名事典. Takeuchi Hiroshi 武内博. Tokyo: Nichigai Asoshiētsu, 1995.

Rekishi jinmei yomikata jiten 歴史人名よみかた辞典. Tokyo: Nichigai Asoshiētsu, 1989.

Rekishi shiryō hozon kikan sōran 歴史資料保存機関総覧. Chihōshi Kenkyū Kyōgikai 地方史研究協議会. Tokyo: Yamakawa Shuppansha, 1990.

Ronbunshū naiyō saimoku sōran 論文集内容細目総覧. Nichigai Asoshiētsu. Tokyo: Nichigai Asoshiētsu, 1993– .

S

Seishi kakei daijiten 姓氏家系大辞典. Ōta Akira 太田亮. Tokyo: Kadokawa Shoten, 1963.

Sekai daihyakka jiten 世界大百科事典. Tokyo: Heibonsha, 1988. Later edition in Web version.

Sengo 50-nen Asahi shinbun midashi dētabēsu 戦後50年朝日新聞見出しデータベース: *CD-ASAX 50 years*. Tokyo: Asahi Shinbunsha, 1995–1996.

Senmon jōhō kikan sōran 専門情報機関総覧 (*Directory of Special Libraries, Japan*). Senmon Toshokan Kyōgikai 専門図書館協議開. Tokyo: Senmon Toshokan Kyōgikai, 1969– .

Shin Nihon Bunken Chizu 新日本分県地図. Kokusai Chigaku Kyōkai. Tokyo: Kokusai Chigaku Kyōkai, 1970– .

Shinshūkyō jiten 新宗教事典. Inoue Nobutaka 井上順孝 et al. Tokyo: Kōbundō, 1990.

Shinshūkyō kyōdan jinbutsu jiten 新宗教教団人物事典. Inoue Nobutaka 井上順孝 et al. Tokyo: Kōbundō, 1996.

Shinchō Nihon jinmei jiten 新潮日本人名辞典. Shinchōsha Henshūbu 新潮社辞典編集部. Tokyo: Shinchōsha, 1991.

Shintei gendai Nihon jinmeiroku; see *Gendai Nihon jinmeiroku*.

Shintei gendai Nihon josei jinmeiroku 新訂現代日本女性人名録. Nichigai Asoshiētsu. Tokyo: Nichigai Asoshiētsu, 2001.

Shintei kokushi taikei 新訂国史大系. Kuroita Katsumi 黒板勝美. Tokyo: Yoshikawa Kōbunkan, 1964–1967.

Shinto-Bibliography in Western languages: Bibliography of Shinto and Religious Sects, Intellectual Schools and Movements Influenced by Shintoism. Schwade, Archadio. Leiden: E. J. Brill, 1986.

Shintō bunrui sōmokuroku 神道分類総目録. Saeki Ariyoshi 佐伯有義. Tokyo: Meicho Fukyūkai, 1988.

Shintō daijiten 神道大辞典. Shimonaka Yasaburō 下中弥三郎. Kyoto: Rinsen Shoten, 1986.

Shintō jinbutsu kenkyū bunken mokuroku 神道人物研究文献目録. Kokugakuin Daigaku Nihon Bunka Kenkyūjo 國學院大學日本文化研究所. Tokyo: Kōbundō, 2000.

Shintō jiten 神道事典. Kokugakuin Daigaku Nihon Bunka Kenkyūjo 國學院大學日本文化研究所. Tokyo: Kōbundō, 1994.

Shintō ronbun sōmokuroku 神道論文総目録. Kokugakuin Daigaku Nihon Bunka Kenkyūjo 國學院大學日本文化研究所. Tokyo: Meiji Jingū Shamusho, 1963 (reprinted 1988, Tokyo: Daiichi Shobō). See also *Zoku Shintō ronbun sōmokuroku*.

Shintō shoseki mokuroku 神道書籍目録 (*A Bibliography of Shinto*). Kato Genchi 加藤玄智. Tokyo: Meiji Seitoku Kinen Gakkai, 1938.

Shintō taikei 神道大系. Shintō Taikei Hensankai 神道大系編纂会. Tokyo: Shintō Taikei Hensankai, 1977– .

Shokuinroku 職員録. Tokyo: Ōkurasho Insatsukyoku, 1886– .

Shōwa no Yomiuri Shinbun 昭和の読売新聞 CD-ROM. Tokyo: Yomiuri Shinbunsha, 2002.

Shōwa nyūsu jiten 昭和ニュース事典. Shōwa Nyūsu Jiten Henshū Iinkai & Mainichi Komyunikēshonzu. Tokyo: Mainichi Komyunikēshonzu, 1990–1994.

Shūkyō nenkan 宗教年鑑. Bunkachō 文化庁. Tokyo: Gyōsei, 1955– .

Shuppan nenkan 出版年鑑. Shuppan Nyūsusha, Tokyo: Shuppan Nyūsusha, 1950.

Sōgō Bukkyō daijiten 総合佛教大辞典. Sōgō Bukkyō Daijiten Henshū Iinkai 総合佛教大辞典編集委員会. Kyoto: Hōzōkan, 1987.

Sonpi bunmyaku 尊卑分脈. In *Shintei kokushi taikei* 新訂国史大系. Tōin Kinsada 洞院公定. Tokyo: Yoshikawa Kōbunkan, 1957–1964.

A Student Guide to Japanese Sources in the Humanities. Makino, Yasuko and Masaei Saito. Ann Arbor, MI: Center for Japanese Studies, University of Michigan, 1994. (Michigan papers in Japanese Studies, no. 24)

T

Taishō no Yomiuri Shinbun 大正の読売新聞 CD-ROM. Tokyo: Yomiuri Shinbunsha, 2002.

Taishō nyūsu jiten 大正ニュース事典. Taishō Nyūsu Jiten Henshū Iinkai and Mainichi Komyunikēshonzu 大正ニュース事典編纂委員会、毎日コミュニケーションズ, eds. Tokyo: Mainichi Komyunikēshonzu, 1986–1989.

Taishō shinshū daizōkyō 大正新脩大蔵経. Takakusu Junjirō 高楠順次郎 et al. Tokyo: Taishō Issaikyō Kankōkai, 1924–1935.

Tenrikyō jiten 天理教事典. Tenri Daigaku Oyasato Kenkyūjo 天理大学おやさと研究所. Tenri: Tenrikyō Dōyūsha, 1997.

Tōkei jōhō indekkusu 統計情報インデックス. Sōmuchō. Tōkeikyoku 総務庁統計局. Tokyo: Nihon Tōkei Kyōkai, 1992.

Tōkyō Daigaku Hōgakubu Fuzoku Meiji Shinbun Zasshi Bunko shozō zasshi mokuji sōran 東京大学法学部付属明治新聞雑誌文庫所蔵雑誌目次総覧. Tōkyō Daigaku Hōgakubu Fuzoku Meiji Shinbun Zasshi Bunko 東京大学法学部付属明治新聞雑誌文庫. Tokyo: Ōzorasha, 1993–1998.

W

Web Oya-bunko. Oya Soichi Bunko. Tokyo: Oya Soichi Bunko, 2003– .

WINE (Waseda University Scholarly Information Network)
WorldCat OCLC

Z

Zasshi kiji sakuin 雑誌記事索引. Kokuritsu Kokkai Toshokan. Tokyo: Kokuritsu Kokkai Tosho-kan, 1948– .

Zasshi kiji sakuin fairu 雑誌記事索引ファイル. Kokuritsu Kokkai Toshokan. Tokyo: Nichigai Asoshiētsu.

Zen Buddhism: A Classical Bibliography of Western Language Publications Through 1909. Gardner, James. Salt Lake City: Wings of Fire Press, 1991.

Zenkoku chimei ekimei yomikata jiten 全国地名駅名よみかた辞典. Tokyo: Nichigai Asoshiētsu, 2000.

Zenkoku daigaku shokuinroku 全国大学職員録. Tokyo; Kojunsha, 1958– .

Zenkoku toshokan Annai 全国図書館案内. Shoshi Kenkyū Konwakai 書誌研究懇話会. Tokyo: San'ichi Shobo, 1990.

Zenshu gasshu shusai honyaku tosho mokuroku 全集合集収載翻訳図書目録. Tokyo: Nichigai Asoshiētsu, 1995–1996.

Zenshū kōza naiyō sōran 全集講座内容総覧. Tokyo: Nichigai Asoshiētsu, 1995–2000.

Zenshū sōsho saimoku sōran: Koten hen 全集叢書細目総覧：古典編. Kokuritsu Kokkai Toshokan 国立国会図書館. Tokyo: Kokuritsu Kokkai Toshokan, 1977–1989.

Zenshū sōsho sōmokuroku 全集叢書総目録 45/90. Tokyo: Nichigai Asoshiētsu, 1992– .

Zenshū sōsho sōran: Meiji shonen-Shōwa 56-nen 全集叢書総覧—明治初年～昭和56年. Shoshi Kenkyū Konwakai 書誌研究懇話会. Tokyo: Yagi Shoten, 1983.

Zoku Gunsho ruijū 続群書類従. Ōta Tōshiro 太田藤四郎. Tokyo: Zoku Gunsho Ruijū Kanseikai, 1928–1934.

Zoku jinbutsu kenkyu, denki hyoden tosho mokuroku; see *Jinbutsu kenkyu denki hyoden tosho mokuroku.*

Zoku Shintō ronbun sōmokuroku 続神道論文総目録. Kokugakuin Daigaku Nihon Bunka Kenkyūjo 國學院大學日本文化研究所. Tokyo: Daiichi Shobō, 1989.

Zusetsu Bukkyōgo daijiten 図説仏教語大辞典. Nakamura Hajime 中村　元. Tokyo: Tōkyō Shoseki, 1988.

APPENDIX 1. USEFUL HOMEPAGE AND OTHER ONLINE RESOURCES

Search engines

Google Nihongo . . . . http://www.google.co.jp
Yahoo! Japan . . . . http://www.yahoo.co.jp
Infoseek . . . . http://www.infoseek.co.jp
goo . . . . http://www.goo.ne.jp

Libraries, etc.

Kokuritsu Kokkai Toshokan (National Diet Library, NDL)
国立国会図書館 . . . . http://www.ndl.go.jp

National Diet Library Web-OPAC . . . . http://opac.ndl.go.jp

The Library of Congress . . . . http://www.loc.gov

The Library of Congress, Asian Reference Room. . . http://www.loc.gov/rr/asian

Council on East Asian Libraries (CEAL) . . http://www.sois.uwm.edu/jeong/ceal

Kokuritsu Jōhōgaku Kenkyūjo (National Institute of Informatics, NII. Formerly
NACSIS) 国立情報学研究所. NACSIS Webcat . . . . http://webcat.nii.ac.jp

Waseda University Scholarly Information Network (WINE)
早稲田大学学術情報検索システム . . . . http://wine.wul.waseda.ac.jp

Kokuritsu Kokubungaku Kenkyū Shiryōkan
国立国文学研究資料館 . . . . http://www.nijl.ac.jp

Tōkyō Daigaku Shiryō Hensanjo
東京大学史料編纂所 . . . . http://www.hi.u-tokyo.ac.jp

Kokusai Nihon Bunka Kenkyū Sentā (Nichibunken)
国際日本文化研究センター . . . . http://www.nichibun.ac.jp

Hōsei Daigaku Ōhara Shakai Mondai Kenkyūjo
(OISR.ORG) 法政大学大原社会問題研究所 . . . . http://oohara.mt.tama.hosei.ac.jp

Government

Shushō Kantei 首相官邸 . . . . http://www.kantei.go.jp

Tōkeikyoku Tōkei Sentā (Statistics Bureau & Statistics Center, Sōmushō)
統計局統計センター . . . . http://www.stat.go.jp

Bookstores, etc.

Kōseisha Database 皓星社 . . . . http://www.libro-koseisha.co.jp

Zasshi kiji sakuin shūsei hoka
雑誌記事索引集成他 http://www.libro-koseisha.co.jp/top01/main01.html

Amazon Japan . . . . http://www.amazon.co.jp

Books.or.jp (Japanese equivalent of Books in Print)
本書籍総目録 . . . . http://www.books.or.jp

Newspapers

Asahi Shinbun 朝日新聞 . . . . http://www.asahi.com
Mainichi Shinbun 毎日新聞 . . . . http://www.mainichi-msn.co.jp
Nikkei Net . . . . http://nikkei.co.jp

APPENDIX 2. COMMONLY USED LIBRARY TERMS

abstract   *yōyaku* / *yōshi* 要約 /要旨
annotation   *kaidai* 解題

author	*chosha* 著者
author/Title catalog	*choshamei / shomei mokuroku* 著者名・書名目録
bibliography	*shoshi* 書誌
book catalog	*sasshitai mokuroku* 冊子体目録
books /Monographs	*shoseki / tankōbon* 書籍・単行本
bulletin board	*keijiban* 掲示板
call number	*seikyū bangō, tōroku bangō* 請求番号 登録番号
catalog	*mokuroku* 目録
CD-ROM	シーディー・ロム
Chinese and Japanese books	*wakansho* 和漢書
circulation desk	*suitōdai* 出納台
closing time	*heikan jikan* 閉館時間
collection	*zōsho* 蔵書
copy machine	*fukushaki* 複写機
copyright	*chosakuken* 著作権
database	*dētabēsu* データベース
director	*toshokanchō* 図書館長
download	*daunrōdo* ダウンロード
exhibit	*tenji* 展示
hold, reserve	*yoyaku* 予約
icon	*aikon* アイコン
interlibrary loan	*toshokan sōgo taishaku seido* 図書館間相互貸借制度
Internet	*intānetto* インターネット
Japanese books	*washo* 和書
journals/periodicals	*zasshi / teiki kankōbutsu* 雑誌・定期刊行物
keyword	*kīwādo* キーワード
librarian	*toshokan'in / shisho* 図書館員 司書
library	*toshokan* 図書館
loan period	*kashidashi kikan* 貸し出し期間
menu	*menyū* メニュー
microfilm	*maikurofirumu* マイクロフィルム
modem	*modemu* モデム
mouse	*mausu* マウス
network	*nettowāku* ネットワーク
online catalog	*onrain katarogu* オンライン カタログ
opening hours	*kaikan jikan* 開館時間
private library	*shiritsu toshokan* 私立図書館
public library	*kōkyō toshokan* 公共図書館
rare books	*kichōsho / kikōsho* 貴重書 稀こう書
reading room	*etsuranshitsu* 閲覧室

reference book	*sankō tosho* 参考図書
renewal	*kigen enchō* 期限延長
reserve, hold	*yoyaku* 予約
return	*henkyaku* 返却
special library	*senmon toshokan* 専門図書館
stacks	*shoko* 書庫
subject catalog	*shudai mokuroku* 主題目録
subject heading	*kenmei hyōmoku* 件名標目
terminal	*tanmatsu* 端末
thesaurus	*shisōrasu* シソーラス
title	*shomei / daimei* 書名 題名
users	*riyōsha / raikansha* 利用者 来館者
www	*webu* ウェブ
yearbooks	*nenkan* 年鑑

APPENDIX 3. RELEVANT NIPPON DECIMAL CLASSIFICATION (NDC) SYSTEM (*NIHON JISSHIN BUNRUIHŌ*)

000	Generalia	
	030	Encyclopedia
	050	Periodicals
	070	Newspapers, Journalism
	080	Collections, Series
100	Philosophy	
	160	Religion
	170	Shintoism
	180	Buddhism
	190	Christianity
200	History	
	210	Japan
	280	Biography
300	Social Sciences	
400	Natural Science	
500	Applied Science and Technology	
600	Industry	
700	Fine Arts	
800	Language	
900	Literature	
910	Japanese Literature	

Brian O. Ruppert

Using Archives in the Study of Japanese Religions

Regardless of one's ethnicity or citizenship, the process of gaining access to and skillfully drawing upon archival materials in Japan can prove daunting. It would not be an exaggeration to say that, regardless of one's field, the social skills required prove difficult for many Japanese, let alone foreigners; at the same time, we might note that the non-Japanese researcher, because of her or his foreignness, may find that, depending on the situation and audience, s/he possesses more or less advantages than Japanese counterparts in the effort to be successful.

I would like to make it clear, from the outset, that all researchers in the study of Japanese religions must accept that the effort to successfully gather evidence in Japanese archives is a life-long project that, regardless of the focus of study, will rarely be completed in a perfectly smooth fashion. At the same time, there are a series of issues that any researcher must address to improve her chances to make the most of the opportunity to gain access to materials that may otherwise not exist in printed form. The results, when generally successful, may not necessarily reshape her understanding of her topic of study, but it will at the very least prove a useful supplement to printed sources she has gathered and offer the hope that she has exhausted materials relevant to the completion of a well-rounded analysis.

FINDING THE MANUSCRIPTS

There are a variety of ways in which one may encounter references to texts that may or may not have been reproduced in printed form. One obvious way is to read secondary sources written by Japanese scholars that contain references to manuscripts which one has not read. Another method is to conduct a search for materials on one's chosen topic, searching through a database or written list of the materials in the manuscript collection of a temple or archive. One's first assignment is to verify that there is no printed version of the text for which one is searching. The first source one must consult is *Kokusho sōmokuroku* (Comprehensive Catalogue of Japanese Sources),[1] which provides details regarding the author and date, the extant versions of the manuscript and where they are housed, as well as information concerning printed versions. The existence of a printed source, of course, does not necessarily preclude the necessity of examining the original document, but it may save the researcher a great deal of energy in the course of collecting multiple manuscripts or even in the reading of the work. Do note, however, that Japanese scholars have on occasion made serious mistakes—e.g., even in works such as *Taishō shinshū daizōkyō* and *Heian/Kamakura ibun*—in their rendering of the original manuscript into the printed text, so caution must be taken in the reading of printed sources. One may also consult "Webcat" online, which offers information on all of the university libraries which offer holdings of printed works as well as manuscripts photographically reproduced in book series. In the case of Buddhist sources, one may also draw on Ono Genmyō's *Bussho kaisetsu daijiten*, which lists and evaluates the character and date of most Buddhist works in Japan, as well as the site where the manuscript is housed.[2]

Issues of Protocol

As with virtually any social situation in which mutually unknown individuals make acquaintance in Japan, the scholar of Japanese religions must avail herself of a workable knowledge of the protocols necessary for successful interaction. It goes without saying that it is important to be dressed in formal attire, to carry a business card, to use honorific language, and to bow with respect upon approaching officials in any institution. However, there are a series of earlier as well as more subtle and formal aspects to the process of which one should be aware.

First, one should ideally attempt to be "introduced" by a scholar who is already known

1. 10 vols., Kokusho Sōmokuroku Kankōkai, ed. Tokyo: Iwanami Shoten, 1976.

2. 13 vols., Tokyo: Daitō Shuppansha, 1933–1936. The entire work has recently been reproduced (1999) in a handy one-volume format, featuring miniaturized reproductions of each page.

to the officials on hand. The effort to engage in *nemawashi* (root-digging) can be arduous and time-consuming, but it is also the most likely approach to succeed. The introducing scholar may, if she is known and respected, be a non-Japanese; for example, I gained access to a private university library collection through an informal introduction by my adviser in graduate school. Indeed, while introduction by a Japanese is presumably the shortest route to access, spoken or otherwise unspoken factional divisions between differing lineages and scholars in Japan sometimes prove impediments rather than advantages. In other words, speak to more than one scholar—at least one scholar experienced in archival research—before using any particular form of introduction. Moreover, if one hopes to obtain photographs of materials, be forewarned that while purchase of photographs is relatively simple at public institutions—albeit often requiring written permission from the temple or shrine that owns the rights to the document—gaining permission to photograph materials is often extremely difficult even for Japanese scholars at shrine or temple archives.

At the same time, depending on the institution, one may or may not have trouble gaining access even without an introduction. During the period of my dissertation research, I gained access to the materials in a major temple merely through a phone call and fax stating that I was a Ph.D. candidate. My position as a non-Japanese seems to have made the process easier in this case; moreover, I unknowingly contacted the temple during its scheduled annual period of access, which made the process all the smoother. At the same time, one cannot necessarily assume that initial access, especially that gained through informal contact, means continued access.

Requirements

One should initially familiarize oneself with the requirements of the particular institution. At minimum, one should be aware that one must always use only pencils when examining original materials, due to serious damage even slight smudges of ink can cause in aged Japanese paper. Unless one can obtain permission to purchase reproductions of the material, one should bring a pad of *genkō yōshi* or a legal pad to copy down the document as faithfully as possible, perhaps a ruler to measure its dimensions, a magnifying glass for close observation, and the so-called *Rekishi techō* (Historical Daily Notebook, Yoshikawa Kōbunkan, published annually) for lists of emperors, reign-dates, and so on. If one plans to examine a large number of documents, note cards or a laptop (with permission) may be appropriate for data entry.

It is important to be as careful as possible in the handling of the materials. We must remember not merely that we are guests but also historical actors who have a responsibility to our profession as well as to the individuals and institutions who permit us to examine dated and fragile manuscripts.[3] This is particularly true for non-Japanese scholars because an inconsiderate step may result in the future inaccessibility of the institution to foreign

---

3. For a useful overview of the basic needs of researchers in the on-site examination of historical materials, see Kodama Kōta, *Komonjo chōsa handobukku* (Tokyo: Yoshikawa Kōbunkan, 1997).

scholars. Seemingly trite matters such as the washing of hands take on real relevance in the handling of fragile paper.

Although it may seem an obvious point, one should ideally acquire some training in the reading of unpublished manuscripts prior to attempting to enter an archival collection or, via some other means, examine unpublished materials. It is of utmost necessity that one consult a *Kuzushiji kaidoku jiten* (Dictionary for Reading Cursive Characters) such as the classic *Gotaijirui* (Five-Form Character Dictionary), and Kodama's well-known work, and Hatano Yukihiko's more recent publication.[4] Hopefully, one has taken a reading course in *kanbun* or *kobun* that includes unpublished materials. In this regard, some useful materials for the reading of non-printed works include series such as Yūzankaku's *Komonjo nyūmon sōsho* (Introduction to Ancient Documents Series) and *Nihon komonjogaku kōza* (Lectures on the Study of Ancient Japanese Documents).

Other well-known overviews of or introductions to the study of documents, whether unpublished or published, include Satō Shin'ichi's *Komonjogaku nyūmon* (Introduction to the Study of Documents), perhaps the most useful work of its kind,[5] as well as more recent works such as a collection edited by Asai Junko, *Kurashi no naka no komonjo* (Documents in Daily Life; Tokyo: Yoshikawa Kōbunkan, 1992), which introduces readers to manuscripts illustrating social life in historical Japan—records concerning matters such as childbirth, children, youth, marriage, divorce, and gambling. There are, finally, also dictionaries for the study of terminology and characters used in manuscripts, such as Ikeda Shichiro's *Komonjo yōji yōgo daijiten* (Great Dictionary of Terminology and Characters used in Documents; Tokyo: Shinjinbutsu Ōraisha, 1995), as well as for the reading of irregular characters. Useful dictionaries of the latter sort include Ariga Yōen's edited volumes *Bukkyō nanji daijiten* (Great Dictionary of Difficult Buddhist Characters; Tokyo: Kokusho Kankōkai, 1986) and *Nanji/itaiji jiten* (Dictionary of Irregular/Difficult Characters; Tokyo Kokusho Kankōkai, 1997), as well as the Nanji Taiken Henshū Iinkai group's *Itaiji kaidoku jiten* (Dictionary for Reading Irregular Characters; Tokyo: Kashiwa Shobō, 1993). Ariga's works are useful for their Buddhist characters, while the last work is useful for its pronunciation index.

MAJOR SITES FOR MANUSCRIPT RESEARCH

We can begin our consideration of major sites for manuscript research by dividing up our survey into sites in or near the Tōhoku, Kantō, Tōkai, and Kansai regions. Although some of these sites include published materials and periodicals, we will con-

---

4. See Takada Chikuzan, ed., *Gotaijirui,* 3rd ed. (Tokyo: Seitō Shobō, 2001), Kodama Kōta, ed., *Kuzushiji kaidoku jiten* (Tokyo: Tōkyōdō Shuppan, 1994), and Hatano Yukihiko, supervisor, and Tōkyō Tegami-no-Kai, ed., *Kuzushiji jiten* (Kyoto: Shibunkaku, 2000).

5. See the 1997 edition (Tokyo: Hōsei Daigaku), though there are a plethora of other relevant works. See, for example, the following: Nihon Rekishi Gakkai, eds., *Gaisetsu komonjogaku* (Tokyo: Yoshikawa Kōbunkan, 1983); Yoshimura Shigeki, *Komonjogaku* (Tokyo: Tōkyō Daigaku Shuppankai, 1974); Iikura Harutake, *Komonjogaku handobukku* (Tokyo: Yoshikawa Kōbunkan, 1993); Ishii Susumu, *Chūsei o yomitoku* (Tokyo: Daigaku Shuppankai, 1990).

centrate on unpublished cursive and, to some extent, rare printed primary sources.[6] (All references made are to works published by the institution under consideration, with the exception of those in which the publisher is expressly given.)

Tōhoku

Kanō Bunko is attached to the main library of Tōhoku University in Sendai, at the northeastern tip of Honshū. The manuscript collection, established by Kanō Kōkichi (1865–1942), includes more than 108,000 volumes of materials, of which some 55,000 can be searched online, including almost 14,000 images. The collection is divided into ten sections based on area of study, of which we can note five particularly relevant for the study of religion: area 2 (philosophy, religion, education), area 3 (history, geography), area 4 (language, literature), area 5 (art, technical arts, ornamental arts), and area 6 (law, politics, economics). It includes a number of Buddhist scriptures and treatises such as a Kamakura-era copy of *Abidatsuma-kusharon* (Sk. *Abhidharma-kośa-śāstra*), as well as Muromachi-era *Hyakuhōmondō shō* and *Shōtoku taishi denryaku*. The collection also features early printed works such as a Korean edition of *Fa-yuan chü-lin*, and part of *Hua-yen ching sui-shu yen-i ch'ao* (T. 35, no. 1735), and Ch'an biographical literature. Most of the collection of Kanō Bunko from the early periods to the Edo era are recorded on microfilm in the *Kanō bunko maikurohan shūsei* (14 reels; Tokyo: Maruzen, 1992–), which almost without exception can be viewed and copied upon the granting of permission. Kanō Bunko's collection is listed in the Tōhoku University catalog of documents, *Tōhoku daigaku shozō wakansho koten bunrui mokuroku* (Tōhoku Daigaku Fuzoku Toshokan, ed., 7 vols.), which also includes works from the early periods to the Edo era. Recently, the Japanese documents on microfilm in the collection have been listed in the *Tōhoku daigaku fuzoku toshokan shozō Kanō bunko mokuroku washonobu* catalog (idem., 11 vols.; Tokyo: Maruzen, 1994).

Kantō

Kokubungaku Kenkyū Shiryōkan (National Institute of Japanese Literature), established through the cooperative effort of a group of universities in Tokyo in 1972, is a large archive for the study of Japanese literature. Given its short history, it is not surprising that the collection consists primarily of microfilm, microfiche, and photographic reprints of a variety of materials from a series of universities, local libraries, and, to some extent, religious institutions. Access to examine the materials comes easily, and copies can usually be obtained, but the process of obtaining permissions from the owner-institution is sometimes time-consuming. Before going on-site, one can inspect its homepage and conduct searches of the microfilm materials catalog and the Japanese ancient works catalog (Kokubungaku Kenkyū Shiryōkan, ed., *Kokubungaku kenkyū shiryōkanzō wakosho mokuroku*, 1982)

6. I would like to thank professors Kikuchi Hiroki and Hayashi Yuzuru of the University of Tokyo Historiographical Institute for their discussions of archives. In addition, I have especially drawn on the "Bunko meguri" series in Nihon Bukkyō Kenkyūkai, ed., *Nihon no Bukkyō*, vols. 1–6 (Kyoto: Hōzōkan, 1994–1996) and Yoshinari Isamu, ed., *Nihon rekishi "Kokiroku" sōran, gekan* (Tokyo: Shinjinbutsu Ōraisha, 1990), "Shuyō 'kokiroku' hozon kikan."

database. Perhaps most useful is the fact that many photographic reproductions can be borrowed overnight. Among the more prominent sets of materials from manuscript collections of temples are included those of the Tendai temples Saikyōji and Shinpukuji (Nagoya). Within the same compound is a separate Historical Archive (Shiryōkan), which includes roughly 500,000 historical documents from throughout Japan (*chihō monjo*) dating from the Edo era (*kinsei*); many of the materials, which may often be copied with permission, can be accessed through searching the relevant catalogs, including *Kokubungaku kenkyū shiryōkan shozō shiryō mokuroku* (74 collections; Kokubungaku Kenkyū Shiryōkan, ed., 1952–), *Kokubungaku kenkyū shiryōkan maikuro shiryō mokuroku* (Kokubungaku Kenkyū Shiryōkan Seiri-Etsuranbu, ed., 1977–2000), *Kokubungaku kenkyū shiryōkan koten seki sōgō mokuroku* (Kokusho Sōmokuroku and Kokubungaku Kenkyū Shiryōkan, eds., 3 vols., Tokyo: Iwanami Shoten, 1990), *Shiryōkan sōsho* (Kokubungaku Kenkyū Shiryōkan, ed., Tokyo: Meicho Shuppan, 1997–), and *Shiryōkan shozō ichiran* (Kokuritsu Shiryōkan, ed., Kokuritsu Shiryōkan, 1980).

Tōkyō Daigaku Shiryō Hensanjo (The University of Tokyo Historiographical Institute) constitutes the leading archive housing historical materials in Japan. Founded as an imperial holding of historical sources by imperial order, Shiryō Hensanjo came under the umbrella of the University of Tokyo in 1888, and received its present name in 1929. Charged with the task of studying, editing, and publishing historical sources of Japan, the scholars there devoted much of the early decades engaged in the painstaking process of attempting to faithfully copy original materials by hand (producing variously *eishabon* through tracing and *tōshabon* through careful copying), in addition to acquiring some other primary sources. As a result, Shiryō Hensanjo not only managed to produce additional copies to preserve that national collection of historical materials, but amassed a massive collection that totals more than 300,000 Chinese and Japanese works. Scholars can, of course, examine original materials, but they can also clarify the contents of manuscripts which may have been eaten by insects at the resident institution after the Shiryō Hensanjo staff copied them. The collection preserves a variety of genres of sources, including materials owned by Shinto shrines and Buddhist temples throughout the country; the number of temples of which documents or copies are held number almost 300, gathered from throughout Japan. Moreover, a catalog of the materials (*Tōkyō daigaku shiryō hensanjo tosho mokuroku*, part 2, *Wakanshoshahon hen*, cursive, 10 vols., Tōkyō Daigaku, 1961–1978; *Kanpon*, printed, 5 vols., Tōkyō Daigaku, 1955–1973) has been published so that scholars can investigate the titles held prior to going on-site; in fact, a relatively large percentage of the materials in the collection are accessible through the Hensanjo website, which sports a useful search function. Perhaps the most famous authentic religious work housed is the fund-raising monk Chōgen's (1121–1206) signed original manuscript of *Namu amida butsu sazen shū*; other authentic materials held include medieval aristocratic diaries, such as Sanjō Sanefusa's *Gumai ki* (early Kamakura era) and Sanjō Sanemi's *Sanemikyō ki* (late Kamakura era). The only difficulty for some might be access to the collection, because an invitation from one of the staff or professors of the Hensanjo is preferred; once access is obtained, however, one finds that the staff is very helpful, and acquisition of copies can, while comparatively expensive and time-consuming, be accomplished with little difficulty. We should also mention the Japan Memory Project (Zenkindai Nihon no Shiryō Isan Purojekuto), which the Hensanjo recently launched; one relevant part of the project is the effort to produce a glossary online of terminology and translations used in the study of premodern Japanese history, and the ongoing presence of religion scholars on the staff has ensured that the glossary, now accessible through the Hensanjo website, provides scholars throughout the world with a valuable resource for research and in the translation of specialized historical and religious terminology.

We may also make note of three collections held by branches of the Japanese government. The Kunaichō Shoryōbu of the imperial household, which holds roughly 340,000 manuscripts and numerous documents concerning the imperial and related aristocratic families (including the Kujō) as well as a superb collection of imperial and aristocratic diaries, also features religious works such as a Sung Dynasty Buddhist canon and *Greater Perfection of Wisdom Sūtra*, the two-fascicle *Hōbutsu shū*, and Kūkai's *Bunkyō hifu ron* (see *Kunaichō shoryōbu wakan tosho bunrui mokuroku*, 4 vols., 1952–1968). The Shoryōbu's famous Kyōto-Higashiyama Go-Bunko collection can potentially be examined on-site, while a large bloc of photographs of the documents are held in Tōkyō Daigaku Shiryō Hensanjo. We should also note that many of its materials concerning palace life have been published in the series *Kōshitsu seido shiryō* (Documents of the Imperial Family System; 15 vols., Tokyo: Yoshikawa Kōbunkan, 1978–2001). Kokuritsu Kokkai Toshokan (National Diet Library) features over 300,000 manuscripts, although it would seem to have few materials distinctly religious in character. To gain access to a manuscript at this library, a letter is required, outlining the day of one's visit, the catalog number of the manuscript (see Kokuritsu Kokkai Toshokan Toshobu, ed., *Kokuritsu kokkai toshokan zōsho mokuroku*, 7 vols. [esp. 1–2]; Kokuritsu Kokkai Toshokan Toshobu, ed., Kokuritsu Kokkai Toshokan, 1959–1968), and the reason why it is necessary to gain access to the special collection. A visit to its website gives further information about its collection, and reproduces one hundred of its famous holdings in its digital archives, including *Hyakumantō darani kyō*. Naikaku Bunko, while famous for its governmental documents, also possesses a large number of medieval manuscripts (see *Naikaku bunko kokusho bunrui mokuroku*, 3 vols., 1974–1976), including Kōfukuji works such as *Daijō'in jisha zōji ki* and *Daijō'in monjo*, as well as a large number of medieval aristocratic diaries.[7]

Taishō University Library (Taishō Daigaku Fuzoku Toshokan) and Komazawa University Library (Komazawa Daigaku Toshokan) represent two of the major university institutions in Tokyo that are useful for archival research. Taishō is well known for its broad collection of materials of a variety of schools of Buddhism such as the Pure Land Schools, Tendai, and Shingon. One can examine its holdings online, although an introducing letter

---

7. In addition, Sonkeikaku Bunko, while perhaps not well known among religion scholars, possesses a superb collection of medieval aristocratic diaries (see *Sonkeikaku kokusho bunrui mokuroku*, 1939). Considering the virtually ubiquitous references to religious practices in many diaries, a glance at *Kokusho sōmokuroku* would indicate if a printed version exists, whereupon a visit may or may not be in order; a letter of introduction from a Japanese scholar, however, is preferred.

from an institution or temple is necessary. Komazawa, famous for its Zen holdings, also requires an introduction.

Established in 1981, Kokuritsu Rekishi Minzoku Hakubutsukan (National Museum of Japanese History) offers a valuable collection of more than 110,000 historical, archaeological, architectural, and artistic materials, and an additional set of photographic reproductions (see Kokuritsu Rekishi Minzoku Hakubutsukan Kanzō Shiryō Iinkai, ed., *Kokuritsu rekishi minzoku hakubutsukan kanzō shiryō mokuroku*, Sakura, Japan: Kokuritsu Rekishi Minzoku Hakubutsukan Kanzō Shiryō Iinkai, 1992–). Among the famous holdings are the Nomura clothing and Akioka historical-map collections. Access to the collection is relatively easy, although a written request to examine the more valuable materials is preferred.

A treasure trove for the study of esoteric Buddhism and, to some extent, kami worship which some foreign scholars are not very aware of can be found in Kanazawa Bunko (Kanagawa Kenritsu Kanazawa Bunko), located in the suburbs of Yokohama. The comparatively easy access any scholar can gain to materials in virtually any prefectural institution in Japan is well demonstrated here. Anyone can enter by paying a small fee, and through examining the catalog on-site (although for distinct works, see Kanagawa-Kenritsu Kanazawa Bunkō, ed., *Kanagawa-kenritsu Kanazawa bunko zōsho mokuroku: shudaibetsu sankō bunken mokuroku*, 4 vols., 1970–1973; idem., *Kanazawa bunko monjo shōgyō fukugen mokuroku*, 1990; idem., *Kanazawa bunko monjo mokuroku*, 1990), acquire photographic reproductions of roughly 20,000 documents for examination. Kanazawa Bunko—originally Kanezawa Bunko—refers to what was once the archive of the Shingon temple Shōmyōji, founded by Hōjō Sanetoki in 1260, which was actually held at first in his residence next door. Scholars of medieval Shingon will find this collection particularly useful, especially insofar as the collection includes variant manuscripts of works such as the well-known *Kakuzen-shō*, and a whole host of ritual texts—even some works of medieval Ryōbu Shinto. We should also note, moreover, that a large number of the documents are included in printed collections published by Kanazawa Bunko; in particular, the ten-volume collection of printed versions of manuscripts held in Kanazawa Bunko (Kenritsu Kanazawa Bunko, ed., *Kanazawa bunko shiryō zensho*, 1974–1991) includes sections on Zen, Kegon, Tendai, Jōdo, Kairitsu, Shingon, as well as on Buddhist music-related works (various *kayō* and *shomyo* as well as *kōshiki* and *kechimyaku*, etc.) and on temple maps. Finally, the journal *Kanazawa bunko kenkyū* (1934–) regularly includes in many of its articles printed reproductions of works held in the archives.

Tōkai

A prominent collection of Buddhist works in the Tōkai region between western and eastern Japan is held by the Shingon temple Shinpukuji (also called Ōsu Kannon and Hōshōin) in Nagoya, which houses a manuscript collection (Shinpukuji Bunko) of more than 10,000 documents that until recently was unknown by many even in Japan. Originally constructed as the Jingūji for Kitanosha, the temple served also as the treasury for the offering documents (*kishinjō*) given to the shrine. Although Kuroita Katsumi of the University of Tokyo Shiryō Hensanjo compiled a list of the more valuable manuscripts in *Shinpukuji zenpon mokuroku* (1935), the list comprises only a small portion of the entire collection. The most famous manuscript is the national treasure *Kojiki* (on loan to the Nara City Museum), but the collection also houses a series of well-known Buddhist works, including *Kōbō Daishi den*, *Nihon ryōiki*, and *Zoku honchō ōjōden*, and another variant manuscript of *Kakuzen-shō*. We should also note the recent publication of the series *Shinpukuji zenpon sōkan* (Kokubungaku Kenkyū Shiryōkan, ed.; Kyoto: Rinsen Shoten, 1998–2000, 12 vols., and the ongoing publication of *Shinpukuji zenpon sōkan dai niki* [Kokubungaku Kenkyū Shiryōkan, ed.; Kyoto: Rinsen Shoten, 2004– , 12 vols.]), which include photographic reproductions of a variety of well-preserved works in the collection as well as their printed reproductions. Among the more relevant works are those that concern the medieval *Nihongi*, represent Ryōbu Shinto, and indicate the extent to which the extensive literature of so-called Kenmitsu Buddhism had infiltrated the gap between Heian-kyō (Kyoto) and Kamakura in the medieval era; others include documents and other manuscripts originally transmitted from Tōdaiji collections. Still other works in the collection can also be viewed at Kokubungaku Kenkyū Shiryōkan, which has continued its efforts at converting photographs of the materials into microfilm. One can potentially gain access to Shinpukuji Bunko, but must first make an appointment with the staff, and pay a fee.

Ise features an invaluable collection for the study of kami worship and modern Shinto at Jingū Bunko, the modern history of which dates to 1648, and which holds roughly 260,000 manuscripts. In addition to its Shinto materials, the holdings include a number of medieval and late premodern diaries (see Jingūshichō, ed. *Jingū bunko tosho mokuroku*, Ise: Jingūshichō, 1922; Jingū Bunko, *Jingū bunko zōka tosho mokuroku*, 5 vols., 1923–1992; *Jingū bunko tosho mokuroku*, Tokyo: Kyūko Shoin, 1973; and Yoshizaki Hisashi, *Jingū bunko Suika Shintō Kikke Shintō kankeisho mokuroku*, Ise: Kōgakkan Daigaku Shintō Kenkyūjo, 1981). Permission to view manuscripts or acquire photographic reproductions requires a letter be written to the head of the archive prior to the visit.

Kansai

Western Honshu also features a series of invaluable archival collections. One of the most useful collections for the study of popular religion is that held in Gangōji Bunkazai Kenkyūsho in Nara, the research institute attached to the temple Gangōji. Gangōji, the Nara-era temple which had moved from the original site (Moto-Gangōji)—the first temple in Japanese history to house a full monastic ground—has had an episodic history. Although it was virtually abandoned during the Heian era, the temple became the site for popular piety in the form of the enshrinement and veneration of the remains of the dead during the medieval era. And while it was virtually forgotten again later, it was restored between the 1940s and 1960s. The occasion was particularly auspicious, because a whole series of remains were discovered: large numbers of wooden memorial stūpas (*sotoba*), funerary five-wheel stūpas (*gorintō*), and other materials. For this reason, Gangōji is the ideal site for research into popular piety of the medieval era, offering scholars artifacts that, especially in the form of inscriptions, provide insight into the lives of medieval people outside of the monastic community, the shogunate, and the imperial court.

We should also note that Gangōji Bunkazai Kenkyūsho has published a large quantity of its materials (*Nihon Bukkyō minzoku kiso shiryō shūsei: Gangōji gokurakubō hen*, 7 vols.;

Tokyo: Chūōkōron Bijutsu, 1974–1980). The Kenkyūsho is famous for its ongoing effort to gather materials concerning the religious life of the populace during the medieval era; it also has conducted research on medieval shrines (*yashiro*) and their relationship with Buddhism (*shinbutsu shūgō*; see *Chūsei sonraku jisha no kenkyū chōsa hōkoku sho*, 1989; *Shinbutsu shūgō o tōshite mita Nihonjin no shūkyōteki sekai*, 1990; and *Shintō kanjō*, 1999). In order to make use of the collection, after contacting the Jinbun/Kōkogaku Kenkyūshitsu, one can take a letter of application (to Gangōji) to obtain entrance into the general collection of Gangōji, and a letter (to Gangōji Bunkazai Kenkyūsho) together with written permission from the original owner of the materials one requests to see. Such letters and written permission should suffice to gain access to the larger collection of materials.

Nearby, Nara Kokuritsu Hakubutsukan (Nara National Museum) features a collection of religious art materials from throughout Japanese history. Although the museum's activities were originally confined to borrowing materials from other institutions, it has collected more than a thousand pieces over the past four decades. Moreover, insofar as its activities have concentrated on Buddhist materials, especially of the Asuka to Kamakura eras, it is the only one among all the national museums to specialize in the collection and display of Buddhist art (see *Nara kokuritsu hakubutsukanzōhin zuhan mokuroku*, 4 vols., 1988–). Moreover, as a public facility, it is generally user-friendly; one can see the collection of books and photographs held in its Bukkyō Bijutsu Shiryō Kenkyū Sentā during public display on certain days of each week. The contingencies accruing to public display of the original collection make private close examination more difficult, but with the proper introductions and completion of special forms for permission to examine objects (*tokubetsu kanran*), one may be granted special access; moreover, present members of the staff are increasingly interested in improving outreach and efforts for international collaboration, so scholars of Buddhist art history are especially encouraged to approach them.[8]

Another resident Nara archive can be found in the Tōdaiji Toshokan (Tōdaiji Library), which features a series of materials held by the famous temple. Originally called Nanto Bukkyō Toshokan, the collection originally housed not only Tōdaiji manuscripts but also those lent by Kōfukuji, Tōshōdaiji, and Hōryūji in response to the anti-Buddhist campaigns of the early Meiji era. Later, the plan did not come to fruition, so during the Taishō era, it was given its current name, and correspondingly, includes primarily Tōdaiji records (*komonjo*) and other sources. The collection (see *Tōdaiji toshokan zōsho mokuroku*, 1977) is divided into four kinds of sources: documents, photographic reproductions and originals of early scriptural and other Buddhist scrolls, Edo-era Japanese-style book-form manuscripts, as well as Meiji and later Western-style books. The collection is, of course, useful for its historical documents, but it is also valuable for its works concerning the teachings of not only Kegon but virtually all of the schools of Nara Buddhism, as well as documents by illustrious Nara figures such as the Kasagidera monk Jōkei (1155–1213). To gain access to the

8. In a related vein, we can make note of the Nara Bunkazai Kenkyūsho, the work of which focuses on archaeological research of the area of the Heijō capital of the early era, and which features databases on *mokkan* tablets and excavated sites.

more valuable original materials, it is necessary to submit a letter asking for permission to the head of the archive; otherwise, one can view materials in the library on any given day.

Saidaiji temple houses materials from as early as the eighth century, although the majority of materials date from either the height of the medieval era, when the Shingon Risshū monk Eison was active, or the Edo era onward. However, if one wishes to understand the larger significance of Saidaiji in the medieval era, before visiting, one should acquaint oneself with the study by Gangōji Bunkazai Kenkyūsho, *Chūsei minshū jiin no kenkyū chōsa hōkoku sho* 1-3 (1989–1991), which analyzes the medieval branch temples of Saidaiji. For a virtually complete list of the Saidaiji manuscript collection, which includes over 3,000 *shōgyō* manuscripts and 600 documents (*monjo*), one must examine *Saidaiji tenseki komonjo mokuroku*. It is possible, albeit not certain, that one can view materials there through introduction by Japanese scholars. At the same time, one should also be aware that photographic reproductions of the Saidaiji document collection (*Saidaiji monjo*, 13 vols.) are held by University of Tokyo Shiryō Hensanjo, and that Saidaiji has been very active for the last several decades in publishing printed versions of a number of its materials.

Tenri Daigaku Fuzoku Tenri Toshokan (The Tenri Library, Tenri University), in nearby Tenri City, includes a large collection of premodern manuscripts, a number of which are Shinto (kami worship) or Buddhist. Aside from the well-known *Fudo ki*, Fujiwara no Teika's diary *Meigetsu ki*, and a number of Edo-era *jōruri* and other works, the library holds collections of the Confucian scholars' *Kogidō Bunko* and *Yoshida Bunko* of Kyoto's Yoshida shrine. The library is also noted for Chinese Buddhist works such as the eighth-century national treasure *Nan-hai-chi-kui-nei-fa-chüan* by I-ching (635–713). In order to view manuscripts directly, one must first send a request to inspect special books (*tokubetsu-bon etsuran mōshikomisho*) that details the title of the work, the time requested, and the reason to the head of the library (*kanchō*) in order to receive permission; copies of some materials are also available for purchase, the details of which can be obtained through contacting the clerk in charge (*fukusei gakari*). If you have no idea as to the materials you would like to examine, you first need to examine the catalog online. We must also note the publication of a series of volumes of photographic reproductions of manuscripts in the collection, entitled *Tenri toshokan zenpon sōsho* (Tenritoshokan Zenpon Sōsho Washonobu Henshū Iinkai, ed., Tokyo: Yagi Shoten, 1970–1986, 103 vols.), which includes a number of Buddhist and other religious works; moreover, the list of works is included on the website.

Kōyasan University Library (Kōyasan Daigaku Toshokan), while in a rural area, offers an excellent collection of manuscripts on Shingon Buddhism. This includes not only manuscripts of the Mt. Kōya *shōgyō* collection such as *Seirei shū* and genres such as *kōshiki*, *kuketsu*, and Ryōbu Shinto materials (some of which have been distributed on CD-ROM), but also a series of temple collections purchased from outside Kōya (see also *Ōyama bunko mokuroku*, 1991). Display of your identification (and, ideally, prior notification) is all that is required to gain entry, and many of the materials are open for view; however, it is difficult to gain access to valuable cultural properties, and permission to purchase reproductions, when granted, are only done so after the manuscripts are sent out to a photographer.

In Kyoto, the prefectural Kyōto Furitsu Sōgō Shiryōkan Archive is particularly useful for the study of medieval religious documents, especially those connected with the Shingon temple Tōji, and for the study of diaries of the medieval and Edo eras. For the study of medieval religious life and practice at Tōji and at the Shingon'in chapel of the larger imperial palace, the large *Tōji hyakugō monjo* (The 100 Boxes of Manuscripts of Tōji) held there is invaluable. The archive purchased the collection from Tōji, which included roughly 24,000 records in 1967, and first opened up the newly organized collection to the public in 1980. Among the rituals recorded in manuscripts in *Hyakugō monjo* are regular ceremonies such as the famous *Go-shichinichi mishiho* (Latter Seven-Day Rite), the semi-regular *Busshari kankei shiki* (Buddha relic inventory) as well as *Godan-hō* (Five Altars Rite), a series of initiation (*kanjō*) rites, and irregular rites such as rain-making, rain-stoppage, and rites to avoid or overcome climatic and physical calamity. *Hyakugō monjo* also includes some records with no direct connection to Tōji, including ones of the Tendai temple Enryakuji and the Shingon-Ritsu monk Eison (1201–1290). If possible, one might examine the five-volume catalog of the *Hyakugō monjo* prior to going to the Shiryōkan; moreover, the library has established a database concerning its most valuable collections online, which proves an invaluable resource for the researcher before her visit. In any event, once there, the Shiryōkan allows anyone access to photographic reprints of the works in the collection and, if the researcher can demonstrate that she cannot complete her study without access to the original manuscripts, she can gain permission to examine the latter on-site; otherwise, it is also possible to purchase photographic reprints of virtually all of the materials, albeit in many cases where the library holds photographs of materials held in other institutions, one can do so only after first gaining permission from them.[9]

Among the university libraries in Kyoto that hold manuscripts, Kyoto University Library (Kyōto Daigaku Fuzoku Toshokan) holds a series of famous collections, two of the most elaborate of which are *Kyōōgokokuji monjo* (~3,500 manuscripts; also published in *Dai Nihon komonjo*) and *Tōji monjo* (~700 manuscripts), both of which are Tōji document collections, and the photographic reproductions of which are also held in Kyōto Furitsu Sōgō Shiryōkan. Since 1994, Kyoto University has made the most exhaustive of efforts not only to put its catalog on its website but also to reproduce its most valuable holdings in digital archives available to the public online (e.g., the national treasure Suzuka-bon *Konjaku monogatari*, and a whole series of literary works, diaries, and other didactic literature), making a trek to the library unnecessary for many scholars, or at least supplementing their research activities there.

Ryūkoku University Library (Ryūkoku Daigaku Toshokan) is also noted not only for its collection of some 60,000 Jōdo Shinshū and other materials, but also for its extensive efforts at digital archivalization. For example, since its digital archives were first opened to the public in the mid-nineties, it has included its holdings of materials of the early twentieth-century Nishi-Honganji abbot Kōzui. Access to the library requires submission of a letter of introduction as well as the completion of a *kichō tosho etsuran kyoka gan* examination

9. Another prominent collection we should make note of is Yōmei Bunko, which has a large collection of medieval imperial and aristocratic diaries. Some photographic reproductions of materials from this collection have been published. One person is in charge of the collection, so a letter (if possible, an introduction) is necessary to view the materials.

application form at the counter; approval requires roughly a week. Another university digital archive includes that of Nara Kyōiku Daigaku, which features *Shukongōjin engi e-maki* and *Nara e-hon* (Momoyama and Edo eras).

Hanazono University International Research Institute for Zen Buddhism and Bukkyō University Library represent two more of the university libraries useful for research in Kyoto. Zenbunka Kenkyūjo features more than 33,500 volumes, including a large microfilm collection of materials of Zen temples, and is accessible to foreign researchers. Bukkyō Daigaku is also extremely user-friendly, albeit with the requirement that one have a letter of introduction for entrance.

The Tendai archive Eizan Bunko, originally the scriptural treasury (Konpon Kyōzō) founded by Saichō (766–822), is located on Mt. Hiei, northeast of Kyoto. However, the modern library, established in 1921, includes collections from fifty temple and other private collections, comprising roughly 130,000 volumes. Enryakuji recently published the catalog *Eizan bunko monjo ezu mokuroku* (Kyoto: Rinsen Shoten, 1994), but it is limited to documents (*monjo*) and illustrations (*ezu*); for Tendai scholastic materials, first see *Eizan bunko Tendaigaku tosho bunrui mokuroku* (Ōtsu: Eizan Bunko, 1933). If one can gain access through introduction by a Japanese institution or a monk resident at Hiei, one can conduct a search on-site of the materials held in each of the collections. Unfortunately, photographic reprints are not available for purchase, so one can only conduct investigation of the materials while on the premises.

Finally, we should make note of the substantial manuscript collections held in a number of other temples. However, we should also bear in mind that these temples, as a general rule, are open for access only during a scheduled period annually, and entry as a member of a regular research group (e.g., officials of Tōkyō Daigaku Shiryō Hensanjo) is generally preferred. Shingon temples such as Daigoji (see *Daigoji kiroku shōgyō mokuroku*, 76 vols.; *Daigoji monjo shōgyō mokuroku*, Tokyo: Benseisha, 2000–),[10] Ninnaji (see Abe Yasurō and Yamazaki Makoto, eds., *Ninnajizō goryū shōgyō*, Benseisha, 1998),[11] Kajūji,[12] and Kōzanji

---

10. The Daigoji research projects are continuing, and the photographs/microfilm of less than 200 of the approximately 800 boxes of the collection are currently held in Tōkyō Daigaku Shiryō Hensanjo; likewise, none of the catalogs are as yet complete. At the same time, articles in the journal *Kenkyū Kiyō (Daigoji Bunkazai Kenkyūjo*, sometimes referred to as *Daigoji Bunkazai Kenkyūjo Kenkyū Kiyō*) often reproduce manuscripts from the collection in printed form, and are sometimes accompanied by photographs of the works under discussion.

11. Ninnaji is the focus not only of research projects of Abe and his associates as well as of the research group that publishes the new journal *Ninnaji kenkyū*, but also of research groups headed by the literature scholar Tsukimoto Masayuki, University of Tokyo, as well as by members of Tōkyō Daigaku Shiryō Hensanjo. Many articles in the journal include reproductions of relevant works in printed and, sometimes, photographic form.

12. We should note that the Kakuzenshō Kenkyūkai has published 14 volumes that reproduce photographically Kajūji's manuscript edition of *Kakuzen-shō*, the famous version of the work, which is printed in *Taishō shinshū daizōkyō zuzōbu* (see the series *Kajūji zenpon eiin shūsei*, Kōyasan: Shinnō'in Gyōei Bunko, 2000–2003). Following this first series, series on commentaries/scriptural collections, documents, and *engi* narratives of the temple are also scheduled for publication.

(see Kōzanji Tenseki Monjo Sōgō Chōsa, ed., *Kōzanji kyōzō komokuroku*, Tokyo: Tōkyō Daigaku, 1985; and idem., *Kōzanji kyōzō tenseki monjo mokuroku*, Tokyo: Tōkyō Daigaku, 1973–1982) in Kyoto have been sites for group research projects for many years, and can potentially be approached, as has Ishiyamadera (see Kyōto Shiritsu Geijutsu Daigaku Ishiyamadera Chōsa, ed., *Ishiyamadera shōgyō mokuroku*, 2 vols., 1972) in nearby Shiga Prefecture. Other Tendai temples that can conceivably be contacted are the cloisters Shōren'in (see Kissuizō [alt. Yoshimizu Zō] Shōgyō Chōsa, ed., *Shōren'in monzeki kissuizō shōgyō mokuroku*, Tokyo: Kyūko Shoin, 1999) and Sanzen'in (see Sanzen'in Monjo Shiryōshitsu, ed., *Sanzen'in enyūzō monjo mokuroku*, 1984). Major Zen temples which might possibly be approached include, for example, Myōshinji in Kyoto and Eiheiji in Fukui Prefecture. We should also remember that large quantities of materials of the late premodern and modern eras are held in local temples throughout the country and in larger complexes such as those on Kōyasan and Konpirasan; the ongoing work of Tamamuro Fumio of Meiji University is a well-known example of continued efforts to photograph and catalog such manuscripts.

CONCLUSION: THEORIES FOR APPROACHING MANUSCRIPTS, AND THE POTENTIAL CONTRIBUTIONS OF NON-JAPANESE SCHOLARS

An introduction to archival research inevitably overlooks some sites for potential study. I leave it to others to improve on the discussion of temple sites through future research, and can only express the hope that temples make a greater effort to establish the requisite number of personnel to both maintain their collections and make them available for researchers, both Japanese and non-Japanese.

We should also note that theories in the study of historical manuscripts have made tremendous strides over the last two decades, due especially to the ongoing efforts of Japanese archivists. Amino Yoshihiko (*Nihon chūsei shiryōgaku no kadai*, Tokyo: Kōbundō, 1996) and Ishigami Eiichi (*Nihon kodai shiryōgaku*, Tokyo University Press, 1997), in particular, have made great contributions in their theoretical analyses of the study of premodern manuscripts, as have scholars at Kokubungaku Kenkyū Shiryōkan and elsewhere more recently (Kokubungaku Kenkyū Shiryōkan, ed., *Ākaibuzu no kagaku*, 2 vols., Tokyo: Kashiwa Shobō, 2003). Nagamura Makoto has recently written a major study of the theory of temple manuscripts, *Chūsei jiin shiryō ron* (Theory of Historical Manuscripts of Medieval Temples, Tokyo: Yoshikawa Kōbunkan, 2000), which provides an exhaustive analysis of the history of manuscript study and attempts to situate temple manuscripts—so-called *shōgyō* (sacred collections) as well as *komonjo* (documents)—within the social environs of medieval temples. Moreover, Kamikawa Michio has written a series of articles in which, based on the theoretical framework established by Kuroda Toshio, he argues for the attention to social context in the study of temple manuscripts.[13] Such works constitute the theoretical starting-points for any serious further research in the study of archival materials.

13. See, for example, his "Monjo yōshiki no shōgyō ni tsuite," in Tōji Monjo Kenkyūkai, ed., *Tōji monjo ni miru chsei shakai* (Tokyo: Tōkyōdō, 1999), pp. 534–58.

Until recently, non-Japanese researchers have very rarely made use of archival materials in Japan, due apparently to the presumed difficulty not only of gaining access to manuscripts but also of reading them. We can only hope that more non-Japanese scholars make the effort to improve their studies of Japanese history and religions through making use of the resources available to anyone interested.

WEBSITES

Bukkyō University Library . . . . www.bukkyo-u.ac.jp/lib/
Gangōji Bunkazai Kenkyūsho . . . . www.gangoji.or.jp
Hanazono Daigaku Kokusai Zengaku Kenkyūjo . . . . iriz.hanazono.or.jp
Jingū Bunko www.isejingu.or.jp/bunka/bunbody4.html
Kanō Bunko www2.library.tohoku.ac.jp
Kokubungaku Kenkyū Shiryōkan . . . . www.nijl.ac.jp
Kokuritsu Kokkai Toshokan www3.ndl.go.jp
Kokuritsu Rekishi Minzoku
    Hakubutsukan . . . . www.rekihaku.ac.jp/search.html
Komazawa University Library . . . . www.komazawa-u.ac.jp/~toshokan
Kōyasan University Library . . . . www.koyasan-u.ac.jp/tosho/
Kunaichō Shoryōbu www.kunaicho.go.jp/15/m15.html
Kyōto Furitsu Sōgō Shiryōkan . . . . www.pref.kyoto.jp/shiryokan/
Kyōto University Library . . . . www.kulib.kyoto-u.ac.jp/homejm.html
Naikaku Bunko www2.archives.go.jp/index.html
Nara Bunkazai Kenkyūsho . . . . www.nabunken.go.jp
Nara Kokuritsu Hakubutsukan . . . . narahaku.go.jp
Nara Kyōiku Daigaku . . . . www.nara-edu.ac.jp/LIB
Ryūkoku University Library opac.lib.ryukoku.ac.jp/nb/c-top6.html
Taishō University Library . . . . www.tais.ac.jp/lib/
Tenri Daigaku Fuzoku Toshokan . . . . www.tcl.gr.jp
Tōdaiji Toshokan . . . . www.nabunken.go.jp/naralib/nptodai.html
Tōkyō Daigaku Shiryō Hensanjo . . . . www.hi.u-tokyo.ac.jp/index-j.html
Webcat . . . . webcat.nii.ac.jp

ADDRESSES

Bukkyō Daigaku Toshokan, 96 Kita Hana-no-bō chō, Murasakino, Kita-ku, Kyoto 603-8301
    603-8301 京都市北区北紫野花ノ坊町96 仏教大学図書館
Dokuritsu Gyōseihōjin Bunkazai Kenkyūsho Nara Bunkazai Kenkyūsho, 2-9-1 Nijō-chō, Nara
    630-8577
    630-8577 奈良市二条町2-9-1 独立行政法人文化財研究所 奈良文化財研究所
Eizan Bunko, 4-9-45 Sakamoto, Ōtsu-shi, Shiga Prefecture 520-0113
    520-0113 滋賀県大津市坂本 4-9-45 叡山文庫
Gangōji Bunkazai Kenkyūsho, 11 Chūin-chō, Nara, 630-8341
    630-8341 奈良市中院町11 元興寺文化財研究所

Hanazono Daigaku Kokusai Zengaku Kenkyūjo, Hanazono Daigaku-nai, 8-1 Nishi-no-kyō tsubo-no-uchi -chō, Nakagyō-ku, Kyoto 604-8456
604-8456 京都市中京区西ノ京壷ノ内町8-1 花園大学内 花園大学国際禅学研究所

Jingū Bunko, 1711 Kanda-hisashi-honchō, Ise-shi, Mie Prefecture 516-0016
516-0016 三重県伊勢市神田久志本町1711 神宮文庫

Kanazawa Bunko (Kanagawa Kenritsu), 142 Kanazawa-chō, Kanazawa-ku, Yokohama, Kanagawa Prefecture 236-0015
236-0015 神奈川県横浜金沢区金沢町142 神奈川県立 金沢文庫

Kanō Bunko, Tōhoku University Library, 27-1 Kawauchi, Aoba-ku, Sendai-shi, Miyagi Prefecture 980-8576
980-8576 宮城県仙台市青葉区川内27-1 東北大学付属図書館 狩野文庫

Kokubungaku Kenkyū Shiryōkan, 1-16-10 Yutaka-machi, Shinagawa-ku, Tokyo 142-8585
142-8585 東京都品川区豊町1−16−10 国文学研究資料館

Kokuritsu Kokkai Toshokan, 1-10-1 Nagata-chō, Chiyoda-ku, Tokyo 100-8924
100-8924 東京都千代田区永田町1−10−1 国立国会図書館

Kokuritsu Rekishi Minzoku Hakubutsukan, 117 Jōnai-machi, Sakura-shi, Chiba Prefecture 285-8502
285-8502 千葉県佐倉市城内町117 国立歴史民俗博物館

Komazawa University Library, 1-23-1 Komazawa, Setagaya-ku, Tokyo 154-8525
154-8525 東京都世田谷区駒沢1−23−1 駒澤大学図書館

Kōyasan University Library, 385 Kōyasan, Kōya-chō, Ito-gun, Wakayama Prefecture 648-0280
648-0280 和歌山県伊都郡高野町高野山385 高野山大学図書館

Kunaichō Shoryōbu, 1-1 Chiyoda, Chiyoda-ku, Tokyo 100-8111
100-8111 東京都千代田区千代田1−1 宮内庁書陵部

Kyōto Furitsu Sōgō Shiryōkan, Hangi-chō, Shimo-Gamo, Sakyō-ku, Kyoto 606-0823
606-0823 京都市左京区下鴨半木町 京都府立総合資料館

Kyoto University Library, Yoshida Honmachi, Sakyō-ku, Kyoto 606-8501
606-8501 京都市左京区吉田本町 京都大学附属図書館

Naikaku Bunko, Kokuritsu Kōbunsho-kan, 3-2 Kitanomaru Kōen, Chiyoda-ku, Tokyo 102-0091
102-0091 東京都千代田区北の丸公園3−2 国立公文書館 内閣文庫

Nara Kokuritsu Hakubutsukan, 50 Noboriōji-chō, Nara 630-8213
630-8213 奈良市登大路町50 奈良国立博物館

Ryūkoku University Library, 125-1 Daiku-chō, Ōmiya Higashi-iru, Shichijō-dōri, Shimogyō-ku, Kyoto 600-8268
600-8268 京都市下京区七条通り大宮東入大工町125-1 龍谷大学図書館

Saidaiji, 1-1-5 Shiba-machi, Saidaiji, Nara 631-0825
631-0825 奈良市西大寺芝町1−1−5 西大寺

Shinpukuji, 2-21-47 Ōsu, Naka-ku, Nagoya, Aichi Prefecture 460-0011
460-0011 愛知県名古屋市中区大須2−21−47 真福寺

Sonkeikaku Bunko, 4-3-55 Komaba, Meguro-ku, Tokyo 153-0041
153-0041 東京都目黒区駒場4−3−55 尊経閣文庫

Taishō University Library, 3-20-1 Nishi Sugamo, Toshima-ku, Tokyo 170-8470
170-8470 東京都豊島区西巣鴨3−20−1 大正大学附属図書館

Tenri University Library, 1050 Soma-no-uchi-chō, Tenri City, Nara Prefecture 632-8577
    632-8577 奈良県天理市杣之内町1050 天理大学附属天理図書館

Tōdaiji Toshokan, Minamidaimon Higashigawa, 406-1 Zōshi-chō, Nara, 630-8211
    630-8211 奈良市雑司町406−1 南大門東側 東大寺図書館

Tōkyō Daigaku Shiryō Hensanjo, 7-3-1 Hongō, Bunkyō-ku, Tokyo 113-0033
    113-0033 東京都文京区本郷7−3−1 東京大学史料編纂所

Yōmei Bunko, 1-2 Udano-Kaminotani-chō, Ukyō-ku, Kyoto 616-8252
    616-8252 京都市右京区宇多野上ノ谷町1−2 陽明文庫

Scott SCHNELL

Conducting Fieldwork on Japanese Religions

Textual analysis is obviously a very important aspect of religious studies. Exclusive reliance on written documents, however, is insufficient for addressing certain problems involving the actual practice and experience of religion.

Indeed, the more localized or "folk" religions often have no written texts, their messages being embodied in ritual activity and oral tradition. If written accounts do exist, they are likely to be biased toward the perceptions of the literary elite or outside observer, inadequately representing the attitudes and opinions of the majority of the population. Furthermore, there is an obvious distinction between the way people describe themselves and what they actually do. By this I do not mean to imply that people are inherently duplicitous, but simply that, in our daily activities, we often fail to live up to the ideals we have established. And while ideals exert an important influence on our behavior, to ignore the way religion is ordinarily *practiced* would be to misrepresent reality, and quite possibly overlook certain highly significant aspects of the religious experience.

When I first became interested in Japan during my undergraduate years, I was deeply impressed by the environmental ethic that various treatises on Zen Buddhism and Shinto appeared to convey. This impression was further encouraged by Lynn WHITE's (1967) famous article claiming that the Western tendency to exploit the environment derives from the Biblical injunction that humans "shall have dominion over the earth." Japanese acquaintances were quick to affirm the White thesis, insisting that their own religious traditions favored harmony with nature. I was therefore greatly disillusioned upon finally arriving in Japan, only to find that people there seemed no less inclined to despoil nature than we were in America.

Though I eventually overcame my initial disappointment, I was left with uncertainties about the relevance of texts. Then one day, while hiking in the mountains of central Japan, I came upon a sign along the trail which led me to an important insight. The sign read "Let us greet each other properly along the trail," referring to the custom of offering friendly words of greeting and encouragement to the fellow hikers one encounters, rather than passing by in icy silence. While this seemed an admirable sentiment, I nevertheless began to wonder: if greeting each other along the trail is such a widely recognized and time-honored custom, why do we need a sign to remind us to observe it? The presence of the sign does not indicate that people are adhering to the custom, but rather that they are failing to do so, and now certain civically minded observers are beginning to worry. This simple incident came to influence (or perhaps epitomize in retrospect) how I view religious texts—not as accurate reflections of daily practice, but as sources of insight into the problems with which society at large is confronted.

For example, the pervasive emphasis on harmony and cooperation in Japanese society might be taken not as an expression of inherent tendencies, but as an indication that conflict, especially within the context of many people living and working in close proximity, is an ever-present or recurring problem. Anyone who has lived for an extended period of time in a Japanese community knows that, despite its calm exterior, conflicts seethe beneath the surfaces, perhaps breaking into the open only on certain prescribed occasions. A drinking bout is one such occasion; the revelry associated with a *matsuri*, or Shinto festival, is another. This, to me, is one of the most interesting aspects of the festival experience—the exciting possibility that, within an atmosphere of temporary license, practically anything might happen. In fact, the momentary release from everyday constraints may well explain the singular appeal of Shinto festivals, not just for me as an anthropologist, but for the regular participants themselves. And while written accounts of *matsuri* do contain vague allusions to this aspect, I have only come to recognize and appreciate its potential through my own firsthand experience. This underscores the value of ethnographic fieldwork for achieving a more complete understanding of religious activity—in Japan and elsewhere.

There are many excellent and detailed books dealing with the particulars of conducting ethnographic fieldwork (see, for example, BERNARD 2002; DENZIN and LINCOLN 2000; SCHENSUL, SCHENSUL, LeCOMPTE 1999; and BESTOR et al., 2003). In what follows I will

RESEARCH

offer a few humble words of advice based on my own experiences, specifically relating to field research on Japanese religion and ritual (see SCHNELL 1999).

THE UTILITY OF CHANCE ENCOUNTERS

Fieldwork is a rather open-ended process, in that some of the most important discoveries stem from chance encounters and random occurrences. The events that led to my choice of a field site, for example, were largely accidental, beginning well before my decision to become an anthropologist. I was living and teaching English in Nagoya at the time and was interested in exploring the Japanese countryside on weekends and vacations. One day while leafing through a travel guide, one of the photographs it contained caught my attention. Taken at nighttime, the photograph showed two semi-naked young men sitting back-to-back astride a large, barrel-shaped drum. Each held a long stick in vertical position high above his head, dramatically poised to strike the drum with a downward arcing motion. The drum itself was perched atop a turret, which was in turn supported by a huge, rectangular framework made of overlapping wooden beams. Several somewhat older men balanced themselves precariously on this framework, positioned in front and back of the big drum as if guarding it from attack. Most curiously of all, the entire structure was being borne by a mass of revelers down a narrow street, while additional masses, each armed with a somewhat smaller drum attached to a stout pole, pressed in upon the framework from behind. This, the caption informed me, was the *okoshi daiko* 起し太鼓, or "rousing drum" ritual, performed every year on the night of 19 April in Furukawa, a small town located in Japan's mountainous interior. The accompanying passage explained that the drum ritual was part of a larger *matsuri* that included bonfires, shrine ceremonies, and various folk performances, all dedicated to a local guardian deity. In my naïve foreigner's mind, the fires, drums, and darkness harkened back to a mystical tribal past, well before the incursion of Western influences. I decided that I must go to see this *matsuri*, which was due to be performed only a few weeks later.

I mentioned my plan to some friends, one of whom immediately recalled an old college classmate who had been from Furukawa. He offered to call her for more information. To our pleasant surprise, the former classmate invited us to stay there with her family, as accommodations would be very difficult to find at *matsuri* time. This was my introduction to the Kamamiya family, my oldest and dearest friends in Furukawa, and to the *matsuri* that eventually became the focus of my doctoral dissertation.

During the months and years that followed I returned to Furukawa several times, got to know its people, and even came to see it as my Japanese "hometown." Despite my initial naïvete about the *matsuri* and all that it entailed, it was nevertheless quite obvious from the beginning that the drum ritual served as the definitive expression of local identity. I was therefore led to wonder: what messages did this ritual convey? How did it develop? How has its meaning changed over time? A few years later, as a graduate student studying anthropology back in the United States, I began to formulate a research project aimed at addressing these questions. On a subsequent return visit during the summer I asked my friends the Kamamiyas what they thought of such a project, and was delighted when they responded with enthusiastic support. They, in turn, began to broach the idea among their neighbors and friends, employing a kind of *nemawashi* 根回し ("root binding") approach to prepare the way for my next arrival, not as a simple visitor this time, but as a long-term resident and researcher.

MOVING IN AND GETTING STARTED

Before initiating my fieldwork, I needed to obtain official recognition and approval from local leaders. From the US, my academic advisor offered to write several letters of introduction on my behalf—one to the mayor of Furukawa, one to the head priest of the shrine to which the *matsuri* was directed, and one to the leader of the parish elders (*ujiko sōdai* 氏子総代) who administered the shrine's affairs. This endorsement from a faculty member at a major American university helped establish my credentials as a serious researcher, and I believe it was particularly advantageous that he could write well in formal Japanese. In retrospect, I wish that I had asked him to also write a letter to the head of the local educational committee (*kyōiku iinkaichō*), who oversaw not only the school system but scholarly activity throughout the town in general.

In any case, all of these individuals were familiar with the gist of my project well before my actual arrival. The head priest and leader of the parish elders were kind enough to reply with letters offering their support. I was told informally that the mayor, too, had no objections. When I arrived in Furukawa, I went to visit each of these officials to present myself in person and ask again for their cooperation.

The importance of proper introductions and consent from the upper levels of authority is almost a truism in Japan, the assumption being that, in a hierarchical society, approval at the highest level ensures the (somewhat obligatory) cooperation of the people lower down. Certainly, gaining permission at the top has symbolic importance and is widely recognized as the "proper" way to proceed. In practical terms, however, relationships with people at lower levels in an organizational hierarchy will often prove more useful. And since people in support positions exercise a certain latitude to grant or withhold their assistance (see, for example, PHARR 1984, KONDO 1990, OGASAWARA 1998), it is highly advisable to treat *everyone* with courtesy and respect, regardless of their status.

Having formal affiliation at a Japanese academic institution is also quite helpful, as it will register greater name recognition among the people you encounter and thereby add legitimacy to your project. For many non-Japanese researchers, it is likely that such affiliation will have been arranged already, as grants and fellowships to conduct research in Japan generally require a Japanese sponsor. I was fortunate in being affiliated with a rather prestigious Japanese university, which greatly enhanced my *meishi* ("name card") and afforded me a kind of symbolic capital in pursuing my research. My Japanese sponsor/advisor, himself a professor of anthropology, was kind enough to introduce me to a number of prominent scholars who had expertise in the topical areas I was addressing. One of these scholars, in fact, had briefly conducted research in Furukawa several years before, and gave me important insights into the structure of the *matsuri*. He was also on friendly terms with the head priest and a number of influential shrine parishioners and helped me to gain their confidence and support.

When it came to finding a place to live, again my friends the Kamamiyas came to my aid. The family operated a small clothing store in one of the older neighborhoods, and offered me the use of a spacious room on the second floor. There was also a small kitchen, restroom, and bath downstairs behind the shop itself, as well as a telephone and copy machine in an adjacent makeshift office. This, to me, was the ideal living arrangement. During the day, I had immediate access to many different people, as the store drew customers from all over town. At night, however, everyone went home, allowing me the privacy I needed to write up my field notes and pursue my own interests.

I realize, of course, that I am drawing mostly from my own individual experiences, and that there is considerable room for variation depending on the topic you have chosen, the type of community in which you will be working, and your own distinctive attributes. It is perhaps another truism that the key to success lies in capitalizing on whatever advantages your situation affords you. If you enter the field as a lone individual, you will have plenty of flexibility to go where and when you choose without having to accommodate the needs of other people—you will be free, in other words, to focus on your research without distraction. Being accompanied by a spouse and/or children, however, has its own distinct advantages, in addition to the obvious emotional support they provide. Marriage, and especially having children, will lend you an air of respectability and make you less an object of suspicion and concern. Through the interaction of your family members with other people in the community, you will be drawn into experiences and relationships that you would not otherwise have had. And while these may not bear directly on your research project, in the long term anything that expands your network of acquaintances is likely to prove beneficial.

Upon moving into your chosen field site, it is wise to inform as many people as possible about what you are trying to accomplish. People are generally quite willing to help and will even go well out of their way to facilitate your project, but they can only do so if they have some idea of what that project entails. A brief mention of your purpose could easily be included with your name and institutional affiliation when introducing yourself to others. This will not appear unusual or presumptuous, as people will quite naturally be interested in the reason for your presence there among them. In fact friends will often provide this information themselves when introducing you to their acquaintances. In my own experience, this has frequently led to helpful responses from the acquaintances themselves, such as "Well, then, have you met Fuse-san in Mukaimachi? He is quite knowledgeable on that subject," or "My father-in-law was riding the drum the year it rammed into the police station. Perhaps you should talk to him." A friend in Furukawa even suggested that I post a notice in the local weekly newspaper, calling for documents, old photographs, oral accounts—any sources of information that people might have to offer. At the time I was reluctant to appear too obtrusive, so I did not follow his suggestion, but in retrospect I have often wished that I had.

In making yourself more accessible to the community, I recommend adopting a pattern favored by many Japanese themselves—namely, stopping in at a favorite coffee shop on a regular basis to get to know the staff and other customers. A coffee shop offers a more relaxed atmosphere where people are inclined to join in conversation. It is a good place to meet people and expand your range of acquaintances. If this becomes a normal part of your routine, people will know where and when to find you and perhaps leave messages for you there with the proprietor. Even if no one else appears on any given day, you can bring your laptop computer along and work on your field notes, thereby easing your anxiety about wasting time. Patronizing local restaurants and drinking establishments is another way of increasing your social encounters, with the added advantage that you are giving something back to the community, namely your money.

Indeed, realizing the extent to which the success of your project is made possible by the people around you, you may look for more substantial ways to reciprocate their kindness. I helped several households with the transplanting and harvesting of their rice, unloaded and stocked boxes at my friends' clothing store, shoveled voluminous amounts of snow from roofs and alleys, and of course prepared for and performed my assigned roles in the *matsuri*. However, even my meager attempts to give something back to the community often seemed to benefit myself more than others. At one point I was asked by the educational committee if I might be willing to teach a weekly English lesson for local residents. Among my "pupils" on the first day of class was none other than the current heir of the largest prewar landlord household in the entire Hida region (though her husband, who had married into the household, is its nominal head). She proved an invaluable source of information on the structure of the *dannashū* 旦那衆 (old landlord class) and the local economy; we remain good friends to this day. Another member of the same English class was very active in the *matsuri* in terms of preparing food, entertaining guests, and engaging in other behind-the-scenes preparations. Her husband was a musician who performed *gagaku* (sacred music) at the shrine, and was familiar with its inner workings. They also introduced me to their son, a recent graduate from a prestigious national university where he had majored in the social sciences. The son proved a useful sounding board for testing my ideas, since he combined the theoretical sophistication of an academic with the insight of a local resident. These are examples of how seemingly irrelevant encounters can develop into a network of useful contacts.

GATHERING DATA

How do we ensure that our research generates reliable ethnographic data— that we "get it right," in other words? My initial advice is to spend as much time in the field and interact with as many different people as circumstance allows; cutting down on either risks jumping to hasty and misinformed conclusions. In the beginning, the people you encounter may be somewhat reticent or suspicious of your motives. The more time you spend among them, the greater opportunity they will have to learn about and accept you, which should translate into more reliable information. I also favor periodic return visits after the initial fieldwork has ended. This will allow you to gather more and different kinds of information as your analysis matures. My research in Furukawa began with an initial fourteen months, followed by several return visits conducted mostly during the summers and ranging in length from one to three months. Each return led me to important new insights and helped refine my thinking.

My field research was roughly divided into three activities: (1) analysis of written documents, including historical accounts, local newspaper articles, police and shrine regulations; (2) interviewing "informants" to gain their individual perspectives; and (3) simply experiencing life in Furukawa by living and working among its people. The latter, of course, included preparing for and performing in the *matsuri* itself. But even the more mundane activities provided insight into my topic. For example, after spending a long, rather confining winter in Furukawa, during which one of the recurring tasks was to shovel massive accumulations of snow from roofs and alleyways, I could better understand the exuberance of finally breaking loose in spring as expressed through lively participation in the *matsuri*.

Many anthropologists come to rely heavily on the knowledge and insight provided by "key informants." Still, it is risky to assume that what two or three people have told you is representative of the entire community. As you interact with a wider range of people, you may find that attitudes and opinions vary with age, gender, neighborhood affiliation, occupation, socioeconomic status, or other attributes. This may lead you to important insights into the various meanings attached to a single text or performance. Shortly after beginning my fieldwork in Furukawa I was subjected to a friendly "intervention" by two local elders. Both were the current heads of prominent prewar landlord households and lived just outside the boundaries of Furukawa in areas protected by other shrines. They were concerned about my focus on the drum ritual, insisting that it was largely a "show" for the amusement of the spectators. The essence of the *matsuri*, they reminded me, was embodied in the rather solemn rituals performed at the shrine to invoke, honor, and supplicate the guardian deity. While I knew this to be true in principle, I nevertheless recognized that the drum ritual, which originated as a rather innocuous preliminary, had at some point in its history undergone a dramatic transformation, growing in scale and intensity to eventually eclipse all the other events. When I began to piece together the story of its emergence as an expression of political opposition issuing from the ranks of the less influential members of the community, I could well understand why the hereditary elite objected to my focusing there.

On the other hand, in many cases the more privileged members of old established households *do* possess superior knowledge about religion and historical events, simply because they have a vested interest in such matters and the time and resources to pursue them. Most people have neither the means nor the inclination to delve so deeply into the past. This does not mean, however, that their opinions are of little value. Popular opinions are important and informative, but in a different sense; they provide insight into how people fashion their own narratives or assign their own special significance to symbols, activities, and events. This may entail an imaginative reconfiguring of the past for present purposes, and therefore conflict with what the scholar deems to be "factual" as revealed through the analysis of texts. If we continually surrender to our own obsession with historical authenticity, however, we may fail to appreciate the vitality of religion as an adaptable presence.

To take a very simple example, a Shinto priest once told me that the word *ine* 稲, meaning "rice plant," is actually an abbreviation of the phrase *inochi no ne* 命の根, meaning "the source of life." This is an example of what linguists refer to as "folk etymology," a popular explanation for the origin of a word, but one that is of dubious authenticity. Nevertheless, the priest's explanation, regardless of whether it is strictly factual, underscores the importance of rice from a Shinto perspective and therefore represents a significant ethnographic finding. The same applies to more complex explanations—those that are used to justify political initiatives, for example. By acting on current needs and reasoning back in time, precedents are "discovered," means and motives legitimized. The past is enlisted for present purposes, making it all the more relevant as a focus of research. In this sense, a single-minded quest for historical authenticity misses the point (see KELLY 1987, ŌTA 1993, HASHIMOTO 1996).

In short, varied and conflicting opinions should not be seen as impediments to your research. Rather, they are to be expected as the natural correlates of social complexity—perhaps even a reflection of your skill as a fieldworker—and will ultimately render your analyses more compelling.

There is yet another reason for establishing contacts with a wide a range of people, however, and that is to enhance our own objectivity. Care must be taken to overcome bias, both in ourselves and in the people who supply us with information. While it may be impossible to completely rid ourselves of bias, it is nevertheless important that we make the effort. Objectivity, it seems to me, lies not in relinquishing our own personal values and attitudes, but in complementing them with other points of view.

As for the data collection process itself, some ethnographers favor structured interviews, following a checklist of questions or topics to address and carefully recording the responses. Others are skilled at embedding their questions in what otherwise appears to be an ordinary conversation. The latter approach is not meant to be deceptive, but rather to make the interview more enjoyable and less intrusive to the other person. This is a skill that is well worth developing. I prefer open-ended questions that allow the other person to elaborate at length, leading the discussion into his or her own areas of interest or expertise. For example, "The *matsuri* as it is performed in the present day—is it largely the same as in the past, or has it changed over the years?" Then I can ask for elaboration or detail on the responses that emerge. If your research involves a particular ritual, location, or group of adherents, it is useful to bring photographs of the facet in question and refer to them during the interview. This will give you some basis for discussion, allow you to focus on specific details, and help to jog your informant's memory. Photographs also help limit people's tendency to embellish the facts or exaggerate conditions when recounting the past.

It is said that a fieldworker is always "on call," as virtually any activity or encounter is a potential source of data. Indeed, some of your most important insights are likely to emerge in ordinary conversation, while sharing a table or riding as a passenger in someone's car. I adopted the habit of carrying a mechanical pencil and folded piece of paper in my shirt pocket at all times so that I could quickly jot down random comments no matter where I happened to be. In time people grew accustomed to my pulling out the paper on the spur of the moment to record a new phrase or piece of information. It seems to have been considered an endearing if somewhat quirky trait, and even enhanced my image as a serious scholar. Too much time spent in copious on-the-spot note-taking, however, can bring a lively and informative conversation to an abrupt halt. For this reason, I often wrote only a few key words to refresh my memory later when I could sit down to write out my notes at length.

Whether in casual conversation or a formal interview, special care should be taken to avoid the use of "leading" questions. This is a particular problem in Japan where proper social comportment often requires the subordination of one's own opinions in deference to others. Your hosts, in other words, are likely to agree with you or affirm what you say simply in the spirit of harmonious interaction. This relates to a more general problem: the impact of the ethnographer's own presence on the data that are obtained. For example, in researching the "rousing drum" ritual I noticed a rather intriguing similarity. In the *Nihon shoki* (Chronicles of Japan, circa 720), there is brief mention of a character named Ryōmen Sukuna 両面宿儺, a local Hida chieftain during the Fourth Century who defies the emperor's authority but is ultimately defeated. As the name "Ryōmen" (両面, literally "two-faced") implies, the Sukuna supposedly had two faces aligned in opposite directions, each with its own set of arms and legs but attached to a single trunk (see ASTON 1972 [1886], p. 298, and INOUE 1987, pp. 362, 611). This, to me, seemed strikingly similar to the position taken by the two young men sitting back-to-back atop the drum, who in fact are bound together at the trunk by a roll of cloth. Ryōmen Sukuna has become a kind of culture hero throughout the Hida region, and I thought that the similarity might have been intentional—a defiant assertion of local identity. I was so excited by this prospect that I began to ask people explicitly whether this might have been the case. The best I could obtain in the way of confirmation, however, was a rather tentative acknowledgment that the two images were strikingly similar; the question remained unresolved. Then during a later return visit, I finally heard some local people, unsolicited by me, alluding to a direct link between the two images. By that time, however, I could no longer be certain that I myself had not "planted" the idea through my suggestive questioning, effectively engaging in folk etymology.

PRODUCTIVE DEPARTURES

As your network of acquaintances expands, you may find yourself being invited to places and to do things that have no apparent bearing on your project. Within reason, it is advisable to allow yourself to be "sidetracked" in this manner. For one thing, it demonstrates that you are genuinely interested in getting to know people and not merely exploiting them in pursuit of your own research agenda. Even so, it is remarkable how often these seemingly irrelevant side excursions lead to new insights or useful contacts. It is often the case, in other words, that the data find *you*, provided that you make yourself available to them. Thus field research should combine careful planning and execution with ample opportunity for spontaneous departures, much in the manner of the *matsuri* experience.

Spending an extended period of time in a small, well-integrated community can sometimes feel like living in a fish bowl, and while the advantages of assistance and support far outweigh the lack of privacy, it may be helpful to escape briefly when you are feeling overwhelmed. During my time in Furukawa, I would occasionally board the train for a getaway weekend in Nagoya (an interesting reversal of the pattern I had adopted while living in that city several years before). My purpose was mainly to visit friends, but it was also enjoyable simply to join the urban masses and be anonymous for a while.

One way of taking a break from the field without feeling guilty about neglecting your research is to schedule a visit with your sponsoring institution to present some of your preliminary findings. This will enhance your relationship with your Japanese colleagues and provide you with valuable feedback on the development of your project. By periodically testing your ideas in this manner, you will be able to discover weaknesses early on in the process while there is still time to correct them.

However, if you have developed a compelling argument that seems to make sense of the data, do not be too quick to discard it at the first hint of a challenge. Knowledgeable as they are, the people at your sponsoring institution will not have the kind of intimate experience with your field site that you yourself possess. And while long-term local residents are highly familiar with their own specific roles within a community or performance, they lack the "big picture" perspective of the distanced observer. Midway through my research, I had come to recognize the "rousing drum" in Furukawa as a ritualized expression of opposition, which emerged during the mid-Meiji period in response to the concentration of wealth and power among the local elite and the increasing imposition of outside authority by the central government. I was therefore somewhat discouraged that my informants consistently described the ritual as a conflict between *neighborhoods*, rather than between socioeconomic and political categories. Eventually I realized that we were talking about *the same thing*. Wealthy merchants and landlords were clustered in certain neighborhoods while tenant cultivators and laborers were concentrated in others. Therefore neighborhood affiliation automatically invoked economic and political disparities. This was borne out in subsequent interviews—informants from the less influential neighborhoods being far more inclined to view the drum ritual as an opportunity to air their grievances and challenge the structure of authority.

In short, while the "insider's" viewpoint is vitally important, the "outsider" brings a fresh perspective that also has much to contribute. Truly insightful research lies in combining the two, and that is what fieldwork should ultimately accomplish.

BIBLIOGRAPHY

ASTON, W. G., tr., 1972 [1886]. *Nihongi: Chronicles of Japan from the Earliest Times to A.D. 697.* Rutland: Charles E. Tuttle Company.

BERNARD, H. Russell, 2002. *Research Methods in Anthropology: Qualitative and Quantitative Approaches*, 3rd ed. Walnut Creek: AltaMira Press.

BESTOR, Theodore C., Patricia G. STEINHOFF, and Victoria Lyon BESTOR, eds., 2003. *Doing Fieldwork in Japan.* Honolulu: University of Hawai'i Press.

DENZIN, Norman K., and Yvonna S. LINCOLN, eds., 2000. *Handbook of Qualitative Research.* Thousand Oaks: Sage Publications.

HASHIMOTO Hiroyuki 橋本裕之, 1996. *Hozon to kankō no hazama de: Minzoku geinō no genzai* 保存と観光のはざまで——民俗芸能の現在. In *Kankō jinruigaku* 観光人類学, ed. Yamashita Shinji, pp. 178–88. Tokyo: Shinyōsha.

INOUE Mitsusada 井上光貞, tr., 1987. *Nihon shoki* 日本書紀, vol. 1. Tokyo: Chūō Kōronsha.

KELLY, William W., 1987. Rethinking Rural Festivals in Contemporary Japan. *Japan Foundation Newsletter* 15: 12–15.

KONDO, Dorinne K., 1990. *Crafting Selves: Power, Gender, and Discourses of Identity in a Japanese Workplace*. Chicago: University of Chicago Press.

OGASAWARA, Yuko, 1998. *Office Ladies and Salaried Men: Power, Gender, and Work in Japanese Companies*. Berkeley: University of California Press.

ŌTA Yoshinobu 大田好信, 1993. *Bunka no kyakutai-ka: Kankō o tōshita bunka to aidentiti no sōzō* 文化の客体化——観光をとおした文化とアイデンティティの創造. *Minzokugaku kenkyū* 57: 383–410.

PHARR, Susan J., 1984. Status Conflict: The Rebellion of the Tea Pourers. In *Conflict in Japan*, ed. Ellis S. Krauss, Thomas P. Rohlen, and Patricia G. Steinhoff, pp. 214–40. Honolulu: University of Hawai'i Press.

SCHENSUL, Stephen L., Jean J. SCHENSUL, and Margaret D. LECOMPTE, 1999. *Essential Ethnographic Methods: Observations, Interviews, and Questionnaires*. Walnut Creek: AltaMira Press.

SCHNELL, Scott, 1999. *The Rousing Drum: Ritual Practice in a Japanese Community*. Honolulu: University of Hawai'i Press.

WHITE, Lynn W., 1967. The Historical Roots of Our Environmental Crisis. *Science* 155: 1203–207.

Chronology

William M. Bodiford

A Chronology of Religion in Japan

This chronology originated as private notes compiled as an aid for my own memory. It is biased, therefore, toward subjects of interest to me. It largely reproduces without modification or critical analysis the format and structure of conventional chronologies produced in Japan. It is a chronology of events, not of processes. Nonetheless, many of the events listed herein might be more accurately regarded as being representative of complex processes that actually spanned many years or decades. Moreover, many other events (usually those with question marks, such as the instatement of Jinmu in 660 BCE) should not be accepted as historical facts, but regarded as historically influential fictions that tell us more about the concerns of the later chroniclers who wrote of them than about the times when they supposedly occurred. Be forewarned: it is not the purpose of this chronology to determine which of these events might be more or less plausible. Entries for these events frequently use the same anachronistic terminology (e.g., *tennō* 天皇 for "sovereign") as found in the later texts cited therein. The use of this terminology does not imply its acceptance, but is meant to draw attention to its influence

I never recorded bibliographic information regarding the original sources and secondary scholarship on which I based my original notes and dates. In the process of preparing this revised edition, I have endeavored to confirm its accuracy by consulting the standard reference works, including (but not limited to) the following:

Asao Naohiro 朝尾直弘 et al., eds., 1996. *Kadokawa Nihonshi jiten* 角川 日本史辞典 (The Kadokawa Dictionary of Japanese History). New edition. Tokyo: Kadokawa Shoten.

Hiraoka Jōkai 平岡常海 et al., eds., 1999. *Nihon Bukkyōshi nenpyō* 日本仏教史年表 (Historical Chronology of Japanese Buddhism). Tokyo: Yūzankaku.

Kasahara Kazuo 笠原一男 and Yamazaki Hiroshi 山崎 宏, eds., 1979. *Bukkyōshi nenpyō* 仏教史年表 (Historical Chronology of Buddhism). Kyoto: Hōzōkan.

Ōno Tatsunosuke 大野達之助, ed., 1979. *Nihon Bukkyōshi jiten* 日本仏教史辞典 (Dictionary of Japanese Buddhist History). Tokyo: Tōkyōdō Shuppan.

Tōkyō Gakugei Daigaku Nihonshi Kenkyūshitsu 東京学芸大学日本史研究室, ed., 1984. *Nihonshi nenpyō* 日本史年表 (Historical Chronology of Japan). Tokyo: Tōkyōdō Shuppan.

During the process of revision this chronology also benefited from numerous suggestions, comments, additions, and corrections provided by many friends and colleagues, including (but not limited to): Karl F. Friday (University of Georgia), Jacqueline I. Stone (Princeton University), John B. Duncan and Donald F. McCallum (University of California, Los Angeles). I am very much indebted to each of them. I alone am responsible for any errors of fact or interpretation.

CONVENTIONS USED IN THIS CHRONOLOGY

ca. (*circa*, "about") is placed before dates that may be inexact or that are based on scholarly conjecture.

? ("questionable") is placed after dates, proper names, and events that might not have existed, that are subject to dispute, or that supposedly occurred prior to 680 but for which the only evidence is later Japanese texts, such as *Kojiki* 古事記 (712), *Nihon shoki* 日本書紀 (720), *Gangōji engi* 元興寺縁起 (747), *Fusō ryakki* 扶桑略記 (ca. 1180), etc.

ⓒ mainland or China

ⓚ the Korean peninsula

ⓞ elsewhere outside the Japanese archipelago

Dates	Events
BCE	Paleolithic period (prior to ca. 8,000 BCE): no archaeological evidence for religious activity
ca. 8,000–	Jōmon 縄文 (Mesolithic and Neolithic) period: sophisticated cord-patterned (*jōmon*) pottery developed among hunter-gatherers inhabiting Japanese archipelago
ca. 5,000–	Agriculture developed as people began to dwell in villages and towns; development of pottery figurines in shapes of animals (and humans?) suggest possible religious symbolism
ca. 1,000–	Archaeological evidence for circles outside villages suggest possible sites (shrines?) for religious rituals; pottery figurines in shapes of heavy-set females suggest possible goddess worship or shamanism
660 ?	Jinmu 神武 (?) became first sovereign (*tennō* 天皇) of Japan (according to *Nihon shoki* 日本書紀, 720)
ca. 400–250 CE	Yayoi 弥生 period: Immigrants from northern Asia swept into archipelago, introduced new culture, new language (which evolved into Japanese), and new technology, especially bronze and iron work; musical instruments, such as bronze bells (*dōtaku* 銅鐸), suggest possibility of sophisticated religious rites; wide regional variations, however, preclude the existence of any uniform cultural or religious milieu
ca. 300s	Irrigated rice paddy cultivation began in Kyushu (southern island of Japan)
221	© Qin 秦 empire (221–206 BCE), having conquered other Chinese kingdoms, established unified state
206	© Han 漢 dynasty (206 BCE–220 CE) replaced Qin, established Confucian Imperial State
CE 57	Chinese Han emperor awarded official seal of investiture to unnamed "king" 王 (chieftain?) of Nu Kingdom 奴國 somewhere (Kyushu?) in Wa 倭 (Japanese islands) (according to *Hou Hanshu* 後漢書)
220	© Han dynasty fell, Chinese continent became divided among many competing kingdoms
ca. 239	Wei 魏 Kingdom in China awarded official seal of investiture to queen "Himiko" 卑彌呼 (a.k.a. Pimiko) of Yamatai 邪馬臺 (somewhere in Japanese islands), who supposedly conquered many warring states and who ruled by *kidō* 鬼道: the Way (or Dao) of Ghosts (according to *Wei Zhi* 魏志); many Chinese mirrors came to Japan around this time
ca. 250–600	Kofun 古墳 period: Emergence of powerful local rulers who were commemorated with massive burial mounds (*kofun*), especially in Miyazaki 宮崎 (Kyushu) and in Okayama 岡山, Gunma 群馬, and central (Nara 奈良, Osaka 大阪, Kyoto 京都) areas of Honshu; goods from continent (Korean and Chinese states) became more widespread; bows and arrows used not just for hunting but also for warfare; terra cotta figurines (*haniwa* 埴輪) and other grave goods from these mounds suggest complex local hierarchies in which underlings, servants, and slaves represented by *haniwa* cared for deceased rulers in the afterlife

Dates	Events
313	ⓚ Luolang 樂浪郡 colony (Han Chinese) in northern Korean peninsula overrun by Koguryŏ 高句麗
367 ?	ⓚ Korean kingdom of Paekche 百濟 sent Confucian scholars (?) to Yamato 倭 court (?) in Japan and requested soldiers (according to *Nihon shoki*)
372	ⓚ Buddhist missionary Sundo 順道 (Shundao) from Former Qin 前秦 kingdom in China introduced Buddhist images and scriptures to King Sosurim 小獸林 (r. 371–384) of Koguryŏ; Confucian academy (T'aehak 太學) also established in Koguryŏ
385	ⓚ Paekche established Buddhist monastery on Mount Han (Hansan Pulsa 漢山佛寺) one year after arrival of Buddhist monk Mālānanda (?, Maranat'a 摩羅難提)
393	ⓚ Koguryŏ established nine Buddhist temples in capital city of P'yŏngyang 平壤
ca. 400s	Seaport around Osaka became more developed than Nara region; burial mounds increased to enormous size and their grave goods become more militaristic, with more iron swords, arrowheads, armor, and saddles; Chinese bronze mirrors with images of buddhas also found; social groups known as *uji* 氏 (clans or tribes based on Korean social models) probably fully emerged during this period
421	Chieftain "San" 讚 (somewhere in Japanese islands) sent tribute to China's Liu Song 劉宋 Kingdom (according to *Songshu* 宋書)
425	Chieftain "San" (somewhere in Japanese islands) sent tribute to China's Liu Song Kingdom
438	Chieftain "Chin" 珍 (somewhere in Japanese islands) sent tribute to China's Liu Song Kingdom, received title: "General (*shōgun* 將軍) who commands the 6 lands of Wa 倭, Paekche 百濟, Silla 新羅, Inna 任那, Jinhan 秦韓, and Mokhan 慕韓" (of which, all except Wa were located on Korean peninsula)
443	Chieftain "Sai" 濟 (somewhere in Japanese islands) sent tribute to China's Liu Song Kingdom, received title: "General who pacifies the East" (*antō shōgun* 安東將軍)
446–452	ⓒ First major persecution of Buddhism (by Northern Wei 北魏 Kingdom) in China
451	Chieftain "Sai" received title: "General who commands the 6 lands of Wa, Silla, Inna, Kala 加羅, Jinhan, and Mokhan" (according to *Songshu*)
462	Chieftain "Kō" 興 (somewhere in Japanese islands) sent tribute to China's Liu Song Kingdom, received title: "General who pacifies the East" (according to *Songshu*)
478	Chieftain "Bu" 武 (somewhere in Japanese islands) sent tribute to China's Liu Song Kingdom, received title: "General who commands the 6 lands of Wa, Silla, Inna, Kala, Jinhan, and Mokhan"
502	Chieftain "Bu" 武 sent tribute to China's Liang 梁 Kingdom, received title of "General" (*shōgun*) (according to *Liangshu* 梁書)

Dates	Events
ca. 500s	Large-scale land clearing and irrigation projects greatly expanded agriculture and wealth (of elites); rulers began to construct residential compounds separate from villages; iron increasingly produced domestically rather than imported; prestige goods (mirrors, crowns, swords, horse trappings) from Korean peninsula used to mark social status; Buddha images began to be worshiped by elites; Yamato hegemony over central region began to be established
507 ?	Yamato hegemon (*tennō*) Buretsu 武烈 (?) overthrown for his depravity; new royal line established by hegemon Keitai 繼体 (?; according to *Nihon shoki*) [legend of Jinmu began about this time?]
513 ?	Paekche 百済 (?) sent Confucian scholars and scriptures to Yamato court (according to *Nihon shoki*)
522 ?	Shiba Tatto 司馬達等 (?) built Buddhist chapel (according to *Fusō ryakki* 扶桑略記, ca. 1180)
528	ⓚ King Pŏphŭng 法興 (r. 514–540) of Silla officially recognized Buddhism one year after death of Ich'adon 異次頓; Silla construction of Taet'ong-sa 大通寺 monastery in 529
538 ?	Paekche (?) presented Buddhist statues to Yamato court (according to *Gangōji engi* 元興寺緣起, 747)
544	ⓚ Silla permits local people to become Buddhist monks and nuns and to build temples
552 ?	King Sŏngmyŏng 聖明 (r. 523–554) of Paekche (?) presented statue of Śākyamuni Buddha to Yamato court (according to *Nihon shoki*) ⓒ Year regarded as beginning of Dharma Decline (*mappō* 末法) by some Buddhists in China
554 ?	Yamato and Paekche (?) armies allied in battle against Silla, and Paekche (?) sent masters of Chinese learning to Yamato court (according to *Nihon shoki*, which perhaps attempts to prefigure 588 events?)
569	ⓒ Zhiyi 智顗 (538–597) began teaching *Lotus Sūtra* and Mahāyāna meditation practices; eventually established Tiantai 天台 (Tendai) school
574, 577	ⓒ 2nd major persecution of Buddhism (by Northern Zhou 北周 Kingdom) in China
577 ?	King Sŏngmyŏng of Paekche (?) sent monks, nuns, meditation masters, and Buddhist artisans to Yamato court in Japan (according to *Nihon shoki*)
579 ?	Silla 新羅 (?) sent Buddhist images to Yamato court in Japan (according to *Nihon shoki*)
584 ?	Soga no Umako 蘇我馬子 (?) obtained two Buddha images from Paekche and erected worship hall for them where daughter of Shiba Tatto served as the "nun" Zenshin'ni 善信尼 (according to *Nihon shoki*)

Dates	Events
585 ?	Mononobe Moriya 物部守屋 (?) blamed outbreak of pestilence on new "buddha-*kami*" 佛神 and burned down Soga's worship hall, disposed of Buddha image in river, and had nuns publicly flogged (according to *Nihon shoki*)
587 ?	Yamato hegemon performed *Niinamesai* 新嘗祭 (or *Daijōsai* 大嘗祭) for first time (?); Soga 蘇我 *uji* (?) defeated Mononobe 物部 *uji*, Buddhism now formally accepted by Yamato hegemon (according to *Nihon shoki*)
588 ?	Soga no Umako (?) established Asukadera 飛鳥寺 (subsequently regarded as origin of the later Hōkōji 法興寺 and of the still later Gangōji 元興寺) as Japan's first major Buddhist temple, invited craftsmen and artisans from Paekche to begin construction, sent Zenshin and other women to Paekche for proper Buddhist ordination as nuns (according to *Nihon shoki*); hereafter, wealthy elites began to abandon custom of burial mounds (*kofun*) and erected Buddhist halls as mausoleums instead
589	ⓒ Sui 隋 Dynasty (581–617) united North and South China into new Imperial State
592 ?	Soga Umako (?) murdered Yamato hegemon (*tennō*) Sushun 崇峻 (?), placed wife of Bidatsu 敏達 (?) on throne as female hegemon Suiko 推古 (?; according to *Nihon shoki*)
594 ?	Shōtoku *taishi* 聖德太子 (?; 574–622) leads court for Suiko (according to *Nihon shoki*); Shōtoku subsequently worshiped as patron saint of Japanese Buddhism and described as "regent" (*sesshō* 攝政)
598	ⓚ Sui armies attacked Koguryŏ 高句麗
600	Japanese king 倭王 sent embassy to China's Sui court in Chang'an 長安 (according to *Suishu* 隋書)
602 ?	Paekche (?) monks introduced books on astronomy, calendar, geography, and military science (according to *Nihon shoki*)
604 ?	Shōtoku *taishi* (?) issued 17 article "Constitution" (*kenpō* 憲法); established Japan's first calendar (according to *Nihon shoki*)
607	Japanese king sent 2nd embassy to Sui court in China (with greetings from "son of heaven in land of rising sun 日出處天子 to son of heaven in land where the sun sets") (according to *Suishu*)
608 ?	Yamato court received official envoy from Sui court in China; in return they sent 3rd embassy to Sui, including several people who stayed in China and became officially ordained as Buddhist monks (according to *Nihon shoki*)
612	ⓚ Sui armies attacked Koguryŏ
618	ⓒ Tang 唐 dynasty (618–907) replaced Sui and inaugurated new flowering of Chinese civilization
623 ?	Yamato court sent embassy (?) to Tang court in China (according to *Nihon shoki*)

DATES	EVENTS
624 ?	Ecclesiastical magistrates (?) of Saṅgha Prefect (*sōjō* 僧正), Saṅgha Provost (*sōzu* 僧都), and Dharma Chief (*hōtō* 法頭) appointed for first time to manage 46 temples (*ji* 寺) with 1,385 male and female residents (according to *Nihon shoki*)
632 ?	Japanese Buddhist monks returned from China
639 ?	Kudara ōdera 百済大寺 constructed as the court's first major Buddhist temple (subsequently regarded as origin of the later Daikan daiji 大官大寺 and of the still later Daianji 大安寺) (according to *Nihon shoki*)
643 ?	Soga Iruka 蘇我入鹿 (?) murdered entire family of Shōtoku's son Yamashiro no Ōe 山背大兄 (according to *Nihon shoki*)
644 ?	Daoist (?) religious movement 常世神信仰 suppressed by Yamato court (according to *Nihon shoki*)
645 ?	Taika coup d'etat 大化改新 (?; according to *Nihon shoki*): Yamato prince Naka no Ōe 中大兄 murdered Soga Iruka; attempted to create "imperial" state based on Tang system: Yamato court supposedly confiscated all rice lands, abolished *uji* control over families, outlawed slavery, and imposed taxation ⓒ Xuanzang 玄奘 (ca. 596–664) returned to China after 15 years in India
ca. 650s	First evidence of literacy and written records among some Yamato ruling elites
653 ?	Dōshō 道昭 (629–700) traveled to Chang'an (capital of Tang China) along with other scholar monks and embassy from Yamato court (according to *Nihon shoki*); Dōshō studied with Xuanzang
654 ?	Four traders from Tokhara (Afghanistan) and a woman from Śrāvastī (northeast India) shipwrecked in Kyushu (according to *Nihon shoki*)
660	Ⓚ Silla (allied with Tang) defeated Paekche First *Ninnō e* 仁王會 (?; chanting ceremony to invoke the protection of 4 heavenly kings) at Yamato court (according to *Nihon shoki*)
ca. 660s	Kawaradera 川原寺 Buddhist temple erected by Yamato hegemon (Tenji 天智 or Saimei 斉明 ?)
661	Yamato court sent embassy to Tang court in China (according to *Xin Tangshu* 新唐書); Dōshō returned from China (according to *Nihon shoki*)
662 ?	Dōshō established Zen'inji 禪院寺 (?) meditation center within Asukadera (according to *Genkō shakusho* 元亨釋書, 1322)
663	Yamato court sent embassy to Tang court in China (according to *Xin Tangshu*); Japanese forces (?) in Korea defeated by Silla (and Tang) (according to *Nihon shoki*)
668	Ⓚ Silla (and Tang) defeated Koguryŏ = beginning of unified Silla dynasty

Dates	Events
669 ?	Nakatomi no Kamatari 中臣鎌足 (?; 614–669) erected Yamashinadera 山階寺 temple (subsequently regarded as origin of the later Kōfukuji 興福寺) (according to *Kōfukuji engi* 興福寺緣起, 900)
670	Yamato hegemon (Tenji ?) sent embassy to Tang court in China, stated that his kingdom should be called "Nippon" 日本 (instead of "Wa" 倭) (according to *Xin Tangshu*); thereafter, no diplomatic relations with China for 30 years (until 701)
672	Jinshin no ran 壬申の乱: Tenmu 天武 (d. 686) became Yamato monarch after bloody succession dispute, established rival royal line, implemented Taika reforms (?)
672 ?	Tenmu appointed *gūji* 宮司 (celebrant) to Ise 伊勢 Shrines (?) for first time (according to *Nihon shoki*)
673 ?	Tenmu ordered Buddhist scriptures copied at Kawaradera and began construction on great temple at Takechi 高市大寺 (subsequently named Daikan daiji 大官大寺) (according to *Nihon shoki*)
674	© Chinese Tang emperor briefly adopted title of "heavenly sovereign" (*tennō* 天皇)
675 ?	Tenmu confiscated land holdings of aristocrats and Buddhist temples; first prohibition of hunting and eating meat (according to *Nihon shoki*)
676 ?	First edict to release all captive animals (*hōjō* 放生); lectures ordered on scriptures of Golden Illumination (*Konkōmyō kyō* 金光明經) and of Humane Kings (*Ninnō kyō* 仁王經) (according to *Nihon shoki*)
679 ?	Tenmu regulated the income and names of all official temples (according to *Nihon shoki*)
680	Tenmu vowed to erect Yakushiji 藥師寺 (The Healing Buddha's Temple) to help his consort recover from an illness (this is the first temple named with a Buddhist term instead of its geographical location)
681	Tenmu ordered compilation of royal history (origin of *Kojiki* 古事記 and *Nihon shoki*); events began to be recorded, dates in *Nihon shoki* become somewhat reliable
682	Gyōki 行基 (668–749) became Dōshō's disciple; draft of *Kojiki* probably written about this time (?)
684	© Zhou 周 dynasty (684–704) of empress Wu 則天武后 briefly took over Tang, used Buddhism to legitimate female rulership (became model for Japanese story of Suiko?)
685 ?	First order that all elite families should construct Buddhist icons and erect Buddhist worship halls; Grand Shrines of Ise rebuilt (or built?) for first time (according to *Nihon shoki*)
687	Buddhist memorial services performed for Tenmu, hereafter Buddhist memorial rites for rulers became established custom

Dates	Events
ca. 690s	Title *tennō* 天皇 began to be used as term for head of royal family (originally a Daoist title for the pole star, *tennō* literally means "heavenly sovereign" and today usually is translated as "emperor")
690	In one ceremony at palace the Yamato court presented gifts to 3,363 (?) monks from 7 major monasteries (according to *Nihon shoki*)
692	Genkareki 元嘉暦 (a luni-solar calendar used in China during 445–509) adopted as official calendar; census recorded 545 Buddhist worship sites (*ji* 寺) (according to *Nihon shoki*)
694	Fujiwarakyō 藤原京 laid out as vast capital city with four major Buddhist temples: Yakushiji, Daikan daiji, Hōkōji, and Kawaradera = complete adoption of Buddhism as state religion
697	Gihōreki 儀鳳暦 (a luni-solar calendar used in Tang China during 665–727) adopted as official calendar
699	En no Ozunu 役小角 (*gyōja* 行者) of Mt. Katsuragi 葛城山 banished to Izu peninsula for practicing black magic (or Daoist rituals?); En no Gyōja later regarded as founder of Shugendō 修験道
700	Dōshō's corpse cremated (Japan's first Buddhist cremation according to *Shoku Nihongi* 續日本紀)
701	*Taihō Law Code* 太寶律令 (not extant) supposedly formally established kingdom called "Nippon" 日本國; divided government into two halves: Jingikan 神祇官 and Dajōkan 太政官, which incorporated monks and nuns as government workers (*kansō* 官僧) governed by the Saṅgha Magistrates (*sōgō* 僧綱); *Sōniryō* 僧尼令 (Saṅgha Regulations) section of *Taihō Law Code* forbade Buddhist preaching to commoners, meditation in the mountains, teaching military tactics, etc. Diplomatic embassy sent to China for first time since 670, included Buddhist monk Dōji 道慈 (d. 744)
710	Nara Period: Nara 奈良 (Heijōkyō 平城京) established as new capital city for Kingdom of Nippon
712	*Kojiki* 古事記 completed (written in Chinese mixed together with Japanese transliterated by Chinese glyphs) as official history of royal house (this text later used to rediscover "ancient Shinto")
713	Gyōki (Buddhist preacher) began missions among rural Japanese
714	Vimalakīrti Ceremony (*Yuima-e* 維摩會) performed at Kōfukuji 興福寺 monastery in Nara for first time
717	Gyōki repressed by government; Genbō 玄昉 (d. 746) traveled to China

Dates	Events
718	Dōji (Buddhist monk) returned to Japan, aided in compilation of *Nihon shoki* (to replace defective *Kojiki*) and new *Yōrō Law Code* 養老令 promulgated (to more closely approximate Chinese model); Buddhist monks again forbidden from living in mountains
720	*Nihon shoki* 日本書紀 completed (written in proper Chinese) as official history of royal family and government (this text used as basis for subsequent "histories" of ancient Japan, BCE 660–697 CE)
729	Court issued new edicts prohibiting Buddhists from training in mountains
733	Government sent 2 monks to China to bring back a vinaya master
735	Genbō returned from China with handwritten copy of entire *Chinese Buddhist Canon* (5,000+ fascicles)
736	Daoxuan 道璿 (Dōsen, 702–760) arrived in Japan, taught vinaya and Chan 禪 (Zen); Bodhisena (from India) and another monk from Champa 林邑 (Vietnam) arrived in Japan
737	Major smallpox epidemic (threatened court); Genbō appointed Official Court Meditation Master (*zenji* 禪師), cared for sick queen (i.e., empress)
740	Revolt by Fujiwara Hirotsugu 藤原廣嗣 in Kyushu directed against Genbō's politics
741	Court established provincial temple (Kokubunji 國分寺) system with Tōdaiji 東大寺 monastery as head; Court officially designated six areas of specialization for Buddhist studies (i.e., Ritsu 律, Kusha 倶舍, Jōjitsu 成實, Sanron 三論, Hossō 法相, and Kegon 華嚴)
743	Gyōki used as fund raiser for Tōdaiji monastery
747	*Gangōji engi* 元興寺緣起 compiled as private history of early Japanese Buddhism
749	Gold discovered in Japan; Hachiman 八幡 (Yahata) enshrined at Tamukeyama 手向山 in Nara
ca. 751	*Kaifūsō* 懷風漢 collection of Chinese verse by Japanese aristocrats compiled
752	Tōdaiji Dedication: Completion of colossal Buddha (*daibutsu* 大佛) image
754	Ganjin 鑑眞 (Jianzhen, 687–763) established Ritsu (Vinaya) in Japan; conducted first proper Buddhist ordinations on special platform at Tōdaiji; government now controlled ordinations
755	© Revolt of An Lushan 安祿山 (d. 757) severely weakened Tang government
758	Court ordered mountain priests (*zenji*) to more than 10 years of "pure practice" to be recognized as ordained
759	Tōshōdaiji 唐招提寺 monastery established for Ganjin as headquarters of vinaya studies

Dates	Events
ca. 760	*Man'yōshū* 萬葉集 (10,000 Leaves) collection of Japanese verse and song (written in Japanese transliterated by Chinese glyphs) compiled
764	Retired female sovereign Kōken 孝謙 (r. 749–758) resumed control under new name 稱德 (Shōtoku, r. 764–770), attempted to found Buddhist theocracy like that of Chinese Empress Wu (d. 704); 1 million+ copies of Buddhist *dhāraṇī* printed in Japan (world's oldest extant printed text?) and distributed throughout the land (now known as *hyakumantō darani* 百萬塔陀羅尼); Dōkyō 道鏡 (d. 772) appointed "Prime Minister Zen Master" (*daijin zenji* 大臣禪師); Taienreki 大衍曆 (a luni-solar calendar designed by the Buddhist monk Yixing 一行, 673–727; used in China during 728–761) adopted as court calendar
765	Dōkyō appointed "Chancellor Zen Master" (*dajō daijin zenji* 太政大臣禪師), indicating that he exercised full control over the court
766	Dōkyō assumed title of Dharma King (*hōō* 法王), indicating that he exercised full control over the clergy; major Buddhist temples built at (future?) site of Ise shrines
769	Dōkyō revealed Hachiman oracle that he should be "Heavenly Sovereign" (*tennō*); subsequent oracle from Hachiman temple in Usa 宇佐 (Kyushu) contradicted Dōkyō
770	Dōkyō banished; Kōnin 光仁 *tennō* established new royal house (which claimed descent from Tenji); court lifted all restrictions on mountain training
772	Court established group of *jū zenji* 十禪師 (10 Meditation Masters) to pray for health of ruler
774–811	Repeated military campaigns to defeat Emishi 蝦夷 kingdoms in northern Japan bring fame to warrior leaders such as Ōtomo no Otomaro 大伴弟麻呂 and Sakanoue no Tamuramaro 坂上田村麻呂 (758–811)
779	Court attempted to defrock all unauthorized (i.e., self-ordained) monks and nuns
ca. 780s	Sovereign (*tennō*) first referred to as *aki tsu mi kami* (manifest god): idea of "divine king"
781	Hachiman awarded status of bodhisattva (*bosatsu* 菩薩)
785	Saichō 最澄 (767–822) ordained in Nara, retired to Mt. Hiei 比叡山 (future site of Enryakuji 延曆寺)
791	Kūkai 空海 (774–835) learned *gumonjihō* 求聞字法 and dropped out of state college
794	Heian Period: Kyoto 京都 (Heiankyō 平安京) established as new capital
797	Saichō appointed court Meditation Master (*zenji*)
799	Court ordered provincial governors to purge provincial temples (Kokubunji) of corrupt monks

Dates	Events
ca. 800s	Aristocrats began to construct shrines for worship of their divine ancestors (*ujigami* 氏神)
800	Ise shrines codified rituals (in *Gishikichō* 儀式帳); Ise shrines identified as Royal State Mausolea (*sōbyō* 宗廟), like mausolea of Chinese noble clans; worship at Ise forbidden to all but sovereign (*tennō*)
804.7	Saichō and Kūkai traveled to China: Saichō studied at Mt. Tiantai 天台山; Kūkai studied at Tang capital of Chang'an 長安
805.7	Saichō returned to Japan: claimed 4 lineages of *en mitsu zen kai* 圓密禪戒 (Tiantai, esoteric, Chan, and bodhisattva precepts); performed esoteric rituals for court
806.10	Kūkai returned to Japan
815	Saichō began mission in eastern Japan
ca. 817	Tokuichi (Tokuitsu) 徳一 (Hossō monk) and Saichō began polemical debate
822	Saichō died; court authorized a Tendai "Mahāyāna Ordination Platform" on Mt. Hiei
ca. 823	Kyōkai 景戒 wrote *Nihon ryōiki* 日本靈異記, recorded early Buddhist folktales and faith in *karma*; Mt. Hiei awarded name Enryakuji 延暦寺; Tendai now an independent school
830	Kūkai wrote *Jūjūshinron* 十住心論, systematized Shingon
834	Kūkai established Shingon'in 眞言院 esoteric training hall inside royal palace, began performing Latter Seven-Day Rite (*Go shichinichi mishiho* 後七日御修法) as annual Buddhist consecration of ruler
838	Ennin 圓仁 (794–864) accompanied the 12th (and last) official trade embassy to Tang China, wrote detailed diary of his travels in China and the Huichang Chinese persecution of Buddhism
845	© Huichang 會昌 persecution of Buddhism in China: beginning of the end of Tang-style Buddhism
847	Ennin returned from China, established superiority of Tendai esoteric rites (*mikkyō* 密教) over Shingon lineage, and introduced new rituals for worship of Amitābha (Amida 阿彌陀) Buddha
850	Ennin established Mt. Hiei as protector of the sovereign (*tennō goji* 天皇護持)
853	Enchin 圓珍 (814–891) journeyed to China
855	Head of colossal Buddha image at Tōdaiji in Nara fell during earthquake; head subsequently reattached

Dates	Events
858	Enchin returned to Japan; founded new Tendai center Onjōji 園城寺 (a.k.a. Miidera 三井寺); Gokireki 五紀暦 (a luni-solar calendar used in Tang China during 762–821) adopted as court's official calendar
860	Hachiman enshrined in Buddhist temple at Iwashimizu 石清水 near Kyoto
862	Senmyōreki 宣明暦 (a luni-solar calendar used in Tang China during 822–895) adopted as court's official calendar; in Japan the Senmyōreki remained the official court calendar until 1684
862–867	Shūei 宗叡 (808–884) journeyed to Tang China (was last renowned Japanese monk to visit Tang)
878	Emishi revolted in northern Japan
ca. 901	Annen 安然 (n.d.) advocated changing name of his own Tendai tradition to "Shingon" since its esoteric rites constitute its most important practices; Annen taught unity of Shingon, Tendai, and Zen
907	ⓒ Tang state collapsed: China entered period of civil warfare that destroyed Buddhist monasteries
918	ⓚ Koryŏ dynasty 高麗 (918–1392) established in Korean peninsula
927	*Engishiki* 延喜式 (Engi-period Regulations) compiled, regulated court support for religious rituals
938	Kōya 空也 (Kūya, 903–972) began to teach *nenbutsu* in the marketplace
939	Emishi revolted in northern Japan
939–940	Taira no Masakado 平 将門 (d. 940) seized control of 8 provincial governments in eastern Japan
947	Tenjin Shrine 天神祠 to appease Sugawara Michizane 管原道眞 (845–903) erected at Kitano 北野
949	Tōdaiji sent monastic militia (*sōhei* 僧兵) to demonstrate in Kyoto (this tactic subsequently adopted by other wealthy temples and shrines)
960	ⓒ Song 宋 dynasty (960–1279) established; Chan and Tiantai became mainstream Buddhism
967	Fujiwara Saneyori 藤原實頼 (900–970) became regent (*kanpaku* 關白); thereafter the head of Fujiwara family ruled court as regent continuously until 1068
968	Open conflict erupted between Tōdaiji and Kōfukuji (2 main Nara monasteries)
971–983	ⓒ Song government printed entire *Chinese Buddhist Canon* 蜀版大藏經 (5,586 fascicles)
983	Chōnen 奝然 (d. 1016) traveled to Song China

DATES	EVENTS
984	Minamoto Tamenori 源 爲憲 wrote *Sanbō e kotoba* 三寶絵詞, recorded annual Buddhist rituals
985	Genshin 源信 (942–1017) wrote *Ōjōyōshū* 往生要集, popularized Pure Land meditation within Tendai
986	Ise Shrines sent militia (*jinin* 神人) to demonstrate in Kyoto; Yoshishige Yasutane 慶滋保胤 (Jakushin 寂心; d. 1002) founded fraternity (called Nenbutsu zanmai e 念佛三昧會) on Mt. Hiei dedicated to deliverance in Amitābha's Pure Land; Yasutane subsequently compiled *Nihon ōjō gokuraku ki* 日本往生極樂記 hagiography of people delivered to Pure Land
987	Chōnen returned to Japan with entire Song Edition of *Chinese Buddhist Canon* and statue of Buddha containing inner organs
993	Open conflict erupted between Enryakuji and Onjōji (both major Tendai monasteries)
994	Main pagoda on Mt. Kōya 高野山 destroyed by fire (and not rebuilt until 1103)
1003	Genshin corresponded with Zhili 知礼 (960–1028) on points of Tiantai doctrine (final installment in Tendai correspondence that began with Chinese teachers in 805, 840, and 845)
1004	© Zhili began campaign to eliminate heretical interpretations of Chinese Tiantai, initiated great controversy between "mountain lineage" 山家 and "outside the mountain" 山外 forms of Tiantai
ca. 1005	Chinese merchants begin introducing Song dynasty wares to Japan
ca. 1008 ?	Murasaki Shikibu 紫 式部 wrote *Genji monogatari* 源氏物語 (Tale of Genji)
1010s	Ⓚ Koryŏ state began printing *Chinese Buddhist Canon* 高麗版 based on 983 Song edition Armed conflict between Tōdaiji and Kōfukuji (2 main Nara monasteries)
1013	Armed conflict between Enryakuji (Tendai) and Kōfukuji (Nara)
1028	Taira no Tadatsune 平 忠常 (d. 1031) seized control of 3 provincial governments in eastern Japan; campaign to capture him devastated the provinces of the Bōsō 房總 peninsula
ca. 1044	Chingen 鎮源 wrote *Hokke genki* 法華驗記, recorded "*Lotus Sūtra* Miracles"
1049	Buddha relics (*shari* 舍利) distributed as offering to all important regional shrines
1051	Former Nine-Years War 前九年の役 started in northern Japan (lasted until 1063)
1052	Year regarded as the beginning of Dharma Decline (*mappō* 末法) by some Japanese

DATES	EVENTS
1072	Jōjin 成尋 (1011–1081) traveled to Song China, wrote diary of visits to Mt. Tiantai and Mt. Wutai 五台山
1073	ⓚ Japanese merchants establish trade agreements with Koryŏ court in Korea
1074	ⓒ Song court permitted export of coins to Japan, thereafter Chinese coins become main currency in Japan
1075	Enryakuji attacked Onjōji to prevent the latter from establishing its own ordination platform
1081	Monastic militia from Enryakuji burned Onjōji (conflicts last until 16th century); monastic militia from Kōfukuji attacked Buddhist monastery at Tōnomine 多武峰
1083	Later Three-Years War 後三年の役 started in northern Japan (lasted until 1087)
1086	Shirakawa 白河 (1053–1129; r. 1072–1086) retired from office of tennō and became Buddhist monk, but still ruled from his temple (in 院); began rule by cloistered sovereign (insei 院政), a practice that continued until 1180; all retired sovereigns continued to become Buddhist monks until 1840
1090	Shirakawa completed religious pilgrimage to Kumano 熊野, marked growing popularity of pilgrimages
1094	Fujiwara Kiyohira 藤原清衡 (d. 1128) established Hiraizumi 平泉 as new Fujiwara capital city to rule over northern Japan
1095	Monastic militia from Enryakuji blackmailed government by bringing portable shrine of the mountain god (Hie 日吉) into the capital (this tactic used repeatedly)
1098	Great fires destroyed much of Kyoto
1102	Monastic militia from Tōdaiji blackmailed government by bringing portable shrine of the bodhisattva Hachiman into the capital (this tactic used repeatedly)
1107 ?	Konjaku monogatari 今昔物語 compiled about this time, recorded popular Buddhist literature
1116	Nara monk Jippan [Jichihan] 實範 (d. 1144) restored Tōshōdaiji, advocated ordinations based on vinaya
ca. 1117	Ryōnin 良忍 (1073–1232) attained vision of Amitābha Buddha, initiated practice of yūzū nenbutsu 融通念佛 (interpenetration of all things through recalling Amitābha Buddha)
1127	ⓒ Northern China fell to Mongols 蒙古; **Southern Song** 南宋 **dynasty** (1127–1279) began
1134	Major famine in Japan
ca. 1141	Kakuban 覺鑁 (1095–1143) wrote Gorin kujimyō himitsu shaku 五輪九字明秘密釋, advocated unity of Shingon and nenbutsu 念佛 (recalling Amitābha Buddha)

Dates	Events
1150 ?	Hōnen 法然 (Genkū 源空; 1133–1212) left Mt. Hiei to live among the *hijiri* 聖 (i.e., ascetics)
1151	Famine in Kyoto
1156	Hogen Incident 保元の亂: warrior bands fought in support of rival candidates for royal (*tennō*) succession and for the Fujiwara 藤原 headship
1159–1161	Heiji Incident 平治の亂: Taira no Kiyomori 平 清盛 (1118–1181) defeated Minamoto 源 warrior bands
1163	Famine in Kyoto
1167	Chōgen 重源 (1121–1206) visited China; studied Tiantai (returned with Eisai)
1168	Eisai 榮西 (1141–1215) visited China for 5 months; studied Tiantai
1172	Hōnen read writings of Shandao 善導 (Zendō, 613–681), began teaching exclusive Pure Land faith
1177	Major earthquake and fire destroyed much of Kyoto again
1180	Genpei War 源平合戰: Minamoto Yoritomo 源 賴朝 (1147–1199) gained supremacy in revolt against Taira no Kiyomori; during course of this conflict Taira no Shigehira 平 重衡 (1156–1185) torched Nara, destroying the great temple complexes of Tōdaiji, Kōfukuji, and Gangōji; Tōdaiji's colossal Buddha image melted, priests slaughtered
ca. 1180	Hachiman enshrined in Kamakura (origin of Tsurugaoka 鶴岡 Buddhist temple complex); *Fusō ryakki* 扶桑略記 (30 vols.) compiled as documentary history of Japan
1181	Famine in Kyoto; court dismissed Tōdaiji and Kōfukuji prelates from offices, confiscated all temple lands; land holdings restored 2 months later
1181	Chōgen began fund-raising campaign to rebuild Tōdaiji; Chōgen invited team of artisans from China to recast colossal Buddha
1185	Kamakura Period: Minamoto Yoritomo established Kamakura *bakufu* 鎌倉幕府 (military administration), immediately donated lands to Grand Shrines of Ise and funds for Tōdaiji; Taira no Shigehira executed in Nara
1186	Chōgen led large group of Buddhist monks to Grand Shrines of Ise to pray for restoration of Tōdaiji; monk-poet Saigyō 西行 (1118–1190) led Tōdaiji fund-raising campaign to northern Japan
1187	Eisai again went to China and studied Rinzai 臨濟 Zen at Mt. Tiantai
1189	Nōnin 能忍 began teaching "Darumashū" 達磨宗 Zen at Sanbōji 三寶寺 temple in Settsu 攝津; Minamoto Yoritomo defeated the Northern Fujiwara
1191	Eisai returned to Japan, taught Zen in Kyushu, advocated observing vinaya precepts
1192	Court granted Minamoto Yoritomo official title of *shōgun* 將軍

Dates	Events
1194	Exclusive Zen of Eisai and Nōnin banned by royal court in Kyoto
1195	Tōdaiji's Main Buddha Hall restored and dedicated
1198	Hōnen wrote *Senchakushū* 選擇集; Eisai wrote *Kōzen gokokuron* 興禪護國論 to defend Zen
1199	Shunjō 俊芿 (1166–1227) went to China, studied Vinaya, Tiantai, Zen, and Pure Land Buddhism
1200	Eisai invited to Kamakura as Kamakura *bakufu* began to patronize Zen teachers
1201	Shinran 親鸞 (1173–1263) became Hōnen's disciple
1202	Eisai allowed to build Kenninji 建仁寺 temple in Kyoto with backing of Kamakura *bakufu*
1203	Kōben 高辨 (Myōe 明惠, 1173–1232) abandoned plan to visit India because oracle of Kasuga 春日 shrine identified Nara as being the Pure Land of the Buddha Śākyamuni; Kōben taught Mantra of Radiant Wisdom (*kōmyō shingon* 光明眞言)
1205	Jōkei 貞慶 (1155–1213) denounced Hōnen in his *Kōfukuji Petition* 興福寺奏狀
1206	Eisai appointed head of Tōdaiji fund-raising campaign
1207	Exclusive Pure Land banned by royal court, Hōnen and Shinran sent into exile outside of Kyoto
1211	Ban on Pure Land teachings lifted; Jōkei vowed to restore vinaya; Shunjō returned from China, built Sennyūji 泉涌寺 temple as Chinese-style center for Tendai, Vinaya, Zen, and Pure Land
1212	*Hōjōki* 方丈記 written by Kamo no Chōmei 鴨長明 (ca. 1155–1216), lamented Dharma Decline (*mappō*); Kōben (Myōe) denounced Hōnen in his *Saijarin* 摧邪輪
ca. 1219	*Kitano tenjin engi* 北野天神緣起 (history of Kitano Shrine) composed about this time, other shrines and temples also begin compiling own legendary histories (*jisha engi* 寺社緣起)
1221	Jōkyū Disturbance 承久の亂: 3 ex-*tennō* (sovereigns) sent into exile, royal lands seized by *bakufu*, power balance shifted to Kamakura
ca. 1224	Shinran wrote *Kyōgyōshinshō* 教行信證, his major statement of Pure Land doctrine
1227	Militia from Enryakuji attempt to suppress Hōnen's followers, destroyed Hōnen's grave site
1231	Major famine
1233	Dōgen 道元 (1200–1253) founded exclusive Zen temple (Kōshōji 興聖寺); event regarded as founding of Japan's Sōtō 曹洞 Zen lineage

Dates	Events
1234	Eison 叡尊 (1201–1290) vowed to restore vinaya, founded Saidaiji 西大寺 temple to propagate vinaya, eventually administered full (*gusokukai* 具足戒) ordinations to 800+ monks and nuns, and lay precepts to tens of thousands of people
1244	Eison and disciple Ninshō 忍性 (1217–1303) began ministry to outcasts (*hinin* 非人), beggars, and lepers
1249	Kenchōji 建長寺 in Kamakura built as first Song Dynasty-style Zen temple by Hōjō 北條 Regents
1251	Ⓚ Koryǒ state reprinted *Chinese Buddhist Canon* 高麗版 (6,558 fascicles) based on 1011 Koryǒ edition plus supplements [this is earliest extant complete printed edition]
1252	Ⓒ Siqi Fabaosi temple printed a new edition of *Chinese Buddhist Canon* 思溪法寶寺版 (5,740 fascicles)
1253	Nichiren 日蓮 (1222–1282) began lecturing on *Lotus Sūtra*, subsequently founds Nichiren School
1259	Famine widespread
1260	Nichiren wrote *Risshō ankokuron* 立正安國論 to admonish the warrior administration (denounced Hōnen's Pure Land teachings), later arrested and exiled to Izu 伊豆
1264	Colossal Buddha (*daibutsu*) image of Amitābha constructed at Kamakura
1268	Mongol envoys visited Japan, demanded tribute
1271	Ⓒ Yüan 元 dynasty (1271–1368): all of China conquered by Mongols
1271–1272	Severe drought throughout Japan; Court asked Ninshō to pray for rain; Nichiren exiled again in wake of his mounting criticisms of other forms of Buddhism
1273	Court asked Eison to pray at Grand Shrines of Ise to repel Mongol threat
1274	Mongol armies attempted to invade Japan 文永の異國合戰 (蒙古襲来); Nichiren released from exile; Ninshō organized campaign to feed starving masses; Ippen 一遍 (Chishin 智眞, 1239–1289) began his travels to popularize practice of *nenbutsu* (recalling Amitābha), subsequently founds Jishū 時宗 School
1276	Gyōnen 凝然 (1240–1321) began teaching at Tōdaiji, lectured on all aspects of Buddhist doctrines and history, wrote 1,200+ volumes, which form basis of subsequent Japanese Buddhist scholarship
1281	Mongol armies again attempted to invade Japan 弘安の異國合戰 (蒙古襲来) and lost 70,000 men
1283	Mujū Dōgyō 無住道曉 (1226–1312) wrote *Shasekishū* 沙石集, recorded popular religious beliefs

DATES	EVENTS
1287	Ninshō founded public hospital to care for sick, said to have healed tens of thousands of people
1291	Nanzenji 南禪寺 in Kyoto built as first Chinese-style Zen monastery sponsored by southern royal family
1293	Earthquake in Kamakura killed over 20,000 people
ca. 1296	Outer Shrine at Ise assumed "Imperial" (*kōtai* 皇太) title (emergence of "Watarai Shinto" 度會神道)
1299	"Five Mountain" (*Gozan* 五山) system of prestigious Zen temples established by *bakufu*
1301	*bakufu* implemented policy of alternate succession among 2 branches (northern-southern) of royal family
ca. 1321	Keizan Jōkin 瑩山紹瑾 (1264–1365) founded Sōjiji 總持寺 monastery on the Noto 能登 peninsula, thereby laid foundation for the subsequent propagation of Sōtō Zen throughout rural areas
1322	Kokan Shiren 虎關師錬 (1278–1346) wrote *Genkō shakusho* 元亨釋書, the first comprehensive history of Japanese religion
ca. 1331	Kakunyo 覺如 (1270–1351) established Honganji 本願寺 temple at Shinran's grave (*byō* 廟) in Ōtani 大谷
1332	Go-Daigo 後醍醐 (1288–1339) sovereign exiled to Oki 隠岐 (Oki no shima) for refusing policy of alternate succession
1333	Go-Daigo escaped from Oki; his forces overthrew Kamakura *bakufu*
1334	Go-Daigo proclaimed "Kenmu Restoration" 建武の新政 (= direct rule by *tennō*); Nichizō 日像 (1269–1342) finally received permission to teach Nichiren's Lotus Buddhism in Kyoto
1336	Ashikaga Takauji 足利尊氏 (1305–1358) deposed Go-Daigo and established Ashikaga *bakufu* 足利幕府; Go-Daigo established rival court at Zaōdō 藏王堂 temple in Yoshino 吉野 (south of Nara): beginning of split between northern and southern lines of royal family 南北朝 (divided courts persisted until 1392)
1338	Ashikaga Takauji officially awarded title of *shōgun*, located his military government (*bakufu*) in Kyoto; trade relations established with Yüan (Mongol) China
1342	"Five Mountain" (*Gozan*) Zen temples in Kyoto, under patronage of Ashikaga *bakufu* and of Northern Court, assumed higher rank than "Five Mountain" temples in Kamakura
1343	Kitabatake Chikafusa 北畠親房 (1293–1354) completed *Jinnō shōtōki* 神皇正統記 (Chronicle of Legitimate Gods and Sovereigns), argued for legitimacy of Go-Daigo's southern line

DATES	EVENTS
ca. 1348	Kōshū 光宗 (1276–1350) compiled *Keiran shūyōshū* 溪嵐拾葉集, recorded Tendai initiations
ca. 1350s	Takuga 託何 (1285–1354) wrote *Kibokuron* 器朴論, systematized Jishū 時宗 Pure Land doctrines
1368	ⓒ Ming 明 dynasty (1368–1644) established in China
1369	Trade relations established with Ming China
1379	Saṅgha Registrar (*sōroku* 僧録) established by Ashikaga *bakufu* to regulate *Gozan* Zen temples
1386	Nanzenji in Kyoto designated #1 *Gozan* Zen temple by *bakufu*
1392	Southern Court (Go-Daigo's line) defeated by Ashikaga *bakufu* ⓚ Chosŏn 朝鮮 dynasty (1392–1910) established in Korea
1397	Trade relations established with Chosŏn Korea
ca. 1400	Yūkai 宥快 (1345–1416) wrote *Hōkyōshō* 寶鏡鈔, in which he denounced as unorthodox the sexual rituals taught in the Shingon lineages that he (falsely) identified as "Tachikawaryū" 立川流
1404	Official tally trade 勘合貿易 began with Ming China
ca. 1418	Tally trade conducted with Chosŏn Korea
1423	Trade relations established with Ryūkyū 琉球 Kingdom (Okinawa)
1431	Major famine
1434	Outer (Watarai) Shrine of Ise rebuilt for last time (until 1563)
1440s	Series of epidemics
1450s	Series of famines; thievery and disorder became increasingly common
1461	Major famine
1463	Inner (Imperial) Shrine of Ise rebuilt for last time (until 1585)
1465	Monastic militia from Enryakuji destroyed the original Honganji temple (site of Shinran's tomb)
1466	*Daijō sai* 大嘗祭 (spiritual-king food offering as part of enthronement ceremony) conducted by royal court for last time until 1687 (abbreviated version will be recreated in 1738 and 1847; revised 1871 version performed as state ceremony in 1915, 1928, and 1990)
1467	Ōnin War 應仁の亂 began: Kyoto left in ruins; traditional rituals and traditional learning of court nobles also largely destroyed; spread of warfare marked beginning of period of regional power struggles

Dates	Events
1474	Pure Land peasant leagues (*ikkō ikki* 一向一揆) formed in Kaga Province
1478	Rennyo 蓮如 (1415–1499) founded a new Honganji temple at Yamashina 山科
1479	Pure Land peasant leagues formed in Etchū Province
1480s	Dōkō 道興 (1465–1501) began to affiliate organizations of mountain guides (*sen-dat-su* 先達) with Kumano 熊野 to form Honzanha 本山派 School of Shugendō; other schools of Shugendō also began to organize
1484	Yoshida Kanetomo 吉田兼倶 (1435–1511) erected Daigengū 大元宮 temple at Yoshida Shrine: marked founding of Yuiitsu 唯一 Shinto (*aka* "Yoshida Shinto" 吉田神道)
1486	Outer (Watarai) Shrine of Ise destroyed by fire (not rebuilt until 1563)
1488	Pure Land peasant leagues began to control part of Kaga Province
1489	Inner (Imperial) Shrine of Ise destroyed by fire (not rebuilt until 1585)
1490s	Famines and epidemics widespread
1491	Major fires in Kyoto
1495	Tsunami destroyed the wooden buildings surrounding the colossal Buddha image at Kamakura
1500	*Gion matsuri* 祇園祭 staged in Kyoto for first time since Ōnin War
1505	*Bon odori* 盆踊り prohibited in Kyoto
1506	Pure Land peasant leagues take control of parts of Kaga, Noto, and Etchū
1531	Fighting and more revolts by Pure Land peasant leagues in Kaga
1532	Nichiren leagues (*Hokke ikki* 法華一揆) seized all of Kyoto; Pure Land leaders moved to Ishiyama 石山
1536	Kyoto burned when forces of Mt. Hiei (Tendai) defeat Nichiren leagues 天文法華の乱
1540	Severe nationwide famine
1542	Yoshida Kanemigi 吉田兼右 (1516–1573) visited Kyushu, began issuing Yoshida Shinto certificates of initiation to celebrants of local shrines (Yoshida Shinto started to expand beyond central regions)
1543	Firearms introduced to Japan by Portuguese traders
1546	Kanazawa Gobō 金澤御坊 established by local Pure Land leagues to govern Kaga province
1549	Francisco de Xavier (1506–1552) led Portuguese Jesuit missionaries to Kyushu (southern Japan)
1560	Jesuit missionaries permitted to proselytize in Kyoto

Dates	Events
1563	Outer (Watarai) Shrine of Ise rebuilt through fund-raising efforts of Buddhist nun Seijun 清順 (d. 1566)
1567	Colossal Buddha Hall at Tōdaiji burned down, second colossal Buddha image also melted
1568	Ōmura Sumitada 大村純忠 (1533–1587) became first regional war lord (*daimyō* 大名) baptized by Jesuits; Tōdaiji fund-raising campaign launched
1569	Oda Nobunaga 織田信長 (1534–1582) provided protection to Jesuit missionaries in Kyoto
1570	Oda Nobunaga began campaign to destroy military power of Buddhist institutions: launched first attack on Pure Land strongholds at Ishiyama
1571	Oda Nobunaga destroyed Tendai center on Mt. Hiei 元亀の兵乱, burned all buildings, killed everyone
1572	Oda Nobunaga attacked Pure Land strongholds at Nagashima 長島 in Ise
1573	Oda Nobunaga expelled *Shōgun* Ashikaga Yoshiaki 義昭 (1537–1597) from Kyoto
1574	Pure Land leagues seized control of Echizen; Oda Nobunaga suppressed Pure Land leagues in Ise
1575	Oda Nobunaga destroyed all Pure Land opposition in Echizen
1578	Oda Nobunaga sponsored building of Christian church (Nanbanji 南蠻寺) in Kyoto
1580	Oda Nobunaga eliminated Pure Land opposition in Kaga, defeated Pure Land stronghold at Ishiyama; first English ships visited Japan
1581	Oda Nobunaga killed more than 1,000 monks on Mt. Koya; Jesuits established Christian academy
1582–1590	◎ Japanese Christians traveled to Europe and visited pope at Vatican in Rome
1585	Toyotomi Hideyoshi 豊臣秀吉 (1536–1598) appointed court regent (*kanpaku* 關白): thereby became de facto ruler of Japan; Inner and Outer Shrines of Ise rebuilt with funds provided by Hideyoshi
1587	Toyotomi Hideyoshi confronted Gaspar Coelho (1530–1590) and ordered all Christian *padres* (*batenren* 伴天連) missionaries out of Japan
1588	Ashikaga *bakufu* officially dissolved; Toyotomi Hideyoshi expelled Christians from Nagasaki 長崎; Hideyoshi initiated "sword hunt" (*katanagari* 刀狩) to prevent peasants from becoming warriors
1589	Toyotomi Hideyoshi destroyed Christian church in Kyoto; Hideyoshi erected colossal Buddha (*daibutsu*) image at Hōkōji 方廣寺 temple in Kyoto; work began to rebuild temples on Mt. Hiei

Dates	Events
1590	Hasshinden 八神殿 (Hall of Eight Deities) at Yoshida Shrine used for official rites of worship by royal court (Yoshida Shinto now enjoyed full court recognition)
1592	Toyotomi Hideyoshi tried to open trade with Spanish
1592	Ⓚ Toyotomi Hideyoshi sent troops to invade Korea 文禄の役 (壬申倭亂)
1593	Ⓚ Toyotomi Hideyoshi entered negotiations with Ming Chinese court over war in Korea Franciscan (Spanish) missionaries came to Japan, Jesuit (Portuguese) mission monopoly broken
1595	Nichiō 日奥 (1565–1630) refused to participate in joint Buddhist services in honor of Hideyoshi at Hōkōji: marked beginning of Fuju-fuse 不受不施 (not accepting, not contributing) branch of Nichiren
1596	Colossal Buddha at Hōkōji temple toppled in earthquake; "San Felipe Incident," Franciscans crucified
1597	Ⓚ Toyotomi Hideyoshi sent more troops to invade Korea 慶長の役 (丁酉倭亂) after negotiations with Ming Chinese broke down
1598	Toyotomi Hideyoshi died, Japanese troops abandoned Korean campaign
1599	Toyotomi Hideyoshi deified as Toyokuni *dai myōjin* 豊國大明神
1600	Battle of Sekigahara 關ヶ原の戰: Tokugawa Ieyasu 徳川家康 (1542–1616) defeated supporters of Toyotomi family and thereby became unrivaled war lord; first Dutch merchant ships arrived in Japan (with Englishman William Adams, 1564–1620)
1601	Jesuits established seminary in Nagasaki Ⓒ Matteo Ricci (1552–1610) established first Jesuit mission in Peking
1602	Tokugawa Ieyasu sponsored the building of two new Honganji temples—Higashi 東 (east) and Nishi 西 (west)— in Kyoto, thereby splitting the Pure Land Shin denomination in two; Hōkōji destroyed by fire; Myōnin 明忍 (1576–1610) advocated vinaya, founded as new "Shingon Ritsu School" 眞言律宗
1603	Edo 江戸 Period: Tokugawa Ieyasu granted official title of *shōgun*, established Tokugawa military administration (*bakufu*) in Edo (Tokyo)
1605	Sweet potatoes introduced to Japan: population increased; Zōjōji 増上寺 (Pure Land) temple built in Edo for Tokugawa family
1607	Hayashi Razan 林羅山 (1583–1657) appointed first Confucian advisor to the *bakufu*, advocated the rational (*kyūri* 窮理) Confucianism of Zhu Xi 朱熹 (Shu Ki, 1130–1200)
1608–1618	*Bakufu* issued regulations (*hatto* 法度) to major Buddhist temples, established strict lines of command, limited conversions, demanded strict discipline and academic study of their own doctrinal lineages; 1608 = regulations (*hatto*) issued for Mt. Hiei and Jōbodaiin 成菩提院 (both Tendai)

DATES	EVENTS
1609	Dutch allowed to establish trading factory at Hirado 平戸 (near Nagasaki); regulations (*hatto*) issued for Onjōji, Shugendō, and for various Shingon temples (e.g., Tōji, Mt. Kōya)
ca. 1610	Hasegawa Kakugyō 長谷川角行 (1541–1646) organized Fujikō 富士講 (Mt. Fuji worship) groups in Edo
1612	Christianity banned (this ban re-issued repeatedly); Christian churches throughout the land destroyed; regulations (*hatto*) issued for Kōfukuji, Hasedera 長谷寺, etc.
1613	Regulations (*hatto*) issued for Tendai temples in eastern Japan, for Shugendō, and for Shingon temples
1614–1615	Osaka campaign 大坂の陣: Tokugawa forces destroyed supporters of Toyotomi family
1615	Regulations (*hatto*) issued for royal family and aristocrats, for Five Mountain Zen temples, for Sōtō Zen, and for Jōdo (Pure Land) temples
1616	Dutch, Portuguese, and European trade restricted to Hirado; regulations (*hatto*) issued for Kuonji 久遠寺 Nichiren school temple
1617	Tōshōgū 東照宮 mausoleum constructed at Nikkō 日光; Tokugawa Ieyasu deified as bodhisattva: Tōshō dai gongen 東照大権現 (subsequently called the divine ruler, *shinkun* 神君)
1619	Christians burned at the stake in Kyoto (52 died)
1620	© Lengyansi 楞嚴寺 temple printed corrected version of Ming edition 明版 of the *Chinese Buddhist Canon* 萬曆版 (6,361 fascicles) Fabian Fucan 不干斎ハビアン (1565–1621) wrote *Deus Destroyed* (*Ha Daiusu* 破提宇子) to refute Christianity; Fabian's treatise became model for subsequent anti-Christian tracts
1621	Overseas travel forbidden
1622	Construction of new Buddhist temples forbidden; persecution of Christians entered most extreme phase
1624	Spanish trade cut off; Spanish ships forbidden to come to Japan
1625	Tenkai 天海 (1536–1643) constructed Kan'eiji 寛永寺 (Tō Eizan 東叡山) temple in Edo as new administrative head for Tendai school
1629	Takuan Sōhō 澤庵宗彭 (1573–1645) exiled to Dewa 出羽 for protesting *bakufu* restrictions on the court's ability to award purple robes (*shie* 紫衣) to the abbots of Nanzenji and Daitokuji 大徳寺 Zen temples
1630	Leaders of Fuju-Fuse 不受不施 branch of Nichiren exiled
1632	Senseiden 先聖殿 Confucian Temple erected at Hayashi's Academy

Dates	Events
1633–1639	Closing of the country (*sakoku* 鎖國): orders issued repeatedly to arrest Christians, to restrict foreign trade, to prevent foreign travel, and to prohibit return of Japanese who went overseas
1635	Regulations (*hatto*) issued to Grand Shrines of Ise (and other shrines); Office of Temples and Shrines (Jisha bugyō 寺社奉行) established; Temple registration (*tera-uke seido* 寺請) initiated
1637	Tenkai started printing *Chinese Buddhist Canon* 天海版 (寛永寺版) in Japan with movable type (completed 1648; total 6,323 fascicles) based on 1252 Siqi Fabaosi temple edition plus supplements; Shimabara 島原 revolt 天草の亂: Christian peasants seize control of Shimabara fortress
1638	Japanese Christians at Shimabara defeated with help of Dutch warships
1639	Portuguese trade cut off; Portuguese ships forbidden to come to Japan
1640	Office of Religious Inspection (Shūmon aratame yaku 宗門改役) established; 61 Christians executed
1641	Dutch trading factory transferred from Hirado to Deshima 出島 island (in Nagasaki harbor)
1642	Severe famine
1644	© Qing 清 dynasty (1644–1912) established in China Hayashi Razan wrote *Shintō denju* 神道傳授, explained local Japanese gods (*shintō*) in terms of Confucian principle (*ri* 理)
1654	Yinyuan Longqi 隱元隆琦 (Ingen Ryūki, 1592–1673) and disciples arrived with supporters of defeated Ming dynasty, taught Chinese-style Zen (with vinaya precepts and Pure Land chanting), eventually established Ōbaku 黃檗 Zen lineage
1657	Edo fires: tens of thousands of people killed
1658	Yamaga Sokō 山鹿素行 (1632–1685) wrote *Bukyō shōgaku* 武教小學, justified warrior rule in Confucian terms; Kumazawa Banzan 熊澤蕃山 (1619–1691) opened academy in Kyoto, advocated the idealistic Confucianism of Wang Yangming 王陽明 (Ō Yōmei, 1472–1528)
1660s	Itō Jinsai 伊藤仁齊 (1627–1705) began advocating return to ancient meaning 古義學 of Confucian texts
1662–1671	Temple registration system fully established so that all families will be affiliated with local Buddhist temples (*dannadera* 檀那寺) that record census, births, deaths, marriages, tax obligations, etc.
1665	Regulations (*hatto*) issued to control all shrines (*shosha* 諸社) and shrine celebrants (*negi* 禰宜); Yoshida family awarded power to license shrine celebrants (i.e., official recognition of Yoshida Shinto)

Dates	Events
1668	Establishment of new Buddhist temples prohibited (but they continued to appear until ca. 1700)
1669	Fuju-Fuse branch of Nichiren shū outlawed by Tokugawa *bakufu*
1670s	Kaibara Ekiken 貝原益軒 (1630–1714) explained Confucian moral teachings in simple terms accessible to ordinary people; his *Wazoku dōji kun* 和俗童子訓 (from which the extremely popular *Onna daigaku* 女大學 later would be extracted) defined the goals of popular education for decades to come
1671	Yamazaki Ansai 山崎闇斎 (1618–1682) proclaimed Suika Shinto 垂加神道 as Japanese version of Confucianism that teaches mental concentration (*kei* 敬) and self-control
1675	Tachibana Mitsuyoshi 橘 三喜 (1635–1704) toured the country to teach Yoshida Shinto to the masses (the 1st of many such efforts by shrine priests to popularize and disseminate Shinto teachings)
1681	Tetsugen Dōkō 鐵眼道光 (1630–1682) and other Ōbaku monks printed *Chinese Buddhist Canon* 黄檗版 (6,771 fascicles) based on 1620 Lengyansi temple Ming edition plus supplements
1684	Jōkyōreki 上享暦 adopted by Tokugawa *bakufu* as official calendar, thereby depriving court of its control over the calendar; Jōkyōreki designed by Shibukawa Harumi 渋川春海 (1639–1715) based on Jujireki 授時暦 luni-solar calendar used in China during 1281–1368
1687	*Daijō sai* (spiritual-king food offering) performed by sovereign (*tennō*) for first time since 1466
1689	Tendai secret doctrines of *Genshi kimyōdan* 玄旨歸命壇 declared heretical; rejection of Tendai traditions of Original Awakening (*hongaku hōmon* 本覺法門) in favor of Zhili's "mountain lineage" orthodoxy
1690	Hayashi family head given hereditary title of College Rector (*daigaku no kami* 大學上), gave Confucian scholars institutional independence from Buddhism: Confucians no longer had to shave their heads Keichū 契沖 (1640–1701), a Shingon monk, wrote *Man'yō daishōki* 萬葉代匠記, his study of the *Man'yōshū*, in which he demonstrated how Buddhist techniques of textual analysis can be applied to Japanese literature; thereby paved the way for the development of Nativist Studies (Kokugaku 國學)
1691	Colossal Buddha image at Tōdaiji completed (temple buildings not until 1705)
1703	Manzan Dōhaku 卍山道白 (1636–1714) successfully petitioned Tokugawa *bakufu* to reform Sōtō Zen lineages, marked beginning of "restoration movement" (*fukko undō* 復古運動) to return to Dōgen
1705	First major *okage mairi* お蔭参り to Ise; other major Ise pilgrimages in 1771, 1803, 1830, and 1855

Dates	Events
1716	Ogyū Sorai 荻生徂來 (1666–1728) began advocating Ancient Learning (古學) and the pragmatic application of Confucian teachings to matters of social policy
1729	Ishida Baigan 石田梅岩 (1685–1744) began teaching "Learning of the Heart Mind" (*shingaku* 心學) and conventional morality (*tsūzoku dōtoku* 通俗道德) to ordinary farmers and townsmen; Itō Jikigyō Miroku 伊藤食行身祿 (1671–1733) wrote sacred texts of Fujikō (Mt. Fuji worship) = started first of Japan's "new religions"?
1736	Yoshimi Yukikazu 吉見幸和 (1673–1761) wrote *Gobusho setsuben* 五部書説辨, a devistating critique of Ise Shinto teachings in which he demonstrated that its "ancient texts" were medieval frauds; also wrote similar critiques of Yoshida Shinto and of Suika Shinto; argued that Shinto must be based on the pre-Buddhist and pre-Confucian practices of ancient Japan
1745	Tominaga Nakamoto 富永仲基 (1715–1746) published *Shutsujōgo go* 出定後語 (Conversations after Emerging from Meditation), a critical study of Buddhist scriptures in which he argued that Mahāyāna could not have been preached by the historical Buddha (*daijō hi bussetsu* 大乘非佛説)
1751	Shirakawa Masafuyu 白川雅冬 established new Hasshinden 八神殿 (Hall of Eight Deities) for official court rites of worship; Shirakawa family (Hakke 伯家) Shinto began to compete with Yoshida
1755	Hōrekireki 寶曆曆 adopted by Tokugawa *bakufu* as official calendar, but it proved to be plagued by errors
1760s	Kamo Mabuchi 賀茂眞淵 (1697–1769) began detailed study of ancient Japanese literature and place names, helped start Nativist (Kokugaku 國學) Movement
1767	Secret (*kakure*) *nenbutsu* 隠れ念佛 groups suppressed in Edo
1787	◎ William Jones (1736–1794) introduced Sanskrit language studies to Europeans
1791	Tsuchimikado 土御門 family granted exclusive authority over all Yin-Yang (Onmyōdō 陰陽道) practitioners; Yoshida family established branch office in Edo to consolidate their control over shrines in eastern Japan; shortly thereafter, Shirakawa family also established branch office in Edo
1792	Russians attempted to open trade relations
1795	Russians occupied Kuril Islands north of Hokkaidō
1798	Kanseireki 寛政曆 adopted by Tokugawa *bakufu* as official calendar: first Japanese luni-solar calendar designed with calculations based on Western astronomy, it used Kyoto as its earthly reference point Motoori Norinaga 本居宣長 (1730–1801) wrote *Kojiki-den* 古事記傳, his deciphering of the *Kojiki*; argued that the *Kojiki* reveals the original ancient Shinto of Japan
1803	First American ship visited Japan

Dates	Events
1804	Jiun Onkō 慈雲飲光 (1718–1804) completed 1,000-volume encyclopedia of Sanskrit studies (grammar, glossary, texts); Russian warship of Admiral N. P. Rezanov (1776–1807) visited Nagasaki
1808	English warship Phaeton visited Nagasaki
1812	Hirata Atsutane 平田篤胤 (1776–1843) wrote *Tama no mihashira* 靈能眞柱, which draws on Western astronomy and Christian ideas (Izanagi and Izanami are Adam and Eve) to argue that ancient Shinto is the only true religion for Japan; helped transform Nativism into Shinto Restoration (*fukko* 復古) Movement
1814	Kurozumi Munetada 黒住宗忠 (1780–1850) attained unity with the morning sun, founded Kurozumikyō 黒住教, one of the first so-called "new religions" 新宗教
1826	ⓞ Eugene Burnouf (1801–1852) published his *Essai sur le Pali*, marked beginning of academic Buddhist Studies in Europe
1838	Nakayama Miki 中山みき (1798–1887) possessed by deity, began teaching Tenrikyō 天理教
1840–1842	ⓒ Opium War 阿片戰爭: British forces won treaty concessions, European powers began to carve out own spheres of influence in China
1841	Hirata Atsutane exiled to Akita 秋田 for anti-Tokugawa religious teachings
1843	Inoue Masakane 井上正鐵 (1790–1849) exiled to Miyake Island 三宅島 for teaching Misogikyō 禊教
1844	Dutch warship Palembang visited Nagasaki, presented news of China's defeat in Opium War; Tenpōreki 天保暦 adopted by Tokugawa *bakufu* as official calendar: last Japanese luni-solar calendar
1846	Warships from America and France toured Japanese ports
1847	Tokugawa *bakufu* suppressed Fuke 普化 Zen, restricted movements of *shakuhachi* Zen priests
1849	Hirata Atsutane published *Shutsujō shōgo* 出定笑語 (Laughs after Emerging from Meditation), a critical attack on all aspects of Buddhism; Tokugawa *bakufu* banned Fujikō worshipers of Mt. Fuji
1849–1852	Warships from England, Rumania, Russia, Holland, etc., toured Japanese ports
1853	Commodore Matthew Perry (1794–1858) arrived in Japan, demanded open ports, forced Tokugawa regime to sign trade treaty
1853–1855	Russia, Holland, France, and England all demanded and received trade rights equal to the U.S.
1856–1860	ⓒ Arrow (2nd Opium) War: British and French forces won additional treaty concessions in China

Dates	Events
1858	Ii Naosuke 井伊直弼 (1815–1860) signed trade treaties between Tokugawa *bakufu* and 5 Western powers (U.S.A., Holland, Russia, England, France), ordered purge 安政の大獄 of all anti-*bakufu* groups
1859	Kawate Bunjirō 川手文次郎 (1814–1883) possessed by deity, began teaching Konkōkyō 金光教
1859	Christian missionaries returned to Japan
1860	Ii Naosuke assassinated outside of Sakurada Gate 櫻田門外の變, marked beginning of wave of terrorism as men of determination (*shishi* 志士) assassinated opponents in name of "revere the king, expel the barbarians" (*sonnō jōi* 尊王攘夷); Ⓚ Ch'oe Che-u 崔濟愚 (1824–1864) began teaching "Eastern Learning" (Tonghak 東學), the first of Korea's "new religions"
1862	Chōshū Domain 長州蕃 ordered shore batteries to fire on American, French, and Dutch ships in Shimonoseki 下關 Straits
1863	British naval fleet bombarded port town of Kagoshima 鹿児島
1864	British and allied fleets bombarded Chōshū shore batteries, reopened Shimonoseki Straits; Tokugawa *bakufu* sent troops to chastise Chōshū but military battles were avoided
1865	British fleet threatened Hyōgo 兵庫 Bay, forced sovereign (*tennō*) to sign trade treaties; Japanese "hidden" (*kakure*) Christians in Urakami Village 浦上村 revealed themselves to Western missionary
1866	Satsuma domain 薩摩蕃 and Chōshū domain reached secret agreement 薩長盟約 to oppose Tokugawa *bakufu* (and received assistance in secret from the British); *bakufu*'s second attempt to chastise Chōshū resulted in major military defeat that exposed *bakufu* weakness; Satsuma domain began systematic destruction of all Buddhist temples
1867	Major "*Ee ja nai ka?*" ええじゃないか riots spread from Nagoya to all major urban areas; Tokugawa *bakufu* reached agreement with French for aid against Satsuma and Chōshu
1868	Meiji Restoration 明治維新 proclaimed after armed forces from domains of Satsuma, Echizen, Owari, Tosa, and Aki seized Kyoto; court moved to Edo (Tokyo); Mutsuhito 睦仁 (1852–1912) enthroned as Emperor Meiji 明治天皇
1868	New Meiji government ordered separation of gods and buddhas (*shinbutsu bunri* 神佛分離); thousands of Buddhist temples destroyed, monks defrocked (*haibutsu kishaku* 廃佛毀釈); deprived of ritual and doctrinal context, newly independent "shintō" 神道 shrines forced to adopt new identities; prohibition of Christianity reconfirmed

Dates	Events
1869	Department of Shinto Affairs (Jingikan 神祇官) established as highest unit within central government in effort to Unify Religion and Government (*saisei itchi* 祭政一致); military forces loyal to Tokugawa *bakufu* defeated (= end of anti-restoration civil war 戊辰戰爭); Emperor Meiji visited Ise Shrines = first time Japanese *tennō* ever visited Ise; Yasukuni Shrine 靖國神社 established to enshrine "heroic spirits" (*eirei* 英靈) of army soldiers who died fighting for *tennō* in civil war
1870	"Great Teaching Promulgation Campaign" (*taikyō senpu undō* 大教宣布運動) launched to create new national ideology; 3,000+ Hidden Christians sentenced to banishment
1871	Department of Shinto Affairs demoted to ministry status (Jingishō 神祇省) with its policies in disarray; government rescinded anti-Buddhist policy; *Outcast Emancipation Edict* 解放令 ended legal segregation of outcasts; government abolished Fukeshū branch of Zen; revised *Daijō sai* (spiritual-king food offering) performed by Meiji *tennō* as state ceremony (financed by taxes); Ministry of Education (Monbushō 文部省) established, implemented nationwide system of compulsory education
1872	Ministry of Shinto Affairs (Jingishō) reformulated as Ministry of [Religious] Instruction (Kyōbushō 教部省); status of Buddhist monks reduced to that of ordinary "imperial subjects" (*kōmin* 皇民); laws forbidding women at religious institutions rescinded; laws forbidding Buddhist monks from marriage and eating meat (*nikujiki saitai* 肉食妻帯) rescinded; private funerals forbidden; government ordered all independent Shugendō orders merged with Tendai or Shingon temples
1872–1876	Buddhist temples declined from 89,914 to 71,962, and monks from 75,925 to 19,490
1873	Christianity permitted; government prohibited shamanistic practices of exorcisms, faith healing, and other folk religious rituals (e.g., 梓巫, 市子, 憑祈禱, 狐下げ, etc.); Gregorian solar calendar adopted with national holidays based on *tennō* mythology (e.g., Jinmu's Founding of Japan, Jinmu's Death, etc.)
1875	Bureau of Shinto (Shintō Jimukyoku 神道事務局) established; Ise Shrine placed in charge of "Great Promulgation Campaign"; all shrines ordered to perform rituals in "ancient style" Ⓚ Japanese warships tried to open trade ports in Korea (concluded trade treaties in 1876)
1876	Nanjō Bun'yū 南條文雄 (1849–1927) and Kasahara Kenju 笠原研壽 (1852–1883) (both leading Buddhist scholars) traveled to England to study Sanskrit under Max Müller (1823–1900): marked beginning of importation of Western methods of academic Buddhist studies
1877	Ministry of [Religious] Instruction replaced by Bureau of Shrines and Temples (Shajikyoku 社寺局) in Ministry of the Interior Ⓚ Japanese Buddhist missionaries sent to Korea to "revive" Korean Buddhism
1878	Edward S. Morse (1838–1920) lectured in Japan on evolution, attacked Christianity as "unscientific"

Dates	Events
1880–1885	"Small Print" (*shukusatsu* 縮刷) edition of the *Chinese Buddhist Canon* published (418 vols., 8,534 fascicles) in Tokyo based on the 1251 Koryŏ edition plus supplements; government forbade military men, police officers, teachers, students, and technicians from attending political meetings
1882	"Shinto" declared a patriotic duty, not a "religion"; government ordered shrine priests to stop all religious instruction; government officially distinguished between "non-religious vs. religious Shinto," which it called "shrine" (*jinja* 神社) and "sect" (*kyōha* 教派) Shinto; government suppressed Tenrikyō, but Nakayama Miki finished writing *Ofudesaki*, her record of Tenrikyō teachings
1886	University of Tokyo 東京大學 established (included first Chair of Indian [Buddhist] and Sanskrit Studies)
1888	Emperor's photo enshrined in all schools and government buildings; following death of Nakayama Miki, Tenrikyō permitted to continue, but only under direct police supervision
1889	*Meiji Constitution* 大日本帝國憲法 promulgated: guaranteed "freedom of religious belief within limits not antagonistic to people's duties as imperial subjects" 臣民タルノ義務ニ背カサル限ニ於テ信教ノ自由, also recognized "Shinto" as foundation of state; granted emperor alone direct control over military; Interior Ministry issued ordinances allowing Christian organizations to register as religions
1890	*Imperial Rescript on Education* 教育勅語 issued, exalted loyalty to the emperor; government began to inspect all school textbooks; Kokugakuin University 國學院大學 established to study Shinto theology
ca. 1890s	Meiji social policy characterized by three slogans: (1) exalt bureaucrats, despise ordinary people (*kanson minpi* 官尊民卑), (2) a racial, family-based state (so that any political change violates native culture; *kazoku kokka* 家族國家), and (3) royal considerations decide all issues (*banki kōron* 萬機公論)
1891	Ministry of Education issued guidelines for "moral indoctrination" (*shūshin* 修身); Uchimura Kanzō 内村鑑三 (1861–1930) denounced for refusing to bow to *Imperial Rescript on Education*
1892	Kume Kunitake 久米邦武 (1839–1931) fired from University of Tokyo for writing scholarly article linking "ancient Shinto" rites to Chinese influences; Deguchi Nao 出口なを (1836–1918) founded Ōmoto 大本
1893	Shaku Sōen 釋宗圓 (1859–1919) and other Buddhist leaders attended ◎ World Parliament of Religions in Chicago, promoted Buddhism as a "scientific" religion; Ministry of Education instituted singing of "Kimi ga yo" 君が代 song in schools
1894	Shinto shrine priests made officers in the government, subject to bureaucratic control; Japan defeated China in Sino-Japanese War 日清戰爭
1895	© Taiwan 臺湾 annexed by Japan; Salvation Army 日本救世軍 established in Japan

Dates	Events
1896	Interior Ministry drafted secret order to suppress new religions, beginning with Tenrikyō
1897	D. T. Suzuki 鈴木大拙 (1870–1966) traveled to United States where he would spend eleven years (until 1908) studying "Science of Religion" from German émigré theologian Paul Carus (1852–1919)
1900	Bureau of Religion (Shūkyōkyoku 宗教局) created (within Interior Ministry) to administer all Shinto institutions = full-fledged establishment of State Shinto ◎ Nitobe Inazō 新渡戸稲造 (1862–1933), a Quaker living in the U.S., published *Bushido, The Soul of Japan*, introduced concept of *bushidō* 武士道 (the warrior's code of honor) to the West, from where it was imported into Japan
1902–1905	*Manji* 卍字 edition of the *Chinese Buddhist Canon* published (347 vols., 7,082 fascicles) in Kyoto
1903	Japanese YMCA 日本基督教青年會 founded
1903–1920	"Shrine Mergers" 神社合祀 (合併): government destroyed more than half of the Shinto shrines in Japan, thereby consolidated power over official Shinto ideology; deprived of links to local religious practices Shinto shrines forced to adopt new identities as "civic centers"
1904–1905	Russo-Japanese War 日露戰爭 fought to extend greater influence over Korean peninsula and Manchuria; fighting ended, after major Japanese naval victory at Tsushima 對島 straights, with peace deal brokered by U.S.
1905	Army adopted policy of relying on fighting spirit (*kōgeki seishin* 攻擊精神) to overcome lack of material resources, began developing curriculum of "spiritual education" (*seishin kyōiku* 精神教育) based on martial arts; supplement (*Zokuzōkyō* 續藏經) to the *Manji* edition of the *Chinese Buddhist Canon* published (750 vols.)
1906	Government began direct economic support of all officially recognized Shinto shrines
1907	Ministers of the Army and Navy required to be active duty officers, effectively handing the general staffs of these organizations veto power over cabinet formation
1908	Ministry of Education issued new textbooks that interpreted *Imperial Rescript on Education* as depicting Japan as organic (*yūkitai* 有機体) "emperor-family state" that must be the supreme entity in the lives of every imperial subject; Tenrikyō permitted as a form of "Sect" Shinto (the last of the officially recognized 13 Shinto sects)
1910	Ⓚ Korean peninsula annexed by Japan; Japanese National Shinto Shrines established in Korea
1911	Lèse Majesté Affair (*taigyaku jiken* 大逆事件): 12 socialists executed, including Uchiyama Gudō 内山愚童 (Sōtō Zen priest); others sentenced to life in prison, including Takagi Kenmyō 高木顯明 (Pure Land priest) and Mineo Setsudō 峰尾節堂 (Rinzai Zen priest); government began repressing left-wing thinkers

DATES	EVENTS
1912	Yoshihito 嘉仁 (1879–1926) enthroned as the Taishō 大正 Emperor; reign of sickly emperor corresponds to brief period of popular demands for democracy
1912	*Dai Nihon Bukkyō zensho* 大日本佛教全書 (premodern Japanese texts on Buddhism) published (151 vols.); Kanada Tokumitsu 金田德光 (1863–1924) founded Tokumitsukyō (beginning of PL Kyōdan PL教団)
1913	Ōnishi Aijirō 大西愛次郎 (1881–1958) split from Tenrikyō, founded Honmichi ほんみち; Bureau of Religious [Control] (Shūkyōkyoku 宗教局) transferred to inside Ministry of Education
1914	Tanaka Chigaku 田中智學 (1861–1939) established the Kokuchūkai 國柱會 (Pillar of the State Society), advocated the unity of Nichiren Buddhism and national structure (*kokutai* 國体, i.e., emperor system) ◎ Great War breaks out in Europe (*aka* World War I)
1916	Ōmoto changed its name to Kōdō Ōmoto 皇道大本 ("Imperial Way Ōmoto")
1917–1918	◎ Communists seized control over Russia: started world-wide "red scare" as governments everywhere became more authoritarian to suppress local communists
1918	Japanese Army sent to Siberia alongside British, French, and American troops to fight against Russian communist forces
1919	Government began campaign against what it labeled "pseudo religions" (*ruiji shūkyō* 類似宗教)
1920	Meiji Shrine 明治神宮 established in Tokyo, deification of Meiji *tennō* complete
1921	D. T. Suzuki founded *The Eastern Buddhist* magazine; Deguchi Onisaburō 出口王仁三郎 (1871–1948), leader of Ōmoto 大本, jailed for treason; Prince Hirohito completed his military education and visited Europe to see first-hand how to suppress anti-monarchy movements
1922	Levelers' Society (Suiheisha 水平社) established to fight discrimination against descendants of outcaste groups; Levelers organized first strike against Jōdo Shinshū (True Pure Land) school to protest Buddhist prejudices
1923	Great Tokyo earthquake 關東大震災 followed by pogroms against Koreans and leftists; government issued declaration on Strengthening the Spirit of Citizenry 國民精神作興に関する詔書, which attacked progressive ideas and encouraged obedience to established social hierarchy
1924	Taishō edition of the *Chinese Buddhist Canon* (*Taishō shinshū daizōkyō* 大正新脩大藏經) published (100 vols., 11,970 fascicles) based on the 1251 Koryŏ edition plus supplements including treatises and ritual manuals composed in Japan

DATES	EVENTS
1925	*Peace Preservation Law* 治安維持法 (first legal use of term *kokutai* 國体 since 1885): empowered police to arrest advocates of communism, socialism, democracy, or religious freedom as well as anyone "disrespectful" of the throne; Kubo Kakutarō 久保角太郎 (1892–1944) founded Reiyūkai 靈友會
1926	Hirohito 裕仁 (1901–1989) enthroned as the Shōwa 昭和 Emperor: first modern emperor; books by Inoue Tetsujirō 井上哲次郎 (1855–1944) banned for suggesting rational (as opposed to mythological) basis for *kokutai* 國体 (emperor system); Ministry of Education introduced new physical education curriculum in which martial arts (*budō* 武道) provide "spiritual education"
1928	Japanese-language translation of *Chinese Buddhist Canon* (*Kokuyaku issaikyō* 國訳一切經) published (222 vols.); Okada Mokichi 岡田茂吉 (1882–1955) founded Sekai Kyūseikyō 世界救世教; government arrested leaders of Tenri Kenkyūkai 天理研究會 (*aka* Tenri Honmichi 天理本道) and 385 followers
1929	Taniguchi Masaharu 谷口雅春 (1893–1985) founded Seichō no Ie 生長の家
1930	Makiguchi Tsunesaburō 牧口常三郎 (1871–1944) founded Sōka Kyōiku Gakkai 創價教育學會 (later Sōka Gakkai 創価学会); Jōdo Shinshū leaders issued permission for followers to worship at Shinto shrines as an expression of virtuous citizenship (*kokumin dōtoku* 國民道德) but not as an act of religious faith
1931	© Japanese Kwantung army 關東軍 seized Mukden (Shenyang 瀋陽) in Manchuria 滿州事變, marked start of 15-Years War 十五年戰爭 (from 1931 to 1945) Followers of Fukada Chiyoko 深田千代子 (1887–1925) formed Ennōkyō 圓應教; famines in Tōhoku and in Hokkaidō
1932	Blood Brotherhood 血盟團 (radical right-wing organization) assassinated finance minister and prime minister for appearing too timid in war against China; Ministry of Education issued order requiring all school children to worship at Shinto shrines as expression of patriotism © Japanese established puppet state of Manchukuo 滿州國 (Manchuria) with Henry Pu Yi 溥儀 (1906–1967; the "Last Emperor") as puppet ruler
1934	Bureau of Thought [Control] (Shisōkyoku 思想局) established inside Ministry of Education
1935	Japanese translation of *Pāli Buddhist Canon* (*Nanden daizōkyō* 南傳大藏經) published (70 vols.); police cite *Peace Preservation Law* to launch campaign to eradicate "evil religious cults" (*jakyō senmetsu* 邪教殲滅): Deguchi Onisaburō jailed for treason again, Ōmoto suppressed
1936.2.26	Junior Army officers attempted *coup d'état* (*ni-ni-roku jiken* 2.26 事件), set stage for policy of permanent military expansion into China

DATES	EVENTS
1937	◎ Indiscriminate bombing of Guernica by German air force introduced new kind of military terror © Shots fired at Marco Polo Bridge 蘆溝橋 (Peking/Beijing) marked beginning of Japanese War of territorial conquest in China 日中戰爭 Ministry of Education issued official textbook on Shinto ideology: *Kokutai no hongi* 國体の本義 (Cardinal Principles of the National Structure); government suppressed Hitonomichi Kyōdan 人道教團; campaign for General Mobilization of the Spirit of the Citizens 國民精神總動員運動 launched to insure blind obedience to government: marked full-scale adoption of fascism © "Rape of Nanking (Nanjing)" 南京大虐殺事件
1938	Government suppressed Tenri Honmichi; © indiscriminate fire bombing of Chungking (Chongqing 重慶) by Japanese air force; in response, U.S. imposed first trade embargo against Japan; Niwano Nikkyō 庭野日敬 (1906–1999) founded Risshō Kōsei Kai 立正佼成會
1939	*Religious Organizations Law* 宗教團体法 allowed government control over religious organizations and authorized government to disband groups deemed incompatible with "The Imperial Way" (*kōdō* 皇道); government disbanded Hitonomichi Kyōdan
1940	Board of Shinto (Jingi-in 神祇院) established: government banned Tsuda Sōkichi's 津田左右吉 (1873–1961) books on Shinto; Jehovah's Witnesses エホバの證人 jailed
1941	◎ U.S. ordered embargo on shipments of oil to Japan Japan attacked Pearl Harbor 眞珠湾空襲, marked beginning of Great Pacific War 太平洋戰爭 (World War II); all religious denominations (Shinto, Buddhist, Christian) ordered to unite in defense of Japan Ⓚ More than 2,000 Korean Christians jailed for refusing to participate in obligatory Shinto ceremonies, more than 200 Korean Christian Churches destroyed
1942	Government ordered Buddhist temples to "donate" all metal images, bells, and decorations to war effort
1943	Sōka Gakkai leaders jailed for disrespect toward Ise shrines (Makiguchi subsequently died in prison)
1944	◎ Indiscriminate bombing of London by German V1 and V2 rockets
1945	◎ Indiscriminate firebombing of Dresden by British and U.S. air forces Japan systematically destroyed: indiscriminate firebombing of Tokyo 東京大空襲, followed by indiscriminate fire bombing of 20 other major cities; Japanese leaders decided national suicide is necessary to preserve *kokutai* of imperial rule
1945.8	Atomic bombing 原子爆彈投下 of Hiroshima 廣島 and Nagasaki 長崎 by U.S. air force; Soviet Union declared war on Japan and began hostilities against Japanese forces in Manchuria and Korea

Dates	Events
1945.8.15	Japan surrendered; SCAP Occupation GHQ-ordered land reforms deprived Buddhist temples of major sources of income; GHQ abolished State Shinto 神道指令: deprived of nationalist and ideological purpose, Shinto shrines forced to adopt new identities as primitive nature cults
1946	Hirohito *tennō* (emperor) publicly denied his divinity 天皇人間宣言; *New "Peace" Constitution* 日本國憲法 promulgated; Constitution guarantees freedom of religion and separation of religion and state; Western Christian missionaries resumed teaching openly; Japanese Christian organizations formally expressed regret for war responsibility; Hitonomichi Kyōdan reformulated as PL Kyōdan; Sōka Gakkai resumed activities
1947	New *National Law Code* 民法 abolished legal basis of Meiji-period family (*ie* 家) system; Kitamura Sayo 北村さよ (1900–1967) founded Tenshō Kōtai Jingūkyō 天照皇太神宮教
1948	*Imperial Rescript on Education* ruled invalid; *Eugenic Protection Law* 優性保護法 legalized abortions
1950	Ⓚ Korean War 朝鮮戦争 began Occupation GHQ in Japan reversed liberal policies, cracked down on leftists
1951	*Religious Juridical Persons Law* 宗教法人法 established; Itō Shinjō 伊藤真乗 (1906–1989) founded Shinnyoen 真如苑
1952	Allied Occupation ended; *Subversive Activities Prevention Law* 破壊活動防止法 enacted; Hirohito visited Ise shrines for first time since end of War
1950s	Rapid urbanization weakened links to traditionally rural-based religious institutions
1954	Yasutani Hakuun 安谷白雲 (1885–1973) founded Sanbōkyōdan 三宝教団, popularized Zen *satori* for lay people Ⓚ Moon Sun-Myung 文鮮明 (1920–) founded Unification Church 統一教会 in South Korea
1955	D. T. Suzuki published Peking edition of *Tibetan Buddhist Canon* (168 vols.); Goi Masahisa 五井昌久 (1916–1980) founded Byakkō Shinkōkai 白光真宏会
1956	19 major temples and shrines in Kyoto stage first major protest against tourism tax
1959	Government established Memorial for War Dead 戦没者墓苑 at Chidorigafuchi 千鳥ヶ淵; Okada Kōtama 岡田光玉 (1901–1974) founded Mahikari 真光; Unification Church introduced to Japan from Korea
ca. 1960	More than half (ca. 70%) of Japanese lived in urban areas
1960	Ikeda Daisaku 池田大作 became 3rd president of Sōka Gakkai
1961	Higashi Honganji formed Dōbōkai 同朋会 (Brotherhood of Faith) Movement

Dates	Events
1964	Sōka Gakkai sponsored formation of Kōmeitō 公明党 (Clean Government Party)
1965	Ministry of Education attacked by media for proposing draft textbook on ethics (*dōtoku* 道徳)
1970	Socialist Party accused Kōmeitō officials of preventing publication of Fujiwara Kōtatsu's 藤原弘達 book, *I Denounce Sōka Gakkai* 創価学会を斬る; after subsequent scandal, Sōka Gakkai agreed to moderate aggressive proselytizing (*shakubuku* 折伏) and Kōmeitō asserted independence; Takahashi Shinji 高橋信次 (1927–1976) founded GLA
1970s	Media began reporting growing popularity of temple pilgrimage and rites for aborted fetuses (*mizuko kuyō* 水子供養)
1971	Okinawa reverted to Japan; Hirohito visited Hiroshima Memorial 原爆慰霊碑 for first time
1974	Japanese Islam Federation founded
1978	Yasukuni Shrine enshrined Class-A war criminals, including Tōjō Hideki 東條英機 (1884–1948); Kiriyama Seiyū 桐山靖雄 (1921–) founded Agonshū 阿含宗
1979	Machida Munco 町田宗夫 proclaimed "social discrimination does not exist in Japan," embroiled All Buddhist Federation and Sōtō Zen in major scandal
1981	Pope John Paul II visited Japan; during the 1980s media began reporting about interest in occult and mysticism among young people
1985	Prime Minister Nakasone Yasuhiro 中曽根康弘 and entire government cabinet performed official act of homage at Yasukuni Shrine = high point in attempt to revive State Shinto
1986	Ōkawa Ryūhō 大川隆法 (1956–) founded Kōfuku no Kagaku 幸福の科学 (IRH); 7 female members of Shinri no tomo 真理の友 set themselves on fire; media began to attack religious "cults" カルト
1989	Akihito 明仁 (1933–) ascended throne as new Heisei 平成 Emperor
	Asahara Shōkō 麻原彰晃 (real name Matsumoto Chizuo 松本智津夫, 1955–) gains legal status for Aum Shinrikyō オウム真理教
1990	Tōdaiji Buddha Hall restored; *Daijō sai* (spiritual-king food offering) performed as state ceremony (financed by taxpayers) for first time since 1926 despite 1946 constitution: ritual based on Meiji-period imperial ordinance that could not have been legal under new constitution; "religion/state" distinction lost; newspapers filled with speculation on religious mysteries of "ancient" ceremony (actually created ca. 1871)
1991	Nichiren Shōshū 日蓮正宗 (temple-based denomination) and Sōka Gakkai (lay organization) broke apart, sparked crisis of legitimization ◎ Soviet Union dismantled: end of communist challenge to democracy and capitalism

Dates	Events
1994	Gas attack in Matsumoto 松本サリン事件: Aum Shinrikyō blamed U.S. military
1995	Aum Shinrikyō used poison gas in attack on Tokyo subway system オウム真理教事件
1996	Aum Shinrikyō disbanded by Japanese government; government proposed invoking for first time in history *Subversive Activities Prevention Law* to suppress Aum; Public Security Investigation Agency 公安調査庁 ordered to provide 24-hour surveillance of all people associated with Aum; government proposed changes in *Religious Juridical Persons Law* (supposedly in response to Aum Shinrikyō, but actually designed to limit political influence of Sōka Gakkai and Kōmeitō)
1999	Government enacted 2 laws (団体規制法 and オウム特例法) to suppress activity by everyone formerly associated with Aum and to seize their assets; all religious organizations now subject to supervision
2000	Aum Shinrikyō's former members reformulated group as "Aleph" アレフ, but public hysteria and police harassment continued unchanged
2001	Prime Minister Koizumi Jun'ichirō 小泉純一郎 worshiped at Yasukuni Shrine to promote "Japanese values" (8.13); ☉ World Trade Center and Pentagon attacked (9.11 terrorism): religion increasingly perceived as threat to public security
2002	Prime Minister Koizumi made second visit to Yasukuni Shrine (4.21)
2003	Prime Minister Koizumi made third visit to Yasukuni Shrine (1.14)
2004	Prime Minister Koizumi made fourth visit to Yasukuni Shrine (1.1); district court ruled that Koizumi's visits to Yasukuni violate constitutional separation of religion and state (but court cannot enforce ruling)

Contributors

Barbara AMBROS is an Assistant Professor of East Asian religions in the Department of Religious Studies at the University of North Carolina at Chapel Hill. She has published several articles on pilgrimage and sacred mountains in premodern Japan and has a monograph on the early modern mountain cult of Ōyama forthcoming with Harvard University Press. She has also filmed a documentary on the contempary Ōyama cult and participated in a documentary on the *Kumano Kanjin Jikkai Mandara* and the Kumano *bikuni*. Her most recent research project is an ethnographic study of the religions of overseas Chinese in Japan.

Trevor ASTLEY is the Nanzan Copy Editor and Lecturer in the Faculty of Foreign Studies at Nanzan University. His main work has been in the field of Japanese new religious movements, including a biography of the founder of a small Nichiren-derived group (unpublished) and a treatment of one of the more recent new religious movements, Kōfuku no Kagaku (1995). His current interest in the field lies principally in the formation of religious biographies, particularly with regard to the interaction between religious leaders and their followers during the formation process and the role of memory and ontologically motivated concerns in creating the life story.

William M. BODIFORD is Associate Professor at the University of California, Los Angeles. He is an associate editor of *Encyclopedia of Buddhism* (Macmillian Reference USA, 2004), editor of *Going Forth: Visions of Buddhist Vinaya* (University of Hawai'i Press, 2005), and author of *Soto Zen in Medieval Japan* (University of Hawai'i Press, 1994) and of many other articles and translations.

Clark CHILSON is Assistant Professor of Religion at Pacific Lutheran University. He is the co-editor of *Shamans in Asia* (with Peter Knecht, 2003) and has published on Kūya and on secretive Shinshū traditions. In 2004 he completed his Ph.D. for Lancaster University with a dissertation on three lay secretive Shinshū associations in contemporary Japan.

Helen HARDACRE is Reischauer Institute Professor of Japanese Religions and Society at Harvard University. Her publications include *Lay Buddhism in Contemporary Japan* (1984),

Kurozumikyo and the New Religions of Japan (1986), *Shintō and the State 1868–1988* (1989), *Marketing the Menacing Fetus in Japan* (1997), and most recently *Religion and Society in Nineteenth-century Japan* (2003). Her current interests include analyzing Japanese society and religion from the perspective of "civil society," and the ramifications of possible constitutional amendments on religion in Japan.

Norman HAVENS is affiliated with the Institute for Japanese Culture and Classics at Kokugakuin University. He holds an MA in the Study of Religion from Princeton University, and has carried out research on modern Japanese religion, with a focus on the history of popular pilgrimage to Ise. He has translated several books from Japanese, including *The World of Shinto* (1985), *Matsuri: Festival and Rite in Japanese Life* (1988), *New Religions* (1991), and *Kami* (1998).

HAYASHI Makoto 林 淳 is Professor in the Department of Religious Studies, Aichi Gakuin University. He is a specialist in the history of Japanese religions, in particular the Onmyōdō tradition during the Tokugawa Period (1600–1868). His publications (in Japanese) include *The World of Hōnen* (1991), *The World of Japanese Religions from a Different Cultural Perspective* (co-edited with Paul Swanson, 2000), and *Lectures on Onmyōdō* (co-edited with Koike Jun'ichi, 2002), and has published numerous essays in academic journals in both Japanese and English.

Thomas P. KASULIS is Professor of Comparative Cultural Studies in the Department of Comparative Studies at the Ohio State University. He is also affiliated with the departments of Philosophy and of East Asian Languages and Literatures. His books include *Zen Action/Zen Person* (1981), *Intimacy or Integrity: Philosophy and Cultural Difference* (2002), and *Shinto: The Way Home* (2004). His current projects include a history of Japanese philosophy and the co-editing of a sourcebook of readings in Japanese philosophy.

KAWAHASHI Noriko 川橋範子 holds a doctorate in Religion from Princeton University and is an Associate Professor of religion at Nagoya Institute of Technology (Nagoya Kōgyō Daigaku). She has published extensively on the subject of women and religion in Japan and Okinawa, both in English and Japanese. She has co-authored with Kuroki Masako a book on religion and postcolonial feminism, *Konzaisuru Megumi* (2004), and co-edited with Kuroki Masako the *JJRS* Special Issue on "Feminism and Religion in Japan" (vol. 30, Fall 2003). She is a member of the Board of Advisors of the International Institute for the Study of Religion.

Robert KISALA is Professor in the Humanities Faculty of Nanzan University. His publications include *Prophets of Peace* (1999) and *Religion and Social Crisis in Japan* (co-edited with Mark Mullins, 2001). His interests are Japanese new religious movements and values in contemporary Japan.

MAKINO Yasuko 牧野康子 is Japanese Bibliographer and Cataloger at the East Asian Library and the Gest Collection of Princeton University. Her major publications are *Japan through Children's Literature: A Critical Bibliography* (1985), *A Student Guide to Japanese Sources in the Humanities* (1994), and *Japan and the Japanese: A Bibliographic Guide to Reference Works* (1996).

MATSUMURA Kazuo 松村一男 is Professor of the History of Religions and Comparative Mythology at Wako University in Tokyo. His publications in English include "Alone among Women" (in *Kami*, Kokugakuin University, 1998) and "The Koki Story and the

Femininity of the Foundress of Tenrikyo" (in *Women and Religion,* Tenri Yamato Culture Congress, 2003). He has also translated books by Georges Dumezil and Mircea Eliade into Japanese.

Robert E. Morrell is Professor Emeritus, Washington University in St. Louis. His publications generally focus on examples in popular literature which reflect accommodation of ideological diversity grounded in the skillful means (*hōben*) ideal of Mahāyāna Buddhism as set forth in the Lotus Sutra: *Sand and Pebbles (Shasekishū): The Tales of Mujū Ichien, A Voice for Pluralism in Kamakura Buddhism* (1985); *Early Kamakura Buddhism: A Minority Report* (1987); and *[Rinzai] Zen Sanctuary of Purple Robes: Japan's Tōkeiji Convent since 1285* (co-authored with Sachiko Kaneko Morrell, 2005).

Mark R. Mullins is Professor of Religion in the Faculty of Comparative Culture, Sophia University, Tokyo. He is the author/co-editor of a number of works, including *Religion and Society in Modern Japan* (1993), *Perspectives on Christianity in Korea and Japan* (1995), *Christianity Made in Japan* (1998), and *Religion and Social Crisis in Japan* (2001). His research focuses on the sociology of religious minorities, particularly new religious movements and Christianity in East Asia.

Richard K. Payne is the Dean of the Institute of Buddhist Studies at the Graduate Theological Union, Berkeley. He is chair of the editorial committee of *Pacific World: Journal of the Institute of Buddhist Studies,* and of the Pure Land Buddhist Studies Series. His publications include *Approaching the Land of Bliss: Religious Praxis in the Cult of Amitābha,* co-edited with Kenneth K. Tanaka; *Language and Discourse in Medieval Japanese Buddhism,* co-edited with Taigen Dan Leighton; and *Tantra in East Asia.* His continuing research interest is tantric Buddhist ritual and the development of a cognitive theory of ritual.

Ian Reader is Professor of Religious Studies at Lancaster University, England. Previously he has worked at academic institutions in Japan, Denmark, Hawaii, and Scotland. Among his publications are *Making Pilgrimages: Meaning and Practice in Shikoku* (2005), *Religious Violence in Contemporary Japan: The Case of Aum Shinrikyō* (2000); *Practically Religious: Worldly Benefits and the Common Religion of Japan* (co-authored with George J. Tanabe, Jr., 1998), and *Religion in Contemporary Japan* (1991). Current interests include gardening, cricket, soccer, drinking beer, rock music, and avoiding any further engagement with academic institutions.

Brian O. Ruppert is Associate Professor of Japanese Religions at the University of Illinois. His publications include *Jewel in the Ashes: Buddha Relics and Power in Early Medieval Japan* (2000), "Sin or Crime? Debts, Social Relations, and Buddhism in Early Medieval Japan" (*Japanese Journal of Religious Studies,* 2001), "Buddhist Rain-making in Early Japan: Dragon Kings and the Ritual Careers of Shingon Monks" (*History of Religions,* 2002), and "Buddhism in Japan" (*The Encyclopedia of Religion,* 2nd ed., 2005). His current projects are on Buddhist discourses and practices of indebtedness in early medieval Japanese society, and on the relationship between Buddhism and communication in premodern Japan.

Scott Schnell is an Associate Professor of Anthropology at the University of Iowa. For several years he has been conducting ethnographic fieldwork in the mountainous Hida region of central Japan. His major works include *The Rousing Drum: Ritual Practice in a Japanese Community* (1999), which explores the use of ritual as an effective medium for negotiating sociopolitical and economic change. He is currently researching local perceptions of the natural environment and their expression through popular religious concepts and ritual activity.

SHIMAZONO Susumu 島薗 進 is Professor in the Department of Religious Studies at the University of Tokyo. He has published extensively on new religious movements, and the role of religion in contemporary Japanese society. In addition to numerous publications in Japanese, his work in English includes *Religion and Society in Modern Japan* (co-edited with Mark Mullins and Paul Swanson, 1993), and a collection of his essays, *From Salvation to Spirituality: Popular Religious Movements in Modern Japan* (2004). He is currently leading a research project on "Death-and-Life Studies."

Jacqueline I. STONE is Professor of Japanese Religions at Princeton University. She is the author of *Original Enlightenment and the Transformation of Medieval Japanese Buddhism* (1999). Her research has focused chiefly on Japanese Buddhism, especially of the medieval period, as well as modern reinterpretations of traditional doctrine. She has published articles on the Tendai, Pure Land, and Nichiren traditions. In addition to her ongoing work on Nichiren Buddhism, she is currently researching deathbed practices in premodern Japan.

Paul L. SWANSON is a Permanent Fellow and Director of the Nanzan Institute for Religion and Culture, Nanzan University. His dual areas of specialization are Japanese Religions (Shugendō) and Buddhist Studies (T'ien-t'ai/Tendai Buddhism), and he is the editor of the *Japanese Journal of Religious Studies*. Publications include *Foundations of T'ien-t'ai Philosophy* (1989), *Religion and Society in Modern Japan* (1993), and *Pruning the Bodhi Tree* (1997). His annotated translation of the Chinese Buddhist classic *Mo-ho chih-kuan* has been provisionally released on CD-ROM as *The Great Cessation-and-Contemplation* (2004).

Duncan Ryūken WILLIAMS is an Associate Professor of Japanese Buddhism at the University of California, Berkeley. His publications include *The Other Side of Zen* (2005), and co-edited volumes, *Buddhism and Ecology* (1997) and *American Buddhism* (1999). His current research interests include Japanese Buddhism in diaspora, Japanese-American Buddhism in the World War II internment camps, and Japanese Buddhism and bathing.

YOSHIDA Kazuhiko 吉田一彦 is Professor in the Graduate School of Humanities and Social Sciences at Nagoya City University. His publications (in Japanese) include *Buddhism and Ancient Japanese Society* (1995) and *The Truth Concerning Shōtoku Taishi* (with Ōyama Seiichi, 2003). He specializes in the study of ancient Japanese history and the history of Buddhism in Japan.

Index